Geryow Gwir

Other Cornish books from Evertype

Tredden in Scath (Jerome K. Jerome, tr. Nicholas Williams 2014)

Gwerryans an Planettys (H. G. Wells, tr. Nicholas Williams 2013)

Ky Teylu Baskerville (Arthur Conan Doyle, tr. Nicholas Williams 2012)

Flehes an Hens Horn (Edith Nesbit, tr. Nicholas Williams 2012)

Phyllis in Piskie-land (J. Henry Harris 2012)

An Beybel Sans: The Holy Bible in Cornish (tr. Nicholas Williams 2011)

Whedhlow ha Drollys a Gernow Goth (Nigel Roberts, tr. Nicholas Williams 2011)

The Beast of Bodmin Moor: Best Goon Brèn (Alan Kent, tr. Neil Kennedy 2011)

Enys Tresour (Robert Louis Stevenson, tr. Nicholas Williams 2010)

Whedhlow Kernowek: Stories in Cornish (A.S.D. Smith, ed. Nicholas Williams 2010)

Henry Jenner's Handbook of the Cornish Language (ed. Michael Everson 2010)

The Cult of Relics: Devocyon dhe Greryow (Alan Kent, tr. Nicholas Williams, 2010)

Jowal Lethesow: Whedhel a'm West a Gernow
(Craig Weatherhill, tr. Nicholas Williams, 2009)

Skeul an Tavas: A coursebook in Standard Cornish (Ray Chubb, 2009)

Kensa Lyver Redya
(Harriette Treadwell & Margaret Free, tr. Eddie Foirbeis Climo, 2009)

Adro dhe'n Bÿs in Peswar Ugans Dëdh
(Jules Verne, abridged and tr. Kaspar Hocking, 2009)

A Concise Dictionary of Cornish Place-Names (Craig Weatherhill, 2009)

Alys in Pow an Anethow (Lewis Carroll, tr. Nicholas Williams, 2009)

Form and Content in Revived Cornish
(Everson, Weatherhill, Chubb, Deacon, Williams, 2006)

Towards Authentic Cornish (Nicholas Williams, 2006)

Writings on Revived Cornish (Nicholas Williams, 2006)

Cornish Today (Nicholas Williams, 2006)

Geryow Gwir

The lexicon of revived Cornish

Second edition
Revised and enlarged

Nicholas Williams

2014

Published by Evertype, Cnoc na Sceiche, Leac an Anfa, Cathair na Mart, Co. Mhaigh Eo, Éire. www.evertype.com.

© 2014 Nicholas Williams and Michael Everson.

Editor: Michael Everson.

Second edition, revised and enlarged 2014.

All rights reserved. No part of this publication may be reproduced, stored in a retrieval system, or transmitted, in any form or by any means, electronic, mechanical, photocopying, recording, or otherwise, without the prior permission in writing of the Publisher, or as expressly permitted by law, or under terms agreed with the appropriate reprographics rights organization.

A catalogue record for this book is available from the British Library.

ISBN-10 1-78201-068-8
ISBN-13 978-1-78201-068-5

Typeset in Baskerville by Michael Everson.

Cover design by Michael Everson.
Photo by Mark Stokes dreamstime.com/nomadimages_info

Printed and bound by LightningSource.

TABLE OF CONTENTS

Raglavar • Foreword xiv
Cot'heansow • Abbreviations xviii
A 1
  About 1
  According to 3
  Accuse 5
  After, afterwards 6
  Against 8
  Agree, agreement 9
  Always 11
  Amend *see* Improve .... (217)
  And 12
  Anger, to anger, to be angry 14
  Animal 17
  Apologize 20
  Appear 20
  Argue, argument 22
  Arise *see* Spring up .... (428)
  Army 22
  Article 22
  As *see* Like .... (262)
  Ascend 24
  At 26
  Attack 28
  Avenge *see* Vengence .... (456)
  Avoid 30
  Award 30
  Away 31
B 35
  Baby 35
  Bad 36
  Battle 39
  Beer 40
  Beg, beggar 41
  Behaviour, conduct 41
  Behind 42
  Big *see* Large .... (250)
  Body 43

GERYOW GWIR

- Bow (down) 45
- Box 45
- Branch 45
- Breast, breastplate 47
- Brush *see* Sweep .... (436)
- Build 48
- Bury 49
- But 51
- Buy 56

C **59**
- Call 59
- Calm 63
- Cease, to stop 64
- Chair 65
- Circular *see* Round .... (394)
- Circumcise 67
- Cloud 67
- Coast 68
- Colour 69
- Comfort, to comfort 70
- Command, commandment 73
- Company 79
- Conceive 81
- Concern 82
- Conclude 85
- Confess, confession, confessor 86
- Conquer, conqueror, conquest 89
- Consecrate, consecration 90
- Converse 92
- Cornish (language) 92
- Country 94
- Courage, courageous 97
- Course 98
- Court 98
- Create, creator, creation 99
- Crime, criminal 104
- Culpable 106

D **108**
- Damnation 108
- Day 108
- Deceit, to deceive 110
- Depart *see* Away .... (31)

GERYOW GWIR

Descend *see* Ascend .... (24)
Desert 113
Desire, to desire 114
Despise 118
Despite *see* Spite .... (426)
Destruction 120
Devonshire 121
Die 122
Disciple 123
Displease, displeasure 125
Down 126
Drink 128
Drive 130
Drop, to drop 131
Duke 132
Dwell *see* Live .... (264)

E 134
Ears 134
Easy 134
Element 135
Emperor, empire 136
England 137
Enjoy 137
Escape 138
Event 139
Ever *see* Never .... (304)
Everything 140
Exalt 140
Examine 141
Example 142
Exile, to exile 143
Experience 144
Eyes 144

F 147
Fan, to fan 147
Face 147
Farewell 149
Father 151
Feed 153
Feet 155
Flint 156
Flock 156

Flower.. 157
Fluent.. 159
Forest.. 161
Form... 162
Forsake... 163
Found.. 164
France.. 165
Free, to free, freedom.. 166
Friend.. 170
Fruit... 174
G **177**
Generous... 177
Gentle *see* Noble .... (308)
Germany.. 178
Get... 179
Glory, glorify, glorious...................................... 181
Gluttony.. 186
Govern, government, governor................................. 186
Grammar, grammarian.. 190
Grape... 191
Great *see* Large .... (250)
Grief, grievance, to grieve 192
Group... 197
H **199**
Hand, hands... 199
Harp.. 203
Hasten, haste 203
Horseman.. 205
Hour.. 208
House, houses... 210
How... 211
Hungry.. 213
Husband... 214
I **216**
I, me... 216
Important, significant.. 216
Impossible *see* Possible .... (337)
Improve, amend.. 217
Increase.. 218
Ireland 220
Irishman, Irish language...................................... 220

GERYOW GWIR

J **221**
   Jaw 221
   Jesus 221
   Jew 223
   Jewel 226
   John, John the Baptist 226
   Join 228
   Joy, joyful 229
   Judge, to judge 236
   Justice 240
K **242**
   Kind 242
   Kingdom 246
   Know 248
L **250**
   Large, great 250
   Later 257
   Lay waste *see* Waste .... (476)
   Lend 259
   Leper, leprosy 260
   Like, as 262
   Lion 264
   Live, to dwell 264
M **268**
   Man, men, people 268
   Marry, marriage 277
   Me *see* I .... (216)
   Mean, meaning 279
   Melt 282
   Mention, to mention 283
   Mercy 284
   Messenger 287
   Million 289
   Miracle 290
   Money 293
   Mortal 295
   Move, movement, motion 296
   Murder, to murder, murderer 298
   Must 299
N **303**
   Nation 303
   Never, ever 304

Noble 308
Nose 310
Number, to number 311
O **313**
   Obey, obedient, obedience 313
   Offend 317
   Offer 318
   Often 320
   Ointment 322
   Only 323
   Open 326
P **329**
   Pain 329
   Paint 332
   Paradise 332
   Payment 334
   People *see* Man . . . . (268)
   Please 334
   Poet 336
   Poison, to poison 337
   Possible, impossible 337
   Power, powerful 338
   Praise, to praise 342
   Presence, present, to present 344
   Priest 346
   Prince 348
   Promise, to promise 350
   Proud 354
   Public house 356
   Punish, punishment 356
   Purse 359
Q **360**
   Question 360
R **362**
   Read, reader 362
   Reason, to reason 364
   Rebel, to rebel, rebellion 370
   Rebuke, a rebuke, reproof 370
   Receive, receiver 373
   Record 375
   Redeemer, to redeem, redemption 377
   Regret *see* Repent . . . . (383)

GERYOW GWIR

Rejoice 378
Remain. 379
Remember, remembrance 379
Repent, regret. 383
Reprove *see* Rebuke . . . . (370)
Require. 385
Reverence. 386
Reward, to reward 388
Rich 390
River. 392
Romans 393
Room 393
Round, circular 394
S. 396
  Sake, for the sake of 396
  Salmon 398
  Salvation. 398
  Sanctify. 400
  Saxons. 401
  Scot, Scotland. 401
  Seagull 402
  Second 402
  Servant 404
  Serve, service 406
  Shake 410
  Shame, to shame 411
  Sharp, to sharpen 413
  Shop 415
  Short. 415
  Sight 417
  Sign. 419
  Significant *see* Important. . . . . (216)
  Small. 421
  Smell. 423
  Snake 425
  Spite, in spite of, despite. 426
  Spring up, to arise 428
  State 429
  Step. 431
  Stop *see* Cease . . . . (64)
  Succeed, success 433
  Swan. 435

Sweep, to brush 436
T **437**
　Table 437
　Talk *see* Converse .... (92)
　Tame 438
　Taste 438
　Tent 439
　Test *see* Try .... (447)
　Thank you 440
　Threaten 442
　Top 442
　Tradition 443
　Transform, transfigure 444
　Tribe 444
　Truth 445
　Try, to test 447
U **449**
　Understand, understanding 449
　Unity 452
　Use 453
V **456**
　Valley 456
　Vengence, to avenge 456
　Very 460
　Victory 462
　Vineyard 463
　Violence 463
　Virgin 464
　Voice 467
W **469**
　Wages 469
　Wales 470
　Wander 471
　Want to 472
　Wage war, warrior, war 474
　Waste, to lay waste 476
　Way 477
　Welcome, to welcome 479
　Work 483
　Worse, worst 487
Y **489**
　Young 489

GERYOW GWIR

Appendix A: The Calendar **491**
   Days of the Week 491
   The Sabbath 492
   Months of the Year 493
   Festivals and Holy Days 495

Appendix B: Unnecessary Coinages **498**
   *Ar 'battle, slaughter' 498
   *Argyans 'argument' 498
   *Arweth 'sign' 498
   *Blasa 'to taste' 498
   *Dampnyans 'damnation' 498
   *Denyon 'men' 498
   *Devnydhya 'to use' 499
   *Dewotty 'public house' 499
   *Dyvroa 'to exile' 499
   *Enwosa 'to circumcise' 499
   *Gos 'is known' 499
   *Gwerthjy 'shop' 499
   *Gwinreunen, *gwinreun 'grape, grapes' 500
   *Gwinlan 'vineyard' 500
   *Gwynsella 'to fan' 500
   *Hebaskhe 'to calm, to soothe' 500
   *Kelghyek 'circular, round' 500
   *Lenna 'to read' 500
   *Pow Sows, *Bro Sows 'England' 500
   *Rôsya 'to wander' 500
   *Sans'he 'to sanctify' 501
   *Sêlya 'to found' 501
   *Talas 'payment' 501
   *Temptyans 'temptation' 501
   *Trodrehy *see* *Enwosa 501
   *Treusfurvya 'to transform, to transfigure' 501
   *Yalgh 'purse' 501
   *Yêdhowek 'Jewish, Hebraic' 501

Appendix C: Loanwords **502**
   Verbs borrowed from Old English 502
   Verb borrowed from Old French 502
   Verbs borrowed from Modern English 502
   Verbs borrowed from Middle English 503

RAGLAVAR
FOREWORD

If one compares the vocabulary laid out in the handbooks of revived Cornish with the lexicon of the traditional texts, one is struck by how different are the two. From the beginnings Unified Cornish in the 1920s it appears that revivalists have tended to avoid words borrowed from English, replacing them with more "Celtic" etyma. Thus Nance, for example, knew that **mona** was the ordinary word for 'money', but used **arhans** instead. He understood that **enep** was absent from Middle Cornish but preferred the word to the attested **fâss** 'face'. Similarly he preferred the unattested ***comolen** 'cloud' to the attested word **cloud**. He preferred **blejen**, respelt from Old Cornish ***blodon***, to **flour**, the only word for 'flower' in the Middle Cornish texts. Two noteworthy coinages by Nance are ***dyvroa** 'to exile', although the verb **exîlya** is in *Origo Mundi* and ***blasa** 'to taste', when **tâstya** is the only word in the texts. Many further examples of Nance's purism could be cited. More recently others have gone a step further and have in their handbooks advised learners, for example, to replace the attested **pors** 'purse' with the unattested ***yalgh** or the attested word **fanya** 'to fan' with the unattested ***gwynsella**. Again such examples could be multiplied greatly.

Nowhere is this purism so noticeable as in the verbs. Since the beginning of Cornish as a written language verbs have been borrowed from the English current at the time. One of the earliest is **redya** 'to read', which was already in Cornish by the time of the *Old Cornish Vocabulary*. Our earliest long text is *Pascon agan Arluth* (PA), written probably at the end of the fourteenth century. PA already contains *inter alia* such obviously borrowed verbs as **acordya** 'to agree', **blâmya** 'to blame'; **comfortya** 'to comfort'; **convyctya** 'to convict'; **decêvya** 'to deceive'; **desîrya** 'to desire'; **dyscomfortya** 'to discomfort'; **grauntya** 'to grant'; **jùjya** 'to judge'; **praisya** 'to praise'; **rebukya** 'to rebuke'; **recêva** 'to receive'; **servya** 'to serve'; **shakya** 'to shake'; **spêdya** 'to succeed'; **strîvya** 'to strive'; **temptya** 'to tempt'; **tackya** 'to nail' and **tùchya** 'to touch'.

It is also worth pointing out that many of the verbs frequently used by revivalists are themselves borrowings from English, although the origin of such items is not always recognized. The following verbs, for example, are all borrowed from English: **ancombra** 'to trouble' (Middle English *encombren*); **assoylya** 'to solve' (Middle English *assoilen*); **crùllya** 'to curl' (Middle English *crullen*); **gordhya** 'to worship' (Middle English *worthien*); **gwaya** 'to move' (Middle English *weien*); **gwedhra** 'to wither' (Early Modern English *wither*); **gwetyas** 'to be careful, to hope' (Middle English *waiten*); **mellya** 'to interfere' (Middle English *medlen, mellen*); **sconya** 'to refuse' (Middle English *schonen*); **sewya** 'to follow' (Middle English *seuen*); **sordya** 'to rise up' (Middle English *sourden*) and **trailya** 'to turn' (Middle English *trailen*).

John Tregear and the author of *Sacrament an Alter* are both fond of using verbs borrowed from English. It should be noticed, however, that verbs like Tregear's ***dryvya*** 'to drive' and ***shynya*** 'to shine' are Middle English in form, that is to say, neither has undergone the Great Vowel Shift. They were thus not adopted from English by Tregear himself, but had been in Cornish since the fourteenth century at the latest. Tregear and *Sacrament an Alter* use **ùnderstondya, ùnderstandya** 'to understand', a verb which is not attested elsewhere. As I attempt to show below, the verb **convedhes**, most commonly used by revivalists to mean 'to understand', does not really mean 'to understand' as much as 'to perceive'. **Convedhes** is an exclusively Late Cornish word, being found only in the *Creation of the World* (1611) and in Pryce (1798). It is a variant of the verb *canfos 'to perceive' (***canfethis, canfethys*** in *Bewnans Ke*). The verb **ùnderstondya, ùnderstandya** was adopted into Cornish probably because speakers believed no native verb expressed the notion of understanding adequately. It is also likely that **ùnderstondya** had been in Cornish long before it first appears in John Tregear's sermons (c. 1555). After all, we know that Tregear's **remembra** 'to remember' and **overcùmya** 'to overcome' were already in use in *Beunans Meriasek* (1504).

If an obvious borrowing is attested in only one text, we have no way of knowing whether the item in question was ever part of the vocabulary of traditional Cornish. If, on the other hand, a borrowing is attested independently in at least two texts, it is very likely that the word was well-known in the traditional language. For example the word **spryngya** 'to spring' is attested both in *Bewnans Ke* and in Tregear's homilies; it is likely therefore to have been a established item of the native lexicon. Similarly the word **profet**, *pl.* **profettys** 'prophet' is attested in Tregear, in *Sacrament an Alter* and in Rowe. It was clearly therefore a well-established word in Cornish as early as the mid sixteenth-century. The word **dysseytya** 'to deceive' is attested once in *Pascon agan Arluth*, but nowhere else, being replaced (even in PA) by **decêvya**. We cannot, therefore, be sure that **dysseytya** was ever an essential element of the Middle Cornish lexicon.

In the following pages I attempt, with examples, to elucidate some small part of the vocabulary of the Cornish texts. We have all been guilty of using words that were never part of the lexicon of traditional Cornish. As a result some Cornish written in recent years has the appearance of a conlang, rather than of a revitalized form of a historical language.

I have suggested elsewhere that the influence of English has been decisive for the phonology of Middle Cornish. It seems to me also that the influence of English has been of the greatest importance for the vocabulary of Cornish. Breton was, naturally enough, largely untouched by English, since the language developed and flourished in the ambit of French. Moreover in modern times French borrowings have often been replaced by more native words. Welsh, because it had so many more speakers than did Cornish, and was not so thoroughly penetrated by English, developed its medieval and early modern vocabulary along native lines. The more Celtic appearance the vocabulary of both Welsh and Breton has been a source of envy to some Cornish revivalists. From Nance onwards such purists have believed that English borrowings disfigured Cornish and in some sense did not belong in the language. They considered that revived Cornish would be more authentic, if as many borrowings as possible were replaced by native or Celtic words. Such a perception is perhaps understandable in the context of the Cornish language as a badge of ethnic identity. From a historical and linguistic perspective, however, it is misplaced. Cornish, unlike its sister languages, had always adopted words from English. Indeed it is these English borrowings which give the mature language of the Middle Cornish period its distinctive flavour. Cornish without the English element is quite simply not Cornish.

Cornish is unlike both Welsh and Breton in that it lacks native speakers. The closest learners of Cornish can come to the traditional language is in

GERYOW GWIR

the Cornish texts in their original spelling. Those should be the touchstone for our own attempts to speak and write Cornish. Where there are gaps in our vocabulary, it may be necessary to devise or borrow terms. Where, however, a suitable borrowing from English is attested in traditional Cornish, that item should be used in preference to an unattested word devised on the basis of Welsh and/or Breton.

If the Cornish speaking community were large and contained many people for whom Cornish were a native language, the situation would be quite different. The language, including its lexicon, would be determined by the linguistic practice of its speakers. The words used by native speakers of Cornish would be decisive. As it is, the number of people fluent in Cornish is pitifully small and does not at present appear able to perpetuate itself. Since there is no sizeable community speaking revived Cornish as a native language, we are compelled to rely on the only native speakers available to us, namely the writers of the traditional texts. We must follow them as closely as we can. It is not legitimate for us at this stage in the revival to attempt to reshape the language according to our own preferences.

In a work of this kind misprints and other errors are bound to occur. If any reader notices typographical or similar errors, the publisher will be very pleased to hear of them. Errata submitted will be made available online at *http://evertype.com/books/ggw-errata.html* before their incorporation into subsequent editions of this work.

I hope that this book will in some small measure assist learners of Cornish to speak and to write a form of the language more closely related to what remains to us of traditional Cornish.

Nicholas Williams
Dublin 2014

COT'HEANSOW
ABBREVIATIONS

AB = Edward Lhuyd, *Archæologia Britannica* (London 1707 [reprinted Shannon 1971])

ACB = William Pryce, *Archaeologia Cornu-Britannica* (London 1790 [reprinted Menston 1972])

BF = O. J. Padel, *The Cornish Writings of the Boson Family* (Redruth 1975)

Bilbao MS = Henry Jenner 'The Cornish Manuscript in the provincial library at Bilbao, Spain', *Journal of the Royal Institution of Cornwall* 21 (1924-25): 421-37

BK = Graham Thomas & Nicholas Williams (editors), *Bewnans Ke : The Life of St Kea* (Exeter 2007)

BM = Whitley Stokes (editor), *Beunans Meriasek: the life of St Meriasek, Bishop and confessor, a Cornish drama* (London: Trübner and Co. 1872)

Bodewryd MS = Andrew Hawke, 'A Rediscovered Cornish-English Vocabulary', *Cornish Studies: Nine* (2001): 83-104.

Bodinar = "William Bodinar's Letter", LAM: 244

Borde = Andrew Borde, cited from J. Loth, 'Cornique moderne', *Archiv für Celtische Lexicographie* 1 (1900): 224-28

Borlase = William Borlase, *Antiquities of the County of Cornwall* (London 1754)

Carew = F.E. Halliday (editor), *Richard Carew of Antony, the survey of Cornwall* (London 1953)

CF = *The Charter Fragment*, text from E. Campanile, 'Un frammento scenico medio-cornico', *Studi e saggi linguistici* 60-80, supplement to *L'Italia Dialettale 26*

CPNE = O. J. Padel, *Cornish Place-Name Elements* (Nottingham 1985)

CW = Whitley Stokes, *Gwreans an Bys: The Creation of the World* (London 1864 [reprinted 2003 by Kessinger Publishing, Montana, USA]

Exeter Consistory Court = Deposition of the Bishop's Consistory Court at Exeter (1572). Quoted from Martyn F. Wakelin, *Language and history in Cornwall* (Leicester University Press 1975): 89

GERYOW GWIR

Geirlyer Kyrnweig = Edward Lhuyd's Cornish glossary, National Library of Wales. MS Llanstephan 84.
GMW = D. Simon Evans, *A Grammar of Middle Welsh* (Dublin 1964)
Gwavas MS = BM Add. MS 28, 554 f. 106, edited by R. Hooper, *Old Cornwall* vol. ix, no. 11, Autumn 1984
HMSB = Roparz Hemon, *A Historical Morphology and Syntax of Breton* (Dublin 1984)
Jago = F. W. P. Jago, *Dialect of Cornwall* (Truro 1882)
JBoson = "Cornish writings of John Boson", in BF
JCH = *John of Chyanhor*, in O.J. Padel, *The Cornish Writings of the Boson Family* (Redruth 1975)
JJenkins = two poems by James Jenkins, quoted in Pryce (1790)
JKeigwin = 1. John Keigwin's translation of the letter of Charles I in Tremenheere MSS, Morrab Library, Penzance, typescript edition by P.A.S. Pool (1995); 2. His translation of *Genesis* 1, from Gwavas collection, British Library Add MS 28554
JTonkin = two poems by John Tonkin (c. 1693 & c. 1695) in LAM: 224-228
KmK = E. G. R. Hooper (ed.), *Kemysk Kernewek* (Camborne 1964)
KS = Kernowek Standard
LAM = Alan Kent and Tim Saunders (editors), *Looking at the Mermaid: A Reader in Cornish Literature 900-1900* (London 2000)
Lh = Edward Lhuyd
Lhuyd MSS = proverbs from Lhuyd's Manuscripts in W.C. Borlase, "A Collection of hitherto unpublished Proverbs and rhymes, in the Ancient Cornish Language", *Journal of the Royal Institution of Cornwall* 1886: 10
Nance = R. M. Nance, *English-Cornish Dictionary* (Marazon, 1952)
NBoson = Nicholas Boson, "Nebbaz Gerriau dro tho Carnoack", in BF
NWB = A. S. D. Smith (Caradar), *Nebes Whethlow Ber* (Camborne [1946])
OCV = Eugene V. Graves, *The Old Cornish Vocabulary* (PhD thesis, Columbia University 1962)
Oliver Oldwanton = Michael Flachman (editor), 'The First English Epistolary Novel: "The Image of Idleness (1555)", *Studies in Philology* 87, No. 1 (Winter 1990). University of North Carolina Press
OM = "Origo Mundi" in Edwin Norris, *The Ancient Cornish Drama* (London 1859 [reprinted New York & London 1968]: i 1-219
PA = Harry Woodhouse (editor), *The Cornish Passion Poem in facsimile* (Penryn 2002)
PC = "Passio Christi" in Edwin Norris, *The Ancient Cornish Drama* (London 1859 [reprinted New York & London 1968]: i 221-479

GERYOW GWIR

Pender = letter by Oliver Pender (August 1711) in LAM: 239

Pryce = ACB

RD = "Resurrexio Domini" in Edwin Norris, *The Ancient Cornish Drama* (London 1859 [reprinted New York & London 1968]: ii 1-199

RSymonds = Charles Edward Long (editor), *Diary of the Marches of the Royal Army during the Great Civil War; kept by Richard Symonds* (Camden Society 1859)

Rowe = J. Loth (editor), 'Textes inédits en cornique moderne', *Revue Celtique* 23, 173-200.

SA = *Sacrament an Alter*, text quoted from an unpublished edition by D.H. Frost (St David's College 2003)

Scawen MSS = proverbs and rhymes from Mr. Scawen's Manuscripts in W.C. Borlase, "A Collection of hitherto unpublished Proverbs and rhymes, in the Ancient Cornish Language", *Journal of the Royal Institution of Cornwall* 1886: 9-10

TH = John Tregear, *Homelyes xiii in Cornyshe* (British Library Additional MS 46, 397) [text from a cylclostyled text published by Christopher Bice (s.l. [1969])

UC = Unified Cornish

UCR = Unified Cornish Revised

Ustick MSS = proverbs and rhymes from Ustick's Manuscripts in W.C. Borlase, 'A Collection of hitherto unpublished Proverbs and rhymes, in the Ancient Cornish Language; from the Manuscripts of Dr Borlase', *Journal of the Royal Institution of Cornwall* 1886: 11-12

WBodinar = P.A.S. Pool & O.J. Padel, 'William Bodinar's Letter, 1776', *Journal of the Royal Institution of Cornwall*, New Series, vol. 7 (1975-76), 231-36

WGwavas = writings by William Gwavas in ACB and LAM.

A

ABOUT *(prep.)*
When this means 'around', it is rendered in Cornish by **adro dhe**:

*guetyeugh bones avorow ov conys yn crys a'n dre war beyn cregy ha tenne **adro the'n temple** hep gow* 'make sure to be working in the middle of the town around the temple on pain of being hanged and drawn indeed' OM 2299-302
*me a thuk curyn a spern nep try our **adro thu'm pen*** 'I wore a crown of thorns about three hours around my head' RD 2554-55
*ha lemen sur golvygyen **adro thym** yma cothys* 'and now indeed radiance has fallen around me' BM 3681-82
*an moar brase yn cutt termyn **adro thom tyre** a vyth dreys rag y wetha pur elyn* 'the great sea will be brought round my land in a short while to keep it very clear' CW 88-90.

When 'about' means 'concerning' 'Revived Cornish has in the past used **in kever** with both nouns and possessive adjectives. This usage is difficult to justify, for several reasons, A) **in kever** is never used with nouns; B) **in kever** does not mean 'about, concerning' but rather 'with respect to, regarding'; C) **in kever** is rare. There are only five examples attested in all Middle and Late Cornish:

*whet kerghough thy'mmo pilat **yn y geuer** del fuef badt* 'still fetch me Pilate, as I have been bad with respect to him' RD 1885-86
*me a vyn pesy gevyans boys mar thyek **yth keuer*** 'I will beg forgiveness for being so lethargic regarding you' BM 3359-60
*maria re buff re logh **in the gever*** 'Mary, I have been too negligent towards you' BM 3798-99
*hag amyndya ef a ra **y'th kevar** del vo reson* 'and he will improve in your regard as is reasonable' BK 916-17
*mal dha va prêv erra e wrêg guitha kympez **et i gever** erra po nag erra* 'that he might establish whether his wife was remaining faithful to him, was she or not' BF: 18.

In traditional Cornish 'around, concerning' can be rendered in four different ways: A) **a** 'from'; B) **adro dhe**, which is a Late Cornish use,

1

presumably in imitation of English 'about'; C) **ow tùchya, ow tùchya dhe** 'touching, concerning' and on occasion the particle **ow** is omitted; D) the English word **tùchyng tùchyng dhe** 'touching, concerning' is used with the sense 'about, concerning', though it can also mean 'with respect to, regarding'. Here are some examples of all four:

A **a** 'concerning, about'
Anotho *marth es preder worth y wythyes govynne* 'If you are anxious about him ask of his keeper' OM 608-09
pur wyryoneth re geusys ***ahanaf*** *re'n geth hethev* 'about me you have spoken very truth by this day today' PC 1587-88
me re glowes ov map wek ***ahanes*** *covs mur thadder* 'I have heard much good spoken about you, my dear son' BM 527-28
yma notijs sur ha covsis mur thadder ***an*** *keth den na* 'there is noted surely and much good spoken concerning that man' BM 2772-74.

B **adro dhe** 'concerning, about'
Nebbaz Gerriau ***dro tho*** *Carnoack* 'A Few Words about Cornish' BF: 25
kar dre vedno why gwellaz urt hemma ***dro tho*** *an emp[iri]ck Angwin* 'as you will see from this about Angwin the empiric' BF: 25
Me a glowaz ***dro tho*** *an karak Mean Omber* 'I heard about the rock Mean Omber' BF: 25
Ma lever bean rebbam ***dro tho*** *an Arlothas Curnow* 'I have a book beside me about the Duchess of Cornwall' BF: 29.

C **ow tùchya** 'touching, concerning'
An kensa tra vgy ***ow tuchia*** *an creacion a mab den* 'The first thing concerning the creation of mankind' TH 1
An re ma ew an very gyrryow agan savyoure ***ow tochia*** *an kerensa agan kyscristian* 'These are the very words of our Saviour concerning the love of our fellow Christian' TH 22
Omma ow ommyttya aucthors erall heb deweth, a dus coyth auncient ***ow tochya*** *an primacie* 'Here omitting countless other authors, of ancient men of yore, concerning the primacy' TH 46
Rag henna, tus vas, why a wore lymmyn pan dra ew an lell crygyans ***ow tochia*** *thyn sacrament an aulter* 'Therefore, good people, you know know what is the true belief concerning the sacrament of the altar' TH 58
hag yth ew in sertan degre a excelency the vos verefies in den rag ***tuchia*** *an estate ay originall innocenci* 'and certainly a degree of excellency is to be verified in man concerning his original state of innocence' TH 3
Whath, rag ***tochya*** *thyn gyrryow ma, hem ew ow corffe vy, onyn vith an Aweylers nyg eus ow cull mencyon na declarasion war hemma* 'Still, concerning these words, This is my body, not one of the evangelists mentions or makes any statement upon this' TH 53

Tuchia *an seconde, ken na vo travith na hene mas an generall cregians an chatholik egglos* 'Concerning the second, though it be nothing other than the general faith of the catholic Church' TH 55.

D **tùchyng**
Me a wor na'th es paraw **tochyng** *hegar benenas* 'I know you have no equal with regard to lovable women' BK 1136-37.
Ny worthebe' thotha **toching** *the'n questons eral* 'I shall not anser him concerning the other questions' BK 2127-28

For 'about, concerning' with nouns Cornish speakers would be well advised to use **a, ow tùchya** (**dhe**) or **adro dhe** rather than **in kever**.

ACCORDING TO

Traditional Cornish has several words to express this idea. The first is **herwyth**:

herwyth *y volungeth ef ov map certan y fyth gurys* 'according to his will, my son, certainly will be done' OM 1320-21
dyth brues y wregh ysethe ol an bys ma rak iugge pup ol **herwyth** *y ober* 'on the day of judgement you will sit to judge all in this world according to their deeds' PC 814-16
ha **herwyth** *agas laha ha concyans guregh y iuggye* 'and according to your law and conscience judge him' PC 1978-79.

A much commoner way of saying 'according to' is **warlergh** (the basic meaning of which is 'after'):

y a ruge aʒesympys oll **war lyrgh** *y arhadow* 'they all immediately did according to his command' PA 247d
rag henna hep falladow ol **warlergh** *the gussullyow bys venytha my a wra* 'therefore without fail I shall always do according to your counsels' OM 2268-70
a tus vas why re welas fetel formyas dev an tas nef ha nor **war lergh** *y vrys* 'good people you have seen that God, the Father of heaven, created heaven and earth according to his intention' OM 2825-27
warlergh *sen luk me an kyff lel thyugh in awell* 'according to St Luke I find it truly for you in the gospel' BM 391-93
kowses **warlerth** *an maner an bobill* 'spoken according to the manner of the people' TH 1
Walkyow ha gwandrow **warlyrth** *an spuris* 'Walk and proceed according to the Spirit' TH 16a

according to   **GERYOW GWIR**

kynsa the wothfes fatell res thyn scripture bos vnderstondyys **warlerth** *an generall menyng a egglos crist* 'first to know that the scripture must be understood according to the general sense of Christ's Church' TH 18

hag yth esans ow pewa **warlerth** *an letterall sens a la moyses mar compis in face an bys* 'and they lived according to the literal sense of the law of Moses so correctly before the world' TH 26a

then stat a den perfect, **warlyrth** *an measure an lene oys a crist* 'to the state of perfect man, according to the measure of the full age of Christ' TH 42

ha keneffra ethan skelle **worler** *go kenda* 'and every winged bird according to their kind' JKeigwin.

Tregear and SA often use the expression **acordyng dhe**:

ny rug du an tas a neff mas commondya ha **according thy** *blonogeth oll creators a ve gwrys gans an ger a thu* 'God the Father of heaven merely commanded, and according to his will all creatures were made by the word of God' TH 1

an very mab du an second person in dryngys **according the** *blonogath y das, a gemeras warnotha an nature a then* 'the very Son of God, the second person in the Trinity according to the will of his Father took upon himself the nature of man' TH 12a

pan ruga colynwell pub tra **according then** *scriptur han prophetes* 'when he had fulfilled everything according to the scripture and the prophets' TH 15

fatell ronns y tewlell drog pobill in prison, kemeras in kerth aga pith, ha treweythow aga bewnans **according then** *la an wlas* 'that they throw evil people in prison, take away their possessions and sometimes their life according to the law of the land' TH 24a

han punysment dew ragtha a vith brassa inweth **according the** *gyrryow crist in v-as chapter a S mathew* 'and the punishment due for it will be greater also according to the words of Christ in the fifth chapter of St Matthew' TH 28a

Inweth awosa y assencion thyn neff, **according thy** *promes eff a thanvonas then dore an spuris sans* 'Also after his ascension into heaven, according to his promise he sent down the Holy Spirit' TH 36

ha wosa henna in dede eff a ros henna **according the** *promysse* 'and thereafter indeed he gave that according to the promise' TH 51a

accordyng the *quantyte aga devotion* 'according to the quantity of their devotion' SA 64.

Since the expression **acordyng dhe** 'according to' is attested in both TH and SA, it is likely that it was well established in the spoken Cornish of the sixteenth century. We need not, however, use it widely in the revived language, where **warlergh** is probably the preposition of choice.

TO ACCUSE

In PA and OM the word for 'to accuse' is **cùhudha, cùhudhas**:

Iȝ esa an venyn ganse paris ens ȝy **huhuȝas** 'There was a woman with them; they were ready to accuse her' PA 33b

pema yn meth crist ȝyȝy neb a vyn ȝe **guhuȝa** 'Where, said Christ, to her, is he who wishes to accuse you?' PA 34b

mur a dus o cuntullys er y byn ȝy **guhuȝas** 'many people had gathered against him to accuse him' PA 88d

Eua ny allaf methes rag ovn ty tho'm **kuhuthe** 'Eve, I cannot say, lest you accuse me' OM 159-60

awos travyth ny wrussen benytha the **gvhuthas** 'I would not accuse you for anything' OM 163-64.

Notice also that **cuhuthioc** 'accuser' is found at OCV §957. The word **acûsya**, however, replaces **cùhudha** in PC:

da vye thy'n mos ganso may hyllyn y **acusye** 'it would be good for us to go in order to accuse him' PC 1624-25

pan fue genough **acusyys** *ef ny gafas fout yn bys* 'when he was accused by you, he found no fault at all' PC 1859-60

lauar thy'mo vy yn scon yv ty myghtern yethewon kepar del fus **acusyys** 'tell me quickly, are you the king of the Jews as you have been accused?' PC 1997-99

towel auel vn bobba a wruk pan fue **acussys** 'he was silent like a fool when he was accused' PC 2385-86.

Lhuyd also uses **acûsya**, which suggests he heard the word used while he was in Cornwall:

Mi a uon en ta lauer boz lîaz tîz (pôrletryz ha pôrskientek en traou erel) a **akiuzya** *ha damnya peb prediryanz adrô kuitha am'àn an Kouzanz Kernûak* 'I know very well that many people (very learned and very wise in other matters) accuse and condemn all thought of preserving the Cornish dialect' AB: 224.

It should also be remembered that the only attested word for 'accusation' in the texts is **acûsacyon**:

ha na vons y oppressys gans fals **accusacion** 'and less they be oppressed by false accusation' TH 25.

In the revived language 'to accuse' can either be **cùhudha** or **acûsya**. 'Accusation' is perhaps best rendered by **acûsacyon**.

after

AFTER, AFTERWARDS

When 'after' is a preposition with temporal sense, e.g. 'after the storm', 'after the meeting', etc., the Cornish equivalent is **wosa, awosa**:

Wose *cous ha lafurye an vaner a vye da kemeres croust hag eve* 'After talking and working it would be a good thing to take a snack and to drink' OM 1899-901

tommans onan dour war tan rag **woge** *soper certan my a woulgh ol agas trys* 'let one heat water on the fire, for after supper indeed I shall wash the feet of you all' PC 833-35

reys yv thy'm agy the lyst emloth worth an antecryst hag ef thu'm gruthyl marow **wose** *try deyth ha hanter bos yn nef yn vhelder gans cryst myghtern hep parow* 'It is necessary for me to fight in the lists against the Antichrist and for him to kill me; after three and a half days I must be in heaven on high with Christ, peerless King' RD 223-28

mar ny rug crist kemeras kygg an wyrhes maria fatell ew an promes ny colynwys, a rug du promysya **wosa** *an towle agan hyndasow adam hag lynnyath eva pan rug an tas aga dryvya in mes a paradice* 'if Christ did not take upon him the flesh of the Virgin Mary, how has the promise fulfilled which God promised after the fall of our forebears Adam and the lineage of Eve, when the Father drove them out of paradise?' TH 13

ha **wosa** *an tyrmyn cut a vethyn ny omma in present ha mortall bewnans ma* 'and after the short time that we shall be here in this present mortal life' TH 26

Ha **wosa** *agan bewnans omma in bys* 'And after our life in the world' TH 35

Inweth **awosa** *y assencion thyn neff, according thy promes, eff a thanvonas then dore an spurissans warben y abosteleth, kepar dell ra S luk scriffa* 'Also after his ascension into heaven, according to his promise, he sent down the Holy Spirit upon his apostles, as St Luke writes' TH 36

An pith o 300 blethan **wosa** *crist* 'The thing was 300 years after Christ' TH 49.

'After that, afterwards, ' is rendered **(a)wosa henna**:

ha **wose henna** *evyn pep ol adro draght a wyn rag comfortye y golon* 'and afterwards let us all about drink a draught of wine to cheer the heart' OM 2626-68

hen yv agan crygyans oll ihesu cryst woge merwel y vones gorrys yn pry **woge henna** *dasserghy the pen try dyth* 'that is the faith of us all, that after his death Christ was put in the earth and afterwards rose at the end of three days' RD 954-58

Ea, lowar c. blethan **awosa henna** *eff a promysyas the viterne Dauid fatell re haes inweth dos anotheff* 'Yea, many hundreds of years thereafter he promised to king David that progeny would come from him' TH 13a

ha kepar dell rug eff nena promysya, in della **wosa henna** *eff a rug y perfumya* 'and as he then promised, so thereafter did he perform' TH 51a

Nenna mose alez tho scole ha **ugge hedda** *mose tho Frenk* 'Then I went away to school and thereafter to France' BF: 29

durt an Romans meskez gen a Brittez, po **ugge hedna** *durt an Sausen* 'from the Romans mixed with the Britons, or thereafter from the Saxons' BF: 29.

'After this, afterwards, later' is rendered **wosa hemma**:

rag sythyn **wose hemma** *dew vgens dyth my a as glaw the gothe awartha* 'for a week from now I will let rain fall from above for forty days' OM 1026-28

ty a wra **woge hemma** *gorre an tus alena bys yn tyreth a thynwa lanwes leyth ha mel kefrys* 'you shall hereafter take the people hence to the land that flows with fullness of milk and honey as well' OM 1427-30

woge hemma *ty a wel map dev sur owth esethe abart dyow th'y lawe the'n tas dev arluth huhel* 'hereafter you shall see the Son of God sitting on the right hand (praised be he) of the Father, high God' PC 1327-30

grammer an geffa deffry y vyea tek ha worshypp **wosa helma** 'if he were to learn grammar indeed it would be nice and honour hereafter' BM 20-22

omma lemen fondya plays dre voth ihesu a vercy sur me a vyn **awose helme** *eglos the worthya crist deth ha nos* 'here now I will found a place through the will of Jesus of mercy surely, hereafter a church to worship Christ day and night' BM 720-24

Bohogogneth abreth du remoconn then cur yth yv **wose helma** 'Poverty for the sake of God is removal to the court of heaven hereafter' BM 2010-12

drens hy ov map dymo vy ha gruens ov servia deyly arta **awose helma** 'let her bring my son to me and let her serve me daily again hereafter' BM 3696-98

Andelna eu pe na veth nab peth gwrez lebben ita, na scant vedna bose gwrez **ugge hemma** 'So it is, if nothing is done now in it, hardly will it be done hereafter' BF: 27

Eahas da why leben ha **vge hema** 'Health to you now and hereafter' BF: 39.

Wosa 'after' is on occasion replaced by **warlergh** 'after':

Ha dew a thuk dustuny yn clewsons ow leuerell pur wyr y fenne terry an tempel cref hay wuʒell **war lyrgh henna** *dre vestry yn tressa dyth heb fyllell dre nerth bras yn drehevy* 'And two bore witness they heard him say indeed he would destroy the mighty temple and build it thereafter by power on the third day; without fail by great strength he would raise it up' PA 91a-d

Rag an traytor a gewsys ha ʒerag leas huny **war lyrgh y vonas** *leʒys ʒen tressa dyth y seuy* 'For the traitor spoke and to many that after being killed he would rise on the third day' PA 240ab

sav me **war lergh drehevel** *a's dyerbyn dyougel yn galile ol warbarth* 'but I after rising will meet them all together certainly in Galilee' PC 896-98

warlergh henna *begythys ty a veth sur ha golhys may fy salov* 'thereafter you will be baptized and washed so that you may be healed' BM 1820-22

rag me an creys sans in neff pur thefry y vones eff **warlergh y ober** *oma* 'for I believe that he is a saint in heaven in very truth after his labour here' BM 4404-06

warlergh henna *leferis gans ancov y voys tuchys* 'thereafter he said that he had been touched by death' BM 4422-23

Mar pewas Christ, me a grys, **warlergh mirwall**, *ow du Jovyn a'n dathorthas der e ras* 'If Christ lived, I believe, after dying, my god Jovyn resurrected him by his grace' BK 316-19

after   **GERYOW GWIR**

Warlyrgh henna *ny a'n myr* 'After that we will look at him' BK 345
Warlyrgh hemma *benary mar petheth mettys i'n pow, re'n nor a'm dog ha re Astrot ha Jovyn in dyspyt the'th nassyoyn, the vaw the honen a'th crog* 'Hereafter for ever if you are found in the land, by the earth that bore me, and by Astrot and Jovyn, in spite of your nation, your own servant will hang you' BK 461-66.

Perhaps the most important point to notice here is that 'later, thereafter' in Cornish is rendered by **wosa henna** and 'later, hereafter' is **wosa hemma**. One cannot use **dewetha** 'later' in either case. **Ev a dheuth wosa hedna** 'he came later' and **me a vydn côwsel orthowgh wosa hebma** 'I will speak to you later' are both correct. **Me a vydn y wil ragowgh *dewetha** is not; see also s.v. '**LATER**' below.

AGAINST

In Middle Cornish the default word for 'against' was ***erbynn***. This combined with possessive adjectives to give ***er ow fynn*** 'against me', ***er dha bynn*** 'against you', etc. By the middle of the sixteenth century ***erbynn*** had given way to ***warbynn***, ***war ow fynn***, etc. In Late Cornish this appears as ***warbydn***:

A **erbyn**

er aga fyn *betegyns crist vn ger ny leuery* 'against them, however, Christ was not saying a word' PA 96d

prag y tolste sy hep ken worth hy thempte the dyrry an frut ***erbyn*** *ov dyfen* 'why did you deceive without cause tempting her to pluck the fruit contrary to my prohibition?' OM 302-04

yma an turant heb mar ***er agis pyn*** *drehevys* 'the tyrant has of course risen up against you' BM 3239-40

an epscop purguir a thuea the certen plas ***er ov fyn*** 'the bishop indeed will come to a certain place to meet me' BM 3902-03

palm ha floris kekyffris ***er y byn*** *degis a ve* 'palm and flowers also were brought to him' PA 29d

eff a rug acceptya paciently pub tra a ve kowsys thotha eff haga russens gull ***er y byn*** *eff* 'he paciently accepted everything that was spoken against him and what they did against him' TH 23.

B **warbyn**

pegh o an pith a rug then kyge stryvya gans an spuris han spuris ***warbyn*** *an kyge* 'sin was what made the flesh strive with the spirit and the spirit against the flesh' TH 3

me a behas warbyn gwlas neff ha ***war the byn*** *ge, ow thas* 'I have sinned agains the kingdom of heaven and against you, my father' TH 9a

GERYOW GWIR agree

war an garrak ma me a vyn byldya ow egglos, han yeattys a yffarne ny ra prevaylya **war y byn** 'upon this rock I shall build my Church, and the gates of hell will not prevail against it' TH 44

an nethewan a ve spitfull **warbyn** *agen arluth Christ* 'the Jews were very spiteful against our lord Christ' SA 61

pyw henna a veth mar vold cowse gear **warbyn** *lucyfer* 'who is that who is so bold as to speak a word against Lucifer?' CW 163-64.

C **warbydn**

envyes ove **war y bydn** 'I am resentful against him' CW 440

Na raz tiah gow **warbidn** *de contrevak* 'You shalt not swear falsehood against your neighbour' ACB: E e 4

Buz, mor mennow direvall **warbidn** *an pow yeine, why dalveya gowas an brossa mine* 'but if you will build against cold country, you must get the biggest stones' ACB: F f 3

Ha ryney vedn dirra **bidn** *mor, ha gwenz* 'And those will survive against sea and wind' ACB: F f 3

Ha neb yn mânah a trailiaz e gein **uarbidn** *an tùll* 'And a certain monk turned his back to the hole' BF: 18

pecare ter era ny gava an pehadurrian **war agen pedne** 'just as we forgive the sinners against us' BF: 41.

In accordance with the principle of *tota Cornicitas* the following ought be allowed in the revived language: **erbynn, er ow fynn**, etc.; **warbynn, war ow fynn**, etc. and **warbydn, wàr ow fydn**, etc.

AGREE, AGREEMENT

The adjective **unver** means 'unanimous' and is attested once:

y fons ***vnver*** *yntreʒe kepar ha del wovyny dek warn ugens a vone yn vn payment y wrens ry* 'they were unanimous among themselves and just as he asked they would give him thirty pieces of money as one payment' PA 39cd

The verb **unverhe** 'to be of one mind, to agree' is a derivative of **unver**. It is attested twice in the form of the verbal adjective:

Vnferheys *kepar del on berth in eglos sent sampson bethens eff consecratis* 'As we are agreed, let him be consecrated in the church os St Samson' BM 2982-84

Erna vony ***unwerhys****, neffra ny veth da ow cher* 'Until we are reconciled, never shall I be content' BK 1035-36.

The word **acord** means 'agreement' and is well attested:

agree   **GERYOW GWIR**

Kyn nag off den skentyll pur par del won lauaraff 3ys yntre du ha pehadur **acord** *del ve kemerys* 'Though I am not a very clever man, as I know so I shall tell you how agreement was adopted between God and the sinner' PA 8ab

my ny dorraf bys vycken an **acord** *vs lemyn gureys yntre my ha lynneth den* 'I shall never break the agreement made between me and the human race' OM 1239-41

honna a vyth tokyn da a'n **acord** *vs gureys hep fal* 'that will be a sign of the agreement made without fail' OM 1247

my a vyr scon orth honna hag a'n **acord** *a vyth cof* 'I shall look at that and there will be remembrance of the agreement' OM 1251-52

gesow ny oll gans vn **accorde** *the ry thotheff agan voyses gans ioy pub vr presya ha magnifya an kyth arluth ma a vercy* 'let us all with one accord give to him our voices with joy always praising and magnifying the same Lord of mercy' TH 11-11a.

The verb **acordya** 'to agree' is derived from **acord** and is attested twice:

yn deweth ny **acordye** *y golon gans y lauar* 'in the end his heart did not agree with what he said' PA 40d

trest am bus boys **acordys** *orth ihesu crist a vercy* 'I have faith that I shall be reconciled to Jesus Christ of mercy' BM 494-95.

'To agree' can also be rendered by use of the verb **assentya**:

a vynnegh ol **assentye** *rak pask my thylyfrye ihesu myghtern yethewon* 'do you agree that I should deliver Jesus king of the Jews to you for Passover?' PC 2037-39

assentye *ol the henna sur me a vyn* 'I will agree to all that' RD 583-84

Henna ol ny a **assent** 'To that we all agree' BM 2926

ena ty a vyth tregys ha myns **assentyas** *genas sche an naw order in paynes bys venary* 'there you shall dwell in pain for ever and as many of the nine orders as agreed with you' CW 246-49

hanter an elath genaffa **assentyes** *yth yns sera thom mayntaynya in spyte thys* 'half the angels are agreed, sir, to support me in spite of you' CW 271-73

poken sertayne venarye why a vyth avell flehys bo yn **assentys** *te a glow* 'otherwise certainly for ever you will be like children, or you agree to hear it' CW 652-54.

The word in TH for to 'to agree' is **agria**:

ny a goth thyn dysky fatell ew an lell diskans han feith a crist hay egglos onyn, ha fatell vsans pub vr ow **hagrya** 'we must learn that the true doctrine and the faith of Christ and of his Church are one, and that they always agree' TH 34a

rag heresy, pub vr a rug hag a ra raynya, ha bys worfan an bys, kepar dell rug athewethas tevy ha raynya, ha inweth lurkya in cornettyow privet, so neffra **agry** *gonsa y honyn* 'for heresy always has and will reign, and until the end of the world, just as it recently arose and reigned, and also lurks in private corners, but never agrees with itself' TH 34a

ha yma S Augustin ow **hagrea** *the hemma in y 102 epistill* 'and St Augustine agrees to this in his epistle 102nd epistle' TH 48

In termyn passyes, pan esans ow **hagrea** *gans an sea ha stall a rome... y a rug, florysshya in religion a crist ha in rychis an bys* 'In time past when they agreed with the see and seat of Rome... they flourished in the religion of Christ and in worldly riches' TH 49a
fatell vsy an iii aweylar, mark, mathew ha luke ow **hagrya** *in vn maner institution an sacrament ma* 'that the three evangelists, Mark, Matthew and Luke agree in one way about the institution of this sacrament' TH 52a.

Lhuyd almost certainly heard the word **agria** in Cornwall, since he uses the derived noun **agreanz** 'agreement, equivalence' AB: 223.

In revived Cornish if one wants to say 'to agree' the obvious choices are **acordya**, **assentya** and possibly **agria** as well. **Bos unverhës** means 'to be of one mind'.

ALWAYS

In his 1952 English-Cornish dictionary s.v. 'always' Nance *inter alia* gives **pùpprës** (UC *pupprys*); **pùb eur oll** (UC *pup ur oll*); **pùptëdh oll** (UC *pupteth-oll*); **prest**; **james** (UC *jammes*) and **in y dhedhyow** or **vêwnans** or **oos** (UC *yn y dhedhyow* or *vewnans* or *os*). *pùpprës*. **Pùpprës, pùb eur** and **prest** are common in the texts. **James** is very rare, being attested twice only (OM 1711, RD 677). **Pùptëdh oll** is attested only once (*Pub teȝoll* PA 228a), although the following also occur: *pup tyth* OM 831; *pup deyth* PC 2549; *pup deth* BM 682, 4444, SA 60.

Curiously Nance has omitted one of the commoner ways of saying 'always', namely (**in**) **pùb termyn**:

molloȝ den ha gour ha gwrek a ȝe poran er ȝe byn peynys ad wra moreȝek yn yffarn down **pub termyn** 'curse of mankind, man and woman, will come against you; torments will grieve you in deep hell always' PA 66cd

beneges re bo an tas a vynnas dysquethes thy'n gvelynny a gemmys ras luen a vertu **pup termyn** *thyworthe magan bo gras* 'blessed be the Father who wishes to show us rods of so great grace, full of power always, so that we might have grace from them' OM 1745-49

gorthyys re bo dev an tas yn y ober **pup termyn** 'worshipped be God the Father in his work always' OM 2075-76

ha nep as tefo gallos a vyth gans yowynk ha los henwys tus vras **pup termyn** 'and those who have any power are always called great men by young and old' PC 788-90

mester bynyges re by rak the thescas tek dy'nny yv parys **yn pup termyn** 'master, may you be blessed, for your fine teaching which is ready for us always' PC 817-19

sav the voth the gy arluth bethens gruys **yn pup termyn** 'but thy wish, Lord, be done always' PC 1039-40

ow thas ker gorthys re bo rak y confort yv thy'mmo fest parys **yn pup termyn** 'my Father, may he be worshipped, for his comfort is always very ready for me' PC 1051-53

always   **GERYOW GWIR**

yma thy'mmo hyreth tyn yn ow colon **pup termyn** 'There is always sharp longing in my heart' RD 747-48

ha the henna me a vyn don dustuny **pup termyn** *bos guyr an cas* 'and of that I shall bear witness always that the matter is true' RD 1052-54

rak the naghe gy lemmyn mercy pysaf **pup termyn** *yn certan a luen golon* 'I beg mercy always from the bottom of my heart for having denied you' RD 1156-68

myns may hyllen sur esyes ty a vyth **yn pup termyn** 'as far as we can indeed you will always be accommodated' BM 140-41

A dyves del redyn ny rych lour o **in pup termen** 'As we read of Dives, he was a very rich man always' BM 446-47

Me yv epscop in breten in conteth gelwys kernov mur yv ov rays **pup termen** 'I am bishop in Brittany in the county called Cornouailles; great is my worth always' BM 511-13

cryst roy dis **in pub termyn** *omguythe prest in glander* 'may Christ grant you always to preserve yourself in purity' BM 532-33

sav me a beys crist ihesus thagys socra **pub termen** 'but I pray Jesus Christ to succour you always' BM 591-92

gallus an iovle **pup termen** *dretho a veth confundijs* 'the power of the devil will always be confounded by him' BM 2032-33

the pup gruegh restorite myns may hallogh **pub termen** 'to everybody make restitution as far as you can always' BM 2179-80

Gallus ha confort an tas re bo genes **pup termen** 'May the power and comfort of the Father be with you always' BM 2735-36

Gwayt e worthya **pub termayn** *ha nagh Astrot ha Jovyn* 'Be careful to worship him always and renounce Astrot and Jovyn' BK 221-22

E coyth thotha gothvas gras ha'y lunworthya **pub termyn** 'It is right to thank him and to worship him worthily always' BK 320-21

Gwayt ma'n gorthy **pub termyn**, *rag gurthuhar ha myttyn nyng es thenny mar tha car* 'Be careful that you worship him always, for we have no better friend evening or morning' BK 826-28

Parys on the'th unadow rag the servya **pub termyn** 'We are ready at your desire to serve you always' BK 2036-37.

Pùb termyn should perhaps henceforward be included in English-Cornish glossaries s.v. 'always'.

AMEND *see* IMPROVE

AND

In revived Cornish for 'and' is **ha** before consonants and **hag** before vowels, although **ha+an** is usually written **ha'n**. In the texts, however, **ha**

GERYOW GWIR — and

is frequently written before vowels other than the **a** of the definite article. Here are a very few examples:

eyll o **ha y** *ny wozyens* 'he was an angel and they did not know' PA 254c
ha poynyn gans mur a grys **ha yn** *dour goryn an pren* 'and let us run with great speed and in the water let us put the timber' OM 2789-90
kemmys a'n crys **ha a** *vo lel vygythys sylwel a wra* 'as many as believe him and are properly baptized he will save' RD 1142-44
ha ene *dre gallarow woge y vos gurys marow* 'and then after he had been killed by torment' RD 1267-69
kynth yv teller guyls **ha yne** 'though it is a wild and narrow place' BM 1145
ha in *henna an drynsys tas a leverys* 'and in that the the Father of the Trinity said' TH 1a
ha in *myrnans heb dywith kyffrys an corffe han ena* 'and in the eternal death also of the body and soul' TH 4
nag o offens adam **ha eve** *mar vras* 'that the offence of Adam and Eve was not so great' TH 4
ha indelma *yma an profet Jheremy worth agan lell gylwall* 'and thus the prophet Jeremiah rightly calls us' TH 7a
ha eff *a drygas in agan mysk ny* 'and he dwelt among us' TH 15
Hemma ew sufficient cawse **ha occacion** *thenny* 'This is sufficient cause and occasion for us' TH 15a
ha in *y tressa chapter the Thimothe in second pistill yma eff ow cowsse indelma* 'and in the third chapter to Timothy in the second epistle he speaks thus' TH 18a
not an ymaginacion a then, mas an very gyrryow **ha exampill** *agan Savioure Jhesu crist* 'not the imagination of man, but the very words and example of our Saviour Jesus Christ' TH 21
ow exortya y yskerens **ha ow** *rebukya aga fautes* 'exhorting his enemies and rebuking their faults' TH 22a
So keneuer a wothfa redya **ha vnderstondia** *a yll gwellas fatell ra ran y vsya gloriusly* 'But as many as can read and understand can see that some use it gloriously' TH 32a
yma ow declarya fatell vs in catholyk egglos orders **ha officers** 'he declares that there are in the catholic Church orders and officers' TH 33a
ha vn *awelle arell a ve gylwis Evangelium Nazareorum* 'and one other gospel was called called *Evangelium Nazareorum*' TH 37a
yma lyas aucthor kyffrys an scriptur **ha a** *dus coth aunciant* 'there are many authors also of the scripture and of ancient men of yore' TH 49a
hemma ew thegys exortia why **ha in** *hanow du thegys requiria* 'this is to exhort you and in God's name to require you' TH 51
bothar **ha omlavar** 'deaf and dumb' TH 57a
ha eweth *in sted a thewas* 'and also instead of drink' SA 59a
neb a theffa dibbry ow kig **ha eva** *ow dewas* 'who happens to eat my flesh and drink my drink' SA 61
ha Christ a commandias **ha y** *a ve creatis* 'and Christ commanded and they were created' SA 61a

13

and GERYOW GWIR

Christ a ve goris in grows, marow **ha inclithis** 'Christ was put on the cross, dead and buried' SA 61a

ha ef *a walkias in kigg na omma war a nore* 'and he walked in that flesh here on the earth' SA 64a

Ke in carharow **ha in** *preson gorys* 'Ke put in shackles and in prison' BK 408 [note]

ha indelma *y leverys an gyrryow ma* 'and thus he said these words' CW 1374-75

Simnen criez Peder, **ha Andrew** *e broder* 'Simon called Peter, and Andrew his brother' Rowe

E ve troublez **ha oll** *Jerusalem gonz eue* 'He was troubled and all Jerusalem with him' Rowe

ha enna *ti an kâv* 'and there you will find him' BF: 17

ha ev *a uelaz golou* 'and he saw a light' BF: 18.

Some revivalists when speaking seem to consider **hag** to be the base form for 'and' in all positions. In the light of the above examples, perhaps it might be more authentic to favour **ha** as the default form.

ANGER, TO ANGER, TO BE ANGRY

The usual word in Cornish for the noun 'anger' is **sorr**. 'To feel anger' is **don sorr**:

Ragon y pesys y das oll y **sor** *may fe gevys gans y gorff dre beynys bras* 'For us he prayed his Father that by his body through great pains all his wrath might be forgiven' PA 9ab

Na thegough **sor** *yn golon war neb a vyn ow sawye* 'Do not bear anger in your heart against her who will salve me' PA 37a

pana dra a ren ny gwettyas theworth du alymma rag mar teny ha peha hay ankevy eff, forsoth, travith mas **sore***, anger, han vingians a thu* 'what shall we expect from God from now on, if we sin and forget him? Nothing forsooth but anger, wrath and the vengeance of God' TH 15a

nyn sevith eff bewnas, mas an **sorre** *a crist a dryg vghta* 'he will not have life, but the anger of Christ will remain over him' TH 40

Don e **sor** *nyng ew mar scaf* 'it is not easy to bear his anger' BK 997

Ny yl den vith don ow **sor** 'no man can bear my anger' BK 1264

y whon gwyre dew agen tas y **sor** *thyn y teig pur vras me an suppose* 'I know that God our Father will bear great anger against us, I suppose' CW 860-62

gallas genaf **sor** *an tase rag latha abell pen braas* 'I have received the anger of the Father for killing the fool Abel' CW 1339-40

Rag me an Arluth thy Dew, yw Dew a **sor***, ha vyn towle pehosow an Tazow war an ffledgiow bys an tresa, ha'n peswerra denythyans* 'for I the Lord thy God am a God of anger, and will cast the sins of the fathers upon the children unto the third and fourth generation' ACB: E e 3.

The related verb is **serry**, *3sg. preterite* **sorras**, which means both 'to be angry' and 'to anger'. The verbal adjective **serrys** is used for 'angry':

*En scherewys a **sorras** rag bonas crist honoris ha bos y ober mar vras* 'the scoundrels were angry that Christ was honoured and that his works were so great' PA 31ab

*eua kyns del vy **serrys** my a wra ol del vynny* 'Eve, rather than that you be angered, I will do just as you wish' OM 245-46

*y won the wyr dev an tas re **sorras** dre wyth benen* 'I know truly that God the Father has been angered by the action of a woman' OM 255-56

***serry** orthyf ny res thy's* 'there is no need for you to be angry with me' OM 2524

*saf yn ban del y'm kerry rak nans yv pilat **serrys** ow crye kepar ha ky* 'get up as you love me, for now Pilate is angry, yelping like a dog' PC 2240-42

*ha ny won pyth eth heb nam ragtho mayth oma **serres*** 'and I do not know where he has gone at all, so that I am angry about it' BM 1942-43

*ty re fue [sic!] napyth redovnt moys the **serry** an turant lemen ty a oyl henna* 'you have been a little too impertinent, venturing to anger the tyrant; you will regret that' BM 3570-72

*Syra, thewgh why lowena! Na **syrrough** kynth oma hil* 'Greetings to you, sir. Do not be angry though I am late' BK 451-52

*in quarel gwyer dris mor ha tyr, yn **serres**, anwek lowan* 'in a true dispute over sea and land, angry, happily harsh' BK 1505-07

*A pes **syrrys** ha'th voth terrys, ny'th wortesa gwyls na whar* 'Were you angry and your will crossed, neither wild nor tame could withstand you' BK 1961-63 & 1969-71

*Mer a foly o prederys mos thu'm **serry*** 'Much folly has been undertaken, venturing to anger me' BK 2178-80

*Suer heb kelas, in **syrrys** neb a'n gwelha ny'n dythursa pyth ellya war ambos e wohelas* 'Truly to be honest, whoever would see him angry, would not care where he went if only he could avoid him' BK 2321-24

*drevan **serry** an taes dew towles ew tha vyshow bras rag drog polat par dell ew ha lenwys a volothowe* 'because he angered God the Father, he has been cast into great misery as an evil fellow which he is and full of curses' CW 1483-86

*Na **sorren** may tefo gueith ha losou* 'Let us not be angry that trees and herbs grow' Lhuyd MSS.

Gradually **sorr**, **serry**, **serrys** began to be replaced by **anger**, **angra**, **engrys** and **angry**:

*aga fen y a sackye hag a gewsy pur debell worth Ihesus rag y **angre*** 'they shook their heads and spoke vilely to Jesus to make him angry' PA 195bc

*mernans trystyns hag **anger** me a wruk aga fethe mayth yw lemmyn da ow cher* 'death, sorrow, anger—I have conquered them so that now my condition is good' RD 499-501

*Yma in pov falge cregyans ov cul dym **angyr** an iovle* 'there is a false belief in the country that is provoking in me the devil's anger' BM 1161-62

anger

*lymmyn mar te cristonyan ha concevya **anger** in aga colonow, ha na rellans by an by suppressia an kythsam **anger** na, mas procedia pella inna ha tyrry charite, henna ew the vttra aga **anger** dre sygne ha tokyn, nena an kythsame fawt ma ew brassa ys y gela* 'now if Christians conceive anger in their hearts, and if they do not soon suppress that same anger, but continue further in it and fracture charity, that is to utter their anger by a sign or token, then that same fault is greater than the other' TH 28a

*fatla wrene ny avoydeya **anger** a thew? rag neg eran cregy nanyle regardia gerryow Dew ha only mab dew* 'how will we escape the anger of God? For we neither believe nor regard the words of God and the only son of God' SA 59

*yma S paul worth agan payntia ny in mes in colors in leas tellar in scriptur, orth agan gylwall ny an flehes a thesplesians hag a **angras** du* 'St Paul paints us in colour in many places in scripture, calling us the children of displeasure and who angered God' TH 7a

*der henna me a **angras** ha pur vskys an lathas* 'I was angered by that and very quickly killed him' CW 1683-84

*Assof **engrys**! The ves omden!* 'How angry I am! Get out!' BK 2156-57

*Nena Herod pe rêg e gwellaz fatal o geaze gwreaze anotha gen an teze feere, yw **engrez*** 'Then Herod, when he saw that the wise men had mocked him, he was angered' Rowe

*Rag vee da Deew bonegath vedn boaze **engros** gen a chee ha compoza cabmwithe an zeera war an flehaz da a'n dridga ha boswerha heeneth a rima neg eeze ort a hara* 'For I, thy God of jealousy will be angry with thee and avenge the wrong of the father upon the children unto the third and fourth generation of those who do not love me' Rowe

*penagoll a vo **angry** gans y brothar, eff a vith in danger a judgement* 'whoever is angry with his brother, will be in danger of judgement' TH 27

*an lya tra a ra den tyrry charite ew bos **angry**, han punysment a henna appoyntys thyn ny gans crist ew judgment* 'the smallest thing by which a man may fracture charity is to be angry and the punishment appointed for us by Christ is judgement' TH 27

*mar crug agan Savyoure agan forbydya ny the vos **angry**, the leverall Racha bo te foolle, onyn ahanan ny the gella* 'if our Saviour forbade us to be angry, to say *racha* or you fool, one of us to his fellow' TH 29a

*Arthor pan vo va **angry*** 'Arthur when he is angry' BK 1412 [note].

No word for 'raging, furious' is attested in Middle Cornish, but *rabidus uel amens uel demens **conerioc*** 'raging, demented' is attested at OCV §392. Borlase gives the corresponding noun **connar** 'rage, fury'. A verb **fernewy** 'to rage, to be furious' < Latin *fornax, fornac-* 'oven, furnace' is attested twice in BK:

*Mar fol e reth **fernewy**, rag own te thu'm reverthy ny vetha' dos athan guyth* 'So madly do you rage, for fear that you will overwhelm me I dare not come out from under the trees' BK 976-78

*rag mar tema ha rowtya ha **ferneuwhy** ha stowtya, ny vith mab den na'm dowtya* 'for if I happen to domineer and rage and brag, there will be no man who does not fear me' BK 1639-41.

In revived Cornish the default word for 'anger' should be **sorr**, for 'to anger, to be angry' **serry** and for 'angry' **serrys**. **Anger**, **angra**, **engrys** and **angry** can perhaps also be used. 'Rage' is **conar**, 'rabid' can be rendered **coneryak** and 'to rage' **fernewy**.

ANIMAL

The default word in revived Cornish for 'animal' has always been **mil**, although the word is wholly absent from Middle Cornish, being attested only once in Old Cornish: *animal* **mil** 'animal' OCV §607. Lhuyd gives **Bêst** as the Cornish word for 'animal', but he adds †***Mîl***, where the obelus indicates that the item has been taken from OCV. It is almost certainly from Lhuyd that John Boson got ***mîl*** in the expression ***mîl an aor*** 'beast of the field' BF: 52. Both Pryce in ACB and Borlase cite ***mîl*** 'animal', where the circumflex indicates that they are both quoting from Lhuyd.

The ordinary word for 'animal' in Middle Cornish is **best**, *plural* **bêstas**. Here is a selection of examples:

yn pympes dyth me a vyn may fo formyys dre ov nel **bestes** *puskes hag ethyn tyr ha mor the goullenwel* 'on the fourth day I wish that through my power be created animals, fish and birds, to fill the land' OM 41-44

hethyw yw an whefes dyth aban dalletheys gonys may rug nef mor tyr ha gveyth **bestes** *puskes golowys* 'today is the sixth day since I began to work in which I made heaven, sea, land and trees, animals, fish, heavenly bodies' OM 49-52

Adam otte an puskes ythyn a'n nef ha'n **bestes** *kefrys yn tyr hag yn mor* 'Adam, here are the fish, the birds of the heavens and the animals as well on land and at sea' OM 117-19

ha margh yw **best** *hep parow the vap den rag ymweres* 'and horse is a peerless animal to assist mankind' OM 124-25

ytho bethyth mylyges pur wyr drys ol an **bestes** *a gertho war an norveis* 'therefore you shall be accursed indeed above all animals that walk the earth' OM 311-13

vn sarf in guethen yma **best** *vthek hep falladow* 'there is a serpent in the tree, a horrible animal without fail' OM 797-98

a bub eghen **best** *yn wlas gor genes dew annethe* 'of every kind of animal in the country take with you two of them' OM 977-78

rag y tue lyf war an bys may fo pup den ol ynno ha pup **best** *warbarth buthys* 'for a flood will come upon the world so that everybody and every animal together will be drowned' OM 1042-44

del yv gorhemmynnys thy'n my a's gor bys yn gorhal kefrys **bestes** *hag ethyn* 'as we have been commanded I will bring them to the ark, both animals and birds' OM 1049-51

kynyver **best** *vs yn tyr ythyn ha puskes kefreys yv gosteth theugh yn pur wyr* 'each animal that is in the land, birds and fish as well are subject to you indeed' OM 1215-17

animal GERYOW GWIR

an dour ha'n eys yv posnys mayth eus mur a tus dyswreys ha **bestes** *certan y'th wlas* 'the water and the corn have been poisoned so that many men and animals indeed have been killed in your land' OM 1559-61

neffre yn dour hedre vo ny thue dresto na varwo gour gruek na **best** 'as long as he is in the water neither man, woman nor animal will ever pass across without dying' RD 2225-27

Best *thys me a worhemmyn thymmo na rylly dregyn na the crystyan benytha* 'Animal, I command you that you shall not harm me ever nor any Christian' BM 1109-11

in hanov crist map guirhas thys **best** *me a worhemyn moys then guelfos* 'in the name of Christ the son of a Virgin, I command you, animal, to depart into the wilderness' BM 1125-27

Pana goys a veth henna na sparyogh **best** *in bys ma* 'What blood will that be? Don't spare any animal in this world' BM 1501-02

*an dragon yv tebel***vest** 'the dragon is an nasty animal' BM 4127

drok nefre gueyt na rylly the **vest** *na den creff na guan* 'be careful not to do any harm to animal or man, strong or weak' BM 4144-45

ha dre an commondment a du an nore a thros in rag **bestes** *peswartrosek han dowre in kepare maner a thros in rag puskas* 'and by the commandment of God the earth brought forth four-footed animals and the water similarly brought forth fish' TH 2

Eff an grug souereign rewler ha pen war oll an pusces in dowre, war an ethen in eyer, ha war oll an **bestas** *in nore* 'He made him sovereign ruler and chief over all the fish in the water, over the birds of the air and of all the animals on the earth' TH 2

Peys! Syth Y hot wyld and tam, den ha **best** *peswartrosak, I say Arthur is my nam, myghtern bras ha galosak* 'Peace! Sith I am called wild and tame, O man and four-footed animal, I say Arthur is my name, a great and powerful king' BK 1397-400

Ny won i'n bys pew a'th feth, den na **best** *peswartrosak, mars an emprowr, agan arluth* 'I do not know in the world who will beat you, man or four-footed animal, except the emperor, our lord' BK 1998-2001

haw hendas cayme whath en bew yn defyth in myske **bestas** *yma ef prest ow pewa* 'and my grandfather Cain is still living perpetually in the wilderness among the animals' CW 1480-82

sera in myske an **bestas** *strange yth ew eve tha welas* 'sir, he is strange to be seen among the animals' CW 1548-49

ken es **beast** *nag ew henna ha strang yw the vos gwelys* 'that is no other than an animal and a strange sight it is' CW 1557-58

Lebben an hagar-breeve o moy foulze avell onen veth ell an **bestaz** *an gweale a reege an Arleth Deew geele* 'Now the evil-serpent was more treacherous than any other of the animals of the field which the Lord God made' Rowe

Ha Deew lauarhaz gwrenz an beaze dry raag an tacklow beawe worler go kendah an chatthall ha a tacklow cramyhaz ha **beasthaz** *an gweale worler go hendah ha an delha eth o* 'And God said, Let the earth bring forth living things according to their kind, the cattle and creeping things and animals of the field according to their kind, and thus it was' JKeigwin

Animal...., An Animal, a Beast. C. **Bêst** AB: 3a.

It is clear from the above selection of examples not only that **best** was the ordinary word for 'animal' in Middle and Late Cornish, but also that **best peswar-trosek** was the accepted way of speaking of a four-footed animal or quadruped. It seems likely that Nance preferred not to use the word **best**, because he believed it to be a borrowing from English *beast*. This is by no means certain, however, for **best** is equally likely to derive from Latin *bestia* 'animal, beast'.

Lodn means 'bullock, steer' but is on occasion used with a more general sense:

v **lon** *bowyn dufunys y a depse in ij deth* 'they would eat five minced beeves in one day' BM 3224-25

a vs kyek an bestas na a veast na **lodn** *in beyse ny wressan bythqwath tastya* 'of the use of flesh of those animals nor of any bullock have we ever tasted' CW 1470-72

me a weall un **lodn** *pur vras hans in bushe ow plattya* 'I see a very large beast yonder crouching in the bushes' CW 1546-47

lead ve quycke besyn thotha may hallan ve attendya pan vanar **lon** *yth ewa* 'lead me quickly to him that I may ascertain what kind of beast it is' CW 1567-69

ke in meas an lester skon thethe wreag hathe flehys keffrys ethyn bestas ha pub **lodn** 'go out of the ark soon, your wife and your children and also birds, animals and every beast' CW 2475-77

Juvencus.... C. **Lodn** 'a bullock or steer; a young ox' AB: 74c

Vervex.... C. *Molz [& Moulz]* **lodon** *davaz* 'A wether sheep' AB: 172c

Lodn 'A bullock' AB: 241b

Ma huî biuh dhodho, dêau marh, ha trei kanz **lvdn** *davaz* 'He has six cows, two horses and three hundred sheep' AB: 244a

chee, ha de mab, ha de merh, de gwaz, ha de maithez, **de lodnow***, ha dean uncouth; lebes gyi de porthow* 'you, and your son, and your daughter, and your servant, and your maidservant, and your animals, and your guest who is withing your gates' ACB: E e 3 *verso*.

The plural **enevales** 'animals' is attested once, referring to the two asses of Palm Sunday: *cowethe thy'm lauerewgh yn scon pragh yth hembrenkygh ov* **enevalles** *the ves* 'friends tell me quickly, why are you leading away my beasts?' PC 204-05. Lhuyd reading this passage appears mistakenly to have taken **enevalles** to be a feminine singular, hence **Enevales** 'a she beast' AB: 241a.

Eneval is too rare and **lodn** too specialized to function as the generic word for 'animal' in revived Cornish. The authentic word is **best**, which should perhaps be used in preference to **mil**. At the same time **morvil**, a derivative of **mil** is the word of choice for 'whale'; cf. *cetus* **moruil** 'whale' OCV §541.

apologize   GERYOW GWIR

TO APOLOGIZE

It seem that there are two attested words in the texts for 'to apologize', **dyharas** and **omdhyvlâmya**:

lemmen tobesy gueras bys may fons ov **teharas** *the gerthes gays an guelan* 'now, Tobesy, help until they apologize. Let the rod go forth' BM 3343-45

Solabrys kynth of cryys, the'n turant ny vetha' mos rag own a drol, saw whath rys ew mos thotha hag **omthyvlamya** *orta* 'Since I am now called, I do not dare go to the tyrant for fear of a drubbing, but still I must go and apologize to him' BK 444-49.

TO APPEAR

In Middle Cornish the word **omdhysqwedhes**, literally 'to show oneself', is attested once only with the sense 'to appear':

ymthysquethas *ny vynna the plussyon auelough why* 'he did not wish to appear to worthless fellows like you' RD 1496-97.

Dysqwedhes can also be used with the reflexive pronoun **honen** to mean 'to appear':

yma eff ow menya na rellan ny cristonnyan ***desquethes agan honyn*** *da ha virtus, war ves in sight an bys only* 'he means that we Christians should not appear good and virtuous externally in the sight of the world only' TH 26a.

Dysqwedhes without either reflexive prefix or reflexive pronoun is also used for 'to appear':

ny wruk dev thy'm ***dysquethas*** *byth ny'n cresons ef neffre* 'God did not appear to me. Never will they believe it at all' OM 1439-40

tokyn thyugh mar ny ***thyswe*** *kyn fe dyswrys an temple the'n dor quyt na safe man me a'n dreha sur arte* 'if no sign appears to you, though the temple were pulled down to the ground so that it did not stand, I will surely build it up again' PC 343-46

Nena Herod, pe reeg e prevath crya an deez feere, e a vednyaz thoranze seer puna termin reeg an steare ***disquethaz*** 'Then Herod, when he had called the wise men privately, he asked them assiduously when the star had appeared' Rowe

Ha po tho angye gellez carr, mero, elez neeue a ***desquethaz*** *ha Joseph a ve hendrez* 'And when they had departed, behold, the angels of heaven appeared when Joseph was dreaming' Rowe.

By far the commonest verb meaning 'to appear', however, is **apperya**:

GERYOW GWIR   **appear**

yma ow **apperya**, *kynthew an gothwas an gwryoneth necessary the attaynya an bewnans heb deweth... yth ew re wan rag y purgya theworth pegh* 'it appears, although the truth is necessary to obtains eternal life... it is too weak to purge him from sin' TH 14

so dre henna yma pleynly ow **apperya** *fatell vsy then Catholyk egglos an kythsam auctorite na only* 'but it appears plainly that only the catholic Church has that same authority' TH 38

yth ew scriffys fatell rug agan Savyour, wosa y resurreccion, **apperia** *in mor in tyllar gylwys Tiberias* 'it is written that our Saviour, after his resurrection, appeared in the sea in a place called Tiberias' TH 42a

kepar dell vsy ow **apperya** *moy largia in xxx-ans chapter an lever a Eusebius* 'as appears more fully in the 30th chapter of the book of Eusebius' TH 47a

ha kyns oll hemma ew the vos notys, fatell rug du thea dalleth an bys lyas tyrmyn **apperya** *the vabden* 'and first of all this is to be noted, that God from the beginning on many occasions appeared to mankind' TH 55

yth ew scriffes fatell rug du ha iii oll gansa **apperia** *the Abraham in hevelep the dus* 'it is written that God and all three with him appeared to Abraham in the likeness of men' TH 55

fatell ylly du po ell **apperia** *in hevelep a den* 'that God or an angel could appear in the likeness of man' TH 55

ha fatell alsans **apperia** *in corfow po na alsans* 'and that they could appear in bodies or could not' TH 55

In trissa lyuer a exodus ny a rede fatell rug du **apperya** *the Moyses in hevelep a flam a dan* 'In the third book of Exodus we read that God appeared to Moses in the likeness of a flame of fire' TH 55-55a

In v-as a Josue yth ew recordys fatell rug onyn sodenly **apperya** *the Josue havall the den ha cletha noith in y dorne* 'In the fifth chapter of Joshua it is recorded that one suddenly appeared to Joshua like a man with a naked sword in his hand' TH 55a

pandra ill den vith leverell, fatell rug Du **apperia** *in flam a dan* 'what can one say? That God appeared in a flame of fire' TH 55a

pana substans a cletha o honna essa in dorne henna a rug **apperia** *the Josue?* 'what substance of sword was that that was in the hand of him who appeared to Joshua?' TH 55a

In xxiiii a luk crist a rug **apperya** *the ii y thissiplis ow mos the Emavs kepar a stranger* 'in the 23rd chapter of St Luke Christ appeared to two of his disciples going to Emmaus like a stranger' TH 56a

girryow an scripture a yll bos easiy vnderstandis (kepare dell vgy **apperia**) *owrth an artickell ma* 'the words of scripture can easily be understood (as appears) from this article' SA 64.

Dysqwedhes, **omdhysqwedhes** and **dhysqwedhes y honen** are the native ways in Cornish of saying 'to appear.' Given, however, that **apperya** is attested 14 times and in two texts, the word can hardly be proscribed.

21

TO ARGUE, ARGUMENT

The word **argya** 'to argue' is well attested:

argye na moy thy'n ny reys na keusel na moy gerryow 'we need not argue any more or speek any more words' PC 2467-68
Ny thue les agen **argya** kyn feny oma vyketh 'Good will not come from our arguing, though we be for ever heare' BM 891-92
raghyl yv in y pemont **argya** orto ny ammont 'he is a rascal in his payment; it is no use arguing with him' BM 3331-32.

Some commentators have suggested using ***argyans** as a derived noun for 'argument'. This is unnecessary, since the attested word is **argùment**, plural **argùmentys**:

me a'n conclud yredy ma na wothfo gorthyby vn reson thu'm **argument** 'I will refute him indeed so that he will not be able to answer a single reason to my argument' PC 1659-61
Na esyn vsya **argumentys**, mas vsya exampels Christ 'Let us not use arguments, but use the examples of Christ' SA 61a.

The attested word **argùment** is surely to be preferred over the unattested ***argyans**.

ARISE see SPRING UP

ARMY

For 'army' Nance suggests both **lu** and **ost**. Lu is very rare and tends to mean 'crowd, collection' rather than 'army':

classis **luu** listri 'fleet of ships' OCV §270
Ihesus a ve hombronkis ha war y lyrgh mur a **lu** 'Jesus was led and behind him a large crowd' PA 163c
ha'm **lu** ervys a vith pals 'and my armed host will be large' BK 2310.

Ost 'host' usually means 'army' in the military sense:

ov tos yma syr pharo hag **ost** bras pur wyr ganso 'Sir Pharaoh is coming and a great army with him indeed' OM 1651-52
Aban yv myghtern faro buthys ha'y **ost** ol ganso 'Since king Pharaoh and his army with him have been drowned' OM 1712-13

GERYOW GWIR article

gor **ost** *genes yrvys da the omlath del y'm kerry* 'take with you a well-armed army to fight as you love me' OM 2141-42

yma duk oma in vlays drehevys sur er the byn ha ganso pur guir **ost** *brays* 'a duke here in the land has arise indeed against you and with him very truly a great army' BM 2301-03

ta a feth meth hath **ost** *defry* 'you will be put to shame and your army indeed' BM 2442-43

attense enos in prays ha ganso **ost** *brays ervys* 'there he is yonder in the field and with him a large army with weapons' BM 3447-48

Ke wyn an duk ha Bithwar a ve lethis in cres **host** *Myghtern Medys, pan ve Lucy debynnys, mayth of cuthys, re Sint Luk!* 'Duke Ke the bright and Bedevere were killed in the midst of the army of the King of the Medes, when Lucius was beheaded, so that I am sorrowful, by St Luke!' BK 3289-93.

TH uses the English borrowing **army**:

Du a rug cawsia sownde a verth, charettys, ha **army** *bras, ha whath ena nyns esa na marth, charet, na* **army** 'God caused the sound of horses, chariots and a great army, but still there was neither horse, chariot nor army' TH 56a.

The ordinary word for 'army' in the revived language should perhaps be **ost**. **Lu** and **army** can also be used as variants.

ARTICLE

For 'article' when referring to a piece of text, some commentators recommend the unattested word ***erthygel**, *pl.* ***erthyglow**, borrowed from Welsh *erthygl* < Latin *articulus*. The attested word, however, is **artykyl**, *pl.* ***artyklys**:

Mar tewhy demandea praga a ruke an egglos dewys mar galys vnderstandyng an keth **ar(t)ickell** *ma girryow an scripture a yll bos easiy vnderstandis (kepare dell vgy apperia) owrth an* **artickell** *ma* 'If you ask, why the church chose such a difficult understanding of this same article, the words of scripture can be easily understood (as is made plain) from this article' SA 64.

The attested form **artykyl** would seem preferable to the unattested ***erthygel**.

AS *see* **LIKE**

ascend   GERYOW GWIR

TO ASCEND, TO DESCEND

The history of the Cornish word for 'to ascend' is intimately related to the word for 'to descend'. In the earliest Middle Cornish, A) 'to ascend' is **iskyna** and B) 'to descend' **dieskyna** (Later **dieskynnya**):

A **iskyna** 'to ascend, to mount (a horse)'

beys vynytha y wharthes rag ioy ha rag lowene kepar yn beys ha dves the'n nef grusses **yskynne** 'for ever you would laugh for joy and happiness; in the world like a goddess you would ascend to heaven' OM 153-56

arluth pan vynny **yskyn** 'lord, whenever you wish, mount [your horse]' OM 1968

In nomine dei patris a nef mennaf **yskynne** 'In the name of God the Father of heaven I will mount' OM 1975-76

lemyn pep ol **yskynnens** *yn hanow a'n tas dev ker* 'now let everybody mount in the name of the Father, beloved God' OM 2001-02

***yskyn** yn ban mars yw prys* 'mount, if it is time' PC 222

rag pan **yskynnyf** *the nef me a fyn cafus gynef kekeffrys eleth ha syns* 'for when I ascend to heaven I shall find with me both angels and saints' RD 188-90

henna ny a vyn notye le mayth yllyn yn pup le certan y vos dasserhys kepar del sevys a'n beth the'n nef gans mur a eleth ny th'y weles **yskynnys** 'that we will declare wherever we can everywhere indeed that he is risen, as he rose from the tomb, we saw him ascended into heaven with a host of angels' RD 663-68

alena yth **yskynnaf** *yn ban bys yn glascor nef* 'thence I shall ascend into the kingdom of heaven' RD 2401-02

hag yn ban the nef the'n ioy ihesu a wruk **yskynne** 'and up into heaven to bliss Jesus ascended' RD 2639-40.

B **dieskyna** 'to descend, to dismount'

***dyyskyn** ha powes ha 3ymo dus nes* 'dismount and rest and come near to me' CF 3-4

ihesus crist a ve mevijs may fynnas **dijskynna** *yn gwerhas ha bos genys* 'Jesus Christ was moved so that he descended into a virgin and was born' PA 4cd

Ihesu crist mur gerense 3e vab den a 3ysweʒas an vghelder mayʒ ese ʒen bys pan **deyskynnas** 'Jesus Christ showed much love for mankind from the height where he was when he descended into the world' PA 5ab

mars os mab du a vur brys **dijskyn** *ha ʒen dor ke* 'if you are the son of God of great worth descend and go down' PA 14d

***dyskynnough** ketep map pron* 'dismount every man of you' OM 1983

lemyn pup **dyyskynnes** 'now let everyone dismount' OM 2029

mars os map dev a mur prys **dyyskyn** *ha the'n dor ke* 'if you are the son of God of great worth descend and go down' PC 99-100

mara sose map dev mvr **dyeskyn** *an vynk the'n lur* 'if you are the son of God, descend from the scaffold' PC 2867-68

lemmyn a'n grous **dyyskyn** *ha ny a wra the worthye* 'now descend from the cross and we will worship you' PC 2983-84

GERYOW GWIR ascend

deyskyn *then dor mata ha the borse mes ath ascra me am beth hath margh uskis* 'dismount, pal, and I will have your purse from your breast pocket and your horse quickly' BM 1887-89

my a⌈s⌉ sone gans ow ganow hag a vyn diskynnya than noore in dan an clowdys 'I will bless them with my mouth and will descend to the earth beneath the clouds' CW 74-76

*rag ʒa oth tha bayne nefra ty a wra **dyiskynya** mahellas ysall* 'for your pride you will descend for ever to pain so that you will be brought low' CW 233-35.

The later form **dieskynnya** was in later texts often reduced to **skynnya**, **skydnya**:

*me an felge adrus then pen may teffo y ompynnen ha **skynnya** avel mottis* 'I will split him across the head so that his brains will come and fall down like motes' BM 1273-75

neb tebel dorne pan vo grueys mas hap [leg. ?*par hap*] *drok orthugh a **skyn*** 'when some evil turn is done, perhaps harm will fall upon you' BM 1284-85

*ha mar te ha gull an dra a ra an perill **skynnya** anotha wosa y bosa gwarnys y fowt ew the vrassa ha the voy* 'and if he does the thing from which danger descends after being warned, his fault is the greater and the more' TH 4

*awosa ny vnwith the **skynnya** in pegh, an golow a nature ynnan ny, na an gothvas han vnderstonding a vlonogath du der speciall dyswythyans innan ny, nyns o abyll thegan gweras ny* 'after we once descended into sin, neither the light of nature in us, nor the knowledge nor the understanding of the will of God by special revelation in us, was able to help us' TH 13a

*martesyn eff a yll **skynnya** in myschew an par na* 'perhaps he may descend into harm of that kind' TH 25a

*mehall **yskydnyow** eall splan hellowgh adam gans cletha dan* 'Michael, go down, splendid angel, so that you can evict Adam with a fiery sword' CW 964-65

*ha then tas gwren oll pegy na **skydnya** an keth vengeans in neb termyn warnan ny* 'and let us all pray the Father that the same vengeance does not descend upon us at any time' CW 2207-09

*ty an oole ha lyas myell kynth ota **skydnys** in wharthe in dewathe heb tull na gyle* 'you will regret it and many thousands, though you have descended into laughing fits, in the end without deceit or guile' CW 2305-07

*mar ny wrewh vengence pur vras a **skydn** warnough kyns na pell* 'if you do not, very great vengeance will descend upon you ere long' CW 2368-69.

The inflected forms of **skynnya** 'to descend' are very similar to the those of **iskyna** 'to ascend', and it seems that as a result, **iskyna** was in part replaced by **ascendya**:

*a ihesu myghtern a nef ty re glewas agan lef yn **ascendys*** 'O Jesus, king of heaven, you have heard our voice ascending to you' RD 173-75

ascend   GERYOW GWIR

a fue marov in grovs pren hag anclethys in beth men then tresse deth dasserrys **assendijs** *then neff in ban* 'who died on the cross and was buried in the tomb; on the third day arisen ascended into the heavens above' BM 4049-52

a fue marov anclethyys dasserrys then tresse deth then neff **assendias** *inweth* 'who was dead, buried, arisen on the third day, ascended also' BM 4083-84

rag eff a leverys fatell rug crist **assendia** *thyn neff* 'for he said that Christ ascended into heaven' TH 33a

ha only mab dew, agyn arluth han saviour, ew **ascendis** *then nef* 'and the only son of God, our Lord and Saviour, has ascended into heaven' SA 59

mas Dew **ascendias** *then neff, hef asas vmma e kig theny* 'but God ascended into heaven, and he left here his flesh for us' SA 60.

The verb **descendya** is attested only once and it means 'to descend, to be a descendant': *Sevys a lydnyathe pur vras heb dowt ythof ha pur leall an sythvas degre* **desendys** *a adam ove* 'Arisen from a very great lineage I am indeed and truly in the seventh degree descended I am from Adam' CW 2097-2100.

If we use **skynnya**, **skydnya** for 'to descend', it is probably better to use **ascendya** rather than **iskyna** for 'to ascend'. Although **ascendya** is used almost exclusively for 'to ascend' in the theological sense, this may reflect the topics of interest in the Cornish texts. If we had more Cornish, we might well find that **ascendya** was also used for 'to mount, to go up' in other contexts. There can, I think, be no objection, for example, to using **ascendya** in the revived language for 'to take off' of an aeroplane.

AT

In his 1938 Cornish-English dictionary Nance glosses *dhe* as 'to, for, at' and in his 1952 English-Cornish dictionary s.v. 'at' he gives *orth, dhe, yn* and *a*. It seems, then, that Nance believed that English 'at' could be translated by *dhe*. This remains the case in the revived language, where one commonly finds expressions like ***dhe cyta Davyth** 'at the city of David', ***dhe Aberfal** 'at Falmouth', etc. It is a mystery where Nance derived this notion. There seems to be no evidence at all in any of the Cornish texts of any period that 'at' could be translated by using **dhe**. When using the names of towns and cities the preposition is always **in**:

rag y feth map **yn bethlem** *genys a thyspreen an bys* 'for a son will be born at Bethlehem who will redeem the world' OM 1934-35

my a wyth an gueel a ras **yn ierusalem** *nefre* 'I shall keep the rods of grace at Jerusalem for ever' OM 2059-60

yma tregys **in cambron** *den ov cul merclys dyson* 'there lives at Camborne a man working miracles indeed' BM 687-88

*Ith off gelwys costentyn **in rome** chyff cyte an beys emperour curunys certyn* 'I am called Constantine, a crowned emperor indeed at Rome, the capital of the world' BM 2513-15

*ha pan deweth ha martirdom a ve va **in Rome*** 'and what end and martyrdom he suffered at Rome' TH 47a

*an gwyr a ve derives a thorne the thorne, may halla ynna bos gothvethis eysy, ea, kefys ha gwethis **in rome*** 'the right was passed from hand to hand, so that it might me known easily, yea, found and kept at Rome' TH 48

*Teutharus a ros the Ke an gwel nessa thu'n goys **in Rosewa*** 'Teudar gave to Kea the field next to the wood at Rosewa' BK 625 [note]

*an letherau war an mean beath ez **en eglez Burian*** 'the letters upon the tombstone at Buryan church' BF: 27

*rag ma dro da deux mill hosket whath **in Falmeth*** 'for there are about two thousand barrels still at Falmouth' LAM: 238.

When **dhe** is used with the names of towns and cities it means 'to':

*a's drens **the ierusalem*** 'let them bring them to Jerusalem' OM 1933

***the venitens** mannaff moys* 'I will go to Vannes' BM 2863

*Na rug Du dynvyn y chyff apostill pedyr **the rome*** 'Did not God send his chief apostle Peter to Rome?' TH 46a

*Leben po ue Jesus gennez en Bethalem a Judeah en deethyow Herod an matern, a reeg doaze teeze veer thor an est **tha Jerusalem*** 'Now when Jesus was born in Bethlehem of Judea in the days of Herod the king, wise men came from the east to Jerusalem' Rowe

*Pes myllder eus alemma **de Londres**?* 'How many miles is it from here to London?' Borde

*Mee rese mos **tha Loundres** mes a thornow* 'I must go to London immediately' Bilbao MS.

If 'at' does not mean in the town or city, but rather near it or just outside, Cornish uses the preposition **ryb**:

*yma pur guir meryasek devethys oma then pov **ryb pontelyne** eredy* 'Meriasek very truly has come here to the region at Pontelyne indeed' BM 1945-46

*In kernov me am beth chy **ryb maria a cambron*** 'In Cornwall I shall have a house at the church of Mary of Camborne' BM 4293-94.

'At' in English is used in such expressions as 'at night' and 'at midnight' and 'at midday'. In Cornish **in**, **in prës** or **in termyn** are used to express these; **dhe** is not used:

*gansa y an hombronkyas **yn prys hanter nos** heb wow bys yn aga fryns annas* 'with them they led him at midnight indeed to their prince Annas' PA 76cd

at GERYOW GWIR

Rag henna pylat a ros ʒen vorogyon aga ro may lavarsans ha dolos yn pub tyller dris an vro ʒe vos tus ynys **yn nos** *warneʒe* 'Therefore Pilate gave the horsemen their commission that they should say and give to understand everywhere throughout the country that armed men came upon them at night' PA 250a-c
Dev then a thuth dym **in nos** *gans nerth bras a wolovder* 'Two men came to me at night with great strength of light' BM 1787-88
Maria thymo **in nos** *purguir a thueth then preson* 'Mary came to me at night indeed to the prison' BM 3766-68
Ma ladran moz **en termen noz** *reb vor Loundres Tur* 'Robbers go at night by the road of the Tower of London' BF: 58.

'At' in English is used after 'to look'. In Cornish 'to look at' is rendered by **meras (w)orth** or **meras wàr**:

hay dew **myr orth** *ov offryn ha ressef thy's ov dege* 'O God, look upon my offering and accept my tithe' OM 505-06
hag a's ty gans plynkennow may fo ioy **myres worte** 'and will roof her with planks so that it will be a joy to look at her' OM 2475-76
me a'n knouk fest dybyte man geffo pup ol bysne ow **myres worth** *y vody* 'I will batter him very pitilessly so that everyone will get a lesson looking at his body' PC 2091-93
myreugh worth *an vorvoran hanter pysk ha hanter den* 'look at the mermaid, half fish and half human' PC 2403-04
na rewgh mas **meras war** *an pow ha gwlasow, ha war an bobyll vs in captiuite gans an turk bras* 'merely look at the land and the kingdoms and at the people who are in captivity by the Great Turk' TH 49a
Na esyn ny **miras wor** *an bara han dewas ew sittys deragen* 'Let us not look at the bread and drink set before us' SA 65a.

Dhe 'at' appears to be without warrant in the texts. With the names of towns and cities 'at' is translated by **in**. For periods of the day **in** or **in prës**, **in termyn** should be used. When 'at' follows **meras** 'to look', the correct preposition is **(w)orth** or **wàr**.

TO ATTACK

It is sometimes suggested that **omsettya** means 'to attack'. This is not borne out by the attested examples:

dallaʒ avar infreʒ darwar oun ma porʒo ef **emsettye** *worʒesy* 'start early; vigorously be careful that he be afraid to set himself against you' CF 27-9
te na yllyth omweʒe vn pres yn geyth na peghy pan **omsettyas** *ʒe demptye guʒyll pegh neb na ylly* 'you cannot keep yourself from sinning even once a day, seeing that he set himself to tempt him who could not sin' PA 20cd

Govern an wlas ha the honester **omset**, *i'n dywath may 'festa gras* 'Govern the kingdom and devote yourself to seemliness, that you may find grace in the end' BK 2781-83.

Settya orth, settya wàr and **settya warbydn** are sometimes suggested as ways to translate 'to attack', but none of these expressions is really sufficiently strong:

Orth pylat *ol y* **setsans** *ha warnoʒo a rug cry rag Ihesus crist ʒen mernans y a vynne porrys dry* 'They all opposed Pilate and made a cry against him, for they urgently wanted to bring him to his death' PA 117ab

y a schaky age barvov neb a **settya er the byn** 'they shake their beards who would oppose you' BM 2313-14

Plos marrek pour dar seposia prest a reta omma **settya orth emperour** 'very vile knight, what, do you presume here to oppose an emperor?' BM 2444-47.

Arveth as a verb seems to mean 'to affront, harass' and as a noun 'affront, harassment':

del vs an yethewon wheth pup vr worth agan **arveth** *hag ow koddros* 'as the Jews still are always insulting us and threatening us' RD 2406-07

ow **arfeth** *byth na whyla ahanas gy vn demma my ny sensaf yn tor ma* 'do not ever attempt to harass me. I do not now value you at a halfpenny' PC 2262-64

A varwo awos **arveth**, *nyng ew guyw the vorogath, in meth an hen* 'whoever dies because of insults, is not worthy to ride to battle, says the sage' BK 928-30.

Again **arveth** is not really strong enough to mean 'to attack'.

The only attested word for 'to attack' is the English borrowing, **assaultya**:

In marver dell ve agan mam sans egglos a thewethas **assaultys** *dre lyas sort ha sect a eryses, ha mar ver shackys ha tossys may rug lyas onyn seperatya aga honyn the worty hay naha (henna o the voy pety) lyas onyn a rug resak ha ponya in stray* 'Inasmuch as our mother Church has recently been attacked by many kinds and sects of heresies, and so greatly shaken and tossed that many separated themselves from her and reject her (that was the great pity), many is the one that has gone astray' TH 30a.

Assaultya is *faute de mieux* probably the best word for 'to attack' in the revived language.

TO AVOID

The inherited word for 'to avoid' is **goheles**:

*ny vyn mernans ov gueles yma orth ov **goheles** drefen ov boys anhethek* 'death will not see me; he avoids me because I am infirm' BM 3070-72

*Num bus esel nag yv mans ha pup vr yma mernans in beys orth ov **gohelas*** 'I have no limb that is not lame and always does death avoid me in the world' BM 4211-13

*Ow yskerans ny vith fuer mar ny rowns ow **gohelas** hag omdenna* 'My enemies will not be wise if they do not avoid me and withdraw' BK 1510-12

*Suer heb kelas, in syrrys neb a'n gwelha ny'n dythursa pyth ellya war ambos e **wohelas*** 'Truly to be honest, whoever would see him anger, would not care where he went if only he could avoid him' BK 2321-24

*Ow thraytor ru'm **gohelas*** 'My betrayer has avoided me' BK 3277.

The English borrowing **avoydya**, **voydya** is also used:

*dre besyon ythoff guarnys mayth ellen mes an pov ma arta the breten uskys han falge tevdar **avodya*** 'I have been warned by a vision that I should leave this country for Brittany quickly and avoid false Teudar' BM 984-87

*Soweth prendreny dotha mur a varth yv annotha **vodya** sur an dynyte* 'Alas, what shall we do to him? It is a great wonder that he shun the dignity' BM 2854-56

*ny a res thy casa an teball ell hay power ha then vttermost thegen gallus **avoydya** y temptacions* 'we must hate the devil and his power and to uttermost of our ability avoid his temptations' TH 3a

*me a dryst why a vith circumspect the **avoydia** oll kynde pehosow ha disobediens* 'I trust you will be circumspect to avoid all kind of sins and disobedience' TH 5

*nyns o mabden abyll the **avoydya** eternal damnacion* 'mankind was not able to avoid eternal damnation' TH 14a

*rag henna an re na ny a res **avoydya**, han discans vgy an egglos ow dysky ny a res thyn y gara* 'therefore we must avoid those and the doctrine which the Church teaches we must love it' TH 19

*fatla wrene ny **avoydeya** anger a thew?* 'how shall we avoid the anger of God?' SA 59

*rag henna gwrens tues dowtya an tase dew tha offendya der neb maner for in beyse rag **voydya** an peril na* 'therefore let men fear to offend God the Father in any way in the world to avoid that danger' CW 2167-70

*an lester a vythe genyn der weras dew vskes gwryes rag **voydya** an danger ma* 'the vessel will be made by us soon by the help of God to avoid this danger' CW 2375-77.

Avoydya can also mean 'to depart, to go away'; see s.v. '**AWAY**' below.

AWARD

Pêwas, **pôwas** 'award, recompense, requital' is attested only twice:

yn meth pylat worth an myns an pegh **peuas** *ris yv ry* 'Pilate said: it is necessary to make the requital according to the extent of the wrongdoing' PA 117c

Bounas heb dueth eu **poes** *karens wei tha pobl bohodzhak Paull han egles nei* 'Life eternal is the reward for your love to the poor people of Paul and to our church' BF: 57.

Since this word appears with [ɛʊ] in Middle Cornish and [oʊ] in Late Cornish, it is spelt **pêwas** or **pôwas** in KS. There is no justification for the spelling *piwas.

AWAY

Some revivalists use **dhe ves** to mean 'away', but **dhe ves** more accurately translates 'off'. It is used of taking off garments or shoes, and when the sense is 'off, to freedom', 'off, to relieve someone of something' and 'off, away for the time being':

the ves *y a thelyffras barabas quyth may3 elle* 'they released Barabbas so that he might depart' PA 150d

gallas an glaw ***the ves*** *gvlan ha'n dour my a gres basseys* 'the rain has quite gone off, and the water, I believe, has reduced' OM 1097-98

dysk the skyggyow quyk ***the ves*** 'take your shoes off quickly' OM 1406

gesough ***the ves*** *croffolas* 'leave off complaining' OM 1662

pyiadow a luen colon a wor ***the ves*** *temptacion* 'earnest prayer takes away temptation' PC 25

ke ***the ves*** *ymskemenys yn defyth yn tewolgow* 'begone from me, accursed one, into the desert into darkness' PC 141-42

cowethe thy'm lauerewgh yn scon pragh yth hembrenkygh ov enevalles ***the ves*** 'companions, tell me quickly, why are you leading my beasts off?' PC 203-05

ow tas mar ny yl bones may treylyo mernens ***the ves*** *sav y wothaf thy'm a reys the volnegeth re bo gures* 'Father, if it cannot be that death cannot be turned away but must be suffered by me, may your will be done' PC 1069-72

gesough ov thus vs gene ***the ves*** *quyt the tremene* 'let the men who are with me go off free' PC 1122-23

ow scoforn treghys myrough quyt ***the ves*** *thyworth ow pen* 'look at my ear cut quite off from my head' PC 1144-45

y gase ***the ves*** *then fo nyns us guel cusyl yn beys* 'to let him go off free, there is no better plan at all' PC 2159-60

y cussylyaf yn certan leuerel dos nerth warnan ha'y thon ***the ves*** 'I recommend indeed that we say that a force came upon us and carried him off' RD 569-71

lemmyn hertheugh hy ***the ves*** 'now push her [the boat] off' RD 2295

pan fue an purpur war skwych kychys ***the ves*** *gans dywthorn worto y glynes hardlych ran a'n kyc bys yn ascorn* 'when the purple robe was with a jerk taken off by two hands, there stuck fast to it some of the flesh to the bone' RD 2595-97

So nyns ew an Spuris sans mar dyligens in travith dell ewa ow tenna then dore haw kemeras ***the ves*** *an goth a vabden gylwys in scriptur Vaynglori* 'But the Spirit is not as diligent in anything else as it is in humbling and removing the pride of mankind, called vainglory in scripture' TH 6

rag pan deffa an welsan ha dalleth seeha an flowre a ra clamdera ha cotha **the ves** 'for when the grass begins to dry up, the flower withers and falls off' TH 7

eff ew an one a thew neb a gemeras **the ves** *an pehosow an bys* 'he is the lamb of God who took away the sins of the world' TH 10a-11

Rag henna the gemeras oll excuses an par na **the ves** 'therefore to remove all excuses of that kind' TH 13a

ha rag kemeras pegh **the ves** *the worthan mab du a ve incarnatys* 'and to remove from us sin the son of God was made flesh' TH 16

Omden **the ves**, *rag own cafas war an pol a behen e reta ges!* 'Take yourself off, lest you discover on your head of what kind of man you are mocking!' BK 2249-51.

It should be noticed also that **dhe ves** is not attested in Late Cornish.

'Away' with the sense 'gone completely, gone for good' is translated in Cornish by **in kerdh**. 'To go away, to depart' therefore is **mos in kerdh**, as can be seen from the following examples:

ke yn kerth *ov map evy ha nefra ov bannat thy's* 'depart, my son, and always my blessing to you' OM 725-26

dvn yn kerth *ow bruder whek* 'let us go hence, dear brother' PC 188

ke yn kerth *ty ihesu plos* 'go away, you foul Jesus' PC 1671

dun yn kergh *gans an prysnes* 'let us depart with the prisoners' PC 2289

ke yn kergh *dywhans hep let na strech* 'go away immediately without delay or waiting' RD 116-17

yn kerth gallas *mes a'n beth* 'he has departed out of the grave' RD 532

ow arluth ***yn kerth gallas*** *mes a'n beth sur* 'my lord has departed indeed from the grave' RD 722-23

ihesu y vos dasserghys hag a'n beth ***yn kergh gyllys*** *the'n nef deffry* 'that Jesus has risen and that he has departed indeed to heaven from the tomb' RD 808-10

dun yn kergh *rak dout pystyk* 'let us depart for fear of injury' RD 2305

ov envy **in kerth galsons** 'my enemies have gone' BM 1069

duen in kerth *scon cowetha* 'let us soon depart, companions' BM 1201

Out ***duen in kerth*** *cowetha* 'Oh, let us depart, companions' BM 1306

der an golen me ath ver mar **nyns eth in kerth** *war nuk quik mes am grond* 'I will pierce you through the heart, if you do not depart immediately quick from my land' BM 2408-10

ty ***a in kerth*** *genen ny* 'you will depart with us' BM 2968

In kerth *sur* ***galles*** *holma* 'that creature has indeed gone away' BM 4148

ymowns ow tos omma thyn bys haw **mos in kerth** *alemma arta ny woryn pyscotter* 'they come here into the world and depart hence again, we don't know how soon' TH 6a

eff a clomder hag ***a in kerth*** *kepar ha skesse* 'he withers and departs like a shadow' TH 7

Ke in kerth *ha lavar thotha y fowt intre te hag eff only* 'Depart and tell him his fault between you and him alone' TH 31a

GERYOW GWIR   away

kewgh in kerth *inweth gonʒa* 'depart also with him' CW 324
ke in ker *eva benyn vas* 'go away, Eve, good woman' CW 712
*quicke **in ker ke** alebma* 'quick, depart hence' CW 1208
deen ny in kerth *kekeffres peldar adro in byes* 'let us go away also a distance around in the world' CW 1383-84
*Nenna e **eath car** rag Frink* 'Then he went away to France' LAM: 226
*Ma materen ni daoze tre beddn wave ha **moaze car** arta pe teffia have* 'Our king will come home by winter and will go away again when summer comes' LAM: 226
*ha angye **eath carr** tha pow go honnen vor aral* 'and they went away to their own country by a different route' Rowe
*Ha potho angye **gellez carr**, mero, elez neeue a desquethaz* 'And when they had departed, behold, angels from heaven appeared' Rowe
*Ha Dzhûan medh hyi, po 'rygo huei **moz ker**, thera vi gillyz trei mîz gen 'hlôh* 'O, Jowan, she said, when you went away, I was three months pregnant' BF: 19.

The word **dyberth, dybarth** means ' to separate, to part' and is mostly found in the phrase **kyns dyberth, kyns ès dyberth** 'before leaving, before departing'. The verbal adjective **dyberthys** is used to mean 'separated, isolated, apart' of lepers or heretics. **Dyberth** can also be used as a full verb to mean 'to leave, to depart, to go away':

*y fy an deues a bel hag ol an flok a **thybarth*** 'the sheep flee afar and the flock scatters' PC 894-95
*morethek ass off defry ov **tyberth** sur theorthys* 'how sorrowful I am indeed departing from you' BM 509-10
*mara tuen ha debatya mas an nyyl party omma ov **teberth** purguir ny warth* 'if we dispute, one party here only here will not laugh on departing' BM 3476-78
*reys yv **dyberth** otyweth kyn fo tek an gowethas* 'we must part at last though the company be pleasant' BM 4255-56
*Arluth fetel vyth dynny mar **teberthyth** eredy* 'Lord, how will it be for us if you depart form us indeed?' BM 4263-64
*in hanov map maria in vvelder **deberthyn*** 'in the name of the son of Mary let us depart in humility' BM 4327-28.

As mentioned above **avoydya, voydya** is often used with the sense 'to depart':

*reys yv **vodya** a vur spas oges yma ov envy* 'I must depart shortly; my enemy is near' BM 1012-13
*ny a vyn polge **avodya** mara kyllyn omguytha orth costentyn in tor ma* 'we will depart a space if we can preserve ourselves from Constantine at the moment' BM 1338-40
*grua then re na **avodya** par del yv mur the galloys* 'make them depart as your power is great' BM 2061-62
***avodia** sur mar ny vyn y woys a resek then luyr* 'indeed if he does not depart, his blood will drip to the ground' BM 2262-63

peys gevyans warna losel bo **voyd** *am syght a pur hond* 'beg me for forgiveness, rogue, or depart from my sight, you utter cur' BM 2413-14

an drok sperys **avodys** *yma sur theortheff vy* 'the evil spirit has departed from me indeed' BM 2657-58

avoyd *ʒeorthef leman* 'depart from me now' BM 4143

Voydough *ha coyth, degowgh an toyt mes a'm golok* 'Depart and quickly take the cup out of my sight' BK 750-52

rag henna **voyde** *alema na whela agen nea* 'therefore depart hence; do not try to annoy us' CW 1276-77

malbew yddrag es thyma an chorle abell [y] *latha* **avoyddama** 'I have damn all regret for killing the churl Abel. I'm off!' CW 1291-92.

Tregear and SA both use the English borrowing **departya** for 'to go away, to depart':

Ken rug oll an x tryb a Israell **departia** *a theworth Roboam mab Salamon* 'Although all the ten tribes of Israel departed from Rehoboam son of Solomon' TH 50a

pan ruga ry y corf tha vos dibbrys ha e gois the vos evys, y a **departias** 'when he gave his body to be eaten and his blood to be drunk, they went away' SA 62a.

For 'to depart' the revived language can use **mos in kerdh**, **dyberth**, **avoydya** or **departya**.

B

BABY

The word **baban** is attested once:

Thum du offrynnyaff pen margh tan ha gore in the argh present worthy yma orto skyrennov eff a dall deneren nov rag **baban** *a welogh why* 'To my god I offer a horse's head; take it and put it in your chest, a worthy present. There are hooks on it. It is worth nine pence as a doll which you can see' BM 3400-05

This occurs in a passage where the tyrant and his three torturers are offering gifts to their god, a bull's head, a ram's head, a horse's head and three ravens. The second torturer here offers his horse's head with the **skyrennow** 'hooks' on it.

The word **baban**, like its Welsh congener *baban*, probably derives from ***maban** 'little boy, small child' < **mab** + **an**. It has probably been contaminated in both languages by the English word 'babe'. Welsh *baban* can mean both 'small child' and 'doll'. Here in the Cornish of BM it appears to have the second sense 'doll, puppet'. In spite of its etymology, there is no evidence that the Cornish word **baban** was ever used to mean 'baby'.

A genuine word for 'baby' in Cornish is **baby**, *plural* **babiow**:

merugh an **babyov** *wek* 'look, the sweet babies' BM 1577.
awoys ovn peryl na pegh eff a dre gena hythyv dus dus a **vaby** 'in spite of peril or sin, he will come home with me today. Come, come, baby' BM 3633-35.

In Cornish, as in the other Celtic languages, the word for 'child' is also used to refer to a baby or infant in arms. This can be seen from numerous examples:

na heb mur lavur defry benytha ny's tevyth **flogh** 'nor without much labour indeed will she ever have a baby' OM 299-300
arluth hen yw re nebes mar quren **flogh** *vyth denythy* 'Lord, that is too little, if we ever have a baby' OM 389-90

baby   **GERYOW GWIR**

*yma **flogh** genaf genys dre voth a'n tas dev inweth* 'I have given birth to a baby through the will of God the Father also' OM 672-73

*yn wethen me a welas yn ban vhel worth scoren **flogh** byen nowyth gynys hag ef yn quethow maylys* 'i'n the tree I saw high up in the tree a little newborn baby and he was wrapped is cloths' OM 804-06

*erbyn reson yv in beys heb hays gorryth thymo creys bones **flogh** vyth concevijs in breys benen heb awer* 'against reason it is in this world, believe me, that any baby be conceived in the womb of a woman truly without male seed' BM 844-47

*In kepar maner yma S Agustyn ow cowse an beseth an **flehis**, ha fatell yll an sacrament na provaylya, lyas onyn a ra decessia kyns y the wothfas an effect anotha* 'In a similar way St Augustine speaking of the baptism of babies and that that sacrament can prevail; many a one will die before they know the effect of it' TH 37

*fatell ra an feith an re na a throlla an **flehis** the vos besitthis ha cristonys preveylya thyn **flogh** a vo drys the receva y cristoneth* 'that the faith of those who bring the babies to be baptized and christened prevails for the baby who is brought to receive his christening' TH 37-37a

*lowarth mamb wore e **flehis** the benenas erall the vaga* 'many a mother sends her babies to other women to be breastfed' SA 59

*me a weall vn mayteth wheake ow setha in pur sertan hag in y devran **flogh** teake* 'I see a sweet virgin sitting indeed and in her bosom a fair baby' CW 1835-37

*Ha Dzhûan medh hyi, po 'rygo huei moz ker, thera vi gillyz trei mîz gen **hlôh*** 'Hey, Jowan, she said, when you departed, I was three months gone with a baby' BF: 19

*saue a man ha kebar an **flô** yonk ha e thama ha ke tha Egyp* 'get up and take the young baby and his mother and go to Egypt' Rowe

*ha thavanaz mehaz, ha lathaz oll an **flehaz** a era en Bethalem, ha oll an dro, en dadn deaw vloth coth, a tho an termen a reeg e gofen thur an teez feere* 'and he sent out and killed all the babies that were in Bethlehem and all around under two years old from the time when he enquired of the wise men' Rowe

*Pa reg e saval, e comeraz an **flô** yonk ha e thama en noaze ha geeth tha Egyp* 'When he rose, he took the baby and his mother and went into Egypt' Rowe.

The word for 'baby' in revived Cornish should perhaps either be **baby**, **babiow** or **flogh**, **flehes**. There is no evidence for **baban** with the sense 'baby' in Cornish, and it would be thus inauthentic to use it with such a sense.

BAD

The default word for 'bad' in Cornish is **drog**. This can be used as a predicative adjective:

***Drog yv** genef gruthyl den* 'I regret having created man' OM 917

GERYOW GWIR   bad

a ihesu whek re iovyn **drok yv** *gyne na venta kammen tryle yn maner tek* 'dear Jesus, by Jovyn I regret that you will not convert nicely at all' PC 1291-94

drok yv *gynef bones mar lyes enef ow mos the'n nef* 'I am sorry that so many souls are going to heaven' RD 298-300

thomas ty yv muskegys hag yn muscokneth gyllys **drok yv** *gynef vy lemmyn* 'Thomas, you are mad and sunken in insanity, I regret' RD 1127-29

thomas ty yv me a grys an gokye den yn beys ha henna **yv drok** 'Thomas, you, I believe, are the silliest man in the world and that is bad' RD 1453-55

drog yv *gena doys oma* 'I regret coming here' BM 457

Drog o *the gan owth owtya* 'Evil was your song as you yelled' BK 27.

If **drog** is used as an attributive adjective, it must be prefixed to its noun:

In meth an lader arall **drok ʒen** *os kepar del ves* 'The other thief said, You are an evil man as you have been' PA 192a

Gans an eʒewon war hast **drok ʒewas** *a ve dyʒgtys* 'By the Jews in haste an evil drink was got ready' PA 202a

A out warnes **drok venen** *worto pan wrussys cole* 'damn you, evil woman, that you paid attention to him' OM 221-22

mar ny fystyn pup huny why as byth **drog vommennow** 'if everyone does not hurry, you will get evil blows' OM 2323-24

kepar hag ef on crousys ha dre wyr vreus quyt iuggys rak agan **drok ober** *kens* 'like him we are crucified and by true judgement condemned for our evil deeds ere now' PC 2900-02

pan ello ow corf yn pry guyth vy rak an joul **drok was** 'when my body goes into the earth, protect me from the devil, the evil fellow' RD 1563-64

vyngens re'n geffo amen ha **drok thyweyth** 'may he suffer vengeance, amen, and an evil end' RD 2085-86

kemereugh corf a'n **drok was** *vgy ow flerye gans blas yw myligys* 'take the body of the evil fellow that is stinking with an accursed odour' RD 2159-61

Ser duk me a weyl tevdar ha parcel a **throk coscar** *pur thevrey orth y sewa* 'Sir duke, I see Teudar and a group of evil fellows indeed following him' BM 2358-60

pan rellens remembra ha lamentya aga pehosow haga **drog bewnans** *esans ow ledya* 'when they remember and lament their sins and their evil lives which they were leading' TH 6a

yma eff ow dysky fatell ra **drog gerryow** *ha* **drog prederow** *deservya condemnacion* 'he teaches that evil words and evil thoughts will deserve condemnation' TH 9

kepar dell ra an laddron, advltrers, denlath, hag oll an **drog pobill** *erell* 'as the thieves do, adulterers, murderers and all the other evil people' TH 24

So rag an wyckyd han **drog requestys** *ma eff a ve grevously rebukys ha reprovys* 'but for these wicked and evil requests he was grievously rebuked and reproved' TH 46a

A **throg thewath** *re wynwhy!* 'May you die an evil death!' BK 473

Thymmo heb mar, te **drog-den**, *ny vethyth gowr* 'To me indeed, you evil man, you will not be a husband' BK 2960-61

bad

Gallas Lucifer **droke preve** 'Lucifer, the evil snake, has gone' CW 335

them shape ow honyn ytama why a weall omma treylys **drog pullat** *ha brase* 'to my own shape, behold me, you see me transformed, an evil fellow and a great one' CW 925-27

gallas genaf ve **droag lam** *poran rag an ober na* 'I have suffered an evil fate precisely for that deed' CW 1687-88.

Drog cannot be used after the adverbial particle **yn**; thus *****yn trog** 'badly' is unattested. 'Badly' in Cornish is most frequently rendered by **drog-** prefixed to verbs:

gueyt an harlot na scapyo **drok handle** *del om kyry pan gyffy dalhen ynno* 'make sure that the scoundrel does not escape being badly treated, as you love me, when you get your hands on him' PC 990-92

dre laha y coth dotho **drok dywethe** 'by law he ought to die badly' PC 1827-28

y thadder yw **drok tylys** *pan y'n lathsons dybyte* 'his goodness has been badly repaid since they have killed him without mercy' PC 3096-97

hy re ruk ov delyfrya mes a preson mam kerra le mayth ena **drokhendelys** 'she has delivered me from prison, dearest mother, where I was being badly treated' BM 3758-60

me a'm bues gallos i'n bys ha'm yskerans a **throkfar** 'I have power in the world and my enemies will fare badly' BK 1411-12.

The English borrowing **bad** 'bad, poor, deficient' is also used as an adjective:

eugh whyleugh thy'mmo pilat gothfetheugh ma na veugh **bad** 'go, seek for me Pilate; mind that you are not deficient' RD 1773-74

whet kerghough thy'mmo pilat yn y geuer del fuef **badt** 'again fetch Pilate to me as I was deficient regarding him' RD 1885-86

mar te cherite requyria the predyry, the cowsse da, ha the wull da the bub den, da ha **bad**, *fatell yll an rewlysy an wlas executia justis war drog pobill gans charite?* 'if charity demands that we think and speak and do good to everybody, good and bad, how can the rulers of the country execute justice on bad people with charity?' TH 24a

an ros a gymmar inny kyffrys an puscas da han **bad** *warbarth* 'the nets takes up in itself both the good fish and the bad together' TH 34

yma lyas sort a bobill ow pewa in dan an catholik egglos, ran da, ran **bad** 'there are many kinds of people living under the catholic Church, some good, some bad' TH 34

[*not*] *ef the recevia pith ew* **badd**, [*eff a*] *recevyas corf Dew warlerth* **badd** *maner* 'not that he received what is bad, he received the body of God in a bad way' SA 65a.

It can also function as an adverb:

*tebel seruont a leuer mar serf ef **bad** y vester ke the honan ha gura guel* 'a wicked servant says, if he serves his master badly, go yourself and do better' PC 2283-85.

And it used as a prefixed adjective:

*whath kenth ew ow hendas cayne pur **bad dean** lower accomptys me an kymmar in dysdayne mar ny vethaf ve prevys whath mere lacka* 'still though my grandfather Cain accounted a very bad man, I will disdain him if I am not proven to be much worse' CW 1446-50.

*Huei òl? mêr a huei aniustîz iou (a medh Dzhûan) gyr ter o an [dhiz-urêg ha manah] 'ryg an **bad-ober**?* 'You all? Look it is an injustice, said Jowan. Know that it was the ale-wife and a monk who did the evil work' BF: 18

*Piu a 'ryg an **bad-ober**? Piu a 'ryg an **bad-ober**? medh Dzhân; mar ny[m ez]dra dheffa previ peu a 'ryg an **bad-ober**; mî a vedn krêg ragta* 'Who did the evil-work? Who did the evil work? said Jowan; if I haven't got something that will prove who did the evil work, I will hang for it' BF: 18.

The most important point to notice here is that **drog** cannot function as an attributive adjective after its noun, but must rather be prefixed to it. Moreover the Cornish for 'badly' is not ***yn trog**, but **drog-** prefixed to its verb.

BATTLE

Nance suggests three words for the noun 'battle': **cas** (UC *cas*) *f.*, **batel** *f.* and ***ar**. ***Ar** is unattested and there is no need for it. **Cas** 'battle' in the texts is sometimes difficult to distinguish from **cas** 'case' (KS **câss**) and **cas** 'hateful'. **Cas** 'battle' is not common outside the expression **senjy cas** 'to fight a battle'. Moreover no plural is attested. The following examples are found:

*tus ven gweskis yn arvow kepar ha del ens 3en **gas*** 'stout men dressed in armour as though they were going to battle' PA 64b

*hag in batal hag in **cas** me a'n socker in pub plas gans ow mebel* 'and in encounter and in battle I will assist him everywhere with my equipment' BK 1439-41

*Mar pyth rys thym synge **cas**, ases lyas myghtern gwlas a the thymmo gans y rowt thu'm gweras smart!* 'If I have to fight a battle, how many kings of kingdoms will come to me with their hosts sharply to assist me!' BK 1863-66

*Lowena ha beawtys the warthyvyas lyas **cas**!* 'Joy and delights to the victor of many battles!' BK 1922-23

*Arthor Gornow, myghtern freth, a vyn orta syngy **cas*** 'Arthur, the Cornishman, an impetuous king, will do battle with you' BK 2502-03

battle   **GERYOW GWIR**

Ny re dueth a lyas gwlas, pan glowsyn the vos serrys, gene' gy rag syngy **cas** 'We have come from many countries, when we heard you were angry, to do battle along side you' BK 2611-13.

Batel *f*, plural **batalyow** is well attested:

rys yv dy'mmo lafurye the vn **vatel** *yredy* 'I must indeed go to a battle indeed' OM 2176-77

arluth cref ha galosek hag yn **bateyl** *barthesek* 'a lord strong and powerful and prodigious in battle' RD 108-09

neb a lath flogh in **batel** *sensys y feth den cruel* 'who kills a child in battle will be considered a cruel man' BM 1630-31

rag henna yma dre reson, **batallyow** *bras theworthan ny requyrys* 'therefore great battles are required from us' TH 28

hag in **batal** *hag in cas me a'n socker in pub plas gans ow mebel* 'and in battle and in encounter I will assist him everywhere with my equipment' BK 1439-41

Ow spous gentyl, Guynuwer, mos the'n **batal** *me a vyn* 'my gentle spouse, Guinevere, I will go into battle' BK 2741-42.

'To do battle, to fight a battle' may be rendered by use of the verb **batalyas**:

Mas lemmyn rys yv porris **batayles** *kyns ys coske* 'But now it is necessary to do battle indeed rather than sleep' PA 51a

in hanov crist thyn yma wans orth escar crist **batalyays** 'in the name of Christ we have a desire to do battle with the enemy of Christ' BM 2473-74.

In the revived language 'battle' should either be **cas** or **batel**, plural **batalyow**. 'To do battle' is either **sensy cas** or **batalyas**.

BEER

The word for 'beer' is attested at all periods:

cervisia **coruf** 'beer' OCV §858

cervisia uel celea **coref** 'beer or ale' OCV §861

corff *bo gvyn a cafen vy dour ny effsen eredy* 'were I to get ale or wine, I should not drink water' BM 661-62

corguela 'best beer' ACB: M 2

Ha why el evah **cor gwella**, *mor seez du brage* 'And you can drink ale if you have malt' ACB: F f 3

Cervisia... C. **Kor**, **kor guelha** 'Ale, beer' AB: 47b

cor 'ale' Borlase.

It seems, therefore, that there are two forms: Old and Middle Cornish **coref**, **corf** and Later Cornish **còr**. There seems to be no warrant for final **v** in this word.

BEG, BEGGAR
There are three different words for 'beggar' in the texts:

A **beggar**
*nynsyv crygy the **beggars** hag a fo aga dyllas cloutys gans dyuers pannow* 'one need not believe beggars whose clothes are patched with various rags' RD 1507-09.

B **begyer**
*In vr na avel **begyer** ty a veth sur heb awer sensys in pov* 'Then you will be considered a beggar in the land indeed and without doubt' BM 416-18

*meth yv gans ol the cufyon tha vones omma dyson avel **begyer** desethys* 'it is an embarrassment to all your dear ones that you indeed should be set here like a beggar' BM 2019-21.

C **gwyll**
*Mendicus... C. **Guilleiu** 'beggar' AB: 88c.

In the last example **guilleiu** is a plural given in error as singular. The singular by rights is **gwyll**, and the plural **gwyllyow** is what is to be understood from **guilleiu**.

There is no attested word for 'to beg (as a mendicant)'. Nance suggest ***beggya** on the basis of **begyer**. One might also say **pesy alusyon** or **pesy alusonow** 'to beg alms', although neither expression is actually attested.

BEHAVIOUR, CONDUCT
Under 'to conceive' below it will be noticed that both **omdhon** and **omdhegyans** are each attested once with the sense 'behaviour, conduct'. There are two further ways of expressing the same idea: A) **fara**, a borrowing from the Middle English noun *fare*, one meaning of which is 'manner of acting, behaviour conduct'; **fara**, **farya** is also a verb 'to fare, to behave, to proceed'. B) **conversacyon**, borrowed from Middle English *conversacioun*, of which the primary sense is 'manner of living, behaviour, conduct.' I have collected the following examples:

behaviour

A **fara** 'behaviour, conduct'

*pan drok vo yn a ver tu a thysquythysta thy'nny pan wreta mar coynt **fara** ow scollye agan guara* 'what evil shortly will you show us, that you exhibit such strange conduct in scattering our wares?' PC 338-41

*me a vyn mose thom sera tha welas pana **fara** a wra ef an nowethys* 'I shall go to my father to see what conduct he will show at the news' CW 1184-86.

B **conuersacyon** 'manner of living, behaviour, conduct'

*Meriasek lowena dys densa ath **conuersascon** pur guir yth oys acontys* 'Greetings to you, Meriasek; very truly you are considered a good man in your conduct' BM 2546-48

*densa dy **conuersasconn** sur in mesk ol y nascon ny a wor guir y vose* 'a good man in his conduct among all his nation I know that he is indeed' BM 2917-19

*Densa ath **conuersasconn** ty yv in meske the nascon* 'A good man in your conduct are you among your nation' BM 2944-45

*Ny wor mas ran pur thyson in beys y **conuersasconn*** 'In truth only a few know his conduct in the world' BM 4440-41

*Han re na a rella indella ymowns in sure in forth a salvacion, mar te va ha folya henna in y **conuersacion*** 'and those who do thus, are on the sure road to salvation, if he follows that in his behaviour' TH 20

*na rens whath na rens ef examnya den vith arell, mas y golan y honyn, y vewnans, y **conuersacion**, ha ny vith eff deceyvys* 'let him not still, let him not examine anyone else, but his own heart, his life, his behaviour, and he will not be deceived' TH 23-23a.

There are thus four expressions for 'conduct, behaviour, way of life' in Cornish: **omdhon**, **omdhegyans**, **fara** and **conuersacyon**. Of these **conuersacyon** is by far the best attested.

BEHIND

The preposition **adrëv** is attested only once in all Cornish literature:

*ny gowsyn yn tewolgow **adryff** tus yn vn hanas* 'we did not speak in the dark, whispering behind people' PA 79d.

To translate 'behind me, you, him' etc. **wàr ow lergh**, **wàr dha lergh**, **wàr y lergh**, etc. are used:

*Ihesus a ve hombronkis ha **war y lyrgh** mur a lu* 'Jesus was led and behind him a great crowd' PA 163c

***war y lergh** guel yv mones* 'it is better to go after him' BM 3248.

There is no evidence for such forms as **adrëv dhymm**, **adrëv dhis**, etc.

BIG see LARGE

BODY

The commonest word for 'body' in the texts is **corf**, plural **corfow**. Here are a very few examples:

*an arghans a gemeras rag **corf** crist ʒe rysseve ef as tewlys dre sor bras ʒen eʒewon yntreʒe* 'the silver which he had received for delivering the body of Christ, he threw it in great anger among the Jews' PA 103bc
*En beʒow yn lower le apert a ve egerys han **corfow** esa ynne a ve yn ban drehevys* 'The graves in many places were opened wide and the bodies in them were raised up' PA 210ab
*my ny vennaf growethe bynytha gans **corf** eva* 'I will never lie alongside the body of Eve' OM 624-25
*ow **corf** yv re'n oferen kepar del leuerys theugh* 'it is my body, by the mass, as I told you' PC 764-65
*syr pilat thy's lowene **corf** Cryst a gysseugh gyne yn beth gallas* 'hail to you, Sir Pilate; the body of Christ which you left with me has gone into the tomb' RD 37-9
*nyns yv onest thys heb nam dones therag arlythy ha ty noth the **corff** ol trogh* 'it is not decent for you without doubt to appear before nobles naked and your body all diseased' BM 3044-46
*the settia agys **corfow** hagys enevow hooll the thu galosek in sacryfice* 'to set your bodies and souls entirely to almighty God in sacrifice' TH 35
*kynth on **corfow** da ha fuer, an myr ha'n wel anotha a'gen teylly* 'though we are bodies good and wise, his look and appearance went through us' BK 2327-29
*in nergh **korf** kemmys a vo in arvow rys ew thotha hastia thu'm arluth uhall* 'as many have the power of their bodies in arms must hasten to my noble lord' BK 2369-71
*agen **corfow** nooth gallas* 'our bodies have become naked' CW 856
*thethoryanz a'n **corf** ha bewnans heb dywath* 'the resurrection of the body and the life without end' ACB: E e 3.

It is noteworthy, however, that the word **body** is commonly used to mean both 'body' and 'person':

*ny a whyth in thy **vody** sperys [may] hylly bewe* 'we will breathe spirit into your body so that you may live' OM 61-2
*Na lader by my vallok kyn fe vyth mar vras quallok na mar hovtyn a'y **vody*** 'he will not steal by my cullion though he be never so great an oaf nor so haughty in his person' OM 2067-69
*marogeth my ny alla yma cleves y'm **body*** 'I cannot ride; there is a sickness in my body' OM 2145-46
*nep a rella yn ketella mernans yv guyw th'y **vody*** 'who ever does thus, death is due to his body' OM 2240-42

body   **GERYOW GWIR**

dew **vody** *tha ough yn guyr* 'you are two good persons' OM 2461

dev yv spirys hep **body** *den yv corf gans ysyly* 'God is spirit without body, man is body with limbs' PC 1732

vnwyth mar pyth den marow y spyrys neffre hep gow byth ny thue yn y **vody** 'once a man is dead, spirit indeed can never enter into his body' PC 1748-50

me a'n knouk fest dybyte man geffo pup ol bysne ow myres worth y **vody** 'I shall strike him very cruelly so that everyone may learn a lesson looking at his body' PC 2091-93

hag y a wyth y **vody** *na potre bys vynary* 'and they will preserve his body from decay for ever' PC 3199-200

me a'n kyf by god ys blod kyn fo an harlot mar wod na mar houtyn y **body** 'I will find him by God's blood, though the scoundrel be so mad and so haughty in his person' RD 543-45

trueth vye del wothogh latha omma iij myl flogh awoys sawya vn **body** 'it would have been a pity, as you know, to kill three thousand children here in order to heal one body' BM 1656-58

Ren ena us om **body** *poren an re na ens y* 'By the soul in my body they were exactly those' BM 1809-10

molleth du war y **vody** *scherevwa yv in meske myl* 'God's curse on his body, he is a scoundrel among a thousand' BM 3279-80

Mer syngys of the'th cara del os **body** *heb paraw* 'Greatly bound am I to love you, as you are a peerless person' BK 395-96

Ow maseger Cuf-e-Das, joy war the vody ha ras! 'My messenger Cuf-e-Das, joy and grace upon your body!' BK 876-77

Atomma losow an gog ha coulregh, (n)y a son drog hearlygh in agys **body** 'Here are lords-and-ladies and water pepper, they will heartily soothe pain in your body' BK 1165-67

Nyng es ewyth in the **vody** *moy ys leugh* 'there is no vigour in your body any more than in a calf' BK 1244-46

Me ew **body** *dyspusond, Augel, myghtern in Scotland* 'I am a powerful body, Augel, king of Scotland' BK1279-80

Ny wyskys pan **body** *a'th par* 'Never did cloth cover a body equal to you' BK 1763-64

Myghtern Grece ove o'm towr, Epystrophus, **body** *flower* 'I am Epistrophus, king of Greece in my tower, a choice person' BK 2417-18

Ny vyth cosolak goyth in ow **body** 'No sinew in my body will rest' BK 2471-72

Me, Ypolyt, duk Creth heb fall, gan bonas mal war e **vody** *a ra spyt* 'I, Hippolytus, duke of Crete, without fail with a will shall inflict harm upon his person' BK 2663-66

me a wra ge dean a bry havall thagan face whare hag a wheth in [th]y **body** *sperys may hallas bewa* 'I will make you, man, of clay like unto my face indeed and will breathe spirit in your body so that you may live' CW 345-48.

Since **body** is so well-attested in the texts with the senses 'body' and 'person', there is no reason to proscribe its use.

TO BOW (DOWN)

For this Nance suggests UC *omblegya, which is unattested. 'To bow (down)' is always simply **plegya** without the reflexive prefix:

*nyng ew ragos se laʒe Cryst yv synsys mur dremas ʒe ʒenwyth awos **plegye*** 'it is not for you to kill Christ, who is considered a good man, because you are yielding to anybody' PA 123bc

*ha'y gras theugwhy re wronntyo nefre the **blygye** thotho yn dalleth hag yn dyweth* 'and may he grant you his grace always to yield to him in the beginning and at the end' OM 1726-28

*rak hedre vyugh ow **pleghye** thywhy byth ny's dysk neffre yn nep maner* 'for while you are yielding he will never take it [his garment] off for you in any way' RD 1950-52

*na re'au **pleghie** dothans na worria dothans* 'thou shalt not bow down to them nor worship them' BF: 55

*Ti na ras **pleghe** dha rina, na gura gurthy* 'Thou shalt not bow down to those, nor worship' Gwavas MS.

***Omblegya** ought perhaps not to be used.

BOX

When 'box' in English means a large wooden or metal container or chest, the default word in revived Cornish is **kyst**. When the box is a small one, the usual word in the revived language is **kysten**. Neither can really be justified. Both derive from Borlase and are ultimately based on Welsh *cist* 'chest'. In the texts, however, 'large box' is rendered by A) **cofyr** and 'small box' by B) **box**:

A **cofyr**

*pur ker ty a veth guythys avel ov flogh ov honyn hag in quethov fyn malys in ov **cofyr** sur gorys* 'very dearly you will be kept like my own child and wrapped in fine cloths and set in my chest' BM 3640-43

*Cista... C. **Kofar** 'Chest'* AB: 48a.

B **box**

*Benyn dyr vur cheryte y **box** ryche leun a yly a vgh crist rag y vntye hy a vynnas y derry corf ihesus rag comfortye* 'A woman through great charity wished to break a box full of rich unguent over Christ to comfort the body of Jesus' PA 35a-c

*Iudas fals a leuerys trehans dynar a vone en **box** oll beʒens gwerthys awos den rag y ranne the vohosogyon yn bys* 'False Judas said: for three hundred pence let all the box be sold for a man to distribute it to the poor of the world' PA 36a-c

box GERYOW GWIR

*ow **box** mennaf the terry a dal mur a vone da war the pen y thenewy ha war the treys magata* 'I will break my box which is worth much money, pour it over your head and upon your feet as well' PC 485-88.

In the interests of authenticity, **cofyr** and **box** are perhaps to be preferred to **kyst** and **kysten**.

BRANCH

The commonest word used in revived Cornish for 'branch' is **scoren** *f.*, *coll.* **scor**, *plural* **scorennow**. This item is well attested:

Ramus, **scorren** 'branch' OCV §685
*warnethy yma gvethen vhel gans lues **scoren** saw noth ol yns hep dylyow* 'upon it there is a tree with many branches but they are all bare without leaves' OM 775-77
*noth yv ol hy **scorennow*** 'all its branches are bare' OM 780
*myr pandra wylly ynny kefrys gwrythyow ha **scoren*** 'observe what do you see in it, both roots and branch' OM 801-02
*yn wethen me a welas yn ban vhel worth **scoren** flogh byen nowyth gynys* 'high up in the tree upon a branch I saw a small newborn child' OM 804-06
*A das ker my a welas yn paradys fenten ras ha warnythy vn wethen hyr gans mur a **scorennow*** 'Dear father, I saw in paradise a blessed spring and growing upon it a tall tree with many branches' OM 835-38
*me a ysten an **skoran** kymmar an frute annethy* 'I will bend the branch; take the fruit from her' CW 687-88
*a reeg e thanen tho an kensa **skoren** an choy na igge trig[az lebben] nez tho an Karrack Glooz an Cooze* 'who sent him from the first branch of the kindred that is not now living near St Michael's Mount' BF: 27.

The word **branch**, *plural* **branchys** is also well attested:

*ha war woles pan vyrys my a welas hy gurythyow bys yn yffarn dywenys yn mysk mur a tewolgow ha'y **branchys** yn ban tyvys bys yn nef vhel golow* 'and when I looked at its base, I saw its roots penetrating into hell in the midst of great darkness and its branches above growing up into high bright heaven' OM 781-86
*dyuythys yv hag yma yn hy myyn **branch** olyf glas* 'she has come and there is in her beak a branch of green olive' OM 1121-22
***branchys** olyf pan kyffyn my a set athyragtho* 'when I get olive branches, I shall set them before him' PC 244-45
*mar ny gaffaf **branchys** vas me a thystryp ow dyllas hagh a's set y dan y treys* 'if I do not find good branches, I shall strip off my clothes and set them under his feet' PC 249-51

ow benneth ol ragas bo ow tos yn onor thy'mmo gans **branchis** *flourys kefrys* 'may you all have my blessing coming in honour to me with branches and flowers also' PC 265-67

Then tase dew rebo grassyes an golam ew devethys ha gensy **branche** *olyf glase* 'Thanks be to the Father, the dove has come with a branch of green olive' CW 2460-62.

BREAST, BREASTPLATE

When 'breast' refers to chest or upper torso in either man or woman, the customary word in revived Cornish is **clos dywvron**. This expression is unattested itself, being respelt from *Pectus,* **cluit duiuron** 'breast' OCV §55. The attested Middle Cornish word for 'breast' in this sense, however, is **brèst**:

my a re gans mur a ras whare lemyn strokyas bras pur evn war an **brest** *arag bys may cothe hy the'n dor* 'I shall give with much grace straightway now great blow exactly on the breast in front until she fall down' OM 2715-18.

For 'breastplate' some commentators recommend the word ***luryk**. This is unattested in the texts although it may occur with the sense 'breastwork, rampart' in the two place-names *Calerik* < ?**ker+luryk** and *Penhalurick* < ?**pen+hal+luryk**. The attested word for 'breastplate' is **brestplât**:

yth o ow fous ha'm **brustplat** *purpur garow thu'm strothe* 'my robe and my breastplate were rough purple to constrict me' RD 2591-92.

Since the form ***luryk** is unattested outside place-names and since there is no evidence that it was ever used in Middle Cornish to mean 'breastplate', there is no need to introduce it into the revived language. The word **brestplât** is quite sufficient.

When 'breast' refers to a woman's breast, the word is **bronn, brodn** and the dual is **dewvron, dywvron**.

pectus, cluit **duiuron** 'breast, chest' OCV §55
may fyth torrow benegis bythqueth na allas e[m]ʒon ha benenas kekyffrys na ve ʒeʒe denys **bron** 'so that wombs will be blessed that never could conceive, and women also whose breasts were never sucked' PA 169cd
govy vyth pan vef genys a dor ov mam dynythys na bythqueth pan denys **bron** 'woe is me that I was born coming from my mother's womb or ever that I sucked breast' OM 1753-55
hag in y **devran** *flogh teake* 'and at her breast a beautiful baby' CW 1837
hay floghe pur semely maylyes vny **defran** 'and her baby beautifully swaddled at her breast' CW 1909-10
BRON, *a breast, a teat* ACB: L 3 *verso*.

breast   **GERYOW GWIR**

'Breasts' in some forms of Cornish is written **diwvronn*, a spelling is based on Breton *divronn*. Since the diphthong <iw> is not found in traditional Cornish, **diwvronn* not a suitable spelling in Cornish.

BRUSH *see* SWEEP

TO BUILD

The default word in revived Cornish for 'to build' has always been **derevel**, **drehevel**, whose essential meaning is 'to raise'. The sense 'to build' is also represented in the texts:

my a vyn gruthyl castel ha **drehevel** *thy'm ostel ynno jammes rag trege* 'I will construct a castle and make for myself a dwelling to live for ever in it' OM 1709-11

moyses whek ny a **dreha** *ragon chy pols the wonys* 'dear Moses, we will build for ourselves a house to work for a while' OM 1715-16

arluth ytho pyw a wra coul **dreheuel** *ol the chy* 'Lord, therefore who will finish building all your house?' OM 2339-40

Salamon the vap kerra a'n coul **threha** *eredy* 'Solomon your dearest son will complete the building of it indeed' OM 2341-42

kyn fe dyswrys an temple yn tri dyth y'n **drehafse** *bythqueth whet na fe ve guel* 'though the temple were destroyed, he would build in three days that never was it better' PC 382-84

pup den yn bys ma a wor den vyth ol na'n **drehafse** *yn try dythwyth war nep cor* 'everybody in the world knows that no one could build it in three days at all' PC 386-68

me a vyn y examyne y **threheuel** *mar a kor* 'I will examine him to see whether he can build it' PC 389-90

Buz mor mennow **direvall** *warbidn an pow yeine* 'But if you wish to build against the cold country' : F f 3

Sera ve reg lavar dhe'm Gomar mab Japhet, mab Noah vo an den reg clapia kernuak en termen an Tur Babel vo **derevalz** 'my father told me that Gomar son of Japhet son of Noah was the man to speak Cornish when the tower of Babel was built' BF: 46.

The verb **gwil** 'to do, to make' is also used to mean 'to build':

Rag henna fystyn ke **gura** *gorhel a blankos playnyys* 'therefore hurry, go, build a ship of planed planks' OM 949-50

Arluth kepar del vynny an gorhel sur my a'n **gura** 'Lord, as you wish, the ship I will surely build it' OM 965-66

Dauid ny **wreth** *thy'mo chy yn certen bys venary* 'David, you will not build a house for me ever' OM 2333-34

rag mur y carsen defry **guthel** *thymmo oratry in herwyth chy maria* 'for greatly I should like to build an oratory for myself near to the church of St Mary' BM 638-40 *hag omma **gul** me a vyn ryb chapel maria wyn thym oratry* 'and here I shall build a oratory for myself by the chapel of Blessed Mary' BM 652-54

*gwarnys of gans dew an tase tha **wythell** an lesster ma* 'I was warned by God the Father to build this ship' CW 2309-10

*now an lester yth ew **gwryes** teake ha da tham plegadow* 'now the vessel has been built fair and good to my satisfaction' CW 2409-10.

This use of the verb **gwil** 'to do, to make' has parallels elsewhere in the Celtic languages.

Increasingly 'to build' is expressed by means of the English borrowing **byldya**:

*Cyte a ve settys bo **byldys** war meneth ny yll bois coveys* 'A city set or built upon a hill cannot be hidden' TH 17a

*an catholyk egglos a rug crist y honyn **byldya** in y abosteleth* 'the catholic Church, which Christ himself built in his apostles' TH 35a

*ha war an power ma eff a rug **buldya** y egglos* 'and upon this power he built his Church' TH 45a

*ha dre reson y vosa mar sure in feith an egglos a ve **buldys** warnotha* 'and because he was so sure in faith, the Church was built upon him' TH 45a

*ha war an garrak ma me a vyn **buldya** ow egglos* 'and upon this rock I shall build my Church' TH 45a

*Ha yma ow **buldya** y feith in myske re erell war an succession an epscobow a rome* 'And he builds his faith among others upon the succession of the bishops of Rome' TH 48a

*An feith a res thyn ny kafus in agan colonow, pan deffan thyn vois a crist, ew the vos **buldys** in kepar maner war an aucthors an scripture* 'The faith which we must have in our hearts when we come to Christ's table is to be built in the same way upon the authors of scripture' TH 51a

*eff a gotha thotha, bos sufficient grounde rag pub den da oll the **byldya** y consciens warnotha* 'it ought to be sufficient ground for all good men to build their conscience on it' TH 55

*praga ew genas she omma **buyldya** lester mar worthy in creys powe thaworthe an moare* 'why have you got to build such a fine ship in the middle of the land far from the sea?' CW 2296-98.

For 'to build' the revived language has three choices: **derevel**, **gwil** or **byldya**.

TO BURY

I list below the attestations of the Cornish verb for 'to bury':

bury

droga galar ev thy'mmo y **anclethyas** *mar uskys* 'what a grievous sorrow it is to me to bury him so quickly' OM 868-69

en keth oynement a scollyas warnaf rak ow **anclythyas** 'the same ointment she poured out upon me for my burial' PC 547-48

me a's kymmer yn lowen hag a gul trank hep worfen thy's y guerthe the **anclethyas** *crystenyon na vons yn mysk yethewon ov fleyrye re* 'I will take them from you gladly and in perpetuity I will sell it to you to bury Christians so that they won't be stinking too much among Jews' PC 1561-66

y **enclethyes** *vye da* 'it would be good to bury him' PC 3103

ro thy'm kummeas me a'th pys a kymeres corf ihesu yv yn pren crous tremenys may hallo bos **anclethys** *yn beth men the voth mars yw* 'give me permission, I beg you, to take the body of Jesus who is dead upon the cross, that he may be buried in a tomb, if it is your wish' PC 3112-16

ef a vyth sur **anclethys** *yn le na fue den bythqueth* 'he will be buried surely in a place where no man ever was' PC 3134-35

iosep vs thy'so cummyas an corf ker the **anclethyas** 'Joseph, have you permission to bury the beloved body?' PC 3139-40

cummyas grantyys thy'm yma th'y **anclethyas** *yn lowen* 'I have been gladly granted permission to bury him' PC 3146-47

otte cendal glan a les parys rag y **enclethyes** 'here is fine clean linen spread out, ready to bury him' PC 3159-60

ihesu a fue **anclethyys** *hag yn beth a ven gorrys* 'Jesus was buried and placed in a tomb of stone' RD 1-2

me a wruk y **anclethyes** *hag a'n gorras yn beth men* 'I buried him and put him in the tomb' RD 439-40

woge y vos gurys marow tus yn beth a'n **anclethyas** 'after he was put to death men buried him in the tomb' RD 1268-69

ny a vyn moys alemma the **anclethyias** *an dus vays us mertherijs del glowa* 'we will go hence to bury the good men who have been martyred, as I hear' BM 1322-24

ihesu crist map maria ha genys a lel werheys a fue marov in grovs pren hag **anclethys** *in beth men* 'Jesus Christ, son of Mary, and born of a true virgin, was dead on the cross and buried in the tomb' BM 4047-50

ihesu crist yth yv henna a fue marov **anclethyys** 'that is Jesus Christ who was dead and buried' BM 4081-82

mones deglos ny a vyn thy **anclethyes** *in certyn an corff uskys* 'we will go to church to bury the body quickly' BM 4470-72

Lemen parusugh an beth in hanov crist del deleth may hallen y **anclethyas** 'Now get ready the grave in the name of Christ, as is fitting, so that we may bury him' BM 4509-12

an lell kig agen arluth Christ a ve goris in grows, marow ha **inclithis** 'the true flesh of our Lord Christ was put on the cross, dead and buried' SA 61a

pen vo dewath y thethyow hag in doer tha vos **anclythys** *goer sprusan in y anowe* 'when his days end and he is to be put in the ground, place a pip in his mouth' CW 1850-52 *ow thas pan ewa marowe me a vyn y* **anclythyas** 'since my father is dead, I will bury him' CW 2078-79

creages war an growse, marrou ha **inclithes** 'hanged upon the cross, dead and buried' BF: 41

gorris war an growse the merrans, marrow, hag **ynclythys** 'put to death upon the cross, dead and buried' ACB: E e 3.

In some forms of Cornish the verb for 'to bury' is spelt **ynkleudhya*. There is no warrant in the texts for such a spelling, since in the texts the second vowel is always **e** or **i/y**.

BUT

The default word for the conjunction 'but' in revived Cornish has always been **mès**. This is fairly well attested, though not in all texts:

Maras ew ʒe voth ow ʒas gura ʒen payn ma ow gasa **mes** *beʒens guris ʒe vynnas arluth du ʒe voth del ve* 'If it is thy wish, my Father, make this torment leave me, but be your wish be done, Lord God, as may be your will' PA 55ab

En eʒewon a vynne porrys y vonas leʒys resons y a rey ragthe **mes** *war fals yʒ ens growndys* 'The Jews wished precisely that he be killed; they gave reasons for it but they were founded on falsity' PA 118ab

a pup plos yth ough glanhys **mes** *ol nyns ough gulan deffry yma onan pur vostyys omma agys company* 'you are cleansed of all stain but you are not all clean indeed; there is one who is very unclean here of your company' PC 865-68

mernans ny wressans tastya **mes** *in pleasure venarye y a wressa prest bewa* 'they would not have tasted death, but in pleasure they would have lived always for ever' CW 995-97

rag henna woʒa hemma nefra ny wren rejoycya **mes** *pub ere oll ow murnya heb ioy vyth na lowena der tha wadn ober omma* 'therefore hereafter we shall not rejoice, but will mourn always without any joy or happiness through your evil work here' CW 1271-74

nyng es tra in bys ma gwryes **mes** *thewhy a wra service* 'there is nothing created in this world but serves you' CW 2515-16.

Mès 'but' is a variant of **màs** 'but', which is slightly commoner in the texts than **mès**:

Ihesus crist leun a bete a leueris ʒen dowʒek wy yv glan a bup fylte **mas** *nyni ough ol da na whek* 'Jesus Christ full of mercy said to the twelve: You are clean of all filth, but you are not all good nor sweet' PA 47ab

Mas *lemmyn rys yv porris batayles kyns ys coske* 'But now indeed it is very necessary to do battle before sleeping' PA 51a *ny fue ragtho y honan yn gothefys ef certan* **mas** *rak kerenge map den* 'it was not for himself that he suffered it indeed, but for the sake of mankind' PC 3226-28

epscop worthy me ath ra chyff peb les oll an pov ma na moy me ny deserya **mas** *gorthya mahum pup preys* 'I will make you a worthy bishop, chief of the whole breadth of this land; I desire nothing more than to worship Mahound always' BM 896-99

Ov flehys eugh why de dre ha thymmo na regh grasse **mas** *only the crist avan* 'My children, go home and do not give thanks to me but only to Christ on high' BM 3150-52

ny vynna an corfe abeya an ena, nan ena ny vynna obeya du, **mas** *pub tra in den o treylys an pith awartha the wolas* 'the body would not obey the soul, nor would the soul obey God, but everything in man was turned upside down' TH 4

ny rug eff leverall in pegh, **mas** *in plurel number, in pehosow, hen ew the venya in mes a onyn y te mere* 'he did not say in sin, but in the plural number, in sins; that means that from one many come' TH 8a

mas *eff a gemeras an nature a then an very substans an wyrhes ker maria y vam* 'but he took the nature of man from the very substance of the Blessed Virgin Mary his mother' TH 12a

ny rug den vith govyn pew a rug hemma na henna, **mas** *cresy an dra* 'no man enquired who did this nor that, but believed the matter' TH 57

nena ne ra an pronter vsya girreow e honyn, **mas** *girreow Christ* 'then the priest does not use his own words, but the words of Christ' SA 62

Na esyny miras wor an bara han dewas ew sittys deragen **mas** *derevall agen mynd ha colan da,* **mas** *cregy faithfully, fatla ew sittis onne Dew war an alter benegas* 'Let us not look upon the bread and drink that is set before us, but raise our minds and good hearts, but faithly believe, that the lamb of God is set upon the blessed altar' SA 65a.

Mès, **màs** is in origin a reduced form of **marnas** 'if not, unless'.

In later Cornish **mès**, **màs** is contaminated by the English conjunction 'but' to give **bùs**:

Christ ew devethis, not dir subtelnath, **bus** *openly the kenever a whelha ha vo o sevall rebta* 'Christ has come, not by subtlety, but openly to all who see or are standing beside him' SA 60

Tee a ill percevia pa vaner a sort esta o qvelas agen saviour Christ, **bus** *e dochya, not only touchia,* **bus** *e thibbry* 'You can perceive in which way you see our saviour Christ, but touch him, not only touch him, but eat him' SA 60a

kins an girryow benegas the vos leveris kyn tra eth o hynvis, **bus** *osa an consecration eth o gwris corf agen arluth Christ* 'beofre the blessed words were said, it was called something else, but after the consecration it has been made the body of our Lord Christ' SA 61a

obba tha gubber; **buz** *mar venta ri them arta; mee a deska deez keen point a skeeans* 'here are your wages; but if you will give them back to me, I will teach you another counsel' BF: 15

rag radden el bose keevez na el skant clappia na guthvaz Curnooack, **buz** *skant den veeth* **buz** *ore guthvaz ha clappia Sousenack* 'for some can be found who can hardly speak or

GERYOW GWIR   **but**

understand Cornish, but hardly anybody who doesn't speak and understand English' BF: 25

Enna a wraze lowar wheal tha weel, bownenge kelles leeas meel, **buz** *materen Willie wraze an wheal ha fesias gy car vez an gweal* 'Then he did much work, lives lost many thousands, but king Willy did the work and put them to flight from the field' LAM: 224

dreffen en tacklow broaz, ma an gymennow hetha go honnen; **bus** *en tacklow minnis, ema an gye suyah hâz go honnen* 'because in big matters they often exert themselves, but in small matters they follow their own nature' ACB: E e 4 *verso*

Buz*, mor mennow direvall war bidn an pow yeine, Why dal veya gowas an brossa mine* 'But if you wish to build against the cold country, you must get the biggest stones' ACB: F f 3.

The commonest word for 'but' in the texts is **saw**:

Tus crist ʒe ves a fyas pep ay du pur voreʒek **saw** *pedyr crist a holyas abell avel vn ownek* 'Christ's people fled away, each one very sorrowful his own way, but Peter followed at a distance like a coward' PA 77ab

ny gewsys ʒe blegadow **saw** *war thu y a vynne dre envy leuerell gow* 'he did not speak to please, but against God they wished through spite to speak falsehood' PA 90bc

War paradys my a'th as **saw** *gvraa vn dra a'm govys* 'I will leave you in charge of paradise, but do one thing for my sake' OM 75-6

sav *an wethen thy'm yma hy bos syghys marthys vras* 'but I am greatly astonished at the tree that it has withered' OM 755-56

Saw *my a greys hy bos segh ha gurys noth ol rag an pegh a pehas ov thas ha'm mam* 'But I believe that it is dry and has been stripped for all the sin which my father and mother sinned' OM 757-59

nyns us den ort ov seruye len ha guyryon me a greys yn ol an beys **sav** *noe ha'y wrek ha'y flehes kefrys* 'no man serves me loyally and innocently, I believe, in all the world but Noah, his wife and his children also' OM 929-32

mergh guarthek mogh ha deves dreugh abervet desempys **sav** *an ethyn byneges y a nyg quyc hag vskys* 'bring in horses, cattle, pigs and sheep immediately, but the blessed birds, they will fly quick and swiftly' OM 1065-68

an bos nos dywy a wra **saw** *nyns ugy ov lesky* 'yonder bush is glowing but it is not burning' OM 1397-98

sav *kyns ys yn tour mones leuereugh thy'm company py le vyth an guel plynsys* 'but before we go into the tower, tell my company where will the rods be planted' OM 2030-32

rys yv dy'mmo lafurye the vn vatel yredy **sav** *dystogh hy a vyth due* 'I must travel to a battle indeed but it will be over very soon' OM 2176-78

gans moreth yth of lynwys war the lergh ov arluth whek **sav** *byner re thewhylly* 'I am filled with sorrow after you, my dear lord, but never may you return' OM 2194-96

ovote vy devethys arte the dre **sav** *syr vrry ev lethys ha the votteler kekyfrys* 'here I am having come back home but Sir Uriah has been killed and your butler as well' OM 2212-15

but   **GERYOW GWIR**

sav *rak peder caradow lyes guyth me re bysys na dreyle y gousesow* 'but for beloved Peter I have often prayed that his resolve would not falter' PC 883-85

sav *me war lergh drehevel a's dyerbyn dyougel yn galile ol warbarth* 'but I after rising will meet them all together certainly in Galilee' PC 896-98

ow tas mar ny yl bones may treylyo mernens the ves ***sav*** *y wothaf thy'm a reys* 'my Father, if it cannot be that death turn away but that I must suffer it' PC 1069-71

mars yv the voth grant an spas na theffo thy'm an mernans ***sav*** *mar ny yl bos nahen the voth prest yn pup hehen y goulenwel yv ow whans* 'if it is your wish, grant the favour that death come not to me, but if it cannot be otherwise, your wish in every way, it is my desire to fulfill it' PC 1088-92

sav *certan nyns o torn da danvon guesyon an par ma gans arvow thu'm kemeres* 'but indeed it was not a good move to send fellows like this with weapons to arrest me' PC 1298-1300

sav *wheth me a leuer thy's woge henma ty a wel map dev sur owth esethe abart dyow th'y lawe the'n tas dev arluth huhel* 'but I tell you hereafter you will see the son of God sitting on the right hand of the Father, Lord God exalted (may he be praised!)' PC 1326-30

me re'n cusullyes myl wyth ***sav*** *ny vyn awos trauyth gage y tebel crygyans* 'I have a thousand times advised him, but he will not abandon his evil belief for anything' PC 1811-13

sav *leuerough cowethe py kefer pren th'y crousye* 'but tell me, companions, where will be found a tree to crucify him?' PC 2534-35

na scrif myghtern yethewen ***sau*** *scryf ynno an bylen the leuerol y vos ef myghtern yethewen certan* 'do not write king of the Jews, but write in it that the scoundrel indeed said he was king of the Jews' PC 2797-800

sav *bytegyns pan y'th welaf bos hep hyreth my ny allaf ha nyns yv marth* 'but when I see you however, I cannot be without longing, and it is no wonder' PC 3175-77

sav *ef ny vew gas the son an dreyn bys yn ympynnyon eth yn y pen* 'but he is not alive; leave of your prattling; the thorns went into his head as far as the brain' RD 1010-12

sav *benen gynef yma dretho the sawye a wra a'th galarow* 'but I have a woman with me; through it she will heal you of your affliction' RD 1682-84

sav *an devgys a vynnays arta y vones prennys the saluascon* 'but the Deity wished that he should be redeemed to salvation' BM 884-86

sav *noswyth athyuvne syght coynt y welys certen* 'but awake at night I saw a strange sight indeed' BM 1785-86

sav *plas aral sur heb mar us then tebel genesek berth in povder* 'but the ill-born fellow naturally has another place indeed in Powdar' BM 2286-88

meryasek yv dewesys ***sav*** *eff ny vyn del glowys y receva eredy* 'Meriasek has been chosen, but he does not wish to accept it, as I have indeed heard' BM 2875-77

kelmys of the vryasek ***sav*** *ny von pur in metyaff* 'I am bound to Meriasek, but I do not know when I shall meet him' BM 4185-86

sow *in creacion a vabden an tas a vsias solempnyty bras* 'but in the creation of mankind the Father used great solemnity' TH 1

GERYOW GWIR   but

Saw *vn kynda a frut an tas du a chargias mabden na rella myllya na tuchia worta* 'But one kind of fruit the God the Father charged mankind that he should not meddle with or touch' TH 2

ny rewgh merwell, ***sow*** *du a wore peskytter may tepprow anythy why a vith kepar ha du* 'you will not die, but God knows as soon as you eat of it you shall be like God' TH 3a

Saw *gyrryow du a worta rag neffra perpetually* 'But the words of God remain for ever perpetually' TH 7

sow *ny rug y wull a pry kepar dell ruga gull an corf a Adam* 'but he did not make him of clay as he made the body of Adam' TH 12a

Saw *an dra ma ew strayng the ran an bobyll, dre reson du the wortas mar bell heb colynwel an promyses* 'But this matter is strange to some people, because God waited so long without fulfilling the promises' TH 13a

yth o gwrys in pub part kepar hag onyn ahanan ny, ***sow*** *pegh only theworth eff exceptys* 'he was made in every respect like one of us, but only that sin was not part of him' TH 15

Walkyow ha gwandrow warlyrth an spuris, ***so*** *na rewgh colynwall lustys an kyge* 'Walk and wander according to the Spirit, but do not fulfill the lusts of the flesh' TH 16a

So *mar ten ha gull ken, y myth crist, nyg esan ow kull bith well agys an pharises, publicans, han hethens* 'But if we do otherwise, says Christ, we do no better than the Pharisees, publicans and heathens' TH 22a

Saw *an deg gormynadow, hag oll an morall preceptys contewnys in testament coth, ny cristonnyan ew kylmys the wetha an re na* 'But the ten commandments, and all the moral precepts contained in the Old Testament, we Christians are bound to keep those' TH 27a

ha fatell o va changys in nature ***so*** *not in forme* 'and that it had been changed in nature, but not in form' TH 56

So *the thu yth ew mater eysy* 'But to God it is an easy matter' TH 56a

Devethys o the dirmyn, ***saw*** *lemmyn un marth a wher* 'Your time had come, but now a miracle is happening' BK 17-8

Anotho te re gowsys, ***saw*** *pew ew ny attendys* 'You spoke of him, but you do not consider who he is' BK 212-13

Nag ew, ow arluth, pur weyr na ny geu galar na gu, ***saw*** *e davas a vyth hyr pub ur ow corthya e Thew* 'No, my lord, he does not suffer pain nor affliction, but his tongue is long always worshipping his God' BK 510-13

Sau *ol theso me a'n gaf rag the vos gyntel ha fre* 'But I forgive you all, because you are gentle and noble' BK 1097-98

Saw *kevennough, del ew a goyth leverys: por theffry ny vith kerys neb mar te va re venowgh* 'But remember that it is said of old, in very truth, if someone come too often, he will not be welcome' BK 1598-600

Saw *gwayt, byth fuer ow nygyssyas, rag ken in suer, thys ny vyth fas omma napel* 'But take care, be shrewd in negotiating, for otherwise surely, you will not have standing here for long' BK 1909-13

Sow *an keth adam yw gwryes* 'But the same Adam has been created' CW 461

Sow *mar callaf der thavys gwyll tha adam thym cola me an drossa tha baynes* 'But if I can by a scheme make Adam harken to me, I would bring him to torments' CW 466-68

sow *pur wyre thymo ve creis* 'but very truly believe me' CW 943

sow *yth ota gy gockye* 'but you are foolish' CW 2324

but   **GERYOW GWIR**

***saw** gans coll a ran tuz a brys neb ny vyth nefra gans ny ankevys* 'but with the loss of some men of importance who will never be forgotten by us' JKeigwin.

In the light of the above examples, it is perhaps curious that **mès, màs** rather than **saw** has become the usual word for 'but' in the revived language. Perhaps it is time for **saw** to be adopted as the usual word for 'but'.

TO BUY

For 'to buy' in his 1952 English-Cornish dictionary Nance gives **prena**. The verb **prena** 'to buy, to redeem, to pay for' is well attested indeed, but it exhibits two differing stems, A) **pren-** and B) **pern-**. Here are some examples:

A **prena**
*Abel a'n **pren** rag henna* 'Therefore Abel will pay for this' OM 524
*kyn fy mar prout ty a'n **pren*** 'be you never so proud, you will pay for it' OM 2669
*gow a leuer an iaudyn ef a'n **pren** re synt iovyn* 'the scoundrel speaks falsehood; he will pay for it by St Jovyn' PC 367-68
*ru'm fay guyr yv agas cous ef a'n **pren** sur wythovt flous* 'upon my faith your speech is true; he will pay for it without doubt' PC 1345-46
*my a'n te thy's war ow feyth ef a'n **pren** kyns tremene* 'I swear it to you upon my faith, he will pay for it before departing' PC 1469-70
*ha my a's **pren** thyworthy's otte an mone parys thy'so the pe* 'and I shall buy it from you; her is the money ready to pay you' PC 1555-57
*y laddre mar whyle den war ow ene ef a'n **pren** may fo dyswrys* 'if somebody tries to steal it, upon my soul he will pay for it so that he will be destroyed' RD 370-72
*rag mar ny'n kefough aplygth sur why a'n **pren*** 'for if you do not find him, of a surety you will pay for it' RD 620-21
*pan dremennogh an bys me agys sperys sur an **pren*** 'when you pass from this word your spirit will pay for it' BM 1892-93
*Suer te a'n **pren*** 'Surely you will pay for it' BK 180
*Me a wostel, te a'n **pren**, awos ol the goyntwyry* 'I bet, you will pay for it, in spite of all your cleverness' BK 924-25
*Mara'n cuthys den, ru'm fay, ef a'n **pren***! 'If any man grieved him, by my faith, he will pay for it!' BK 2461-62
*Y a'n **pren** un gyth a the* 'They will pay for it someday' BK 2549
*Ragon y pesys y das oll y sor may fe gevys gans y gorff dre beynys bras agan pegh may fo **prennys***
'For us he prayed to his Father that all his wrath be fogiven by his body through torments, that our sin might be redeemed' PA 9ab
*hen o 3030 calys feyn agan pegh ny ow **prenne*** 'that was a hard end to him redeeming our sin' PA 196d

GERYOW GWIR   **buy**

ha ganse oynment heb par rag corf Ihesus o **prennys** 'and with them unequalled ointment which had been purchased for the body of Jesus' PA 252c

benythe ny thof a'n plen erna'n **prenne** *an guas na* 'I shall never leave the field of battle until that fellow pay for it' OM 2151-52

del vyth gans the gorf **prennys** *adam hag eva kefrys* 'as Adam and Eve also will be redeemed by your body' OM 2638-39

ny goth aga bos gorrys yn arghov rak bos **prennys** *ganse mernans den bryntyn* 'they ought not be put in the treasury because the death of a fine man was bought with them' PC 1540-42

me a gesul bos ganse **prennys** *da gwon yn nep le rag anclathva crystunyon* 'I advise that with them be bought a good field somewhere as a cemetery for Christians' PC 1543-45

dasserghy sur ef a wra par del **prennas** *an bys ma gans y gyk ha gans y wos* 'he will certainly rise again as he redeemed this world with his flesh and with his blood' RD 61-63

dre ov fegh ty a'm collas ha gans the wos a'm **prennas** 'by my sin you lost me and by your blood you redeemed me' RD 146-47

th'agas **prenne** *me a ros gos ow holon* 'to redeem you I surrender the blood of my heart' RD 165-66

cryst agan **prennas** *yn tyn* 'Christ painfully redeemed us' RD 830

rag a'n **prenna** *y fyrwy hag arte y tasserghy woge henna* 'for whoever would redeem us would die, and again would rise again thereafter' RD 1192-93

sav an devgys a vynnays arta y vones **prennys** *the saluascon* 'but the Godhead wished again that he be redeemed unto salvation' BM 884-85

me a comond der ov gluas naha dewov nag yv vas ha gorthya crist luen a ras agen **prennas** *in grovs pren* 'I command throughout my kingdom that evil gods be rejected and Christ full of grace be worshipped, who redeemed us on the cross' BM 2518-21

nyns yv y voth boys kelys an peth a ruk the **prenna** 'it is not his will that that which he bought be lost' BM 2745-46

der vyrtu a pyjadow te a dryl heb faladow dyl vyn Du a'th **prennas** *ker* 'by virtue of prayer to you will return without fail as God wishes who redeemed you dearly' BK 18-20

ha'm bos parys the sconya pub cam der weras Jesu a'n **prennas** *tyn* 'and that I am ready to reject all wrong by the help of Jesus who redeemed us painfully' BK 2028-30.

B **perna**

ihesus crist a ve mevijs may fynnas dijskynna yn gwerhas ha bos genys gans y gyk agan **perna** 'Jesus Christ was moved that he wished to descend in a virgin and be born to redeem us by his flesh' PA 4b-d

Pehadoryon rag **perna** *o desevijs dre satnas* 'To redeem sinners who had been deceived by Satan' PA 5c

Dew ʒen crist a ʒanvonas ʒe **berna** *boys ha dewas* 'Two men Christ sent to buy food and drink' PA 42a

buy   **GERYOW GWIR**

*ow horf ave yw henma yn meth crist sur ragough wy **pernys** a berth yn bysma dyspresys haneth a vyth* 'my body this is, said Christ, for you, redeemed in this world, which will be dispised tonight' PA 44bc

*an geffo pows as gwyrȝyns ha ȝoȝo **pernas** cleȝe* 'whoever has a cloak let him sell it and let him buy a sword for himself' PA 51b

*Han eȝewon a gewsys pandrew henna ȝynny ny ny an **pernas** ȝeworȝys* 'And the Jews said: What is that to us? We bought him from you.' PA 105ab

*me a vyn gul drynk dywhy mar cafa stoff the **perna*** 'I will make a draught for you if I get stuff to buy' BM 1462-63

*ha me a vyn then benenes ry mona boys ha dewes the **perna*** 'and I will give to the women money to buy food and drink' BM 1671-73

*Ef a'm **pernas** gans e wos* "He redeemed me by his blood" BK 429

*Rag kerensa Marya ha'y Mab a'th **pernas** i'n pren* 'For the sake of Mary and her Son who redeemed you on the tree' BK 788-89

*Kepar del e'th **purnas** ker, Jesu re bo the vethak a'n leper cref anhethek* 'Just as he bought you dearly, may Jesus be your physician for the chronic leprosy' BK 804-06

*Der gras Christ a'gen **pernas*** 'By the grace of Christ who redeemed us' BK 1486

*ha ru'm Arluth a'm **pernys**, thynny ef a leverys, e vos guyryak y'th ympyr* 'and by my Lord who redeemed me, he said to us that he had rights in your empire' BK 2235-27

*ru'm Arluth a'n **pernas** ker!* 'by my Lord who redeemed us dearly!' BK 2545

*Gans the woys te a'n **pernas*** 'By your blood you redeemed him' BK 2837

*ha'n Arluth a'th **pernas** ker re'th lowenha sulvegyns* 'and the Lord who redeemed you dearly, may he gladden you immediately' BK 3152-53

*Ru'm Arluth a'm **pernas** ker! ny wortaf omma pelha* 'By my Lord who redeemed me dearly! I shall not remain here any further' BK 3275-76

*Re Christ a'm **pernas** i'n pren!* 'By Christ who redeemed me on the tree!' BK 3280-81

*Dry dre an mona, ha **perna** muy* 'To bring the money home and buy more' ACB: F f verso

*Na dalle deez **perna** kinnis war an sawe* 'You ought not buy firewood by the load' ACB: F f 3

*Gwell eye veyha **perna** nebas glow* 'It would be better to buy some coal' ACB: F f 3

*Na 'reuh e **berna*** 'Do not buy it' AB: 244c.

It would seem from these examples that 'to buy', the verbal noun is usually **perna**, the 3rd singular present-future is invariably **pren**, the verbal adjective is either **pernys** or **prenys** (written ***prennys***), and the 3rd singular preterite is either **pernas** or **prenas** (written ***prennas***). Perhaps these preferences should be made explicit in future grammars of the language.

58

C

TO CALL

The English verb 'to call' has at least four meanings: A) 'to cry out'; B) when 'for' follows 'to beg for'; C) 'to call, to summons'; D) 'to call by name, to name'. The Cornish verb **gelwel** 'to call' can be used in all these four senses:

A **gelwel** 'to cry out'

Otte voys mernans abel the vroder prest ov **kelwel** *a'n dor warnaf pup teller* 'Behold the voice of the death of Abel your brother is always calling to me everywhere from the earth' OM 577-79

ny fyn an guas **gelwel** *tru na pygy cafus merci* 'the fellow will neither call out alas nor beg to get mercy' PC 2089-90

pendra reuy dar napya ay num clewugh ov **kelwel** 'what are you doing? Eh? Napping? Do you not hear me calling?' BM 958-59

Dun ahanan, Pen Tarow. 'Ma ow arluth ow **kelwal** 'Let go, Bull Head. My lord is calling' BK 338-39

pan e'th clowas ow **kylwal***, meskegys moy ys gwenhal* 'when I heard you calling, I became more ecstatic than a swallow' BK 1108-09.

B **gelwel** 'to call for, to beg for'

moyses sur my re beghas hag a henna a **elow** *mersy war dev agan tas may affo an peghosow* 'Moses, surely I have sinned and therefore call for mercy from God our Father, that he may forgive the sins' OM 1863-66

thotho ef me a'n gafse a menne **gelwel** *gyuyans* 'I would forgive if he were to call for forgiveness' PC 1815-16.

C **gelwel** 'to summon'

vthyk mur yv the areth leman worth agan **gylwel** 'dreadful is your speech now summoning us' PC 953-55

yth egen yn cres almayn orth vn prys ly yn pur wyr pan fuf **gylwys** 'I was in the middle of Germany at lunchtime indeed when I was summoned' RD 2148-50

pur vth o clewas an cry genef orth agas **gylwel** 'sheer horror it was to hear my cry as I summoned you' RD 2244-45

call   **GERYOW GWIR**

galwy *dis bras ha munys hag ol the varogyen keth hath arlythy* 'summon to you great and small and all your knights, commons and lords' BM 2432-34

*thotho eff agen **gelwys** ha thynny a comondyas doys oll dotho the amma* 'he summoned us to him and commanded us all to kiss him' BM 4428-30.

D **gelwel** 'to call, to name'

*Onon esa yn preson barabas yth o **gylwys*** 'One who was in prison was called Barabbas' PA 124a

*peghadores es hep gow an brassa ege yn pow gans pup ol ty o **gylwys*** 'you were a sinful woman; indeed you were called the greatest in the land by everybody' RD 1094-96

***Gelwys** y3 of conany mytern yn bryten vyan* 'I am called Conan, king in Brittany' BM 168-69

*Lymmyn ny vanna ve na moy agys **gylwell** why servantes, mas cothmans* 'Now I will no longer call you servants, but friends' TH 35a

*Rag an cawses ma nyg us feithfull colonow vith greviis war y **gylwell** bara in scriptur* 'For this cause no faithful hearts are grieved to call it bread in scripture' TH 57a.

'To call, to name' can also be rendered in Cornish by **henwel**:

*a glewsyugh why cowethe del vgy an vyl hore ov **thenwel** an pyth na vyth* 'did you hear, comrades, that the vile whore is naming that which does not exist?' OM 2727-29

*ha nep as tefo gallos a vyth gans yowynk ha los **henwys** tus vras pup termyn* 'and those who have power are always called great men by young and old' PC 787-90

*hag in meske ol the nasconn **henwys** oys pronter grassijs* 'and in all your nation you are called a gracious priest' BM 2549-50

*kyn rug an heretickys y **henwall** papisticall egglos* 'though the heretics named it papistical church' TH 32a

*an tas a rug der entent in myske oll prevas in bys formya preve **henwis** serpent* 'the Father has deliberately among all reptiles in the world created the reptile called snake' CW 496-98

*ha mean orrol en Madern en Gunneau Bosolo **henwez** Mean Scriffez* 'and another stone in Madron in Bosullow Downs called the Inscribed Stone' BF: 27.

The Cornish verb **cria** is a borrowing from English 'cry'. Although the word is written with ***y*** in Middle Cornish, the stressed vowel appears as ***ey*** as early as BM, which is presumably the same vowel as that seen in Lhuyd's ***kreiez*** 'called' (see below). **Cria** can mean A) 'to call out, to cry out'; B) 'to call for, to beg for'; C) 'to call, to summons, to invoke'; and D) 'to call, to name'. The last of these senses is attested in Late Cornish only:

GERYOW GWIR   **call**

A **cria** 'to call out'

*ymons thy'mo ov **crye** rag an lafur vs thethe byth ny yllons ymmeres* 'they call to me for they cannot manage the work they have' OM 1418-20

*rak nans yv pilat serrys ow **crye** kepar ha ky* 'for now is Pilate angry, crying out like a dog' PC 2241-42

*ma stryf yntre an thev cam ny wrons vry my the **crye*** 'there is conflict between the two scoundrels; they do not notice that I am calling' PC 2248-49

*ny a vyn the requyrye ha warbarth ol sur **crye** crucifige* 'we shall demand and indeed all cry out Crucify him' PC 2475-76

***cryeugh** fast gans mur a grys may fo an ihesu crousys* 'call out firmly and with great vigour that the Jesus fellow be crucified' PC 2477-78

*me a vynse y wythe ha ny yllyn cammen vyth pup ol ese ow **crye** y lathe awos trauyth* 'I would have wished to protect him and I couldn't do anything; everyone was crying out for him to be killed for nothing' PC 3125-28

*ymons ow **crye** huthyk dun yn kergh rak dout pystyk scon hep lettye* 'they are crying out joyfully; let us go away immediately without delay for fear of being injured' RD 2304-06

*owt in ov dythyov **creyaff** warnogh ladron drues* 'Out! in my days I cry upon you, perverse thieves' BM 1046-47

*maria me a weyl neys am **creya** vy fors ny reyth* 'Mary, I see clearly you do not take any notice of my crying out' BM 3619-20

*Heyl ser emperour costentyn ha warnes ny a **cry** out* 'Hail, Sir Emperor Constantine, and upon you we cry out' BM 3960-61

*Ea, han pore creaturs a crist gesys the famya rag fowt bos, dewas, hag ethom dyllas, ow **crya** out* 'Yea, and the poor creatures of Christ left to starve for lack of food, drink and need of clothes, crying out' TH 40a

*Dowtya a ren ha **crya** ha parugy the fya* 'I feared and called and got ready to flee' BK 25-26

*henna o gwan obar gwryes may ma dew han noer keffrys warnas pub ere ow **crya*** 'that was bad work done, so that God and the earth as well are always crying out to you' CW 1268-70

*Ha an Arluth Deew a **gerias** tha Adam, ha lavarraz thotha peleha estha?* 'And the Lord God called to Adam and said to him, Where are you?' Rowe.

B **cria** 'to call for, to beg for'

*y gelmy fast why a wra gans louan ha chaynys yen ha mar ny fyn dynaghe y gow ha mercy **crye*** 'you shall bind him firmly with rope and cold chains, if he will not deny his falsehood and call for mercy' PC 2059-62

*mercy war crist y **creya** boys crystyan menna heb wov* 'I shall call for mercy from Christ; I wish without a lie to be a Christian' BM 1816-17

*Y ij luff y trehevys war guir thu mercy **creyays*** 'He raised his two hands, he called for mercy from the true God' BM 4431-32 *ha gesow ny the repentya ha mekya ha humblya agan honyn hartely ha **crya** mercy war thu* 'and let us repent and heartily make ourselves meek and humble and call upon God for mercy' TH 9-9a

*whansack nyng ew tha drevyth mes pub eare ma ow **crya** warlerth an oyle a vercy* 'he desires nothing but is always crying out for the oil of mercy' CW 1794-96.

C **cria** 'to call upon, to invoke'

*ha me a vyn y pesy mar pe y voth indella na rella den peryllya in tyr na mor in bys ma mar **creya** war crist ha my* 'and I shall pray him, if so be his will, that no man should be in danger on land of at sea, if he call upon Christ and upon me' BM 613-17

*oma yth on devethys del grese awoys gul da ny russugh agen **creya*** 'here we have come; as I believe, you would not have called for us for having done well' BM 1529-31

*Penys purguir yv ov luyst ha **creya** pur vr war crist* 'My desire is to fast and always to call upon Christ' BM 1824-25

*na ve **creya** warnogh why kellys ol y fyen ny yowynk ha loys* 'had it not been for invoking you, we all young and old would have been lost' BM 2166-68

*Solabrys kynth of **cryys**, the'n turant ny vetha' mos rag own a drol* 'Although I have long been summoned, I do not dare go to the tyrant for fear of torture' BK 445-47

*Nena Herod, pereeg e prevath **crya** an deez feere, e a vednyaz thoranze seer puna termin reeg an steare disquethaz* 'Then Herod, when he had summoned the wise men privately, he asked them assiduously when did the star appear' Rowe

*Ha e ve enna terebah mernaz Herod; malga boaz composez a ve cowsez gen Arleth neue der an prophet, o laule a vez a Egyp me vedn **crya** a mâb* 'And he was there until the death of Herod, so that what was spoken by the Lord of heaven through the prophet might be fulfilled, saying Out of Egypt I shall call my son' Rowe.

D **cria** 'to call, to name'

*En termen ez passiez thera trigaz en St. Levan; dean ha bennen en tellar **creiez** Chei an Horr* 'In time past there lived in St Levan a man and a woman in a place called House of the Ram' BF: 15

*En termen ez passiez thera trigaz en St. Levan, dên ha bennen en teller **kreiez** Tshei an Hor* 'In time past there lived in St Levan a man and a woman in a place called House of the Ram' BF: 16

*Ha Deu a **kries** an ebron neve, ha gethihuer ha metten vo nessa jorna* 'And God call the firmament heaven, and evening and morning were the second day' BF: 52

*Ha Deu **kriez** an teer zeth an aor, ha kentel varbar an dour e **kriez** mor* 'And God called the dry land the earth, and the collection of the water he called sea' BF: 52

*An tiz Germo (**kriez** Stynnorian)* 'the men of Germoe, called tinners' BF: 46

*An lyzûan bîan ʒen i'ar nedhez, ez a tivi en an halou nei, ez **kreiez** Plêth Maria* 'The small plant with the twisted stalk, which grows on our hills, is called Lady's tresses' AB: 245a.

In Cornish 'to call' in most senses is **gelwel**; **henwel** means 'to call' to name'. **Cria** (pronounced *creia*) is common at all periods. It can mean 'to call out, to summons, to invoke, to beg for' and to 'to call, to name'. There are no examples of this last sense, however, until the Late Cornish period. For the other senses, however, there is no reason to avoid **cria** in revived Middle Cornish

CALM

For the adjective meaning 'calm, serene, quiet' some commentators recommend using ***hebask** or ***coselek**. The word ***hebask** is not attested and cannot be recommended. ***Coselek** is an error; the word should be written *cosolek*—a form which is attested once:

Ny vyth **cosolak** *goyth in ow body* 'No sinew in my body will be quiet' BK 2471-72.

Commoner words for 'calm, serene, meek' in the texts are *cosel* and *clor*.

A cosel

Cosel *my re bowesas ass yw whek an hun myttyn* 'Quietly I have rested; how sweet is a sleep in the morning' OM 2073-74

indelle ty gargesen drok thym ty a russa a mennen vy pur guir sevel in **cosel** 'so, you glutton, you would have done me harm, had I wished indeed to stand calmly' BM 2423-26

Cusal *ha têg, sîrra wheage, Moaz pell* 'calm and gentle, sweet sir, go far' ACB: F f.

B clor

Adam saf yn ban yn **clor** *ha treyl the gyk ha the woys* 'Adam stand up meekly and turn to flesh and blood' OM 65-66

dus yn **clor** *torr'e ha ke the gerthes* 'come meekly, pluck it and go on your way' OM 203-04

ha'y brewy guyls yndar **clor** *mar venys avel skyl brag* 'and bruise her wildly, not mildly, as small as malt sprouts' OM 2719-20

me a'n guyth sur deth ha nos awos y dysciplys plos kyn teffons y vyth mar **clor** 'I will guard him indeed day and night in spite of his disciples, though they come never so quietly' RD 390-92

Ihesu a ruk neff ha nor me a peys omma in **clor** *re therbara dis ʒehes* 'Jesus, who made heaven and earth I beseech her quietly; may he grant you health' BM 4219-21

A'y lavarow sul ew stowt, my a'n gwra **clor**, *rag ef a verew, nyng es dowt, mar pith kevys ugh an dor* 'Whoever is obstinate in his words, I will render him meek, for he will die, there is no doubt, if he is found above ground' BK 2790-93.

'The Pacific Ocean' should be called **An Mor Cosel** in Cornish.

calm　　　　　　　　**GERYOW GWIR**

The Cornish word meaning 'tranquility, peace, calmness, stillness' is either **calamynjy** or **cosoleth**:

A **calmynjy**
Tranquillitas… Tranquillity, quietness, stillness, a calm. C. ***Kallaminsi*** AB: 166a
KALLAMINGI 'quietness, stillness' ACB: R 3 *verso*
Kallaminghi 'Tranquillity, Calm' Borlase.

B **cosoleth**
rag bos abel gvyr thege ef a'n gefyth yn dyweth an ioy na thyfyk nefre yn ov gulas ha **cosoleth** 'because Abel is a true tithe, he will in the end get the joy that never fail in my kingdom an peace' OM 515-18
banneth a'n tas ragas bo hag ef prest ragas gvytho benytha in **cosoleth** 'may you have the blessing of the Father and may he always keep you in quietness' OM 1723-25
pokene benytha ny ny gefyn cresse, **cosoleth** *ha powesva a consciens in agan colonow* 'otherwise we will never have peace, tranquility nor quietness of conscience in our hearts' TH 10a
Rag eff ew an tas a vercy ha du a **cosoleth** *ha confort* 'For he is the Father of mercy and the God of peace and comfort' TH 10a
Concordia… Peace, concord, agreement. C. ***Kÿzalath*** AB: 50b
Pax… Peace, quietness;… C. ***Kyzalath*** AB: 115a
Kÿzvleth 'Peace, peaceableness, tranquillity' AB: 240c
Kÿzaleth 'Peace' AB: 243b.

'To calm' is **coselhe**:

The ihesu re bo grasseys hag inweth ʒe veryasek thyn ol yth yv **coselheys** *rych ha bososek purguir a yll lemen mones then feryov* 'Jesus and Meriasek be praised; to us all it has been made calm; rich and poor indeed can now go to the fairs' BM 2180-85

'To pacify, to reconcile' is **coseletha**: *Concilio… to make friends, or reconcile;* C. *Dho* ***kÿzalatha*** AB: 50b.

TO CEASE, TO STOP

In revived Cornish the customary word for 'to cease' has always been **hedhy**. This word, however, is poorly attested as a full verb. It is more commonly found in the fossilized expression **kyns ès hedhy** 'straight away, without delay':

del wascaf y peydrennow may fo gos y vlewennow ha'y corf ol ***kyns ys hethy*** 'as I strike his buttock, so that his sides may be blood and all his body without delay' PC 2094-96

GERYOW GWIR   chair

me a vyn **kyns es hethy** *mos alema* 'I will depart hence without delay' CW 1217-18

hag y teaf thewhy arta gans gorryb **kyns es hethy** *der both an tas awartha* 'and I shall return to you with an answer without delay by the will of the Father above' CW 1760-62

me a wra then horsen cam boos calassa presonys mar callaf **kyns es hethy** *drefan terry gorhemyn* 'I will have the devious scoundrel more severely imprisoned if I can without delay because he broke the commandment' CW 2037-40.

Outside the set phrase **kyns ès hedhy**, the verb **hedhy** is apparently attested only in OM:

guyn veys ha quellen an gyth may fe yrhys thy'm **hethy** 'happy I would be if I could see the day when I should be told to stop' OM 1013-14

orden the'th tus hy knoukye gans meyn na **hethens** *nefra erna varwa eredy* 'order your men to strike her with stones; let them not cease until she is dead indeed' OM 2675-77

ha gans myyn gureugh hy knoukye erna wrello tremene benytha na wreugh **hethy** 'and with stones strike her until she dies; never cease' OM 2694-96.

Cessya 'to cease' is well attested:

ha homma byth ny **sestyas** *aban duthe yn chy thy's pup vr ol amme thu'm treys* 'and this woman has never ceased, since I came into your house, continually to kiss my feet' PC 523-25

rag henna eff ny rug **cessia** *dre crefte ha dre questonow adro the eva neb o an gwanha in power han medalha vessell bys may rug gull thethy terry commondment an tas* 'therefore he did not cease by craft and by questions around Eve, who was the weaker in power and the softer vessel, until he made her break the commandment of the Father' TH 4

yma S Cyrill ow commondya thetha **sessia** *heb gull marthussyan crist the ry power an par na* 'St Cyril commands them to cease marvelling that Christ gave such power' TH 38a.

Although **cessya** is a borrowing, there is no reason to avoid using it in the revived language.

CHAIR

The ordinary word for 'chair' in Cornish has always been **cader** *f.*, **caderyow**. This word is unattested, however, in either the *Old Cornish Vocabulary* or the Middle Cornish texts

65

[Note: in *Desky Kernowek*, page 275, I say that *cader* is found in OCV and place-names. This statement should be corrected by omitting the reference to OCV.]

Cader is certainly found in place-names; cf. **Cadar, Gadar** '*a chair*'; **chapel an gadar** in *St Peran Sabulo* ACB: L 4 *b*. We have no evidence, however, that **cader** 'chair' was ever part of the lexicon of spoken Middle Cornish. In modern English place-names, for example, one frequently finds the elements *chipping, hurst* and *leigh,* but none of these is a living word in modern English. Similarly the presence of the element **cader** in a Cornish place-name does not mean that the word was in daily use for 'chair' in the Middle and Late Cornish period. Indeed the texts suggest otherwise, since the only attested word for 'chair' in them is **chair**, *plural* **chairys**:

me a's ordyn though wharre **cheyrys** *ha formys plente ysethough syre iustis* 'I will order them for you straight away, chairs and many benches; be seated, Sir Justice' PC 2228-30

Na govs thyn geryov vfer dus oma ese yth **cheer** *guyske the dylles yth kerhyn* 'Do not speak idle words; come here; sit in your chair; put your garments on' BM 3001-03

So, ny vynys colynwall an la, a rug agan savyour, a supposta, inivry ha cam an par na then stall po **cheare** *an scribys han phariseis* 'But you will not fulfil the law, which our Saviour gave. Do you presume wrong and hostility of that kind to the chair of the scribes and pharisees?' TH 48a

Mar pith den vith ioynys the **chear** *pedyr, po sensy then stall a pedyr, yth ew ow servont ve* 'If a any man is joined to the chair of St Peter, or keeps to the stall of St Peter, he is my servant' TH 49.

Notice in the last two examples chair is used metaphorically to mean 'seat of authority, ecclesiastical chair'. This is the equivalent of the Latin word *cathedra* (< Greek *kathedra* 'chair'), which is the origin both of **cader** and **chair**. **Chair** was probably used for a wooden seat with arms. A low armless seat, bench or stool seems to have been called **scavel** *f.* This word is well attested both by itself and in the expression **scavel droos** 'footstool':

Scabellum, **scauel** 'bench' OCV §773

gwregh honora **scavall** *e dryes* 'honour his footstool' SA 64a

thesa ve ow covyn, mith ef, pandrew an **scavall** *e drys eff* 'I ask, he says, what is his footstool?' SA 64a

an grond ew an **skavall** *ow thrys ve* 'the ground is my footstool' SA 64a

han noore inwethe awollas scon worthe compas a vyth gwryes honna a vythe ow **skavall** *droose* 'and the earth beneath soon will be made completely; that shall be my footstool' CW 18-20

Nessa, vrt an **skauoll** *crackan codna iggeva setha war en crees an aules ewhall* 'Next by the break-neck stool he sits upon in the middle of the high cliff' BF: 9

Nessa, urt an **skavoll** *crack-an-codna iggava setha war en cres an awles ewhall* 'Next by the break-neck stool he sits upon in the middle of the high cliff' BF: 12

C. **Skaval**, *A Stool* AB: 46c

Sella... A seat, a chair, a bench C. **Skaval** AB: 148a

†**Scavel**, *a bench, a stool. Hod*[*ie*] **Skaval***; skaval an gow, the bench of lies;* **skaval** *droasa, a foot-stool* ACB: Y

Scavel, *a Bench;* **skaval** *id. Lh*[uyd] Borlase.

In revived Cornish the word for a chair with arms is best translated **chair**. A bench, stool or chair without arms is probably best rendered by **scavel**.

CIRCULAR see ROUND

TO CIRCUMCISE

For 'to circumcise' Nance devised **enwosa* on the basis of Welsh *enwaedu* 'to circumcise'. Other commentators have devised **trodrehy* on the basis of Breton *amdroc'hañ*. Neither neologism is necessary, since the word for 'to circumcise' is attested in traditional Cornish:

Rag nyg one ny kylmys the vos **circumcisis***, na the offra in ban the thew ley oghan, devas, ha gyffras* 'For we are not bound to be circumcised, nor to offer up to God calves, oxen sheep and goats' TH 27a.

An attested borrowing is always to be preferred to an unattested coinage. It is clear therefore that the ordinary word for 'to circumcise' is best rendered by **cyrcùmcîsya** in the revived language.

CLOUD

For 'cloud' Nance recommended ***comolen** f., coll. *comol*. This word is unattested anywhere in Cornish and can be deduced only from the Welsh and Breton congeners and the word ***komolek*** glossing *Tenebrosus* 'dark or close', given by Lhuyd at AB: 162a for both Cornish and Breton. The word for 'cloud' in Cornish is attested twice only, both times in the plural:

Ego sum Alpha et Omega heb dallath na dowethva pur wyre me ew omma agy than **clowdes** 'I am Alpha and Omega, without beginning nor end truly I am here within the clouds' CW 1-4

cloud   **GERYOW GWIR**

hag a vyn diskynnya than noore in dan an **clowdys** *hag ow both gwethill ena* 'and will descend to the earth beneath the clouds and do my will there' CW 75-77.

The only attested word for 'cloud' in the Cornish texts is *cloud, plural cloudys. This should perhaps be the ordinary word in the revived language.

COAST

In some varieties of Cornish the default word for 'coast' is *arvor. Unfortunately such a word is unattested. Lhuyd uses the word ***Arvorek*** to mean 'Breton, Armoric' but neither a proper noun ****Arvor*** nor a common noun ****arvor*** is attested either in Lhuyd or in traditional Cornish. Lhuyd gives Cornish ***Torneuan*** s.v. *Litus* 'shore, sea-side, bank' (AB: 81a), but this is merely a variant of **ternewen** 'side', cited here presumably for 'river bank' or 'sea-side'.

The word **âls** means 'seashore' and 'cliff' as well. In Old Cornish we find *litus* **als** 'seashore, strand' OCV §733. This also attested in *en crees an* **aules** *ewhall* 'in the middle of the high cliff' BF: 9. In place-names the element may mean either 'cliff', 'shore' or 'slope'.

***Morrep** 'seashore' occurs in place-names, but it is unattested in the texts.

The word **cost**, plural **côstys**, is well attested and it seems to mean both 'coast, shore' and 'border, area, region', exactly like the word *coste* in Middle English from which the Cornish word was borrowed:

cost, côstys

lauar thy'mmo kyns mones py tyller yma moyses ha py **cost** *yma trygys* 'tell me before you go where is Moses and in what area does he live' OM 1550-52

Henn ew the leverell Jhesus a theth then **costes** *a cesarye philippi* 'That is to say, Jesus came to the region of Cesarea Philippi' TH 43a

nena eff a gemeras owne a drega na fella in **cost** *na, henn o in Samarya* 'then he became afraid to dwell any longer in that region, that is to say in Samaria' TH 46a

Pan nowothou, pan guestlow us genowgh why a'n **cost** *west?* 'What news, what pledges have you from the west coast?' BK 2222-23

Ke souyth ha north ha gura cry cref in pub **cost***, ow soccors may teffons tost* 'Go south and north and make a loud cry in each coast, that my allies may come soon' BK 2350-52.

If we are talking about the coast or litoral as distinct from inland, we use **âls**. If, on the other hand, we are talking about a maritime region or area, we can use **cost**, *plural* **côstys**.

COLOUR

The word **lyw** in Cornish means 'colour', in particular of a person's complexion or of the brightness of the sun:

*Color **liu*** 'colour' OCV §481

*rag own y a gangyes **lyw** rag gwander y a goʒas* 'for fear they changed colour; for weakness they fell' PA 68c

*hay mab as gorth del vyn ef tecke ys houl yv y **lyw*** 'and her son honours her as he wishes; fairer than the sun is her colour' PA 226d

*an hovl y **lyw** re gollas me a grys ny re peghas* 'the sun has lost its brightness; I believe we have sinned' PC 2992-93

*an houl ny golse y **lyw** awos map den the verwel* 'the sun would not have lost its brilliance had a human being died' PC 3083-84

*rag an houl y **lyw** golow a gollas pan eth a'n beys* 'for the sun lost its bright colour when he passed from the world' PC 3123-24

*gorryn ef yn beth arte du yw y **lyw*** 'let us put him in the grave again; black is his colour' RD 2100-01

*an eleth omma yv guyn avel an houl pan thywhyn yn ken **lyw** ny's guylys wheth* 'the angels here are as bright as the sun when it shines; I have not yet seen them in a different colour' RD 2532-34

*ena yth esa flowrys ha frutes teke aga **lew** thagan maga* 'in that place there were flowers and fair-coloured fruits to feed us' CW 1050-52.

With OC ***liu*** compare *deformis **disliu*** 'discoloured; multicoloured' OCV §§126, 489; *minium **liu melet*** 'ochre, raddle' OCV §363; *unus color **unliu*** 'of one colour' OCV §488.

In the later texts ***lyw***, ***lew*** is the regular spelling for the word for 'deluge, flood'. Perhaps to avoid any confusion ***lyw*** 'colour, complexion' appears to be yielding somewhat to **colour**, **colourys**:

*heil syr lord and emperour heil now kyng of kynggys flour arluth dres ol an bys ma fayr an suyt bryte of **colour*** 'hail, sir lord and emperor, hail now king, of kings the flower, lord over all this world, fair and sweet, bright of colour' PC 1681-84

*yma S paul worth agan payntia ny in mes in **colors** in leas tellar in scriptur* 'St Paul paints us in colour in many places in scripture' TH 7a

*Hayl, arluth ker! Pehan tectar! **Colorys** cler, lun a whekter a caradow arluthesow a'th hoyl pupprys!* 'Hail, dear lord! What beauty! Clear colours, full of the sweetness of delightful ladies follow you always!' 1710-16

*Rag kueth, pan i'n canfethis, me re jangyas ow **holor*** 'For grief when I perceived it, I changed my colour' BK 3129-30.

There are two words for 'colour' in Cornish, **lyw**, *****lywyow** and **colour**, **colours**. Either can be used.

comfort   **GERYOW GWIR**

COMFORT, TO COMFORT

The word **hebasca** 'comfort, solace' is attested once only:

Hebasca *thywhy ov mam mur reverons the varia thynny prest y fye cam mar ny rellen y gorthya* 'Comfort to you, my mother; great reverence to Mary. It would be a great wrong if we did not worship her' BM 3752-56.

The ordinary words for 'solace, comfort' are A) **solas** and B) **comfort, confort**:

A **solas**

Nu'm let **solas** *war an bys erna theffyf theugh arta* 'no solace in the world will delay me until I come to you again' BK 899-900

Dun, ow amors ha'm cuvyon, gans **solas** *hag eglynnyon* 'Come, my loves and my dear ones, with solace and verses' BK 2060.

B **comfort, confort**

Gans an ioul kyn fy temptijs ano30 na ro dymme rag **comfort** *yw henna ʒys* 'Though you are tempted by the devil, do not give a fig for him, for that is a comfort for you' PA 22a

yndelma **comfort** *ʒyʒy y map a vynnas dygtye* 'thus her son wished to arrange comfort for her' PA 199d

byth lemmyn a **confort** *da pan yv both dev yndella* 'be now of good comfort since the will of God is thus' OM 1341-42

mur a **confort** *ef o thy'n* 'he was much comfort to us' RD 688

thagas fastye yn crygyans theugh **confort** *a spyrys sans a thanfonaf* 'to confirm you in faith I shall send you the comfort of the Holy Spirit' RD 1174-76

yn **confort** *thyugh my a as an spyrys sans* 'as a comfort to you I leave the Holy Spirit' RD 2371-72

A bethugh a **confort** *da crist agen gueres a ra* 'Oh, be of good comfort; Christ will assist us' BM 611-12

Yv helma ol an **confort** *am bethe deworthugh wy* 'Is that all the comfort I shall have from you?' BM 1054-55

Gallus ha **confort** *an tas re bo genes pup termen* 'May you have the power and the comfort of the Father always' BM 2735-36

Ith ew benefyt ha **confort** *bras ragan ny* 'It is a benefit and great comfort for us' TH 1a

Sow innove only yma gweras **confort** *ha succure* 'But in me only is help, comfort and succour' TH 11a

ynweth rag **confort** *in kythsame part ma* 'also for comfort in this same part' TH 30a

a rug appoyntia hag ordenya thenny the vos kerengyak mam thegan gwetha ha preservia rag **confort** *hag eghas the enevow* 'who appointed and ordained her for us to be a loving mother to keep and preserve us for the comfort and health of souls' TH 30a *oll pub pleasure an bys ma yn plas ma yta tevys mayth ew* **confort** *ʒa wellas* 'every pleasure in this world behold is growing in this place so that it is a comfort to see' CW 540-42.

For the verb 'to comfort' Nance recommended **chêrya** and ***hebaskhe**. **Chêrya** is a derivative of *cher* < English 'cheer' and means 'to cheer, to cherish, to assist', rather than 'to comfort'. There are a few examples:

maria numbus flehys marnes vn map thum ***cherya*** 'Mary, I have no children but one son to cheer me' BM 3192-93
an re ew da ny a res thyn aga ***cheria*** *rag aga dadder* 'those who are good, we should cherish them for their goodness' TH 26
The wethel gist settys of rag the ***gerya****, ha dyswul ha conquerya the yskerans der gras Christ* 'I am determined to do the deed to cheer you, and to destroy and conquer your enemies by the grace of Christ' BK 1482-85
Why a'm ***cher*** *hag a'm dythan* 'You cheer and amuse me' BK 1591
Ol the'th talant an bys a'th ***cher*** 'All the world according to your ability cherishes you' BK 1744.

***Hebaskhe** 'to comfort, to soothe' is unattested, having been devised by Nance himself. The commonest word for 'to comfort' in traditional Cornish is **confortya, comfortya**:

hy a vynnas y derry corf ihesus rag ***comfortye*** 'she wished to break it, to soothe the body of Jesus' PA 35bc
yn meth crist vn pols golyas ny yllough ʒum ***comfortye*** 'said Christ, Can you not watch a little to comfort me?' PA 55d
war ben dewlyn pan ese an nef y fe danuenys el ʒoʒo ʒy ***gomfortye*** 'when he was on bended knee, an angel was sent to him to comfort him' PA 58ab
Gensy prest ij venyn len esa worth y ***homfortye*** 'With her always two women, who were comforting her' PA 167a
Gans henna y a drylyas ***confortis*** *ha lowenek hag eth tus crist rag whelas* 'Thereupon they turned, comforted and joyful and went to seek Christ' PA 257ab
ha wose henna evyn pep ol adro draght a wyn rag ***comfortye*** *y golon* 'and afterwards let us all about drink a draught of wine to cheer the heart' OM 2626-28
mar ny thue thu'm ***confortye*** *ow mornyngh vyth ogh ha tru* 'if he does not come to comfort me, my mourning will be Oh! and Alas!' RD 437-38
ota gy ow map ihesu dyuythys thu'm ***confortye*** 'there you are, my son Jesus, come to comfort me' RD 463-64
me yv ihesus the vab ker me re thuth the'th ***confortye*** 'I am Jesus, your beloved son; I have come to comfort you' RD 472-73
confortys *yv ow colon pan clewys ow teryfas bones leghys the pascyon* 'my heart is comforted when I heard that your suffering was lessened' RD 503-05

comfort   **GERYOW GWIR**

y grassaf lemmyn an cas ty the vynnes thy'm danfon thu'm **confortye** *the vap ras* 'I give thanks now for the fact that you will send me your gracious son to comfort me' RD 508-10

ha dres henna porth cof lauar **confort** *yn ta thymmo pedar mur yu kyrys* 'and more than that remember, speak, comfort well Peter for me, who is greatly loved' RD 890-92

Densa benyges re by dovr oma ov try thynny mar dek thagen **confortya** 'Good man, may you be blessed bringing us water here so beautifully to comfort us' BM 672-74

broder povle duen alema the **confortya** *costenten* 'brother Paul, let us go hence to comfort Constantine' BM 1696-97

aleys ol y wolyov theragoff sur disquetheys ys guelys cleth a dyov ha tek eff am **confortyeys** 'I saw before me all his wounds displayed before me, left and right, and fairly he comforted me' BM 1848-51

Meryasek lowena dys omma duthen theth vereys hag inweth theth **confortia** 'Meriasek, joy to you. We have come here to see you and to comfort you as well' BM 1980-82

tevdar drok lor eff a ra y **confortya** *mar menyn* 'Teudar, he will do badly enough, if we comfort him' BM 2333-34

Meryasek gorthys re by genes **confortis** *on ny ese in mur a ponfos* 'Meriasek, may you be revered; we who were in great affliction have been comforted by you' BM 2670-72

may hyllen pur eredy moys ganso thy **confortya** 'that we may go indeed with him to comfort him' BM 3273-74

kynth os gyllys feynt ha guan wath ty a veth **confortys** 'though you have become faint and weak, you shall be comforted' BM 3672-73

crist ker regyn danvoneys oma prest theth **confortya** 'beloved Christ has sent us here readily to comfort you' BM 3883-84

gueyt in tek y **confortye** *ha gans henne y desky* 'be sure to comfort him beautifully and also to teach him' BM 4019-20

me ny won thum **confortia** *pyv us oma devethys* 'I do not know who has come here to comfort me' BM 4038-39

lues den guan in bys ma pur guir eff a **confortyas** 'many weak men in this world he comforted in very truth' BM 4480-81

Eff a ra agys **confortya**, *eff a ra agys ledya in oll gwryoneth* 'he will comfort you, he will lead you in all truth' TH 38

Arluth nef re bo gorthys, mar deke eth of **confortys** *der wryans an caradow* 'May the Lord of heaven be revered; so beautifully am I comforted by the actions of the beloved' BK 829-31

Arluth, re by **confortys***!* 'Lord, may you be comforted' BK 1183

Arluth Du re'th **confortya***!* 'May the Lord God comfort you!' BK 3193b

Rachal wholo rag e flehaz ha na venga hye boaze **comfortyes**, *rag tho angye lathez* 'Rachel weeping for her children and she will not be comforted, for they have been killed' Rowe.

Comfortya should perhaps be the default word in revived Cornish for 'to comfort, to console'. There is no need for the neologism ***hebaskhe**.

TO COMMAND, COMMANDMENT

A common way of translating 'to command' in Cornish is **erhy**, *preterite* **erhys**:

*In er na ʒen menyʒyow why a **ergh** warnough coʒe* 'On that day you will bid the mountains fall upon you' PA 170a

*ʒen marreg worth y hanow y a **yrhys** may whane yn corf Ihesus caradow* 'they commanded the soldier by name to pierce the body of beloved Jesus' PA 218bc

*hys the baal luen the drehy thy's yth **arghaf** a dyreyth* 'I command you to cut land to the length of your spade' OM 380-81

*Adam an tas dev guella a **yrghys** thy's growethe gans the bryes ker eva* 'Adam, the best Father has commanded you to sleep with Eve, your dear spouse' OM 644-46

*guyn veys ha quellen an gyth may fe **yrhys** thy'm hethy* 'happy were I to see the day in which I were commanded to stop' OM 1013-14

*dev thy'mmo vy a **erghys** may fy thegy offrynnys thotho ef war an alter* 'God has commanded me that you be offered to him upon the altar' OM 1326-28

ha thy'so dev a yrghys may fe y tus ol gesys the wul thotho sacryfys 'and God has commanded you that all his folk be allowed to make sacrifice to him' OM 1491-93

*dev a **erghys** thy's moyses the welen ay kemeres ha guyskel an mor gynsy* 'God commanded to Moses to take up the rod and to strike the sea with it' OM 1663-65

*kepar del fue thy'n **yrhys** gans y das kyns tremene* 'as it was commanded us by his father before he died' OM 2375-76

*woge ow da oberow dywes a **yrhys** dethe* 'after my good deeds, I bade them give me a drink' RD 2599-600

*the costyntyn an emperour reys yv dygh lafurya dour eff a **erhys** indella* 'it is necessary to travel to the emperor Constantine immediately; he commanded thus' BM 1748-50.

The verb **gorhemmyn**, **gorhebmyn** is also used, though in the later language it can mean 'to greet':

*hag yn tyr **gorhemennaf** may tefo gveyth ha losow* 'and on the land I command that trees and plants grow' OM 27-28

*thethe me a **worhemmyn** encressyens ha bewens pel* 'to them I command: let them encrease and live long' OM 47-48

*del yv **gorhemmynnys** thy'n my a's gor bys yn gorhal* 'as we have been commanded, I will put them in the ark' OM 1049-50

*my a **worhemmyn** whare the'n glaw na moy na wrello* 'I will command soon to the rain that it fall no longer' OM 1091-92

*Noe my a **worhemmyn** thy's ke yn mes a'th worhel scon* 'Noah, I command you, go out of your vessel soon' OM 1157-58

*botler my a **worhemnyn** ha'th cowyth guytheugh why y ma na vons yn nep maner remmvys the gen tyller* 'butler, I command you and your companion; guard them that they are not removed in any way to another place' OM 2042-45

command   GERYOW GWIR

ke **gorhemmyn** *the'n cyte may teffons omma whare war beyn aga bos dyswrys* 'go, command to the city, that they come here immediately upon pain of being executed' OM 2407-09

an myghtern a **worhemmyn** *the ol an karpentoryon masons ynweth tyorryon may fons y ganso myttyn omma the wul an temple* 'the king commands to all the carpenters and masons, and roofers also, that they be with him tomorrow to build the temple' OM 2421-25

ha thethe prest **gorhemmyn** *gruthyl wheyl dek ha prive* 'and command them directly to do fair and private work' OM 2439-40

my a **worhemmyn** *yn scon* 'I shall soon command' OM 2625

fystynyn fast alemma del **gorhemynnys** *deffry* 'let us hasten firmly hence as he commanded us indeed' PC 645-46

Best thys me a **worhemmyn** *thymmo na rylly dregyn na the crystyan benytha* 'Beast, I command you that you do no harm to me or any Christian ever' BM 1109-11

thys best me a **worhemyn** *moys then guelfos gans mab den na ra mellya* 'you, beast, I command to go into the wilderness; do no interfere with mankind' BM 1126-28

In y hanov dus in mes par del yv **gorhemynnes** *gans crist dymo in bys ma* 'In his name, come out as has been commanded to me by Christ in this world' BM 4088-90

me ath **worhemmyn** *dragan then guylfos quik math ylly* 'I command you, dragon, that you should go quickly to the wilderness' BM 4141-42

me a **worhemyn** *whare than glawe namoy na wrella* 'I shall command immediately to the rain that it fall no more' CW 2458-59

Dh'ens **karebma** *dh'eu* 'They greet you' BF: 46

ma gi **karebma** *dha vi* 'they greet you' BF: 46.

In the texts the verb **comondya**, **comandya** becomes an increasingly common way to translate 'to command':

me a **commonnd** *scon dotho th'y teller kyns ens arte* 'I command it soon: let it return to its former place' OM 1094-95

moyses me a **commond** *thy's ha the aron kekyfrys mayth ylleugh yn mes a'm glas* 'Moses, command you and Aaron also to go out from my kingdom' OM 1585-87

hag arta perthugh coff guel pendr'ellen the **comondya** 'and in the future remember better what I may command' BM 1064-65

del yv dynny **comondys** *lel pup vr ol y feth grueys* 'as has been commanded to us always truly shall be done' BM 1296-97

dres an gluas y **comondyaff** *du mas crist gorthys na ve* 'throughout the kingdom I command that no God but Christ be worshipped' BM 1862-63

me a **comond** *der ov gluas naha dewov nag yv vas* 'I command throughout my kingdom to renounce gods that are no good' BM 2518-19

dyso gy y **comondyaff** 'to you I command' BM 3293

ha pyle bohosogyon y **commondias** *thyn defry* 'and he commanded us to rob the poor indeed' BM 3430-31 *han dares dym egoras hag vfel am* **comondyas** *thum mam the dre mayth ellen* 'and she opened the door for me and commanded me to go to home humbly to my mother' BM 3773-75

eff as led avel on doff ha der gallus du in proff as **comond** *then dysert dovn* 'he will lead it like a tame lamb and to prove the power of God will command it into the deep desert' BM 4028-30

thotho eff agen gelwys ha thynny a **comondyas** *doys oll dotho the amma* 'he called us to him and bade us all kiss him' BM 4428-30

ny rug du an tas a neff mas **commondya** 'the Father of heaven merely commanded' TH 1

An kynsa, an pith a rug du mab den the refraynya theworta 'the first, the thing that God commanded mankind to refrain from' TH 4

Du a **commondyas** *an profet Ysay the wull proclamacion the oll an bys* 'God commanded the prophet Isaiah to make proclamation to all the world' TH 6a-7

so yma cherite ow **commondia** *thyn rebukya malefactors ha drog tus* 'but charity commands that we rebuke malefactors and evil people' TH 30

kepar dell levar S powle, ow scriffa the Tyte, eff a **commondias** *Tite the exortya ha rebukya* 'as St Paul says, writing to Titus, he commanded Titus to exhort and to rebuke' TH 33a

Ima omma ow exortia ha ow **commondya** 'Here he exhorts and commands' TH 37

An pyth vsy an egglos ow **commondya** *gans auctorite* 'That which the Church commands with authority' TH 37a

yma S Cyrill ow **commondya** *thetha sessia heb gull marthussyan* 'St Cyril commands them not to wonder' TH 38a

han pith ew performys in telythow erell ew omma **commondys** *in gyrryow ma a crist* 'and that which is performed in other places is here commanded in these words of Christ' TH 44

rag henna eff as **commondyas** *y kynsa thy gemeras, ha na vonsy ownek the dybbry hag eva anotha* 'Therefore he commanded them, his fellows to take it, and that they should not be afraid to eat and drink of him' TH 52a

ha Christ a **commandias** *ha y a ve creatis* 'and Christ commanded and they were created' SA 61a

an arluth a **commandias** *ha nef a ve gwreis; an arluth a* **commandias***, an nore a ve gwreis; an arluth a* **commandias** *han more a ve gwreis, an arluth a* **commandias** *ha pub creature a ve gwreis* 'the Lord commanded and heaven was made; the Lord commanded, the earth was made; the Lord commanded and the sea was made; the Lord commanded and every creature was made' SA 62

ef a **commaundias***, y a ve creatis* 'he commanded, they were created' SA 62

ha pub onyn thy thecree a vyth gorris thom service pan vidnaf ve **comanndya** 'every one to his degree will be put to serve me when I command' CW 34-36

me a **gomannd** *war bub tew myns es yn neif thom gworthya* 'I command whoever is in heaven on every side to worship me' CW 138-39

vskys **commandyaf** *henna* 'swiftly I command that' CW 245

*re***commaundias** 'did comaund' Bodewryd MS.

command   **GERYOW GWIR**

In Cornish 'command, commandment' is either A) **arhadow**; B) **gorhemmyn/gorhebmyn ~ gorhemynadow**; or C) **comondment**:

A **arhadow**

y a ruge aʒesympys oll warlyrgh y **arhadow** 'they did immediately all according to his command' PA 247d

Arluth cuf the **arghadow** *y wruthyl res ev thy'mmo* 'Dear Lord, I must do your command' OM 997-98

a das benyges del os the **arhadow** *me a wra* 'O Father, as thou art blessed, I will do your command' OM 1033-34

Kepar del vynny a das my a wra the **arhadow** 'As you wish, O father, I will do your command' OM 1133-34

arluth ker the **arhadow** *my a'n gura hep falladow* 'dear Lord, your wish I shall do withour fail' PC 185-86

me a genes yn lowen ha'm dyscyblyon kettep pen the'th **arhadow** 'I will go with you gladly and all my disciples at your command' PC 461-63

Arluth a ver ryelder, the **arghadow** *a vith gwrys* 'Lord of great majesty, your command will be done' BK 402-03

Ow arluth, heb falladow me a ra the **arhadaw** 'My lord, without fail I will do your command' BK 551-52

Ny a rug the **arghadaw** 'We did your command' BK 726

Arluth ker, the **arhadow** *a vith gwreys ha'th worhemyn* 'Dear lord, your command and your instruction will be done' BK 2034-35

Gwrys ew sotal, war ow lowta, the **arghadow** 'Your command has been craftily done, upon my loyalty' BK 2914-16

Me a wor theso mer gras rag the thos thu'm **arhadow** 'I am very grateful to you for coming to me at my command' BK 3073-74

arluthe kref tha **arhadowe** *me a ra so mot y go* 'powerful Lord, your wish I shall do, so mote I go' CW 2278-79.

B **gorhemmyn, gorhemynadow**

ro thethe aga hynwyn y a thue the'th **worhemmyn** 'give them their names; they will come at your command' OM 120-21

nefre gustyth th'y gorty me a orden bos benen may mohghaho hy huth hy dre wul ow **gorhemmyn** *trogh* 'ever obedient to her husband I ordain that woman shall be, that her affliction be increased, since she broke my commandment' OM 295-98

Ellas gveles an termyn ov arluth pan wruk serry pan ruk drys y **worhenmyn** [sic] 'Alas that I have seen the time when I angered my Lord, when I transgressed his commandment' OM 351-53

gorhemmyn *dev dres pup tra res yv y vas coullenwys* 'God's command above all things, it is necessary that it be fulfilled' OM 654-55

A das ker the'th **worhemmyn** *my a th'y athysempys* 'O dear father, at your command I shall go there immediately' OM 696-97

GERYOW GWIR command

Arluth del os dres pup tra the **worhemmyn** *a vyt gureys* 'Lord, as you are over all things, your command shall be done' OM 1255-5

my a wra ol del vynny the **worhemmyn** *yn pup plas* 'I shall do, all as you wish, your command everywhere' OM 1940-41

syr arluth re synt gylmyn my a wra the **worhenmyn** *ol yn tyen* 'Sir lord, by St Colman, I will do all your command' OM 2413-15

syr cayfas re synt iouyn me a wra the **gorhemmyn** *fest yn lowen* 'Sir Caiaphas, by St Jovyn, I shall do your command very gladly' PC 1364-65

pur parys th'y **worhemmyn** *ny a thy a ver termyn* 'very readily at his command we will go thither shortly' PC 1653-55

longys reys yv thy's gyne vn pols byan lafurye dre **worhemmyn** *a'n iustis* 'Longinus, it is necessary for you to walk a little by the command of the justice' PC 3003-05

gorhemmyn *dev a terrys dre henna y fuf dampnys* 'I broke the commandment of God; through that I was damned' RD 212-13

reys yv gul ow **gorhemmyn** *athesempys* 'need is to do my command without delay' RD 1993-94

Arluth ker, the arhadow a vith gwreys ha'th **worhemyn** 'Dear lord, your instruction and your command will be done' BK 2034-35

An **gorhemmyn** *ew henna, ha ris ew gul ethevys war bayn cregy ha tenna* 'that is the command, and it must be done precisely on pain of hanging and drawing' BK 2373-75

may moyghea y lavyer hy der weyll ow **gorhemen** *troghe* 'that her labour might increase through breaking my commandment' CW 897-98

me a ra heb falladowe tha **worhemmyn** *yn tean* 'without fail I will do all your commandment' CW 1077-78

me a wra then horsen cam boos calassa presonys mar callaf kyns es hethy drefan terry **gorhemyn** 'I will made the treacherous scoundrel be more grimly imprisoned, if I can, withot delay, since he broke the commandment' CW 2037-40

worthibmen 'commandment' Bodewryd MS

Caym whek preder a'd enef awos an tas dev a'n nef gvra y **worhemmynnadow** 'Dear Cain, think of your soul because of the Father of heaven; do his commandment' OM 479-81

Serafyn the adam ke hag argh thotho growethe dre ov **gorhemmynnadow** *wheth gans eva y wreghty* 'Seraph, go to Adam and order him through my commandment again to sleep with his wife' OM 634-7

the **gorhemynnadow** *prest sur ny a wra* 'your commandment surely we will always do' PC 158-59

Saw an deg **gormynadow**, *hag oll an morall preceptys contewnys in testament coth, ny cristonnyan ew kylmys the wetha an rena* 'But the Ten Commandments, and all the moral precepts contained in the Old Testament, we Christians are bound to keep them' TH 27a.

C **comondment**

The constentyn me a due thy **comondment** *benythe* 'To Constantine I shall come always to his commandment' BM 3991-92

ha dre an **commondment** *a du an nore a thros in rag bestes peswar trosek* 'and by the command of God the earth brought forth four-footed animals' TH 2

Praga a rug du ry thewhy **commondment** 'Why did God give you a commandment?' TH 3a

bys may rug gull thethy terry **commondment** *an tas* 'until he made her break the commandment of the Father' TH 4

beva dre **commondment** *du* 'whether it be by the commandment of God' TH 5

ha specially dre **commondment** *du* 'and especially by the commandment of God' TH 5

ny a rug mos war thellar, arluth, theworth oll the preceptys hath **commondementys** 'we have retreated, Lord, from all your precepts and commandments' TH 10

dre agan mortall yskar an teball ell, dre transgression ha tyrry an **commondementys** *a thu* 'through our mortal enemy the devil, by transgression and breaking of the commandments of God' TH 10

panadra ew an brassa **commondment** *in la?* 'which is the greatest commandment in the law?' TH 20a

Hag in nese an ü **commondment** *ma yma oll an la han prophetys ow hangya* 'and by these two commandments hang all the law and the prophets' TH 20a

Hem ew, y myth crist, an brassa han kynsa **commondement**, *han second ew havall the hemma* 'This is, says Christ, the greatest and first commandment, and the second is like to this' TH 20a

ny a gottha thyn omry agan honyn the wetha ha the colynwall y **commondment** *eff* 'we ought to submit ourselves to keep and fulfil his commandment' TH 21a

mas omry aga honyn the ernystly the thu, the wull oll y blonogath hay **commondementys** 'but submit ourselves earnestly to God, to do all his will and his commandments' TH 23a

Mars esow worth ow cara ve, gwethogh ow **commondementys** 'If you love me, keep my commandments' TH 23a

Rag neb a wore ow **commondmentys**, *hag a rella aga gwetha, henna ew, y myth crist, neb vgy worth ow cara ve* 'For whoever knows my commandments and keeps them, that man is, says Christ, he who loves me' TH 23a

indella y dre an **commondment** *a S powle, a rug ordeynya re erall* 'thus they through the commandment of St Paul ordained others' TH 33a-34

mar teffa an holl brodereth obeya according then **commondmentys** *a thu* 'if all the brotherhood had obeyed according to the commandments of God' TH 42a

pell therag an tyrmyn a rug crist ry an **commondementys** *arell the pedyr* 'long before the time that Christ gave the other commandments to Peter' TH 44

kepar ha **commondementys** *ha taclenow forbyddys, etc.* 'like commandments and forbidden things, etc.' TH 50a

hay **gommandement** *pur thefry a rose straytly dres pub tra na wrellan mellya worty* 'and indeed he gave his commandment strictly above all things that we should not interfere with it' CW 632-34

mara gwren terry vn ieit y **gomanndement** *thyn reyse par hap in efarne neffra ny an bythe agen trygva* 'if we break any jot of his commandment given to us, perhaps we will have our dwelling in hell for ever' CW 659-62

Syrra, me a vyden gewel ages **commaundement** *why* 'Sir, I will do your commandment' Borde.

We can see that 'to command' in Cornish is either **erhy**, **gorhebmyn** or **comondya** and that **comondya** becomes increasingly common. 'Commandment' is either **arhadow, gorhebmyn/gormynadow** or **comondment**, *plural* **comondmentys**. **Comondment** was clearly used in later spoken Cornish and is the only one of the three substantives whose plural is attested.

COMPANY

The default word for 'company' in revived Cornish has always been **cowethas** *f.*, *plural* *****cowethasow**. This word is not common in the texts, however, and is difficult to distinguish on occasion from **cowethes** 'female companion'.

A **cowethas** 'company'

gase farwel me a vyn molleth du in **cowetheys** 'I will take my leave. God's curse in the company' BM 1286-87

an **cowethes** *peseff dour the venetens moys a regh* 'the company I beg earnestly; you will go to Vannes' BM 2885-86

reys yv dyberth otyweth kyn fo tek an **gowethas** 'it is necessary to leave at last, though the company be pleasant' BM 4255-56

peys da off an **cowethas** *in tor ma pur eredy* 'I am pleased now in very truth with the company' BM 4381-82.

B **cowethes** 'female companion'

pur luen yma thy'm ow whans a'n ven **cowethes** *ordnys* 'very full is my desire for the one female companion arranged for me' OM 91-2

Nyns yw da yn pur certan bones vn den y honan heb cowyth py **cowethes** 'It is not good in very truth that one man should be alone without a companion or female companion' OM 93-5

ke growet war an dor gvlan ha cosk byth na saf yn ban er na fo **cowethes** *gvres* 'go, lie upon the clean ground and sleep; do not arise until a female companion has been made' OM 96-8

company   GERYOW GWIR

a das ty re thros thy'mmo ascorn a'm kyk ha corf o par may fo ow ***howethes*** 'Father, you have brought me bone of my flesh and she was body so that she may be my female companion' OM 112-13

dues ov ***howethes*** *eva, groweth yn gvyly ahys* 'come, my spouse Eve, lie at length on the bed' OM 652-53

tra morethack ew serten gwellas adam y honyn heb ***cowethas*** 'it is a sad thing indeed to see Adam alone without a female companion' CW 381-83.

The English borrowing **company** is much commoner than **cowethas**:

sav kyns ys yn tour mones leuereugh thy'm ***company*** *py le vyth an guel plynsys* 'but before entering the tower, tell me, company, where shall the rods be planted' OM 2030-32

yma onan pur vostyys omma agys ***company*** 'there is one very impure of your company' PC 867-68

ha me ynweth a'n guelas ha ganso ef ***company*** *bras* 'and I also saw him and a large company with him' RD 555-56

worth an iaul ha'y ***company*** *ra'gas guytho yn pup le ha'y vennath theugh pup huny* 'against the devil and his company may he keep you everywhere and his blessing to you all' RD 2641-43

ha not ***company*** *vith arell mas an catholyk eglos, an jevas an gothfas a pub tra oll necessary rag salvacion* 'and not any other company but the catholic Church, which has the knowledge of everything necessary for salvation' TH 17

An kythsame catholyk egglos ma a res bos guthvethis in pub ois oll a vabden hag in myske ***company*** *an par na may halla an gwyr bos pregowthis ha gothvethis openly* 'This very same catholic Church must be known in all ages of mankind and among company of that kind so that the truth may be preached and known openly' TH 17a

So not warlerth an priveth interpretacion a then vith severall, na ***company*** 'But not according to the private interpretation of any man, several nor company' TH 18

yma crist omma ow menya certan ***company*** *a bobill esa in myske an Jewys* 'Christ here means certain company of people who existed among the Jews' TH 26a

the thesernya ha the aswon an lell egglos a crist theworth oll an ***company*** *han congregacion an heretickys han scismatickys* 'to discern and to recognize the true Church from all the company and assembly of the heretics and schismatics' TH 31a

kepar dell rug an scismaticall ***company*** *gull omma athewethas* 'as the schismatic company did here recently' TH 32

ny vynsa den vith styrrya na gwaya warbyn an colleges po ***company*** *a prontyrryan* 'nobody would have stirred or moved against the colleges or the company of priests' TH 42a

an re na ew an coleg po ***company*** *a prontyryan* 'those are the college or company of priests' TH 48a

Evyn an dewetha nois a rug eff bos in ***company*** *gans y aposteleth the rag y virnans* 'Even the last night that he was in the company of his apostles before his death' TH 51a-52

ny bydgyaf gwelas mabe dean gans ow both in neb termyn mes **company** *leas gwyth a bub beast* 'I cannot tolerate to see mankind willingly at any time but rather often the company of every beast' CW 1670-73.

It cannot be denied, I think, that **company** was an integral part of the lexicon of Middle Cornish. It is also probable that **company** in Cornish was stressed on the second syllable.

TO CONCEIVE

For 'to conceive' in the reproductive sense Nance gives **omdhon** and **concêvya**. A) **O·mdhon** is stressed on the prefix and is thus distinguished from B) **omdho·n** 'to behave', with stress on the second syllable. **O·mdhon** means 'to breed, to be pregnant' as much as 'to conceive'. **Omdho·n** 'to behave' is well attested

A **o·mdhon** 'to conceive'

en dezyow a vyth guelys hag a ze sur yntrezon may fyth torrow benegis bythqueth na allas e[m] zon
'the days will be seen and are coming among us when wombs that were never able to conceive will be blessed' PA 169bc
Me vedn meare cressha tha dewhan ha **humthan** 'I will greatly increase your anguish in bearing children' Rowe
an Arleth ny leb vye a **humthan** *der an Speryz Sanz* 'our Lord who was conceived by the Holy Spirit' ACB: E e 2 *verso*
Ma hy a **humthan** 'She is breeding' ACB: F f *verso*.

B **omdho·n** 'to behave'

ny a gren agen barvov mar ny **omthegen** *the guel* 'we shall shake our beards if we do not behave better' BM 3450-51
Coyth ew e ben ha'y **omthon** *ha'y antall* 'Clever are his head and his behaving and his snares' BK 998-99
Ow holan ew crackys quyt drefen why th'y lowenhe der lewd **omthon** 'My heart is utterly broken by your delighting him by lewd behaviour' BK 2339-41.

And compare: *The* **omthegyans** *ew worthy* 'Your behaviour is proper' BK 1607, 1605.

The word **concêvya** is better attested and means 'to conceive' in a reproductive sense as well as 'to conceive in the mind, to imagine, to comprehend':

conceive

erbyn reson yv in beys heb hays gorryth thymo creys bones flogh vyth **concevijs** 'it is contrary to reason in the world that any child was conceived without male seed, believe me' BM 844-46

der an sperys sans kerra **concevijs** *y fue the guir* 'conceived by the most beloved Holy Spirit he was indeed' BM 858-59

an map a fue **concevijs** *ha densis a kemereys* 'the son was conceived and took manhood' BM 887-88

pew a yll gull glan, neb ew **conceyvys** *in mostethes* 'who can make clean him who is conceived in filth?' TH 7

Mark inta me a ve **conceviis** *in pehosow* 'Mark well: I was conceived in sin' TH 8a

nyns ew ottrys na settys in mes dre signn vith, mas only **conceviis** *secretly in golan* 'it is not uttered or set forth by any sign but only conceived secretly in the heart' TH 28

lymmyn mar te cristonyan ha **concevya** *anger in aga colonow* 'now if Christians conceive anger in their hearts' TH 28a

Christ mab an ughella Tas ew Du pur wyer ha den heb nam, a'n Spurys Sans **concevyys** *hag a Varya genys, kekeffrys mayghtath ha mam* 'Christ the Son of the highest Father very truly and sinless man, conceived by the Holy Spirit and born of Mary, both maid and mother' BK 170-75

An Tas Du ha'n Mab ker emouns bythquath unoys prest ow kysober, a 'fuys furneth th'e **concyvya** 'God the Father and the beloved Son they are coeval, always working together, did you have the wisdom to conceive it' BK 240-44.

Since it is far better attested than **omdhon**, has a wider semantic range and is unambiguous in sense, **concêvya** could perhaps be the default word for 'to conceive' in the revived language.

CONCERN

If one wishes to say 'it is of no concern, no matter' in Cornish, one says A) **na fors** or B) **nyns eus fors**:

A **na fors**

na fors *kyn na threhetho ken tol ny vyth gurys ragtho* 'it does not matter though it does not reach; another hole will not be made for him' PC 2758-59

ay serys yma thyugh sport pan vs dewen dymmo vy wel wel **na fors** 'Oh, sir, you are amused when I suffer affliction. Well, well, no matter' BM 1056-58.

B **nyns eus fors**

Nyns us fors *awos henna my a wor wheth cusyl tha* 'That does not matter; I know yet a good plan' OM 2801-02

nyns us forse *kyn fens can moy* 'it does not matter if they were a hundred more' BM 1540.

'It is of no concern to me' can be rendered A) **ny'm deur** or B) **ny vern dhybm**:

GERYOW GWIR   concern

A ny'm deur

*kyn whrylly flattre mar mur ahanas tra uyth **ny'm dur** kynth os bysy* 'though you try to wheedle me so greatly, you are of no concern to me, though you endeavour' RD 1058-60

*Na govsugh a chevalry byth moy rychys **num dur** man* 'Speak not of chivalry; greater richers are of no concern to me at all' BM 442-43

*A peth an beys **num dur** man* 'Worldly riches are of no interest at all to me' BM 2563.

Cf. *cryst ow sylwyas clev **mara'th dur** thy's daryvas del garsen mur* 'Christ my saviour, listen if you are concerned that I should greatly like to tell you' RD 845-46. Notice that the related verb ***ny'm dethur** 'It does not matter to me' is attested once in the conditional: *in syrrys neb a'n gwelha ny'n **dythursa** pyth ellya war ambos e wohelas* 'whoever saw him angry, would not care whither he went if only he could avoid him' BK 2322-24.

B ny vern

***ny vern** tra vyth assaye* 'it does not matter to try' OM 2477

*myghtern yethewon heil thy's rak the sallugy **ny vern*** 'hail to you, king of the Jews, for it is of no importance to salute you' PC 2125-26

*rag myghtern nep a ymwra er byn cesar cous yma ha'y lathe travyth **ny vern*** 'for whoever claims to be a king is speaking against Caesar and it is of no importance to kill him' PC 2222-24

*Ry peth dyso thym **ny vern*** 'It is of no importance to me to give you something' BM 2586.

To say 'I consider of no importance' one can use an expression like A) **ny sensaf/setyaf X a**; B) **ny rov X a**; or C) **ny wrav vry/fors a**:

A ny sensaf... a

*me **ny sensaf vn bram plos** an cas yn geth nagh yn nos* 'I do not care a dirty fart for the case by day or by night' PC 2268-69

ny senseff** ath geryov bolde **vn faven kuk 'for your brave words I do not care an empty bean' BM 3480-81

*na anothans y byth voye me **ny settyaf gwaile gala*** 'nor do I care any the more for them than a stalk of straw' CW 1354-55

*y vos lathys me ew heare **ny sensaf poynt*** 'for his being dead—I am heir—I care not a jot' CW 1137-38.

B ny rov... a

*kyn feue map dev a'n nef na map an iaul **ny rof bram*** 'though he be the son of God or the son of the devil I don't give a fart' PC 1460-61

*an promas me **ny roof oye*** 'for the promise I don't give a damn' CW 1379.

83

concern GERYOW GWIR

C ny wrav vry/fors a

Pan welas en ethewon bos crist au cuthyll meystry ow care eʒomogyon hag aneʒe **na wre vry** 'When the Jews saw that Christ was acting forcefully, loving the needy and of them taking no heed' PA 26ab

Pandra ny vyn dev **gul vry** *ahanaf* 'What? God will not consider me' OM 519-20

ken fe y golon terrys a henna my **ny wraf vry** 'though his heart be broken, of that I take no heed' PC 2243-44

ny **wrons vry** *my the crye* 'they take no heed of my calling' PC 2249

tormentoris dugh dym scon ay ay ay dar **ny regh vry** 'executioners, come here to me immediately. Oh, oh, oh, damn! you take no notice' BM 952-53

Ne ren vry *pew a's pewa, kyn fe va arluth mar vras* 'I took no heed who owned it, be he never so great a lord' BK 100-01

me **ny wraf vry** *a henna* 'I do not give a fig for that' CW 1282

kyn fo porthov neff degeys wath y ferne a veth aleys peneyl ellen **fors ny raff** 'though the gates of heaven be closed, still hell will be wide open; I don't care where I go' BM 1255-57

am creya vy **fors ny reyth** 'for my crying you do not give a jot' BM 3620.

In the revived language one sometimes comes across expressions like **mater *a vern** 'matter of concern', **nowodhow *a vern** 'news of importance'. The expression ***a vern** is without warrant in the texts. The noun **bern** is never so used after the preposition **a**:

yn ov colon as yw **bern** *pan welaf ov map ihesu a dro th'y pen curyn spern* 'what a great concern it is in my heart when I see my son Jesus and a crown of thorns about his head' PC 2932-34

lauar thy'mmo vy pyv os rag omma awos the vos gynef vy by nyns yw **bern** 'tell me who you are for your being here with me is not a concern' RD 262-64

hy frenne byth nyns yw **bern** 'to buy it is no concern at all' RD 2234

The worthyb stowt thym ew **bern** 'Your stubborn answer is a concern to me' BK 52

Pan ew ow dewan mar drus, ef the vynnas bysmeras thym eth yw **bern** 'When my anxiety is so vexing it is a matter of concern that he wishes to disgrace me' BK 412-14

Mars ew **bern** *thys an whetlow* 'If the tales are of a concern to you' BK 2224

me a vyn gul indella, gans ow ownter ken fe **berne** 'I will do so, though it be a concern to my uncle' BK 3010-11.

The verbal form **ny vern** 'it does not matter' is well attested, as is the noun **bern** 'concern'. The expression ***a vern** 'of concern' is attested nowhere in traditional Cornish and cannot be recommended.

TO CONCLUDE

'To conclude' in English can mean both 'to bring to a conclusion, to finish' and 'to decide, to deduce'.

'To finish, to end, to come to an end, to conclude' can be translated in several ways in Cornish: A) **gorfenna**; B) **dewedha**; C) **fynyshya**; and D) **conclûdya**:

A gorfenna
*prederys peb a'y worfen fettyl allo **gorfenne*** 'let everybody think of his end, how he may end up' OM 227-28

*As ew coyth y'n **gorfensen**, a'n caffan arag ow fas* 'How quickly I would finish him off, if I got him in front of me' BK 2291-92.

B dewedha
*guyn veys a quellen vn wyth an termyn the **thewethe*** 'how happy I would be if I could see the time to finish' OM 685-86

*dre laha y coth dotho drok **dywethe*** 'by law he ought to end miserably' PC 1827-28

*aban na fyn **dewethe** me a vyn y curune auel myghtern yethewon* 'since he will not finish, I shall crown him as king of the Jews' PC 2115-17

*roy the pup vs yn bys ma yn bevnans gulan **dywethe*** 'grant to everyone in this world to end in a state of grace' PC 3215-16.

C fynyshya
*an iovle agis acectour re bo pan vowhy marrov mar quregh **fynsya*** 'may the devil be your attendant when you die, if you finish' BM 3523-25.

D conclûdya
*Rag henna the **concludia** rag an present termyn ma helma a vith rag agys exortia why* 'Therefore to conclude for the present time, this will be to exhort you' TH 5

*Rag henna lymmyn the **concludia**: why a glowas pana kerensa pana perfect charite vsy agan saviour ow requiria the vos ynnan ny* 'Therefore to conclude: you have heard what love, what perfect charity our Saviour requires to be in us' TH 30

*rag **concludia** in mater ma hemma ew thegys exortia why* 'to conclude in this matter, this is to exhort you' TH 51.

Conclûdya can also mean 'to determine, to deduce.'

*Indelma yma oecumenius ow **concludia** fatell res thyn ny cristonnyan, gans mer a payne ha nerth omleth warbyn agen ysker an teball ell* 'Thus Oecumenius determines that we Christians, with much effort and strength must fight agains our enemy, the devil' TH 28 *determys ove 3a vn dra ha* **concludys** *magata tha wythyll vn dean omma a thore ha sleme 3om servia* 'I am determined and decided as well to make a man here from earth and slime to serve me' CW 236-30.

It should be remembered, however, that **conclûdya** in the earlier texts means 'to silence in argument':

me a wra by god ys fo y **concludye** *war vn lam* 'I shall by God's foe silence him at a stroke' PC 1463-64

ny a thy a ver termyn agan dev wythoute fal hag a'n **conclud** *an iaudyn a leuer y vos dev thy'n* 'we two shortly will go thither without fail and will silence the scoundrel who says he is God to us' PC 1654-57

me a'n **conclud** *yredy ma na wothfo gorthyby* 'I shall silence him in argument indeed so that he won't be able to answer' PC 1659-60

bysy vye thy's gothuos yn certan mur a scryptours mara mynnyth gorthyby hytheu **concludys** *na vy* 'it would be necessary for you indeed to know much scripture, if you want to answer today, lest you be silenced in argument' PC 1672-75

dout an ieues an losel mar keus y vos **concludyys** 'the scoundrel fears that if he speaks, he'll be silenced in argument' PC 1776-77.

Probably, therefore, the best attested words for 'to finish, to end up, to finish off' in Cornish are **dewedha**, followed by **conclûdya**.

TO CONFESS, CONFESSION, CONFESSOR

In his 1952 English-Cornish dictionary Nance gives: 'confess' **avowa**; 'confess sins' **yes**, **meneges**; 'confession' *****cofes**, **yessans** and 'confessor' **yesser**. These entries give a rather false picture of the position in traditional Cornish.

Avowa 'to admit, to acknowledge' is certainly attested:

myns a wruk me a'n **avow** *hag a gyf dustynyow ty the govs er byn laha* 'all I did I admit, and will produce witnesses that you spoke contrary to the law' PC 1301-03

yn tokyn y vos goky ha myns a geusys foly ma na veath y **avowe** *hethough cercot a baly thotho me a vyn y ry* 'as a sign that he is a fool and all he has spoken folly, so that he dare not admit it, bring a surcoat of silk; I will give it to him' PC 1781-85

An trubut pan ve tochys, e worthyb o tyn ha freth hag ef garaw hag owth **avowa** *forsoyth a'y wlascor trubut na goyth, mars agys pen, ow arluth* 'When the tribute was mentioned, his answer was sharp and vigorous and he was violent, acknowledging indeed that his kingdom owed no tribute, other than your head, my lord' BK 2262-67

me a wore yma in pow leas dean a gowse an tase tues perfyt me an **advow** *yth yns i ha polatis brase* 'I know there are many men in the land who speak of the Father, perfect men, I admit, are they and great fellows' CW 2351-54.

GERYOW GWIR — confess

Yes 'to confess, to obtain absolution' is confined to *Beunans Meriasek*, where it is attested five times:

*ens pub the **zeys** thy gela* 'let each man go to confess to his fellow' BM 607
*guetyogh may fegh glan **zesseys** na dreylogh the pegh na moy* 'take care to be fully absolved; turn no more to sin' BM 2162-63
*insol bethugh glan **zesseys** avodyogh pegh in bys ma* 'up! get full absolution; avoid sin in this world' BM 2747-48
***zesseys** vnctis communijs off lemen the ihesu grays* 'I have now been shriven, anointed and housled, to Jesus be thanks' BM 4272-73
*ihesu arluth gront dethy gallus boys **zesseys** oma kyns es merwel eredy* 'Jesus grant to them the power to be absolved from sin indeed before dying' BM 4278-80.

Meneges means 'to admit, to acknowledge, to declare' rather than merely 'to confess sins':

*mar ten ha **menegas** agan pehosow du ew lene a vercy, just ha fethfull the gava thyn agan pehosow* 'If we confess our sins, God is full of mercy, just and faithful to forgive us our sins' TH 8
*yma eff worth agan dysky ny in agan golahes the **meneges** agan honyn pehadorryan ha the whelas gyvyans* 'he teaches us in our worship to acknowledge we are sinners and to seek forgiveness' TH 8a
*The negys them **menag** a, py te a 'fyth edrega* 'Your business, declare it to me, or you will regret it' BK 43-4
*A bele teta the'n tyr? **Menyk** the bow whath ha'th tyman!* 'Whence did you come into the land? Declare your country and your domain!' BK 80-2.

The commonest word for 'to confess; to acknowledge' is **confessya**:

*Indella yma S Pawle ow **confessia** y honyn pandra o eff anotha y honyn* 'Thus St Paul confesses himself, what he was of himself' TH 8
*so nyns o ef methek the **confessia** y pehosow, pan lowar turne a rug eff ernestly ha lamentably desyrya an mercy a thu* 'but he was not ashamed to confess his sins, how often he earnestly and lamentably desired God's mercy' TH 8a
*Inweth fatell rug an den benegas ma **confessia** y pehosow fattell ens mar ver in number* 'Although that this holy man confessed his sins, that they were so great in number' TH 8a
*gesow ny oll the **confessia** gans ganow ha gans colan fatell ony len a imperfeccion* 'let us all confess with mouth and with heart that we are full of imperfection' TH 9a
*na esow ny the vos methek the **confessia** an stat agan vnperfectnes. Ha na esow ny the vos methek the **confessia** nag ony mar perfect dell vea res thyn in oll agen oberow, na esow ny the vos methek the **confessia** agan foly ha leverell kepar dell rug pedyr Me ew pehadure* 'let us not be ashamed to confess the state of our imperfection. And let us not be ashamed

to confess that we are not as perfect as we ought be in all our works, let us not be ashamed to confess our folly and to say as Peter did, I am a sinner' TH 9a

ow menya dre henna fatell vynna eff worth oll an bys gothvas, ha **confessia** *an auctorite an catholyk egglos* 'meaning by that that he would for all the world recognize and acknowledge the authority of the catholic Church' TH 35a

ha henna yma pub lell cristian ow **confessia** *pub dith in y credo, ow leverall, me a crys in Catholyk eglos* 'and that every true Christian confesses every day in his creed, saying: I believe in the catholic Church' TH 39

ha gwren **confessia** *agan transgressyon ha humbly desyre may hallan bos recevys gans crist in y chy* 'and let us confess our transgression and humbly desire that we may be received by Christ in his house' TH 40a-41

may ruga in y lyver gylwys RESOLUTION LUTHERIANA SUPER PROPOSITIONE SUA .13. DE POTESTATE PAPE **confessya** *plenly kepar dell vsy omm*[a] *ow folya* 'so that in his book called *Resolutio Lutheriana super propositione sua 13 de potestate Pape* he confessed plainly as follows here' TH 49a

gas an mynd **confessia** *da achy, an pith a whrella an ganow cows, gas an golan percyvia da, an geer a vo soundis* 'let the mind confess well inside what the mouth speaks; let the heart perceive well, the word that is uttered' SA 61a.

For 'confession' Nance suggest ***yessans** < **yes** 'to confess' and ***cofes**. Neither is attested. ***Yessans** is formed on the basis of **yes** 'to confess'. ***Cofes** is Nance's suggestion on the basis of Breton *kofez* 'confession' and Welsh *cyffes* 'idem' < Latin *confessio*. The vocalism of *cofes is not certain. If Latin *commendo* 'I commend' has given Cornish **kemmyn** (PC 2985, BK 2831; cf. Welsh *cymyn* 'legacy'), one might expect Latin *confessio* to give Cornish ***kefes** rather than ***cofes** (cf. Welsh *cyffes*).

The only attested word for 'confession' is **confessyon**:

Gesow ny oll the wull agan **confession** *kepar dell rug an flogh prodigall leverall thy das pan o spendys oll y substans* 'Let us all make our confession as the prodigal son said to his father when all his wealth had been spent' TH 9a.

For 'confessor' Nance suggests ***yesser**, a word of his own devising. Breton for 'confessor' has both *kofesour* and *koñfesor* for 'confessor', Welsh has *cyffeswr*. The attested word in Cornish is **confessour**:

tus vas owhy ha tus fuer, ha'm **confessors** 'you are goodly men and wise, and my confessors' BK 1619-21.

In traditional Cornish 'to confess, to acknowledge' is either **avowa**, **meneges** or **confessya**. 'To confess (one's sins)' is **yes** and **confessya**; 'confessor' is **confessour**, plural **confessours**.

TO CONQUER, CONQUEROR, CONQUEST

For 'to conquer' Nance suggests **fetha**, ***tryhy** (UC *tryghy*) and **conqwerrya** (UC *conquerrya*). ***Tryhy** is unattested. **Fetha** means 'to defeat, to withstand' and is not common:

> *evgh alemma ahanan the seruye ow map kerra re **fethas** an fals ievan hythyw tergwyth yn certan* 'go hence from here to minister to my dearest son, who has three times today defeated the false demon' PC 152-55
>
> *Dell eugh tus fuer, ordnowgh aragof uskis peswar myghtern curunys gans clethythyow a owr per in tokyn me the **fetha** ow yskerans in pub tu* 'As you are wise men, array before me four crowned kings with swords of pure gold as a sign that I have conquered my enemies on all sides' BK 2021-27.

Conqwerrya is attested:

> *adam plos a thesefse warnan **conquerrye** neffre lemyn ef yv agan guas* 'dirty Adam presumed to overcome us for ever. Now he is our servant' OM 908-10
>
> *The wethel gist settys of rag the gerya, ha dyswul ha **conquerya** the yskerans der gras Christ* 'To do great deeds I am determined to assist you and to destroy and to conquer your foes by the grace of Christ' BK 1482-85.

The commonest word for 'to conquer', however, is **overcùmya**:

> *mar qureth y **ouercummya** the crist ny a vyn treyla* 'if you conquer her, we will turn to Christ' BM 4012-13
>
> *gwren ny kemeras with hay avoydia inweth y **ouercommya** gans oll y traynes hay antylly* 'let us be careful and also overcome him with all his snares and temptations' TH 5a
>
> *Eff a promysyas fatell vetha onyn genys mes an stok han has a Eva, a re **overcommya** agan eskar ny an teball ell* 'He promised that one would be born of the stock and seed of Eve, who would conquer our enemy the devil' TH 13
>
> *ha gwregh incessantly omlath warbyn agys yskar an teball ell, neb ew **overcummys** dre Jhesu crist* 'and incessantly fight against your enemy the devil, who has been overcome by Jesus Christ' TH 16
>
> *nyns ew eff lymmyn abyll thegan **ouercommya** ny* 'he isn't now able to overcome us' TH 16
>
> *an egglos catholyk neffra ny vith **ouercommys** gans error* 'the catholic Church will never be overcome by error' TH 17a
>
> *neb a rug confondya Symon magus ha y **ouercommya*** 'who confounded Simon Magus and defeated him' TH 46a
>
> *Eff a theth the Rome the **ouercommya** Symon magus* 'He came to Rome to overcome Simon Magus' TH 47
>
> *whath hemma a vea sufficient lowre the **ouercummya** an re a vynna gull resystens* 'still this would be sufficient to defeat those who wish to resist' TH 50a.

conquer

For 'conqueror' Nance suggests **tryhor** (UC *trygher*), ***fethor** (UC **fether*) and **conqwerrour** (UC *conquerour*). **Tryhor** is attested once: *ambosow orth tryher gureys annethe nynses laha* 'promises made to a victor, there is no law to keep them' OM 1235-36. ***Fethor** is unattested. The commonest word for 'conqueror' in the traditional language is **conqwerrour**:

Me yv empour ha governour **conquerrour** *tyr* 'I am an emperor and governor, a conqueror of territory' BM 930-32

conquerrour *off corff da in proff dovtijs in meske arlythy* 'I am a conqueror, a good body in trial, feared among lords' BM 2403-05

I say Arthur is my nam, myghtern bras ha galosak ha **conquerror** 'I say, Arthur is my name; a great and powerful king and conqueror' BK 1399-401.

For 'conquest' Nance suggests ***tryhans** (UC *tryghans*) and **conqwest** (UC *conquest*). Of these only **conqwest** is attested:

ty re fue fest lafur bras dre **conquest** *a thylyfras mes a payn an enefow* 'you have had very great labour, which through conquest has delivered the souls from torment' RD 2628-30.

'To conquer, to defeat, to overcome' in Cornish is either **fetha**, **conqwerrya** or **overcùmya**. The default word for 'conqueror' is **conqwerrour** and for 'conquest', **conqwest**.

TO CONSECRATE, CONSECRATION

There are two words for 'to consecrate' (a bishop, the Eucharist) in traditional Cornish: A) **sacra** and B) **consecrâtya**. A can also be used more widely to mean 'ordain (as priest)':

A **sacra**

y **sacra** *scon my a wra* 'I shall consecrate him soon' OM 2600

the epscop guraf the **sacre** *kymmer the vytour whare* 'I consecrate you as a bishop; take your mitre immediately' OM 2614-15

ry dys ordys me a vyn in hanov ihesu lemyn **sacrys** *gena betheth suer* 'I will give you holy orders; in the name of Jesus now you shall be consecrated by me' BM 529-31

oma danvenys ovy a vreten pur eredy rag weles sur arluth wek gallus may fo meryasek epscop **sacrys** *pur defry in venetens cyte dek* 'I have been sent here from Brittany in very truth to seek indeed, dear lord, power that Meriasek may be consecrated bishop of Vannes, a fair city' BM 2756-61

pyv a vo epscop **sacrys** 'who should be consecrated bishop?' BM 2869 *meryasek yv dewesys the vones epscop **sacrys** sav eff ren nahas dyson* 'Meriasek has been chosen to be consecrated bishop, but he has refused it indeed' BM 2905-07

*The dre mar tuth yv vollys epscop eff a veth **sacrys*** 'If his bulls have come home, he shall be consecrated bishop' BM 2908-09

*in venetenes the **sacre** epscop gallus thyn yma* 'I have power to consecrate you bishop of Vannes' BM 2951-52

*Lemmen oll ny yv plesijs meryasek y voys **sacrys** epscop thynny* 'Now we are all pleased that Meriasek should be consecrated bishop for us' BM 3019-21.

B consecrâtya

*berth in eglos sent sampson bethens eff **consecratis*** 'in the church of St Samson let him be consecrated' BM 2983-84

*an kigg ew anoyntis, may halla an nenaf bos **consecratis*** 'the flesh is anointed that the soul may be consecrated' SA 60a

*nyng o corf Christ kyns ef the vos **consecratis**, bus osa the vos **consecratis**, me a laver the gee, e thew lymmen corf agen arluth Jesus Christ* 'it was not the body of Christ before it was consecrated, but after its being consecrated, I tell you, it is now the body of our Lord Jesus Christ' SA 62

*Kyns an bara the vos **consecratis**, ith thew bara* 'Before the bread is consecrated, it is bread' SA 62

*indella eth ew disquethas thyn [an] bois the vos **consecratis** dir geir a pesadow* 'thus it is demonstrated to us that the food is consecrated by the word of prayer' SA 63

*Neg eran ny ow kemeras hemma rag common bara ha dewas, mas kigg ha gois agen Saviour Jesus Christ, thaken sawya ny, pan vo va **consecratis*** 'We do not take this for common bread and drink, but the flesh and blood of our Saviour Jesus Christ, to save us, when it is consecrated' SA 63a.

For 'consecration' Nance suggests *sacrans. But such a form is unattested. The only attested Cornish word for 'consecration' is **consecracyon**:

*bus osa an **consecration** eth o gwris corf agen arluth* 'but after the consecration it was made the body of our Lord' Christ SA 61a

*pan o an girreow an **consecration** devethis then bara, an bara ew gwres kig agen arluth Christ* 'when the words of the consecration came to the bread, the bread is made the flesh of our Lord Christ' SA 62

*fatla ew an bara Corf Christ dir **consecration** an girreow. **Consecration** ew gwris dir girreow agen arluth Jesus* 'how is the bread the body of Christ by consecration? Consecration is made by means of the words of our Lord Jesus' SA 62

*dir **consecration** an geir dew benegas e thew gwris gois* 'by consecration of the word of blessed God it is made blood' SA 63.

In the revived language 'to consecrate' can be either **sacra** or **consecrâtya**. 'Consecration' should probably be **consecracyon**.

TO CONVERSE

The verb **kescôwsel, keskêwsel** 'to talk together, to converse' is well established in the revived language. It should be pointed out, however, that this word was devised by Nance and is not found in the texts. The only attested word is **kestalkya** 'to talk together, to converse' which occurs once:

me re deth omma defry drefen agen bos vnwoys 3e **kestalkye** 'I have come here indeed, because we are closely related, to converse' BM 234-36.

Kestalkya is a compound of **kes-** and **talkya** 'to talk, to speak', which latter is attested more than once:

Eua prag na thuete nes rag cous orthyf ha **talkye** 'Eve, why do you not come near to speak to me and to talk?' OM 149-50

whath pan esa eff in myske tus dyskys, rag **talkya** *an mater ma in aga mysk y ha gansans y* 'still when he was among learned men to talk of this matter among them and with them' TH 49a

Ha whath dre reson ran a thewethas a rug **talkya** *vaynly ha curiously an kythsam seconde part ma* 'And moreover since some recently have talked vainly and curiously of this same second part' TH 55

eva prage na theta nes rag cowse orthaf ha **talkya** 'Eve, why do you not come near to speak to me and to talk?' CW 543-44.

Kestalkya and **talkya** should perhaps both be part of the lexicon of the revived language.

CORNISH (LANGUAGE)

For 'Cornish (language)' Nance used **Kernewek*, which he based on *Cernewec*, the headword in Williams' Lexicon. **Kernewek* is unattested, since all the occurring forms have either **o** or **û** as the stressed vowel. I have collected the following examples:

Cycely called Agnes Davey whore and whore bitch in English and not in **Cornowok** Exeter Consistory Court (1572)

Gun tavaz **Carnoack** *eu mar pel gwadnhez* 'Our Cornish language is so weakened' BF: 25

ma mouy Sousenek clappiez dre eza **Curnooack**, *rag radden el bose keevez na el skant clappia na guthvaz* **Curnooack** 'there is more English spoken than Cornish, for some can be found who can hardly speak or understand Cornish' BF: 25

mar pith tra vith gwrez tho gwetha **Curnooack** 'if anything is done to preserve Cornish' BF: 25

GERYOW GWIR — Cornish

Rag me a hunnen ve gennez en collan an pow na eu an **Curnooack** *moyha cowsez* 'For I myself was born in the heart of that country where Cornish is most spoken' BF: 27

nag ez ko them tho guthva[z] *meer en tavaz* **Curnooack** 'I do not remember knowing much of the Cornish language' BF: 29

dro tho an tavaz **Curnooack** 'about the Cornish language' BF: 29

buz me a aore hemma urt e hoer an **Curnoack** 'but I know this from her sister, the Cornish language' BF: 31

radden olga bose parrez tho leverol drerama gweel nebbaz [ena] *a* **Curnoack** 'some might be prepared to say that I am making little there of Cornish' BF: 31

ul an sompel rag an **Curnooack** 'all the example for Cornish' BF: 31

Gomar mab Japhet mab Noah vo an den reg clapia **kernuak** 'Gomer son of Japhet son of Noah was the man who spoke Cornish' BF: 46

ha rag hedna ni el guelas ha adzhan an tavaz **kernuak** *dha boz tavaz koth* 'and therefore we can see and understand that the Cornish language is an ancient tongue' BF: 46

Ha dotha tavaz **Kornooack** *vo res* 'And to him the Cornish language was given' BF: 48

Dadn an mean ma deskes brose dean en tavaz **Kernooak** *gelles* 'Under this stone a mighty learned man in the Cornish language is gone' BF: 48

En tavaz Greka, Lathen ha'n Hebra, en Frenkock ha **Carnoack** *deskes dha* 'In the Greek language, Latin and Hebrew, in French and Cornish well learned' BF: 59

Deske **Cornoack** 'to learn Cornish' WGwavas

Menja Tiz **Kernuack** *buz gasowas* 'If Cornish men would only listen' LAM: 224

Rag na algia ea clappia na screffa **Curnoack** *precarra why* 'For he could not speak nor write Cornish like you' LAM: 238

Me rig deskey **Cornoack** *termen me vee mawe* 'I learnt Cornish at the time when I was a boy' LAM: 244

No rig avee biscath gwelles lever **cornoack** 'I never saw a Cornish book' LAM: 244

Cornoack *ewe all neceaves gen poble younk* 'Cornish is all forgotten by young people' LAM: 244

Elo why clapier **Kernuack**? 'Can you speak Cornish?' ACB: F f *verso*

Kernûak 'Cornish' Borlase.

It seems that Nance believed that **Kernewek* was the earlier form of **Cornoack**, **Kernûak**, etc., just as **clewes** 'to hear' is an earlier form of *clowes* and **dewthek** an earlier form of **dowthek** 'twelve'. It must be admitted, however, that **clowas** 'to hear' is already common in BM and **dowthek** for **dewthek** 'twelve' is attested as early as PA (ʒen **dowʒek** PA 47a, 61a). Moreover the form **Cornowok** is attested in 1572, i.e. well within the Middle Cornish period. Since **Kernewek* is unattested, and since forms with a rounded vowel are universal in the texts, it might be advisable to replace **Kernewek* with **Kernowek**.

COUNTRY

There are four different words used for 'country' in the revived language: A) **bro**; B) **gwlas**; C) **tireth** and D) **pow**. These four items differ in both frequency and usage.

Bro has a general sense of 'country' but it is very rare indeed, being attested once only in the traditional texts:

A **bro**

*Rag henna pylat a ros ʒen vorogyon aga ro may lavarsans ha dolos yn pub tyller dris an **vro** ʒe vos tus yrvys yn nos warneʒe* 'Therefore Pilate gave their present to the soldiers that they should say and claim everywhere in the land that armed men came upon them' PA 250 a-c.

It also occurs in the toponym *Penbro* in Breage.

The word **gwlas** is common. It means 'country' in the political sense, and can often be translated 'kingdom'. Indeed **gwlas nev** is the usual expression for 'kingdom of heaven':

B1 **gwlas**

*out out out ellas ellas bos wharfethys yn ov **gulas** myshyf an par-ma cothys* 'Oh, oh, oh! Alas, alas! that it has happened that misfortune like this has fallen upon my kingdom' OM 1547-49

*re'n kyrho thotho th'y **wleth*** 'may he fetch him to him in his kingdom' OM 2370

*the worthyby me a wra nyns yv ow **gulas** a'n bys ma* 'I will answer you: my kingdom is not of this world' PC 2009-10

*my an dysk na vo yn **gvlas** gramarion vyth ay parov* 'I shall teach him so that there will not be a grammarian to equal him in the kingdom' BM 91-2

*ty re wores mes an **gluas** meryasek neb o dremas acontis certen a ʒus* 'you have put out of the kingdom Meriasek who was considered a good man indeed by men' BM 2374-76

*me a comond der ov **gluas** naha dewov nag yv vas* 'I command throughout my kigdom to deny gods that are not good' BM 2518-19

*ny a yll vnderstondya fatell ew lell feith ha discans an egglos an pith ew only vniversall in pub **gwlas** dyskys ha cresys* 'we can understand that the true faith and teaching of the Church is that which is only universally taught and believed in every kingdom' TH 34a.

B2 **gwlas nev**

*An dus vas a ʒeserya ʒeʒe **gulas nef** o kyllys* 'The good men desired for themselves the kingdom of heaven which had been lost' PA 4a

*ha gevys may fe ʒoʒo kyffrys y begh hay fyltye degis na ve ʒe worto **gulas nef** [h]a roys ʒe gen re* 'and that also he might be forgiven his sin and his impurity, so that the kingdom of heaven would not be taken from him and given to others' PA 23cd *ha thywhy me re ordynas* **glas nef** *ynny rak tryge* 'and for you I have ordained the kingdom of heaven to dwell therein' PC 807-08

Da dym yth yv nesse the du hay gorthya eff guthel y voth kepar del goth may hallen dendyl **gluas neff** 'I am glad to approach God and to worship him, to do his will as is fitting, that I may deserve the kingdom of heaven' BM 1998-2003

Rag ny neg on abyll ahanan agan honyn the wull agan honyn an erryan a **wlas neff** 'For we are not able of ourselves to make ourselves the heirs of the kingdom of heaven' TH 10a

Mas agys lelldury a vo vght lelldury an scribis han pharysys, ny illowgh intra in **gwlas neff** 'Unless your faithfulness is above the faithfulness of the scribes and pharisees, you cannot enter into the kingdom of heaven' TH 26a

mas Dew ascendias then neff, hef asas vmma e kig theny ha e weth ef a woras e kig gansa the **gwlas neff** 'but God ascended into heaven and he left here his flesh for us and also he brought his flesh with him to the kingdom of heaven' SA 60

try fersons yns pur worthy ow kysraynya in joyes in **gwlase nef** *es awartha* 'they are three very worthy persons reigning together in the joys of the kingdom of heaven above' CW 1960-62

Glaze neave *than enna ni veath aheaze* 'The kingdom of heaven we will have for the soul at length' LAM: 228.

Tireth means 'country' from a geographical point of view, i.e. hill country, wooded country. The word is not common, however:

C tireth

thy's yth arghaf a **dyreyth** *gas adam the'th egery* 'to you, O land, I command: let Adam open you' OM 381-82

ty a wra woge hemma gorre an tus alena bys yn **tyreth** *a thynwa lanwes leyth ha mel kefrys* 'you will after this lead the people thence into the country in which flows a fullness of milk and honey also' OM 1427-30

gallas ef the ken **tyreth** *ha ganso mur a eleth ellas lemmyn rak moreth* 'he has gone to another country and with him many angels. Alas now for sorrow' RD 763-65

Devethys off in **tereth** *ha squeth me yv ow kerthes* 'I have come to the country and I am tired walking' BM 632-33

ha war an **tyreth** *vhel thym yma castel arel a veth gelwys tyndagyel* 'and in the high country I have another castle called Tintagel' BM 2212-14

An mens **tyrath** *a barkys, hedre ven ow cul tronkys, me a ro thys perpetual in dyswyllyans an trespas* 'As much land as you enclose while I am bathing, I will give you as a perpetual gift as restitution for the wrong' BK 1087-90.

The commonest word for 'country' in the texts is **pow**, *plural* **powyow**:

D pow

Ihesu crist yn **pow** *adro pub eroll pregoth a wre* 'Jesus Christ in the country round about always used to preach' PA 23a *kepar ha del vena ve an purra lader yn* **pow** 'as though I were the veriest brigand in the country' PA 74d

ha hy a wra aspye mars us dor segh yn nep **pow** 'and she will see whether there is dry land in any country' OM 1114-16

ny vynnyth the pobel dev gase cres thy'n yn nep tv awos tryga yn **pov** *ma* 'you will not leave the people of God in peace for us on any side because they dwell in this country' OM 1597-99

mar ny fethe ef guythys gans y tus y fyth leddrys ha'n corf yn mes kymerys ha gorrys ef the ken **pow** 'if he is not guarded he will be stolen by his men and the body taken out and brought to another country' RD 353-56

A vreten sur then **pov** *ma dres en mor me re dufa* 'From Brittany surely to this country I have come over the sea' BM 649-50

Indelma oll gouernans gwlasow, an **pow***, an trevow marras, han trevow trygva, y a vea res thetha iently correctia oll an re ew offenders in dan aga gouernans* 'Thus all governments of kingdoms, of the country, of the market towns and the inhabited towns, they have gently to correct all those who are offenders under their governance' TH 25a

thyn Jewys neb ow dispersys a leys in lyas **pow** 'to the Jews who were scattered in many countries' TH 47

My a'n helgh in mes a'n **pow** 'I will chase him out of the country' BK 545

me a vyn kyns es hethy mos alema ha gwandra adro in **powe** 'I will straight away go hence and wander around in the country' CW 1217-19

Rag me a hunnen ve gennez en collan an **pow** *na eu an Curnooack mouyha cowsez* 'For I myself was born in the heart of that country where Cornish is most spoken' BF: 27

ha angye eath carr tha **pow** *go honnen vor aral* 'and they went away to their own country another way' Rowe

Buz, mor mennow direvall war bidn an **pow** *yeine* 'But if you will build against the cold country' ACB: F f 3.

Pow also occurs as the first element in place-names. The following, *inter alia*, are attested **Pow Ameryca** 'America', **Pow an Brethon** 'Britain', **Pow an Fleman** 'Flanders', **Pow an Sowson** 'England', **Pow Densher** 'Devonshire', **Pow Jûda** 'Judaea'.

To sum up, **gwlas** means 'country' in a political sense, and can also be translated 'kingdom'; cf. **gwlas nev** 'the kingdom of heaven'. **Bro** is so rarely attested, that it was hardly an element of the Middle and Late Cornish vocabulary at all. **Tireth** means 'country' in a rather specialized sense. The default word for 'country' in Cornish is **pow**, and this should be reflected in the revived language.

See further *s.v.* '**ENGLAND**', '**FRANCE**' and '**KINGDOM**'.

COURAGE, COURAGEOUS

For 'courage' Nance recommends **colon dhâ** (UC *colon dha*) and ***colonecter** (UC **colonnekter*). **Colon dhâ** appears to be attested once, but it seems to mean 'good heart, kind heart' rather than 'courage':

*Gofen ha gwrâ gans **colon da** 'Ask and act with a good heart' Gwavas MSS.*

***Colonecter** (UC **colonnnekter*) is unattested. The word **coraj** is attested once:

*ma[s] the ry thetha **corag** the wull da ha the contynewa in dadder* 'but to give them courage to do good and to continue in goodness' TH 25.

The word **colonnek** is attested, but it seems for the most part to mean 'good-hearted, willing, eager.' The sense 'courageous' is confined to two citations in Lhuyd:

*Beneth du 3ys meryasek pup vr ty yv **colonnek** parys rag dysky dader* 'God's blessing to you, Meriasek, you are always eager, ready to learn goodness' BM 31-3
*Banneth crist 3ys meriasek ham benneth pur **colonnek*** 'The blessing of Christ to you Meriasek and my blessing very willingly' BM 201-02
*pybugh menstrels **colonnek** may hyllyn donsia dyson* 'Pipe, minstrels, eagerly, that we may straightway dance' BM 2511-12
*mones dotho **colonnek** mannaff the weles gueres* 'I will go to him eagerly to seek assistance' BM 3105-06
*nena eff a suffras myrnans **colonnek**, henno myrnans in crowsse* 'then he suffered willing death, that is death upon the cross' TH 15
*rag crist a suffras y virnans ragan ny **colonnek** rag agan pegh ny* 'for Christ suffered his death for us willingly, for our sin' TH 15a
*Ha penagull a cause an geffa den in contrary, whath bette thewetha the thon blonogath da ha **colonnek** the pub den* 'And whatever cause a man may have to the contrary, nonetheless he must bear good and good-hearted will to all men' TH 21a
*Animosus... Stout, courageous; C. **Kolannak** AB: 43a*
*Magnanimus... Valiant, stout, courageous, of a great spirit, adventurous. C. **Kalonnek** AB: 84a.*

Bold is a commoner word for 'courageous, brave' in the texts:

*En prins scon a leueris te crist lauar 3ym plema 3e dus mar **voldh** re 3yssys* 'The prince soon said, You Christ, tell me, where are your men you taught so boldly?' PA 78ab
*Guelwys off mytern massen arluth **bolde** in ov dethyov* 'I am called king Maxen, a brave lord in my days' BM 3156-57

courage GERYOW GWIR

ny senseff ath geryov **bolde** *vn faven kuk* 'for your brave words I do not care an empty bean' BM 3480-81

Hayl, arluth **bold**, *del os sauns per!* 'Hail, brave lord, as you are without peer!' BK 1720-21

Ef ew an **bolta** *mab den a gampoller gans ganow* 'he is the bravest man who is mentioned by mouth' BK 2319-20

pyw henna a veth mar **vold** *cowse gear warbyn lucyfer* 'who is that who is so brave as to speak a word against Lucifer?' CW 163-64.

The abstract noun **bolder** is also attested, but it means 'rashness, temerity' rather than 'courage':

Ihesus a ve hombronkis ha war y lyrgh mur a lu dre **volder** *tebel Iustis rag y chasye kynȝ o du* 'Jesus was led and after him a large crowd through the temerity of a wicked justice to pursue him though he was God' PA 163cd.

The only attested word for 'courage' in the texts is **coraj**. For 'courageous' **bold** and **colonnek**, **colodnek** are probably the best words to use.

COURSE

There are three words in use for 'course' in revived Cornish, **resegva**, ***steus** and **cors**. **Resegva** is a respelling of Old Cornish **redegua** (*cursus redegua* 'course' OCV §9). ***Steus** (*stus, stes* in UC) was devised by Nance on the basis of Welsh *ystod* 'course' and Breton *steud* 'file, rangée'. The only attested word is **cors**:

powesough lymmyn vn **cors** *me agas pys* 'rest now a course, I beg you' PC 2146-67
Py du y syngough an **cours**? 'In which direction are you holding course?' BK 1380.

Cors is probably, therefore, the best way to render 'course' in the revived language.

COURT

The word **lys**, **lës** 'court' is not attested in the texts, being known only from place-names, e.g. *Liskeard, Lesnewth, Gadles*, etc. The compound ***breuslys** (UC *bruslys*) 'court of law' was devised by Nance on the basis of Welsh *brawdlys*.

There are two words for 'court' in the Cornish texts: A) **cur** and B) **cort**.

create

A **cur**

scon yn mes quyk a'm golok na tryk y'm **cur** 'get out of my sight quick sharp. Stay not in my court!' OM 1530-31

a nef vhel an tas mer re'th ordene ty ha'th wrek pan vy marow yn y **cver** 'may the great Father from heaven on high order you and your wife into his court' PC 684-86

Bohogogneth abreth du remoconn then **cur** *yth yv wose helma* 'Poverty for the sake of God is removal hereafter to the court of heaven' BM 2010-12

Re Syn Jovyn a'n **cur** *loys!* 'By St Jovyn of the bright court heaven' BK 107

re Syn Jovyn a'n **cur** *loys!* 'by St Jovyn of the bright court of heaven' BK 1040.

B

me a vyn mones heb bern lemen the **corte** *an mytern* 'I will go willingly to the king's court' BM 3176-77

Duen ny oll gans procession thy **curte** *syluester dysonn gruen y gora* 'Let us all go with a procession; let us bring Silvester to his court' BM 4174-76

Ma tha vee treall en **cort** *an vaternes* 'I have a trial in the queen's court' Bilbao MS.

As can be seen from the above examples, the word **cur** is used chiefly of the court of heaven. It is not perhaps therefore the most apt word for 'court' in the sense of 'royal court' or 'court of law'. That is best translated by **cort**.

TO CREATE, CREATOR, CREATION

The ordinary word for 'to create' in the texts is **formya**:

ha hethyv me a thesyr dre ov grath dalleth an beys y lauaraf nef ha tyr bethens **formyys** *orth ov brys* 'and today I desire through my grace to begin the world; I say heaven and earth, let them be created according to my wish' OM 5-8

lemmen pan yv nef thy'n gwrys ha lenwys a eleth splan ny a vyn **formye** *an bys par del on try hag onan* 'now that heaven has been made for us and filled with glorious angels, we will create the world, as we are three and one' OM 9-12

bethens ebron dreys pup tra rak kvthe myns vs **formyys** 'let the heavens be over everything to cover all that has been created' OM 21-2

yn pympes dyth me a vyn may fo **formyys** *dre ov nel bestes puskes hag ethyn* 'on the fifth day I wish that through my power animals, fish and birds be created' OM 41-3

map den a bry yn perfyth me a vyn y vos **formyys** 'mankind from clay perfectly I wish him to be created' OM 55-6

A das map ha spyrys sans gorthyans the'th corf wek pup prys ow **formye** *tek ha dyblans ty ru'm gruk pur havel thy's* 'O Father, Son and Holy Spirit, worship to your dear person always, creating me fair and clear you have made me like you' OM 85-8

benytha gorthyys re by del russys moy a'm govys worth ow **formye** *haval thy's* 'always may you be adored, as you have done more for me creating me like you' OM 107-09

create   **GERYOW GWIR**

Rag bones ol tek ha da in whed dyth myns yw **formyys** *aga sona ny a wra* 'Since all is fair and good, everything that has been created, I will bless them' OM 141-43

an tas a wruk ov **formye** *a'm offryn re woffe gras* 'the Father who created me may he be grateful for my offering' OM 529-30

ellas vyth pan yu kyllys Abel whek ov map kerra na bythqueth pan vef **formys** 'alas that Abel my dearest son was lost at all, or ever I was created' OM 614-16

a das del on the wythres a bol hag a lyys **formys** 'O Father, as we are your handiwork created of mire and mud' OM 1069-70

a ny vynta obeye the thev a wruk the **formye** *hag a formyas nef ha'n beys* 'will you not obey your God who created you and who created heaven and earth?' OM 1505-07

a tus vas why re welas fetel **formyas** *dev an tas nef ha nor war lergh y vrys* 'good people, you have seen how God the Father created heaven and earth according to his will' OM 2825-27

both the vap yw yndella rak selwel kemmys yv da aban fue adam **formys** 'your son's wish is thus to save all that is good since Adam was created' PC 2952-54

a tas ker yn huhelder ty a **formyas** *nef ha beys* 'O dear Father in the height, you created heaven and earth' RD 423-44

by ny geusy ken ys wyr nep a **formyas** *mor ha tyr* 'never did he speak other than truth, he who created sea and land' RD 1195-96

kens ol ef agan **formyas** *ha gans y wos a prennas gour ha benen* 'first of all he created us and by his blood redeemed man and woman' RD 2430-32

in hanov du dy lawe neb a **formyas** *neff ha novr in bys ma gans y dule map den a pry* 'in the name of God, praised be he, who created heaven and earth, in this world mankind from clay' BM 1313-16

Ith ew benefyt ha confort bras ragan ny the consydra agan bos ny creatys ha **formys** *havall then ymag a thu y honen* 'It is a great benefit and comfort to us to consider that we were made an created in the image of God himself' TH 1a

Du an **furmyas** *han shappyas in mes an nore* 'God created and shaped him out of the earth' TH 2

Rag ny ren ny redya in teller vith in scripture fatell rug du schappya na **furmya** *mabden* 'For we do not read in any place in scripture that God shaped or created mankind' TH 2

rag a henna te a ve **furmys** *in dalleth* 'for from that you were created in the beginning' TH 6

onyn ew Christ, Du ha den, ow Arluth guew, neb a **formyas** *nef ha'n bys* 'one is Christ, God and man, my worthy Lord, who created heaven and the earth' BK 203-05

An Du a **formyas** *pub tra, ru'n droy thymmo in poynt ta!* 'May the God who created all things, bring him to me in good health!' BK 2757-58

neb an **formyas** *ev omma an deform arta predar* 'he who created him here, will deform him again, mind' CW 173-74

pra na wreta predery y festa **formys** *devery der y wreans eve omma* 'why do you not consider that you were created indeed by his activity here?' CW 207-09

me a vyn heb falladowe vn dean **formya** 'I will without fail create a man' CW 338-39

my a wore yma **formys** *gans an tas vn dean a bry* 'I know that there has been created by the Father a man of clay' CW 435-36 *an tas a rug der entent in myske oll prevas in bys **formya** preve henwis serpent* 'the Father by design among all reptiles in the world created a reptile named serpent' CW 496-98

*fensan ow bosaf marowe soweth bythqwathe bos **formys*** 'I would that I were dead; alas that I was ever created' CW 1264-65

*me a servyas pell an beyse aban vema kyns **formys*** 'I have served the world a long time since I was first created' CW 1974-75

*del o ef an kensa dean a ve gans an tas **formyes*** 'as he was the first man that was created by the Father' CW 2089-90.

Creatya 'to create' is found in TH, SA and CW:

*An kyth cyrcomstans ma a alse bos geses in part du an tas rag eff a alsa **creatya** ha gull mab den hebtha* 'The same circumstance could have been omitted on God's part for he could have created and made man without it' TH 1

*Ith ew benefyt ha confort bras ragan ny the consydra agan bos ny **creatys** ha formys havall then ymag a thu y honyn* 'It is a great benefit and comfort to us to consider that we were created and made like the image of God himself' TH 1a

*dre henna yth esa du ow notya ha shappya mabden vgh oll an creatus erall myng a rug du **creatya** ha gull* 'by that God was distinguishing and shaping mankind above all other creatures that God created and made' TH 2

*lymmyn pan rug du in maner an par ma **creatya** ha gull den, eff an grug souereign rewler* 'now when God in a manner of this kind created and made man, he made him sovereign ruler' TH 2

*I fe deswethys thewgh... in kynsa homely fetell ve agan hendasow ny, adam hag eve, dre an singular daddar han speciall favoure a thu golosek, **creatis** nobyll ha worthy creaturs* 'It was demonstrated to you... in the first homily that our ancestors Adam and Eve by the singular goodness and special favour of mighty God were created noble and worthy creaturs' TH 12

*Rag henna gwregh drehevall in ban agas colonow, hag egerogh y aleis, the receva abervath inna kerensa bras the thu, neb a rug mar notably agan **creatya** ny* 'Therefore lift up your hearts and open them wide to receive into them the great love of God, who so notably created us' TH 16

*ha Christ a commandias ha y a ve **creatis*** 'and Christ commanded and they were created' SA 61a

*ef a commaundias, y a ve **creatis*** 'he commanded, they were created' SA 62

***creatys** nobell omma yth ota [a] nature creif* 'you have been created noble here of a strong nature' CW 150-51.

The Old Cornish word for 'creator' was **creador** OCV §493. It is not attested in Middle or Late Cornish, which prefer A) **formyor**; B) **creator**; C) **gwrior**; and D) **maker**:

create   **GERYOW GWIR**

A **formyor**

*En tas a nef y'm gylwyr **formyer** pup tra a vyt gvrys* 'I am called the Father of heaven, creator of all things that are made' OM 1-2

*dotho megyans degen dyblans theorth an **formyer** guella* 'let us take him nourishment clearly from the most worthy creator' BM 3879-81

*mearworthyans theis ow **formyer*** 'great worship to you, my creator' CW 1414.

B **creator**

*the reiosya in sight agan **creator** ha redemar* 'to rejoice in the sight of our creator and redeemer' TH 1

*ny wore gull ken ys ry honor, lawde ha preysse the du neb o y gwrer ha **creator*** 'he cannot do other than give honour, laud and praise to God who was his maker and creator' TH 1

*Indella in agan part ny du agan **creator** ha gwrer a rug agan gull gans perfeccion* 'Thus for our part God our creator and maker made us with perfection' TH 2a

*ha the servia du agan gwrer ha **creator** kerngeek* 'and to serve God our maker and loving creator' TH 3

*fatell russens dysobaya aga gwrear, aga **creator** henn o an tas a neff* 'that they disobeyed their maker and creator, that is to say the Father of heaven' TH 12.

C **gwrior**

*hag eff ew agan **gwrer** ny* 'and he is our creator' TH 1

*ny wore gull ken ys ry honor, lawde ha preysse the du neb o y **gwrer** ha creator* 'he cannot do otherwise than give honour, laud and praise to God, who was his maker and creator' TH 1

*Indella in agan part ny du agan creator ha **gwrer** a rug agan gull gans perfeccion* 'Thus for our part God our creator and maker made us with perfection' TH 2a

*ha the servia du agan **gwrer** ha creator kerngeek* 'and to serve God our maker and loving creator' TH 3

*ha du an **gwrer** han factor anotha* 'and God the creator and maker of it' TH 56a

*dre reson y bos du an **gwrear** anetha* 'since God is the creator of them' TH 57

*na ren ny in mar vhell mater predery nag ewa possyble thagyn **gwrear*** 'let us not in such a high matter consider that it is not possible for our creator' TH 57

*nyng o ef only deane ew sacrificed mas agen arluth christ e honyn, an **gwrerer** a pub tra oll* 'it was not only a man sacrificed, but our Lord Christ himself, the creator of all things' SA 61

*An Mab ema i'n Tas ha'n Tas ynno ef, un Du yns, **gwrer** nor ha nef* 'The Son is in the Father and the Father in him, they are one God, creator of earth and heaven' BK 236-38

*mars ew bothe dew y honyn neb ew **gwrear** noer ha neef tha slackya an kyth lyw brase* 'if it is the wish of God himself, who is the creator of earth and heaven, to lessen the same great flood' CW 2468-70.

D maker

*te creature unkinda warbyn ʒa **vaker** ow cowse* 'you unnatural creature, speaking against your creator' CW 155-56

*te lucifer vnkinda meer yth os ortha **vaker*** 'you, Lucifer, are most unnatural towards your creator' CW 202-03

*gwrew grasse thagen **maker*** 'give thanks to our creator' CW 1310.

The Cornish play CW (*Creation of the World*) refers to God's creation of the heaven and earth as follows:

*why a wellas pub degre leas matters gwarryes ha **creacon** oll an byse* 'you have seen every degree many matters played and the creation of all the world' CW 2533-35.

John Keigwin's version of this reads:

*Hag oll an bys ma an **gwreans** ynweth why a welys.*

Following Keigwin subsequent commentators have used the word **gwrians** to mean 'creation'. This is unfortunate, since it is clear from the rest of Cornish literature that the word **gwrians** does not mean 'creation,' but 'activity, behaviour', and is an abstract collective noun without a plural:

*tormentores deugh yn scon may huththaho ow colon agan **guryans** na'm bo meth* 'executioners, come quickly that my heart may rejoice, that I may not be ashamed of our activity' RD 1876-78

*duen then emperour costentyn ha dotho eff leveryn y **vryans** eff yv helma* 'let us go to teh emperor Constantine and let us tell him that this is his doing' BM 3957-59

*ha moy worthy y **vryans** yv the kemendya dyblans* 'and more worthy his behaviour is to be commended indeed' BM 4389-90

*ow affirmya playn fatell wothya an bobyl mer an **gwrythyans** a thu* 'affirming plainly that the general people knew the activity of God' TH 14

*may teffans ha tenna re erell dre aga teball examplis ha **gwrythyans*** 'so that they may lead others by their bad examples and behaviour' TH 25a

*han rulle ew holma, kemerys in mes an **gwrythyans** a awncyent den dyskys in discans an egglos crist* 'and the rule is this, taken from the practice of an ancient doctor of the teaching of Christ's Church' TH 34a

*Lemmen me a wor in ta orth the worthyb ha **gwryans** the vos cle'gys* 'Now I know from your answer and behaviour that you are diseased' BK 603-05

*Arluth nef re bo gorthys, mar deke eth of confortys der **wryans** an caradow* 'May the Lord of heaven be glorified, so beautifully am I consoled by the activity of the beloved' BK 829-31

*pra na wreta predery y festa formys devery der y **wreans** eve omma* 'why do you not consider that you were created indeed by his activity here?' CW 207-09

create

*yn bys ma rag tha **wreans** ty a berth sure gossythyans* 'in this world for your behaviour you will surely have punishment' CW 1121-22
*me a wore hag a leall gryes **gwreans** dew y vos hemma* 'I know and truly believe that this is God's doing' CW 2127-28.

The word for 'creation' in traditional Cornish is **creacyon**:

*Rag in dede neb a rella predery an **creacyon** a vabden ha pondra in ta in y remembrans a behan o agan dallath* 'For indeed whoever considers the creation of mankind and ponders well in his remembrance what was our beginning' TH 1
*Rag in **creacion** a bub tra arell visible ny rug du an tas a neff mas commondya* 'For in the creation of all other visible things God the Father merely commanded' TH 1
*sow in **creacion** a vabden an tas a vsias solempnyty bras* 'but in the creation of mankind the Father used great solemnity' TH 1
*An kensa tra vgy ow tuchia an **creacion** a mab den* 'The first thing concerning the creation of mankind' TH 1
*lemmyn merkyow tus vas pandra rug du an tas ragan ny in agan **creacion*** 'now notice, good people, what God the Father did for us in our creation' TH 1a
*Whath rag procedia pelha rag descernya an **creacion** a then* 'Still to proceed further to discern the creation of man' TH 1a
*pendra alsan ny predery fatell ylly du gull moy ragan in agen **creacion** dell ruga gull* 'what could we think, that God could do more for us in our creation than he did?' TH 2a
*gwrys da ha perfect in aga **creasion*** 'made good and perfect in their creation' TH 2a
*An dra ma ew lell generall in oll creaturs consernya agan **creacion*** 'This matter is truly general in all creatures concerning our creation' TH 3
*ena mabden o enduwyes in dalleth in y **creacion*** 'there mankind was endowed in the beginning in his creation' TH 12
*ha vnderstondys dre an oberow an **creacion** an bys* 'and understood through the works of the creation of the world' TH 14
*why a wellas pub degre leas matters gwarryes ha **creacon** oll an byse* 'you have seen every degree many matters played and the creation of all the world' CW 2533-35.

In the revived language the ordinary word for 'to create' should probably be **formya**. 'Creator' should be either **formyor** or **gwrior**. 'Creation' is best rendered **creacyon**.

CRIME, CRIMINAL

'Crime, criminality' in Cornish may be rendered A) **drog-ober** or B) **gwadn-ober**

GERYOW GWIR   crime

A

*kepar hag ef on crousys ha dre wyr vreus quyt iuggys rak agan **drok ober** kens* 'like him we have been crucified and by right verdict completely judged for our previous criminality' PC 2900-01

*ty a wruge pur **throog ober** that latha abell dean da* 'you committed a serious crime in killing Abel, a good man' CW 1298-99.

B

*moy ew ow **gwan oberowe** hag inwethe ow fehasowe es tell ew tha vercy dew thym tha ava* 'greater are my crimes and also my sins than is thy mercy, O God, to forgive' CW 1169-72

*a te cayne omskemunys ow molath thezo henna o **gwan obar** gwryes may ma dew han noer keffrys warnas pub ere ow crya* 'O you accursed Cain, my curse upon you; that was a crime committed so that God and the earth also are always crying against you' CW 1265-70

*heb ioy vyth na lowena der tha **wadn ober** obma* 'without any joy or happiness through your crime here' CW 1274-75

*prag ye rusta ye latha hag eve tha vrodar nessa henna o **gwadn ober** gwryes* 'why did you kill him and he your closely related kinsman? That was a crime committed' CW 1677-79.

In Late Cornish **drog-ober** and **gwadn-ober** are replaced by **bad-ober**:

*Huei òl? mêra huei aniustîz iou (a medh Dzhûan) gyr ter o an [dhiz-urêg ha manah 'ryg] an **bad-ober**, medh Dzhûan. Piu a ôr medh an dzhei? Piu a 'ryg an **bad-ober**? Piu a 'ryg an **bad-ober**? medh Dzhûan; mar nyz mar [nym yz a dra 'dheffa previ] peu a 'ryg an **bad-ober**, mî a vedn krêg ragta* 'You all? Look it is an injustice, said Jowan. Know that it was the ale-wife and a monk who committed the crime, said Jowan. Who knows? they said. Who committed the crime? Who committed the crime? said Jowan; if I have not got something which will prove who committed the crime, I will hang for it' BF: 18.

'Criminal' is **drog-oberor** in Old Cornish: *maleficus **drochoberor*** 'criminal' OCV §313, but the word is not attested in Middle or Late Cornish. 'Criminal' in the Middle Cornish texts is **felon**, *plural* **felons**:

*ny degoth thy'nny lathe den vyth ol yn norvys ma **felon** na lader kyn fe hep brus iustis bynytha* 'we ought not ever execute any man in all the world, even a robber or criminal, without the verdict of a justice' PC 1981-84

*ha dun coyt war an Vretons ha prosternyn an **felans** the'n myrnans dyhow ha cleth* 'and let us attack the Britons quickly and bring the criminals down to death right and left' BK 2805-07.

105

crime

It can also be translated by the word **offender**, *plural* **offenders**:

*y a vea res thetha iently correctia oll an re ew **offenders** in dan aga gouernans* 'they should gently correct all those who are offenders under their governance' TH 25a

*han **offendars** a res bos rebukys ha correctys in dew tyrmyn* 'and the offenders must be rebuked and corrected in due time' TH 25a

*oll **offenders** an parna warbyn du, ha war byn an welth an pow yma charite ow requyrya eff the vos deberthis theworth an commonwelth* 'all offenders of that kind against God and against the wellbeing of the country, charity demands that he should be separated from the commonwealth' TH 25a

*dre hemma ny a yll gwelas ha persevya fatell ew kynde an par na an rebukys an re an jevas auctorite may thillans rebukya an drog pobyll han trespasces han **offendars** a lays du* 'by this we can see and perceive that rebukes of this sort are kind from those who have authority to rebuke evil people, and crimes and offenders agains the laws of God' TH 29a.

CULPABLE

The first translation given by Nance is **cablus**, a word which is attested twice:

*del heuol thy'mmo ynwys conciens da na syv certan lathe den nag yw **cablys*** 'as it seems to me, a good conscience will not follow from killing a man who is not culpable' PC 2433-34

*Me a wor ow bos **camblys**, saw pur wyer rag an tryspys ema thymmo eddrag tyn* 'I know I am culpable, but in very truth I regret the wrongdoing greatly' BK 1072-74.

For 'culpable, guilty' the author of SA uses **gylty** twice:

*ef ew **gilty** an corf han gos agen arluth Christ* 'he is guilty of the body and blood of our Lord Christ' SA 61

*eth ew ef **gilty** an gos agen arluth Dew kepar a ve Judas* 'he is guilty of the blood of our Lord God, as was Judas' SA 61.

The commonest way of translating the adjective 'culpable, guilty', however, is to use the phrase **dhe vlâmya**:

*thy'mmo vy why a ros gvrek honna yw ol **the vlamye*** 'you gave me a wife; she is entirely culpable' OM 265-66

*Ny yv plesijs hag a vyn boys revlijs drethogh certeyn ha meriasek kekefrys ken **the vlamya** y fyen* 'We are pleased and will be ruled by you indeed, and Meriasek as well; otherwise we would be culpable' BM 314-17

GERYOW GWIR culpable

yma ree ov leferel heb ty vyth na govlya delyfrys der varia fetel ywa dyogel hagis boys wy **de vlamya** *war vohogo[g]yon cruel* 'some are saying without oath nor perjury that he has been delivered by St Mary truly and that you are culpable, cruel to the poor' BM 3739-44

gansa pan wres comparya mer **tha vlamya** *yth osta* 'when you compare with him you are very culpable' CW 160-61

thyma ve why a rose gwreag hona yw all **tha vlamya** 'you gave me a wife; she is wholly culpable' CW 877-78

yn henna yth os **tha vlamya** 'for that you are wholly culpable' CW 1371

ow boya o **tha vlamya** *ef a ornas thym tenna* 'my servant was culpable; he ordered me to shoot' CW 1651-52.

D

DAMNATION

Some commentators recommend the word ***dampnyans*** for 'damnation'. This form is unattested. The Cornish word for 'damnation' is **dampnacyon**:

*byth na thovtyogh **dampnasconn*** 'never fear damnation' BM 1184

*remembrogh agis sperys rag dovt cafus **dampnasconn*** 'remember your spirit lest you revceive damnation' BM 1250-51

*Pegh o an cawse a rug the oll an vssew a Adam ha Eva the vos genys in state a **thampnacion*** 'Sin was the reason that caused all the offspring of Adam and Eve to be born in a state of damnation' TH 3

*ha rag henna y a thros aga honyn hag oll lynyath mabden then stat a **thampnacion*** 'and therefore they brought themselves and all the lineage of mankind to the state of damnation' TH 12

*ha whath mabden yth esa ow mois pelha ha pelha in **dampnacion*** 'and still mankind was going further and further into damnation' TH 13a

*nyns o mabden abyll the avoydya eternal **damnacion*** 'mankind was not able to avoid damnation' TH 14a

*Indella ny vith nagonyn sawys theworth **dampnacion**, mas an re vsy in vnite an egglos a crist* 'Thus no one will be saved from damnation, but those who are in the unity of the Church of Christ' TH 39a

*Y a's tevith **damnassyon**, kyn fe rys thym mos drys mor th'aga welas* 'They will receive damnation, though I shall have to go overseas to see them' BK 1447-49

*Du roy thymmo **dampnassyon** hag eselder ha passyon, mar ny's tevith myrnans tyn* 'God give me damnation and lowness and suffering, if they do not receive bitter death' BK 3140-42.

***Dampnyans** is an unnecessary coinage which is perhaps best avoided in the revived language.

DAY

The ordinary word for 'day' in Cornish is **dëdh**, **dÿdh**, which is variously spelt *dyth*, *dith*, *deth*, *deyth* in the texts. Although spellings with **i** or **y** may indicate a long [iː] and spellings with **e** or **ey** may indicate [eː], this is by no means certain. It is noteworthy, for example, that Treger writes ***dith*** 'day' with **i**, but ***an jeth*** 'the day' with **e**. It is unlikely that the word was pronounced with a different vowel from that in the unmutated form when the initial consonant was assibilated. It is more like that the difference in spelling is simply orthographic rather than phonetic. Presumably **jith** (earlier ?**iith**) was a form which Tregear had been taught to avoid:

A **dith**

*rag agys exortia why na rellogh fillall pub **dith*** 'to exhort you that you should not fail every day' TH 5
*bys in **dith** hethew* 'until this day' TH 17
*bys an present **dith** ma* 'until this present day' TH 34
*ow confessia pub **dith** in y credo* 'confessing every day in his creed' TH 39
*vn **dith**, arluth, ew gwell spendyys in the chy ge* 'one day, Lord, is better spent in thy house' TH 41
*pub **dith** moye ha moy appla the procedia* 'every day more and more able to proceed' TH 41
*thea nyna bys in **dith** hethow* 'from then until today' TH 41a
*the suffra in vn **dith**, in vn tyller* 'to suffer in one day, in one place' TH 47
*ha in iii **dith** me a ra y wull arta* 'and in three days I will build it again' TH 53.

B **an jeth**

*An den gwyrryan a goth vii trovath **in Jeth*** 'The just man falls seven times in the day' TH 8
*bys may teffa **an Jeth** hag egery* 'until the day happens to dawn' TH 18
*hethew **in Jeth*** 'nowadays' TH 27a
*ha pell ew mer an bobill resys hethow **in Jeth** theworth an kithsam rulle ma* 'and many people nowadays have run far from this same rule' TH 37
***An Jeth** o rag aga merite* 'The day was for their merit' TH 47
*lymmyn hethew **in Jeth*** 'now these days' TH 48.

It is possible, therefore that the spellings *dyth* and *deth* in the texts may have represent the same pronunciation.

In Later Cornish, starting with CW, the word **dëdh** is in some contexts replaced by **jorna**.

*lebmyn pan ew thymo gwryes neve ha noore orth both ow bryes han naw order collenwys han kynsa **jorna** spedyes my a[s] sone gans ow ganow* 'now that I have made heaven and earth to my desire and the nine orders finished and the first day successfully accomplished, I shall bless them with my mouth' CW 70-4
*lebmyn yn second **jorna** gwraf broster athesempys* 'now on the second day I shall straightway create a firmament' CW 80-1

*an kethe **jorna** ma ew de 3en tase dew re bo grassyes* 'the same day is finished, may the Father be praised' CW 2531-32

*ha mean orrol en Madern en Gunneau Bosolo henwez Mean Scriffez tho an **jorna** ma* 'and another stone in Madron, in Bosullow Downs called Mean Scriffez to this day' BF: 27

*an kensa **journa** a messe Heddra an centle, en plew Paule, in Cernow teage en Blooth Creste an Arleuth whege meele sithcans ha hanter deege* 'the first day of the month of October was the meeting, in the parish of Paul in fair Cornwall in the year of Christ the dear Lord one thousand, seven hundred and five' BF: 38

*ro do ny an **journa** ma gen bara **journa*** 'give us this day our daily bread' BF: 41

*ha an gothihuar ha metten vo an kenza **jorna*** 'and the evening and the morning were the first day' BF: 51

*ha gethihuer ha metten vo nessa **jorna*** 'and evening and morning were a second day' BF: 52

*weeah **jorna** ra whei gwra weal* 'six days shall you do labour' BF: 55

*Rag en whee'ah **jorna** an Arleth gwraz a neue an aor a môre* 'For in six days the Lord made the heaven, the earth and sea' BF: 55

*Rag Deew a ore, a en **jorna** reah debre nothe, n'ena agoz lagagow ra bos geres* 'For God knows on the day when you eat of it, then your eyes will be opened' Rowe

*Ha pereeg e penes doganze **jorna** ha doganze noze, e ve ouga nena gwage* 'And when he had fasted forty days and forty nights, he was thereafter hungry' Rowe.

Jorna 'day' itself was not borrowed directly from Modern English, but must derive from Middle English *journei* < Old French *journee* 'day, day's travel'. This suggests that **jorna** 'day' had been in Cornish since the medieval period, but did not appear in the texts until much later. It also means that the replacement of **dëdh** by **jorna** was not provoked by the prevalence of **jorna** in English, but rather by factors inside Cornish itself. The increasing popularity of **an jorna** may conceivably have something to do with the emergence in Later Cornish of the new third person plural pronoun **anjy**, **angye** [ɔnˈdʒɔɪ]. **Anjy a dhros** 'they brought', for example, would have been phonetically very similar in rapid speech to **an jëdh a dhros** 'the day brought.' This might have led speakers to replace **an jëdh** with the less ambiguous **an jorna**. Certainly **jorna** may replace **dÿdh**, **dëdh** in the singular in the revived language. The plural 'days', however, should probably be **dedhyow** or **dydhyow**.

DECEIT, TO DECEIVE

There are two words for 'deceit' in the texts: **tùll** and **dysseyt**. The first is known mostly in the phrase **tùll na gil** 'deceit nor guile':

GERYOW GWIR   deceit

aspyeugh yn ov cossow pren the gyst hep **tol na gyl** 'look out in my forest for wood for a beam without deceit or guile' OM 2558-59

ynweth dewthack warn ugans a virhas in pur thibblans my am be heb **tull na gyll** *a thalathfas an bys ma* 'also very clearly I have had 32 daughters since the beginning of this world without deceit or guile' CW 1984-87

kynth ota skydnys in wharthe in dewathe heb **tull na gyle** *why a weall deall vskys* 'although you have started to laugh, in the end without deceit or guile, you will soon see vengeance' CW 2306-08.

Since **tùll** is attested only in the phrase **tùll na gil**, there is no evidence **Tùll** by itself to mean 'deceit' is apparently attested once only:

Unwath a'y **doll** *ha cryfter elhas bos rys thym kyny* 'Alas for his deceit and might that I should ever have to weep!' BK 3146-47.

Dysseyt 'deceit' is attested only in TH:

I a vsse crafft ha **deceyt***, an poyson a serpons yma indan aga tavosow* 'They practise craft and deceit, the poison of serpents is under their tongues' TH 7a

hag in y ganow eff ny ve bythqueth kyffys **deceypt** *vith na gyll* 'and in his mouth no deceit or guile was ever found' TH 11.

It is probable, however, that **dysseyt** was in use in Cornish at a much earlier period, since the verb **dysseytya** occurs in PA:

ragon ny wor omweze na gans olly tretury ny yll agan **dyssaytye** 'he cannot protect himself from us, nor with all his treachery can he deceive us' PA 194cd.

There are two words for 'to deceive' in Cornish: A) **tùlla** and B) **decêvya**

A **tùlla**

Gans gloteny ef pan welas cam na ylly y **dolla** 'When he saw that by gluttony he could in no way deceive him...' PA 13a

a debel venyn hep ras ty ru'm **tullas** *sur hep ken* 'O evil woman without grace, you have deceived me without reason' OM 251-52

Eua prag y whruste sy **tulle** *the bryes hep ken* 'Eve, why did you deceive your husband without cause?' OM 277-78

lauar thy'mmo cowyth mas py vr a tun th'y gerghas ha guet na veny **tollys** 'tell me, good friend, when shall we come to get him and be careful that we are not deceived' PC 602-04

rak ef a wor lyes cast rak the **tolle** 'for he knows many tricks to deceive you' PC 1884-85

deceit   **GERYOW GWIR**

yn y geuer del fuef badt y fuf **tollys** 'as I was bad in his regard, I was deceived' RD 1886-87

a thensa nyns on **tollys** *danvenogh rag y vollys* 'O good sir, we are not deceived; send for his bulls' BM 2719-20

molleth du the tobesy eff re ruk agen **tolla** 'God's curse on Toby; he has deceived us' BM 3247-48

Ny dal **tolla** *Arthur, agen arluth flower* 'We must not deceive Arthur, our best of lords' BK 2955-56

in for ma mar pyth **tullys** *me a vyth compes ganso* 'in this way if he is deceived I shall be even with him' CW 491-92

rag ty tha gulla ortye ha **tulla** *tha bryas leel nefra gostyth thy gorty me a ordayne bos benyn* 'because you listened to her and deceived your faithful husband, ever I ordain that woman shall be obedient to her husband' CW 892-95

an hager-breeve a **thullas** *ve, ha ve reeg debre* 'the serpent deceived me and I ate' Rowe.

B **decêvya**

Ihesu crist mur gerense ze vab den a zyswezas an vghelder mayz ese zen bys pan deyskynnas pehadoryon rag perna o **desevijs** *dre satnas* 'Jesus Christ showed great love to mankind when he came down from the heights where he was to redeem sinners who had been deceived by Satan' PA 5a-c

yth esan ow **desyvya** *agan honyn han gweroneth nys ugy genyn* 'we deceive ourselves and the truth is not in us' TH 8

na ny yll bos **decevys** *in maner vith* 'nor can he be deceived in any way' TH 17

ha ny vith eff **deceyvys***, mas eff a ra lell iugia ha descernya mars uga in perfect charite* 'and he will not be deceived, but he will correctly judge and discern if he is in perfect charity' TH 23a

ny res the then vith bos **deseviis** 'we must not be deceived' TH 25a

ha honna ny ra agys **desevia** 'and that will never deceive you' TH 34a

ny ra neffra fyllell, na decaya, na agys **decevya***, han rulle ew holma* 'nor will it ever fail nor decay, nor deceive you, and the rule is this...' TH 34a

hag ena Symon magus a rug **desevya** *an bobyll dre y enchontementys ha falsenes* 'and there Simon Magus deceived the people by his enchantments and falsity' TH 46a

Symon magus a rug **decevya** *ha dalla an bobyll* 'Simon Magus deceived and blinded many people' TH 46a

ow **tesevya** *an bobyll kepar dell rug eff* 'deceiving the people as he did' TH 50a

ymowns ow **desyvya** *aga honyn, ow myskemeras an significacion an ger ma* 'they deceive themselves, misunderstanding the meaning of this word' TH 57a

Ima lowarth onyn o bostia, fatla vgy faith an tasow coth a vam egglys inansy, but **decevis** *ens sy* 'many is the one who boasts that the faith of the ancient fathers of mother church are in them, but they are deceived' SA 59a.

For the noun 'deceit' **tùll** and **dysseyt** can both be used. For the verb 'to deceive', however, **tùlla**, **decêvya** and **dysseytya** can be used in the revived language.

DEPART see AWAY

DESCEND see ASCEND

DESERT
There are three words in the texts for 'desert, wilderness': A) **gwylfos**; B) **dysert**; and C) **defyth**:

A gwylfos
thys best me a worhemyn moys then **guelfos** 'I command you, beast, to go into the wilderness' BM 1126-27

Me a vyn moys then **guylfoys** 'I will go into the wilderness' BM 1132

omma yth ese tregys avel hermyt in **guelfos** 'here I am dwelling like a hermit in the wilderness' BM 1963-64

lemmen ens tus then **guelfos** *the kerhes dyn meryasek* 'now let people go into the wilderness to fetch Meriasek to us' BM 2794-95

yma eff prest in **guylfos** 'he is always in the wilderness' BM 2802

then **guylfoys** *in pur certen me a vyn mones deyow prest the helghya* 'I will very truly indeed go on Thursday into the wilderness to hunt' BM 3158-60

then **guylfos** *mones lemen ny a vyn sur ze sportya* 'we will now go into the wilderness to hunt' BM 3203-04

moys the[n] **guelfos** *me a vyn the sportya pur guir lemyn* 'I will not go to the wilderness to hunt indeed' BM 3213-14

parys rag moys then **guelfoys** *ny yv genogh alema* 'we are ready to go with you hence into the wilderness' BM 3218-19

galles pur guir an turent then **guelfoys** *del glowys vy* 'the tyrant has indeed gone into the wilderness, as I have heard' BM 3246-47

myr an turant then **guelfoys** *mara mynna lafurya* 'see whether the tyrant wishes to go into the wilderness' BM 3270-71

dugh genevy desempys alemma then **guelfos** *snel* 'come with me immediately quickly into the wilderness' BM 3367-68

me ath worhemyn dragan then **guylfos** *quik math ylly* 'I command you, dragon, to go quickly into the wilderness' BM 4141-42.

B dysert
ha der gallus du in proff as comond then **dysert** *dovn* 'and in proof by the power of God he will command it into the deep desert' BM 4029-30

dre gras ihesu us avan then **dysert** *me as gor hy* 'by the grace of Jesus above I shall send it into the desert' BM 4137-38.

desert

C **defyth**

Ke ʒe ves omscumvnys ʒe ȝyveyth veth yn tewolgow 'go away, accursed one, into the wilderness into darkness' PA 17c

ke the ves ymskemenys yn defyth yn tewolgow 'depart, accursed one, into the wilderness in darkness' PC 141-42

cuntell warbarth ow fegans me a vyn mos pur vskys ha woʒa hemma dewans pell in devyth tha wandra 'Gather together my possessions I will very quickly and after this immediately go into the desert to wander' CW 1293-96

haw hendas cayme whath en bew yn defyth in myske bestas yma ef prest ow pewa 'and my grandfather Cain, still alive, in the desert among beasts he lives always' CW 1480-82.

Several points are to be noticed here. In the first place both **gwylfos** and **dysert** are confined to BM. This probably reflects the subject matter of the play as much as anything. **Gwylfos** is much commoner than **dysert**, and is used particularly of a wild uninhabited place, where game animals abound and where a hermit leads his solitary life. It is also worth noting that the medial consonant group in **gwylfos** is always **-lf-** and never **-lv-**. **Gwylfos** is an old compound, created before the final **t** in OC **guilt* 'wild' was assibilated to **s**; cf. Welsh *gwyllt* 'wild'. Old Cornish **guilt+bod* which gave **guilfod*, where the final **t** in **guilt* devoiced the lenited initial of *bod*: **b** > **v** > **f**. This was later assibilated to *gwylfos*. In some forms of Cornish 'desert, wilderness' is written **gwylvos*. This is a mistake; the word should be **gwylfos**. **Dyfeth** derives from Latin *defect(us)*; cf. Welsh *diffaith* and the medial **v** in PA and CW is unexpected.

It is also worth noting that no word for 'wilderness' survived into Late Cornish. When translating the fourth chapter of St Matthew's gospel Rowe resorts to the English word:

*Nena ave Jesus humbregez abera tha **wilderness** tha voaze temptez geen an Joule* 'Then Jesus was led into the wilderness to be tempted by the Devil' Rowe.

DESIRE, TO DESIRE

The two chief words for the noun 'desire' in Cornish are A) **whans** and B) **desîr**:

A **whans**

*Re wronte ʒeugh gras ha **whans** ʒe wolsowas y basconn* 'May he grant you grace and desire to listen to his passion' PA 1b

*Ffest yn tyn hy a wole ʒe wherʒyn nys teva **whans*** 'Very sorely she wept; she had no desire to laugh' PA 222a

GERYOW GWIR   desire

pur luen yma thy'm ow **whans** *a'm ben cowethes ordnys* 'fully I have a desire to have ordained for me a companion' OM 91-2

a'y frut dybry ny'm bes **whans** *dres dyfen ov arloth ker* 'of its fruit I have no desire to eat contrary to the prohibition of my dear Lord' OM 171-72

ha pedyr streyth vras defry ov resek adyworty worte myres mayth o **whans** 'and four great streams indeed running from it, so that it is an object of desire to look at them' OM 772-74

An tas a'n nef dre y gras a donvon theugh agas **whans** 'The Father will by his grace send from heaven to you your desire' OM 1805-06

sav mar ny yl bos nahen the voth prest yn pup hehen y goulenwel yv ow **whans** 'but if it cannot be otherwise, my desire in every respect always is to fulfil your will' PC 1090-92

kettel thueth er agan pyn ny gen bo **whans** *guariow ales ol y wolyow athyragon pan guylsyn* 'as soon as he met us, we had no desire for games when we saw before us all his wounds spread open' RD 1330-32

ny'm bus a'th lauarow **whans** *aga clewas* 'I have no desire to hear your words' RD 1517-18

rak thythy yma thy'm **whans** 'for I have great desire for it' RD 1938

in hanov crist thyn yma **wans** *orth escar crist batalyays* 'in the name of Christ we have a desire to battle against the enemy of Christ' BM 2473-74

hay floghe pur semely maylyes vny defran wondrys **whans** 'and her child wrapped beautifully in her bosom, a wondrous cause for desire' CW 1909-10.

B **desîr**

henna ol yw y **thysyr** 'that is all his desire' PC 18

clewys vyth agas **desyr** *why a vyth aquyttys da* 'your desire will be heard; you will be well rewarded' PC 309-10

arluth agan dewlagas yv marthys claf ow colyas golyas o agan **dysyr** 'Lord our eyes are wondrous sick with watching; to watch was our desire' PC 1066-68

yma thy'mmo mur **dysyr** *a wothfes ortheugh an guyr* 'I have a great desire to know from you the truth' RD 194-95

ihesu map ras clew ow **dysyr** 'Jesu, son of grace, hear my desire' RD 858

thy's y y whon gras rak the **thesyr** *ioy yn ow gulas y fyth pur wyr* 'I thank you for your desire; joy in my kingdom you will have very truly' RD 869-70

cryst agan prennas yn tyn ef the thos the gous worthy'n th'agan **dysyr** 'Christ who redeemed us painfully, our desire is that he should come to speak to us' RD 1204-06

andrev mur yv the **thysyr** *an dra na na yl bos guyr gul thy'm crygy* 'Andrew, great is your desire to make me believe that which cannot be true' RD 1460-62

dun ganso dywhans touth bras rak y worre yn dour glas yv ow **dysyr** 'let us go immediately with him at speed; to put him in the blue water is my desire' RD 2192-94

mar ny wre fa ow **desyr** *y fyth dampnys the peynys* 'if he does not do my desire he will be condemned to torments' RD 2473-74

kegy in tyr a dremas in kernov the ihesu gras theth **desyr** *ty re dufa* 'go ashore, good man, to Cornwall. To Jesus thanks, you have come to your desire' BM 621-24

desire　　　　　　　　　GERYOW GWIR

*lemen quik thagis **desyr** grueghwy londia meryasek* 'now quickly to your desire bring Meriasek ashore' BM 1092-93

*han gela veth mys est certen orth ov **deser** an viijth deth* 'and the second will be in August indeed the eighth day according to my desire' BM 2072-75

*thum **desyr** in ketelma in meys est an viijves deth an secund feer sur a veth* 'to my desire in the same way the second fair will indeed be in the month of August the eighth day' BM 2196-98

*ihesu pup vr ol ov **desyr** yv in bys ma the plesia* 'Jesu, always in this world my desire is to please you' BM 2544-45

*grua the **desyr** ha both the vreyes* 'do your desire and the wish of your mind' BM 3657-58

*Theorth crist y ruk pesy certen **desyr** eredy the kenever an gorthya* 'he besought a certain desire indeed from Christ for as many who would worship him' BM 4425-27

*ihesu re grontias detha age **desyr** eredy* 'Jesus has granted them their desire indeed' BM 4555-56

*nyg esa inna foude vith, na lust, **desyre** concupiscens, na lust vith the throgkoleth* 'there was no fault in him nor lust, desire, concuspiscense nor lust for wickedness' TH 2a

*henna ew ow **thesyre** ew gans oll ow holan, the dibbry an pask onn ma genogh* 'that is: my desire is with all my heart to eat this pascal lamb with you' SA 64a

*ef rag henna a ruge protestia myre a **thesyre** the thybbry e bask* 'he therefore protested much desire to eat his passover' SA 64a

*nyng ew ken the accowntya agys guthyl e **thesyr*** 'it is to be considered nothing but doing his desire' BK 540-41

*Freth y feth gweregys, mar peth rys dos the henna, ol the'th **desyer*** 'He will be vigorously helped, if it is necessary to come to that, all according to your desire' BK 1846-48

*The leud **desyr** a'm cuth por wyer* 'Your lewd desire disturbs me' BK 2952-53

*a cuffan y voʒa gwyre me a sewsye tha **thesyre** drefan te tha thos an nef* 'if I could be certain it was true, I would follow your desire, because you have come from heaven' CW 672-74

*mar ny vethaf ow **desyre** neffra nyn gwellaf omma* 'if I do not get my desire, never shall I see him here' CW 824-25

*haw **desyre** ny wres fillall* 'and you will not fail in my desire' CW 1755.

It can readily be seen that **desîr** is much more common than **whans**.

The verb **whansa** 'to desire' is very rare. It is attested twice, once as a verbal noun and once as a verbal adjective:

A **whansa**

*Rag an kyge a ra **whanse** contrary then spuris han spuris contrary thyn kyge* 'For the flesh desires contrary to the spirit and the spirit contrary to the flesh' TH 16a

*ema Tertullian ow leverall, pana pask onn o Christ **wensys** tha thibbry gans e apostelath* 'Tertullian says, Which paschal lamb was Christ wishing to eat with his apostles?' SA 64a.

GERYOW GWIR — desire

The verb **yewny** 'to desire' is better attested:

B yewny

folle yn ta y whela ys del wra lyon y pray drey den yn peyn a calla neffre ny **vnsa** *moy ioy* 'more madly by far he seeks than does a lion his prey to bring man into torment. If he could he would not desire more joy' PA 21cd

ken agesough benytha ny **ȝensen** *somot y go* 'I would never desire other than you, so mote I go' OM 2357-58

mars yv hemma an ihesu wolcom yv re'n arluth dev y weles my re **yevnys** 'if this is the Jesus, he is welcome by the Lord God. I have longed to see him' PC 1699-701

yensen *ov bones marow yndella y voth a pe* 'I should long to die, if such were his wish' PC 3167-68

Laver an pyth a vynhy gans the golan the **uny**, *ha te a vith ef heb mar* 'Say what you will desire in your heart, and of course you will have it' BK 1075-77.

The verb **desîrya** 'to desire' on the other hand is common at all periods:

C desîrya

An dus vas a **ȝeserya** *ȝeȝe gulas nef o kyllys* 'The good people desired for themselves heaven which had been lost' PA 4a

ha kemmys a **theseryas** *3030 eff a ve grontis* 'and as much as he desired was granted to him' PA 9d

ha hethyv me a **thesyr** *dre ov grath dalleth an beys* 'and today I desire by my grace to begin the world' OM 5-6

my re **thysyryas** *fest mer dybry genogh why haneth* 'I have very greatly desired to eat with you tonight' PC 718-19

na'y **dysyrye** *nyns yw thy's* 'nor is it for you to desire it' RD 1926

the pygy me a vynse na wrylly y **dysyrye** *yn tor ma thyworthyf vy* 'I would beg you not to desire it from me at the moment' RD 1932-34

Coyl ortheff vy meryasek me ath **desyr** *dre tekter bonyl ty a feth edrek* 'Listen to me, Meriasek, I desire you, by fairness or you will have regret' BM 407-09

na moy me ny **deserya** *mas gorthya mahum pup preys* 'nor do I desire anything more but to worship Mahound always' BM 898-99

mones dotho ny a vyn hay **deserya** *pur ylyn pesy crist dyny gava* 'we will go to him and desire him very clearly to pray Christ to forgive us' BM 2136-38

ha ny fellyth annotha kyn **teseryas** *punsov cans* 'and you will not fail of it though you desire hundreds of pounds' BM 2578-79

yma rych ha bohosek ov **teserya** *meryasek epscop pur guir may fo va* 'rich and poor desire that Meriasek should be bishop in very truth' BM 2695-97

pan lowar turne a rug eff ernestly ha lamentably **desyrya** *an mercy a thu rag y offencys hay pehosow* 'how many times he earnestly and lamentably desired the mercy of God for his offences and sins' TH 8a

hag eff a **thesyrryas** *na rella du entra the jugment ganso eff* 'and he desired that God should not enter into judgment with him' TH 8a

desire   **GERYOW GWIR**

whath me a vyn agys **desyrya** *why the vynnas dylygently merkya, notya, ha done in kerth genowgh vn rulle* 'yet I will desire you to wish diligently to mark, note and take away with you one rule' TH 34a

So my a vyn agys **desyrrya** *why, tus tha oll, the settia agys corfow hagys enevow hooll the thu galosek* 'But I will desire you, all good people, to set your bodies and your souls wholly to almighty God' TH 35

me a vyn agys **desyrrya** *why oll an lell cristonyyan, why the vynnas resortya thegys mam egglos catholik* 'I will desire you all the loyal Christians to wish to resort to the catholic Church, your mother' TH 38

na ankevy an pith a rella **desyrya** *theworta lafull* 'nor forget that which he desires lawfully from him' TH 39a

Ken, pen rellan **desyrrya** *du in agan PATER NOSTER, the ry thynny agan dayly foode* 'Otherwise, when we beseech God in our PATER NOSTER to give us our daily food' TH 57a

rag nyng o met, ef the **deserya** *mas e bask e honyn* 'for it was not meet that he should desire only his own Passover' SA 64a

Pe reege a vennin gwellas tro an wethan da rag booze, ha der o hi blonk tha'n lagagow, ha gwethan tha voaze **desyryes** *tha gwelle onen feere* 'When the woman saw that the tree was good for food, and that it was pleasing to the eyes, and a tree to be desired to make one wise' Rowe.

For the noun 'desire' both **whans** and **desîr** are acceptable in the revived language. For the verb 'to desire' **desîrya** is clearly the word of choice.

TO DESPISE

For 'to despise' Nance suggests A) **defia** (UC *defya*); B) **fia** (UC *fya*); and C) **dysprêsya** (UC *dyspresya*). All three are attested. **Defia** really means 'to defy':

A **defia**

Out warnes ty fals jugleer **defya** *ov dewov flour ty a crek in cloghprennyer* 'Damn you, false trickster! To defy my peerless gods! You will hang on the gallows' BM 921-23

te neb vgy ow **defya** *ydols yth esas ow robbya sans egglos* 'you, who despise idols, are robbing holy Church' TH 14a

A, owt warnas, te rybot, pan reta ow cusullya the gasa cres the'n harlot a vyn prest ow **defya** *ha'm duwow mas* 'Oh, damn you, you scoundrel, when you advise me to leave the villain in peace who will continually defy me and my goodly gods' BK 987-91

Defyys *suer ew Moddras* 'Modred indeed has been defied' BK 3295.

Fia, on the other hand, really means 'to say "fie" to' and thus 'to repudiate':

B fia

*Mur a varth yv genevy pan **fyghyth** rychyth an beys* 'I am greatly astonished that you repudiate worldly wealth' BM 428-29

*Saw refrens ahanogh why, orthowgh kefrys ef a **fy** re'n keth Du a woneth a* 'But saving your reverence, he continually repudiates you by the same God that he serves' BK 945-47.

The verb **dysprêsya** does seem to mean 'to despise':

C dysprêsya

*Ragon menough rebekis ha **dyspresijs** yn harow yn growys gans kentrow fastis peynys bys pan ve marow* 'For us often reproached and cruelly despised, on the cross fastened with nails, tortured until he died' PA 2cd

*ow horf ave yw hemma yn meth crist sur ragough wy pernys aberth yn bys ma **dyspresys** haneth a vyth* 'my body is this, said Christ, Surely for you redeemed in this world it will be despised tonight' PA 44bc

*moy pegh o pan **dyspresyas** ys del o pan yn guerʒe* 'it was a greater sin when he despised him than when he betrayed him' PA 104cd.

The commonest word for 'to despise', however, is **despîsya**, which is found in TH and SA:

*ha penagull a rella tyrry an rena, aga **despisia**, po aga deneya, eff a ra deneya ha forsakya an very gwryoneth* 'and whoever breaks those, despises or denies them, he denies and forsakes the very truth' TH 33a

*ha neb a rella agys **despisia** why, yma worth ow **despisia** ve* 'and whoever despises you, despises me' TH 35a

*kynth usy ran an bobill worth aga **despisia**, ha gora the drevith, yma S Cyrill ow commondya thetha sessia heb gull marthussyan crist the ry power an par na* 'and though some of the people despise them and set them at naught, St Cyril commands that they should cease to wonder that Christ gave power of that kind' TH 38a

*Ha ny drog pobyll a rug **despisia** oll y decreys hay ordynans eff ay justys* 'And we, evil people, have despised all his decrees and the ordinance of his justice' TH 40-40a

*Ha rag na rella den vith **despisya** an auctorite ay appostlis, yma crist ow leverell in xiii-as chapter a Jowan* 'And lest anyone despise the authority of his apostles, Christ says in the 13th chapter of St John' TH 41a

*ha neb a rella agys **despisia** why, yma worth ow **despisia** ve, ha neb a rella ow **despicia** ve, yma ow **despicia** henna a rug ow dynwyn ve* 'and whoever despises you, despises me, and whoever despises me, despises him who sent me' TH 41a

*ow scriffa warbyn onyn, Petilianus, neb a rug **despisia** an sea han stall a rome* 'writing against one, Petilianus, who despised the see and stall of Rome' TH 48

*Pella yma an martyr benegas S. Ciprian in tressa epistill yn y kynsa levyr ow cowse warbyn sertayn re a rug dysobeya ha **despisia** Cornelius, an epscop a rome in vaner ma* 'Moreover the blessed martyr, St Cyprian in the third epistle in his first book speaks agains

despise   **GERYOW GWIR**

certain people who disobeyed and despised Cornelius, the bishop of Rome as follows' TH 48a

*Nens ew nahene cowse y bos hereses drehevys ha scismes springes ha tevys, mas rag y bos an prounter a thu **despisiis** ha nag ewa obeys* 'There is no other reason that heresies have arisen and schisms have sprung up other than that the priest of God is despised and not obeyed' TH 48a

*In aga oberow an par ma fatell yllans gwetias favowre a thewleff aga thas a neff hag I mar spyttefull, ow **despisia** an corfe han gois agan saviour crist y vab eff?* 'In their works of this kind how can they expect favour from the hands of God, their heavenly Father, when they so spitefull despise the body and blood of Christ our Saviour, his son?' TH 55a

*ha yn weth ow gwelas pew vge ow **despisea** ha gwetha y erriow benegas ef* 'and also seeing who despises and who keeps his blessed words' SA 59.

Dysprêsya and **despîsya** are both borrowed from English. Given that **despîsya** is much the commoner of the two, there is little reason to proscribe it.

DESPITE *see* SPITE

DESTRUCTION

There are two attested words for 'destruction' in the texts: A) **dyswrians** and B) **dystrùcsyon**. The first is confined to two instances in BK. The second is the commoner, as can be seen from the following attestations:

A **dyswrians**

*ha mer thuwon ew heb queston (ha del erhyth) **dyswryans** mab den i'n bys* 'and great anguish is without question (and as you order it) the destruction of mankind in the world' BK 1027-30

*Ny alsa moy **dyswryans** wharvos neffra er ow fyn* 'Greater distruction could not happen ever against me' BK 3138-39.

B **dystrùcsyon**

*ow whylas rag agan dry the **thestruccion*** 'seeking to bring us to destruction' TH 5a

*yma **destruccion** hag anken in aga furthow* 'destruction and misery are in their ways' TH 7a

*yma an **destruccion** ahanowhy ow tos ahanow agys honyn* 'your destruction is coming from you yourselves' TH 11a

*Ha neb nan Jevas dyscans a ra trelya an dra, kepar dell rongy the oll scripturs erall, thega **destruccion** aga honyn* 'And whoever hasn't instruction turns the matter, as they do with all other scriptures to their own destruction' TH 18

yma tus an par na ow trelya an scriptures thega **destruccion** *aga honyn* 'men of that kind turn the scriptures to their own destruction' TH 18a

an decay a cherite ew an **destruction** *an bys* 'the decay of charity is the destruction of the world' TH 21

yma Egesippus ow recordya, an den auncient, in y tryssa lever, an **Destruccion** *a Jherusalem* 'Hegesippus, an ancient author, records in his third book the destruction of Jerusalem' TH 47a

cotha in devision ha in stryff agy thetha aga honyn, ha wosa henna in **destruccion** 'fall into division and strife among themselves and after that into destruction' TH 49a

distructyon *yma ornys pur serten war oll an beise* 'destruction has been ordained indeed for all the world' CW 2150-51

han **distructyon** *a vyth bras may fyth an byes destryes* 'and the destruction will be great so that the world will be destroyed' CW 2162-63

sera tha radn an ry na ef a vynsa disclosya an **distructyon** *brase han lywe* 'sir, to some of those he would disclose the great destruction and the flood' CW 2356-58

distructyon *vythe an par na* 'there will be destruction of that kind' CW 2506.

In the revived language both **dyswrians** and **dystrùcsyon** can legitimately be used.

DEVONSHIRE

The Cornish revival has always called 'Devonshire' **Dewnans**, but this name is unattested in traditional Cornish, being found only in Lhuyd's preface to his Cornish grammar:

(pan 'ryg Kadụaladar an Mȳtern Brethonek deụetha a'n Enez-ma môz dha Rev) ha dazkemeraz Ḵernou ha **Deunanz** 'when Cadwalader, the last British king of this island, went to Rome and reconquered Cornwall and Devon' AB: 224

Hag aụôz an dzhȳi rygkuitha **Deunanz** *mer a dermen ụdzhe hemma* 'And after they kept Devon for a long time after this' AB: 224

nag yu mîlo en Kernou ha lîaz en **Deunanz***, deskennyz dhort an Tregòryon kenza* 'there are not thousands in Cornwall and many in Devon descended from the first inhabitants' AB: 224.

Cornish **Kernow** 'Cornwall' derives from the plural **Kornowî (Cornovii)*, the name of the Brythonic people who inhabited the region. Similarly the Brythonic people *Dumnonii* gave their name to Devon. In Cornish, however, *Dumnonii* would have developed to something like ***Dewnyn***. Lhuyd's *Deunanz* is likely to have been his Cornicization of Welsh *Dyfnaint* 'Devon', rather than a native Cornish name. Welsh *Dyfnaint* seems to be from *Dumnonii*, but reshaped as though from *dwfn, dyfn-* 'deep' and *naint* 'streams'.

Devonshire

There is no evidence that ***Dewnans** was ever part of the native lexicon of Cornish.

The only name for Devon, Devonshire in traditional Cornish is found once in the writing of Nicholas Boson:

lavar war cota dean brose en arg[h]anz hunt tho canz bloath coth lebben, marrack en pedden west **pow Densher** 'a motto upon the coat of arms of a great man in silver more than 100 years old now, a knight in the far west of Devonshire' BF: 27.

Pow Densher should perhaps be the term of choice in everyday speech. Poetry and official use are a different matter.

TO DIE

The default word for 'to die' in Cornish is **merwel**. Here are some examples of the verbal noun from various Middle and Late Cornish texts:

yndella ef a vynne may halle dre baynys bras **merwel** *rag 3e gerense* 'thus he wished that he might by great torments die for love of you' PA 70cd

my a'd peys arluth vhel the'n tyr ty a ry cummyas ma'm gasso kyns ys **myrwel** *ynno bos thy'm the welas* 'I beseech you, exalted Lord, to the land you will give permission that it will allow me to seek food for myself in it before I die' OM 375-78

mar tha yv genef a brys **merwel** *kyns dos drok ancow* 'it is as well for me to die betimes before an evil death comes' OM 1229-30

ef a goth thotho **merwel** 'he must die' PC 2408

byth ny yl awos an bys den vyth bones dasserhys wose **merwel** 'never can anyone for all the world rise again having died' RD 938-40

ihesu grond thyn saluasconn rag oma reys yv **merwell** 'Jesus grant us salvation for here me must die' BM 1259-60

No ny rewgh **merwell** 'No, you shall not die' TH 3a

dre henna mayth o res thotha prys **merwell** 'so that through that a time to die was given to him' TH 12

pan vo an dewetha gyrryow clowis a onen a vo in y gwely marnance: ha paris the **verwall** 'when the last words have been heard by someone on his deathbed, and he is ready to die' SA 59

Mar pewas Christ, me a grys, warlergh **mirwall**, *ow du Jovyn a'n dathorthas der e ras* 'If Christ lived, I believe, after dying, my god Jovyn raised him by his grace' BK 316-19

dew a therfyn bos gwerthyes gans an gwella frute pub preys me an gwra avs **merwall** 'God deserves to be worshipped with the best fruit always; I shall do it though I die' CW 1097-99

rag ugge an teez goth tho **merwal** *akar, ny a wele an teez younk tho e clappia le ha le, ha lacka ha lacka* 'for after the old die out, we see the young speaking it less and less and worse and worse' BF: 25

GERYOW GWIR   **disciple**

na eue liklod dre vidn ava bose trigaz pel hep **merwal** *akar ha dose tho travith* 'it is not likely that it will survive long without dying out and coming to nothing' BF: 29

why na'ra seere **merwall** 'you will surely not die' Rowe.

It should also be noted, however, that the collocation **bos marow**, literally 'to be dead' is often used as a periphrasis for 'to die':

yn growys gans kentrow fastis peynys bys pan **ve marow** 'fixed on the cross with nails, tormented until he died' PA 2d

den vyth ny yl amontye na leuerell war anow oll myns peynys an geve kyns ys y **vonas marow** 'no man can calculate nor say by mouth all the torments he suffered before he died' PA 59cd

me a'th pys scryf ow ene pan **vyf marow** *yn the rol* 'I beseech you, write my name in your list when I die' PC 421-22

my re thysyryas fest mer dybry genogh why haneth boys pask kyns ov **bos marow** 'I have very greatly desired to eat the Paschal meal with you before I die' PC 718-20

mars oge cryst map dev ker ymsav scon yn nep maner na **vy marow** 'if you are Christ the son of beloved God, save yourself somehow soon so that you do not die' PC 2891-93

out dethy **bethen marov** *gans flam tan mes ay ganov* 'curse it, we shall die from the fire out of its mouth' BM 3945-46

ihesu crist yth yv henna a **fue marov** *anclethyys dasserrys then tresse deth then neff assendias inweth* 'that is Jesus Christ who died, buried, risen on the third day, ascended into heaven also' BM 4081-84

bethyth marow *a wel the'n pow* 'you shall die in the sight of the people' BK 259-60.

Indella me a vynsa, kyn fe rys thym **bos marow** 'Thus I should, though it be necessary for me to die' BK 433-34

Potho Herod **maraw**, *mero elez neue theath tha Joseph en cuska en Egyp* 'When Herod died, behold angels from heaven came to Joseph in his sleep in Egypt' Rowe.

Bos marow is a useful alternative to **merwel**. Moreover saying, for example, **ev a veu marow** 'he died' is exactly parallel with Welsh *bu farw* 'he died' and Middle Irish *ba marb* 'he died'.

DISCIPLE

There are two words for 'disciple' in Cornish: A) **dyskybel**, *plural* **dyskyblyon, dyskyblon, dyscabels**; B) **dyscypel**, *plural* **dyscypels, dyscyplys**.

A **dyskybel**
Discipulus, **discebel** 'disciple' OCV §371

disciple   GERYOW GWIR

*Eugh yn fen ʒy **ȝyschyblon** ha leuerough wy ʒeʒe* 'Go swiftly to his disciples and tell them' PA 256a

*thyvgh lauara ow **dyskyblyon*** 'to you, my disciples, I say' PC 1

*syre arluth me a'th peys a thybry gynef vn prys dre the voth ha'th **dyskyblon*** 'sir, lord, I beseech you to eat with me by your will and your disciples' PC 455-57

*py plas yth ylle dybry ef hag ol y **tyskyblon*** 'where he can eat, he and all his disciples' PC 635-36

*ef hag ol y **thyskyblon*** 'he and all his disciples' PC 677

*pyv an brasse den senges yn mysk ol thy **thyskyblon*** 'who is considered the greatest man among all your disciples?' PC 773-74

*leuerough ow **dyskyblon** mara fyllys theugh tra wyth* 'tell me, my disciples, if anything was lacking to you' PC 911-12

*ow **dyskyblon** ysethough* 'my disciples, be seated' PC 1011

*ow scoforn treghys myrough quyt the ves thyworth ow pen gans onan a'y **thyskyblon*** 'my ear cut quite away from my head, behold by one of his disciples' PC 1144-46

*lauar thy'mmo vy yn scon ple res eth the **thyskyblon*** 'tell me quickly where your disciples have gone' PC 1245-46

*ha mar ny wrer y wythe y **thyskyblon** yn pryve a'n lader yn mes a'n beyth* 'and if he is not guarded, his disciples will steal him surreptitiously out of the tomb' RD 341-43

*a maria eugh yn scon leuereugh th'y **thyskyblon** ha the pedar* 'O Mary, go quickly; tell his disciples and Peter' RD 793-95

*the **thyskyblon** yv serrys mur* 'your disciples are very angry' RD 884

*ran prophetes, ran aweilers, ran sheppardys, hen ew bugula devas, ha **discabels*** 'some prophets, some evangelists, some shepherds, that is pastors of sheep, and disciples' TH 33a

B **dyscypyl**

*ʒen meneth olyff yʒ eth hay **ȝyscyplys** an sewyas* 'he went to the Mount of Olives and his disciples followed him' PA 52a

*ʒy **ȝyscyplys** y trylyas* 'to his disciples he turned' PA 55c

*me a'n guyth sur deth ha nos awos y **dysciplys** plos* 'I will guard him day and night indeed inspite of his dirty disciples' RD 390-91

*nyns ew worthy the vos **dissipill** na seruant thym* 'he is not worthy to be my disciple or servant' TH 21a

*an **disciples** han folowers a crist* 'the disciples and the followers of Christ' TH 24

*ny a redd fatell rug lyas onyn an **disciplis** a crist a scryffas aweylys* 'we read that many of the disciples of Christ wrote gospels' TH 37a

*agan Savyoure a rug specially, pan esa eff omma war an bys, appoyntya y aposteleth hay **disciplis*** 'our Saviour specially, when he was here on the earth, appointed his apostles and his disciples' TH 41a

*hag a rug y dyrry han ros thy **disciplis*** 'and broke it and gave it to his disciples' TH 52

*crist a rug apperya the ü y **thissiplis** ow mos the Emavs* 'Christ appeared to two of his disciples going to Emmaus' TH 56a

*An **discipels** nyng o abel thy gyrreow age arluth Christ* 'The disciples were not able for the words of their Lord Christ' SA 62a

*e ruk e distributia the e **discipels*** 'he distributed it to his disciples' SA 64a.

Both **dyskybel** and **dyscypyl** are authentic terms for the revived language. It should be noted, however, that the singular ***dyskybel** is unattested in either Middle or Late Cornish.

TO DISPLEASE, DISPLEASURE

'To displease' in Cornish is **dysplêsya**, which is well attested:

*Me a lever 3yvgh mester ha na vewy **dysplesys*** 'I tell you, master, and do not be displeased' BM 118-19

*ha na vewy **dysplesijs** peseff aragogh omma ov ascusia* 'and do not be displeased, I beg you before you to excuse me here' BM 322-24

*genes yth off **dysplesijs*** 'I am displeased with you' BM 400

*yma pensevyk an gluas **dysplesijs** pur guir genas the days hath vam kekefrys* 'the prince of the land displeased very truly with you and your father and your mother also' BM 489-91

*Kynth ogh geneff **dysplesijs** yth yv ol am anvoth vy* 'though you are displeased with me it is all against my will' BM 492-93

*ha tyrry blonogath y soveran hay **displesya*** 'and break his sovereign's wish and displease him' TH 4a

*...na **dysplaysys*** '...nor displeased' BK 708

*Ny'n **dysplaysyth**, mars os fuer, hedre vo bys in e le* 'You will not displease him, if you are wise, while the world lasts' BK 985-86.

Not unnaturally 'displeasure' in Cornish is either A) **dysplêsyans** or B) **dysplesour**:

A **dysplêsyans**

*yma S paul worth agan payntia ny in mes in colors in leas tellars in scriptur, orth agan gylwall ny an flehes a **thesplesians*** 'St Paul paints us in colour in many places in scripture, calling us the children of displeasure' TH 7a.

B **dysplesour**

*rag ny ew dre nature an flehas a **thespleasure** han wroth a thu* 'for we are by nature the children of displeasure and the wrath of God' TH 10-10a

*pana commodite a vethyn ny dretha, ha pana **displesure** rag gull contrary* 'what advantage we will have by it and what displeasure for acting contrary' TH 22a

displease   **GERYOW GWIR**

So *lyas tyrmyn an froward nature a then a ra lyas tyrmyn predery an offencys han* **displesure** *gwrys thotha dre y yskerans* 'But often the disobedient nature of man often thinks of the offences and displeasure wrought on him by his enemies' TH 24

pana **displesure** *a rug eff receva the worth y yskare* 'what displeasure he received from his enemy' TH 24

naneyll ow receva plesurs theworth agan yskar, na ow ryndra thotha **displesurs** *arta* 'neither receiving pleasures from our enemy, nor rendering displeasures to him thereafter' TH 24

whath gesow ny the remembra pana **displesure** *a russyn ny gull warbyn du* 'still let us remember what displeasure we have committed against God' TH 24

dowt yth ow theis rag henna gawas meare y **displeasure** 'therefore you fear greatly receiving his displeasure' CW 204-05

saw dew thyma a wrontyas war y **thysplesure** *ef ryes ny vethan in keth della* 'but God granted to me given upon his displeasure that I should not be in that same way' CW 1638-40

na wra dean vyth ow latha warbyn y **thysplesure** *leel* 'that no man will kill me against his true displeasure' CW 1534-35

ha dew thothef a awas y **thyspleasure** *hay sor bras* 'and God relented to him of his displeasure and his great anger' CW 2044-45.

In the revived language **dysplesour** is perhaps to be preferred to **dysplêsyans**.

DOWN

When 'down' means 'downwards, to a lower position', either literally or metaphorically, with motion implied **wàr nans** may be used, though this expression is very rare in the texts. Until the discovery of BK it was attested once only in the entire corpus of Cornish:

> ...*rag gwan spyrn hag ef yn ten caman na ylly gwyʒe* **war nans** *na bosse y ben rag an arlont a vsye* '... for thorn pricks, and he stretched out, so that he could not at all keep his head from leaning downwards, because of the wreath he was wearing' PA 205ab
> *Lemmyn nyng ew vas an towl mayth esave ow towtya, y tuan* **war nans** 'Now the thing planned is not good so that I fear we will go down' BK 769-71.

The commoner expression, however, is **dhe'n dor**, literally 'to the ground':

> *mars os mab du a vur brys dijskyn ha* **ʒen dor** *ke* 'if you are the son of God of great worth, descend and go down' PA 14d
> *the gryst y tons ʒy syndye ha ʒe dry* **ʒen dor** *gans meth* 'Christ they come to hurt him and to bring him down with shame' PA 97d

rag y thry ȝen dor gans meth yn ges y a leueris mur a onour te a fyth te yw mygtern cvrvnys 'to bring him down with shame they said in mockery: Much honour shall you have; you are a crowned king' PA 136bc

veyll an tempyll a squardyas yntre dew ȝen dor coȝys 'the veil of the temple tore in two, falling down' PA 209c

ha ȝen dor an goys han lyn annoȝo dell deueras 'and that blood and liquid poured down from him' PA 221c

toul an welen ol yn tyen the'n dor vskys 'cast the rod down down quick wholly' OM 1447-48

saw vn marrek a'n lathas ha the'n dor scon a'n goras hag a'n hakyas the dymmyn 'but a knight killed him and soon pulled him down and hacked him to pieces' OM 2226-28

hethe the'n dor my a'd pys scon ef a vyth amendyys 'hand it down, I beg you; it will soon be repaired' OM 2521-22

my a re gans mur a ras whare lemyn strokyas bras pur evn war an brest arag bys may cothe hy the'n dor 'I will land with great grace large blows upon the breast in front until she falls down' OM 2715-18

mars os map dev a mur prys dyyskyn ha the'n dor ke 'if you are the son of God of great worth, descend and go down' PC 99-100

kyn fe dyswrys an temple the'n dor quyt na safe man me a'n dreha sur arte 'though the temple be knocked down entirely so that it did not stand, I will build it again' PC 344-46

lyes guyth y wruk bostye thy'so gy del lauara terry the'n dor an temple yn try geth y wul arta 'often he boasted, as I will tell you, to knock the temple down, in three days to build it again' PC 2439-42

ellas dre kveth yn clamder the'n dor prag na ymwhelaf 'alas, through anguish why do I not fall down in a faint?' PC 2593-94

toul an grous the'n dor hep gow the wrowethe 'cast the cross down indeed to lie on it' PC 2661-62

cothys then doyr attonsy age corff warbarth yv trogh 'they have fallen down; their bodies together are bruised' BM 1278-79

deyskyn then dor mata ha the borse mes ath ascra me am beth hath margh uskis 'get down, mate, and your purse from your bosom and your horse I'll have quickly' BM 1887-89

So nyns ew an Spuris sans mar dyligens in travith dell ewa ow tenna then dore haw kemeras the ves an goth a vabden gylwys in scriptur vaynglori 'But the Holy Spirit is not as diligent in anything as in pulling down and removing the pride of man called vainglory in scripture' TH 6

yma an lyver a skyantoleth ow remembra thyn may teffan ha tenna then dore an pryde vs ew raynya ynnan 'the Book of Wisdom reminds us that we should pull down the pride which reigns in us' TH 6a

Gesow ny the veras war agan treis, ha gwren leverall, then dore, lost peacok (vel payon) prowt, then dore, colonow prowt, then dore brytyll prye ha dore 'Let us look upon our feet, and let us say, down, peacock's (or Pavo's) proud tail, down proud hearts, down feeble clay and earth' TH 9

down GERYOW GWIR

*My a vyn settya envy intre te ha haes an venyn hag eff a putt **then dore** theth pen in dan y dros* 'I will set hatred between you and the seed of the woman, and he will put down your head under his foot' TH 13

*ha nena eff a vith compellys the gotha **thyn dore** in corfe hag in ena therag du* 'and then he will be compelled to fall down in body and in soul before God' TH 30a

*Eff a thanvonas **then dore** an spurissans war ben y abosteleth* 'He sent down the Holy Spirit upon his apostles' TH 36

*hag eff a suffras an drog pobyll the denna **thyn dore** an paell han kee ay vyneyarde* 'and he allowed the evil people to pull down the pailing and the fence of his vineyard' TH 40a

*pana abbys a ve twolys **thyn dore**, pana colyges, pana chauntreys a ve towlys **then dore**?* 'what abbeys were thrown down, what colleges, what chantries were thrown down?' TH 40a

*gesow ny the gotha **thyn dore** flatt therag du agan tas* 'let us fall down flat before God our Father' TH 40a

*y ben a ve treylys **thyn dore** in crowse, ha y dreys in ban* 'his head was turned down on the cross and his feet up' TH 47

*ny a rede in xx chapter a Exodus, fatell ve clowys sownde a trompet pan rug du dos **thyn dore** thea neff in mownt Sinai* 'we read in the 20th chapter of Exodus that the sound of a trumpet was heard when God came down from heaven on Mount Sinai' TH 56a

*ha angye a cothaz **en doar**, ha gorthaz tha eue* 'and they fell down and worshipped him' Rowe

*Na rase plegy **en dore** dothans* 'You shall not bow down to them' BF: 41.

When 'down' is an adverb meaning 'downwards, to a lower position', the default expression in the revived language should perhaps be **dhe'n dor**.

DRINK

The noun 'drink' in Middle Cornish is **dywes**, **dewes**, **dewas** and the plural is **dewosow**:

*Dew ʒen crist a ʒanvonas ʒe berna boys ha **dewas*** 'Christ sent two men to buy food and drink' PA 42a

*mas re war gryst a ynnyas yʒ o **dewas** a yrghy* 'but some urged against Christ that he was asking for a drink' PA 201d

*Gans an eʒewon war hast drok **ʒewas** a ve dyʒgtys* 'By the Jews in haste and evil drink was prepared' PA 202a

*the thev ploste gey ny re na'n nyl thy'n bos na **dewes*** 'your worthless God will give us neither food nor drink' OM 1809-10

*rag **dewes** mar nys tevyth yn certan y a dreyl fyth* 'for if they do not get drink indeed they will change their faith' OM 1816-17

*rag gvel **dewes** bytteth vyn nyns a yn agas ganow* 'for a better drink of wine will never enter your mouths' OM 1912-13

GERYOW GWIR   **drink**

*an **dewes** yv da ha cler* 'the drink is good and clear' OM 1918
*otta **dywes** thys omma* 'here is a drink for you' PC 2980
*woge ow da oberow **dywes** a yrhys dethe* 'after my good deeds I asked them for a drink' RD 2599-600
*rag neffra nahen **dewes** nyns a om ganov defry* 'for never will any other drink go into my mouth' BM 656-57
*arta me a thue deth yov oma dygh gans **dewosov** a relle agis sawye* 'I shall come again on Thursday here with drinks which will cure you' BM 1472-74
*ha me a vyn then benenes ry mona boys ha **dewes** the perna* 'and I will give the women money to buy food and drink' BM 1671-73
*ny eve cydyr na gwyn na **dewes** marnes dour pur* 'I do not drink cider nor wine nor any drink but pure water' BM 1969-70
*boys na **dewes** na regh ry then guas a ruk vy orna the preson pur eredy* 'give neither food nor drink to the fellow I ordered to be put in prison' BM 3603-05
*schant yv an **dewes** han boys* 'scanty is the drink and the food' BM 3929
*ha tan dis **dewes** ha boys* 'and help yourself to drink and food' BM 4243
*rag neb a vynna, a yll eva ha kemeras an **dewas** a vewnans theworth an egglos* 'for whoever wishes, may drink and receive the drink of life from the Church' TH 19
*rag fowt bos, **dewas**, hag ethom dyllas* 'for lack of food, drink and need of clothes' TH 40a
*ha ow gois ew verely **dewas*** 'and my blood is truly drink' TH 51a
*A ra tus vsya offra bois ha **dewas** the re, rag purpos vith arall, mas may teffans dybry hag eva anotha?* 'Do men usually offer food and drink to people for any other purpose, than that they should eat and drink of them?' TH 52a
*in sted a **thewas**, e may vrth agan maga gans e woos* 'instead of drink he feeds us with his blood' SA 59a
*ha ow gois ew verely **dewas*** 'and my blood is truly drink' SA 61
*neb a theffa dibbry ow kig, ha eva ow **dewas**, ema ef ow trega innaff ve* 'whoever eats my flesh and drinks my drink, he dwells in me' SA 61
*Neg eranny ow kemeras hemma rag common bara ha **dewas*** 'We do not take this for common bread and drink' SA 63a
*Na esyny miras wor an bara han **dewas** ew sittys deragen* 'Let us not look at the bread and the drink that is set before us' SA 65a
*Rag pruvya **dewas** ha boys, harlygh robyowgh yonk ha loys* 'To provide drink and food, stoutly rob young and old' BK 2377-78
*Mathtath, [ro de vy] barow ha **dewas*** 'Mayde, give me bread and drinke' Borde
*Potus... Drink C. **Deuaz*** AB: 125a.

In some forms of Cornish 'drink' appears as **diwes*. It is apparent from the above examples that such a spelling is unattested. The word for 'drink' in revived Cornish is best spelt **dewas** and the plural **dewosow**.

There are incidentally two further attested words for 'drink' in the texts: **draght** and **drynk**:

drink

ha wose henna evyn pep ol adro **draght** *a wyn* 'and after that let's all round drink a draught of wine' OM 2626-27
me a vyn gul **drynk** *dywhy mar cafa stoff the perna* 'I will make a drink for you, if I get stuff to buy it' BM 1462-63.

The first of these is a borrowing of English 'draught'. The second seems to mean 'drink' in a medicinal sense, i.e. potion.

TO DRIVE

In English the verb 'to drive' is most frequently used when speaking of cars, lorries, buses and trains. Clearly this is a recent usage, which derives from the earlier use of the verb with horse-drawn or even ox-drawn vehicles. This second usage is probably related to the employment of 'to drive' with the driving of cattle, given that the etymological sense of 'to drive' is 'to urge forward'; cf. the related German verb *treiben* 'to herd, to urge'. In English also one frequently applies the metaphor of steering a ship to that of a car or lorry, and speaks of 'steering' a car by means of its 'steering wheel', for example.

Since there is no reference in Cornish to the driving of either trains or motorized vehicles, to translate the idea of driving a car Nance used the metaphor from the steering of a boat or ship. The entry *gubernator uel nauclerus,* **leuuit** 'pilot or steersman' occurs at OCV §274. Moreover Pryce gives **Lêuiader** 'master or pilot of a ship' ACB: S 2 b *verso* as the modern Cornish word. On the basis of these two forms Nance derived a verb **lewyas* 'to steer, to guide', a verb which has been used for driving a vehicle. In some forms of Cornish this verb appears (incorrectly without vocalic alternation) as **lywya*.

The basic sense of the English verb 'to drive' is 'to urge on, to push, to compel' and with this sense the English was borrowed into Cornish:

wosa an towle agan hyndasow adam hag eva pan rug an tas aga **dryvya** *in mes a paradice* 'after the fall of our ancestors, Adam and Eve, when the Father drove them out of paradise' TH 13
Rag luther in especiall ha vth oll aga hensa o aga gyder ha penleder an besow in mater ma, whath pan esa eff in myske tus dyskys, rag talkya an mater ma in aga mysk y ha gansans y, eff a ve **dryvys** *war thyller* 'For Luther in particular and above all his fellows was their guide and overall leader of the worlds in this matter, and yet when he was among learned men, to speak of this among them and with them, he was driven back' TH 49a.

Since **drîvya** is the only attested word in Cornish for 'to drive', it seems preferable to use it for 'to drive (a vehicle)' than to adopt a wholly unattested word *lewyas, *lewya or whatever. With Cornish **drîvya** one might compare Welsh *dreifio, dreifo* 'to drive (a vehicle)'

DROP, TO DROP

Borlase gives *loum* 'a drop of water'. This rather looks as though it derives from Breton *lomm* 'goutte'. Borlase also gives *dewerryan* 'drop'. This Nance respells as *deveren* and suggests that it has been taken from Breton. Borlase further gives *dryppan* 'a drop', which Nance respells as *dryppyn*. In view of the verb **droppya** 'to drop', which is well attested in Cornish, *dryppyn* is likely to be a genuine form. It is, however, not attested in the texts. In the texts themselves the only word for 'drop' is **banna**, **badna**, which can also be used in an extended sense to mean 'jot, anything', often of seeing.

Gutta uel stilla, **banne** 'drop' OCV §729
Gans queth y ben y queȝens guelas **banna** *na ylly* 'With a cloth they covered his head so that he could not see anything' PA 96a
dal o ny wely **banna** 'he was blind; he saw nothing' PA 217b
bythqueth whet tebel na mas ny wylys ganse **banne** 'never good or ill have I seen anything with them' PC 397-98
iudas ny gosk vn **banne** *lymmyn dywans fystyne thu'm ry the'n fals yethewon* 'Judas does not sleep a jot now, but hastens to betray me to the false Jews' PC 1078-80
kyn na wore hy cowse **banna** *me as rowle hy del vannaf* 'though she cannot speak at all I shall rule her as I wish' CW 506-07
skant ny welaf vn **banna** 'I can hardly see anything' CW 1461
na gwyne ny vsyan **badna** 'nor do we consume a drop of wine' CW 1474
banna *ny allaf gwellas* 'I cannot see anything' CW 1622
ha me ny wellyn **banna** 'and I could see nothing' CW 1653
nyng es omma dean in wlase a greys thybm malbe **vanna** 'there is not here anyone in the land who believes me one whit' CW 2327-28
Dho gware peliow, rag gun ehaz; Dibre tabm dah, hag eva **badna** 'To play bowls, for our health, to eat a good bit and drink a drop' ACB: F f 4.

The intransitive verb 'to drop' is translated **droppya** in PA:

ma teth an goys ha **dropye** *war y fas an caradow* 'so the blood happened to drop upon his face, the beloved' PA 59b
goys ay ben ay ysely a **ȝroppye** *war y ȝewver* 'blood from his head and his limbs was dropping upon his legs' PA 173c.

drop

It is very probable that **droppya** 'to drop' remained part of the lexicon of Cornish thereafter, since the word reappears in the Late Cornish period the compound **pendroppya** 'to nod':

Quinisco... C. Dho pendruppia 'To nod or shake the head' AB: 135a.

In revived Cornish the default word for 'drop' should perhaps be **banna**, **badna**. For the intransitive verb 'to drop' one should use **droppya**.

DUKE

In some forms of Cornish 'duke' is **dug*, plural **dugys*. There is no warrant for such forms, since in traditional Cornish the singular is always **dûk**, and the plural is **dûkys**; there is no instance of **dug* anywhere:

del ose pryns ha chyf **duk** 'as you are prince and chief duke' PC 1926
Me yw gylwys **duk** *bryten* 'I am called the duke of Brittany' BM 1
Honour 3yvgh master worthy ha benytha mur reuerens **duk** *conan pur yredy* 'Honour to you, worthy master, and always much reverence indeed, Duke Conan' BM 82-4
mones y fannaf lemmyn the̹[n] **duk** *pen an chevalry* 'I will go now to the duke, the head of chivalry' BM 173-74
orlyans **duk** *a galloys* 'Orleans, duke of power' BM 282
Ov lich kyng bethugh mery inweth oll an kyffuywy **dukis** *3urlys marogyon* 'My liege king, be merry, also all the guests, dukes, earls, knights' BM 292-94
Farwel ser **duk** 'Farewell, Sir Duke' BM 474
Me yv **duk** *in oll kernow* 'I am duke in all Cornwall' BM 2205
Parys on dywhy sur **duk** 'We are ready for you, Sir Duke' BM 2264
yma **duk** *oma in vlays* 'there is a duke here in the country' BM 2301
y an prenvyth by my sovle an **duk** *hay dus rum ene* 'they will pay for it upon my soul, the duke and his men, I swear it' BM 2320-21
Ser **duk** *me a weyl tevdar* 'Sir Duke, I see Teudar' BM 2357
pendra deseff an map devle dar vyngya war **thuk** *kernov* 'what is the devil's son presuming? What! to be avenged on the Duke of Cornwall?' BM 2395-96
Duk *kernov hag oll y dus in dan ov threys me as glus* 'The Duke of Cornwall and all his men, I shall pulp them underfoot' BM 2397-98
Ser **duk** *ty a nagh the fay* 'Sir Duke, you will deny your faith' BM 2460
an **duk** *yv corff heb parov* 'the duke is a person without equal' BM 2492
Me yv arluth heb parov **duk** *inweth astronymer* 'I am a lord without equal, a duke and also an astronomer' BM 3896-97
y tethewys nans yv meys mones inhans then prasov erbyn **duk** *magus a breys* 'I promised a month ago to go beyond the meadows to meet worthy Duke Magus' BM 3918-20
Heyl dyugh **duk** *nobil magus* 'Hail to you, noble Duke Magus' BM 3930
Me ew **duk** *Kernow Cador* 'I am Cador, duke of Cornwall' BK 1263

GERYOW GWIR　　　　　　　　　　　　　　　　　　　　**duke**

Pax nunc, prelyatores, prynsys, ***dukys****, marrogyon* 'Peace now, prelates, princes, dukes, knights' BK 2380-81

Duk *Borgayn, awos e frap, ny yl poral thymmo scap* 'The duke of Burgundy, for all his strikes, a pig cannot escape from me' BK 2449-50

Me, Ypolyt, ***duk*** *Creth heb fall* 'I, Hippolytus, the duke of Crete indeed' BK 2664

Me, Ethyon, ***duk*** *Boecy, war the enmy a rys gans lune devocyon* 'I, Ethyon, duke of Boetia, upon your enemy will run with full devotion' BK 2673-76

rag me, Teuthar, ***duk*** *Phrygy suer* 'for I, Teuthar, the duke of Phrygia indeed' BK 2683-84

Me, Evander, ***duk*** *Syry, a'n dyelha* 'I, Evander, the duke of Syria, will avenge him' BK 2693-94

duk *Bitini, Pollitetes, gwerryor stowt* 'Pollitetes, the duke of Bithynia, a doughty warrior' BK 2705-06

duk *an Saxens, Chellery* 'Childerich, the duke of the Saxons' BK 3230

An ***duk*** *a'n gevith pur wyer rag e laver ol an tyr a Thowr Hombyr the Scotland* 'The duke will have indeed for his labour all the land from the River Humber to Scotland' BK 3235-37

Ke wyn an ***duk*** *ha Bithwar a ve lethis* 'Fair Kay, the duke, and Bedevere were killed' BK 3289-90

now adam ma ow lordya avell ***duke*** *in paradise* 'now Adam is lording it like a duke in paradise' CW 456-57.

There is no attested word for 'duchy' in Cornish. Since, however, **dûk**, **dûkys** is clearly borrowed from Middle English, it seems likely that the word for 'duchy', if it were attested, would have been based on Middle English *duchee, duchie* 'duchy'. The word ***conteth*** 'county' is attested at BM 512. 'Duchy' in Cornish should probably therefore be ****dùcheth***. In the same way 'duchess' should probably be ****dùches***, *plural* ****dùchesow***.

DWELL *see* **LIVE**

E

EARS

For 'ear' Nance gives **scovarn** *f.*, *plural* ***scovarnow**, *dual* ***dywscovarn**. The following are the attested plural forms:

*pur ankensy gans dornow thotho war an **scovornow** reugh boxsesow trewysy* 'very painfully with fists strike him blows wretchedly on the ears' PC 1360-62

*ha ren thotho boxsusow gans dornow ha guelynny war an **scovornow** bysy* 'and let us strike blows with fists and rods assiduously upon his ears' PC 1389-91

*Me a glowt e **skovornow*** 'I will thump his ears' BK 1657

*Gwel corf in tent nag in towr whath ny glowys **skovernow*** 'A better man in tent or tower ears never heard' BK 1916-17

*y a vynsa stoppya aga **scovurnow*** 'they would stop up their ears' TH 19

*gans agan lagasow ha **scovornow*** 'with our eyes and ears' TH 21a

*skovarn, **skovornow*** 'eare, eares' Bodewryd MS.

Apart from the one example ***skovernow*** in BK, all the plural forms have a back vowel, **o** or **u** in the stressed syllable. There is no justification for Nance's *scovarnow. Moreover Nance's dual *dywscovarn is wholly unattested. In the revived language the 'ear' should be **scovarn**, *plural* **scovornow**. Since a dual ***dywscovarn** is unattested, there is no need to introduce it into the revived language.

EASY

For 'easy' Nance recommends *es*, which he believed was attested in:

*nyns yw thy's tyller pur **es*** 'it is not a very easy place for you' PC 85

He also suggests that the comparative of *es* was *esya*, a form seen in:

*sowe Eva manaf saya hy ew **esya** tha dulla es adam in gwyre yn ta* 'but I will try Eve; she is easier to deceive than Adam very truly' CW 471-72.

The UC pair *es* 'easy', *esya* 'easier', however, may well be based on a misunderstanding. The common word for 'easy' in the texts is **êsy**:

yth o tra **eysy** *lowre the forberya* 'it was easy enourgh to forebear' TH 4
Rag an kythsame ü cawse ma ny cristonyan a res thyn supposia an yocke a crist the vois wheg, hay sawe the vos scaffe hag **eysy** 'For these same two reasons we Christians must suppose the yoke of Christ to be sweet, and his burden to be light and easy' TH 28
mas ny a yll **eysy** *lowre discernya* 'unless we can discern easily enough' TH 31a
whay a yll gwelas **eysy** *ha vnderstondia* 'you can see easily and understand' TH 33a
han kythsam tra ma a alsa **eysy** *y prevy* 'and this same thing is easily proved' TH 34a
may halla ynna bos gothvethis **eysy** 'that it may easily be known among them' TH 48
yth ew **eysy** *lowre* 'it is easy enough' TH 54
ha thotheff the wull pub tra ew **eysy** 'and to make everything easy for him' TH 54
So the thu yth ew mater **eysy** 'But for God it is an easy matter' TH 56a
girryow an scripture a yll bos **eaisy** *vnderstandis* 'the words of the scripture can easily be understoood' SA 64.

The word **es** is usually a noun with the sense 'ease':

may hyl pup map bron ef hag ol y thyskyblon cafus y **es** *hep danger* 'so that every single man, he and his disciples, may take their ease without hindrance' PC 676-77
nyns ew an yoke a crist gilwys wheg, ha y sawe scaff, awois **eays** *vith na remission* 'the yoke of Christ is not called sweet, and his burden light because of any ease or remission' TH 27a.

In which case, the expression **tyller pur es** at PC 85 quoted above, may not contain the adjective *es 'easy', but rather a substantive **es** 'ease'. *Nyns yw thy's tyller pur* **es** may not be 'It is not a very easy place for you' but rather 'It is not a place of pure ease for you'. If *es* here really is a substantive, not an adjective, *es 'easy' disappears from the language. Moreover the comparative **êsya** is the expected comparative of **êsy**. **Êsya** as the comparative of *es 'easy' is harder to explain. In the interests of authenticity *es 'easy', **êsya** 'easier, easiest' should perhaps be replaced by **êsy**, **êsya**.

ELEMENT

For 'element' Nance recommends **elven** *f.* This word is cited by Borlase who gives **Elven** 'an element, a spark of fire'. The origin Borlase's entry is not clear. He may have derived **elven** from Breton *elfenn* 'étincelle; élément'. This is in origin the same word as Welsh *elfen* 'element' < Latin *elementum*. The etymon also survives in Cornish dialect *elvan* 'porphyry', a kind of rock which contains large crystals.

element GERYOW GWIR

The word for 'element' is attested in the Cornish texts, however:

ha yth ew gwrys a ü part, henew an visible formes an **elementys**, *ha an invisible corfe ha gois agan savyour Jhesus crist* 'and it is made of two parts, that is the visible forms, the elements, and the invisible body and blood of our Saviour Jesus Christ' TH 56
Bara ew trylys theworth vn **elyment** *the gela* 'Bread is converted from one element to another' SA 66a.

The second quotation translates the Latin *Panis transelementatur* 'bread is converted as to its element'.

Since **elven** is attested in Borlase and is found, albeit with a change of sense, in Cornish English, it cannot be proscribed. The plural would be ***elvednow**. **Element** 'element', *plural* **elementys** is perhaps to be preferred.

EMPEROR, EMPIRE

For emperor Nance gives **emperour**, **emprour**. This is well attested as can be seen from the following selected examples:

imperator uel cesar uel augustus, **emperur** 'emperor' OCV §167
Emperour *na myghtern glas* 'an emperor or king of a country' OM 2055
heil syre **emperour** *a'n wlas* 'hail, sir emperor of the land' PC 1705
genef yth os dynerghys gans cesar an **emperour** 'by me you are greeted by Caesar, the emperor' RD 1628-29
ty a crek in cloghprennyer rag perel prence hag **emperour** 'you will hang on gallows for peril of prince and emperor' BM 923-24
in deu[e]tha blethan a reign a cruell **Emperour** *Nero* 'in the last year of the reign of the cruel emperor Nero' TH 47
Lowena the berhan ras, avel **empror** *desethys* 'Hail to a lord of grace, enthroned like an emperor' BK 1896-97.

For 'empire' Nance recommends ***emperoreth**, which he says is based on Breton. The only attested word, however, is **empîr**:

thynny ef a leverys, e vos guyryak y'th **ympyr** 'he told us he had rights in your empire' BK 2236-37
In myth Arthur ema gwyer thotha ef in e **ympyer** 'Arthur says that he has the right in his empire' BK 2425-26.

Since it is attested, **empîr** is perhaps preferable to ***emperoreth**.

ENGLAND

For 'England' Nance recommends ***Pow Sows** (UC *Pow Saws*), **Pow an Sowson** (UC *Pow an Sawson*) and ***Bro Sows** (UC *Bro Saws*). Of these three items only **Pow an Sowson** is attested: *Anglia... England; C.* ***Pou an Zouzn*** AB: 42c.

The commonest attested name for 'England' in Cornish is in fact **Inglond**, which is attested three times:

*lymmyn the drelya the gen pow ny a **ynglonde**, hemma a yll bos lell cowsys* 'now to turn to our country of England, this can be said' TH 50a-51

*nyns es onyn an gevas mar ver cawse the favera an sea han stall a rom dell gevas **englond*** 'there is not one that has such a great reason to favour the see and stall of Rome as has England' TH 51

*ha y fe danvenys omma the **Englond** an moyba notabill ha auncyent tus dyskys rag progath* 'and there were sent here to England the most notable and ancient learned men to preach' TH 51

With **Inglond**, compare **Scotland** 'Scotland', q.v. **Inglond** is unlikely to find favour with revivalists. In which case **Pow an Sowson** can be used. The unattested forms ***Pow Sows** and ***Bro Sows** should perhaps be avoided.

TO ENJOY

For 'to enjoy oneself' Nance suggests **omlowenhe*. No such form is attested. *Lowenhe* itself without the prefix *om-* is used intransitively to mean 'to rejoice, to be joyful' as can be seen from the following examples:

*ov colon yv marthys claf **lowenhe** me ny allaf gouy vyth pan y'n neghys* 'my heart is wondrous sick; I cannot be joyful. Alas ever that I denied him' PC 1426-28

*Innan agan honyn, ny yllyn ny **lowenhe**, rag ahanan agan honyn nyg on mas peghadorryan* 'In ourselves we cannot be joyful, for of ourselves we are only sinners' TH 10a

*Ny **lowenhaf** o'm tyrmyn* 'I shall not be joyful in my time' BK 1209

*Ny **lowenhaf** in ow dythyow neffra lam* 'I will not rejoice in my days ever one bit' BK 2930-31

*Ny **lowenhis** war neb us, aban clowys kyns e gows* 'I have not been joyful for any time since I first heard his speech' BK 3131-32.

If one wishes to say 'to enjoy' in Cornish one must paraphrase:

*moye es vn wreag thym yma **thom pleasure rag gwyll ganssy*** 'I have more than one wife for me to enjoy' CW 1451-52.

an pleasure es thym *in beyse yth ew gans gwaracke tedna* 'what I enjoy in the world is to hunt with the bow' CW 1465-66

enjoy   **GERYOW GWIR**

Alternatively one can use the English borrowing **enjoya**:

*eff a rug oll an re na keverennak ganso eff in lowendar, myns a vynna **inioya** an merits ay pascion* 'he made all those partners with him in joy, as many as wish to enjoy the merits of his passion' TH 12a

*oll an re na a rella commyttya tra an parma, ny rowng **enioya** gwlas neff* 'all those who commit such a thing, they will never enjoy the kingdom of heaven' TH 16a

*rag **enioya** an myrnans han pascion a crist, an kythsam ü poynt ma ew the vos requyrys in agan part ny* 'to enjoy the death and passion of Christ these same two points are required on our part' TH 16a.

One thing is certain, *****omlowenhe** is unattested and cannot be recommended.

TO ESCAPE
The native word **diank** 'to escape' is attested in the texts:

A **diank**
*kelmeugh warbarth y thywvreg na allo **dyank** dre wal* 'bind together his two arms so that he cannot escape through lack of care' PC 1179-80

*mars yv **dyenkys** ellas* 'if he has escaped, alas!' RD 520

*why a feth purguir marov maras ywe **dyenkys*** 'you will indeed die, if he has escaped' BM 3731-32.

Commoner, however, is the borrowing **scappya** 'to escape':

B **scappya**
*marow vethyn kettep pen nyns us **scapya** thy'nny ny* 'we shall all die; there is no escaping for us' OM 1655-56

*ellas govy buthys on ny ny wren **scapye*** 'alas, woe is me; we are drowned; we shall not escape' OM 1705-06

*gueyt an harlot na **scapyo*** 'make sure that the villain doesn't escape' PC 990

*gueyt y wrennye prest yn tyn byth na **scapye*** 'be sure to grip him very firmly so he doesn't escape' PC 1887-88

*mar **scap** yth eugh the'n mernans* 'if he escapes, you will be put to death' RD 378

*dalhen mar cafaf ynno pur wyr ny **scap** kyn fynno* 'if I get hold of him, he will not escape, though he wishes' RD 382-83

*ny **skap** kyn fo byth mar fur na'n geffo drok* 'he will not escape though he be never so wise from receiving harm' RD 2019-20

*teulyn grabel warnotho scherp ha dalgenne ynno byth na **schapye*** 'let us cast a grapnel sharply upon him and seize him so that he won't ever escape' RD 2268-70

*tevder mes y skyans a pan glowe y vos **scappys*** 'Teudar will go out of his mind, when he hears he has escaped' BM 1029-30

GERYOW GWIR event

lemen sovdoryen waryogh na **schappya** *benen in beys* 'now, soldiers, be on your guard that no woman at all escapes' BM 1558-59

malbev an flogh a **scappyas** 'not a single damn child escaped' BM 1581

byth ny **schappyons** *heb mernans re thu arluth mur a rays* 'never will they escape without dying, by God, Lord of grace' BM 2469-70

Kyn fe vyth mar ver e nyel, ny **scap**, *ru'm pen!* 'Though his strength be never so great, he will not escape, by my head!' BK 2605-06

Marow ew Lucy heb gyl ha'y werrors in katap myl, mars an cowars re **scapyas** 'Lucy and his warriors are dead every thousand, unless the cowards have escaped!' BK 2832-34

nyg eas **scappya** 'there is no escaping' CW 1972.

It is quite apparent that the writers of traditional Cornish in general preferred **scappya** to **diank**. Revivalists might do well to imitate them in their preference.

EVENT

For 'event' Nance recommends **wharvos** (UC *wharfos*) and **darvos** (UC *darfos*). The verbal noun ***darvos** is not attested. **Wharvos** 'to happen' is attested but only as a verbal noun; it is never used as a noun with the sense 'happening, event'. I have collected the following examples:

wharvos 'to happen'

ny won fatel yl **wharfos** *ty a then omma the vos dyuythys yn kyc yn knevs* 'I do not know how it can be that you, O man, have come here as flesh and skin' RD 229-31

arluth mar calle **wharfos** *gynen ty the vynnes bos omma pup vr* 'Lord, if it could only be that you should wish to be here with us always!' RD 2439-43

den na gresso dyougel an keth den-na the selwel cammen vyth na yl **wharfos** 'a man who does not believe truly, it can in no way happen that that same man be saved' RD 2478-80

Ny alsa moy dyswryans **wharvos** *neffra er ow fyn* 'More destruction could not ever happen against me' BK 3138-39.

Wharvos is a compound of **bos** 'to be' and its verbal adjective is **wharvedhys** (*wharfethys* OM 883, 1542; PC 1943; RD 1260; BM 775; *wharvethys* OM 620, 2082; *warvethys* OM 2547). Since there is no evidence that **wharvos**, the verbal noun itself, was ever used as a noun, it might have been better to derive a well-formed abstract noun 'happening, event' from the verbal stem **wharvedh-**; cf. **devedhyans** 'coming, descent' (**devethyans** BM 439, 830; **thevythyans** BM 1625) < **devedhys** 'come'. In which case ***wharvedhyans** would have been a better formation than **wharvos** for 'occurrence, event'.

EVER *see* **NEVER**

EVERYTHING

The expression **kenyver tra** 'everything' might be considered a Late Cornish phrase. It is, however, found as early as PA:

a vernans crist pan welse **kynyuer tra** *marthusy han enef del dascorse erbyn natar gans vn cry y leuerys heb scornye hem yw mab du yredy* 'when he had seen everything remarkable of Christ's death and that he had given up the ghost, contrary to nature with a cry he said without scorn, This indeed is the Son of God' PA 208b-d

Ha thera an bez heb composter, ha heb **kanifer tra** 'And the world was without shape and without everything' BF: 51

Ha Deu gwras an pusgaz broz, ha **kanifer tra** *es guaya* 'And God made the big fishes and everything that moves' BF: 52

ha **kanifer tra** *es kramia var an aor* 'and everything that crawls upon the earth' BF: 52

ha dres **kanifer tra** *es bounas ha guaya var an aor* 'and over everything that has life and moves on the earth' BF: 53

Ha Deu guelles **kanifer tra** *vo gwres gen e vonnin, ha mero tho vo perth da* 'And God saw everything made by Himself, and behold it was very good' BF: 53.

Since **kenyver tra** 'everything' is found in Middle Cornish, there is no need for revivalists to avoid it.

TO EXALT

Nance *inter alia* recommends **uhelhe** for 'to exalt', a verb which is attested twice only. One of those attestation is in BK, of which Nance was perforce not aware:

A **uhelhe**

ha genaf eth ew tecter i'n bys ma perthy anken hag eselder, in nef may fyf **ughelhys** 'and it is a pleasure in the world for me to suffer misery and lowness, that I may be exalted in heaven' BK 437-40

Dew a 'wras an nef, ha'n oar, ha'n more ha myns es ythens y, ha powesas an seytheras dyth, hag an **ughelchas** 'God made the heaven, the earth and the sea and all that is in them, and he rested on the seventh day and exalted it' JKeigwin.

In the texts, however, the ordinary word for 'to exalt' is **exaltya**:

B **exaltya**

y karsen y **exaltya** *may fo perhennek gwlasow* 'I should like to exalt him that he might be a possessor of lands' BM 15-6

GERYOW GWIR   **examine**

Arluth henna yv gwrys da y **exaltye** *yredy* 'Lord, that is well done to exalt him indeed' BM 17-8

dotho degogh lytherov del ma guelheven an pov orth y **exaltya** *pur dek* 'bring him letters that the nobles of the country are exalting him beautifully' BM 2796-98

ny re duth oma a dre in govenek **exaltye** *meryasek in pur certen* 'we have come here to from home in the hope of exalting Meriasek in very deed' BM 2899-901

lemmen der the vvelder **exaltijs** *the reelder ty yv dremas rag the voas* 'now through your humility, you have been exalted to nobility, because you are a good man' BM 2941-43

eff a rug **exaltia** *y mester crist hag a leverys fatell o eff vnworthy rag bocla y skyggyow* 'he exalted his master Christ and said that he was not worthy to buckle his shoes' TH 8

ha the **exaltia**, *glorifia, presia, ha honora Du vth pub tra* 'and to exalt, glorify, praise and honour God above all things' TH 10

ha drethaf serten pub eare ty a ve **exaltys** *breyf* 'and by me indeed you have always been exalted splendidly' CW 228-29

ty foole prag na bredersys a thorn dew y festa gwryes ynweth ganso **exaltys** 'you fool, why did you not consider that you were made by the hand of God and exalted by him also?' CW 308-10

der henna yth of grevys y wellas eve **exaltys** *ha me dres 3a yseldar* 'by that I am grieved to see him exalted and me brought low' CW 445-47

kooll ge thym men tha gesky mar mynta bos **exaltys** 'listen to me, able to advise you, if you wish to be exalted' CW 650-51

na vea me theth cara ny vynsan awos neb tra yn ban tha vos **exaltys** 'if I didn't love you, I should wish for anything that you be high exalted' CW 699-701.

In everyday speech **exaltya** 'to exalt' is perhaps preferable to the much rarer verb, **uhelhe**.

TO EXAMINE

The default word in revived Cornish for 'to examine by questions' has always been **apposya**. This word, however, is found only once:

A apposya

pronter boys me a garse corff iheus thy venystra mar myn ov descans servya genogh pan ven **apposijs** 'I should like to be a priest to administer the body of Christ, if my learning is considered enough when I am examined' BM 522-26.

The verb **examnya** 'to examine' is much commoner with this sense:

B examnya

me a vyn y **examyne** 'I will examine him' PC 389

me a vyn y **examne** *ha'y dus ha'y deskes wharre* 'I will examine him, his men and his teaching immediately' PC 1210-11

examine GERYOW GWIR

*dun warbarth th'y **examnye** an vyl brybor* 'let's go together to examine him, the vile vagabond' PC 1451-52

*dreugh an profus aberueth rak me a vyn yn pryueth whet vnwyth y **examnye*** 'bring in the prophet for I will examine him once more in private' PC 1465-67

*me a fyn y **examnye** athysempys* 'I will examine him straight away' PC 2149-50

*mara leuerys henna y **examnye** my a wra wheth yn pryue* 'if he said that, I shall examine him still in private' PC 2175-77

*whath na rens ef **examnya** den vith arell, mas y golan y honyn* 'yet let him not examine anyone else, but his own heart' TH 23a

*yma eff ow ry thyn kusyll diligently rag **examyna** ha trya agan honyn* 'he diligently advises us to examine and try ourselves' TH 53a-54

*ty chet gwraf tha **examnya** prage y fyn dew ow damnya ha me mar gollowe ha creif* 'you fellow, I will examine you. Why will God condemn me when I am so bright and strong?' CW 302-04.

Both **apposya** and **examnya** are borrowed from Middle English. The difference between them is that **examnya** is the ordinary word in Cornish for 'to examine'. There does not, incidentally, appear to be any attested word for 'examination'.

EXAMPLE

Nance gives ***ensompel** as the default word for 'example' and also gives **sampel** as a Late Cornish variant. The picture in the texts is a little more complicated than that. There is one example each of **ensampel**, **sompel** and **sampel**:

A ensampel, sompel, sampel

*ha eff a assas **ensampill** thynny, may teffen hay folya eff pella* 'and he left an example to us that we might follow him further' TH 24

*bus 'ma bose gwellez gun ollez gen panna collan da 'th erama leverol ul an **sompel** rag an Curnooack* 'but it is seen ?by all with what good heart I mention all the example as far as the Cornish is concerned' BF: 31

*Rag **sampl**; pan uelon neith tridzhan an ʒerrio Ʒouznak* 'For example, when we see the ?translation of the English words' AB: 223.

Pace Nance, there is thus no attested example of ***ensompel**. Indeed the commonest word by far for 'example' is none of the above, but **exampyl**, *plural* **examplys**:

B exampyl

*dre **exampyll** a henna me a dryst why a vith circumspect the avoydia oll kynde pehosow* 'through the example of that I trust you will be careful to avoid all kinds of sin' TH 5

*Dre an kyth **exampil** ma ny a yll gwellas in ta hag asswon agan honyn* 'Through this same example we can well see and recognize ourselves' TH 6

*merkyow an **exampill** ma in ta* 'notice this example well' TH 6a

*ny a yll disky in scriptur the vos vvell ha myke warlerth an **examplys** a dus tha* 'we can learn in scripture to be humble and meek according to the examples of good men' TH 10

*not an ymaginacion a then, mas an very gyrryow ha **exampill** agan Savioure Jhesu crist* 'not the imagination of man, but the very words and example of our Saviour Jesus Christ' TH 21

*Indelma me a rug dysquethas thewgh pandra ew charite, maga ta dre an discans a crist vell dre an **examples** a crist y honyn* 'Thus I have shown you what charity is, both through the teaching of Christ as through the examples of Christ himself' TH 23

*martesyn y eff a yll skynnya in myschew an par na may teffans ha tenna re erell dre aga teball **examplis** ha gwrythyans* 'perhaps he may fall into harm of that kind if they happen through their bad examples and deeds to attract others' TH 25a

*dre an **exampill** ma surly ny russa an egglos a crist dos then dishonor han disordyr a wylsyn ny* 'through the example the Church of Christ would not have come to the dishonour and disorder which we have seen' TH 39

*Ha mars owhy desyrus the gafus **exampill** in matyr ma* 'And if you are desirous of obtaining an example in this matter' TH 49a

*Merowgh inweth war germany, ha kemerogh **exampyl** anethy* 'Look also at Germany and take example of her' TH 49a

*In oll an kith **examples** ma ny a well maga strang tra dell ew transsubstantiation* 'In all these same examples, we see how strange a thing is transubstantiation' TH 56a-57

*Na esyn vsya argumentys, mas vsya **exampels** Christ* 'Let us not use arguments, but use the examples of Christ' SA 61a.

The default word for 'example' in the revived language should perhaps be either **ensampel**, *****ensamplys** or **exampyl**, **examplys**.

EXILE, TO EXILE

The word ***diures*** *exul* 'exile' occurs at OCV §301. On the basis of that and by analogy with Breton, Nance devised *****dyvro** 'exiled', *****dyvroa** 'to exile', *****dyvroeth** 'exile'. None of these items is attested in the texts. The only word relating to 'exile' in the texts is the verbal adjective of *****exîlya** seen in OM:

*bethens yn mes **exilyys** na theffo onan yn beys the tryge omma neffre* 'let them be exiled away, lest anyone in the world come ever to dwell here' OM 1576-78.

To express the idea of 'exile, person exiled' in Cornish **den exîlys** would be more authentic than **dyvro**. Similarly for 'exile, state of being exiled' would be better rendered *****exîlyans** than *****dyvroeth**.

EXPERIENCE

For 'experience' Nance suggests A) ***prevyans** and B) **skians pernys** (UC *skyans pernys*). **Prevy** 'to prove, to test, to experience' is certainly attested, but not ***prevyans**. Both **skians** 'knowledge' and **pernys** 'bought' are attested, but the phrase **skians pernys** is not. Nance also suggests **experyens** (UC *experyens*) for 'experience by observation'. **Experyens** is well attested and is used to mean 'experience, proof by experience'.

experyens

*ha moy worthy y vryans yv the kemendya dyblans del welys vy **experyans** gonethys ganso certen* 'and more worthy his actions are to be commended certainly as I saw by experience wrought by him indeed' BM 4389-92

*According the henna Ith esa thyn profet Job **experience** an miserabyll stat a mab den* 'According to that the prophet Job had experience of the miserable state of mankind' TH 7

*Surely ny vynsan cresy an aweyll, nave an catholyk egglos the ry thym **experiens*** 'Surely I would not believe the gospel, if the catholic Church did not give me the experiential proof' TH 37a

*Ena ny a yll gwelas an pith a ren ny the aswone dre **experiens*** 'Then we can see that which we recognize by experience' TH 40.

EYES

The dual **dewlagas** is common in earlier Middle Cornish both when referring to the eyes of one person and to the eyes of a group of people:

*Ena mur a vylyny pedyr ʒe gryst a welas y scornye hay voxscusy trewe yn y **ʒewlagas*** 'Then Peter saw much wrong done to Christ, his being scorned and cuffed, men spitting in his eyes' PA 83ab

*y wholhas y **ʒewlagas** gans y eyll leyff o gosys* 'he washed his eyes with his one hand which was bloody' PA 219c

*hay dagrow a ʒevera hay **dewlagas** pur ʒewhans* 'and her tears flowed from her eyes very quickly' PA 222b

*yn dyspyt th'y **thewlagas** my a wyth an gueel a ras* 'in spite of his eyes I will keep the rods of grace' OM 2058-59

*me a'th pys yn cheryte a sawye ow **dewlagas*** 'I beg you in charity to heal my eyes' PC 395-96

*lemyn gans ow **devlagas** sur me a wel* 'now with my eyes indeed I see' PC 410-11

*arluth agan **dewlagas** yv marthys claf ow colyas* 'Lord, our eyes are wondrous sick through watching' PC 1066-67

*hag a'th wor bys yn cayphas yn dyspyt the'th **devlagas*** 'and will send him to Caiaphas in spite of your eyes' PC 1192-93

GERYOW GWIR eyes

me a vyn y thyscuthe hag yn spyt thotho true war y fas ha'y **devlagas** 'I will uncover him and in spite of him spit on his face and eyes' PC 1394-95

me a tru sur vn clotte bras ware yn y **theulagas** 'I will spit surely a great clot upon his eyes' PC 1399-400

hag ath whyp war an wolok may whylly guryghon ha mok the **thevlagas** *a dre dro* 'and will whip you on the face so that you see sparks and smoke around your eyes' PC 2100-02

ha henna ny a'n guylvyth gans **devlagas** 'and that we will see with eyes' RD 53-54

yn sur gans ow **devlagas** *ow syuel me a'n guelas* 'surely with my eyes I saw him rise' RD 529-30

me a'n guelas dre mur ras a'n beth gans ov **devlagas** *ow mos the'n nef* 'I saw him through great grace with eyes rising from the grave going to heaven' RD 616-18

kepar del yv mur y ras roy thy'm gans ow **dewlagas** *y weles wheth* 'as his grace is great, may he grant me to see him again with my own eyes' RD 791-92.

Later, however, the dual **dewlagas** is replaced by the plural **lagasow**, **lagajow**

a rak agan **lagasow** *a les ol y wolyow ny a welas* 'before our eyes we saw all his wounds spread wide' RD 1492-94

why a vith kepar ha du hagys **lagasow** *a vith clerys* 'you will be like God and your eyes will be made clear' TH 3a

an venyn a welas y bos an frut da the thybbry ha teg the sight y **lagasow** *ha pleasant the veras warnetha* 'the woman saw that the fruit was good to eat and fair to the sight of her eyes and pleasant to look at' TH 3a

ha gans henna ow dalhe **lagasow** *an bobyll* 'and also blinding the eyes of the people' TH 19a

henew the venya gans agan dewleff ha treys, gans agan **lagasow** *ha scovornow, gans agan ganowow ha tavosow* 'that means with our hands and feet, with our eyes and ears, with our mouths and tongues' TH 21a

syttys the rag agan **lagasow** 'set before our eyes' TH 42

ow quelas gans aga **lagasow** *kyge* 'seeing with our eyes of flesh' TH 56

Ne ve the bar, re Gasak! na ny'n gwelvith **lagasaw** *i'n bys hagan* 'There was never your equal, by Cadoc! nor will eyes ever see in the world' BK 1974-76

E weflow ha'y **lagasow** *ha'y goyntnans o mar fasow, mayth egan owth umgelly ol clamderak* 'His lips and his eyes and his countenance was so intimidating, that we were swooning and faint' BK 2328-32

Arthor a gel e rasow in spyt in e **lagasow** 'Arthur will lose his graces in spite of his eyes' BK 2710-11

gans tha **lagasowe** *alees ty a weall pub tra omma* 'with your eyes wide open you will see everything here' CW 694-95

n'ena agoz **lagagow** *ra bos geres* 'then your eyes will be opened' Rowe

145

eyes   **GERYOW GWIR**

Pe reege a vennin gwellas tro an wethan da rag booze, ha der o hi blonk tha'n **lagagow** 'When the woman saw that the tree was good for food and that it was pleasant to the eyes' Rowe

Ha **lagagow** *angie ve gerres ha angie oyah teler an gye en noath* 'And their eyes were opened and they knew that they were naked' Rowe

lagas, **lagasaw** 'eye, eyes' Bodewryd MS.

For those revivalists who prefer Tudor or Late Cornish forms, the plural **lagasow**, **lagajow** is clearly preferable to the obsolescent **dewlagas**.

F

FAN, TO FAN

Lhuyd gives the noun *guinzal* s.v. *Flabellum* 'fan' at AB: 60a, This Nance respells as *gwynsel f.* 'a winnowing fan'. On the basis of *gwynsel* Nance devised *gwynsella 'to fan', a word that is not otherwise attested. The traditional verb for 'to fan' is **fanya**:

> *neb na whytho grens **fannye** gans y lappa worth an eth* 'whoever does not blow, let him fan with his lappet at the hearth' PC 1243-44.

There is no need to introduce the unattested ***gwynsella** into the revived language.

FACE

Nance used *enep* for 'face' because he believed that the word was still widely used in Late Cornish. His based this belief on a single sentence in an unpublished manuscript of William Borlase. Such evidence is not necessarily trustworthy. We also have the following entry: *pagina*, **eneb** 'page' OCV §751, where **eneb** means 'page of a book', rather than 'face'. Lhuyd gives the following entries:

> *Contra... Against C.* **Enap**, *bidn* AB: 51a
> *Facies... A face, a visage... C.* **Enap** AB: 58a
> *Vultus... The face, the countenance or visage. C.* **Enap** AB: 179a
> *Facies... C.* **Enap** AB: 292b.

John Keigwin also writes **enapp** in his translation of Genesis 1: *Ema reaze gennan thu keneffra lazoan toane haaz a eze wor **enapp** an noare* 'We have given you every herb bearing seed that is upon the face of the earth,' though we do not know Keigwin's source for this word.

It must be admitted, however, that the noun **enep** or **enap** is not attested elsewhere in the Middle or Late Cornish texts. The word for 'face' is always either A) **fâss** or B) **bejeth** (< *visage*):

face

A **fâss**

*ma teth an goys ha dropye war y **fas** an caradow* 'so that the blood happened to drop upon his face, the beloved' PA 59b

*yn y **fas** y a drewe* 'they were spitting in his face' PA 196c

*ny a'd wra ty then a bry haval d'agan **face** whare* 'we will make you, man, of clay, like unto our face immediately' OM 59-60

*drog yw genef gruthyl den precyous ha haval thu'm **fas*** 'I am sorry to have made man, finely wrought and like my face' OM 417-18

*the lef arluth a glewaf saw the **face** my ny welaf* 'your voice I hear, O Lord, but I do not see your face' OM 587-88

*ty re thyswrug eredy hevelep tho'm **face** vy vrry nep o marrek len* 'you have killed indeed a likeness to my hace, Uriah, who was a loyal knight' OM 2336-38

*gans queth me a vyn cuthe y **fas** hag onan a'n guysk* 'I shall cover his face with a cloth and someone shall strike him' PC 1370-71

*me a vyn y thyscuthe hag yn spyt thotho true war y **fas** ha'y devlagas* 'I shall uncover him and in spite of him spit upon his face and eyes' PC 1393-95

*a harlot yn spit the'th **fas** gans ov scorge tys ha tas me a'th wysk may fo drok pyn* 'O scoundrel, in spite of your face with my scourge I shall strike you back and forth so as to give you nasty pain' PC 2106-08

*arluth ro thy'mo an gras vnwyth the weles the **fas*** 'Lord, give me the grace of seeing your face just once' RD 826-27

*arluth ihesu ro thy'm an gras par may feyf gvyw the gafos spas gynes hythev sur yn nep plas may bome vu ha guel a'th **fas*** 'Lord Jesus, give me grace that I may be worthy to find a place with you today indeed somewhere, that I may have a view of your face' RD 839-42

*form a'y **fas** a thysquethaf* 'I will show the form of his face' RD 1692

***fas** ihesu gynef yma yn hyuelep gurys a'y whys* 'I have the face of Jesus in an image made of his perspiration' RD 1704-05

*in ov **fays** cothys yma cleves vthyk* 'a dreadful disease has fallen upon my face' BM 728

*in ov **fays** cleves yma* 'there is a disease on my face' BM 738

*sur orth fysmens age **fays** crustunyon yth havalsens* 'indeed by the features of their faces they would seem to be Christians' BM 1205-06

*ny gar den gueles ov **fas*** 'no man wishes to see my face' BM 1361

*nyns yv purguir rag clevyen dones in **fays** arlythy* 'it is not in truth for lepers to come before the face of lords' BM 3114-15

*maria del yth peseff sav an re ma corff ha **fays*** 'Mary, as I beseech you, heal these men in body and face' BM 3138-39

*ov cowyth ty yv sawys cler ha tek knesen ha **fays*** 'my friend, you have been healed cleanly and fairly in skin and face' BM 3143-44

*I[n] wysce ath **face** te a thebbyr the vara* 'In the sweat of your face shall you eat your bread' TH 6

*eff a ve gylwys ell gans ran gyllwis mer therag an **face** a Du* 'he was called an angel by some called great before the face of God' TH 8

GERYOW GWIR					farewell

hag yth esans ow pewa warlerth an letterall sens a la moyses mar compis in **face** *an bys* 'and they lived according to the literal sense of the law of Moses so perfectly in the face of the world' TH 26a

In xvii a mathew, ny a rede fatell ve crist transfiguris, ha fatell rug y **face** *shynya kepar han howle* 'In the 17th chapter of Matthew we read that Christ was transfigured, and that his face shone like the sun' TH 56a

Caradowder ema y'th **fas** *ha golowder* 'There is kindliness in your face and brilliance' BK 1755-57

Asew coyth y'n gorfensen, a'n caffan arag ow **fas** 'How quickly would I put an end to him were I to get him before my face' BK 2291-92

Ego sum Alpha et Omega heb dallath na dowethva pur wyre me ew omma agy than clowdes war **face** *an dower in sertan* 'Ego sum Alpha and Omega, without beginning or end indeed I am, here within the clouds upon the face of the waters truly' CW 1-5

me a wra ge dean a bry havall thagan **face** *whare* 'I will make you, man, of clay like to our face presently' CW 345-46

ha pur vskes gwraf an pratt then serpent in spyte thy **face** 'and very swiftly I'll do the trick to the serpent in spite of your face' CW 518-19

nyng es owne thym ahanas drefan bose mar deake tha **face** 'I am not afraid of you, because your face is so beautiful' CW 562-63

theth voice arluth a glowaf saw tha **face** *me ny wellaf sure er ow gew* 'I hear your voice, Lord, but your face indeed I cannot see to my misfortune' CW 1166-68.

B **bejeth**

ha tewlder wor **bedgeth** *an downder* 'and darkness upon the face of the deep' JKeigwin

Pelea era why moaz, moz, fettow, teag, Gen agaz **bedgeth** *gwin, ha agaz blew mellyn?* 'Where are you going, going, fair maid, with your pale face and your yellow hair?' ACB: F f 4 *verso*

ha spiriz Deu reeg guaya var **budgeth** *an dour* 'and the spirit of God moved upon the face of the water' BF: 51

mero ma res gennam do vy kanifer lushan gen haz, pe es var ol **budgeth** *an aor* 'behold I have given you every plant with seed, which is upon all the face of the earth' BF: 53.

Pace Nance, the evidence of the texts suggests that **fâss** and **bejeth** should be the ordinary words for 'face' in Cornish.

FAREWELL

In the revived language it is common to say **Duw genowgh** or **Duw genes** for 'goodbye, farewell'. This expression is found twice in Borde:

Dew genawhy 'God be with you' Borde
Dew gena why 'God be with you' Borde.

farewell GERYOW GWIR

An alternative form is **Bednath Duw genowgh**, though this is used for both 'Greetings, hail' as well as 'goodbye, farewell':

Banneth du genough *tus vays* 'Greetings, good sirs' BM 534
Banneth du genogh *re bo an dynnyte us dymmo reys oma sur drethogh why me an grontse dyogel lowenhe the den arel du dustuny* 'Hail to you; the dignity which has been given to me here by you, I would have certainly granted more willingly to another man, as God is my witness' BM 3093-98
Bena tew gena *why, hostes da* 'God be with you, good hostess' Borde
Benetu gana 'Farewell' Carew.

It must be admitted, however, that the commonest and the most unambiguous expression in the texts for 'goodbye, farewell' is ***farwèl***:

farwel *ov arluth guella* 'farewell, my excellent lord' OM 2165
farwel *ov arluth guella* 'farewell, my excellent lord' OM 2289
farwel *ow benneth gynes* 'farewell, my blessing with you' PC 560
ny strechyaf pel genes ***farwel*** 'I shall not long delay; farewell to you' RD 1625
Farwel *ser duk re crist am gruk the vap yv fol* 'Farewell, Sir Duke; by Christ who created me, your son is foolish' BM 474-76
gase ***farwel*** *me a vyn* 'I shall say goodbye' BM 1286
a tekter rychys ***farwell*** 'beauty, riches, goodbye' BM 1366
mones a raff uskis ha schaff genogh ***farwel*** 'I shall go quickly and swiftly; goodbye to you' BM 2732-34
ov mam wek genogh ***farwel*** 'my dear mother, goodbye to you' BM 3178
farwel *genes maria* 'goodbye to you, Mary' BM 3636
Genas ***farwell!*** 'Goodbye to you!' BK 646
Farwell, *canhas plegadaw!* 'Goodbye, pleasant messenger' BK 2409
Canhas, ***farwel!*** 'Messenger farewell' BK 2443
Farwel, *suffran mas!* 'Goodbye, good sovereign' BK 2476
Genough ***farwel***, *gowr gentyl mas!* 'Goodbye to you, gentle good sir' BK 2884-85
Farwell, *ru'm fer! ow cosyn whek* 'Goodbye, by my fair, my dear cousin!' BK 2892-93
ow arluth, genowgh ***farwell!*** 'my lord, goodbye to you!' BK 3047
Farewell *ow hothman an nef* 'Goodbye, my friend from heaven' CW 718.

In the light of all the above examples, it might be sensible for revivalists to give **farwèl** parity with **Duw genes**, **Duw genowgh**.

FATHER

The ordinary word for 'father' is **tas**, *plural* **tasow**. Unexpectedly perhaps, the plural **tasow** does not show lenition of the initial consonant after the definite article. This can be clearly seen from the examples in the texts:

Ima lowarth onyn o bostia, fatla vgy faith **an tasow** *coth a vam egglys inansy* 'many boast that the faith of the ancient fathers of mother Church is in them' SA 59a

dir girryow **an tasow** *a vam egglos* 'through the words of the fathers of mother Church' SA 64

lowarth onyn erall **an tasow** *coeth* 'many others of the ancient fathers' SA 64

Lowena theugh, a vyghterne, hag onors drys **an tasow***!* 'Joy to you, O king, and honours beyond the fathers!' BK 1956-57

ha vyn towle pehosow **an tasow** *war an ffledgiow bys an tresa han peswera denythyans* 'and will visit the sins of the fathers upon the children unto the third and fourth generation' Keigwin

Rag vê guz Arleth Deiu o'm Deiu guir a vonyn tha tralia peha **an tazow** *vor an fleaz than tridgia ha padjurra hinneth* 'For I your Lord God am a true God to visit the sins of the fathers upon the children to the third and fourth generation' BF: 55.

In Late Cornish **tas** is sometimes replaced by **sîra**, particularly, though not exclusively, in the phrase *sîra ha dama* 'mother and father'. **Sîra** is not found in the plural, where **tasow** is still used (see the example from Keigwin above).

Telhar a **seera** 'my father's place' BF: 29

Worria guz **seera** *ha dama el guz dethiow beth pel vor an tir es res thees gen guz Arleth Deiu* 'Honour your father and mother that your day will be long in the land given to by your Lord God' BF: 55

Ti guras gurthy dha goz **sira***, ha dama, rag goz dydhiou bos pel var an tir es res dh'ys gans Arleth Deu* 'Thou shalt honour your father and mother that your days may be long in the land given to you by the Lord God' Gwavas MS

Seerah *dama ha vee honan* 'Father, mother and I myself' Bilbao MS

Ha madra ta, Pandrig **seera***, ha damma* 'And consider well what father and mother did' ACB: F f 3

Pew vedn a why gawas rag **seera** *rag guz flo?* 'Who will you get as father for your child?' ACB: F f 4 *verso*.

Pryce, however, has a sentence in which **dama** occurs with **tas** rather than **sîra**: *En metten pan a why sevel, why rez cawse tha guz* **taz***, ha guz damma* 'In the morning, when you rise, you must say to your father and mother' ACB: E e 4 *verso*.

father   **GERYOW GWIR**

It should incidentally be understood that **sîra** is not the same word as **sera**, plural **serys** 'sir'. **Sera** is the equivalent of English 'sir', whereas **sîra** corresponds to English 'sire'.

The ordinary word for 'grandfather' is **hendas**, plural **hendasow**, which may also mean 'ancestor':

auus **hendat** 'grandfather' OCV §129

Rag kepar maner dell rug eff temptia agan **hendasow** *ny Adam hag eva* 'For in the same way that he tempted our ancestors Adam and Eve' TH 3a

the wonys innan ny an pith a ruga gonys in agan **hendasow** *adam hag eva* 'to work in us what he wrought in our ancestors Adam and Eve' TH 5a

Ny a rug peha kepar hagan **hendasow** 'We sinned like our ancestors' TH 9a

I fe deswethys thewgh, tus vas, kyns lymma[n] in kynsa homely fetell ve agan **hendasow** *ny, adam hag eve, dre an singular daddar han speciall favoure a thu golosek, creatis nobyll ha worthy creaturs* 'It was demonstrated to you, good people, ere now in the first homily that our ancestors, Adam and Eve by the singular goodness and special favour of almighty God were created noble and worthy creatures' TH 12

ha henna o dre pehosow agan **hendasow** *ny* 'and that was through the sins of our ancestors' TH 12

kenth ew ow **hendas** *cayne pur bad dean lower accomptys* 'though my grandfather Cain is reckoned a pretty bad man' CW 1446-47

me a ra dyllas thyma par del wrug ow **hendasow** *haw* **hendas** *cayme whath en bew* 'I will make clothes for myself as my ancestors and my grandfather Cain [is] still alive' CW 1478-80

me ny allaf convethas y bosta ge ow **hendas** 'I cannot understand that you are my grandfather' CW 1609-10

am corf yth os devethys hag a adam tha **hendas** 'you derive from my body and from Adam your grandfahter' CW 1612-13

a soweth gwelas an pryes genaf y bosta lethys mars ew ty cayne ow **hendas** 'alas that I see the time that you are killed, if you are Cain my grandfather' CW 1648-50

cayne whath kenth ota ow **hendas** *tha aswon me ny wothyan* 'Cain, though you are my grandfather, I was not able to recognize you' CW 1660-61

der temptacon an teball ow **hendas** *adam pur weare eave re gollas der avall an place gloryous pur sure* 'through the temptation of the evil one my ancestor Adam indeed has lost through the apple the glorious place very truly' CW 2133-36.

Lhuyd, however, also cites **tas gwydn** and **sîra wydn** as Cornish words for 'grandfather':

Corn **Taz gwydn** [& ***Sira wydn***] 'a grandfather' AB: 3b
Avus… A Grandfather … †C. **Hendat, sira ṳidn** AB: 44b.

Although Lhuyd cites ***Taz gwydn*** once, it is probable that the actual form had been *****tas wydn**, where the adjective showed permanent lenition. The permanent lenition of the initial consonant of the adjective probably came about through the frequent use of the phrase in the vocative case, i.e. pre-British **tate winne*. It is likely that later **sîra wydn** is based on *****tas wynn**, *****tas wydn**.

Lhuyd has a further word for 'ancestors', namely **ragdasow**: *Majores... Ancestors, predecessors, forefathers. C. **Rhagdazu*** AB: 84ab. Borlase (page 404), presumably from Lhuyd gives: ***Ragdazu*** *Forefathers or **rhag-dazu***. Pryce, on the other hand, gives **RHAGADAZ**, *pl.* ***Ragadazu***, *an ancestor, a forefather* ACB: X 3 *verso*. Pryce's form is almost certainly a misreading. **Ragdasow** is etymologically correct and *****ragadasow** (**ragadazow*) should be emended to **ragdasow** (*ragdazow*).

TO FEED

For 'to feed' Nance gives **maga**. This is the commonest word in the texts for 'to feed' both human beings and animals; it can be used intransitively also:

*lemmyn ny a yll gwelas lauar du **maga** del wra neb a vynno y glewas* 'now we can see that the word of God feeds him who hears it' PA 12cd

*leman why a yl gueles laver dev **maga** del wra neb a yl y kemeres* 'now you can see that the word of God feeds him who can receive it' PC 70-2

*oma ty a veth **megys** gans boys eleth in tor ma* 'here you will be fed with angelic food now' BM 3886-87

*ihesu dyso y crasseeff gans boys neff pan of **megys*** 'Jesus, I thank you that I am fed with heavenly food' BM 3892-93

*ny a vith **megys** gans an bos a lell feith ha bewek* 'we shall be fed with the food of a true and lively faith' TH 41

*Eff a leverys, gwra **maga** ow eyne ve* 'He said: Feed my lambs' TH 43

*Eff a leverys the pedyr, gwra **maga** ow devis* 'He said to Peter, Feed my sheep' TH 43

*henn o the **maga** y flok* 'that was, to feed his flock' TH 44

*Gwra **maga** ow eyn ha **maga** ow deves* 'Feed my lambs and feed my sheep' TH 44

*Pan ve an vhella aucthorite the pedyr reys rag **maga** an devas a crist* 'When the highest authority was given to Peter to feed the sheep of Christ' TH 45

*ow gwetha inweth an succession an epscobow a ve thea pedyr an apostell han tyrmyn a rug agan Savyour wosa y thethyrryans commyttya y thevas the vos **megys*** 'keeping also the succession of the bishops that have been since the time of Peter the apostle and the time that our Saviour after his resurrection committed his sheep to be fed' TH 49

*eff a rug affyrmya fatell o an kyg a vynna eff ry thynny the **vaga** warnotha, fatell vetha an kithsam kyge na a vetha rys rag an bewnans a oll an bys* 'he affirmed that the flesh he would give

feed

for us to feed upon, was the very same flesh that would be given for the life of all the world' TH 52

Indella eff a ylly y ry in kith banket benegas ma thynny the **vaga** *warnotha* 'Thus he could give it to us in this same blessed banquet to feed upon it' TH 54

may teffa pub naturall mam ha **maga** *y flehes gans an substans ay corfe y honyn* 'so that every natural mother might feed her children with the substance of her own body' TH 54a

rag henna ew an foode a ren ny **maga** *warnotha pan rellon receva an sacrament* 'for that is the food that we feed on when we receive the sacrament' TH 57a

lowarth mamb wore e flehis the benenas erall the **vaga** 'many mothers send their children to other women to feed them' SA 59

rag eth ony **megys** *gans an keth sam tra vgy an elath ow gwelas* 'for we are fed by the same thing that the angels see' SA 59

mes ef agan **magas** *ny gans e gorf e honyn* 'but he fed us with his own body' SA 59

a ra an mam **maga** *e flogh gans e leath?* 'does the mother feed her child with her milk?' SA 59

Indella emay Christ vrth agyn **maga** *ny gans e kiyg ha gos e gorf* 'So does Christ feed us with his blood and his body' SA 59

ema ef agyn **maga** *gans e kegg e honyn* 'he feeds us with his own flesh' SA 59a

emay vrth agan **maga** *gans e woos* 'he feeds us with his blood' SA 59a

an corf ema tibbry rag malla an enef bos **megys** 'the body eats so that the body may be fed' SA 61

fatla vgy an bobell ow leverall an kigg na ill recevia gifte Dew, henna ew bewnans heb dewath, ew **megis** *gans corf ha gois agen saviour Christ* 'how do people say that the flesh cannot receive the gift of God, that is everlasting life, which fed by the body and blood of our Saviour Christ?' SA 63a

gwra marvgian pan vosta devethis in ban then reverent alter the vos **megis** *gans an spirituall bois* 'be amazed when you come up to the sacred altar to be fed with the spiritual food' SA 63a

tho ni an parah ma eaue gon **maga** 'we are his flock; he feeds us' BF: 39.

Nance also cites **bosa**, which is cited once by Lhuyd as **buza** 'to feed' at AB: 276a. Lhuyd's form is suspect, since the expected shape of a verb based on **boos** 'food' < Old Cornish **buit**, might be ***bosa** rather than ***busa**.

The noun **sùsten** 'food, sustenance' is well attested in the texts and from it derives the verb **sùstena** 'to feed, to nurture'. The verbal noun was probably stressed on the first syllable and there are a three of examples, all from OM:

my ha'm gurek ha'm flogh byhan bysy vyth the **sostene** 'me and my wife and my little child, it will be necessary to feed' OM 397-98

rag **sustene** *beunans thy'n rys yw porrys lafurrye* 'to sustain life it is very necessary for us to labour' OM 682-83 *rag may fewgwhy* **sostoneys** *eugh the wonys guel ha ton* 'that you may be fed, go to cultivate field and meadow' OM 1163-64.

Tregear also uses **noryshya**:

ow talleth gans myraclis, **norysshys** *gans govenek, encresshys gans charite* 'beginning with miracles, nourished by hope, increased with charity' TH 49.

The default word for 'to feed' is **maga**. **Sùstena** and **noryshya** are also legitimate. ***Bosa** is a *hapax legomenon*; it is not cited in context and its phonology is unexpected. It is perhaps best avoided.

FEET

The Cornish word for 'foot' is **troos**, and the plural **treys**. A dual form **dewdros** occurs in earlier Middle Cornish:

A **dewdros**

ij droys Ihesus caradow hay ij leyff y a delly 'they were penetrating the two feet of Jesus and his two hands' PA 159c

kenter scon dre the **devtros** *my a's guysk may fo drok lam* 'I will soon strike a nail through your two hands so you will get a shock' PC 2781-82

me a's ten athysempys an thyv yn mes a'y thywle hag a'y **thewtros** *kekyffrys* 'I will pull them both straightway out of his two hands and his two feet' PC 3152-24.

In later texts, however, **dewdros** is replaced by the plural **treys**. **Dewla** 'two hands', however, always appears in the dual. Thus the phrase **treys ha dewla** 'hands and feet' is universal in Cornish:

B **treys**

hag ena ij an scorgyas yn tebel gans ij scorgye ha hager fest an dygtyas corf ha pen **treys ha dewle** 'and then they scourged him evilly with two whips and very grimly they treated him, head, feet and hands' PA 130cd

me a vyn mos the vre ow arluth **treys ha devle** 'I shall go to anoint my lord, feet and hands' PC 473-74

ha'n kelmyns **treys ha dule** *ha'n hembrynkys bys thy'nny* 'and let them bind him hands and feet and let them bring him to us' PC 583-84

yma ow **trys ha'm dule** *thyworthef ow teglene* 'my feet and hands are shaking off me (with the cold)' PC 1216-17

ha kelmys **treys ha dule** *ynny hy bethens taclyys* 'and bound feet and hands let him be fixed to it' PC 2163-64

yn pren crous bethens gorrys ha **treys ha dyulef** *kelmys* 'let him be put on the cross and his feet and hands bound' PC 2374-75

feet

treys ha dyvlef *a pup tu fast tackyes gans kentrow hern* 'feet and hand on both sides fixed with iron nails' PC 2937-38

scorgis gans an ʒethewon kentrewys ***treys ha dula*** 'scourged by the Jews, feet and hands nailed' BM 2602-03

treys ha dule *kentreweys berth in grovs inter ladron* 'feet and hands nailed on the cross between thieves' BM 3035-36

spykys bras a horne dre an ***treys ha dewleff*** 'great spikes of iron through the feet and hands' TH 15a.

This corresponds to the usage in both Welsh and Irish, where the word for 'hands' usually appears in the dual form but 'feet' in the plural.

In the revived language 'feet' should be **treys** in preference to **dewdros**. 'Hands and feet' should always be translated **treys ha dewla**.

FLINT

For 'flint' Nance suggests **flynt**, **men flynt** and ***callester**. This last is attested once: *A peble... [Pebles] C. †**Cellester*** AB: 283a. Lhuyd adds a query after †***Cellester***, asking whether it is to be identified with Latin *Silex, Silicis* 'flint'. †***Cellester*** is a congener of Weslh *callestr* 'flint' and Breton *kailhastr* 'silex, flint'. Although Lhuyd puts an obelus before †***Cellester***, thus suggesting that the word is Old Cornish, the word does not occur in OCV.

The only unambiguous word for 'flint' is **men flynt**:

pan yllyn ny yntrethon drey dour a'n ***meen flynt*** *garow dre grace a'n tas a vghon* 'when we can among us bring water from the rough flint stone through the grace of the Father above' OM 1859-61

Silex... A flint-stone. C. ***Maen flent*** AB: 150b

maen flent 'a flint-stone' ACB: T.

Men-flent 'a flint-stone' Borlase.

The entries in both ACB and Borlase presumably derive from Lhuyd. **Men flynt** is the authentic word for 'flint stone'.

FLOCK

For 'flock' referring specifically to sheep Nance gives A) **para**, B) **tonek** and C) **flock** (UC *flok*). A and B are attested once each. **Para** appears indeed to mean 'flock of sheep', but the sense of **tonek** is less clear. It may derive from **tonn, todn** 'turf, grass' and thus mean 'animals at pasture, herd, flock'. There is no indication that it referred specifically to sheep. The best attested word for 'flock of sheep; flock of a Christian pastor' is C) **flock**:

A para

*tho ni an **parah** ma eaue gon maga ha rag e theuaz eave gon kibmeare* 'we are the flock, he feeds us; and for his sheep he takes us' BF: 39

B tonek

*y lauarsons ol an cas yz ezons yn vn **tonek** bys yn galyle zy whelas ha ze gows worth Ihesus wek* 'they told all the matter; they went in one flock to Galilee to seek and to speak to dear Jesus' PA 257 cd

C flock

*pan vo guyskys an bugel y fy an deues abel hag ol an **flok** a thybarth* 'when the shepherd is struck, the sheep flee away and all the flock departs' PC 893-95

*In kepar maner S Poull a cowsys then brontyryan ha then eleders in Ephesus yma eff worth aga gwarnya the gemeras with thetha aga honyn, ha the oll an **flocke*** 'Similarly St Paul spoke to the priests and the elders at Ephesus; he warns them to take care of themselves and of all the flock' TH 32

*ha oll an re na a ve in ministers in egglos a crist thea nyna bys in dith hethow han charg anetha ow rewlya an **flok** a crist* 'and all those were as ministers in the Church of Christ thereafter until today and their charge was to govern the flock of Christ' TH 41a

*Rag yma an scriptur ow prevy fatell rug agan savyour appoyntya Pedyr thyn kyth vhell rome ma, ha thotheff a ve res ha delyuerys an charge war oll an **flok** a crist* 'For the scripture proves that our Saviour appointed Peter to this same high office, and to him was given and delivered the charge over all the flock of Christ' TH 42a

*An gyrryow ma a crist a ve cowsys pell theragan tyrmyn a rug crist ry an commondementys arell the pedyr, henn o the maga y **flok*** 'These words of Christ were spoken long before the time that Christ gave the other commandments to Peter, that is, to feed his flock' TH 44

*yma res thetha an rule han gouernement an holl **flok** a crist, dre blonogath Du, oma in bys* 'to them is give the rule and government of all the flock of Christ by the will of God here on earth' TH 47a.

It is clear from the above that the usual word in Cornish for 'flock of sheep; Christian flock' was **flock**.

FLOWER

Nance taught that the customary word for 'flower' was either ***blejen** f.*, plurals **blejyow**, **blejennow** or **blejyowen** *f.*, plural **blejyow**. None of this is really true. The word ***blejen** is unattested in Middle Cornish. *Flos **blodon*** 'flower' occurs at OCV §670 and Lhuyd gives ***bledzhan*** AB: 60b, 240c and ***bledzhîan*** AB: 10b as words for 'flower'. Moreover the plural **blejyow** occurs in the fossilized phrase ***Dewsull blegyow*** 'Palm Sunday' (literally 'Flower Sunday') at PA 27a. In the texts, however, the word for

flower

'flower' is **flour**, *plural* **flourys**, with a variant singulative **flouren**. **Flour**, **flouren** can function also mean 'the choicest member of a as a class' or it can function as a quasi-adjective meaning 'flower of, best of'. Here are the attested examples:

A **flour**, **flouren** 'flower'

*palm ha **floris** kekyffris er y byn degis a ve* 'palm and flowers also were carried to meet him' PA 29d

*ny dyf guels na **flour** yn bys yn keth forth na may kyrthys* 'neither grass nor flower grows in that same path where I walked' OM 712-13

*ol an tekter a wylys ny yl taves den yn bys y leuerel bynytha a frut da ha **floures** tek* 'all the beauty I saw no tongue in the word can ever describe of good fruit and of fair flowers' OM 766-69

*yma gynef **flowrys** tek* 'I have with me beautiful flowers' PC 258

*ow benneth ol ragas bo ow tos yn onor thy'mmo gans branchis **flourys** kefrys* 'may you all have my blessing coming to me in honour with branches and flowers as well' PC 265-67

*ha fatell ew oll an glory an broghter han lowender a vabden kepar ha **flowres** in prasow* 'and that all the glory, the splendour and the joy of mankind are like flowers in the meadows' TH 7

*rag pan deffa an welsan ha dalleth seeha an **flowre** a ra clamdera ha cotha the ves* 'for when the stalk begins to wither the flower fades and falls away' TH 7

*kepar dell ra an gwels seha, an **flowre** a glomder* 'as the grass withers, the flower fades' TH 7

*eff a deffe in ban kepar ha **flowren*** 'he grows up like a flower' TH 7

*an tryssa dyth me a wra may fo than gwyth sevall yn ban ha doen dellyow teke ha da ha **flowres** wheag in serten* 'the third day I shall contrive that the trees arise and bear fair and good leaves and sweet flowers indeed' CW 92-5

*lower **flowrys** a bub ehan yn place ma yta tevys* 'behold many flowers of every kind growing in this place' CW 363-64

*me a vyn mos tha wandra omma yn myske an **flowrys*** 'I will go to wander here among the flowers' CW 538-39

*ena yth esa **flowrys** ha frutes teke aga lew* 'there were there flowers and fruits of fine colour' CW 1050-51.

B **flour**, **flouren** 'choicest person or thing; choicest'

*lowene the **flour** an beys yma cas bras wharfethys ha cothys war the pobel* 'hail to the flower of the world; a great happening has occurred and has fallen on your people' OM 1541-43

*Bersabe **flour** ol an bys certus rag the gerense syr vrry a fyth lethys* 'Bathsheba, flower of the world, without doubt for your sake Sir Uriah shall be killed' OM 2121-23

*ov holon ger caradow dew rvth ros **flour** hy hynse* 'my dear beloved hear, God has made you flower of all your contemporaries' OM 2135-36 *thotho gueyt may tanfenny cryst bys yn daras y chy dres pup methek del yv **flour*** 'be sure to send to the door of his house Christ, as he is the flower above all doctors' RD 1630-32

*Out warnes ty fals jugleer defya ov dewov **flour*** 'Damn you, you false schemer, for defying my choicest gods!' BM 921-22

*y a veth pur guir marov rag cafus sur age goys an empour **flour** they golhy* 'they shall indeed be killed to get their blood indeed to wash the flower of emperors' BM 1598-600

*Lowena thu'm arluth stowt, lowena the **flowr** an bys* 'Joy to my brave lord, joy to the flower of the world' BK 378-79

*Keugh ahanan, cannas **flowr!*** 'Go hence, flower of messengers!' BK 1031

*ow arluth, **flowran** an bys, a Gyllywyk* 'my lord, flower of the world, of Kellywyk' BK 1285-86

*Gromersy, arluth cortys, **flowran** ol an arlythy* 'Thank you, courteous lord, flower of the nobility' BK 1594-95

*Trystyough thynny, **flowran** an bys, na berthowgh dowt* 'Trust us, flower of the world, do not fear' BK 1677-79

*Eth os **floran** drys peb i'n noer* 'You are the flower above everyone in the world' BK 1765-66

*Lowena ha ryelder the **flowren** an vyghterneth!* 'Joy and nobility to the flower of kings' BK 1930-3

***Flowran** a skyentolath ha gallosak in leawte os war pub ous* 'Flower of wisdom and mighty in loyalty are you beyond every age' BK 1940-42

*Welcum os, **flowr** canhasow, welcum melwith, ru'm ena'!* 'Welcome are you, flower of messengers, a thousand times welcome upon my soul!' BK 2530-31

*Ow unadow, a garadow, ew mos genas, **flowr** benegas, thy'th scothva in privecter* 'My desire, beloved, is to go with you, blessed flower, to your boudoir in privacy' BK 2947-51.

Whether a botanical flower or a metaphorical one is meant, the word in the revived language should probably be **flour**, **flouren**, *plural* **flourys**. There is no reason to use **blejen**, **blejyowen**, *plural* **blejyow**, except in certain set phrases.

FLUENT

In his 1951 dictionary Nance suggests **freth** to translate 'fluent.' This was a mistake. **Freth** does not mean 'fluent', but rather 'assiduous, impetuous, eager, bold, impudent.' The following are all the examples of **freth** I have been able to find:

*In vn stevya oll y eth bys yn pylat o Iustis vn e3ow 3030 yn **freth** yndelma a leuerys* 'Hurryingly they all went to Pilate who was a justice; a Jew emphatically spoke thus to him' PA 239ab

fluent

*lyuyreugh whet pan theugh mar **freth** pyv a whyleugh* 'say again, since you come so eagerly, who is it you seek' PC 1115-16

*otte lour kunys gyne whythyns lemmyn pup yn **freth** neb na whytho grens fannye* 'here I have a lot of firewood; now let everyone blow assiduously. Let him who doesn't blow, fan' PC 1241-43

*syr doctors rys yv theugh whet bys ma fo gurys an dywet certan gynen laufurye rak an harlot a geus **freth*** 'sir doctors you must still, until the end be achieved, indeed travel with us, for the scoundrel talks glibly' PC 1829-32

*myl weth a uyth an dyweth me a'n te re synt iouyn ha hakere es an dalleth rak henna tus ervys **freth** gor th'y wythe atermyn* 'a thousand times worse, I swear by St Jovyn, and nastier than the beginning, therefore send alert armed men to guard him in time' RD 348-52

*duen scon in ban then meneth ha why covsugh arluth **freth** dotho agis galarov* 'let us go up the mountain soon and you, vigorous lord, tell him your grief' BM 2533-35

*Gwayt bos war a'th lavarow, fatel rylly gorthyby, rag **fregh** ew eff* 'Take care of your words, how you will answer, for he is impetuous' BK 555-57

*Bethans mar **freth** del vynho, nu'm bues owne a gows orto gans gweras Christ, arluth nef* 'Let him be as insistent as he wishes, I am not afraid to speak to him with the help of Christ, Lord of heaven' BK 558-60

*pur welcum ough genan ny del on guer **freth** in casow* 'you are very welcome here with us as we are effective men in battles' BK 1363-64

*Me ew myghtern in Island, maga **freth** avel turand, corf ankengy ha dylys* 'I am king in Iceland, as impetuous as a tyrant, a grim and unrestrained man' BK 1449-52

*Fers of ha **freth**. Penagel a'm sorr gans cam, ef a'n gevyth tebal-lam* 'I am fierce and impetuous. Whoever angers me wrongly will get a nasty shock' BK 1473-75

*Der gras Christ a'gen pernas, me, Modreth, a lever **freth**: Arthur a vyth guarthevyas ha'y yskerans ef a feth* 'By the grace of Christ who redeemed us, I Modred, speak emphatically: Arthur will be victorious and he will vanquish his foes' BK 1486-89

*Hail, arluth fers, **freth** gans cletha!* 'Hail, fierce lord, vigorous with the sword!' BK 1771-72

*Hayl, arluth **freth** ha gallasak!* 'Hail, impetuous, powerful lord!' BK 1780-81

*Kynth ewa **freth**, settyough e coyt (elhas, soweth!) in dan e doyt* 'Though he be bold, set it quick (alas and alack) under his cup' BK 1821-24

***Freth** y feth gweregys, mar peth rys dos the henna, ol the'th desyer* 'He will be vigorously helped, if it is necessary to come to that, all according to your desire' BK 1846-48

*Kyn fe mar **freth** du Halan an vlethan i'n kynsa deyth, me a gows war mab Malan ha ny'n sparya', wor ow fayth!* 'Though he be so bold at the Calends of the year, the first day, I will speak by the son of the Devil, that I shall not spare him, upon my faith!' BK 1880-84

*Lowena this, myghtern **freth**, gwerror fers ha galosak!* 'Joy to you, bold king, a fierce and powerful warrior!' BK 1996-97

*The gyrryow **freth** in tyhogal a'th set in nans* 'Your impudent words in truth will bring you down' BK 2148-50

*An trubut pan ve tochys, e worthyb o tyn ha **freth** hag ef garaw* 'When the tribute was discussed, his answer was sharp and impudent and he was grim' BK 2264-64

*Arthur Gornow, myghtern **freth**, a vyn orta syngy cas* 'Arthur the Cornishman, a truculent king, will join battle with him' BK 2502-03

*Lowena thu'm arluth **freth**, gallosak drys tus an bys!* 'Joy to my impetuous lord, powerful beyond all men in the world!' BK 2554-55.

It is clear from the above examples, that **freth** does not mean 'fluent of speech'. This means that one cannot, for example, translate 'He speaks fluent Cornish' either as ***Yma va ow côwsel Kernowek yn freth** or ***Freth yw y Gernowek**. Instead one must say something like the following:

Yma va ow côwsel Kernowek heb hockya
Yma y gows Kernowek ow resek.

Possibly for a general adjective meaning fluent of speech one might coin an adjective ***frosek** 'flowing, fluent'. If we wish to imitate the writers of traditional Cornish, we should certainly refrain from using **freth** to translate 'fluent'.

FOREST

For 'forest' Nance recommends **coos** (UC *cos*), ***coswyk** and **forest**. **Coos** means 'wood' and refers to something smaller than a forest. ***Coswyk** is unattested in the texts and is apparently unknown in place-names also, being formed on the basis of Welsh *coedwig* 'forest, wood'.

Cosow, the plural of **coos**, is used sometimes used to mean 'primaeval forest':

A **cosow**
*rag henna dune alema yn peldar thaworthe ow thase yn **cosow** mannaf bewa po in bushes ha brakes brase* 'therefore let us go hence far from my father; I will live in the forest or in the bushes and great thickets' CW 1360-63

*ages gweracke ha sethow genaf ytowns y parys me as lead bez yn **cosow** hag ena y fythe kevys plenty lower in pur thefry* 'your bow and arrows behold, I have got them ready; I will lead you into the forest and there plenty [of game] will be found in very truth' CW 1493-47.

Notice that after the second quotation from CW above, the English stage direction reads: *depart lameck. his servant leadethe hem to the Forest near the bushe*. The ordinary word for 'forest' in the Cornish texts, however, is **forest**:

forest   GERYOW GWIR

B **forest**

*Wel we met, cosyn, forsoth 'barth in **forest** ow arluth* 'Well we meet, cousin, indeed in the forest of my lord' BK 40-41

*An keth gwas ma us gena', me a'n cafas, ru'm ena! i'n **forest** ha'n yet degys* 'This same fellow here with me, I found him upon my soul, in the forest and the gate was shut' BK 75-77

*Nyng ew repref tho'm ehan hag awos own, me a dyrhas i'n **forest** a Rosewa* 'I am not ashamed of my family, and because I was afraid, I landed in the forest of Rosewa' BK 96-9

*me a vyn mos pur vskes than **forest** quyck alema ha latha an strange bestas* 'I shall go very quickly to the forest hence and kill the strange animals' CW 1467-69.

Forest should perhaps be the default word for 'forest' in the revived language.

FORM

The default word for 'form' in the Revival has always been **furv** (UC *furf*). This is based on the single entry *forma **furf*** 'form' at OCV §490. In the Middle Cornish texts, however, 'form' is always **form**. One of the examples of the plural **formys** bears the sense 'forms, benches'. This is etymologically speaking the same word as **form** 'form, shape':

*me a's ordyn though wharre cheyrys ha **formys** plente ysethough syre iustis* 'I will order them immediately for you, chairs and forms aplenty; be seated Sir Justice' PC 2228-30

***form** a'y fas a thysquethaf thy'm del y'n ros yn lyen* 'I will show you the form of his face as he gave it to me in the cloth' RD 1692-93

*ha lemen sur golvygyen adro thym yma cothys hag yma **forme** a vynen myternes pur in y greys* 'and now indeed light has fallen around me and there is the form of a woman, a pure queen, in the middle' BM 3681-84

*ha te a wore dre an la an **forme** a sciens ha gwryoneth* 'and through the law you know the form of science and truth' TH 14a

*Rag eff the accontya y honyn nag o va worthy the vos crowsyys in kepar maner ha **forme** dell ve y mester* 'For he considered that he was not word to be crucified in the same way and form as was his master' TH 47

*Indella eff a ylly y ry in kith banket benegas ma thynny the vaga warnotha may halla eff bos oll in oll corfe agan savyour crist the vos in very dede in neff, in visibill **forme** a then, ha in sacrament an alter, invisibli in dan an visibill **forme** a bara ha gwyne* 'Thus he was able to give it to us in that same banquet to feed upon him, so that he might be all in all the body of our Saviour Christ, being in very truth in heaven, in the visible form of a man, and in the sacrament of the altar, invisibly in the visible form of bread and wine' TH 54

*gesowgh ny the persuadya agan honyn y bos in sacrament an aulter in dan an **form** a bara ha gwyne* 'let us persuade ourselves that he is in the sacrament of the altar under the form of bread and wine' TH 54a

*An neyll ew an corfe han gois agan Savioure Jhesu crist ena ryally conteynys, y gela ew an **forme** a bara ha gwyn* 'the one is the body and blood of our Saviour Jesus Christ really contained therein, the other is the form of bread and wine' TH 55
*in visibill shap a then ha **forme** a then* 'in the visible shape of man and form of man' TH 56
*eff ew present in sacrament in dan an **forme** a bara ha gwyne indella mayth ew sertifyes (vel crefeis) agan seyght ny warves hagan perseverens, gans an **formes** han qualites sencible* 'he is present in the sacrament under the form of bread and wine thus, so that our outward sight is assured or corroborated and our perseverance by the sensible forms and qualities' TH 56
*yma cristonyan ow honora in dan an **forme** a bara ha gwyne an pith vsans ow quelas gans aga lagasow kyge* 'Christians honour under the form of bread and with that which they see with their bodily eyes' TH 56
*hen ew an visible **formes** an elementys, ha an invisible corfe ha gois agan savyour Jhesus crist* 'that is, the visible forms of the elements, and the invisible body and blood of our Saviour Jesus Christ' TH 56
*yma clerly ow leverell fatell o an bara a rug crist ry the abostoleth, fatell o va gwrys kyge dre an galus han power a thu, ha fatell o va changys in nature so not in **forme*** 'he clearly says that the bread which Christ gave to his apostles, that it had become flesh throught the power and potency of God, and that it had been changed in nature but not in form' TH 56
*Chang a vn substans the arell, na nyns ew the vos contys vnfitty the vos in sacrament an aulter an **forme** a bara, ha not an an substans a bara* 'The change of one substance to another, nor is it to be considered unfit that the form of bread is in the sacrament of the altar, and not the substance of bread' TH 56a
*An iii-a, rag y bos an **forme** a bara ow remaynya whath in henna yma respect inweth gylwys bara* 'The third, since the form of bread remains in that respect it is still also called bread' TH 57a
*Ny a ra honora in dan an **forme** a bara ha gwyn an pith a welyn* 'we honour under the form of bread and wine that which we see' TH 58.

Notice also that the ordinary word for 'form' in Breton is *furm*.

In view of all the above the ordinary word for the noun 'form' in the revived language in all senses should perhaps be **form** *f*., plural **formys**. This would, of course, mean speaking of **an Form Scrifys Savonek**, rather than **an Furv Scrifys Savonek**.

TO FORSAKE

The verb **forsâkya** 'to forsake' is attested in three different texts:

*Crist indelma a leuer ov sywa neb a vynna **forsakyans** byen ha muer teryov trefov an bys ma y days hay vam y nessevyn hay cothmans hag eff a gvayn roov cans* 'Christ thus says, Whoever wishes to follow me, great and small, let him forsake lands, houses of this world,

forsake　　　　　　　　　　**GERYOW GWIR**

his father and mother, his family and friends and he will get a hundred gifts' BM 382-88

In crist ihesu ny a greys awos ovn a then in beys ny **forsakyn** *y hanow* 'In Christ Jesus we believe; we will not forsake his name for fear of any man in the world' BM 1210-12

in kerth galles **forsakis** *y das hay vam ha ny won pyth eth heb nam ragtho mayth oma serres* 'he has gone, and his father and mother forsaken and I do not know whither he has gone at all, so that I am angry because of it' BM 1940-43

hagan hooll bewnans res thy servia eff a vght pub tra, gansa eff the vewa, ha gansa eff the verwall, ea, ha the **forsakya** *pub tra oll in bys rag kerensa du* 'and all our whole life we must serve him above everything, to live with him and to die with him, yea, and to forsake everything in the world for the sake of God' TH 21a

ha penagull a rella tyrry an re na, aga despisia, po aga deneya, eff a ra deneya ha **forsakya** *an very gwryoneth* 'and whoever breaks those, or despises or denies them, he will deny the very truth' TH 33a

Ha genz an krei a 'ríg Dzhûan guîl, an ledran a **forsakiaz** *an vertshants* 'And with the cry that Jowan made, the robbers forsook the merchants' BF: 17.

It has been suggested that **forsâkya** should be replaced by **gasa** 'to leave'. This is not a sensible recommendation, since **forsâkya** is stronger in sense than **gasa**. A word meaning 'to leave, to let, to allow' is clearly not really synonymous with a verbs whose sense is 'to forsake, to abandon'. Since, moreover, **forsâkya** is attested in both Middle and Late Cornish, it was clearly an integral part of the lexicon of the language. There is no need to avoid it.

TO FOUND

For 'to found' Nance recommends A) **fùndya**; B) **grôndya** and C) ***sêlya**. ***Sêlya** is unattested, being derived by Nance on the basis of *fundamentum* **sel** 'foundation' OCV §758. The word **selya** occurs, but it means 'to seal: *an kigg ew* **selis**, *may halla an nenaf bos defendis* 'The flesh is sealed, that the spirit may be defended' SA 60a.

The two verbs **fùndya** and **grôndya**, however, are well attested:

A **fundya**

omma lemen **fondya** *plays dre voth ihesu a vercy sur me a vyn* 'here now I shall by the will of Jesus of mercy found a place' BM 720-22

Omma me re **fundyas** *plas ryb maria a cambron* 'Here I have founded a place beside Mary of Camborne' BM 990-91

ov chy **fundia** *sur ha grondya manneff uskyes* 'I will swiftly found and establish my house' BM 1150-52

GERYOW GWIR France

*Eff a **fowndyas** y egglos, ha nans ew na moy mas onyn* 'He founded his Church, and there is no more than one' TH 45a
*han brassa assonys a oll egglosyow, ha fatell ve hy **foundyes** dre an auncient appostles Pedyr ha powle* 'and acknowledged the greatest of all Churches and that it was founded by the ancient apostles Peter and Paul' TH 47a-48.

B **grôndya**

*reson[s] y a rey ragthe mes war fals y3 ens **growndys*** 'they gave reasons for it but they were founded upon falsehood' PA 118b
*Nans yw **groundyys** genef vy sol[a] brys gans horbenow* 'it has been founded by me long ago with hand-rammers' OM 2321-24
*ov chy fundia sur ha **grondya** manneff uskyes* 'I will swiftly found and establish my house' BM 1150-52
*Rag oll an congregacion an scismatyk[s] kyn rellens y **groundya** aga honyn apparantly war an scriptur benegas, whath yma thethy aga profession kemerys severally theworth neb drog then ha noghty person* 'For all the congregation of the schismatics, though they apparently ground themselves upon holy scripture, yet their profession is taken severally from some evil man and worthless person' TH 32a
*An owne a res the tus cafus, pan rellens preparia aga honyn the thos then Sacrament ma, a res bos **groundys** war an terribill sentens a S paule in xi chapter in kynsa pistill then Corinthians* 'The fear which men should feel when they prepare themselves to approach this sacrament, should be based upon the terrible sentence of St Paul in the 11th chapter of the first epistle to the Corinthians' TH 51a
*Rag an cawses ma nyg us feithfull colonow vith greviis war y gylwell bara in scriptur, mas ow **groundia** aga honyn war an gyrryow agan Savyour Jhesu crist* 'For these causes no faithful hearts are grieved to call it bread in scripture, but basing themselves upon the words of our Saviour Jesus Christ' TH 57a.

There is no need to use the neologism ***sêlya** 'to found'. **Fùndya** and **grôndya** are quite adequate.

FRANCE

In revived Cornish 'France' is sometimes called ***Pow Frynk**. This is a mistake. In traditional Cornish **Frynk** is never used with the word **Pow**, and indeed ***Pow Frynk** is syntactically incorrect. **Frynk**, like Welsh *Ffrainc*, derives from the plural **Franki* 'Franks'; cf. **Kembra**, Welsh *Cymru* < **Kombrogî* 'fellow countrymen'. If **Pow** were used in Cornish in the name for 'France', one would expect the second element to be an adjective ***Pow Frank** or a plural ***Pow an Francas**. The following are the attested occurrences of the name of France in Cornish:

France   GERYOW GWIR

Eth ough ow nerth ha'm socckers, kepar dell ough ow amors. War tua **Frynk** *fystynnyn* 'You are my strength and my assistance, as you are my friends. Let us hasten to France' BK 2733-35

Nenna mose alez tho scole ha ugge hedda mose tho **Frenk** 'Then I went away to school and after that I went to France' BF: 29

Nenna e eath car rag **Frink** *rag debre an tacklow ewe per trink* 'Then he went away to France to eat the very bitter things' LAM: 226

Materen **Frink***, thera vi a menia, na venja hedda whath gun grevia* 'I mean the King of France; that still would not grieve us' LAM: 226

Juglans… A walnut. C. Kynÿphan **frenk** [lit. 'nut of France'] AB: 74a

Pokkys **Frenk** 'The pox' [*lit.* 'the pox of France'] AB: 82a

Brethonek Pou Lezou en **Vrink** 'the Brythonic of Brittany in France' AB: 222.

There are no examples of ***Pow Frynk** in either Lhuyd's writing or in the traditional texts. It might therefore be sensible to discontinue the use of such a term.

FREE, TO FREE, FREEDOM

Nance recommended the word ***rydh** (UC *ryth*) for the adjective 'free', that is to say 'free, unencumbered, at liberty'. This would have been a congener of Welsh *rhydd* 'free'. Nance believed *ryth vcould be seen in place-names like *Goon Reeth, Wheal Reath*, etc. Unfortunately the element *reath, reeth* in such toponyms is better understood as a spelling for *rudh* 'red' (CPNE: 204), than for an otherwise unattested ***rydh** or ***ryth** 'free'.

There are, however, two attested words for the adjective 'free': A) **frank**; B) **fre**.

Frank is confined to the single example in the Godolphin motto: ***Frank ha leal etto ge*** [i.e. ***Frank** ha lel eth oge*] 'Free and loyal art thou' ACB: E e 4 verso.

Fre is better attested, though it means 'liberal, generous; freely':

*Surly ny russa an egglos a crist dos then dishonor han disordyr a wylsyn ny, na ny vea vices ha drokoleth mar **fre** vsyys* 'Surely the Church of Christ would not have come to the dishonour and disorder which we have seen, nor would vices and wickedness be so freely practised' TH 39

*Te a rug ow dyuan claf, sau ol theso me a'n gaf rag the vos gyntel ha **fre*** 'You made my jaws ache, but I forgive it all to you, because you are noble and liberal' BK 1096-98

*Hayl, arluth **fre**! ha'n gwelha gour, bythquath a ve gwelys in towr na whath a vyth* 'Hail, liberal lord! and the best warrior that ever was seen in a tower or ever will be' BK 1680-84.

Cf. *oll an royow ma ew res thynny dre y vercy eff **frely** ha rag kerensa agan saviour Jhesus crist* 'all these gifts have been given to us freely through his mercy and for the sake of our Saviour Jesus Christ' TH 10a.

For the verb 'to free' there are two possibilities: A) **delyfrya**, **delyvra**; B) **fria**.

Delyfrya, **delyvra** really means 'to deliver, to release' and can sometimes be translated 'to hand over' as well as 'to free'. I have collected the following examples:

A **delyfrya**, **delyvra**

*tresse gwyth hag ef yn cren y pesys du **delyr** vy* 'a third time as he was trembling he prayed, God deliver me' PA 57c

*In meth Ihesus nyng vgy ow mesternges yn bys ma hag a pe ow thus ʒewy nym **delyrfsens** yndelma* 'Jesus said, My kingdom is not of this world, and if it were, my men would not have delivered me thus' PA 102ab

*maner o ʒen eʒewon war dyth pasch worth an Iustis an preson govyn onon ha bos henna **delyffrys*** 'it was a custom of the Jews on the day of the Passover to ask the governor of the prison for one prisoner and that he be freed' PA 124cd

*lemmyn merough pe nyle an dus a vyth **delyffris*** 'now look, which of the men shall be freed' PA 125c

*En eʒewon a armas dre bur envy me a gris **dylyver** ʒynny barabas* 'The Jews cries out for sheer spite, I think, free Barabbas for us' PA 126ab

*mar mynnough me an chasty ol warbarth y[n] nycyte hag an **delyrf** ʒe wary* 'if you wish I will scourge him all together in his ignorance and will set him free' PA 127cd

*a ny woʒas ow mestry bos ʒymmo may fes leʒys bo **delyffris** ʒe wary* 'do you not know that I have authority that you may be killed or set free?' PA 144cd

*pylat pan glewas henna a whelas y ʒ**elyffra*** 'when Pilate heard that he tried to free him' PA 145d

*Camen pylat pan welas na ylly crist **delyffre** ma nan geffo ef sor bras ʒeworth ol an goweʒe* 'When Pilate saw that he could not release Christ without getting great anger from all the company' PA 150ab

*Han grous a ve drehevys ha Ihesus fasteys ynny han pen golas **delyffrys** yn tol o tellys rygthy* 'And the cross was raised and Jesus fixed on it and the base of it delivered into the hole which had been made for it' PA 184ab

*awottense ow kelwel hely ʒoʒo ʒy wyʒe myrugh mar te drehevell ay beynys ʒy **delyffre*** 'Lo, he is calling Elijah to him to protect him; look to see whether he rises up to free him from his torments' PA 203bc

*an golom glas hy lagas yn mes gura hy **delyfre*** 'do release out [of the ark] the blue-eyed dove' OM 1109-10

*my a wra hy **delyfre** whare a das caradow* 'I shall release her straightway, O dear father' OM 1113-14 *hy **delyfre** my a wra yn mes yn hanow a'n tas* 'I shall release her forth in the name of the Father' OM 1117-18

*ha mara leuer den vyth er agas pyn why tra vyth ware guregh y gorthyby the'n arluth ethom yma the wruthyl gans an re-na ef a's **dylyrf** genogh why* 'and if anyone says anything against you, immediately answer him, The Lord has need to use those, he will release them to you' PC 179-84

*pan y'n danfonas ef thy'n mara mynne amendye guel vye y **thylyfrye** hep drocoleth thyworthy'n* 'since he sent him to us, if he is willing to change his ways, it would be better to release him without harm from us' PC 1861-64

*a vynnegh ol assentye rak pask my [the] **thylyfrye** ihesu myghtern yethewon* 'will you all agree that I release at Passover Jesus, king of the Jews?' PC 2037-39

*rak henna my a gosse alemma y **thylyffrye** hep gul dotho na moy gref* 'therefore I should release him hence without doing him any more harm' PC 2216-17

*mara'n **dyllyfryth** hep mar nyns os cothman the cesar* 'if you free him, of course you are no friend to Caesar' PC 2219-20

*mara pythe **dylyfrys** the ihesu pendra vyth gurys* 'if he is freed, what will be done to Jesus?' PC 2371-72

*yma ow kelwel ely aspyugh lemmyn bysy mara tue the **thylyffre** mar a'n **dylyrf** yredy ny a wra ynno crygy hag a'n gorth pur wyr neffre* 'he is calling on Elijah. Watch carefully now if he happen to deliver him. If he does deliver him indeed we will believe in him and will revere him for ever' PC 2959-64

*Nov wel far the gentel knyght eff a pee purguir y wyght a our kyn boys **dylyfrys*** 'Now farewell, gentle knight; he shall truly pay his weight in gold before being freed' BM 3549-51

*maria wyn rag ov les y colmennov gura terry maria mara mynnes **delyfrys** bya surly* 'blessed Mary, for my sake break his bonds; Mary, if you wished, he would surely be freed' BM 3597-600

*me ath **dylerff** an preson oma y tuth rag the leys* 'I shall release you from prison; I have come here for your advantage' BM 3675-76

*Lemen ov map ke theth vam ha lafer dethy heb nam maria theth **delyfrya*** 'Now, my son, go to your mother and tell her plainly that Mary freed you' BM 3692-94

*an horsens re bue methov ha re ases tus an pov me a wor thy **delyvrya*** 'the sons of bitches have been drunk and have let the locals, I know, release him' BM 3734-36

*yma ree ov leferel heb ty vyth na govlya **delyfrys** der varia fetel ywa dyogel* 'some people are saying without oath or perjury that he has been freed by Mary indeed' BM 3739-42

*hy re ruk ov **delyfrya** mes a preson mam kerra* 'she has freed me from prison, dearest mother' BM 3758-59

*fetel vusta **delyfrys** laver thymo me ath peys ov map kerra* 'tell me how you were freed, I beg you, my dearest son' BM 3764-66

*In methy lauer theth vam me theth **delyfrye** heb nam* 'She said, Tell your mother that I freed you without doubt' BM 3776-77

*pobyl rome orth ij vernans **delyfrys** yth yns oma* 'the people of Rome have been delivered here from two deaths' BM 4168-69

GERYOW GWIR   free

why a ra clowas an exceding mercy a thu fatell ruga **delyuera** *mabden dre mervelous maner, thean stat a thampnacion* 'you will hear the great mercy of God, that he freed mankind wonderfully from the state of damnation' TH 5

rag innan agan honyn, na drethan agan honyn ny geffyn travith vas, dretha may hallan bos **delyuerys** *theworth an miserabill stat ha captiuite a veny ynna towlys dre agan mortall yskar an teball ell* 'for in ourselves, or by ourselves, we get nothing good, by which we might be freed from the wretched state and captivity into which we have been cast by our mortal enemy, the devil' TH 10

Rag theworth an daynger an teball ell ha pegh ny wothya mabden bos ryddys ha **delyuerys** *mas dre an cruell ha paynfull mernans a vab du* 'For mankind was not able to be rid and freed from the power of the devil and from sin except by the cruel and painful death of the Son of God' TH 15a

ny a vea res thyn nena sewya an order in tradicions, **delyuerys** *drethens y then re a rellany commyttya an ordyr an egglos thetha* 'we ought to follow then the order in the traditions delivered by those to whom we commit the regulation of the Church' TH 19

indella y, dre an commondment a S powle, a rug ordeynya re erall, in aga thyrmyn y a **thelyueras** *thetha inweth an discans a russens y the receva theworth S paule* 'thus they, through the commandment of St Paul ordained others in their time; they delivered to them also the doctrine which they had received from St Paul' TH 33a-34

pubonyn a rug **delyuera** *an feith a russons y receva theworth an abosteleth* 'everyone delivered the faith that they had received from the apostles' TH 34

ha thotheff a ve res ha **delyuerys** *an charge war oll an flok a crist* 'and to him was delivered the charge over all the flock of Christ' TH 42a

arall bethans **delyverys** *does ny vydnas an vrane vras neb caryn hy a gafas* 'let another be released; the great raven did not wish to return; she has found some carrion' CW 2463-65.

B **fria**

Ha genz hedna an vartshants a vî **frîez**: *ha an vènin ha'n manah a vî kemeryz ha kregyz* 'And thereupon the merchants were freed, and the woman and the monk were taken and hanged' BF: 18.

The word **lyfrêson** means 'release, liberation': *ty a fyth the* **lyfreson** *hag an our the weryson* 'you will get your release and of the gold your reward' RD 1676-77.

There appears, however, to be no attested word for 'freedom, liberty'. Some commentators have suggested ***frêdom**. In the light of **frank** in the Godolphin motto, perhaps **franchys** might be a reasonable alternative.

To sum up: the adjective 'free' in the revived language is best rendered by **frank** or **fre**; 'to free' is either **delyvra** or **fria**. 'Freedom' can be rendered either ***frêdom** or ***franchys**.

friend

FRIEND

For many revivalists the ordinary word for 'friend' has always been **car**, *plural* **kerens**. **Car**, however, in the texts does not mean 'friend', so much as 'relative, kinsman':

In vr na avel begyer ty a veth sur heb awer sensys in pov hag ol the **kerens** *blamys* 'Then you will be considered to be a beggar in truth without doubt and all your relatives will be blamed' BM 416-19

meryasek in certan o thymo pur oges **car** *in kerth galles* 'Meriasek indeed who was a very close relative has gone' BM 1938-40

Ny reys thyn fors pyth ellen rag bener re thewellen! menogh y rer y pesy gans agen **kerens** *nessa* 'It is not necessary to bother where we go, for never may we return; he will often be sought by our nearest kinsmen' BM 3438-41

fatell res the thu bos kerys ha honoris dre lell cherite a vght pub tra, ha pub den a res bos kerys, **kerens** *ha cothmans hag yskerenns* 'that God must be loved and honoured by pure charity above all things, and all men must be loved, relatives and friends and enemies' TH 26.

Car does mean 'friend' in Old Cornish: *amicus* **car** 'friend' OCV §157 but it also means 'relative': *affinis uel consanguineus* **car ogos** 'relative' OCV §156. These entries were noted by Lhuyd who gives:

Amicus... A friend... C. **Kâr** AB: 42bc
Cognatus... Kin, of the same bloud †C. **Karogos** [*fortè quasi* **kâr agos**] AB: 48c
Consanguineus... A cousin, a kinsman; C. **Kar** [*pl.* **keranz**] AB: 50c.

This use of **car** to mean 'friend' may have been adopted from Lhuyd by both John Boson and Gwavas, who write:

Kar *ve, Me ri marci dh'eu rag goz Neudhou vorth an kenza Den Kernuak* 'My friend, I thank you for your news about the first Cornishman' BF: 46
A weth thort gus **Kar** *gwîr* 'Also from your true friend' Bilbao MS.

It is possible, however, that in both or either case **Kar** is being used to mean 'Kinsman'. There are two instances in the texts where **car** seems indeed to mean 'friend':

Trueth mur yv ahanas den yv sevys a lyne bras ty the vynnes mar sempel bones omma in ponvos the **car** *the honen nyns os me a veth y leferel* 'It is a great pity for you, a man that springs from a great lineage, that you wish so simply to be here in misery. You are not your own friend. I shall dare to say it' BM 1992-97

GERYOW GWIR friend

*Gwayt ma'n gorthy pub termyn, rag gurthuhar ha myttyn nyng es thenny mar tha **car*** 'Be sure to worship him always, for evening and morning we have no better friend' BK 826-28.

This usage, however, appears to be archaic. Overwhelmingly the ordinary word for 'friend' in the texts is **cothman**, *plural* **cothmans**:

A **cothman**

*a **gothman** da prak y wreta thy'mmo amme* 'my good friend, why do you kiss me?' PC 1105-06

*mar a'n dyllyfryth hep mar nyns os **cothman** the cesar* 'if you release him of course you are no friend to Caesar' PC 2219-20

*thotho ef nyns os **cothman** del heuol th'mmo ynwys conciens da na syv certan lathe den nag yw cablys* 'to him you are not friend, it seems to me; a good conscience will certainly not follow killing a man who is not guilty' PC 2431-34

*ov sywa neb a vynna forsakyans byen ha muer teryov trefov an bys ma y days hay vam y nessevyn hay **cothmans** hag eff a gvayn roov cans* 'whoever wishes to follow me, let him, small or great, forsake lands, houses of this world, his father and his mother, his kinsmen and his friends, and he will gain a hundred gifts' BM 383-88

*meryasek crist denaha ha the **cothmen** me a veth* 'Meriasek, deny Christ and I shall be your friend' BM 893-94

*Me a vyn mones dotha hay **cothmens** pur guir gena y temptya mara kyllyn rag treyla thy eretons* 'I shall go to him and his friends indeed with me, if we can tempt him to turn to his inheritance' BM 1950-53

*mar te den ha receva royow bras theworth y **gothman** po y soveran, mar te in by an by ha tyrry blonogath y soveran hay displesya, an fowt han disobediens dretho ew gwrys the vrassa* 'if a man receive great gifts from his friend of his sovereign, if he soon thereafter violates his sovereign's wishes and displeases him, the fault and the disobedience committed by him are all the greater' TH 4a

*Rag henna ow **cothmans**, dre reson y bosow gwarnys therag dorne, bethow ware rag dowt why gans tus erall the vos tynnys dre error gans an wyckyd han drog pobyll* 'Therefore, my friends, because you have been warned in advance, beware lest you are led with other men to error by the wicked and evil people' TH 18

*Rag charite ew inweth the gara pub den oll tha ha bad, **cothman** hag yskar* 'For it is charity also to love everyone, good and bad, friend and foe' TH 21a

*why an clowes dyskys an tyrmyn res eth, te a ra cara the **cothman** ha casa theth hyskar, so me a levar theugh gwregh cara agys yskerens* 'you heard it said in past times, you shall love your friend and hate your enemy, but I say to you, Love your enemies' TH 21a-22

*mar tewgh why ha cowse da only an re na neb ew agys brederath ha **cothmans**, pana vattar bras ew henna?* 'if you speak well only of those who are your brothers and friends, what great matter is that?' TH 22

*fatell gotha thynny pub den cara y gilla **cothman** ha yskar* 'that we should, everybody, love each other, friend and foe' TH 22

friend   GERYOW GWIR

ow tysky fatell ra an kerensa han cherite ma (ow) pertaynya the **cothman** *den, ha fatell o va sufficient rag den the cara y* **gothman***, han re a rella y gara eff, ha the casa y yskar* 'teaching that this love and charity pertains to the friend of a man, and that it was sufficient for a man to love his friend, and those who love him, and to hate his enemy' TH 22

Indelma an lell charite crist an discas may teffa pub den ha benyn cara du drys pub tra, ha cara peb y gyla, kyffris **cothman** *hag yskar* 'Thus the true charity of Christ taught us that every man and woman should love God above all things, and everyone should love one another, both friend and foe' TH 22a

In kepar maner neb a rella don colan tha ha mynde, hag vsya inta y tavas, hay oberow the bub den, **cothman** *hag yskar, eff a yll gothfas dre henna, fatell vs thotha cherite* 'In the same way whoever has a good heart and mind, and controls his tongue well and his works with respect to all men, friend and foe, he can perceive by that, that he has charity' TH 23a

cara agan **cothmans** *nyns ew mas kepar dell ra an laddron, advltrers, denlath, hag oll an drog pobill erell* 'to love our friends is only like what thieves, adulterers, murderers and all other evil people do' TH 24

Han kyth sam kerensa ma, neb a rella y wetha keffris the thu neb ewa kylmys vgh pub tra, ha the gentrevek, magata y **cothman** *avell y iskar, hay iskar a vell y* **cothman** 'And this same love, which he keep both for God, which he is bound to do above all things, and to his neighbour, both his friend like his foe, and his foe like his friend' TH 25a

Lymmyn ny vanna ve na moy agys gylwell why servantes, mas **cothmans** 'Now no longer will I call you servants but friends' TH 35a

na illen denaha an nenevow tha vos y relevis dir an devotion aga **hvthmans** *ew bew* 'we cannot deny that the souls are relieved by the devotion of their friends who are alive' SA 66

Ow **cothmans** *da, del ough in suer, lemmyn, why a bys in Arthur gans lether clos* 'My good friends, which you are indeed, now you will go to Arthur with a sealed letter' BK 1816-20

ha bethough war na glowo agys dolors onyn vith a'gys amors, **coythman** *vith car* 'and be sure that none of your loved ones, friend or kinsman, hears your sorrows' BK 3261-64

na vannaf tha theskyvra ow **hothman** *a tra in bys* 'I shall not betray you, my friend, for anything in the world' CW 578-79

Farewell ow **hothman** *an nef me ath kare bys venary* 'Farewell, my friend from heaven, I shall love you for ever' CW 718-19

me am be wondrys fancye orth y wellas in weathan ha thevy in curtessye y profyas avell **cothman** *mere a dacklow ram lowta ha pur worthy* 'I had a wonderful delight seeing him in the tree and to me he offered as a friend many things and worthy ones, upon my faith' CW 761-66

ow **hothman** *na gybmar marthe ty an oole ha lyas myell* 'my friend, do not be astonished; you will regret it and many thousands' CW 2304-05

A Mate or Companion; a Friend **Kӳdhman** AB: 14a

Socius… A companion, a mate, a fellow C. **Kӳdhman** AB: 151b.

The word **mâta**, *plural* **mâtys** is used more colloquially to mean 'mates, chums, fellows':

B **mâta**
*nov **mata** make fast the rop yma an gwyns ov wetha* 'now, mate, make fast the rope. The wind is blowing' BM 600-01
*Hov hov pyth esogh **matis** y bescherev your patis* 'Hey, hey, where are you, mates? I curse your pates' BM 956-57
*ten an gol in ban **mata** an gwyns thagen corse dufa* 'pull the sail up, mate. The wind has veered to our course' BM 1085-86
*In sol **matis** duen in kerth aspyogh gans mur an nerth py fo marchont ov quandra* 'Up, mates, let's depart. Look with great attention where a merchant may be wandering' BM 1878-80
*deyskyn then dor **mata** ha the borse mes ath ascra me am beth hath margh uskis* 'dismount, mate, and I'll have your purse from your bosom and your horse quickly' BM 1887-89
***mata** orthen ny na set sav dascor ol the vona* 'mate, do not withstand us but hand over all your money' BM 1916-17
*Nov **matis** merugh adro mar quelogh so mot y go den ryb an coys ov quandra* 'Now, mates, look about, if you see, so may I live, a man wandering beside the wood' BM 2086-88
*Lavar thotha: mara myn trylia th'agan du Jovyn, ef a vith ow **mata** guew* 'Tell him if he will turn to our god, Jovyn, he will be my worthy friend' BK 891-93
*Bonas **mata** the bagan nyng ew rago'* 'It is not for me to be the chum of a pagan' BK 919-20
*Nyng ew ragtha in certain bos **mata** thew', e meth a* 'It is not for him indeed to be your chum, he says' BK 943-44
*Lemmyn, Ke, ow **mata** guyu, an ambos kepar del ew, ke ge duwans the barkya* 'Now, Ke, my worthy chum, as is the agreement, go forthwith to enclose land' BK 1150-52
*Mee's desyer why comende [v]e the o[d]e **matas** da* 'I pray you, commend me to all good fellows' Borde.

The word **sos** was used to mean 'friend(s), companion(s), but it was apparently used only as a vocative. **Sos** survives in Cornu-English dialect e.g. 'Woll'ee, soas?' i.e. 'Now will you' or 'Do'ee soas' i.e., 'Come now do' (see Jago, page 270). Cf. *Rea reva, rea rea, rea **sûas**, repharîa* 'O strange' AB: 249a. These seem to be variants of *Re Varia, **sos** 'By Mary, friend'.

The default word for 'friend' in the revived language should perhaps be **cothman**, *plural* **cothmans**. **Mâta**, **mâtys** can be used in a more colloquial register. **Sos** can be used when addressing someone or some people.

fruit   **GERYOW GWIR**

FRUIT

The entry *fructus* ***fruit*** 'fruit' occurs at OCV §681. Nance respellt OC ***fruit*** as UC *fruyth*. In KS it would be **frooth**. Other forms of Cornish render the word *frooth*; and there are other spellings. John Boson writes the same word as ***ffrueth***, ***frueth*** and uses it twice in his translation of the first chapter of Genesis:

Ha Deu laveraz, gwrens an aor dri meas gwelz ha lushan dro meas hâz, ha gwethan dri meas ***ffrueth*** 'And God said, let the earth bring forth grass and herb producing seed, and tree bearing fruit' BF: 52

Ha Deu lavaras, mero ma res gennam do vy kanifer lushan gen haz, pe es var ol budgeth an aor, ha kanifer guethan menz es ***frueth*** guethan gen haz, do vy enz ra bos rag boaz 'And God said, behold I have given you every herb with seed, which is upon all the face of the earth, and every tree which is a fruit tree bearing seeed; for you they will be for food' BF: 53.

This word has almost certainly come from OCV itself; cf. Boson's use of *avain* 'image' < ***auain*** 'imago' OCV §366.

As Nance himself points out, *frooth* is replaced in Middle Cornish by the word **frût** (UC *frut*), plural **frûtys**. Here are a few examples:

hag ynny bonas gorys ragon ny cryst a vynne ha war an pren ***frut*** degis may fe sur ʒagan sawye may teth ***frut*** may fen kellys rag adam ʒe attamye 'and on it Christ was willing to be put and that he might be borne as a fruit on the tree truly to save us from which came the fruit by which we were lost since Adam took the first bite of it' PA 153b-d

pup gwethen tefyns a'y saf ov ton hy ***frvt*** ha'y delyow 'let every tree grow upright bearing its fruit and leaves' OM 29-30

War bup ***frut*** losow ha has a vo ynny hy tevys saw a'n frut ny fyth kymmyas yw pren a skeyens hynwys 'To every fruit, herb and seed that grows in it, but to the fruit of what is called the tree of knowledge you shall not have permission' OM 77-80

frut a'n wethen a skyans dybbry byth na borth danger 'never hesitate to eat of the fruit of the tree of knowledge' OM 167-68

a'y ***frut*** dybry ny'm bes whans dres dyfen ov arloth ker 'I have no desire to eat of its fruit against the prohibition of my beloved Lord' OM 171-72

a'y ***frut*** hy nep a theppro a wovyth cvsyl a'n tas 'whoever eats of its fruit will know the Father's counsel' OM 187-88

mvr a foly ew thotho an keth ***frut*** na mara'n gas 'it is a great foolishness for him, if he leaves untouched the same fruit' OM 191-92

ty re gamwruk eredy ha re'n dros the vur anken pan russys thotho dybry ha tastye ***frut*** a'n wethen 'you have sinned indeed and have brought him to great misery, when you made him eat and taste the fruit of the tree' OM 281-84

ffrut da bynerre thokko na glase bys gorfen beys 'may it never bear good fruit nor put forth leaves till the end of the world' OM 583-84

GERYOW GWIR   fruit

*ol an tekter a wylys ny yl taves den yn bys y leuerel bynytha a **frut** da ha floures tek menestrouthy ha can whek* 'all the beauty I saw the tongue of no man in the world could tell of goodly fruit and beautiful flowers, sweet music and song' OM 766-70

*ena yth esa plenty a bup kynde a **frutys**, beautyfull tege ha wheg the veras warnetha, ea ha delicius the thebbry ha the then rag maga warnetha. Saw vn kynda a **frut** an tas du a chargias mabden na rella myllya na tuchia worta war bayne merwall a vernans* 'in that place there was plenty of every kind of fruits, beautiful fair and sweet to look upon, yea and delicious to eat and for man to feed upon. But one kind of fruit God the Father charged mankind not to interfere with or touch upon pain of dying the death' TH 2

*an **frut** vs in paradys ny a thebyr, mas an **frut** an wethan vs in nes in cres paradis du agan defennas na rellan tuchia na myllia gynsy* 'of the fruit which is in paradise we may eat, but of the fruit of the tree which is near the middle of paradise God forbade us to touch or interfere with' TH 3a

*In nena an venyn a welas y bos an **frut** da the thybbry ha teg the sight y lagasow ha pleasant the veras war netha, hy a gemeras ran an **frut** hag an debbras hag a ros part then gwerrer Adam hag eff a thebbras* 'Then the woman saw that the fruit was good to eat and fair to the sight of her eyes and pleasant to look upon, she took some of the fruit and ate it and gave some to her husband Adam, and he ate' TH 3a

*ny ew gwyth crabbys, na thora **frut** da vith, ahanan agan honyn ny thryn in rag mas dreys, sperne lynas ha spethas* 'we are crab-apple trees, that bear no good fruit; of ourselves we bring forth nothing but brambles, briars, nettles and thorns' TH 9

*Agan **frutys** ny ew declaris in v chapter a S pawle then galathians. Nyns es thyn naneyll feith, govenek, charite, paciens, chastite, na tra vith arell ew da, mas theworth du oll ymons ow toys ha [rag h]enna an virtues ma ew gylwys in scriptur an **frutys** an spuris sans ha not an **frutys** a vabden* 'Our fruits are declared in the fifth chapter of St Paul to the Galatians. We have neither faith, hope, charity, patience, chastity, or any other good thing, but they all come from God, and therefore these virtues are called in scripture the fruits of the Holy Spirit, not the fruits of man' TH 9

*ow blonogath yw henna may tockans vnna pur splan **frutes** thom both rag maga seyl a theyg bewnans hogan* 'my wish is this that they may bear in them splendid fruits to my desire to feed whoever in time to come will have life' CW 96-99

*ha **frutes** war bub gwethan y teyf gwaf ha have keffrys* 'and fruits upon every tree grow in winter and in summer as well' CW 368-69

*mar pyth y **frute** hy tastys te a vyth dampnys ractha* 'if its fruit is tasted, you will be damned for it' CW 377-78

*mar gwreth tastya an **frute** ma es oma war an wethan maga fure te a vea avell dew es awartha* 'if you taste this fruit, which is here on the tree, you will be as wise as God above' CW 619-22

*sow pur wyre thymo ve creis worth tha wreak drefan cola rag terry an keth **frutes** a wrug defenna 3uwortes spearn y teg thy[s] ha speras* 'but in truth believe me, since you listened to your wife to pluck the same fruits that I forbade to you, it will bear you thorns and briars' CW 943-47

*dew a therfyn bos gwerthyes gans an gwella **frute** pub preys* 'God deserves to be worshipped with the best fruit always' CW 1097-98

fruit   **GERYOW GWIR**

*ena yth esa flowrys ha **frutes** teke aga lew thagan maga* 'in that place there were fair-hued fruits to feed us' CW 1050-52

*ye lysky ny vannaf ve an eys nan **frutes** defrye* 'I will not burn it, the grain nor the fruits indeed' CW 1088-89

***frute** da bydnarre thocka na dadar avall neb preise* 'may it never bear good fruit nor goodness of apple at any time' CW 1162-63

*me a heath ran an **frutyes** hag a thro parte anetha avall pur vras* 'I will hand some of the fruits and will bring some of them, a very large apple' CW 1841-43.

In the revived language the ordinary word for 'fruit' should perhaps be **frût**, *plural* **frûtys**.

G

GENEROUS

For 'generous' Nance suggests **hel**, which he knew from OCV and which is now attested in BK:

largus **hail** 'bountiful' OCV §408
Heel *oge ha plentethus ha guyw the wormoladow dris yonk ha loys* 'You are generous and bountiful and worthy of praise beyond young and old' BK 1628-30
Hayl, arluth **heel** *drys pub huny!* 'Hail, generous lord beyond everybody' BK 1700-01.

Lhuyd lists Old Cornish **Hâil** 'liberal' among words that are disused by the Cornish but still understood by the Welsh (AB: 4c).

In the texts, however, the customary word for 'liberal, generous' is **larych**, **larjy**, comparative **larchya**, **larjya**. As can be seen from the examples below it **larj**, **larjy** often has metaphorical senses 'wide, extensive; liberally'. Moreover the comparative **larjya** is also used as a positive form.

Sul voy ancov a rellogh the **larchya** *preysys fethogh kemendis wose helma* 'The more deaths you achieve the more generously will you praised, commended afterwards' BM 2351-53
han kythsam tra na me a alsa eysy y prevy ha **largy** *lowre y thysquethas thewhy dre pleyn ha manyfest demonstracyon* 'and that same thing I could easily prove and liberally enough show you through plain and manifest demonstration' TH 34a-35
ena yma eff ow kull **largy** *processe a pedyr, ha in myske re erell ow cows a pedyr deniall y vester in vaner ma* 'there he makes a generous discussion of Peter, and among things speaking of Peter's denial of his master thus' TH 46
kepar dell vsy ow apperya moy **largia** *in xxx-ans chapter an lever a Eusebius* 'as appears more liberally in the 30th chapter of Eusebius' book' TH 47a
Pella agys oll an rema, yma in xi chapter a S paul then Corinthians goodly ha **largy** *processe ow tochia thin sacrament ma* 'Further than all these, in the 11th chapter of St Paul to the Corinthians there is a good and liberal discussion of this sacrament' TH 53a
Why a vith, me a trust, instructys ha diskys, in dra na **largy** *lowre* 'You will be, I trust, instructed and taught, liberally enough in that matter' TH 55

generous GERYOW GWIR

*hay bromas yth o **largya** mar gwrean tastya an frut na avell dew ny a vea* 'and his promise was so generous, if we tasted that fruit, we should be like God' CW 780-82

*an leverow ytowns y omma why as gweall wondrys **largya** ha pub tra oll in bys ma skryffes yma yn ry ma* 'the books, behold them here; you see them wonderfully extensive and everything in this world has been written in these' CW 2175-78.

The abstract noun **larjes** 'largesse, generosity' is also found. It seems to be used when thanking someone for his liberality:

*ha **largys** ha gromersy ny a yl bos fest mery rag cafus ro an par-na* 'Oh, generosity, and thank you! We can be very merry for having received such a gift' OM 2465-67

*ha **larges** epscop cortes ha **larges** pup ol gylwes **larges** warbarth leuereugh* 'Oh generosity, courteous bishop; oh generosity let everyone cry; generosity say you all together' OM 2773-75.

In the revived language 'generous' can be either **hel** or **larych/larjy**. 'Generosity' is best rendered by **larjes**.

GENTLE *see* **NOBLE**

GERMANY
There are two words for 'Germany' in the texts: A) **Almayn** and B) **Jermany**:

A
*arluth ow tevos a spayn yth egen yn cres **almayn** orth vn prysly yn pur wyr pan fuf gylwys* 'Lord, coming from Spain I was in the middle of Germany at lunchtime, when I was summoned' RD 2147-50.

B
*ran in **Germany** a levery, omma yma crist, omma yma an egglos, ran in Bohem a lleuery, omma yma crist, oma yma an egglos* 'Some in Germany were saying, Here is Christ, here is the Church, some in Bohemia were saying, Here is Christ here is the Church' TH 32

*Merowgh inweth war **germany**, ha kemerogh examply anethy* 'Look also at Germany, and take an example from her' TH 49a

*Me re thanvanas deffry duk an Saxens, Chellery, the whelas myns a geffa a bagans in **Germany*** 'I have sent indeed Childerich, the duke of the Saxons, to seek as many pagans as he can find in Germany' BK 3229-32.

Jermany is probably to be stressed on the second syllable. Since it is better attested than **Almayn**, there is no reason to proscribe the name **Jermany**.

TO GET

In the earliest texts 'to get, to find, to receive' is *cafos*, *cafus*, *caffus* where the intervocalic segment is clearly voiceless. Here are a very few examples:

A *cafos*

*yn meʒens nyn gorʒyn na ny goth thyn y worʒye na ken mygtern ny venyn ys Cesar **caffos** neffre* 'they said, We do not honour him nor should we worship him nor will we ever have another king apart from Caesar' PA 148cd

***Cafes** moy thy's aban res try heys the bal kemery* 'Since you need to receive more, three lengths of your spade, take them!' OM 391-92

*Caym ny lettys saw vn lam ov **kafus** banneth ov mam ha banneth ov thas kefrys* 'Cain, I stopped only a while to receive the blessing of my mother and of my father also' OM 470-72

*na allons **caffus** cheson the wruthyl crothval na son warnas a das beneges* 'that they may not find a reason to complain or murmer against you, O blessed Father' OM 1835-37

*yma ow kul maystry bras rak mennas **cafos** enor* 'he is making great bravado because he wishes to receive honour' PC 377-78

*me a vyn **caffus** an queth* 'I will get the garment' RD 1875

*yn vr na ny reys thy'nny na den byth ol yn teffry **caffus** neffre na moy ovn* 'then it will not be necessary for us or anyone else indeed ever to have any more fear' RD 2168-70

*nyns o mabden abyll the avoydya eternal damnacion, mas a rese thotha **kafus** ken gweras* 'mankind was not able to avoid eternal damnation, but he had to get further help' TH 14a

*Mara tesyer **cafas** drog, me a'n to, by Godys brow! nyng ew henna mars pen cog* 'If he wishes to receive pain, I swear it by God's brow! that fellow is nothing but a fool' BK 542-44.

In the Later texts a form with intervocalic *-v-* is also found:

B *cavos*

*drefan henna in neb place ny allaf **cavos** powas* 'because of that in no place can I find rest' CW 1514-15

*Dreth 'guz kibmias beniggas why ra **cavas** dr'eeu an gwas Harry ma poddrack broas* 'By your sacred leave you will find that this fellow Harry is a great wizard' BF: 9

*Mar kressa an dean deskez feer na gwellaz hemma [ev] a venga **kavaz** fraga e ouna en skreefa-composter* 'If that learned wise man had seen this, he would have found cause to correct it in orthography' BF: 27

*Ma ko them **cavaz** tra a'n par ma en lever Arlyth an Menneth dro tho e deskanz Latten* 'I remember finding something like this in Lord Montaigne's book about his Latin education' BF: 29

*Huei 'ra **kavaz** an guâz brvz ziʒir-na kusga uvr an gòrha* 'You will find that great lazy fellow sleeping on the hay' AB: 248a.

get   GERYOW GWIR

A commoner variant of **cavos** is **cawas**:

C cawas

me a vyn ***cawys*** *an povs kyn fy mar pyth* 'I will get the coat however grudging you may be' RD 1957-58

y vab rag ***cawas*** *dyskans sur danvenys ateva ȝyugh doctor wek* 'his son to receive education indeed behold he has been sent to you, dear doctor' BM 85-87

Welcum omma lych ryall del ogh pen ha princypall dreson ny ol yn tyan worthy rag ***cawas*** *reuerens* 'Welcome here, royal liege, as you are head and principal over us altogether, worthy to receive reverence' BM 252-45

the canevar den gwyrrian a vo desyrius e ***gowis*** 'to every virtuous man who is desirous to receive it' SA 60

me a yll bos lowanheys kyns es bos dewath an bys ***cawas*** *an oyle a vercy* 'I may well exult before the world ends to receive the oil of mercy' CW 957-59

me a vyn dallath palas rag ***cawas*** *susten ha boos thymo ve ha thom flehys* 'I shall begin to dig to get sustenance and food for myself and for my children' CW 1033-35

rays yw purryes lavyrrya ha gones an beise omma tha ***gawas*** *theny susten* 'it is very necessary to work and to cultivate the world here to obtain food for us' CW 1079-81

tha thew nyng eis otham vythe awoos ***cawas*** *agen pythe* 'God has no need that he should get what belongs to us' CW 1132-33

na wreugh terry an deffan a vyth gans dew thugh vrnys dowte tha ***gawas*** *drog gorfan* 'do not violate the prohibition that God will give you lest you get an evil end' CW 2139-41

kebmys yw an molothowe dowt yw thym ***cawas*** *trygva* 'so great are the curses that I am afraid to get a dwelling-place for myself' CW 1220-21

Deez ubba do ***gawaz*** *an dega?* 'Do you come here to have the tithe?' ACB: F f *verso*

Rag na vedn an Arleth gon ***cawas*** *en paraves rag comeras e hannow en vaine* 'For the Lord will not receive us in paradise for taking his name in vain' Rowe.

Because the verbal noun **cafos**, **cavos**, **cawas** was so frequently used after **dhe** 'to' and **y** 'his, its', it appears in some later texts to have acquired a permanently lenited initial consonant:

D gafos, gawas

Ny yll henna ***gafus*** *du thy das, mas eff a aswonna an egglos the vos y vam* 'That man cannot receive God as his Father, unless he recognises the Church as his mother' TH 39a

han speciall purpose o crist the vynnas ***gafus*** *aucthorite an parna in vn den* 'and the special purpose was that Christ wished that authority of that kind should be found in one man' TH 46

Na'ra chee ***gowas*** *na hene Deew poz vee* 'You shall have no other God but me' Rowe

Ha et eye ollaz, hye dalveath ***gowas*** *tane* 'And on her hearth she ought to get fire' ACB: F f 3

*Ha whaeh an Sousen metessen olga **gawaz** maga nebbaz skeeanz* 'And yet the English perhaps could find as little knowledge' BF: 31.

Like Cornish Middle Welsh exhibits the two stems of the verb 'to get, to receive', i.e. *caff-* and *cav-* (GMW §161). Similarly Middle Breton has both *caffout* and *kavout* 'to get' (HMSB §172b). Since the two stems **caf-** and **cav-**/**caw-** in Cornish have parallels elsewhere in Brythonic, either may be used in the revived language.

GLORY, GLORIFY, GLORIOUS

In the Middle and Late Cornish texts the default word for 'glory, adoration, worship' is the masculine noun **gordhyans**:

*may fo ȝe thu ȝe **worthyans** ha sylwans ȝen enevow* 'that it may be glory for God and salvation for souls' PA 1d

*A das map ha spyrys sans **gorthyans** the'th corf wek pupprys* 'O Father, Son and Holy Spirit, glory to thy sweet person always' OM 85-86

*gorre the'n meneth tabor yn **gorthyans** thy'm th'y lesky* 'take it to Mount Tabor to burn it as worship to me' OM 429-30

*my a'th worth gans ol ov nel y'm colon pur trewysy hag a offryn thy's whare warbarth ol ov gvyrthege yn **gorthyans** thy's y lesky* 'I worship you with all my strength very seriously in my heart and I offer to you altogether my true tithe to be burnt for you as worship' OM 510-14

***gorthyans** ha gras thy's a das dyseghys yv an norveys* 'Glory and grace to you, O Father, the world is left dry' OM 1149-50

*dege ol agan ethyn bestes ynweth megata warnythy my a offryn yn **gorthyans** the'n tas guella* 'a tithe of all birds and beasts also upon it I offer as worship to the most excellent Father' OM 1181-84

*my a offrynn mallart da yn **gorthyans** the tas dev ker* 'I shall offer a goodly mallard as worship to the God, the beloved Father' OM 1199-200

*yn **gorthyans** thotho omma offrynnye an keth mols ma* 'as worship to him here I offer this same wether' OM 1383-84

***gorthyans** the tas dev a'n nef* 'glory to the Father of heaven' OM 2026

***gorthyans** the'n tas arluth nef a'm luen golon my a bys rag luen gallosek yw ef hag yn pup ober marthys* 'glory to the Father, Lord of heaven, I pray with all my heart, for he is almighty and wondrous in all his works' OM 2087-90

*aban vynnyth yndella y resseve my a wra yn **gorthyans** the'n tas a'n nef* 'since you wish it so, I will receive it as glory to the Father of heaven' OM 2617-19

*peb ol war pen y dev glyn a gan yn **gorthyans** dotho* 'everyone on bended knee will sing in worship to him' PC 247-78

*a arluth crist nef ha bys **gorthyans** thy'so gy pupprys* 'O Christ, Lord of heaven and earth, glory to you always' RD 1739-40

glory GERYOW GWIR

Drok yv gena war ov ena meryasek wek gul dis mas da ha **gorthyans** *grua thum dewov tek* 'I regret upon my soul, dear Meriasek, to do anything but good to you and give glory to my lovely gods' BM 909-14

Gorthyans *the crist map maghteth* 'Glory to Christ, son of a maiden' BM 1146

Sylvester **gorthyans** *dywhy* 'Silvester, worship to you!' BM 2755

Maria lowene dis ha **gorthyans** *bys venytha* 'Mary, joy to you and glory for ever' BM 3188-89

Gorthyans *thu'm Arluth a nef a vynnas clowas ow lef* 'Glory to my Lord of heaven, who deigned to hear my voice' BK 1-2

The Jesu **gorthyans** *ha gras eth esaf ynhe tho'm plas ys del desefsan ow bos* 'To Jesus glory and grace; I am nearer to my place than I would have thought I was' BK 28-30

Hayl, syr emprour, y'th ryawta! gans mer honowr ha beawta ha **gorthyans** *bras!* 'Hail, sir emperor, in your majesty! with much honour and pomp and great glory!' BK 1690-94

yn **gorthyans** *tha thew an tase gwren agen sacrafice leall* 'as worship to God the Father let us make our proper sacrifice' CW 1095-96.

Gordhyans frequently appears in the compound **meur-wordhyans** 'great glory, great worship, great honour':

Arluth ker thy's **mur worthyans** *rag hyr lour ev ov bewnans kemmer dy'so on enef* 'Dear Lord, to you great glory, for my life is long enough. Take to yourself my soul' OM 847-49

lemmyn cryst agan arluth **mur worthyans** *thy's del theguth worth agan dry alemma* 'now, Christ our Lord, great glory to you, as is right, for bringing us from here' RD 149-51

then arluth du **murworthyens** *ha grays thym jy ventine re tharbarre* 'great glory to God and may he provide grace to me to maintain it' BM 2684-86

The crist ihesu **mur worthyans** *ha thys meryasek nefra* 'To Christ great honour and to you, Meriasek, for ever' BM 3846-47

An arlythy, kepar dell goyth, a the deffry pen ow arloyth th'y anterya, gans melody ha **mer worthyans**, *empror worthy in e vewnans par del o va* 'The Lords, as is right, will come indeed to bury the head of my lord, with music and great honour, as he was a worthy emperor in his lifetime' BK 2902-10

mear worthyans *theis ow formyer ha gwrear a oll an beyse* 'great glory to you, my Maker, and Creator of all the world' CW 1414-15

mere worthyans *than drenges tase ow crowntya thymmo sylwans* 'great glory to the the Father of the Trinity for granting me salvation' CW 1940-41

meare worthyans *thyes arluth nef te a weras gwadn ha creaf in othom sure pan vo reys* 'great glory to you, Lord of heaven; you help weak and strong in need when it is necessary' CW 2478-80.

Probably as a result of the frequent occurrence of the lenited form **wordhyans** in this compound, the simplex itself acquired perpetual lenition of the initial consonant. **Wordhyans** thus appears in the later language to be a feminine noun:

Arta an Jowle an comeraz eu mann wor hugez meneth euhall ha disquethaz thotha oll an gwellasketh an beaze, ha'n **worriance** *nonge* 'Again the Devil took him up upon a huge high mountain and showed him all the kingdoms of the earth and the glory of them' Rowe

rag an geulaze te beaue, ha ul an nearth, ha **worriance**, *rag nevera venitho* 'for you own the kingdom and the power and glory for ever and ever' BF: 41

Rag gans te y[u] an mighterneth, an creveder, hag an **'worryans**, *byz a venitha* 'For thine is the kingdom, the power and the glory for ever' ACB: E e 2 *verso*

Rag an mychteyrneth ew chee do honnen, ha an crêvder, ha an **'worryans**, *rag bisqueth ha bisqueth* 'For the kingdom is your and the power and the glory for ever and ever' ACB: E e 2 *verso*.

Gordhyans can mean both 'honour, worship' towards a human being and 'glory' of God alone. In some texts **gordhyans** in this second sense is replaced by **glory**:

an tas, an mab, han Spuris sans, thethans y re bo oll honor ha **glory** *bys vyckan* 'the Father, the Son and the Holy Spirit, to them be all honour and glory for ever' TH 16

An pith ew preparyys ragan ny, dre agan Savyowre Jhesu Crist, thotheff, gans an tas, han Spuris sans re bo honor, preysse ha **glory** *heb deweth* 'that which has been prepared for us by our Saviour Jesus Christ; to him with the Father and the Son and the Holy Spirit be all honour, praise and glory without end' TH 41

an very corfe ha gois a crist, worthy the gafus oll an honor han **glory** *a alla bos gans colan prederys* 'the very body and blood of Christ, worthy to receive all the honour and the glory which can be conceived by the heart' TH 54

thotheff, gans an tas han spuris sans re bo oll honor ha **glory** *heb deweth* 'to him with the Father and the Holy Spirit be all honour and glory without end' TH 54a

thotheff re bo oll honor ha **glory** *in gwlas heb deweth* 'to him let there be all honour and glory in the kingdom without end' SA 66a

dell wrama raynya omma yn trone wartha gans **glorye** 'as I shall reign here on the throne above with glory' CW 190-91

henna vea hager dra den a vynta gule a bry 3a thos omma then plas ma neb es lenwys a **glorye** 'that would be an evil thing, that a man you intend to make of clay should come hither to this place which is full of glory' CW 259-63.

Notice incidentally that the initial consonant of **glory** does not appear to undergo lenition.

Further Cornish words for 'honour, worship' of people and groups of people are A) **roweth**; B) **worshyp**; and C) **reverons**. These are discussed s.v. '**REVERENCE**' below.

glory   GERYOW GWIR

The default word for 'to worship, to honour, to glorify' is **gordhya** (Middle English *worthien*), from which **gordhyans** 'glory' derives. **Gordhya** is followed either by A) a direct object; or more rarely, and apparently in Late Cornish only, by B) the preposition **dhe** 'to':

A **gordhya** + direct object

lowene ʒys te yw ʒeyn mygtern rys yw ʒe **worʒye** 'Hail to you, you are king to us; it in necessary to worship you' PA 137c

pysk ragof ny wra skvsy mar **corthyaf** *dev yn perfyth* 'no fish shall escape me if I glorify God perfectly' OM 139-40

ken arluth agesso ef ny'n **gorthyaf** *bys vynary* 'another lord apart from him I shall never worship' OM 1789-90

a gadlyng god yeue the wo ty re **worthyas** *war nep tro an fals losel* 'O vagabond, God give you woe! You have worshipped the false scoundrel at some time' PC 2691-93

iheus arluth cuff colyn the teller da rum gedya **gorthya** *crist ker may hallen han werhes flour maria* 'Jesu, beloved Lord, may he guide me to a suitable place, so that I may glorify Christ and Mary, the flower of virgins' BM 628-31

thy **worthya** *ny yv senses hag a vyn awos peryl* 'we are bound to worship him and we will in spite of danger' BM 716-17

ow **gwerthya** *oll why a wra pare dell ywe owe bothe nefra omma pub pryes* 'you all shall worship me as is my wish here always for ever' CW 42-4

gwayte ow **gworrya** *war bub tew ʒeso gy par del gotha* 'be careful to worship me on every side as you ought' CW 49-50

dew a therfyn bos **gwerthyes** *gans an gwella frute pub preys* 'God deserves to be worhsipped with the best fruit always' CW 1097-98

y bosta arluth heb pare in pub place re b[y] **gwerthys** 'that you are Lord without equal in all places may you be glorified' CW 1416-17

ha rag henna y coth thyma gans colan pure aga **gwerthya** 'and therefore it behoves me to glorify them with a pure heart' CW 1963-64

Worria *guz seera ha dama el guz dethiow beth pel vor an tir es res thees gen guz Arleth Deiu* 'Honour your father and your mother, that your days may be long in the land which your Lord God has given you' BF: 55.

B **gordhya** + **dhe**

Ha potho an gye devethez en choy y a wellaz an flô yonk gen Mareea e thama, ha angye a cothaz en doar, ha **gorthaz tha eue** 'And when they had entered the house, they saw the young child with Mary his mother, and they fell to the ground and worshipped him' Rowe

na re'au pleghie dothans na **worria dothans** 'you shall not bow down to them nor worship them' BF: 55.

For 'to glorify' Tregear uses **gloryfia**:

C **gloryfia**

*Indelma ny a yll disky in scriptur the vos vvell ha myke warlerth an examplys a dus tha, ha the exaltia, **glorifia**, presia, ha honora Du vth pub tra* 'Thus in scripture we can learn to be humble and meek according to the examples of good men, and to exalt, glorify, praise and honour God above all things' TH 10

*Kemmar wyth te ew Jew hag yth esas ow crowetha in la, hag yth esas ow **glorifia** in du, ha te a wore y blonogath hay plesure* 'Take care, you are a Jew and you rest in the law and you glorify in God, and you know his will and his pleasure' TH 14a.

The verb **exaltya** 'to exalt, to elevate, to glorify' is also well attested; s.v. '**EXALT**':

The Cornish for 'glorious' is **gloryùs**, spelt *glorijs*, *gloryes*, *glorius*:

*ihesu crist mytern **glorijs** roy y syght dotho heb fal* 'Jesus Christ, glorious king, give him his sight without fail' BM 548-49

*benyges the peyadov me a wor bones oma ha **glorijs** prest the geryov* 'I know here that your prayer is holy and your words are indeed glorious' BM 560-62

*Iheus arluth galosek re bo gorthys benytha han sans **glorijs** meryasek* 'May Jesus, powerful lord, be worshipped for ever and Meriasek, the glorious saint' BM 2620-22

*Y leferys offeren du guener vetten certen **glorijs** ha tek* 'He said mass on Friday morning indeed, beautifully and gloriously' BM 4419-21

*ena eff a rug contynewa Epscop in kythsame rome na xxv-ans a blethynnyow hag ena ef a rug suffra y **glorius** martyrdum in dewtha blethan a reign an cruell Emperour Nero* 'then he continued bishop in that same Rome 25 years and their he suffered his glorious martyrdom in the final year of the reign of the cruel emperor Nero' TH 46a-47

*Gramersy, arluth **glorius**, the peb eth os plegadow* 'Great thank, glorious lord; to all you are pleasant' BK 1626-27

*hag yny y fythe gorrys neb am gorth gans ioye ha cane naw order elath **gloryes*** 'and in it will be put nine orders of glorious angels who worship me with joy and song' CW 25-7

*henna degowhe destynye om bosof prynce pur **gloryous*** 'bear witness of that, that I am a very glorious prince' CW 127-28

*y flattering o mur **gloryes** ny wothyan guthell nahean* 'his flattery was so glorious, I could not do otherwise' CW 1023-24

*me a weall an place **gloryes** han eall yn yet ow sevall* 'I see the glorious place and the angel standing at the gate' CW 1773-74

*specyall vn gwethan **gloryes** ow hethas in ban pur stowte bes yn nef sure me a gryes* 'and in particular one glorious tree reaching up vigorous into heaven indeed, I believe surely' CW 1899-901

*eave re gollas der avall an place **gloryous** pur sure* 'he has surely lost by an apple the glorious place' CW 2135-36.

Notice that the initial consonant of **gloryùs** does not appear to undergo lenition.

To sum up 'glory' when applied to God is **gordhyans** or **glory**. 'Glory, honour' referring to people and things is **gordhyans** m. (Late Cornish f.); in some cases **worshyp** and **reverons** may be used. 'To glorify, to worship' is **gordhya** (followed by **dhe** in Late Cornish), but **exaltya** can be used in some contexts; Tregear uses **gloryfia**. 'Glorious' is rendered **gloryùs**.

GLUTTONY

For 'gluttony' Nance suggests **gloteny** (**glotny**) and ***cowlegneth**. ***Cowlegneth** is not attested, **gloteny** on the other hand, is attested in three texts:

Gans ***gloteny*** *ef pan welas cam na ylly y dolla en tebell el a vynnas yn ken maner y demptye* 'When he saw that he could not deceive him by gluttony, the devil wished in another way to tempt him' PA 13ab

my a vyn mos th'y tempye mar a callaf y tenne the wuel ***glotny*** *war nep tu* 'I will go to tempt him, if I can, to draw him to commit gluttony in some place' PC 50-52

Sorre, stryf sedicion, sectes, envy, murdyr, methewnep, ***glotny*** *ha re an par ma* 'Anger, strife, sedition, sects, envy, murder, drunkenness, gluttony and thing of this kind' TH 16a.

Since **gloteny**, **glotny** is attested, it should perhaps be the word of choice in the revived language.

TO GOVERN, GOVERNMENT, GOVERNOR

For 'to govern' Nance suggests **rêwlya** (UC *rewlya*), **rowtya** and **governya**. **Rêwlya** means 'to rule, to guide, to govern' and is well enough attested:

war the lergh bethens ***revlys*** 'according to you let them be governed' OM 1434

heil syre emperour a'n wlas iouyn roy thy's bos den mas ha len ***reulye*** *the wlasco*r 'hail, sir emperor of the land, may Jovyn give the to be a good man and rightly rule your kindgdom' PC 1705-07

an fer a fue dallethys dre tus vas berth yn tempel ena ***rewlys*** *o an beys ha lyes onan the wel* 'the fair was started by good men in the temple; there the business was guided and many a one the better for it' PC 2409-12

a'n ***rewlens*** *ef an iustis hag ol an comnors a'n pow* 'let the justice decide it and all the commoners of the country' PC 2469-70

drefen agis governans ***rewlys*** *on brays ha byan* 'by your governance we are ruled great and small' BM 256-57

GERYOW GWIR govern

*Ny yv plesijs hag a vyn boys **revlijs** drethogh certeyn* 'We are pleased and will be guided by you indeed' BM 314-15

*ellas ragos ov map rays na vennyth dre onester bones **revlys*** 'alas for you, my son, that you will not be ruled by seemliness' BM 486-88

*nefre me ny fanna cur marnes a vn ena sur du roy thym y lel **revlya*** 'never do I wish the cure of any but one soul; God grant that I may rule it well' BM 2845-47

*ha oll an re na a ve in ministers in egglos a crist thea nyna bys in dith hethow, han charg anetha ow **rewlya** an flok a crist* 'and all those who were ministers in the Church of Christ from then until the present, and their task was to rule the flock of Christ' TH 41a

*Gweth ve y'th cof ha'm noe a ra the **rewlya*** 'Keep me in remembrance and my nephew shall govern you' BK 2745-46

*kyn na wore hy cowse banna me as **rowle** hy del vannaf* 'though she knows not how to say anything, I shall rule her as I wish' CW 506-07

*gorta ha byth thym **rowlys** gas ve tha entra agye rag ty ny vethys dowtyes drefan y bosta mar deke* 'Stay and be ruled by me; let me enter in, for you will not be feared because you are so fair' CW 520-24

*yn er na re sent deffry yth halsan **rowlya** pur gay ha bos stately 3om deuyse* 'then by St Verily I could rule very nobly and be stately to my heart's content' CW 607-09

*me a vyn thewhy poyntya service tha[n eal] hay gela rage **rowlya** eys ha chattell* 'I will appoint for you service for the one and the other, to govern grain and cattle' CW 1062-64

*Ha Deew gwraz deau gollo broaz: an brossa tha **rowlya** han deeth ha an behattna tha **rowlyah** an noaz* 'And God made to great lights, the larger to rule the day and the smaller to rule the night' JKeigwin

*Ha tha **rowlyah** drez an deeth ha drez an noaz* 'And to ruler over the day and the night' JKeigwin

*ha tha dezeria ra voaze tha goore, ha e ra tha **rowlya*** 'and your desire shall be for your husband and he shall rule you' Rowe.

Rowtya means 'to domineer, to swagger' as much as 'to govern, to rule':

*Gweyr ew henna, by my sowl! Un pols y hylsyn **rowtya*** 'That is true, by my soul! For a while we were able to rule the roost' BK 767-68

*Bethans pur glor, rag mar tema ha **rowtya** ha ferneuwhy ha stowtya, ny vith mab den na'm dowtya* 'Let them be very quiet, for if I happen to domineer and to rage and brag, there will be no man who does not fear me' BK 1638-41

*Drys an gwlasow scon heb ardag, rys ew **rowtya** sherp avel spern* 'Across the kingdoms quickly without delay it is necessary to swagger sharp as thorn' BK 1662-65

*râg a mez a che e ra doaz matern rag **rowtya** tha pobel Ezarel* 'for out of you will come a king to rule your people, Israel' Rowe.

The commonest and most apt verb is **governya**, **governa**:

govern   **GERYOW GWIR**

*rag **governye** ow bewnans yma loer orth both ow brys* 'to conduct my life there is enough at my pleasure' OM 89-90

*pur wyr lour yv an re na rak **governye** ol an beys* 'very truly those are enough to govern all the world' PC 928-30

*an kyth sam catholyk eglos ma, indelma **governys** dre an spuris sans, ha gweresys pub vr gans crist y honyn* 'this same catholic Church, thus governed by the Holy Spirit and assisted always by Christ himself' TH 17

*ha fatell ra an spuris sans rag neffra **geverna** an egglos catholyk* 'and that the Holy Spiris will for ever govern the catholic Church' TH 20

*Pan rug eff gull lawes rag **gouerna** an famos cyte a Athens ny rug eff in oll y lawys apporcion punysment vith rag parricide* 'When he made laws to govern the famous city of Athens, he did not in all his laws apportion any penalty for parricide' TH 29

*yma S agustin ow leverall na rug an spuris a thu, henew an spuris a wrioneth han spiris a vnite promysys dre crist then egglos catholyk, na ruga ledia na **gouerna** sectes an par na* 'St Augustine says that the Spirit of God, that is the Spirit of truth and the Spirit of unity promised by Christ to the catholic Church, did not lead nor govern sects of that kind' TH 32-32a

*mas y a vetha in tyrmyn na rag gull aga duty, dobyll honor ha feithfully **gouerna** an egglos, kepar dell levar S powle, ow scriffa the Tyte* 'but they had at that time double honour to do their duty and faithfully to govern the Church, as St Paul says writing to Titus' TH 33a

*ha rag henna agan Savyoure a rug specially, pan esa eff omma war an bys, appoyntya y aposteleth hay disciplis, han re a theffa war aga lyrth y, the kafus an cure ha the ouerwelas ha **gouerna** y egglos bys gorfen an bys* 'and therefore our Saviour when he was on earth here, specially appointed his apostles and disciples, and those who would come after them, to receive the cure of and to oversee and govern his Church until the end of the world' TH 41a

*ha fatell ve an appostres, aweilers, prophettys, dyscars, ha progothorryan y ffe rys gans crist thy bobyll rag aga **gouerna*** 'and that the apostles, evangelists, prophets, teachers and preachers, they were given by Christ to his people to govern them' TH 42

***Govern** an wlas ha the honester omset, i'n dywath may 'festa gras* 'Govern the kingdom and devote yourself to seemliness that you may find grace in the end' BK 2781-83

*pennagel ew (n)a lavara nagew lucyfer worthy omma thagan **governa** ha bos pedn in nef defry a lavar gowe* 'whoever says that Lucifer is not worthy here to govern us and to be chief in heaven speaks untruth' CW 179-83.

'Government' is usually rendered **governans**:

*drefen agis **governens** rewlys on brays ha byan* 'by your governance we are ruled great and small' BM 256-57

*ken nyns ugensy ow regardya du nan re vsy in dan aga **governans**, mar towns y ha suffra du the vos offendys rag lak a coreccion han re vsy in aga **gouernans** the vos perisshys kepar del ra pub naturall tas ha correctia y naturall flogh* 'otherwise they do not regard God nor those who are under their governance, if they happen to allow God to be offended through lack of correction and those in their governance to become corrupted, as every natural father corrects his own child by nature' TH 25

Indelma oll **gouernans** *gwlasow, an pow, an trevow marras, han trevow trygva, y a vea res thetha iently correctia oll an re ew offenders in dan aga* **gouernans** 'thus all government of kingdoms, of the country, of the market towns and the townships, they ought gently correct all those who are offenders under their government' TH 25a

mar pethans y respect vith the thu ha thega office, bo kerensa thyn re vsy in aga **gouernans***, han offendars a res bos rebukys ha correctys in dew tyrmyn* 'if they have any respect for God and for their office, or love towards those under their government, and the offenders must be rebuked and corrected in due time' TH 25a

An kyth sam text ma a S paulle pleynly syttys therag agan lagasow an auctorite han **gevernans** *a rug agan savyour appoyntia the contynewa bys gorfen an bys in y egglos* 'This same text of St Paul sets in front of our eyes the authority and the government which our Saviour appointed to continue until the end of the world in his Church' TH 42

In dede nyns es tra vith moy a yll supressy heresy ys an **gouernans** *an egglos, mar petha estemys accordyng the henna, hag obeyys* 'Indeed there is nothing which can more suppress heresy than the government of the Church, if it is esteemed accordingly and obeyed' TH 42

Lowena ha sansolath th'agan arluth pub seson, ha fues ha skeantolath ha **governans** *ha reson, sertan heb mar* 'Joy and sanctity to our lord at all seasons, and prosperity and wisdom and government and reason' BK 1538-42

Me a dryst this nos ha dyth. Sicut noui te barum omnium Galliarum, an **governans** *te a vith* 'I trust you night and day. As I have known you to be a stout fellow of all the Gauls, you shall have the government' BK 3207-10.

Tregear also uses the word **government** three times:

gans henna yma S paulle in kythsam tyllar ma ow dysquethas rag pan a purpos ew **gouernement** *an par na hag auctorite instytutys* 'moreover St Paul in this same place shows for what purpose government of that kind and authority are instituted' TH 42

Dre hemma why a yll percevya fatell o an conclusyan a S Cyprian, po judgment an **gouernement** *an egglos amyttys the onyn, ha henna the vos reputyes kepar ha vicar crist* 'Thus you can see that the conclusion of St Cyprian or the judgement of the government of the Church granted to one, and that man was to be reputed Christ's vicar' TH 42a

ha the Pedyr han re a ve thea nena, yma res thetha an rule han **gouernement** *an holl flok a crist dre blonogath Du* 'and to Peter and those who were thereafter the rule and government of the whole flock of Christ has been given by the will of God' TH 47a.

Some revivalists will doubtless find **government** too English and will prefer **governans**.

govern

The ordinary Cornish term for 'governor' is **governour, governours**:

*Salmon lemen ke y'th tour rag ty a vyth **governour** whare myghtern kervnys* 'Solomon, go into your tower, for you will be a governor soon, a crowned king' OM 2389-91

*wy yv pen agen ehen **gouerner** lich a fur rays* 'you are chief of our kindred, governor, liege of great grace' BM 318-19

*Me yv empour ha **governour** conquerrour tyr* 'I am emperor and governor, a conqueror of land' BM 930-32

*an pregowther gans an gere han **gouernor** gans an cletha* 'the preacher by the word and the governor by the sword' TH 25

*pew ew an guyde han **gouernar** an egglos henew the vnderstondya an spuris sans* 'who is the guide and governor of the Church? That is to be understood, the Holy Spirit' TH 36

*ha eff a ros thethe **gouernars** da hag orders, dretha may alsans bewa ha plesya du* 'and he gave them good governors and orders, through them that they might live and please God' TH 40

*Kepar ha in pub naturall core polytyk, indella in egglos militant (an pith ew mystical corfe), in vhelder ha in eselder a res kafus **gouernors** in myske an mymbers anethy* 'As in every natural body, so in the Church militant, which is a mystical body, both above and below governors must be found among its members' TH 41a

*the lettya ha suppressya hereses, han **gouernar** na the vos obeyys gans oll an cristonnyan* 'to hinder and suppress heresies, and that governor should be obeyed by all Christians' TH 42a.

To sum up: for 'to govern, to rule' is best translated either **governya**, **governa** or **rêwlya**. 'Government' should be rendered **governans**, and 'governor' is **governour**, *plural* **governours**.

GRAMMAR, GRAMMARIAN

Lhuyd devised the word **gramatek*, plural **grametekyow* on the basis of Welsh *gramadeg* < Latin *grammatica* '(science) of grammar'.

*Lemmyn pan na veva na ydn lïvan **'rammàtek** na huâth ʒerlevran vêth rag uÿnyn a'n Tavazoma* 'Now when there was not a single sheet of a grammar nor any dictionary for any of these languages' AB: 222

*pÿ kèn e vendzha dazargrafa hy **Grammatèkio** hay ʒerlevro e honan* 'otherwise he would have reprinted its own grammars and dictionaries' AB: 222

*an della 'ryg me (ʒen an Trayllyanz reizyz) dazargraf a an raggoryz **'rammatek** ha'n ʒerlevran Arvorek pÿ Gal-Vrethonek* 'so I reprinted, with the necessary translation the prefixed grammar and dictionary of Armorican or Gaulish-British' AB: 222.

This **gramatek** Nance further Cornicized as ***gramasek**, and gave it the adjectival sense 'grammatical'. There are a number of problems here. In the first place, Lhuyd's form should probably have been ***gramadek**. It would not have assibilated to ***gramasek**, since the **r** in the initial cluster **gr-** would have helped to maintain the intervocalic **-d-**; cf. ***prydyth*** 'poet' at BK 2497. Moreover, it seems from Lhuyd's usage (***Grammetèkio*** and ***an raggoryz 'rammatek***) that Lhuyd believed his coinage to have been a noun, not an adjective.

The word **gramatek**, ***gramasek** are unattested in tradiitonal Cornish and there is thus no need to use either form in the revived language. The attested word is **gramer**:

*perfect ef a wore redya **grammer** an geffa deffry y vyea tek* 'he can read perfectly; if he had grammar indeed it would be fine' BM 19-21

*ke gy gans ov mab kerra bys yn mester a **grammer*** 'go with my dearest son to the master of grammar' BM 35-6.

Gramer means 'grammar' as a subject. A grammar (book) can be translated **lyver gramer**. The attested word for 'grammarian' is **gramaryon**:

*Messeger na zovt an cas my an dysk na vo yn gvlas **gramarion** vyth ay parov* 'Messenger, have no doubt in the matter; I shall teach him so that in the kingdom there is no grammarian equal to him' BM 92.

Since **gramer** is attested, it should perhaps be the item of choice.

GRAPE

In his 1938 dictionary Nance recommended ***gwinreunen**, *coll*. ***gwinreun** for 'grape' (UC **gwynrunen*, **gwynrun*). This was on the basis of Welsh *gwinronyn*, coll. *gwinrawn*. Since the discovery of Tregear's Homilies, however, we have an attested word for 'grape': ***grappa**, **grappys**:

*Yma agan meister, redymer ha Sovyour Jhesu crist, in aweyll a S Jowan, ow comparya ha ow hevely y honyn the wethan **grappys**, ha ny oll thyn barrow* 'Our master, redeemer and saviour Jesus Christ in the gospel of St John compares himself to the vine [*literally* grape tree] and us all to the branches' TH 39a.

Given that the plural ***grappys*** 'grapes' of singular ****grappa*** is found in traditional Cornish, there is no need to adopt the unattested form ***gwinreunen**, ***gwinreun**.

grief

GREAT see LARGE

GRIEF, GRIEVANCE, TO GRIEVE

There are several words in Cornish to translate 'grief'. When the sense is 'grief, woe, sorrow', **tristans** is the word of choice:

A **tristans**

Pedyr androw ha Iowan yn meth crist deugh holyough ve bys yn meneth ha me gwan **trystyns** *vs worth ow bluʒye* 'Peter, Andrew and John, said Christ, Come follow me into the mountain for I am weak; sadness is enervating me' PA 53ab

hay holon whek a ranne me a leuer rag **trystans** *rag an grayth ynhy ese nas gweʒe an spyrys sans* 'and her dear heart would have broken, I say, for sorrow, for because of the grace that was in her the Holy Spirit had not preserved her' PA 222cd

guyn y vys a vo trigys yn the seruys ragh **tristys** *nyn dygemmer vynytha* 'happy is he who dwell in your service for grief will never overtake him' PC 122-24

hedre vy yn beys gynen nefre **trystyns** *ny gen byth* 'as long as you are with us in the world, never shall we have sorrow' PC 730-31

agas try deugh why genef rak yma yn ov enef **trystyns** *fast bys yn ancow* 'come with me you three, for there is in my soul sadness unto death' PC 1021-23

ellas pendra wreth yn bys ena anken ha **trystys** *prest ow bones* 'alas, what will you do in the world, anguish and grief being always there?' RD 203-05

mernans **trystyns** *hag anger me a wruk aga fethe* 'death, sorrow and anger, I defeated them' RD 499-500

ren arluth then beys am ros me a ra pur cot y guyns kyns ys dumerher the nos eff a deerbyn **trestyns** 'by the Lord who brought me into the world, I will shorten his wind; before Thursday evening he will experience grief' BM 2252-55

Dyswrys ove ha lethys rag **tristyns***, ogh, in goval!* 'I am destroyed and killed for grief, Oh, in anxiety!' BK 965-66

Re'n geffa **tristyns** *an tyllak ways!* 'May the shabby scoundrel suffer grief!' BK 2288-89

A Thew, gohy ow holan rag **trystyns** *ha gallaraw!* 'O God, woe is my heart for sorrow and affliction!' BK 3287-88.

When 'grief' is synonymous with 'pain, affliction', **grêf** is the commonest noun:

B **grêf**

an grows I a rug gorre war scoth Ihesus ʒy don ʒy ʒe Ihesus crist may teffe ol an **greff** *han belyny* 'the cross they placed his shoulder for Jesus to carry, so that all the grief and pain should afflict Jesus Christ' PA 162cd

ytho prag na leues ef kafus y thege hep **gref** 'thus why should he not presume to get his tithe without pain?' OM 495-96

GERYOW GWIR   grief

Am thethe athesempys yn hanow a'n tas a'n nef try person vn dev henwys ha sur y lyha the **gref** 'Kiss them immediately in the name of the Father of heaven, three persons called one God, and surely they will lessen your suffering' OM 1769-72

Pur wyr mar lyha ov **gref** *my a'n afyth dyso sy ken arluth agesso ef ny'n gorthyaf bys vynary* 'In truth if it lessen my grief, I confide in you that I shall never worship another Lord apart from him for ever' OM 1786-1790

rak henna my a gosse alemma y thylyffrye hep gul dotho na moy **gref** 'therefore I should release him hence without causing him any more grief' PC 2216

genes yth off dysplesijs gul theth tus bones gesijs kemeres duen ha **greff** 'I am displeased with you that you cause your people to be jeered at and to suffer anguish and grief' BM 400-02

Rag kerense crist an neff me a vyn agis pesy na gemerre den vyth **greff** *na duwen am govys vy* 'For the sake of Christ of heaven I shall beg you that no man suffer grief or anguish for my sake' BM 403-06

henna thymo ny ra **greff** *mar calla cafus tyr neff fy the plos lustis an beys* 'that will not cause me grief, if I can attain the kingdom of heaven. Fie to the dirty lusts of the world!' BM 425-27

yagh yv ov corff ham garrov kerthes heb **greff** *me a yll* 'whole are my body and my leg; I can walk without grief' BM 711-12

Ima lues den heb **greff** *a theseff mones then neff ha wath a gar peth an bys* 'There are many men who without grief expect to attain heaven but still love the riches of the world' BM 2036-38

eff am kemer gans schoris may wothaffsen boys leskis le **greff** *es perthy orta* 'it overtakes me with fits so that I should rather be burnt, a lesser grief, than to tolerate them' BM 2633-35

Rag kerense arluth neff gueres dyn orth agen **gref** 'for the sake of the Lord of heaven help us in our affliction' BM 3128-29

Maria myternes neff peys gena the crist a rays maria orth age **greff** *an othomogyan guerays* 'Mary, queen of heaven, pray for me to Christ of grace; Mary, give aid to the needy in their grief' BM 3134-37

ihesu crist nyn sefeth **greff** *in bys ma ath lelwonys* 'Jesus Christ, he will not have affliction in this world who faithfully serves you' BM 3890-91

ha gras the ihesu heb **greff** *meryasek am sawyes* 'and thanks to Jesus, without grief Meriasek healed me' BM 4399-400

Ha mylwyth purguir in geth war ben y ij lyn purfeth y fynna moys awoys **greff** 'And a thousand times indeed in the day he would go down on his knees in spite of pain' BM 4455-57

Na'n cryssa a'n gevith **gref** 'Whoever does not believe it, will suffer grief' BK 143

Mannaf **gref** *penys ha nawn* 'I want affliction, fasting and hunger' BK 428.

The word **grêvons** is attested and derives from Middle English *grevaunce*. In Cornish the sense is 'complaint, illness':

grief

C grêvons

***Grefons** ha cleves seson mar an geveth lel crystyan hav remembra in plas ma ihesu arluth cuff colan y **grefons** gura sewagya* 'If a true Christian suffer complaint and ague and remember me in this place, Jesus, beloved Lord, cure his complaint!' BM 1000-04
*ov cleves prest wy a weyl nyns yv **grefons** in dan geyl a wothogh gul dym guereys* 'my sickness you see; it is no hidden complaint; can you help me?' BM 1437-39.

For 'to grieve' Nance suggests ***trist'he** (UC *trysthe*), **cudhy**, **dysconfortya/dygonfortya** and **grêvya**. ***Trist'he** is not attested. **Cudhy** is attested as a transitive verb, whose verbal adjective means 'sorrowful, miserable'. Note that the 3rd person singular of the preterite appears to be **cudhys** rather than ***cudhas**, presumably to distinguish this verb from **cudha** 'to hide':

A cudhy

*a vap whek yth of **cuthys** ow colon yv marthys claf* 'O dear son, I am sorrowful; my heart is wondrous sick' OM 1336-37
*ellas lemmyn rak moreth yth of **cuthys*** 'alas, now for sorrow I am miserable' RD 765-66
*gon guyr y fethaf marow mur yv ow fyenasow yth of **cuthys*** 'I know truly I shall die; great is my anxiety; I am sorrowful' RD 2030-32
*Ny won a raf, del ru'm **cuthys** an traytor. Galsaf in claf* 'I do not know what to do, as the traitor has grieved me. I have become sick' BK 331-33
*Asa allaf bos **cuthys** pan yl loral ow gesya* 'How sorrowful I can be, when a rascal can mock me' BK 1009-10
*saw e golan ew **cuthys** rag galaraw* 'but his heart is afflicted with sorrow' BK 2391-92
*Mara'n **cuthys** den, ru'm fay, ef a'n pren!* 'If anyone aggrieved him, by my faith, he will pay for it!' BK 2461-62
*Neb a'th **cuthys** a'n tynbren, may welly an ankenak* 'Whoever aggrieved you, shall pay dearly for it, so that you may see him as penitent' BK 2661-62
*Neb a'th **cuthys** in sertan a veth "goef" er e ran!* 'Whoever aggrieved you surely Woe is him will be his share!' BK 2700-01
*Ke wyn an duk ha Bithwar a ve lethis in cres host Myghtern Medys, pan ve Lucy debynnys, mayth of **cuthys**, re Sint Luk!* 'Duke Ke the bright and Bedevere were killed in the midst of the army of the King of the Medes, when Lucius was beheaded, so that I am sorrowful, by St Luke!' BK 3289-93.

Dygonfortya and **dyscomfortya** are attested once each:

B dygonfortya, dyscomfortya

*Ihesus crist **dygonfortys** war ben dewlyn pan ese an nef y fe danuenys el 3030 3y gomfortye* 'When Jesus Christ was on his knees afflicted, an angel was sent to him thither from heaven' PA 58ab

GERYOW GWIR   grief

*En eyll a gewsys ȝeȝe na veȝough **dyscomfortis** Ihesus crist a naȝary del welsough a ve lethys sevys gallas ȝe gen le* 'The angel spoke to them: Do not be grieved. Jesus Christ of Nazareth, who was killed as you saw, has risen. He has gone to another place' PA 255a-c.

For the verb 'to mourn', which has a similar semantic range to 'to grieve', Nance recommends ***galary**, **duwanhe** (UC *dughanhe*), **kyny** (UC *kyny*) and **mùrnya** (UC *mornya*). ***Galary** seems unattested, having been devised by Nance by analogy with Welsh *galaru* and Breton *glac'hariñ*. Though note that *Ha me rig clowaz an poble **galarou*** 'I heard the people complaining' occurs in ACB: F f 3.

Duwhanhe is not uncommon and means 'to grieve, to afflict' in an active sense:

C duwhanhe

*ov bos serrys nyns yw marth ages bones ol warbarth porrys worth ov **duwenhe*** 'it is no wonder that I am angry that you all together are intent on grieving me' RD 1411-13

*gans gwas eth of **deuwenhys** ha'm du Jovyn eselhys!* 'by a fellow I am afflicted and Jovyn, my God despised!' BK 123-24

*War ow fay! ny thesefsan e fenna an pac-casak bonas mar hyll ha kemmys **dewenhys*** 'Upon my faith, I should not have thought that the pack-mare would be so slow and so afflicted' BK 388-91

*Mara pethaf **dywenhys**, me a'm bues gallos i'n bys ha'm yskerans a throkfar* 'If I am afflicted, I have power in the world and my enemies will fare badly' BK 1410-12

*Kyn fe dowthak **dewenhys**, both e golan a vith gwrys, e honyn kepar del vyn* 'Though twelve men be grieved, the desire of his heart shall be done, just as he himself wishes' BK 1434-36

*A traytors, re'gas bo spyt kemmys orth ow **duwenhe*** 'You traitors, may malice be upon you, when you afflict me so greatly' BK 2337-38

*In ow holan tyn reg eth the vos kemmys **duwhenhys*** 'Pain has entered my heart that you are so afflicted' BK 2556-57

*yth oma pur **dewhanhees** ortha welas in state ma* 'I am very grieved to see you in this state' CW 1225-26.

Kyny is well attested:

D kyny

*nu'm cloweth neb ow **kyny** i'n bys warlergh uhelder* 'you will not hear me lamenting in the world for nobility' BK 623-24

*Unwath a'y doll ha cryfter, elhas bos rys thym **kyny!*** 'Alas that I ever had to lament for his deceit and his might!' BK 3146-47

*attoma hager vyadge ma hallaf **kyny** ellas* 'behold a dreadful business, for which I must grieve, alas!' CW 918-19

grief

*rag henna paynes pur vras yma ornes ragan ny may hellyn **kyny** dretha* 'therefore great pain have been ordained for us, so that we must grieve because of them' CW 1014-16.

In CW 'to mourn, to grieve' is sometimes **mùrnya**:

E **mùrnya**

*rag henna woʒa hemma nefra ny wren rejoycya mes pub ere oll ow **mornya** heb ioy vyth na lowena der tha wadn ober omma* 'therefore hereafter we will never rejoice but always will mourn without joy or gladness through your evil work here' CW 1271-75

*agen tase ha mamm eva lower ymowns y ow **murnya** gansa y ny vyth ankevys an murder bys venary* 'our father and mother Eve, they mourn greatly; never will the murder be forgotten by them' CW 1346-49

*kebmys ew ganssy **murnys** aga holan ew terrys rag cavow methaf y dy* 'so much have they mourned, their heart is broken by sorrow, I can swear it' CW 1350-52.

When 'to grieve, to afflict' is transitive in sense, the best attested word in the texts is **grêvya** and this is attested at all periods:

F **grêvya**

*mab du o kymmys **grevijs** rag tomder ef a wese* 'the Son of God was so pained; he perspired for fever' PA 58c

*koscough lemmyn mars ew prys powesough wy yv **grevijs*** 'sleep now, if it is time, rest; you are grieved' PA 61b

*Han ʒew na bys pan vons squyth war crist y fons ov cronkye manna geve goth na leyth na gesa worth y **grevye*** 'And those two until they tired they were striking Christ, so that he had neither vein nor limb that did not pain him' PA 132ab

*pows Ihesus a ve dyskis y dysky mur an **grevye*** 'Christ's garment was taken off; greatly it was grieving him' PA 176b

*mar posse a neyll tenewen rag y scoth hy a **grevye** Ha whath gweth a wre an pren war ʒellargh maran gorre* 'If he leant sideways it would hurt him because of his shoulder and still worse it would, if he put it backwards from the wood' PA 205cd

*natur scyle me a syns arluth da mar pyth peynys ol y sogete kyn fons syns rag y beyn ʒe vos **grevijs*** 'Nature causes, I believe, if a good lord is pained, all his subject though they be saints, to be afflicted for his torments' PA 211cd

*han anken mur as **grevye** pan vyre worth y woly yn tenewen yʒ ese dre an golon as tylly* 'and the great sorrow afflicted her when she looked at his wound; it was in the side, it pierced her through the heart' PA 231cd

*thy'nny ny travyth ny **gref** aban yw sur y voth ef y lesky hep falladow* 'to us nothing shall be grievous, since his will surely is to burn it without fail' OM 482-84

*a das dev dre the versy danfon jehes thy'mmo vy a'm cleves mayth of **grevyys*** 'O Father, God, by your mercy send me health from my disease by which I am grieved' OM 2629-31 *parys fest yv an spyrys ha'n kyc yv marthys* **grevyys** *gans cleues ha govegyon* 'the spirit is very ready and the flesh is wondrous grieved by sickness and care' PC 1060-62

ow colon yv mur huthys nyns us peyn orth ow **greffya** 'my heart is greatly cheered; no pain is grieving me' RD 483-84

vs whet the'th corf galarow na torment orth the **greffye** 'is there still pain in your body or torment grieving you?' RD 487-58

ny'm **gref** *peyn yn nep maner a wrello thy'm drok neffre* 'no pain afflicts me in any way that will ever do me harm' RD 497-98

nyns us tra orth ow **greffye** 'nothing afflicts me' RD 502

ny yv dev then bohosek me **grefijs** *gans an febyr han keth den ma sur yv mans* 'we are two poor men; I am afflicted by the fever and this same man here is lame' BM 693-95

A thu asoma **grefijs** *rag na wela tra in beys pendra dale ol ov rechys* 'O God, how grieved I am, for I cannot at all in the world what value are all my riches' BM 2522-24

A thu assoma **grefijs** *mans ov esely aheys mas orth dev croyth ny gerthaff* 'O God, how grieved I am; all my limbs are crippled; I can walk only upon two crutches' BM 4181-83

hereth us orth ov **grefya** *ha lues heboff oma purguir hythyv* 'longing is grieving me and indeed many apart from me here today' BM 4544-46

Rag an cawses ma nyg us feithfull colonow vith **greviis** *war y gylwell bara in scriptur* 'For these reasons faithful hearts are not grieved calling it "bread" in scripture' TH 57a

gans dew yth ew apoyntes warden war oll paradys der henna yth of **grevys** *y wellas eve exaltys ha me dres 3a yseldar* 'he has been appointed warden over all paradise by God; I am grieved therefore to see him exalted and me brought low' CW 443-47

me a gryes ty mar pe hemma terrys mes an wethan defennys ragtha me a vyth **grevys** 'I believe, you see, if this was plucked from the forbidden tree, I shall be grieved because of it' CW 749-52

Materen Frink, thera vi a menia, na venja hedda whath gun **greevia** 'The King of France I mean; that would still not grieve us' LAM: 226.

'Grief' is probably best translated as **grêf** or **tristans**. **Grêvons** means 'complaint, illness'. 'To grieve, to afflict' is **cudhy**, **duwhanhe** or **grêvya**. 'To grieve, to mourn is probably best rendered **mùrnya** or **kyny**.

GROUP

The ordinary word for 'group' in the revived language is *****bagas**, a word which is not actually attested. Lhuyd gives: *C[ornish]* ***Bagat*** under *Concilium, A council or assembly* AB: 50b. The word in form is apparently Old Cornish, but is not found in OCV. Indeed it is not certain that **bagat** 'council, assembly' was ever Old Cornish at all. It is possible that the ascription to Cornish by Lhuyd is a misprint. On the other hand the only evidence we have for the word **bagas** with assibilated final, as in Middle Cornish, is ***Bagaz***

group   **GERYOW GWIR**

'A bush'; ***Bagaz*** *eithin* 'a Bush of furze' AB: 33b. It appears therefore that we have no evidence that the word **bagas** ever meant 'assembly, group' in Middle Cornish. On the other hand it should be pointed out that in Middle English the word *bush* means both 'bush' and 'crowd of people', and that when borrowed into Cornish **bùsh** means both 'bush' and 'crowd'; cf., for example:

Aspyen orth en ***buschys*** *hag orth an karrek kefrys* 'Let us look at the bushes and at the rock also' BM 1023-24
me a weyll ***busch*** *brays a dus* 'I see a great crowd of people' BM 3232.

It must be admitted, however, that the evidence for **bagas** 'group' is really very tenuous. The only attested words for 'group, party of people' appear to be **felshyp** and **party**:

der henna y fuff sawys ha part am ***felschyp*** *gena* 'by that I was saved and some of my party with me' BM 2154-55
mara tuen ha debatya mas an nyyl ***party*** *omma ov teberth purguir ny warth* 'if we debate, only one group here will be laughing as they leave' BM 3476-78.

H

HAND, HANDS

In the earliest Middle Cornish the word for 'hand' is **leuv** (UC *luf*). Because the vowel **eu** was liable to unrounding, **leuv** became identical in pronunciation with **lev** 'voice'. It seems that in order to avoid ambiguity, the singular **leuv** *f.* was largely replaced by **dorn** *m.*, which originally meant 'fist'. The plural of **dorn** 'hand', however, was **dywla**, **dewla**, i.e. the dual of **leuv**.

A leuv

*Heys crist y a gemeras an neyll **lef** bys yn y ben* 'They measured Christ's width from one hand to the other' PA 178a

*gvlan ef re gollas an plas a'm **lef** thyghyow a wrussen* 'he has quite lost the place which I made on my right hand' OM 420-21

*gulan ef re gollas an plas a'm **luf** thyghyow a wrussen pan wruge dres ov defen* 'he has quite lost the place that I made upon my right hand when he transgressed by prohibition' OM 920-22

*pandra synsyth y'th **luef** lemyn lauer moyses* 'what are you holding in your hand now? Tell me, Moses' OM 1442-43

*doro kenter er the fyth ha me a tak y **luef** gleth gans ol ow nel* 'bring a nail upon your faith, and I will fasten his left hand with all my strength' PC 2746-48

*ny thue y **luef** sur the'n tol* 'his hand won't surely reach the hole' PC 2755

*an **luef** a'm gruk me a wel ha'y odor whekka ys mel ow tos warnaf* 'I see the hand that made me and its fragrance sweeter than honey coming upon me' RD 143-45

*neffre ny fynnaf crygy ken ben vyth mar mur duwon er na hyndlyf y golon gans ov **luef** dre y woly* 'never shall I believe, though I suffer never so much anguish, until I feel his heart with my hand through his wound' RD 1529-32

*a thomas doro the **luef** yn woly guynys may fuef dre an golon* 'Thomas, put your hand in the wound where I was pierced through the heart' RD 1539-41.

B dorn

*Lemen y3 **torn** my as re ha war an grey3 my an te nag usy far an bar3 ma 3e pons tamar* 'Now I give her into your hand and upon the faith I swear that there is not her equal from here to the Tamar bridge' CF 18-21

hand   **GERYOW GWIR**

Adam ystyn thy'm the **thorn** *tan henna theworthef vy* 'Adam, stretch out your hand to me; take this from me' OM 205-06

a'n lost kymmer thethy yn ban y'th **torn** *hep ger sens the honan thy's lauaraf* 'by the tail pick her up; hold her in your own hand without a word, I tell you' OM 1454-56

me a gergh dour thy's wharre otte ow fycher gyne yn ov **dorn** *rak y gerghas* 'I will fetch water for you immediately. Here I have my pitcher in my hand to fetch it' PC 655-57

com forth ihesu yn ow **dorn** *heil myghtern an yethewon ty a fyth cowal anken* 'come forth, Jesus, led by my hand. Hail, king of the Jews; you will have utter misery' PC 2528-30

tan syns y'th **dorn** *an giu na ha herthy'e gans nerth yn ban* 'here, hold that spear in your hand and thrust it powerfully upwards' PC 3010-11

lemmyn pup ol settyes **dorn** *yn keth schath ma th'y tenne* 'now let everyone put his hand in that same boat to pull it' RD 2351-52

hag eff an jeva an **thorne** *vhella han victuri* 'and he had the upper hand and the victory' TH 34

ha dre an succession an epscobow a rome thea tirmyn pedyr bys in dith hethow, an gwyr a ve derives a **thorne** *the* **thorne** 'and by the succession of the bishops of Rome from the time of Peter until the present the truth has been explained from hand to hand' TH 48

In v-as a Josue yth ew recordys fatell rug onyn sodenly apperya the Josue havall the den ha cletha noith in y **dorne** 'In the 5th chapter of Joshua it is recorded that one suddenly appeared to Joshua like a man with a naked sword in his hand' TH 55a

ha pana substans a cletha o honna essa in **dorne** *henna a rug apperia the Josue?* 'and what substance of sword was that which was in the hand of him who appeared to Joshua?' TH 55a

Du re'th wela mes a'y **dorn***!* 'May God see you out of his hand!' BK 2097

ty foole prag na bredersys a **thorn** *dew y festa gwryes* 'you fool, why did you not consider that you were made by God's hand?' CW 308-09

nymbes yddrag vythe yn beise [gans] owe **doarn** *keth ewe lethys par del oma gwicker coynt* 'I have no regret at all though by my hand he is slain, as I am a smart dealer' CW 1141-43

me a lead an voos am **dorn** 'I shall lead the girl by my hand' CW 1390

drog polat ove rom lowta na mere a **dorn** *da ny wraf* 'I am an evil fellow, upon my faith; I do not turn my hand to much good' CW 1441-42

Ha po 'ryg e doz dhon darraz, ev a vendzha klouaz dhên aral en guili: Ev a uaske e **dorn** *uar e dhâgier dho dhestrîa an dhêau* 'And when he came to the door, he would hear another man i'n the bed. He struck his hand upon his dagger to kill them both' BF: 19

Ha leben lez e ora rag e **dorn** *a raage ha komeraz weeth dore an gwethan bownaz, ha debre, ha bowa râg nevra* 'And now lest he stretch out his hand forward and take also from the tree of life and live for ever' Rowe

Thurt an termen notha Jesus reeg dalla a boroga, ha tha laale, Greew gwel, râg ma gulasketh neue tha **dorn** 'From that time Jesus began his preaching and to say, Make amends, for the Kingdom of Heaven is at hand' Rowe

An lavar kôth yu lavar guîr, Bedh **dvrn** *rê ver, dhvn tavaz rê hîr* 'The proverb is a true saying: the hand is too short for the too longue tongue' AB: 251c.

Notice incidentally that in TH the word **dorn** appears to be feminine, presumably by analogy with **leuv**.

The expression **dhyrag dorn** 'beforehand' is also attested:

pana othom vea cowse hemma severally the pedyr, hag eff the cowse in generally thethans y oll **therag dorne** 'what need would there have been to say this severally when he spoke generally to them all before hand?' TH 44a

ow menya dre an dall, effreg, bothar, ha omlavar, an re a ve **therag dorne** *indella* 'meaning by the blind, lame, deaf and dumb those who had been thus beforehand' TH 57a

Rag henna mars ees marver gallus in geir agen arluth Christ tha gwiel pith nyn go **derag dorne**, *paseil moy gallus, the gonys, ha changya an pith nag o* **derag dorne** 'Therefore if there is such great power in the word of our Lord Christ to create that which was not beforehand, by how much the more power to work and to change that which was not beforehand' SA 62a.

C **dewla**

yn meth an goff clevas bras es om **dewleff** *deveȝys* 'the smith said, A great sickness has come upon my hands' PA 156c

Reys o ȝoȝo dysqueȝas ȝe pur treytours a **ȝewle** 'He was obliged to show his hands to the utter traitors' PA 157a

In meth gurek an goff ȝeȝe kentrow ȝewy why ny fyll awos bos claff y **ȝewle** 'The smith's wife said to them, You will not lack nails, even though his hands are sick' PA 158ab

worth an les y a dollas ij doll yn an [sic]*grows heb ken mayȝ ello an kentrow bras dre y* **ȝewleff** *bys yn p[r]en* 'they bored two holes in the cross only so that the great nails could pass through his hands into the wood' PA 178bc

ow eneff me a gymyn arluth yntre ȝe **ȝewle** 'my soul I commend, O Lord, into your hands' PA 204d

gew a ve yn y **ȝewle** *gans an eȝewon gorris* 'a spear was put into his hands by the Jews' PA 217c

An golon yȝ eth stret bras dour ha goys yn kemeskis ha ryp an gyw a resas ȝe **ȝewle** *neb an gwyskis* 'From the heart there poured a great stream of water and blood mixed and along the spear it ran to the hands of him who smote him' PA 219ab

ov **dywluef** *colm ha'm garrow gans louan fast colmennow na allan seuel am saf* 'bind my hands and my legs with a firm rope, bonds so that I won't be able to stand up' OM 1346-48

me a vyn mos the vre ow arluth treys ha **devle** *gans onement ker yn certan* 'I shall go to anoint my Lord, feet and hands, indeed with expensive ointment' PC 473-75

treys ha **dyvlef** *a pup tu fast tackyes gans kentrow hern ellas* 'feet and hands firmly fixed on both sides with iron nails, alas!' PC 2937-39

me a's ten athysempys an thyv yn mes a'y **thywle** *hag a'y thewtros kekyffrys* 'I will draw them straightway, the two out of his hands and from his two feet as well' PC 3152-54

ellas bones the treys squerdys ol the yscarn dyscavylsys tel y'th **dyvluef** 'alas, that your feet were all torn, all your bones dislocated, with holes in your hands!' PC 3172-74

hand   **GERYOW GWIR**

vfereth yv thy's govyn pyth yv an marth a wharfe a vn profus bynyges yn grous ha thywvregh ales squerdys y treys ha'y **thywle** 'it is futility for you to ask what is the wonder that has occurred concerning a blessed prophet on the cross with his hands outstretched, his hands and his feet torn' RD 1263-66

a thomas doro the luef yn woly guynys may fuef dre an golon hag yn treys hag yn **thyvle** 'O Thomas put your hand in the wound where I was pierced through the heart and in feet and in the hands' RD 1539-42

y fue ow manegow plat spygys bras dre ow **dywle** 'my gauntlets of plate were great spikes through my hands' RD 2589-90

Inter **dula** *du avan ov map gruaff the kemynna* 'Into the hands of God above, my son, I commend you' BM 502-03

scorgis gans an ʒethewon kentrewys treys ha **dula** *gans gu lym in tenewon del russons y y guana* 'scourged by the Jews, nailed feet and hands, as they pierced him with a sharp spear in the side' BM 2602-05

spykys bras a horne dre an treys ha **dewleff** 'great spikes of iron through the feet and hands' TH 15a

Gans agan gallus ha power, hen ew the venya gans agan **dewleff** *ha treys, gans agan lagasow ha scovornow, gans agan ganowow ha tavosow* 'With our might and power, that is to say with our hands and feet, with our eyes and ears, with our mouths and ears' TH 21a

ha in tyrmyn na eff a gemeras bara in y **thewla**, *hag a leueris grace, hag a rug y dyrry han ros thy disciplis* 'and at that moment he took bread in his hands, and said grace, and broke it and gave it to his disciples' TH 52

O mirkell, ha blonogath da a thew, disquethis theny, vgy setha in gwlas neff, vgy intyr **dowla** *tus an beis in tirmyn an sacrifice* 'O miracle shown to us and good will of God, who sits in the kingdom of heaven, who is in the hands of the men of the world at the time of the sacrifice' SA 60

an kigg ew touchis gans **dowla**, *rag malla an nenaf bos golowis gans an spiris sans* 'the flesh is touched by hands, that the soul may be enlightened by the Holy Spirit' SA 60a

Indella emowns y [o] dishonora Christ pan vonsy y recevia ef ha e corf benegas ef gans **dowla** *mustethas* 'Thus they dishonour Christ when they receive him and his blessed body with unclean hands' SA 61

Phoceus ema o leverall: neb vge o recivia corf Dew gans **dowla** *mustethas, eth ew ef gilty an gos agen arluth Dew, kepar a ve Judas* 'Phoceus says: who receives the body of God with unclean hands, is guilt of the blood of our Lord, as was Judas' SA 61

ef a ve degys inter e **thowla** 'he was brought into their hands' SA 65

benegas ema inter **dowla** *an pronter* 'it is blessed in the hands of the priest' SA 66

y varck warnaf y settyas poran gans y owne **dewla** 'he set his mark upon me with his very own hands' CW 1530-31

ha mar petha indella me a vidn ye requyrya a **thewla** *an kethe dean na y woose a theffa scullya* 'and if it be so, I shall require it from the hands of that same man, who should spill his blood' CW 2519-22

ha de scunha leh d'r essa lever an Have an Arlothas Kernow bose kevez en **dula** *a flehaz ugge hemma* 'and the sooner lest that were the book of the Summer of the Duchess of Cornish to be found in the hands of my children after this' BF: 31

E ra ry tha e eelez an pohar anhanesta et ago **doola** *y ra tha doone man leez a turn veth al chee ra browe tha drooze bedn mean* 'He will give his angels power over you; in their hands they will bear you up, lest at any time you injure your foot against a stone' Rowe.

As has been mentioned above under 'feet' and as can be seen in the above examples, the regular way of saying 'hands and feet' in Cornish is **treys ha dewla**.

HARP

The UC word for 'harp' is *telyn f.*, a word that is not attested in Middle Cornish, being respelt from *cithara*, **telein** at OCV §250. The only attested word in Middle Cornish is **harp**, **harpys**, seen in:

whethoug menstrels ha tabours trey hans **harpes** *ha trompours cythol crowd fylh ha savtry psalmus gyttrens ha nakrys organs inweth cymbalys recordys ha symphony* 'Blow minstrels and drums, three hundred harps and trumpets, dulcimer, viol, fiddle and psaltery, shawms, zithers and kettle drums, organs, also cymbals recorders and symphony' OM 1995-2000.

Since the word **harpes** occurs in a list of musical instruments, it is likely that the author of OM was himself familiar with musical instruments and their names. In which case, **harp** was almost certainly the Cornish word current at the time for 'harp'.

The word **telynyor** 'harpist' is a respelling of ***teleinior*** at OCV §249. Nance also suggest ****harpour***, although such a word is not attested.

TO HASTEN, HASTE,

'To hasten, to hurry' is usually **fystena**, which is attested over 60 times. Here are some examples:

A **fystena**
eug alema ha ***fystynyug*** 'go hence and hurry' CF 26
Indelma crist pan wresse ʒe iudas y leueris te ke yn vn ***fystene*** *ʒe voth may fo colenwys* 'When Christ had done thus he said to Judas, You, go in a hurry, that your wish may be fulfilled' PA 48ab
Cherubyn kemmer clethe ***fystyn*** *trogha parathys* 'Cherub, take a sword; hasten to paradise' OM 331-32
lemyn pep ol yskynnens yn hanow a'n tas dev ker ha war tv tre ***fystenens*** *kefrys marrek ha squyer* 'now let everybody mount in the name of the Father, beloved God, and let them hurry home, both knight and squire' OM 2001-04

hasten   **GERYOW GWIR**

ha mowysy gans golow yn lanterns hep falladow ***fysteneugh*** *fast alemma* 'and maids with lighted lanterns, hasten quickly hence' PC 944-46
fystyn *ov duf whek avy gueyt an harlot na scapyo* 'hurry, my dear son-in-law; make sure the rogue does not escape' PC 989-90
lowen henna me a vyn ha thu'm arluth ***fystynyn*** 'gladly I will do that and let us hurry to my lord' RD 1673-74
my ny garaf streche pel na nyl the wyth na the sul ***fysteneugh*** *ow leuerel pendra reys thy'n the wuthul* 'I do not wish to delay for long either on a weekday or Sunday; hurry and say what we need to do' RD 2249-52
Fysten *dewhans, me a'th pys* 'Hurry quickly, I beg you' BK 1034
Dun warbarth. ***Fistenyn*** *scaf* 'Let us go together. Let us hasten quickly' BK 1353
adam attoma dyllas hag eva thages quetha ***ffystenowgh*** *bethans gweskes* 'Adam, here are clothes, and Eve, to dress you. Hurry, let them be put on' CW 977-79
an lywe nang ew devethis may thew da thyne ***fystena*** 'the flood now has come, so that it is good for us to hurry' CW 2431-32
Festino… To mke hast, to hasten or do a thing speedily. C. Dho ***festinna*** AB: 59b.

Festyna, however, does not seem to occur in either BM or TH.
The verb **fysky** 'to hurry, to rush' is attested twice:

B **fysky**

yma moyses pel gyllys yn mor del heuel thy'mmo a rag dywhans ov kerthes an dour ov ***fysky*** *a les pup vr ol a thyragtho* 'Moses has gone far into the sea, as it seems to me, walking quickly ahead, the water rushing apart continually before him' OM 1682-86
Ay tav an iovle theth lesky prag pendryv an ***fesky*** *us genes han terlemel* 'Hey, silence! The devil scald you. Why, what is this hurry of yours and this jumping about?' BM 2098-100.

The verb **hâstya** 'to hasten' is attested twice in BK:

C **hâstya**

Pan wellys e thowlugy, na vynha ***hastia*** *thyuwhy, marthys coyth me a'n settyas a vargh thotha pan gowsen* 'When I saw his devilment, that he would not haste to you, exceedingly quickly I set him on horseback as I spoke to him' BK 383-86
Seglowyns pobel adro, in nergh korf kemmys a vo in arvow rys ew thotha ***hastia*** *thu'm arluth uhall* 'Let people around listen: whoever is able-bodied, must hasten in arms to my noble lord' BK 2368-71.

The Cornish word for the substantive 'haste' is **hast**, which is used mostly in the expressions **wàr hast**, **in hast** and **gans hast** 'in haste, hastily':

En debell wrek casadow gans mur a doth eth yn chy war ***hast*** *ʒe weʒyll kentrow* 'The evil hateful wife went very quickly into the house in haste to make nails' PA 159ab

Gans an eʒewon war **hast** *drok ʒewas a ve dyʒgtys* 'An evil drink was prepared in haste by the Jews' PA 202a

lemyn yn **hast** *me a'th kelm fast a ver termyn* 'now in haste I will bind you in a short time' OM 1361-62

my a ten by god ys fast may hetho the'n tol yn **hast** 'I will pull, by God's fast, so that it may reach the hole in haste' PC 2767-68

mars us kuth war the colon the both a vyth gurys yn scon genen yn **hast** 'if there is sorrow in your heart, your wish will be accomplished soon by us in haste' RD 2156-58

Arthur a vyn e vettya in **hast** *ha'y oversettya ef re dos in ger maraw* 'Arthur wishes to meet him in haste and to overcome him he has sworn with a fruitless word' BK 2393-95

In ol **hast** *ef a'th pegys a thos thotha* 'In all haste he asked you to come to him' BK 2423-24

Pen the yskar, ren ow thas! in ol **hast** *a vith terrys der vras colan* 'The head of your enemy, by my father! will in all haste be cut off by a sturdy heart' BK 2614-16

Me a lever thys, Modres, keffrys te ha'n viternas in ol **hast** *a vith marow* 'I tell you, Modred, you and your queen together will be killed in all haste' BK 3179-81

Kyn fe in cres menath horn, me a'n devyn a deu thorn in **hast**, *by Godys body!* 'Though he were in the middle of a mountain of iron, I will tear him in two pieces in haste, by God's body!' BK 3220-22

Ea, an crothak, in **hast** *e fyth dielhys* 'Yea, the big belly, will be punished in all haste' BK 3254-55

Mar wyr dell oui Jacca, ef a'n gevyth an lacka hag in **hast** *a vith maraw* 'As true as I am called Jack, he will get a worse fate and in haste will be dead' BK 3297-99

na gymmar marth vyth benyn vas me a theth [th]a the wheras mes a neif gans **hast** *pur vras* 'do not be astonished, good woman; I have come with very great haste from heaven to assist you' CW 554-56.

In the revived language 'to hasten, to hurry' should be **fystena**, **fysky** or **hâstya**. 'In haste' on the other hand is best rendered **wàr hast**, **in hast** or **gans hast**.

HORSEMAN

The the expected word for 'horseman, rider, knight' in Cornish is ***marhek**. This form, however, is not attested. In all the attested examples the medial consonant group **-rh-** appears as **-rr-** or **-r-**. It is probable, however, that the medial segment **-rr-** or **-r-** may in fact represent a voiceless **r**. It also appears that the devoiced **r** in certain instances dissimilated the final **-k** to **-g**.

Marrek < ***marhek** has an expected plural ***marhogyon**, **marrogyon**; cf. **bohosek** BM 438, 693, 736, etc. but plural **bohosogyon** BM 2551, 2641, 3430. In the texts, however, **marhek** has acquired an analogical plural **marhegyon**. Moreover the reduced final syllable of **marhek** is frequently written with **-ak** rather than **-ek**. In traditional Cornish, therefore, we find the following forms: (*singular*) **marrek**, **marreg**; **marrak**; (*plural*) **marogyon**; **maregyon**.

Here are all the examples of the word as attested in the texts (note that in PA in particular **marhek** means 'soldier' rather than 'horseman, knight'):

A1 Singular forms in -*ek*, -*eg*

Dyllas crist a ve rynnys pedar ran guris a neȝe gans peswar **marreg** *a brys ȝe bub* **marreg** *ran may fe* 'Christ raiment was divided, four parts made of it by four important soldiers so that each soldier might have a share' PA 190ab

In aga herwyth yȝ ese vn **marreg** *longis hynwys* 'among them there was a soldier called Longinus' PA 217a

ȝen **marreg** *worth y hanow y a yrhys may whane yn corf Ihesus caradow* 'they bade the soldier by his name to pierce the body of beloved Jesus' PA 218bc

y eth yn vn fystene peswar **marrek** *yrvys ens* 'they went off hurriedly; they were four armed soldiers' PA 241d

Pan deȝens y bys yn beth yȝ eth vn **marrek** *ȝy ben hag arall ȝy dreys ynweth* 'When they came to the tomb, one soldier went to his head and another to his feet also' PA 242ab

Pan o pur holergh an gyth y tefenas vn **marrek** 'When the day was very late one soldier awoke' PA 244a

En **marrek** *na a sevys oll yn ban y goweȝe ha ȝeȝe a leuerys a Ihesus fatell vye* 'That soldier aroused all his comrades and he told them how it had been with Jesus' PA 245ab

ha war tu tre fystenens kefrys **marrek** *ha squyer* 'and let them hasten home both knight and squire' OM 2003-04

vrry ov **marrek** *guella my a vynsa the pysy gor ost genes yrvys da the omlath del y'm kerry* 'Uriah, the best of my knights, I would beg you to take a well-armed host with you to fight, as you love me' OM 2139-42

ha del oma **marrek** *len benythe ny thof a'n plen er na'n prenne an guas na* 'and as I am a loyal knight, never will I come from the field until that fellow pay for it' OM 2150-52

my a'd pys may fy asper avel **marrek** *fyn yrvys* 'I beg you to be savage like a fully armed knight' OM 2203-04

saw vn **marrek** *a'n lathas ha the'n dor scon a'n goras hag a'n hakyas the dymmyn* 'but one knight killed him and pulled him to the ground and hacked him to pieces' OM 2226-28

ty re thyswrug eredy hevelep tho'm face vy vrry nep o **marrek** *len* 'you have destroyed a likeness of my own person, Uriah who was a loyal knight' OM 2336-68

ov bolnogeth purguir yv rag gorthia crist galosek bones sacris **marrek** *du* 'my wish indeed in order to worship might Christ is to be consecrated a knight of God' BM 350-52

Plos **marrek** *pour dar seposia prest a reta omma settya orth emperour* 'You utter dirty knight, what, do you presume here to oppose an emperor?' BM 2444-47.

A2 Plural forms in -*egyon*

marregyon *me agas pys gorreugh ef the erod scon* 'knights, I beg you, take him to Herod immediately' PC 1613-14

heil doctors ha mestrygi ***marregyon*** *heil heil thywhy* 'hail, doctors and masters; knight, hail, hail to you' PC 2346-47

eugh lemmyn ow ***marreggyon*** *bys yn beth alemma scon del owgh tus ven* 'go now, my knights, to the tomb quickly hence as you are stalwart men' RD 361-63

out warnough fals ***marregion*** *pyth yw an whethlow ha'n son a glewaf aberth yn pow* 'damn you, false knights! What are the stories and rumours I hear about the land?' RD 607-09

marregyon *theugh ny won blam rak thy'mmo y fye scham gul drok thywhy* 'knights, to you I impute no blame, for it would be an infamy for me to do you any harm' RD 657-59.

B1 Singular forms in -*ak*

Marrak *arall a gowsas gony vyth pan veyn genys* 'Another soldier spoke: Alas that we were born' PA 246a

Elider eth of hynwys, the Arthor ***marrak*** *gostlys, y anmy rag debenna* 'I am called Elider, a knight pledged to Arthur for beheading his enemy' BK 1513-15

Aban dallathas an bys, noble ***marrak****, me a grys, ny ombrevys in dan scoys* 'Since the beginning of the world, a more noble knight, I believe, was never proved beneath a shield' BK 1631-33

Marrak *lym, orth both ow brys, uhal-worthyys of i'n bys* 'A keen knight to my heart's desire, highly revered am I in the world' BK 1648-49

marrack *en pedden west pow Densher* 'a knight in the western part of Devonshire' BF: 27.

B2 Plural forms in -*ogyon*

En ***varogyon*** *a guskas myttyn han gyth ow tarʒe* 'The soldiers slept at morn when the dawn was breaking' PA 243a

Rag henna pylat a ros ʒen ***vorogyon*** *aga ro* 'Therefore Pilate gave the soldiers their reward' PA 250a

En ***varogyon*** *pan glewas pylat ov cows yndella mur a ioy as kemeras* 'When the soldiers heard Pilate speaking thus, great joy seized them' PA 251ab

dun alemma ***marrouggyon*** *kefrys ynweth squyerryon* 'let us go hence, knights and also squires as well' OM 1639-40

marrogyon *parusugh wy haneth omma yredy mytern connan sur a thua* 'knights, get ready here tonight indeed. King Conan is surely coming' BM 221-23

Ov lich kyng bethugh mery inweth oll an kyffuywy dukis ʒurlys ***marogyon*** 'My liege the king, be merry; and also all the guests, dukes, earls, knights' BM 292-94

Duen ny in kerth gans mur a nerth ov ***marogyon*** 'Let us depart with great strength, my knights' BM 813-15

marogyen *duen alema me ny won in fays py ma an keth meneth na certyn* 'let us go hence, knight; I do not well know indeed where that same mountain is' BM 1742-44 *galwy dis bras ha munys hag ol the **varogyen** keth hath arlythy* 'summon to you great and small, and all your knight, base and lords BM 2432-34

*dugh gena ow **marogyon** thy wore in doyr dyson ny a vyn mones lemmen* 'come with me, my knights; to bury him in the ground straightway we will now go' BM 4359-61

***Marrogyon** flowr, wylcum o'm tyr, i wer onowr thewhy pub wyer mar tyrffynnowgh* 'Choicest knight, welcome to my country, to great honour in very deed if you deserve it' BK 1946-50

***Marrogyan**, leverugh why pan worshyp, er agys fith, a wothya Arthor the ry rag an trubut solathyth a stoppyas ef?* 'Knights, tell me what compensation by your faith was Arthur able to give in lieu of the tribute which he has stopped rendering?' BK 2252-56

*Pax nunc, prelyatores, prynsys, dukys, **marrogyon**, autem debiliores* 'Peace now, prelates, princes, dukes, knights, and also poorer men' BK 2380-82

*I o chyf ow **marogyon*** 'They were my chief knights' BK 3286.

In view of the above examples, it the revived language should perhaps allow both **marhek**, **marhegyon** and **marhak**, **marhogyon**. Although forms with medial **-rh-** are not attested, it is probably best write the word with **-rh-** to remind speakers that the medial consonantal segment is a voiceless **-r-**.

The verbal noun **marhogeth** has **-og-** in its stem:

*an asen a ve kerghys warneʒy rag eseʒe dyllas pan a ve gorrys rag **morogeth** a vynne ʒen cyte ʒe vos gorthijs* 'the ass was fetched, upon it for sitting cloth garments were put, for he wished to ride to the city to be acclaimed' PA 28b-d

*my a vyn a thysempys **marogeth** ware bys t'y* 'I will at once ride thither' OM 1970-71

***marogeth** my ny alla yma cleves y'm body* 'I cannot ride; there is a sickness in my body' OM 2145-46

*A varwo awos arveth, nyng ew guyw the **vorogath*** 'Whoever would die because of insults, is not worthy to ride out' BK 928-29

*A varwa awos arveth, nyng ew guew the **varogath*** 'Whoever would die because of insults, is not worthy to ride out' BK 3226-27.

HOUR

The word **eur** (UC *ur*) does not really mean 'hour', but rather 'time' in adverbial phrases, e.g. A) **py eur, p'eur** 'when?'; B) **pub eur** 'always' and C) **i'n eur-na** 'then'. Moreover **i'n eur-na** is often reduced to **nena**, **nyna**. Here are some examples of all three expressions:

A **py eur, p'eur** 'when?'

***py vr** fuf vy y wythes* 'when was I his guardian?' OM 576

***py vr** a tus th'y gerghas ha guet na veny tollys* 'when will men go to fetch him and be sure we are not deceived' PC 603-04

GERYOW GWIR   hour

pur *a wylsta war an kee gesys yn bysma enaff* 'when did you see in this world a soul left on the hedge?' BM 1253-54

*kelmys off the vryasek sav ny von **pur** in metyaff* 'I am bound to Meriasek but I do not know when I shall meet him' BM 4185-86.

B **pub eur** 'always'

*wy a gyff bohosogyon **pub er** warnough ow carme* 'you will have the poor crying out to you always' PA 37c

*mes y ȝeuȝys o mar feyn **pub vr** an trylya ȝeȝa* 'but his godhead was so fine, always it turned him to them' PA 54c

*ty a vyth genen nefre ha dewolow hep nyuer **pup vr** orthys ov scrynkye* 'you will be with us always with innumerable devils always snarling at you' OM 568-70

***pup vr** ty yv colonnek parys rag dysky dader* 'you are always hearty to learn goodness' BM 32-33

*han vohosogyen **pub vr** bethugh sokyr an re na* 'and the poor, always assist those people' BM 4261-62

*Rag yth ewa very expedient ha necessary the gafus **pup vr** oll an kythsam kerensa ma* 'For it is very expedient and necessary to exhibit this same love always' TH 20a

*may ma dew han noer keffrys warnas **pub ere** ow crya* 'so that God and the earth also are always crying out against you' CW 1269-70

*bewa yth esaf **pub eare** in tomdar ha yender reaw sure nos ha dyth* 'I live always in heat and frosty cold indeed night and day' CW 1667-69.

C **i'n eur-na** 'then'

***In er na** ȝen menyȝyow why a ergh warnough coȝe* 'Then you will command the mountains to fall upon you' PA 170a

***yn er na** y fe dorgis ha dris ol an bys ef eth* 'then an earthquake occurred and it went through all the earth' PA 200b

***yn vr na** y fyth clewys del ony ganse brewys hag elf at es* 'then it will be heard that we are wounded by them an ill at ease' RD 572-74

***In nena** an venyn a welas y bos an frut da the thybbry* 'Then the woman saw that the fruit was good to eat' TH 3a

*ha oll an re na a ve in ministers in egglos a crist thea **nyna** bys in dith hethow* 'and all those were ministers in Christ's Church from then until today' TH 41a

***Nena** an Jowle an comeraz e man abera en cyte venegaz* 'Then the Devil took him up into the holy city' Rowe.

When referring to an hour, i.e. a period of 60 minutes, Cornish uses the word **our**:

*me a thuk curyn a spern nep try **our** adro thu'm pen* 'I bore a crown of thorns some three hours around my head' RD 2554-55

hour GERYOW GWIR

vnpossyble nyng ew tra tha wrear all an bys ma awos destrowy an beyse agy tha **ower** 'it is not impossible for the Creator of all this world to destroy the world within an hour' CW 2386-89.

There is unfortunately no example in traditional Cornish of telling the time of day. We can use expressions like **udn eur** 'one o'clock', **dyw eur** 'two o'clock', **teyr eur** 'three o'clock', **peder eur** 'four o'clock', etc. but there is no actual warrant for them in the traditional language.

Notice incidentally the expression **pùb our** is attested once with the sense 'every hour':

helma a vith rag agys exortia why na rellogh fillall pub dith ha pub **owre** *the ry grace the du golosek rag y thaddar thynny disquethis* 'this will be to exhort you not to fail every day and every hour to give thanks to almighty God for his goodness shown towards us' TH 5.

HOUSE, HOUSES

The Cornish word for 'house' is **chy**, and the plural is a suppletive one, **treven**.

Neb a garra y das po y vam, y vab po y virth, chy, **trevyn** *po tyrryow, moy agesa ve, y myth crist, nynsew worthy the vos dissipill na seruant thym* 'Whoever loves his father or his mother, house, houses or lands more than me, says Christ, is not worthy to be my disciple or servant' TH 21a

Ny dale dien gwile **treven** *war an treath* 'You should not build houses upon the sand' ACB: F f 3

Ko anberra der e derggawe gen mear a worianze Ko oagoaze tha e **drevon** *ha bethow why looan* 'Enter through his doors with great worship; approach his dwellings and be joyful' BF: 39

Domus... An house, a lodging, a dwelling. C. Tshyi [*plur.* **Treven**] AB: 55c.

Note that **treven** 'houses' is to be distinguished from **trevow** 'towns':

yn le mayth en yn **trevow** *yn splan me as derevas* 'wherever I went in the towns I declared them openly' PA 79c

myr lowene ol an bys cytes rych **trevow** *a brys castilly bras hagh huhel* 'behold joy of all the world, rich cities, important towns, great and high castles' PC 131-33

Indelma oll gouernans gwlasow, an pow, an **trevow** *marras, han* **trevow** *trygva, y a vea res thetha iently correctia oll an re ew offenders in dan aga gouernans* 'Thus all governments of the country of the market towns, of the country towns, they should gently correct all those who are offenders under their governance' TH 25a *yma ow leverell fatell rug Du plagia cities,* **trevow**, *ha pow, rag y receva vnworthy gans lyas kynde a plagys, gwannegreth, clevas* 'he tells how God plagued cities, towns and country for receiving it unworthily with many kind of plagues, weakness, sickness' TH 53a *scoothyes gans mar gay* **trevow** *lean a tuz* 'support by many fine town full of men' JKeigwin.

Although ***chiow** 'houses' is unattested, it must be used as a formant for the plurals of compounds of **chy**; thus **clâvjy** 'hospital' has a plural ***clâvjiow** 'hospitals', and the plural of **lêty** 'dairy' in the revived language is ***lêtiow**.

HOW

The ordinary word for 'how' in direct and indirect questions is **fatell**, which was probably stressed on the second syllable.

A **fatell** 'how'

lauar cowyth da del os ***fatel*** *yllyn aswonvos en harlot yn mysk y tus* 'tell us, as you are a good friend, how can we recognize the scoundrel among his men' PC 965-67

creators a brys benen yn yfarn na feugh gynen ***fatel*** *thutheugh why omma* 'creatures from the womb of woman, who were not with us in hell, how did you arrive here?' RD 191-93

sevugh in ban a tus vays ***fetel*** *omglowugh omma* 'stand up, good men; how do you feel here?' BM 708-09

fetel *vusta delyfrys laver thymo me ath peys ov map kerra* 'how were you freed? tell me, I beg you, my beloved son' BM 3764-66

Arluth ***fetel*** *vyth dynny mar teberthyth eredy meryasek theorthen* 'Lord, how will it be for us, if you, Meriasek, depart from us?' BM 4263-65

Gwayt bos war a'th lavarow, ***fatel*** *rylly gorthyby, rag fregh ew eff* 'Take care of your words, how you will answer, for he is impetuous' BK 555-57

Mar kyl gul e volenta, nyns us thym joy ow pewa. ***Fatyl*** *vyth, elhas, a Thew!* 'If he can do as he wishes, I have no joy in living. How will it be, alas, O God!' BK 2517-19.

Fatell was increasingly used to introduce indirect statement:

B **fatell** introducing indirect statement:

fatel *fue cryst mertheryys rak kerenge tus a'n beys why a welas yn tyen* 'that Christ was martyred for the sake of the men of the world you have seen completely' PC 3220-22

ha deug avar avorow my agas pys the welas ***fetel*** *sevys cryst mes a'n beth cler ha war* 'and come early tomorrow, I beg you, to see that Christ rose from the tomb clear and gentle' PC 3239-42

how   GERYOW GWIR

ty a wor yn pup maner **fatel** *fue ow map lethys yn grous* 'you know in every way that my son was killed on the cross' RD 427-28

yth ew scriffes in second chapter in Genesis, **fatell** *rug du anella in corff den* 'it is written in the second chapter of Genesis that God breathed into the body of man' TH 2

ha yth esas ow tristya **fatell** *ota gydyar then re ew dall ha golow then re vs in tewolgow* 'and you trust that you are a guide to the blind and a light to those in darkness' TH 14a

Nena Herod perêg e gwellaz **fatal** *o geaze gwreaze anotha gen an teze feere, yw engrez* 'Then Herod, when he saw that he had been mocked by the wise men, he was enraged' Rowe.

Fatell in such syntax was sometimes reduced to **tell**, and then further to **ter**, **tr'**.

C tell, ter, tr' < fatell

Ha lagagow an gie ve gerres ha an gie oyah **tel** *eran gye en noath* 'And their eyes were opened and they knew that they were naked' Rowe

pu reg laule theese **tell** *estah en noath?* 'who told you that you were naked?' Rowe

hei a dhalasvaz dho 'wîl krei **ter** *dha e thermîez hei destrîez* 'she began to make a cry that her husband had been murdered' BF: 18

Bez e brederaz **ter** *gotha dhodho boz aviziyz dhiueth ken guesgal enueth* 'But he thought that he should be advised twice before striking once' BF: 19

ha Deu guellas, **tr**o *va da* 'and God saw that it was good' BF: 52.

Possibly because of this increased use of **fatell** as a conjunction introducing indirect speech, the interrogative adverb 'how' was differentiated by using the variant **fatla**. **Fatla** may well have arisen through false division of earlier **fatell** + the leniting particle **a**. Here are some examples:

D fatla

fatla *wrene ny avoydeya anger a thew?* 'how will we avoid anger from God?' SA 59

henna ew the leverall, gas ve the remembra **fatla** *or ve in ta tha honora* 'that is to say, let me remember how I may honour you well' SA 59

henna ew **fatla** *ill hemma bos vnderstandis the vos gwrys* 'that is, how can this be understood to be done' SA 65

na berth dowte me an prevent hag e thro lower tha paynes me a lavar 3es **fatla** 'fear not; I shall go before him and bring him sufficiently to torments. I will tell you how' CW 493-95

y praytha lavar **fatla** *perthy ny allaf pella* 'I beg you, tell me how. I cannot bear it any longer' CW 609-10

Fatl'*u gan a why* 'How do you do?' Carew.

Fatla *gûra ve agaz gorra why en dowr, Gen agaz bedgeth gwin, ha agaz blew mellyn?* 'How will I lay you upon the ground, With your pale face and your yellow hair?' ACB: F f 4 *verso*.

Pana vaner is used sometimes in the texts to mean 'what manner, what kind, what sort?' On occasion we find **in pana vaner** 'in which way' used to translate 'how':

rag me a'n guelas dufvn dresof ef a tremenas hag a wor **yn pa vaner** 'for I was awake and saw him—he passed over me—and I know how' RD 524-26
me a levar thys mar pleag **yn pan vanar** *yn bema* 'I will, if you please, tell you how I came by it' CW 755-56.

HUNGRY

For 'hungry' the word ***nownek** 'hungry' has been suggested for the revived language, but it is not actually attested. To say 'I am hungry' Nance recommends **yma nown dhybm** (UC *yma nown dhym*) or **ewl debry a'm beus** (UC *ewl dybry a'm bus*). Neither expression is actually attested, however, though **nown a'm beus** is attested once (see below). Remarkably the word **nown** 'hunger' itself is rather rare:

Famis, **naun** 'hunger' OCV §941
mar tue moy nystevyth man rag **nown** *y wrons clamdere* 'if more come, they will get nothing; they will faint for hunger' OM 399-400
Christ ew ow bewnans ha'm boys. Mannaf gref penys ha **nawn** 'Christ is my life and my food. I want grief, fasting and hunger' BK 427-28
Me a'm byth drog **neun** *hanath gans Teuthar pan vo clowys* 'I shall have nasty hunger tonight when Teuthar hears of it' BK 488-89.

In traditional Cornish, 'to be hungry' is most usually rendered by using the adjective **gwag** 'empty':

ny wothen rag ponvotter pyth een yn gveel py yn cos ow holen **gvak** *dyvotter ru'm kymmer hag awel bos* 'we do not know for wretchedness whither we shall go in field or forest. With my belly hungry, famine and desire for food is like to seize me' OM 363-66
lemyn dyfreth of ha **gvak** *pur wyr dres ol tus a'n beys* 'now I am weak and hungry beyond all men in the world' OM 593-94
gvak *yv thym an pengasen a molleth du in gegen schant yv an dewes han boys* 'hungry is my stomach. Oh God's curse in the kitchen. Meagre is the drink and food' BM 3927-29
lemyn deffryth ove ha **gwag** *pur wyre drees oll tues in byes* 'now I am weak and hungry in very truth beyond all men in the world' CW 1173-74
Ha pereeg e penes doganze jorna ha doganze noze, e ve ouga nena **gwage** 'And when he had fasted forty days and forty nights, he was thereafter hungry' Rowe
Gwag *o ve, ra ve gawas haunsell?* 'I am hungry, shall I have breakfast?' ACB: F f *verso*.

hungry   GERYOW GWIR

In the revived language the default way of saying 'I am hungry' should probably be **gwag ov vy** or **me yw gwag**.

HUSBAND

The ordinary word for 'husband' in the revived language is **gour**, plural **gwer**. **Gour**, however, can be variously translated 'man', 'husband', 'male' and even 'hero':

A **gour** 'husband, man, hero'

*mollo3 den ha **gour** ha gwrek a 3e poran er 3e byn peynys ad wra more3ek yn yffarn down pub termyn* 'the curse of man, both male and female, will come upon you; torments will make you perpetually wretched in deep hell' PA 66cd

*Thy **gour** hy a 3anonas a crist kepar del welse yn kerdh delma dre gannas nyng ew ragos se la3e Cryst* 'She sent a message to her husband, as she had seen thus by a messenger, It is not for you to kill Christ' PA 123ab

*rof thy's ov thour hel ha chammbour bethaf the **wour** warbarth ny a dryg nefre* 'I will give you my tower, hall and chamber; I shall be your husband; we will live together forever' OM 2109-12

*leuereugh the **gour** a'n chy agas mester the thanvon py plas yth ylle dybry* 'tell the man of the house that your master is sending to enquire where he can eat' PC 633-35

*ow corf yv re'n oferen kepar del leuerys theugh guyrthys lythys yn grovs pren dretho ef prynnys bytheugh ol ow tus **gour** ha benen* 'my body it is, by the mass, as I told you, betrayed, killed on the cross; by it you, all my people, man and woman will be redeemed' PC 764-68

*leuereugh athysempys the wrek pilat an iustis certan y tue vyngeans bras war y **gour** mar pyth lethys ihesu cryst an lel profys hag ynweth war y fleghas* 'tell the wife of Pilate the justice immediately that certainly great vengeance will come upon her husband if Jesus Christ, the true prophet is killed and also upon her children' PC 1919-24

*pur wyr a lauaraf thy's certan mar pythe lethys y tue wyngeans war the **wour** ha war the fleghys keffrys* 'the very truth I tell you, if he is killed, vengeance will come upon your husband and on your children as well' PC1947-50

*drou e thy'mmo the tackye a vgh y pen gans mur greys may hallo pup y redye **gour** ha benen kekyffrys* 'bring it to me to fix above his head with great speed so that everyone can read it, man and woman also' PC 2807-10

*mur fest y'gen lowenhas dotho ny thyalwhethas **gour** ha benen* 'greatly did he gladden us. To him neither man nor woman unlocked' RD 1444-46

*neffre yn dour hedre vo ny thue dresto na varwo **gour** gruek na best* 'never, while he is in the water, will either man, woman or animal cross over without dying' RD 2225-27

*kens ol ef agan formyas ha gans y wos a prennas **gour** ha benen* 'first of all he created us and with his blood redeemed us, male and female' RD 2430-32

*hy a gemeras ran an frut hag an debbras hag a ros part then **gwerrer** Adam hy hoth hag eff a thebbras* 'she took part of the fruit and ate it and gave part to the man, Adam her partner, and he ate' TH 3a

214

GERYOW GWIR **husband**

Inweth S poull a commodias an **gwer** *the cara aga gwregath kepar dell ra crist cara y egglos* 'St Paul also commanded the husbands to love their wives as Christ loves his Church' TH 31

Me a vyn abarth an Tas mos ahanan toyth garaw the le na thyfyk penlas, the chy an **gour** *hep paraw a Gyllywyk* 'I will go in the name of the Father quickly hence to the place where liquor does not fail, to the house of the hero without equal from Kellywyk' BK 1266-70

Me a gest the'n ughelha arluth us a-ugh an loer, ystyn quaral na relha erbyn Myghtern Bretyn Veor, Arthor, **gour** *mas* 'I declare to the highest Lord, who is above the moon, that he should not dispute with the King of Great Britain, Arthur, a goodly hero' BK 1421-25

Lowena thu'm arluth mas, lowena the'n gwelha **gour** 'Joy to my goodly lord, joy to the best of heroes' BK 1570-71.

I discuss further the expression **gour ha benyn** *s.vv.* 'man, men, people' below.

If one wants expressly to indicate that the man in question is the male partner of a married couple, the correct term is **gour ty**, literally 'man of house':

B **gour ty** 'husband'

a ttebres ty ha'th ***worty*** *a'n wethen ha'y avalow y fyeugh yn surredy yn vr na avel dewow* 'were you and your husband to eat of the tree and of its apples, you would indeed be then like gods' OM 175-78

Neb a'm gruk vy ha'm ***gorty*** *ef a ruk agan dyfen aual na wrellen dybbry* 'He who made me and my husband, he forbade us to eat any apple' OM 181-83

torr'e yn ow feryl vy heb hokye fast haue y do hag inweth gwra the'th ***worty*** *may tebro ef annotho* 'pluck it at my risk without hesitation. Be done quickly and also make sure that your husband eat of it' OM 197-200

Rag ty the gola worty ha tolle the bryes len nefre gustyth th'y ***gorty*** *me a orden bos benen* 'Since you listened to her and misled your faithful spouse, I ordain that woman shall always be obedient to her husband' OM 293-96

rag ty tha gulla ortye ha tulla tha bryas leel nefra gostyth thy ***gorty*** *me a ordayne bos benyn* 'Since you listened to her and misled your loyal spouse, I ordain that woman shall always be obedient to her husband' CW 892-95.

215

I

I, ME

The disjunctive first person singular pronoun meaning 'I, me' in Cornish is usually **my, me**:

*Pedyr androw ha Iowan yn meth crist deugh holyough ve bys yn meneth ha **me** gwan* 'Peter, Andrew and John, said Christ, come, follow me into the mountain since I am weak' PA 53ab

*rag henna my a'n temptyas the behe may fe ellas aga han kepar ha **my*** 'therefore I tempted him to sin that their song should be Alas, like me' OM 308-10

*h'agas myghtern ef synseugh hedre vyugh byv yn bys ma kepar ha **my** ef gorthyeugh* 'and consider him your king while you are alive in this world; like me worship him' OM 2348-50

*ha me a vyn y pesy mar pe y voth indella na rella den peryllya in tyr na mor in bys ma mar creya war crist ha **my*** 'and I will pray him that if it be his will that no man should be at risk on land or at sea in this world if he call upon Christ and me' BM 613-17

*dare ov fobyl yv marov ha **me** tebelwolijs* 'what! my people are dead and I badly wounded' BM 2489-90.

In Late Cornish the pronoun is more often **vee, ve** rather than **my, me**:

*Ne re'au gauas Deiu veth aral buz **vê*** 'You shall have no other God than me' BF: 55
*Na'ra chee gowas na hene Deew poz **vee*** 'You shall have no other God than me' Rowe
*Seerah dama ha **vee** honan* 'Father, mother and I myself' Bilbao MS
***Vee** o gwrege ha flehes* 'I my wife and children' Bilbao MS.

It seems, however, that **ve, vy** rather than **my, me** is much older than the Late Cornish period. I have noticed one example in the earliest Middle Cornish:

*Hag a pe yndella **ve** neffre ny vean fethys* 'And had it been thus, I, never would I be conquered' PA 73a.

IMPORTANT, SIGNIFICANT

In the revived language the expression ***a vry** is often used to mean 'important, significant'. Unfortunately the phrase ***a vry** is without warrant in the texts. The authentic expression for 'important, significant' is **a bris** (UC *a brys*), literally 'of price':

Dyllas crist a ve rynnys pedar ran guris a neʒe gans peswar marreg **a brys** *ʒe bub marreg ran may fe* 'The clothes of Christ were divided, four parts made of them by four soldiers of importance, that each soldier might get a share' PA 190ab

In aga herwyth yʒ ese vn marreg longis hynwys dal o ny wely banna ef rebea den **a brys** 'Among them was a soldier called Longinus; he was blind; he saw nothing. He had been a man of importance' PA 217ab

gromersy arluth **a brys** *rag the roow prest yv da* 'Thank you, lord of importance, for your gifts are always good' OM 2313-14

myr lowene ol an bys cytes rych trevow **a brys** *castilly bras hagh huhel ol an re ma ty a fyth ow gorthye mara mennyth* 'Behold the joy of all the world, rich cities, important towns, great and high castles. All these you shall have if you will worship me' PC 131-35

y tethewys nans yv meys mones in hans then prasov erbyn duk magus **a breys** *den fur in y worthebov* 'I promised a month ago to go yonder to the meadows to meet Duke Magus of importance, a wise man in his answers' BM 3918-21

ha gans an merthus sawynans o both Dew olgallouseck saw gans coil a ran tuz **a brys** *neb ny vyth nefra gans ny ankevys* 'and with the miraculous salvation by the will of God Almighty, but with the ?loss of some men of importance, which we will never forget' JKeigwin.

In the interests of authenticity the unattested expression ***a vry** should perhaps be replaced by **a bris**.

IMPOSSIBLE *see* POSSIBLE

TO IMPROVE, TO AMEND

For 'to improve' Nance recommends A) **gwellhe** and B) **amendya**. **Gwellhe** may be attested once. **Amendya**, **mendya** 'to improve, to amend, to ameliorate' is fairly common. **Omamendya** 'to improve oneself, to do better' is also attested:

A **gwellhe**

me a leuer the plemyk thywy nowothov nowyth **guelheys** *yv ages nygys* 'I will speak bluntly to you of new news: your business has been improved' BM 3314-16.

B **amendya**

mar ny wreth **ymamendye** *ef a wra tyn the punssye may leuerry ogh ellas* 'if you do not improve, he will severely punish you, so that you will cry Oh, alas!' OM 1526-28

improve   **GERYOW GWIR**

*hethe the'n dor my a'd pys scon ef a vyth **amendyys** my a'n scarf yn ta whare* 'hand it down, I beg you; it will soon be set to right' OM 2521-23

*mara mynne **amendye** guel vye y thylyfrye hep drocoleth thyworthy'n* 'if he is willing to improve, it would be best for us to release him without harm from us' PC 1862-64

*ha mar ny fyn dynaghe y gow ha mercy crye hag **amendye** y treyson gans spern guregh y curene* 'and if he does not deny his lies and beg for mercy and amend his treason, crown him with thorns' PC 2060-63

*vnwyth a caffen hansell me a russa **amendie*** 'if I could only have breakfast, I should improve' BM 110-11

*yth ew gwris da aga rebukya, may hallans bos methek ha kemeras sham aga fawtys ha dre rebukys **amendia** aga lewde bewnans* 'it is well done to rebuke them, that they may be embarrassed and be ashamed of their faults and through rebukes amend their wicked life' TH 29a

*Christ re'th **amendya** der ras ha roy thys gwel esethva* 'May Christ improve you by his grace and give you a better place to sit' BK 296-97.

*kebmys pehas es in byes gwrres gans tues heb **amendya** math ew dew an tas serrys bythquath gwyell mabe dean omma* 'so much sin has been committed by men in the world without improvement, that God the Father is angry ever to have created mankind here' CW 2146-49

*kemmys pehas es in beyse ha nyng es tam **amendya** mayth ew an tas dew serrys gans oll pobell an bys ma* 'there is so much sin in the world and there is not a jot of improvement that God the Father is angry with all the people of this world' CW 2335-38

*hag eddrag thothef yma bythquath mabe dean tha vos gwryes rag henna gwrewgh **amendya*** 'and he regrets that ever mankind was created, therefore improve' CW 2339-41

*rag henna theth cregye me ny vannaf moy es kye na **mendya** ny venyn ny awoos theth gyrryau wastys* 'therefore I will not believe you any more than a dog, nor will we improve for all your wasted words' CW 2359-62.

It is not completely certain that ***guelheys*** at BM 3316 is the verbal adjective of **gwellhe**. Given this uncertainty and the prevalence of **amendya**, perhaps it might be wise to replace *****gwellhe** with **amendya** in the revived language as the customary word for 'to improve, to amend, to ameliorate'.

TO INCREASE

When 'to increase' means 'to intensify' the Cornish word is **moghhe**:

A **moghhe**

*nefre gustyth th'y gorty me a orden bos benen may **mohghaho** hy huth hy dre wul ow gorhemmyn trogh* 'always obedient to her husband I ordain that woman shall me, so that her anguish be increased because she broke my commandment' OM 295-98

GERYOW GWIR   increase

the greffe y fyen ny y voys maryys eredy ha **moghheys** *agen roweth* 'we should be the stronger if he were married indeed and increased would be our influence' BM 311-13

Lemen pan vsons in crok vskys **moghheen** *age drok* 'now that they are on the gallows, let us quickly intensify their pain' BM 1264-65

kyn nag o ov poscessyon bras in meske sur ov nascyon me ren **moghheys** *eredy* 'though my property was not large surely among my nation, I have increased it indeed' BM 2400-02

re vahom du a galloys **moghheys** *thymo ov awer* 'my Mahound, god of power, my grief has been increased for me' BM 3305-06

Moyhes *ow fyanhasow!* 'Increased my anxiety!' BK 2346.

When 'to increase' means 'to multiply, to become more numerous, to make more numerous' the usual expression is **encressya** or **cressya**, though this verb can mean 'to intensify' also:

B **encressya**, **cressya**

thethe me a worhemmyn **encressyens** *ha bewens pel* 'to them I command: let them increase and live long' OM 47-8

cresseugh *coullenweugh an beys* 'multiply; fill the world' OM 1161

cresseugh *collenweugh keffrys an nor veys a dus arte* 'increase, fill the world also with people again' OM 1211-12

ow talleth gans myraclis, norysshys gans govenek, **encresshys** *gans charite, ha confyrmys gans antiquite* 'beginning with miracles, nourished by hope, increased by charity and confirmed by antiquity' TH 49

sor dew ha trub[e]ll pub tew yma pub ower ow **cressya** 'the wrath of God and trouble on every side is always increasing' CW 1256-57

han bys yth ew **incresshys** *drethaf ve hag ow flehys heb number tha vos comptys* 'and the world has been increased by me and my innumerable children' CW 1988-90

cressowgh *collenwouh keffrys an noer vyes a dus arta* 'increase, fill the world also with people again' CW 2510-11

ha deew lauaraz thonze grew **cressha** *ha lenno an beaaze* 'and God said to them, increase and fill the world' JKeigwin

Me vedn meare **cressha** *tha dewhan, ha tha humthan* 'I will great increase your pain and your labour' Rowe

betho lean gen haz, ha **kressia** *ha lenal an dour en môr* 'be full of seed and increase and fill the water in the sea' BF: 52

ha gwrens an hethen **kressia** *en aor* 'and let the birds increase in the earth' BF: 52

ha Deu lavaras dothans, bethou lean gen haz, ha **kressia** *ha lenal an aor* 'and God said to them, be full of seed, and increase and fill the earth' BF: 53.

Both **moghhe** and **encressya** can be used in the revived language.

IRELAND

For 'Ireland' Nance suggested ***Iwerdhon** (UC **Ywerdhon*). This form is nowhere attested. The attested form is **Wordhen**:

*Ha e tha **worthen** eath e whonnen rag cowas gen e gare Trip-Cunnen* 'And he himself went to Ireland to talk to his friend Tyrconnell' LAM: 224.
*en Ehual-dir an Alban hag en G'laskor **Uordhyn*** 'in the Highlands of Scotland and in the kingdom of Ireland' AB: 222

In the interests of authenticity, **Wordhen** *f.* should perhaps replace any other form of the Cornish name of Ireland.

IRISHMAN, IRISH LANGUAGE

The attested word for 'Irishman' is **Godhal**, and the attested plural is **Gwydhyly**:

*Pes, seniors, je vow commaund, yonk ha loys, **Gothal** ha Scot!* 'Silence, sirs, I command you, young and old, Irishman and Scotsman' BK 1258-59
*The Second Plural ends in i, as **Guidhili**, Irish-men* AB: 242c.

The word used by Lhuyd for 'Irish language' is **Godhalek**:

*mi rykavaz me honan Kelmez dho skrefa neb 'ramàtek ha zerlevar rag 'oz Tavaz huei ha rag an **Godhalek*** 'I found myself bound to write a grammar and dictionary for your language and for Irish' AB: 222
*mar peue zerlevar &c. Kernûak ha **Godhalek** skrefyz arâg ny vendzha vesga argrafa an papyrio hemma* 'had there been written before a Cornish and Irish dictionary etc., I would never have printed this papers' AB: 222.

Although **Gwydhyly** and **Godhalek** are both confined to Lhuyd, they seem genuine enough, particularly in the light of ***Gothal*** in BK. It would therefore perhaps be wise in the revived language to use **Godhal** *m.*, **Gwydhyly** for 'Irishman, Irishmen' and **Godhalek** *m.* for 'Irish language'.

J

JAW

For 'jaw' Nance recommends **grudh** (UC *gruth*), which is attested once in Old Cornish: *maxilla*, **grud** 'jaw' OCV §35. **Grudh** is related to Welsh *grudd* 'cheek' and Old Irish *gruad* 'cheek', so we cannot be sure what was the exact sense of OC **grud**. The only word for 'jaw' in the texts is **challa**, a borrowing, it seems, from Middle English *chaul*.

*venytha na sowyny tan hemma war an **challa*** 'that you may never thrive take that on the jaw' OM 539-40

*kymar henna te ploos adla war an **challa** gans askern an **challa*** 'take that, you dirty rogue, on the jaw with the bone of the jaw' CW 1115-17.

In the light of those two examples, **challa** should perhaps be the default word for 'jaw' in the revived language.

JESUS

In some forms of Cornish the default form of the Saviour's name is ***Yesu**. This is, I believe, a mistake. It is true that the place-name Pantersbridge in St Neots is attested as ***Pontyesu*** 'the bridge of Jesus' in 1241, but the name ***Pontyesu*** is a fossilized form containing ***Iesu***, ***Yesu*** inherited from British directly from Latin in the period before the Saxon conquest of Cornwall. During the Saxon period, however, it seems that inherited names like ***Iesu*** 'Jesus', ***Meyr** 'Mary', **Yowan** 'John' were lost. They were replaced after the Norman conquest by forms borrowed from Breton, i.e. **Jesu**, **Maria** and **Jowan**. The earlier form **Yesu/Iesu** is attested only in **Pontyesu**; **Yowan** 'John' occurs only in **Golowan** < **Gol+yowan** 'St John's Eve, Midsummer' found in *Guâve en Hâve terebah* **Goluan** *Ha Hâve en Guâve terebah Nedelack* 'Winter in summer till Midsummer/ And Summer in Winter till Christmas' Ustick MSS.

In the texts the name **Jesù(s)** is most frequently written *ihesu*, *Ihesu*, *ihesus*, and *Ihesus*, forms which together are attested almost 400 times.

We can be certain, however, that the initial segment in this name is intended to be **j** [dʒ] not **y** [j] for five separate reasons:

1) The Middle Cornish scribes spell the name Jesus in a variety of ways: *ihesu, jhesu, ihesus, iesu*. If the initial segment in this name had really been **y** [j], one might expect the name on occasion to be written **yesu* (cf. the toponym **Pontyesu** mentioned above). No such spelling is attested. It would seem then that *yesu* in **Pontyesu** and *ihesu, jhesu, iesu* in the texts were pronounced differently.

2) In Cornish several words begin with **ye** [jeː] ~ [jɛ], for example **Yêdhow** 'Jew', plural **Yêdhewon**; **yêhes** 'health', **yêth* 'language', **yêwny** 'to desire', **yêwnadow** 'desire', **yêyn** 'cold'. In all cases there is a strong tendency for the initial **y** in the sequence **yê** to be lost. Here are some examples:

yethow PC 2003, 2027; *yethewon* PC 1080, 1098, 1252, but *ethow* PA 131a, 152a; *eʒow* PA 145c, 259b; *eʒewon* PA 124c, 126a, 140d, *Ethewan* Rowe.
yehes PC 1150, BM 701, 2013, 2537; *yeghes* RD 1716; *yehas* TH 2a, 46, BK 3111, but *ehas* TH 51a; *eghas* TH 30a; *ehaz* AB: 242a, ACB: F f *verso*.
yenes 'desire' OM 2125; *yevnys* 'I desired' PC 1701, but *unadow* 'desire' BK 574, 628, 730
*yeth 'language', the expected form is not attested; cf. Welsh *iaith* 'language' and Breton *yezh* 'language', but *eyth* TH 1, 19, 21, 40, 57a.
yeyn 'cold' PC 1209, 1215, 2729; *yeyne* CW 1262, *yeine* JJenkins, but *eyn* PA 207d, 235d, *yne* BM 1145.

If the name for 'Jesus' had really been **Yêsu* or **Yêsus*, we should expect occasional instances of **Esu* or **Esus*; cf. **Yethow** ~ **Ethow** and **yehes** ~ **ehes**. No such forms are found.

3) The later Cornish writers spell the name in a variety of ways: *Jhesus, Jhesu* TH *passim*; *Jesus* SA *passim*; *Jesus* Rowe *passim*; *Jesu* BF: 41; *Ihesu Chriest* BF: 56; *Jesus Christ* ACB: E e 2 *verso*; *Jesu Chrêst* ACB: E e 2 *verso*. Not once in the later writers do we find the name written with initial **Y**.

4) In Middle Cornish 'Jesus' is most frequently written *ihesu*(s), *Ihesu*(s) where the initial **Ih** has apparently been suggested by IHS, the Christogram in use since the seventh century. In origin the three letters IHS are the first three of the Greek name IHCOYC 'Jesus', but in the western Church were usually understood as the Latin initials of *Iesus Hominum Salvator* 'Jesus

Saviour of Men'. Twice in BM the **h** is omitted and the name appears as *iesu* BM 144, 146. This means that the name is spelt with the same initial as *ioy* 'joy' BM 4284, 4412; *ienkyn* 'Jenkin' BM 1417, 1449; *iubyter* 'Jupiter' BM 2327, all three of which were pronounced with **j**, not **y**. We must, I think, conclude therefore that *iesu* in BM has an initial [dʒ]. Since this is the same name as *ihesu(s)* elsewhere in BM and the rest of Middle Cornish, it is safe to assume that the Middle Cornish name of our Saviour was **Jesù** or **Jesùs**, not **Yesu* or **Yesùs*.

5) Lhuyd spells the name *Dzeziu̯* at AB: 67b. This looks like a misprint for **Dzheziu̯*, where the initial segment is clearly [dʒ].

6) In his translation of Matthew 2 and 4 as well as *Jesus* 'Jesus' Rowe writes *James* 'James', *Jerman* 'Jeremiah', *Jerusalem* 'Jerusalem', *Jordan* 'Jordan', *Joseph* 'Joseph', *Jowan* 'John', *Judah* 'Judah' and *Judeah* 'Judaea.' It is clear from *Jerman* 'Jeremiah' and *Jowan* 'John' that Rowe is not just following the English forms, but rather using names which were current in his Cornish. This suggestion is corroborated by Rowe's use of *Alale* 'Galilee', *Bethalem* 'Bethlehem', *Egyp* 'Egypt', *Ethewan* 'Jews', *Ezarel* 'Israel' and *Yzias* 'Isaiah', which are all different from the corresponding English names. If then Rowe writes *Jesus* with an initial *J* as well as *James*, *Jerman*, *Jerusalem*, *Jordan*, etc., it is fair to assume that the name *Jesus*, in Rowe's speech was pronounced with an initial [dʒ] and that this was a continuation of the form found as *ihesus* in Middle Cornish.

The Middle and Late Cornish form of the Saviour's name was **Jesù** or **Jesùs**, not **Yesu*.

See further **John the Baptist** below.

JEW, JEWISH

As has been noted above the Middle Cornish for 'Jew' was *Yedhow* or *Edhow* and the plural was *Yedhewon* or *Edhewon*.

Here are some examples from the texts:

A **Yedhow**

lauar mars of vy ***yethow*** 'say whether I am a Jew' PC 2003

pepenag vo a'n barth wyr a cleufyth ov voys yn tyr sarsyn py ***yethow*** *kyn fo* 'whoever shall be on the right side will hear my voice in the land, though he be a Saracen or a Jew' PC 2025-27

Nefre ny nehyn an fay awos ovn ahanes gy nag ȝethov ongrassyas 'Never will we deny our faith for fear of you, nor of a graceless Jew' BM 3515-17

sovdrys dehesugh detha the ȝethov sur obaya nefre ny vanna orthogh 'soldiers, fire at them; I will never want you to obey a Jew indeed' BM 3534-36]

yma ran sur kemerys gans an ȝethov ongrassys 'some have been taken by the graceless Jew' BM 3540-41.

B **Edhow**

In scorgijs prenyer esa yn dewle an ij **ethow** 'As scourges there were rods in the hands of the two Jews' PA 131a

mestry vyth te ny vea waraff ve drok vyth na da ken onan ȝys nan rolla byth moy ys **eȝow** *yn ta a beghas orth ov ȝrayta* 'you would have had no authority over me for good or ill had not someone else given it to you, any more than any Jew indeed who sinned in betraying me' PA 145a-c

Vn **ethow** *a brederys hag a leuerys theȝe bonas pren yn dour tewlys* 'A certain Jew considered and told them that a certain tree had been thrown into the water' PA 152ab

vn **ethow** *avell pyth foll a wyskis kenter ynhy* 'a Jew like a made thing struck a nail into it' PA 182b

vn **eȝow** *ȝoȝo yn freth yndelma a leuerys* 'a Jew spoke eagerly to him thus' PA 239b.

A1 **Yedhewon**

iudas ny gosk vn banne lymmyn dywans fystyne thu'm ry the'n fals **yethewon** 'Judas is not sleeping a wink now but is hurrying quickly to deliver me to the perfidious Jews' PC 1078-80

ov nesse yma an preys may fyth map dev ynno reys the'n fals **yethewon** *dygnas* 'the time is approaching when the Son of God will be delivered to the perfidious and cruel Jews' PC 1096-98

apert vythqueth y tyskys ow dyskes the'n **yethewon** 'I always openly taught my doctrine to the Jews' PC 1251-52

na scrif myghtern **yethewen** *sau scryf ynno an bylen the leuerol y vos ef myghtern* **yethewen** *certan* 'do not write King of the Jews, but write on it that the scoundrel said he was indeed the king of the Jews' PC 2797-800

luen tregereth me a pys del vs **yethewon** *pupprys omma worth agan baghe* 'I beg complete mercy as the Jews are always here entrapping us' RD 1148-50

cryst myghtern an **yethewon** *yv dev hep par* 'Christ the king of the Jews is God without equal' RD 1618-19

Me ath peys a luengolon ty the vynnes ov sawya rag kerense an passconn a thuk ihesu in bys ma scorgis gans an **ȝethewon** *kentrewys treys ha dula* 'I beseech you from the bottom of my heart that you will heal me for the sake of the passion, which Jesus bore in this world, scourged by the Jews, nailed feet and hands' BM 2598-603

Rag kerense an pasconn a thuk ihesu ragon ny kentrewys gans **ȝethewon** *treys ha dule eredy* 'For the sake of the passion which Jesus suffered for us, nailed by the Jews in his feet and hands indeed' BM 2988-91.

B1 **Edhewon**

*En **ethewon** dre envy a gewsys crist rag syndye* 'the Jews spoke in spite in order to harm Jesus' PA 107a

*An **ethewon** a grogas lader ʒe gryst an barth cleth hag aʒyghow lader bras cregy a russons ynweth* 'The Jews hanged a robber on the left side of Jesus and a great robber they hanged on his right also' PA 186ab

*an **nethewan** a ve spitfull warbyn agen arluth* 'the Jews were spiteful against our Lord' SA 61

*Indella emowns y dishonora Christ pan vonsy y recevia ef ha e corf benegas ef gans dowla mustethas, ha pecar a ruk an **nethewan** e sensy, ha e recevia ef lymmyn, gans mustethas ganaw* 'Thus they dishonour Christ when they receive him and his blessed body with impure hands, and as the Jews arrested him and receive him now with impure mouth' SA 61

*Lavaral, peleah ma e yw gennez matern an **Ethewan**?* 'Saying, Where is he who is born king of the Jews?' Rowe

*kebar an flô yonk ha e thama, ha ke tha pow an **Ethewan** rag ma Herod maraw* 'take the young child and his mother and go into the land of the Jews, for Herod is dead' Rowe

Edheu̯on 'Jews' AB: 73c
Idheu̯on 'The Jews' AB: 242c.

Curiously, although the word **Edhewon** is used is used in *Sacrament an Alter* and by Rowe and was known to Lhuyd, Tregear himself prefers to use the English borrowing **Jew, Jewys**:

*Pub den oll keffrys **Jew** ha Jentyll ew pehadoryon* 'All men, Jew and Gentile alike, are sinners' TH 7a

*te ew **Jew** hag yth esas ow crowetha in la* 'you are a Jew and you rest in the law' TH 14a

*Rag ny yll an turkys, an **Jewys**, an infideles, neb nan jevas perfect crygyans, cafus dadder na benefit in myrnans na in pascion a crist* 'For the Turks, the Jews, the unbelievers, who have not perfect faith, cannot derive advantage or benefit from the death and passion of Christ' TH 16a

*yma crist omma ow menya certan company a bobill esa in myske an **Jewys**, hag yth esans ow pewa warlerth an letterall sens a la moyses* 'Christ here means a certan group of people who were among the Jews and they lived according to the literal sense of the Mosaic law' TH 26a

*nyns es mar stroyt bewnans na mar calys travill wheles theworthan ny, dell esa theworth an **Jewys*** 'such a strict life and such hard effort are not sought from us as were sought from the Jews' TH 27a

*An neyll ew an abundance a grace lymyn rys in tyrmyn an testament nowith, pell ow excedia an measure a grace res then **Jewys**, ow folya an la moyses, han gela ew an braster a rewarde, promysys thynny vght an **Jewys**, kepar dell vsy Oecumenius inweth ow recordia* 'The one is the abundance of grace now granted in the time of the New Testament, far exceeding the measure of grace given to the Jews, following the law of Moses,

Jew   GERYOW GWIR

and the second is the greatness of the reward promised to us above the Jews, as Oecumenius also records' TH 27a

*S Johan ena a rug aga expondia haga leveris, fattell rug crist, dre y tempill, menya y corfe, an pith a vetha dre an **Jewes** gorys then mernans* 'St John there expounded them and declared how Christ by his temple meant his body, that which would be put to death by the Jews' TH 53.

In view of the Late occurrence of **Edhewon**, there is no need to adopt **Jew**, **Jewys** in the revived language.

For 'Jewish' Nance suggests ***Yedhowek** (UC *Yedhowek*), which is based on Welsh *Iddewig*. There is no need for this word, since the attested adjective **Ebrow** is quite sufficient:

*fleghes **ebbrow** dvn yn vn rew scon hep lettye er byn ihesu neb yv guyr dev ow tos the'n dre* 'Hebrew children, let us go in procession soon without delay to meet Jesus, who is true God, coming to the town' PC 239-42.

Yêdhowek is useful, however, to translate 'Yiddish', both the noun and the adjective.

JEWEL
William Gwavas in his manuscript glossary gives **Jowhall** 'Jewell'. The earlier attested form, however, is **jewall**:

*Praga na russyn ny kyns y ymbrasia, ha ry grace the thu ragtha, rag y bosa an moyha precius **Jewall**, han brassa, bythqueth a ve in myske pobill mortall?* 'Why did we not first embrace it, and give thanks to God for it, since it is the most precious jewel and the greatest that was ever among mortal people?' TH 54a

Since, however, the word is usually pronounced **jowal**, there is no need to introduce a spelling **jewal**, ***jêwal** into the revived language.

JOHN, JOHN THE BAPTIST
Although a form **Yowan** existed in the Old Cornish period, and survives vestigially in the term **Golowan** 'St John's eve, midsummer', the Middle and Late Cornish name **Jowan** was borrowed from French via Breton and has an initial **J**, not **Y**. The name is invariably spelt with initial **J**, or **I** (the medieval equivalent), and Lhuyd writes **Dzhûan** 'John' more than 30 times. It is generally agreed that the Cornish name **Jamys** 'James' is pronounced with an initial **J**, since it appears to have been borrowed from

Middle English and does not derive directly from Latin through British. Significantly the two names **Jamys** and **Jowan** are often mentioned together and invariably they are spelt with the same initial:

> *ow dyskyblon ysethough hag omma pols powesough hedre vyma ov pygy ol sav peder ha **jamys** ha **johann** an try a reys mones gynef yredy* 'my disciples, sit and rest a while here while I am praying, all except Peter and James and John; the three must go with me indeed' PC 1011-16
>
> ***iohan** nynsos lemmyn flogh… **iamys** thy'm na wra duon* 'John, you are only a child… James, do not grieve me' RD 1363 and 1375
>
> *Ha… alenna e a wellaz moy deaw broderath, **Jamez**, mâb Zebde ha **Jowan** e brodar en goral gen Zebde go zeerah owna go rôza* 'And departing thence he saw further two brothers, James the son of Zebedee and John his brother in the ship with Zebedee their father mending their nets' Rowe

We can be quite sure that the name **Jowan** 'John' in Middle and Late Cornish was pronounced with an initial **j**, not **y**. In the interests of authenticity, outside the term **Golowan** < **Gool Yowan**, the form **Yowan** for 'John' in the revived language should be discontinued.

The name 'John the Baptist' has been translated into Cornish as **Yowan an Besydhyer**. As we have seen **Yowan** is without warrant and should be discontinued. As it stands, however, **Yowan an Besydhyer** means 'John of the Baptist', not 'John the Baptist'. Jenner more accurately suggested *Jûan Bejedhyor* for 'John the Baptist' (*Handbook*: 204), presumably basing the term on Middle Breton *Ian Vadezour* and Welsh *Ioan Fedyddiwr*. The Cornish term for 'John the Baptist', however, is well attested:

> *Havel o ov corthy crist prest orth sen **iowen baptyst** guyn na syder ny vsya* 'He was like John the Baptist in worshipping Christ always; he drank no wine nor cider' BM 4449-51
>
> *S. **Johan baptist**, a ve benegas in breis y vam ha gormelas kyns y bos genys* 'St John the Baptist was blessed in his mother's womb and worshipped before he was born' TH 8
>
> *Rag in mar ver dell rug S **Johan baptist** gyllwall an scribis han pharases in iii-a chapter a mathew, An broud a neddras* 'For inasmuch as St John the Baptist called the scribes and the pharisees in the third chapter of Matthew, The brood of vipers' TH 29a
>
> *Ha y a leveris, Ran **Jowan baptist**, ran helyas, ran Jheremyas, po onyn an prophetes* 'And they said, Some John the Baptist, some Elijah, some Jeremiah or one of the prophets' TH 43a.

John   GERYOW GWIR

In the traditional language the name for John the Baptist is **Jowan Baptyst** or **Sen Jowan Baptyst**. This should perhaps be the name in the revived language also.

TO JOIN

For 'to join' Nance suggests both **jùnya** (UC *junnya*) and ***omjùnya** (UC **omjunnya*). This was a mistake, since ***omjùnya** is not attested. **Jùnya**, however, can be used both A) transitively meaning 'to connect (to), to attach (to)' and B) intransitively 'to adhere to, to be connected with':

A **jùnya** as a transitive verb

*henna eff a gemeras han **jonyas** then dugys heb dewathfa* 'that he received and joined it to the eternal Godhead' TH 12a

*hag anethe hy kemeras dynsys ha **joynyas** y honyn then dusys in vnite a person* 'and from her he took manhood and joined himself to the Deity in unity of person' TH 12a

*mes ef agan magas ny gans e gorf e honyn, han **jvnyas** ny thotheffe e honyn* 'but he fed us with his own body and joined us to himself' SA 59

*an kigg yma causya an ena the vos **junys** the dew an neff* 'the flesh causes the body to be joined to the God of heaven' SA 60a

*indella eth eny **jvnis** thagan Saviour Christ dir an keth bara na* 'thus we are joined to our Saviour Christ by that same bread' SA 65.

B **jùnya** as an intransitive verb

*haneth sur an keth guel ma yn dor ymons ol gurythyys ha'n thyr the onan **yvunyys** aban etheugh alema* 'tonight indeed these same rods have all rooted in the ground and the three have joined into one since you departed hence' OM 2083-86

*na nahaf epscop goky rag an thyyr guelen defry a ve gans dauyd plynsys hag a **ivnnyas** the onan yu token da yn certan a'n try person yn drynsys* 'I will not recant, foolish bishop, for the three rods indeed which were planted by David and which joined into one, are a fine symbol of the three persons of the Trinity' OM 2655-60

*Mar pith den vith **ioynys** the chear pedyr, po sensy then stall a pedyr, yth ew ow servont ve, ha me an pewe, ha me a ra y receva ha **joynea** gonsa* 'If any man is joined to the chair of Peter, or holds to the stall of Peter, he is my servant and he is mine, and I will receive him and join myself with him' TH 49.

Since there is no verb ***omjùnya**, one must use **jùnya**. If in the revived language one wants to say, for example, 'He joined the society recently' one would say **Ev a jùnyas dhe'n gowethas agensow** or **Ev a jùnyas gans an gowethas agensow**.

JOY, JOYFUL

There are three main ways of expressing the idea 'joy' in Cornish 1) **lowena**; 2) **lowender**; 3) **joy**. All three are well attested.

Lowena is the commonest of the three words, being attested about 160 times. It can often be translated 'bliss', particularly of the joys of heaven. It is also frequently used in the greetings **Lowena dhis**, **Lowena dhywgh** 'Hail, Greetings':

A **lowena** 'bliss'

*I helwys a leun golon gans mur ioy ha **lowene** yn hanow du yntreȝon benegas yw neb a the* 'There was a cry from sincere hearts with much joy and bliss, In the name of God blessed is he who comes among us' PA 30ab

*ena crist an kuf colon wy an kyff yn **lowene** del leuerys y honon yn kyg yn goys ow pewe* 'there Christ, the beloved, you will find in joy, as he said himself, living in flesh and blood' PA 256bc

*Omma ny wreugh why tryge eugh yn mes athysympys why a geyl of **lowene** a rys thyugh yn parathys* 'Here you shall not dwell; go forth immediately; you will forfeit my bliss which I gave you in paradise' OM 307-10

*arluth dev ker klew ov lef ha gor vy the **lowene** ha'm spyrys thy'so ressef* 'Lord God, hear my voice and bring me to bliss and receive my spirit to yourself' OM 1895-97

*ow tas ynny wolowys re bo gueres theugh pupprys worth temptacyon a'n tebel ma gas bo **lowyne** nef* 'may my Father in his splendour be assistance to you always against the temptation of the evil one so that you may enjoy the bliss of heaven' PC 223-26

*yn lyfryow scryfys yma bos collenwys **lowene** a ganow a'n fleghys da ha'n re mvnys ow tene* 'in the scriptures it is written that joy is fulfilled out of the mouths of good children and of sucklings' PC 435-38

*ef yv gallosek yn cas ha myghtern a **lowene*** 'he is mighty in the case and a king of bliss' RD 122-23

*a arluth mur gras re'th fo rak **lowene** ny gen bo yn le may fuen lemmyn potvan ha lesky* 'Lord, much thanks may you have, for we had no bliss in the place where we were but scorching and burning' RD 167-70

*y a due de **lowena*** 'they shall come to bliss' BM 1296

*genes confortis on ny ese in mur a ponfos ha dreys sur the **lowena*** 'we are comforted by you, who were in much trouble and brought indeed to bliss' BM 2671-73

*then neff ty a the **lowena** rag trega in ioy a beys* 'you will go to heaven to bliss, to dwell in everlasting joy' BM 4346-48

*pan e'th clowas ow kylwal, meskegys moy ys gwenhal i'n forth orth hi **lawana*** 'when I heard you calling, I was more delirious than a swallow on the road in her bliss' BK 1108-10

*Jesu, kymmar e ena ha graunt thotha **lowena*** 'Jesu, receive his soul and grant him bliss' BK 2835-36

*Mar ny asentyyth gena', te a hebcor **lowena** war bur nebas lavaraw* 'If you do not agree with me, you will forfeit all joy in very few words' BK 3087-89

joy   **GERYOW GWIR**

ow folly yth ew mar vras haw holan inweth pur browt ny vanaf thaworth an tase whylas mercy sure heb dowte kyn nam boma **lowena** 'my folly is so great and my heart also so proud, that I will not seek mercy from the Father, though I may not have bliss' CW 1522-26

an chorll adam y drygva a vyth abarth awartha in onyn an clowster[s] na neb na vyth tam **lowena** *mes in tewolgow bras ena ow kelly presens an tase* 'the churl Adam, his dwelling will be at the top in one of those cloisters where there will be no bliss, but in great darkness there forfeiting the Father's presence' CW 2024-29.

B **lowena dhis, lowena dhywgh** 'hail, greetings, good day'

lowene ȝys *a vester yn meth Iudas an brathky* 'Greetings to you, master, said Judas the savage cur' PA 65b

hag y kewsens ȝe scornye hag a gamma aga meyn pub onon rag y eysye **lowene ȝys** *te yw ȝeyn mygtern rys yw ȝe worȝye* 'and they spoke to scorn him and twisted their mouths, everyone to mock him. Greetings to you, you are our king; we must honour you' PA 137a-c

lowene the *flour an beys yma cas bras wharfethys ha cothys war the pobel* 'greetings to the flower of the world. Great trouble has happened and has fallen upon your people' OM 1541-43

lowene thy's *salamon dus genen ny quyc the tron the das dauid* 'greetings to you, Solomon; come with us quickly to the throne of your father David' OM 2377-79

ihesus crist **lowene thy's** *myghtern os war nef ha'n bys* 'Jesus Christ, greetings to you. You are king of heaven and the earth' PC 163-64

mester whek **thy's lowyne** *otte an asen gene ha'n ebel thy'so keffrys* 'dear master, greetings to you. Look, I have the ass with me and the foal for you also' PC 217-19

map dauid **thy's lowyne** *me a'th pys agan sawye ha'ghan dry the wlascor nef* 'son of David, greetings to you. I beg you to save us and bring us the the kingdom of heaven' PC 271-73

lowene thy's *map dauid map dev os ha den ynweyth* 'greetings to you, son of David. You are God and man also' PC 277-78

a vap dev **thy's lowyne** 'O son of God, greetings to you' PC 288

lowyne *sur* **the**'*n dev yv pur ha den keffrys* 'greetings indeed to the true God and man also' PC 293-94

ihesus whek a natharet **lowyne thy'so** *hep let ha mur onor yn teffry* 'dear Jesus of Nazareth, greetings to you immediately and great honour indeed' PC 301-03

mygthern yethewon y'th se heil **thy'so** *ha* **lowene** 'king of the Jews in your seat, hail to you and greetings' PC 2835-36

lowena ȝyvgh *arlothes ha ȝen map ker vs genes* 'greetings to you, lady, and to the dear son who is with you' BM 237-38

Ser epscop **thyugh lowena** 'Sir bishop, greetings to you' BM 519

Lowene dys *meriasek ny yv dev then bohosek* 'Greetings to you, Meriasek, we are two poor men' BM 692-93

Lowene dis *meryasek thymo vy den bohosek awoys crist lemen gueres* 'Greetings to you, Meriasek, help me now, a poor man, for the sake of Christ' BM 735-37

GERYOW GWIR   joy

Ser deyn **lowene** *dywy ha the oll agys colgy* 'Sir dean, greetings to you and to all your college' BM 2698-99

Maria **lowene dis** *ha gorthyans bys venytha* 'Mary, greetings to you, and worship evermore' BM 3188-89

Lowena thys*, Syr Teuthar, abarth y'th towr!* **Lowena thys***, corf heb par, ha mer honour drys peb i'n bys!* 'Greetings to you, Sir Teudar, within your tower. Joy to you, a peerless person, and great honour above everyone in the world' BK 70-74

Syra, **thewgh why lowena!** *Na syrrough kynth oma hil* 'Sir, greetings to you! Do not be angry, though I am late' BK 451-52

Lowena thys*, Syr Tewdar,* **lowena thys***, corf heb par, an gwelha gowr* 'Greetings to you, Sir Teudar, joy to you, a peerless person, the best of heroes' BK 881-83

Ow arluth, **theugh lowena***. Nawothow ema gena' na pleg thewhy, me a grys* 'My lord, greetings to you. I have news which you will not like, I believe' BK 933-35

Arluth, **thewhy lowena!** 'Lord, joy to you!' BK 1105

Lowena thewhy*, Augel! Mos the Arthor dyougal a ren, agen arluth ol* 'Greetings to you, Augel. We are going to Arthur indeed, the lord of us all' BK 1382-844

Lowena thys*, flower an bys, arluth myl bow ha gwlasow!* 'Greetings to you, flower of the world, lord of a thousand countries and kingdoms!' BK 1530-31

Lowena thu*'m gwelha gour a ve bythquath a Gurnow!* 'Greetings to my best hero who ever came from Cornwall!' BK 1914-15

Lowena theugh*, a vyghterne, hag onors drys an tasow!* 'Joy to you, O king, and honours beyond the ancestors!' BK 1956-57

Lowena thewhy *ha ras, hag honor ha beawta! Deg myl* **lowana thu***'m tas, del ew mer the reawta* 'Greetings to you and grace, and honour and pomp. Ten thousand greetings to my father, as your majesty is great' BK 2562-65

eall dew an nef awartha **theis lowena** *ha mear ioy* 'O angel of God from heaven above, greetings to you and much joy' CW1778-79

Lowena thewhy *ow thas devethis a paradice yth of lemyn tha thew gras* 'Greetings to you, my father; I have now come from paradise, may God be praised' CW 1880-82.

As can be seen, **Lowena dhis**, **Lowena dhywgh** are so well attested that they could legitimately be used instead of **Dùrda dhywgh why**, **Dùrda dhis** 'Good day to you' or **Dëdh dâ**, **Dÿdh dâ** 'Good day'. It is noteworthy incidentally that **Dëdh dâ**, **Dÿdh dâ** 'Good day', though common in the revived language, is nowhere attested in the traditional texts.

The word **lowender** is not as well attested as **lowena**, and tends to mean 'cheerfulness, jollity' as much as 'bliss, joy'

C **lowender**

Ima an profet Dauit in peswar vgans ha nownsag psalme ow exortya oll an bobyll the ry prayse hag honor the du ha thy servya in **lowendar** *ha gans perfect colonow the reiosya in sight agan creator ha redemar* 'The prophet David in Psalm 98 exhorts all people to give praise and honour to God and to serve him in cheerfulness and with perfect hearts to rejoice in the sight of our Creator and Redeemer' TH 1

joy

*Du a commondyas an profet Ysay the wull proclamacion the oll an bys fatell ew mabden gwels, ha fatell ew oll an glory an broghter han **lowender** a vabden kepar ha flowres in prasow* 'God commanded the prophet Isaiah to proclaim to all the world that mankind is grass, and that all the glory, brilliance and jollity of mankind is like flowers in the meadows' TH 6a-7

*eff a rug oll an rena keverennak ganso eff in **lowendar**, myns a vynna inioya an meritys ay pascion* 'he made all those to share with him in joy, as many as would enjoy the merits of his passion' TH 12a

*maym bo me grace woʒa hemma theth welas in **lowendar** gans tha elath awartha vhull in neyf* 'that I may have grace hereafter to see you in joy with your angels above high in heaven' CW 1427-30

*Perêg an gye gwellaz an steran, thonge loan gen meare a **loander*** 'When they saw the star, they were joyful with much joy' Rowe.

The word **joy**, *plural* **joyes**, is not as common as **lowena**, but it is frequently found, nonetheless. It has the same semantic range as the English word 'joy':

D **joy** 'joy'

*folle yn ta y whela ys del wra lyon y pray drey den yn peyn a calla neffre ny vnsa moy **ioy*** 'Much more madly he seeks than does a lion his prey to bring man into pain; were he able, never would he wish more joy' PA 21cd

*I feynys o bras ha creff yn **ioy** ʒeʒy trylys yw rag mygternes yw yn nef ʒe vos gorʒijs hy yv gyw* 'Her pains that were great and strong have been turned into joy for her, for she is queen in heaven; she is worthy to be adored' PA 226ab

*En varogyon pan glewas pylat ov cows yndella mur a **ioy** as kemeras y ʒe ʒeank yndella* 'when the soldiers heard Pilate talking thus, great joy overcame them that they should thus escape' PA 251ab

*rag bos abel gvyrthege ef a'n gefyth yn dyweth an **ioy** na thyfyk nefre yn ov gulas ha cosoleth* 'because there is true tithe from Abel, he will get in the end the joy that never fails in my kingdom and peace' OM 515-18

*abram me a leuer thy's el a'n nef of danfenys rag guythe na ve lethys the vap ysac yw the **ioy*** 'Abraham, I tell you: I am an angel sent from heaven to prevent your killing Isaac your son, who is your joy' OM 1371-74

*kowyth profyyn an styllyow marsens compes the'n fosow may haller age lathye gans corbles lasys tennow hag a's ty gans plynkennow may fo **ioy** myres worte* 'companions, let us test the rafters, whether they are right for the walls, so that they may be fixed with corbles, struts and beams, and we will cover them with planks so that it may be a joy to look upon them' OM 2471-76

*ha me a pys ragovgh ow thas may fevgh sylwys dre y luen ras hagh ol kerghys dotho th'y wlas yn **ioy** a pys hep stryf ha kas yn certan gans an eleth* 'and I shall beseech my Father for you, that you may be saved by his abundant grace and all brought to him in his kingdom in joy, which will last without strife or dissension indeed with the angels' PC 27-31

GERYOW GWIR joy

hag yndella mara qureth neffre ny fyth scham na meth saw mur a **ioy** 'and if you do thus never will you be embarrassed or ashamed, but will have much joy' PC 1901-03

kymereugh eveugh an guyn rag ny evaf bys deth fyn genough annotho na moy bys mayth yllyf yn ow gulas ha why gynef gans ow tas hep dywethva prest yn **ioy** 'take, drink the wine, for I shall not drink of it with you any more until the last day, when I enter my kingdom and you with me with my Father without end for ever in joy' PC 723-28

o salve sancta parens the nep yv **ioy** *ow colon ha'm melder kepar ha kens* 'greetings, O holy parent, who are the joy of my heart and my delight as before' RD 455-57

ha kemmys an gorthyo ef gans mur **ioy** *y tue the'n nef dre y thadder oberys* 'and whoever worships him with great joy will come to heaven, accomplished by his goodness' RD 1222-24

yma thy'mmo cowyth da mur a **ioy** *sur yn tor ma a'th tyryvas* 'I have much joy, good companion, now from your account' RD 1306-08

A enevov mertherijs **ioy** *neff yma dyugh grontys gans crist ihesu awartha* 'O martyred souls, the joy of heaven has been granted to you indeed by Jesus Christ above' BM 1300-02

a tekter rychys farwell nebes **ioy** *am bus an beys mensen stak omma merwell in meske tus na ven guelys* 'Ah, beauty, riches, farewell, little joy have I in the world. I should like to die right here on the spot so that I be not seen among men' BM 1366-69

peys da du thym dustuny nyns off y cafus defry a **ioy** *an bys me num duer* 'well satisfied, as God is my witness, I am not to get it indeed; I am not concerned for the joy of this world' BM 3028-30

hen ew the leverell, may fo agan chiff **ioye**, *ha delite settys in du, hag in y honor* 'that is to say, that our chief joy and delight should be set on God and on his honour' TH 21-21a

Ha wosa agan bewnans omma in bys, the vos kevrennek an **joyes** *vs in neff, dre an kythsame arluth na Jhesus crist* 'And after our life here in the world to share in the joys of heaven through that same Lord, Jesus Christ' TH 35

Joy *e golan ew them passion war an norvys* 'The joy of his heart is suffering to me in this world' BK 733-35

Joy *warnowgh ha ryelder, a vyth galaunt retenu, ha devethis a belder* 'Joy to you and majesty, who are always a galant retinue, and who have come from afar' BK 2005-007

Mar kyl gul e volenta, nyns us thym **joy** *ow pewa. Fatyl vyth, elhas, a Thew!* 'If he is able to do his will, I shall have no joy in living. How will things be, alas, O God!' BK 2516-18

ha der pegh a coveytes oll y **joye** *yth ew kellys may fetha paynes ragtha* 'and through the sin of avarice all his joy is lost, so that he will have pains for it' CW 1000-02

mayth ew kellys thyn an place o ornes thyn lean a **ioye** *tha vewa omma neffra* 'so that the place is lost to us that was ordained for us, to live here for ever full of joy' CW 1009-11

try fersons yns pur worthy ow kysraynya in **joyes** *in gwlase nef es awartha* 'they are three worthy persons reigning together in the joys of the kingdom of heaven which is above' CW 1960-62.

joy GERYOW GWIR

Interestingly, **lowender** is attested in Late Cornish, but neither **lowena** nor **joy** appears to be attested during the late period.

In the texts there are three words for 'joyful, happy, merry', A) **lowen**; B) **lowenek**; and C) **mery**.

Lowen and **yn lowen** are attested at all periods and tend to mean 'glad, gladly':

A **lowen**

Letus, ***louen*** 'glad' OCV §939

ha leuerough bos gevys ol ow sor beʒens ***lowen*** *ham gallus y vos grontijs ʒoʒo ʒe urusy an den* 'and tell him all my wrath is remitted; let him be happy and that my power has been granted to him to judge the man' PA 113cd

my a wra fest yn ***lowen*** *the nygys bys yn gorfen* 'I will very happily perform your business to the end' OM 719-20

my a gynes yn ***lowen*** *hagh a thoro an asen genen ha'n ebel keffrys* 'I will go happily with you and will bring the ass with us and the foal as well' PC 191-93

a arluth yth of ***lowen*** *ty the vynnes dos gynen omma th'agan lowenhe* 'Lord I am happy that you were willing to come with us here to make us glad' RD 1165-67

geneugh why mos ny drynyaf thu'm arluth ***lowen*** *yth af tyber cesar* 'I will not hesitate to go with you; to my lord I will go gladly, Tiberius Caesar' RD 1797-99

arluth ny vyen ***lowen*** *mar fur torment a cothfen y bones thy's* 'Lord, I should not have been happy, had I know you suffered such great torment' RD 2541-43

Ty then gylleth boys ***lowen*** *sawys tek oys in certen grasse the meryasek wek* 'You man, can be happy; you have been healed beautifully indeed, thanks to dear Meriasek' BM 747-49

trueth am bus ov queleys age mammov ovth ola ha ***lowen*** *certen ʒeheys thum corff me a gemersa* 'I am filled with pity seeing their mothers weeping and gladly indeed would I get health for my body' BM 1608-11

nyns a the ena the gol ragtho yma thymo tol inweth rag the sovdrys ol bethugh ***lowen*** 'your soul will not be lost; I have a hole for it; also for your soldiers. Be joyful!' BM 2347-50

settyn muter war y ben ny a yll bones ***lowen*** *y thoys then cur* 'let us set a mitre on his head; we may be joyful that he is coming to the cure' BM 3010-12

Ny a yl bonas ***lowan*** 'We can be joyful' BK 863

Byth ***lowen*** *ha da the cher!* 'Be glad and good your mood!' BK 2631

Ewa yagh? ewa ***lowan****? Me a thotha, re Jowan! athesempys; ny raf let* 'Is he well? Is he happy? I'll go to him, by St John! Immediately, I shall not dawdle' BK 3040-42

mars ew an oyle a vercy dres genas omma theth tas pur ***lowan*** *me a vea* 'if you have brought with you here the oil of mercy to your father, I should be very happy' CW 1887-89

Ha po chee & tha wreag an moiha ***looan*** *varbarr; nenna g'reu trea an dezan ha na henz* 'And when you and your wife are the most happy together, then cut the cake and not before' BF: 16

Ha Jooan, a meth an chei, deeow genna nei: ***looan*** *oan nei tha goz guellaz whey* 'Ho, John, they said, Come with us. we are glad to see you' BF: 16

*ha lebmen ma kaz dho nei rag boz **lûan*** 'and now we have cause to be happy' BF: 19

*Ol poble eze war an oare a treegaz keno than Arleth gen gannaw **looan** gormollow Eaue gen owyn preezyo eaue a rage deeaaw why deracta ha beatho **looan*** 'All people that dwell on the earth, sing to the Lord with joyful mouth; praise him with fear; laud him forth; come before him and be joyful' BF: 39.

Lowenek is found in both Middle Cornish and Late Cornish and means 'joyful, merry':

B **lowenek**

*ef a welas golow tek han meyn vmhelys ynweth ese a vgh Ihesus whek ha warnoʒo a yseth ell benegas **lowenek*** 'he saw a fair light and the stone overturned also which had been above Jesus and upon it sitting a blessed joyful angel' PA 244b-d

*Gans henna y a drylyas confortis ha **lowenek** hag eth tus crist rag whelas hag as cafos moreʒek* 'With that they turned comforted and joyful and went to seek Christ's people and found them sorrowful' PA 257ab

*Ov broder pur **lowenek** my a genes the'n meneth saw kyns ys mos ov thas whek ro thy'm the vanneth perfeth* 'My brother I shall be very happy to go with you to the mountain, but before going, my dear father, give me your perfect blessing' OM 449-52

*agan arluth lucifer ny a'n kyrgh thy's hep danger pur **lowenek*** 'our lord Lucifer, we will fetch him to you without demur very happily' OM 547-49

*ov tas fest **lowenek** vyth mar scon a'n bys tremene* 'my father will be very happy to depart from the world so soon' OM 833-34

*ny a yl bos **lowenek** guelas ihesu galosek arluth a ras* 'we may be joyful to have seen Jesus, the mighty lord of grace' RD 1333-35

*warlergh Cryst maras os trest lemmyn pur **lowenek** fest bos ty a yl* 'if you are sad for the loss of Christ, now you may be very happy' RD 1417-19

*pan thueth yn rak an plosek ef a geusys **lowenek** thy'm gruk plekgye* 'when the foul fellow came forward, he spoke joyfully; he made me give way' RD 1848-50

*thotho yth af **lowenek** del yv arluth gallosek ha den ryal* 'I will go to him joyfully as he is a mighty lord and a regal person' RD 1905-07

*trompys cleryons wethugh wy lemen then fest **lowenek*** 'trumpets, clarions, blow you now right merrily' BM 276-77

*bones sacris marrek du an order mur thym a plek benitha hedre ven byv me a garse **lowenek*** 'to be consecrated a soldier of God of the great order that pleases me, always as long as I live, I should gladly desire' BM 350-53

*Banneth du thys meryasek ny a vya **lowenek** a mynnes oma treġa]* 'God's blessing to you, Meriasek, we should be happy if you would dwell here' BM 581-83

*Ty a yl boys **lowenek** kynth este claff anhethek grasse the crist yth oys sav* 'You can be happy; though you were an incurable leper, thanks to Christ you are healed; BM 1852-54

*Ny yv certen **lowenek** rag cafus dyn meryasek the voys revler* 'We are certainly happy to find for ourselves Meriasek to be ruler' BM 2716-18

joy   **GERYOW GWIR**

Ha wosa henna in destruccion, ha agy the proces a dyrmyn arta bos **lowenek** *the trelya thega dew obediens* 'And after that in destruction, and within the course of time to be happy again to return to their due obedience' TH 49a

vn dra a won a[n] gothvas pur **lowenake** *a[th] gwressa cola orthaf a mennas* 'one thing, if you knew it, would make you very happy, were you to listen to me' CW 545-47

Betha why **lawannack** 'Be you merry' Carew.

The word **mery** is clearly borrowed from English 'merry' and is not particularly common:

C **mery**

ha largys ha gromersy ny a yl bos fest **mery** *rag cafus ro an par na* 'Oh generosity, Oh thanks! We can be very merry for getting a present like that' OM 2465-67

Ov lich kyng bethugh **mery** *inweth oll an kyffuywy dukis ȝurlys marogyon* 'My liege king, be merry, and also all the guests, dukes, earls, knights' BM 292-94

mar num kemer du certen an iovle a ra pur lowen mage **fery** *avel hok* 'if God will not take me, the Devil will indeed very gladly, as merrily as a hawk' BM 1899-901.

To sum up: there are three words for 'joy, gladness', namely **lowena**, **lowender** and **joy**. **Lowena dhis**, **Lowena dhywgh** can be used to mean 'Greetings'. For 'joyful, glad' one can use **lowen**, **lowenek** and **mery**, all three of which have different semantic ranges.

JUDGE, TO JUDGE

For the noun 'judge' Nance recommends **jùster** (UC *juster*), ***brusyas**, **brusyth**, and **jùj** (UC *juj*). **Jùster** is Nance's emendation of *iucter* 'judge, ruler, governor' (< ME *justicer*) which is attested twice:

A **jùster**

gansa y an hombronkyas yn prys hanter nos heb wow bys yn aga fryns annas o vn **lucter** *bras yn pow* 'thye led him with them at midnight indeed to their prince Annas, who was a great ruler in the land' PA 76cd

Gans mur a **lucters** *yn wlas ef a ve veyll rebukis kavanskis ef a whelas rag own y vonas leȝys* 'By many rulers in the kingdom he was vilely rebuked. He tried to evade for fear of being killed' PA 156ab.

***Brusyas** is unattested, having been devised by Nance on the basis of **brusy** 'to judge'.

Brusyth is Nance's respelling of *iudex*, **brodit** 'judge' OCV §177. It is not certain, however that OC **brodit** would have developed as **brusyth** in Middle Cornish. In spite of **brusy** 'to judge', it is quite possible that the

236

r in ***brodit*** would have prevented the assibilation of the medial **-d-**; cf. ***prydyth*** 'poet' at BK 2497, not *****prysyth***.

Borlase gives ***Barner*** 'Judge', but this word is almost certainly based on Welsh *barnwr*, and there is no evidence that it ever formed part of the Cornish lexicon.

The word **jùj** is attested in both the singular and the plural:

B jùj

*nep a tawo yn pow ma thyrag **iug** ny fyth iuggys ytho dre pup reson da ny goth thotho bos crousys* 'whoever in this land is silent before a judge shall not be judged. Therefore for every good reason he should not be crucified' PC 2387-90

*Rag lymmyn athewethas pub den sempill heb understonding na skyans a re supposia fatell yllens y bos **iudges** in maters a contrauercite* 'For recently now all simple people without understanding or knowledge believe that they can be judges in matters of controversy' TH 37

*an egglos an jevas an lell sens an scriptur ha yth ew **iudg** a henna* 'the chuch has the true sense of the scripture and is judge of that' TH 36 fn.

*ha in pub oys ha tyrmyn eff a ve kemerys ha recevys gans tus da disposis ha tus diskys rag lell **Judge** a henna* 'and in every age and period he was taken and accepted by well disposed men and learned men as the true judge of that' TH 38

*Rag an tyrmyn an prontyr, ha rag an tyrmyn an **Judge**, in stede a crist* 'For the time being the priest and for the time being the judge in place of Christ' TH 42a

*ha rag an tyrmyn the vos **ivdge** in stede a crist* 'and for the time being to be judge in stead of Christ' TH 48a.

In view of the above, it seems that **jùj**, **jùjys** ought perhaps be the ordinary word for 'judge' in the revived language.

For 'to judge' Nance recommends A) **brusy** and B) **jùjya** (UC *jujja*). **Brusy**, **brujy** is certainly attested:

A brusy

*Ihesus a ve danvenys haʒeworth an prins annas gans tus ven aʒesempys bys an ebscop cayphas dreʒo crist may fe **bresys*** 'Jesus was sent from Prince Annas by strong men immediately to Caiaphas the bishop, that he might be judged by him' PA 88ac

*ha leuerough bos gevys ol ow sor beʒens lowen ham gallus y vos grontijs ʒoʒo ʒe **urusy** an den* 'and tell him that all my anger is abated, let him rejoice, and that my authority has been granted to him to judge the man' PA 113cd

*hag a leuer the pup prout certan y vones map dev neb a thue th'agan **brugy** yn ayr deth brus pup huny* 'and he tells everyone proudly that he is the Son of God, who will come in the heavens to judge everyone of us on the day of judgement' PC 1666-69

*an prysners kettep onan drewhy yn rak dyssempys dismas iesmas baraban may hallons bones **brugys*** 'bring forth the prisoners, every one immediately, Dismas, Jesmas, Barabbas, that they may be judged' PC 2231-34

judge

*ke ty pilat mylyges ena yn dour the woles certan ty a ha genes mollat pup plu drefen fals **brugy map dev map maria*** 'Go, accursed Pilate, there to the bottom of the water you will certainly go and the curse of every parish over you because you falsely judged the Son of God, Son of Mary' RD 2195-200
*deth brus eff a thue certan thagen **brusy** kyk in kneys* 'on the day of judgement he will certainly come to judge us flesh in skin' BM 4053-54
*deth brus eff a thue purfeth the **vrusi** an drok han mays* 'on the day of judgement he will come perfectly to judge the evil and the good' BM 4086-87.

The verb **jùjya** 'to judge', however, is much commoner:

B **jùjya**

*Ha ʒeso y tanvonas y allus crist rag **iudgye*** 'And he has sent you his authority to judge Christ' PA 116a
*rag henna aʒesympys bys yn cayphas ʒy ʒey **yvggye** ef a rug may fe gorrys* 'therefore immediately he had him sent thither to Caiaphas to judge him' PA 118cd
*rag henna ef a **iuggyas** Ihesus ʒeʒe ʒy laʒe the ves y a thelyffras barabas quyth mayʒ elle* 'therefore he adjudged Jesus to them to execute him; they released Barabbas that he might go free' PA 150cd
*bresell cref a ve sordijs en grows pu elle ʒy don dre vur stryff y fe **iuggijs** ys degy crist y honon* 'a vigorous argument arose who might carry the cross thither. By great strife it was judged that Christ should carry it himself' PA 160cd
*dyth brues y wregh ysethe ol an bys ma rak **iugge** pup ol herwyth y ober* 'on the day of judgement you will sit to judge all this world, everyone according to his conduct' PC 815-16
*ha deyth brues theugh ef a thue ha why a'n guylwyth certan yn yer worth agas **yugge*** 'and on judgement day he will come to you and you shall see him indeed in the heaven judging you' PC 1331-33
*ef re thyndyles yn ta gothaf mernens yn bys ma mara pethe lel **iuggys*** 'he has certainly deserved to suffer death in this world if he is properly judged' PC 1342-44
*ytho why kemereugh e ha herwyth agas laha ha concyans guregh y **iuggye** the'n mernans mar coth henna* 'so take him and according to your law and conscience judge him to death if that is necessary' PC 1977-80
*ordnough bar the ysethe ha me [a] wra y **iugge** aban reys thy'mmo porrys* 'arrange a tribunal to sit at and I will judge him since I absolutely must' PC 2225-27
*en prysners bras ha byan drewhy thy'm kettep onan may haller aga **iugge*** 'the prisoners great and small, bring everyone to me that they may be judged' PC 2250-52
*nep a tawo yn pow ma thyrag iug ny fyth **iuggys*** 'whoever is silent in this land before a judge shall not be judged' PC 2387
*syr pylat nans yv hy prys whar ihesu Cryst a rey brueys rak y **iugge*** 'Sir Pilate, it is now time to give verdict on Christ that he may be judged' PC 2471-73
*kepar hag ef on crousys ha dre wyr vreus quyt **iuggys** rak agan drok ober kens* 'like him we have been crucified and by true judgement completely judged for our evil deeds before now' PC 2900-02

GERYOW GWIR judge

*lader of a fue **iuggys** ha ryp ihesu cryst gorrys yn crous a pren* 'I am a robber who was judged and beside Jesus put on a wooden cross' RD 265-67

*ny **iuggyn** mones nep pel lemmyn bys yn vn castel henwys emmavs* 'we do not determine to go far but only to a village called Emmaus' RD 1294-96

*dus thu'm arluth dyssempys ha scon ty a fyth **iuggys** the peyn garow* 'come to my lord immediately and soon you will be condemned to savage torment' RD 1902-04

*ty a wra y worre scon athesempys yn pryson an casadow bys may hallo bos **iuggys*** 'you will soon straightway put him in prison, the hateful fellow, until he can be judged' RD 1977-80

*lemmyn omma ty a dryk bys pan pottro ol the gyk **iuggys** may fey* 'now here you will stay until all your flesh rot, that you may be judged' RD 2021-23

*an haccre mernans a vo war ow fay ty a vetho **iuggys** yv thy's* 'it has been judged for you that you are to get the nastiest death possible upon my faith' RD 2033-35

*ef a whylas ihesu Cryst myghtern a nef ha falslych y'n **iuggyas** ef gans cam pur bras* 'he sought Jesus Christ, the king of heaven, and falsely judged him with a great injustice' RD 2261-64

*Arluth esta ge ow **jugia** mett the veras war onyn an parna ha the thry the vos **jugys** genas ge* 'Lord, do you judge me fit to look upon one of those and to bring him to be judged by you?' TH 7

*neb na garra y gyscristian warlyrth an kyth sort ma ew **judgys** the vos in myrnans dre an wytnys ma a S Johan* 'whoever does not love his fellow-Christian in this way is judged to be in death by this witness of St John' TH 20a

*ha dre gwryoneth, mar mynnyn ny **judgia** compis, hag inta* 'and in truth, if we judge correctly and well' TH 21

*han pith a russans y gull, ny yll bos **judgys** vncharitable* 'and what they did cannot be judged uncharitable' TH 29a

*mar pith mater vith a discorde, kyn fe in mater a nebas valew, na rellan ny warlyrth agan fantasy agan honyn **iudgia** an dra* 'if there is any matter of dispute, even in a matter of small importance, let us not judge the matter according to our own imaginings' TH 37

*An power han auctorite na, kepar dell ve va fuguris in la goyth thyn ordyr a prontereth, the **judgia** lypers ha the punyssya oll an re na na vynna obeya an prontirion* 'That power and authority, as it was configure in the old law for the order of priests, to judge lepers and to punish all those who would not obey the priests' TH 38a

*oll an Epscobow a rome a ve thea tyrmyn Pedyr estymys, **iudgys**, ha kemeris rag an successors han folyars a Pedyr* 'all the bishops of Rome since the time of Peter have been esteemed, judged and accepted as the successors and followers of Peter' TH 47a

*ha ef a vyn dos the **judgia** oll an bobell* 'and he will come to judge all the people' SA 59.

In the revived language either **brusy/brujy** or **jùjya** can be used for 'to judge'.

239

JUSTICE

The word **jùstys** in Middle Cornish means 'justice, magistrate' and is not uncommon:

A **jùstys** 'magistrate'

*pu a woras yt colon cows yndelma worth **iustis*** 'who put it into your heart thus to speak to a magistrate?' PA 81d

*Neb o mester ha **Iustis** worth ihesus ef a gowsas myns vs omma cuntullys pur apert y ret flamyas* 'He who was master and magistrate to Jesus he spoke, All those who are gathered here have quite openly accused you' PA 92ab

*Herodes a leuerys ʒen eʒewon eugh yn fen ʒe bylat agis **Iustis** rag me an syns pur ʒen len* 'Herod said to the Jews: Go straightway to Pilate your magistrate, for I consider him a very trustworthy man' PA 113ab

*ot an **iustys** ow tos thy'n anotho ef grens del vyn pan glevfo y lauarow* 'Look, the magistrate is coming to us; let him do with him as he wishes, when he hears what he says' PC 370-72

*longys reys yv thy's gyne vn pols byan lafurye dre worhemmyn an **iustis*** 'Longinus, you must walk a little way with me by command of the magistrate' PC 3003-05

*saw pyw a vyn leuerel the vewnans ef the seuel hythew yn mes a'n beth pry nag a feth mos the'n **iustys** rag dout y vones lethys* 'but who will say that he has risen today from the tomb of earth or will dare go to the magistrate for fear of being killed?' RD 589-93.

The expression **gwirvreus**, literally 'true judgement' is close in sense to the abstract 'justice':

B **gwirvreus**

*my a wortheb thy's whare yn certan na vy lettyys dre **guyrvrus** sur y cothe dotho gothaf bos lethys yn pur defry nep a rella yn ketella mernans yv gvyw th'y vody* 'I will answer you straightway indeed lest you be delayed; by justice indeed he ought to suffer death; in very truth whoever does thus, death is fitting for his person' OM 2235-42

*certan **guyrvres** yv honna ty a wel an venen ma whet aban thuthe y'th chy golhy ow treys ny hyrsys homma gans daggrow keffrys re's golhas yn surredy* 'certainly that is a right verdict; you see this woman; since I came into your house you did not enjoin my feet to be washed; she with tears also has washed them indeed' PC 515-20.

Tregear, however, uses **jùstys** for 'justice' in the abstract sense:

C **jùstys** 'justice'

*Rag henna ny wothya du dre gwryoneth ha **iustus**, receva mabden arta thy favowre, ha then stat an bewnans heb deweth* 'Therefore God could not by rights and in justice receive mankind back into his favour and to the state of eternal life' TH 12

GERYOW GWIR justice

*ha the restoria mabden arta then stat a ras, the vos glane kyffrys in corffe hag in ena, ha henna dre an forth a **justyce**, ha the wull lene amyndys* 'and to restore mankind again to the state of grace, to be cleansed in both body and soul, and that by the means of justice and to make full amends' TH 12a

*dre paynys an par na gans cammensyth procurijs warbyn an teball ell rag raunsona mabden hay thelver thea ponow ha thea captiuite gwythys gans an teball ell dre **justys*** 'by torments of that kind procured unjustly against the devil to ransom mankind and to deliver him from pains and from captivity, held by justice by the devil' TH 15

*Omma me a vyn govyn vn questyon the vos assoyles, mar te cherite requyria the predyry, the cowsse da, ha the wull da the bub den, da ha bad, fatell yll an rewlysy an wlas executia **justis** war drog pobill gans charite?* 'Here I shall ask a question to be answered: if charity requires us to think, to speak well and to do well to all men, good and bad, how can the rulers of the kingdom execute justice upon evil people with charity?' TH 24a

*Rag an lell vnderstonding an gyrryow ma, yth ew the vos notys, fatell ma gwryoneth ha **justice** in kysam text ma ow signifia pub kynde oll a virtu ha daddar* 'For the full understanding of these words, we should note that righteousness and justice in this same text mean all kind of virtue and goodness' TH 26a

*Rag henna pan vsy agan Savyowre ow requyrya theworthan ny may teffan ny ha passia an scribes han pharises in gwryoneth ha **iustice**, yma eff ow menya na rellan ny cristonnyan desquethes agan honyn da ha virtus warves in sight an bys only* 'Therefore, when our Saviour requires from us that we should excel the scribes and pharisees in righteousness and justice, he means that we Christians should not show ourselves good and virtuous externally only in the sight of the world' TH 26a

*Ha ny drog pobyll a rug despisia oll y decreys, ha y ordynans eff ay **justys*** 'And we, evil people, despised oll his decrees and the ordinance of his justice' TH 40-40a.

The corresponding negative abstract **anjùstys** seems to be attested in Jowan Chy an Hordh. Lhuyd's text at JCH §31 reads: *Huei ol? mêr a huei an Iutiziou (a medh Dzhûan) gyr tero an dhiz rag riman a 'ryg an bad-ober?* (BF: 18), This I should emend slightly to: *Huei ol? mera huei **aniustiz** iou (a medh Dzhûan) gyr ter o an dhiz-reg ha mana a 'ryg an bad-ober* 'You all, look it is an injustice (said John); know that it was the ale-wife and a monk who committed the crime'. If this is correct, then **anjùstys** 'injustice' is attested in Cornish.

To sum up: although **gwirvreus** 'true judgement' can in some cases translate 'justice' in the abstract sense, the best word to translate 'justice' in Cornish is **jùstys**. **Anjùstys** can be used for 'injustice'.

K

KIND

To translate the noun 'kind', i.e. 'sort, variety', there are three Cornish words: A) **ehen** *f.*; B) **kynda** *m.*; and C) **sort** *m.* **Ehen** essentially means 'kindred, kind'; **pùb ehen** can mean 'everything':

A ehen

Ihesus crist a leueris ȝe thu ny goth thys temptye yn neb **ehan** *a seruys lemmyn prest y honore* 'Jesus Christ said, You ought not tempt God in any kind of service, but always honour him' PA 15ab

Ha spycis leas **ehen** *ef a worras yn y veth ȝe gryst a bub tenewen hag aȝyghow hag agleth* 'And spices, many kinds he put in his tomb on either side of Christ, both on the right and on the left' PA 236ab

lauar thy 'mmo ty venen an frut ple russys tyrry mara pe a'n keth **eghen** *o dyfynnys orthyn ny* 'tell me, you woman, where did you pluck the fruit, if it was of the same variety that had been prohibited to us' OM 209-12

ha myr a pup tenewen aspy yn ta pup **eghen** 'look on every side; observe everything well' OM 746-47

a bub **eghen** *best yn wlas gor genes dew annethe* 'of every kind of animal in the land, bring with you two of them' OM 977-78

mar tue nep guas ha laddre en gueel theworthyn pryve meth vyth ol d'agen **ehen** 'if some fellow should happen to steal the rods from us privily, it will be a disgrace to all our kindred' OM 2064-66

sav ma[r] ny yl bos nahen the voth prest yn pup **hehen** *y goulenwel yv ow whans* 'but if it cannot be otherwise, it is always my desire to fulfil your will in everything' PC 1090-92

lyes torn da yn bys ma re wruk the vohosugyon sawye pup **eghen** *clefyon a vewhe yn bewnans da* 'many a kindness he has done in this world for the poor, healing every sort of sick person who lived a good life' PC 3107-10

wy yv pen agen **ehen** *gouerner lich a fur rays* 'you are the head of our kindred; a liege lord of great grace' BM 318-19

nyns yv worschyp theth **ehen** *the conseyt in pur certen* 'your whim is no honour to your kindred in very truth' BM 361-60

ov hanov in guir heb mar yv costyntyn the nobil emprour worthy map then vyternes helen neb yv pen ol y **ehen** *del glowas lues huny* 'my name indeed of course is Constantine the Noble, a worthy emperor, son to Queen Helena, who is head of all his kindred, as many have heard' BM 1155-60

prag na vyn y kemeras dretho y hyl gul gueras ha les the oll y **ehen** 'why will he not accept it? Through it he can bring aid and advantage to all his kindred' BM 2911-13

Nyng ew repref tho'm **ehan** *hag awos own, me a dyrhas i'n forest a Rosewa* 'There is no rebuke to my kindred and in spite of fear, I landed in the forest of Rosewa' BK 96-99

lower flowrys a bub **ehan** *yn place ma yta tevys* 'many flowers of every kind, behold they are growing here' CW 363-64

yma peyke thym provyes ha lavonowe pub **ehan** 'I have provided pitch and ropes, all kinds' CW 2290-91

a bub **ehan** *a vestas drewhy quick ȝym orthe copplow* 'do you bring quickly to me in pairs of all kinds of animals' CW 2411-12

pub **ehan** *ha beast in byes puskas in moer magata a vyth thewgh susten omma* 'every kind of animal in the world, fishes in the sea also, will be food for you now' CW 2512-14

yn dyth na te nyn 'wra **ehan** *a whêl* 'on that day you shall do no kind of labour' ACB: E e 3 verso

Enna chee na wra **ehan** *a wheel* 'Then you shalt do no kind of labour' ACB: E e 3 verso.

Ehen can also be used to mean 'one's natural ability, one's utmost' and is found in several idioms:

bost a wrens tyn ha deveth yn gweȝens **worth y ehen** 'they bitterly and shamelessly boasted that they would guard him in spite of all he might do' PA 242d

kychough ef yn vryongen ha dalynnough mur cales ma na allo pertheges **yn dyspyt ol th'y eghen** 'catch him by the through and hold him so hard that he won't be able to rant, in spite of all his efforts' PC 1007-10

me a'n clewas ov tyffen na vo reys **awos heghen** *trubit vyth the syr cesar* 'I heard him forbidding that there was any need on any account to render any tribute to Lord Caesar' PC 1573-75

rag tha garenga lemyn me a vyn gwyll paradice place delicyous **dres ehan** 'for your sake I will make paradise, an exceedingly delightful place' CW 359-61

me a levar thys eva ha coole orthaf **os ehan** 'I tell you, Eve, and listen to me to your utmost' CW 594-95.

Kynda means 'kind, kindred' also and thus **warbydn kynda** means 'contrary to one's nature, unnatural, cruel':

B kynda

a bup **kynde** *ethen vas y'th worhel guet dew gorre* 'be sure to put two of every kind of useful bird into your vessel' OM 979-80

A arluth ker my a'n kymer yn ban wharre an welen ma yn hy **kunda** *treylys arte* 'Dear Lord, I take it up straightway, this rod, turned into its own kind again' OM 1454-60

kind   **GERYOW GWIR**

*y feth othom annethe the **gvnde** mab den defry may fo rys vn deyth a due guthyl crous annethe y* 'the kindred of man indeed will have need of them, when it will be necessary some day to make a cross of them' OM 1949-52

*me a bref bos gow henna rak dev ha den yv dev dra pur contraryus yn **kende*** 'I shall prove that to be a lie, for God and man are two things very contrary in kind to each other' PC 1729-31

*ena yth esa plenty a bup **kynde** a frutys, beautyfull tege ha wheg the veras warnetha* 'there there were plenty of all kinds of fruits, beautifully fair and sweet to look upon' TH 2

*Saw vn **kynda** a frut an tas du a chargias mabden na rella myllya na tuchia worta war bayne merwall a vernans* 'But one kind of fruit God the Father charged mankind not to meddle with or touch on pain of dying the death' TH 2

*me a dryst why a vith circumspect the avoydia oll **kynde** pehosow ha disobediens kyn fe an dra vith mar nebas in y nature y honyn* 'I trust you will be careful to avoid all kinds of sin and disobedience though it be a matter so small in its own nature' TH 5

*an corfe a ve gwrys gwan ha drys the vos gustith the lyas **kynda** a cleves ha gwannegreth* 'the body became weak and brought to be subject to many kinds of sickness and weakness' TH 12

*eff a suffras lyas **kynde** ha sorte a kammynsoth ha paynys intollerabill ha turmontys yn y pur ha innocent corffe* 'he suffered many kinds and sorts of iniquity and unbearable pains and torments in his pure and guiltless body' TH 15

*fatell ma gwryoneth ha justice in kysam text ma ow signifia pub **kynde** oll a virtu ha daddar* 'that truth and justice in this same texts means all kinds of virtues and goodness' TH 26a

*yth ew gwris da aga rebukya, may hallans bos methek ha kemeras sham aga fawtys ha dre rebukys amendia aga lewde bewnans han kithsame **kende** ma a rebukys ew da ha lawfull gans cherite* 'it is well done to rebuke them, so that they may be ashamed and embarrassed for their faults and by rebukes mend their immoral lives and this same kind of rebukes is good and lawful in all charity' TH 29a

*theth owne vrodar yth o va haw brodar ve magata rag henna warbyn **cunda** yth o theis motty latha* 'he was your own brother and my brother also; therefore it was against nature for you to venture to kill him' CW 1300-03

*pub beast oll ymma gyllys in lester thaga **kynda** dell yw ornys thymo ve* 'every animal has gone into the vessel to their kind, as was ordered to me' CW 2433-35

*Ha Deew wraez bestaaez an beaz wor ler go **kenda**, ha an Chattall worler go **kenda** ha keneffra tra ez a cramyhaz wor an beaze worler go **henda**; ha deew a wellhaz treuah dah* 'And God made the animals according to their kind, and the cattle according to their kind and everything that crawls upon the earth according to their kind, and God saw that it was good' JKeigwin.

Ehen and **kynda** are used together in *A bub **eghen** a **kunda** gorow ha benow yn weth aga gore ty a wra yn the worhel aberveth* 'Of every kind of species male and female also you shall put into your ship' OM 989-92 and *a bub **ehan** a **gynda** gorrow ha benaw inwethe aga gorra ty a wra in tha lester abervathe* 'Of every

244

kind of species male and female also you shall put into your ship' CW 2270-73.

Sort is similar in use to English 'sort'; **warlergh an sort-ma** can be used to mean 'according to this, in this manner':

C sort
in vn noys mar lefara me a russe dywhy ix an keth **sort** *ma* 'in one night, if I say it, I should make for you nine of this same kind' BM 1647-49

eff a suffras lyas kynde ha **sorte** *a kammynsoth ha paynys intollerabill ha turmontys yn y pur ha innocent corffe* 'he suffered many kinds and sorts of iniquity and unbearable pains and torments in his pure and guiltless body' TH 15a

neb na garra y gyscristian warlyrth an kyth **sort** *ma ew judgys the vos in myrnans dre an wytnys ma a S Johan* 'whoever does not love his fellow Christian in this sort is judged to be in a state of death by this witness of St John' TH 20a

In marver dell ve agan mam sans egglos athewethas assaultys dre lyas **sort** *ha sect a eryses* 'In so far as our mother, holy Church, has recently been assaulted by many kinds and sects of heresies' TH 30a

in kepar maner yma lyas **sort** *a bobill ow pewa in dan an catholik egglos* 'in a similar way many sorts of people live under the catholic Church' TH 34

ha kyns oll hemma ew the vos notys, fatell rug du thea dalleth an bys lyas tyrmyn apperya the vabden, pare tyrmyn in vn **sort**, *ha pare tyrmyn in* **sort** *arell* 'and first of all this is to be noted: that God since the beginning of the world often appeared to mankind, at one time in one sort, at another time in another sort' TH 55

Tee a ill percevia pa vaner [h]a **sort** *esta o qvelas agen saviour Christ, bus e dochya, not only [e] touchia bus e thibbry* 'You can see how and in which way you [not only] see our Saviour Christ, but touch him, but eat him' SA 60a

in pympas dyth orth ow breis an puskas heb falladowe hag oll an ethyn keffrys me a gwra thom plegadow hag oll an bestas yn beyse gans prevas a bub **sortowe** 'on the fifth day, as I am minded, the fish without fail and all the birds as well I shall make according to my pleasure, and all the animals in the world with creeping things of every sort' CW 106-11

me ew onyn an **sort** *na* 'I am one of that sort' CW 678

a bub **sort** *oll a leverow egwall vnna ew gorrys pekare yth ew an* **sortow** *gorrys vnna der devyes in diffrans ha kehavall* 'of every kind of book a copy is put into them; in the same way the sorts are put into them by a plan, different and similar' CW 2197-201

deffrans **sortowe** *a wernow yma parys pur effan* 'different sorts of masts have been prepared most amply' CW 2292-93

me a vidn gwythyll canow ha sacryfice lebmyn radn ehan a bub **sortowe** *keffrys bestas hag ethyn gans henna thy honora* 'I will raise hymns and make sacrifice now, a share of every kind, both animals and bird, to honour him therewith' CW 2486-90

Ha Jesus geth oll adro der Alale, deske et ago eglezow an gerryow Deew an gulasketh, sawyah oll **sorto** *clevas, ha oll pesticks mesk an boble* 'And Jesus went all about Galilee, teaching in their churches the words of God of the kingdom, healing all sorts of disease and all sickness among the people' Rowe

kind GERYOW GWIR

*ha angy droaze thotha oll an glevyan, ha rimah o comerez gen pub **sort** clevyas, ha tormentyaz ha ri meh o comerez gen an jowloo, ha ri mah o frantik, ha ri nah o palgeaz ha e o sawyaz* 'and they brought to him all the sick and those who were suffering from all kinds of illness, and tormented and those who were seized by devils, and those who were deranged, and those who were palsied, and he healed them' Rowe.

Ehen and **kynda** both mean 'sort, variety' and 'kindred' as well. **Sort** can mean 'sort, variety', but it also means 'manner.' **Sort** is the only one of the three etyma for which a plural (**sortow**) is attested.

KINGDOM

In Old Cornish the word for 'kingdom' is ***ruifanaid***: *regnum*, ***ruifanaid*** 'kingdom' OCV §104; *sceptrum, guailen **ruifanaid*** 'royal sceptre' (literally 'rod of kingdom') OCV §165. This Nance converted into Middle Cornish as *revaneth. In other forms of Cornish the word is spelt *ruvaneth. Although ***ruifanaid*** is found twice in OCV, it is unknown elsewhere in Cornish.

The ordinary word for 'kingdom' in Middle and Late Cornish is **gwlascor** *f*., which is well attested:

*ov colon yv claf marthys bos drog an par ma cothys yn ov **glascor** yn tor ma* 'my heart is remarkably sick that evil of this kind has fallen upon my kingdom now' OM 1568-70

*mar mynnyth bones yn eys reys yv thy's gorre moyses aron a'th **wlascor** yn meys ha'ga pobel ol ganse* 'if you wish to be at ease, you must put Moses, Aaron out of your kingdom and all their people with them' OM 1571-74

*map dauid thy's lowyne me a'th pys agan sawye ha'ghan dry the **wlascor** nef* 'Hail, son of David. I beg you to save us and to bring us to the kingdom of heaven' PC 271-73

*ef yv an profus jhesu a leuer y vos map dv a nef huhel diwithys a nazare tre a **wlascor** galile pur thyowgel* 'he is the prophet Jesus who says he is the son of God of high heaven; having come from Nazareth, a town in the kingdom of Galileee in very deed' PC 325-30

*yma ov treyle deffry ol an **wlascor** a iudi ov talleth yn galile* 'he is turning indeed all the kingdom, starting in Galilee' PC 1593-95

*heil syre emperour a'n wlas iouyn roy thy's bos den mas ha len reulye the **wlascor*** 'hail, sir emperor of the land. Jovyn give you to be a good man and to rule your kingdom faithfully' PC 1705-07

*ytho dre henna yth yv the vos myghtern war nep cor pan leuerta thy'm ihesu thy'so gy bones **gulascor*** 'So, therefore it means that you are in some way a king, when you tell me, Jesus, that you have a kingdom' PC 2015-18

*arluth cryst me a'th pysse a prydiry ahane pan vyse yn the **wlascor*** 'Lord Christ, I would beg you to think of me when you are in your kingdom' PC 2906-08

GERYOW GWIR   **kingdom**

y'n gylwys map dev yn prof ahanaf may portho cof pan deffe th'y **wlascor** *ef* 'I called him the son of God as evidence that he should remember me when he came to his kingdom' RD 271-73

the'th **wlascor** *pan deffyn ny clew agan lef* 'when we come to your kingdom, hear our voice!' RD 772-74

the'n crystynnyon ol adro yntrethe gasaf ow ras yn ow **gulascor** *ma['s] teffo bewnans neffre ioy hep cas* 'to the Christians all around, among them I leave my grace, that they may have life always, joy unalloyed in my kingdom' RD 1583-86

mars cryst a weres deffry ef a lath gans fleyryngy ol ow **glascor** 'unless Christ help indeed, he will kill all my kingdom by a stench' RD 2132-34

an carn [n]a a ygoras del o destnys thotho ef rak pur wyr yth hepcoras dre y ober **glascor** *nef* 'that mass of rock opened as had been destined for him, for indeed he forfeited by his deed the kingdom of heaven' RD 2335-38

the'n keth plas na thyugh yth af alena yth yskynnaf yn ban bys yn **glascor** *nef* 'to that same place I shall go to you; thence I shall ascend up into the kingdom of heaven' RD 2400-02

Me yw gylwys duk bryten ha seuys a goys ryel ha war an **gwlascur** *cheften nessa ʒen myterne vhell* 'I am called the Duke of Brittany and descended from royal blood and next to the lofty king chieftain over the kingdom' BM 1-4

Gelwys yʒ of conany mytern yn bryten vyan han **gvlascor** *pur yredy me a bev ol yn tyan* 'I am called King Conan in Brittany, and I possess all the kingdom in very deed' BM 168-71

parusse ovy dethy es then brasse arlythy us in **gluascour** *thymo creys* 'I am more ready for them than for the greatest lords which are in the kingdom, believe me' BM 3122-24

hennew the vos excludys ha debertis theworth an number an elect, pobill dewysys, ha deberthis theworth an **wlascur** *a neff heb dewethfa* 'that is, to be excluded and separated from the number of the elect, chosen people, and separated from the eternal kingdom of heaven' TH 22a

Indelma an ii office a vynsa bos diligently executys, rag avoydya **gwlaskur** *an teball ell* 'Thus the two offices would be diligently executed to escape from the kingdom of the devil' TH 25

rag lymmyn nanelle possessyon an bys, na pith an bys, na bewnans here, na gweras a flehes, na victory warbyn agan gostly eskerens, ew promysys, mas an **wlascore** *a neff, dre an gweras a thu* 'for now neither possession of the world, nor worldly possession, nor long life, nor the advantage of children, nor victory against our spiritual enemies are promised, but the kingdom of heaven by the assistance of God' TH 28

ha nena ny a dryg in du ha gans du, ha du a dryg innan ny ha genan ny ha in **walascore** *heb deweth in neff* 'and then we shall dwell in God and with God, and God will dwell in us and with us and in the kingdom of heaven without end' TH 30

Hen ew the leverall, an corffe a crist misticall, an spowse a crist, an **wlascore** *a neff* 'That is to say, the mystical body of Christ, the spouse of Christ, the kingdom of heaven' TH 31

In kepar maner in aweyll yma agan savyour crist ow hevely y egglos the lyas tra, indan an hanow a regnum celorum, henew **gwlascore** *neff, kepar ha the viterne a rug gull ha provya mariag*

247

kingdom   GERYOW GWIR

rag y vab 'Similarly in the gospel our Saviour Christ likens his Church to many things unde the name of *regnum coelorum,* that is the kingdom of heaven, like a king who made and provided a marriage for his son' TH 31

theso ge me a vyn ry an alwetho a **wlascore** *neff* 'to you I shall give the keys of the kingdom of heaven' TH 44

Ith ew impossybyll the then rych entra in **gwlascur** *neff* 'it is impossible for a rich man to enter into the kingdom of heaven' TH 53

Marrak lym, orth both ow brys, uhal-worthyys of i'n bys, moy agys Du, me a grys, in e dron in **gwlaskor** *nef* 'A keen knight, to my hearts desire, highly revered am I in the world, more than God, I believe, sitting on his throne in the kingdom of heaven' BK 1648-51

Rys ew thotha e thoscor, awos e nerth ha'y **wlascor**, *mar myn bewa in dan nef* 'He must hand it over in spite of his power and his kingdom, if he wishes to live under heaven' BK 2257-59

An trubut pan ve tochys, e worthyb o tyn ha freth hag ef garaw, hag owth avowa forsoyth a'y **wlascor** *trubut na goyth, mars agys pen, ow arluth* 'When the tribute was mentioned, his answer was sharp and impetuous and he was harsh, and he claimed forsooth that no tribute was owed from his kingdom, except your head, my lord' BK 2262-67

Arta an Jowle an comeraz eu mann wor hugez meneth euhall ha disquethaz thotha oll an **gwellasketh** *an beaze, ha'n worriance nonge* 'Again the devil took him up upon a huge high mountain and showed him all the kingdoms of the world and their glory' Rowe

Thurt an termen notha Jesus reeg dalla a boroga, ha tha laale, Greew gwel, rág ma **gulasketh** *neue tha dorn* 'From the time when Jesus began his preaching and to say, Improve, for the kingdom of heaven is at hand' Rowe

en Ehual-dir an Alban hag en **G'laskor** *Uordhyn* 'in the Highlands of Scotland and in the Kingdom of Ireland' AB: 222

Ma breez dho **g'laskor** *yw* 'My mind to me a kingdom is' Lhuyd MSS

gwrênz doz thy **gulasker** 'thy kingdom come' ACB: E e 2 verso

gurra de **gulasketh** *d[o]az* 'thy kingdom come' ACB: E e 2 verso.

The ordinary word for 'kingdom' in the revived language should perhaps be **gwlascor**. 'The United Kingdom' is probably therefore best rendered **An Wlascor Unys**.

TO KNOW

Godhvos, the Cornish verb 'to know; to know how to, to be able' is for the most part a compound of **godh-** < Celtic *****weid-** 'knowing' and the verb **bos** 'to be'. The third person singular of the present is **gor**; cf. Welsh *gwyr* and Breton *goar*; this is probably an old deponent form < **widri*; cf. Irish *-fitir* 'knows'. Starting in the sixteenth century, the inherited present paradigm, **gòn**, **godhes**, **gor**, **godhyn**, **godhowgh**, **godhons**, is being replaced by an analogical tense on the basis of the third person singular **gor**. Of this new analogical formation, however, only **goraf**, **gorama** 'I know' and **goryn** 'we know' are attested, although a new second person singular imperative **gor** also seems to occur:

gas ve the remembra fatla **or ve** *in ta tha honora* 'let me remember how I may honour you well' SA 59

Na **ora vee** *drel an Kembreean gweel rag tho gwytha ge tavaz* 'I do not know what the Welsh can do to maintain their language' BF: 29-31

*N'***ora vi** *skrefa na muî* 'I can write no more' AB: 250b

rag nag enz buz nebbas, buz deu po try a **orama** *anetha* 'they are only a few, but two or three that I know of' BF: 25-7

leb ma leverres gena [vee an peth] a **orama** *dro tho an tavaz Curnooack* 'where I have said what I know about the Cornish language' BF: 29

ymowns ow tos omma thyn bys haw mos in kerth alemma arta ny **woryn** *pyscotter* 'they come here into the world and go away again hence, we do not know how soon' TH 6a

an letherau war an mean beath ez en eglez Burian, na **oren** *pendra tho weel anotha* 'the letters on the tombstone which is in Buryan church, we do not know what to make of them' BF: 27

po res dal an vor, na **oren** *pan a tu, Thuryan, houl Zethas, go Gleth, po Dihow* 'when it is necessary to keep to the road, we don't know which way, east, west, north or south' ACB: E e 4 *verso*

gyr *ter o an dhiz rag* [leg. *dhiz-urêg*] *riman a* [leg. *ha manah*] *'ryg an bad-ober* 'know that it was the ale-wife and a monk who committed the crime' BF: 18.

Since **goraf vy**, **gorama** and **goryn ny** were part of the traditional language from the sixteenth century onwards, there is every reason to allow them in the revived language as well.

L

LARGE, GREAT

Meur- is widely used A) as a prefixed adjective 'large great' and B) as a prefixed adverb 'greatly'. Here are some examples of both:

A **meur** *prefixed adjective* 'large, great'
*Ihesu crist **mur gerense** ʒe vab den a ʒysweʒas* 'Jesus Christ showed great love towards mankind' PA 5a
*nyng ew ragos se laʒe Cryst yv synsys **mur dremas*** 'it is not for you to kill Christ, who is considered a great saint' PA 123bc
*kyn wylly **mur wolowys** na thout ny fyth ken ys da* 'though you see great lights, do not fear; it will not be other than good' OM 717-18
*The'n tas dev yn **mur enor** war y alter my a wor grugyer tek hag awhesyth* 'To God the Father in great honour I shall put upon his altar a fair partridge and a lark' OM 1201-03
*ihesus whek a natharet lowyne thy'so hep let ha **mur onor** yn teffry* 'Dear Jesus of Nazareth, greetings to you without restraint and great honour indeed' PC 301-03
*a a arluth ker bynyges yma thy'm **mur varthegyon** pyv a yl henna bones* 'Oh, sweet blessed Lord, I am in great wonder who that can be' PC 769-71
*lemmyn cryst agan arluth **mur worthyans** thy's del theguth worth agan dry alemma* 'now, Christ our Lord, great worship to you, as is fitting, for bringing us hence' RD 149-51
*thu'm tybyans wheth ef ny grys bos ihesu cryst dasserghys dre y **mur ras*** 'in my opinion, he still does not believe that Jesus Christ has risen again by his great grace' RD 1213-15
***mur trueth** y kemerys latha prest kemys flehas awoys vn den* 'I felt great pity to kill indeed so many children for one man' BM 1781-83
*Lowena thys, corf heb par, ha **mer honour** drys peb i'n bys!* 'Greetings to you, person without peer, and great honour beyond all men in the world!' BK 72-4
*may moyghea y lavyer hy der weyll ow gorhemen troghe na heb **mear lavyer** defry benytha nys tevyth floghe* 'so that her labour may increase because she broke my command, nor without great travail indeed shall she ever have a child' CW 897-900
***meare worthyans** thyes arluth nef* 'great glory to you, Lord of heaven' CW 2478.

B **meur** *prefixed adverb* 'greatly, very'
*ow colon yv **mur huthys** nynsus peyn orth ow greffya* 'my heart is greatly cheered; there is no pain afflicting me' RD 483-84

GERYOW GWIR large

*thomas ty yv dyscrygyk pur wyr ha **mur anfusyk*** 'Thomas, you are unbelieving in truth and very unfortunate' RD 1519-20

*ass o **mur tyn** ow passyon pan eth dreyn yn empynnyon a pup parth dre a grogen* 'how very sharp was my passion when thorns went into the brains on all sides through the skull' RD 2555-57

*du as ota **mur presijs** dres ol breten heb awer* 'God, how greatly are you praised without doubt through all Brittany' BM 230-31

Mearthysaysys *of drys pub gyst* 'Greatly afflicted am I beyond all jest' BK 1227-28.

The adjective **meur** is used after its noun to mean 'great' C) in titles of persons and in place-names, e.g. **Duw meur** 'great God', **Breten Veur** 'Great Britain'. It occurs in the expression **tir meur** 'mainland'; **anken meur** 'great grief' and **cleves meur** 'serious disease' are also attested.

C **meur** 'great' *after its noun*

*han **anken mur** as grevye pan vyre worth y woly yn tenewen y3 ese dre an golon as tylly* 'and the great grief that afflicted her as she looked at his wound, it was in the side, was piercing her through the heart' PA 231cd

*yn enour bras d'agan **dev mur** an guel a ras thyworth an lur guraf the drehy* 'in great honour to our great God the rods of grace I shall cut from the ground' OM 1986-88

*maras ose map **dev mvr** dyeskyn a'n vynk the'n lur ha dyswe ran a'th veystry* 'if you are the son of great God, descend from the stand to the ground and show some of your power' PC 2867-69

*a'n dour y fue drehevys ha dreys arte the'n **tyr mur** hag yn gorhel bras gorrys gynen may teffo the'n lur* 'he was lifted from the water and brought to the mainland and set in a large ship that he might come down with us' RD 2327-30

*dymo y a covsis cler donfon warlergh seluester may rellen quik heb awer eff ath wolgh pur lan kyn moys may fo sav the **cleves mur*** 'to me they spoke clearly that I should quickly without grief send after Silvester: He will wash you very clean before going so that your serious disease may be healed' BM 1792-96

*Me a gest the'n ughelha arluth us a-ugh an loer, ystyn quaral na relha erbyn Myghtern **Bretyn Veor**, Arthor, gour mas* 'I declare to the highest Lord who is above the moon that he should not urge a dispute against the King of Great Britain, a goodly hero' BK 1421-25

*ha coyt gwrens pe ow thrubut a **Vretyn Veer*** 'and quickly let him pay my tribute from Great Britain' BK 1840-41.

Notice that in **Breten Veur** the adjective is necessary to distinguish the island of Britain from **Breten Vian** 'Brittany':

*nyns us in **breten vyen** ov parov pur guir heb dovt* 'there are not in Brittany my peers truly without doubt' BM 517-18.

Meur can be used D) predicatively to mean 'great, of importance':

D **meur** 'great' *as a predicative adjective*

mur *o an payn dar ken ʒe vab du mur y alloys* 'great was the pain beyond any other for the Son of God, great his power' PA 135cd

mur *yv ow fyenasow war y lergh ef* 'great is my longing for him' RD 1071-72

gaf thy'mmo vy ow trespys rak ***mur*** *yv ow govygyon* 'forgive me my trespass for my remorse is great' RD 1153-54

Me yv epscop in breten in conteth gelwys kernov ***mur*** *yv ov rays pup termen* 'I am bishop in Brittany in a county called Cornouaille, great is my grace always' BM 511-13

S. Johan baptist, a ve benegas in breis y vam ha gormelas kyns y bos genys, eff a ve gylwys ell gans ran gyllwis ***mer*** *therag an face a Du* 'St John the Baptist, who was blessed in his mother's womb and gave praise before he was born, he was called an angel by some called great before the face of God' TH 8

Me a vyn mos heb gortas, abarth Du in uheldér, the ge ow arluth cortys, neb ew ***mer*** *e ryelder ha'y gallus bras* 'I will go without hesitating in the name of the most high God, to the house of my noble lord, whose majesty is great and great his power' BK 1330-34

Mylwyth welcum ough gena'! As yw ***mer*** *ou lowena a thevythyans ou amors!* 'You are welcome a thousand times with me! How great is my joy at the coming of my friends' BK 1623-25.

Meur is also used in expressions like **meur y ras** 'gracious, of great grace':

E **meur y ras**, etc.

Gans an eʒewon war hast drok ʒewas a ve dyʒgtys tebell lycour ***mur y last*** *eysyll bestyll kemyskis* 'In haste an evil drink was prepared by the Jews, a liquor, great its distastefulness, vinegar and gall mixed' PA 202ab

my a pys dev ***mer y ras*** *danwon gras thy'nny omma* 'I beseech gracious God to send grace to us here' PC 117-18

ytho thy'nny yth heuel dre honna war ow laute the vos map dev ***mur y nel*** *luen a vercy ha pyte* 'therefore it seems to us by that upon my faith that you are the son of God, great his power, full of mercy and pity' PC 1489-92.

Meur is also used as a noun in the phrase F) **meur a** 'much, many':

F **meur a** 'much, many'

Mur a *dus ha benenas a ierusalem yn dre erbyn crist rag y welas y eth* 'Many men and women from Jerusalem in the town went to meet Christ to see him' PA 29ab

lowene ʒys te yw ʒeyn mygtern rys yw ʒe worʒye hen o 3oʒo ***mur a*** *bayn* 'greetings to you, you are king to us. It is necessary for us to revere you. That was great pain for him' PA 137cd

GERYOW GWIR large

Lemmyn ny a yl gwelas hag ervyre fest yn ta cryst ȝe woȝaff dre ȝensys **mur a** *benans yn bys ma* 'Now we can see and determine quite well that Christ through manhood suffered much penance in this world' PA 60ab

mvr a *foly ew thotho an keth frut ne mara'n gas* 'it is much folly for him if he leaves that same fruit' OM 191-92

ha war woles pan vyrys my a welas hy gurythyow bys yn yffarn dywenys yn mysk **mur a** *tewolgow* 'and when I looked down, I saw its roots penetrating into hell in the midst of much darkness' OM 781-84

ov arluth myghtern salmon yma **mur a** *varthogyon a'n keth gyst ma warvethys* 'my lord, King Solomon, many marvels have occurred concerning this same beam' OM 2545-47

penys a reys ragh y terros may fo leheys **mvr a** *y gallos* 'much penance is necessary against his distruction, that much of his power be lessened' PC 43-4

wolcom pilat by thys day ef re wruk **mur a** *theray* 'Welcome, Pilate, by this day; he has wrought much disorder' PC 379-80

Meriasek yv kerys anotha yma notyes **mur a** *ȝadder yn pov ma* 'Meriasek is loved; of him much goodness is noted in this country' BM 187-89

Tevdar dyugh me a leuer **an** *keth den na grueys yv* **muer** *purguir yn pov* 'Teudar, I tell you, much has been made of that man in the country indeed' BM 807-09

dretha may hillyn gwelas ha percevya fatell esa the crist **mer a** *garensa worthan* 'through which we can see and perceive that Christ had much love for us' TH 15a

Pan vo hy culdewethys, hy a ustun **mer a** *dyer* 'When it is fully complete, it will encompass much land' BK 1187-88

mear a *rase thewhy sera ow ry cusyll ȝym mar stowte* 'much thanks to you, sir, for giving me such sound advice' CW 702-03

mear a *ras thewhy eall due ow tysqwethas thym pub tra* 'much thanks to you, angel of God, for showing me everything' CW 1871-72

Perêg angye gwellaz an steran, thonge loan gen **meare a** *loander* 'When they saw the star, they were joyful with great joy' Rowe.

On occasion the preposition **a** in **meur a** is suppressed:

F1 **meur** *for* **meur a**

ota cowes pur ahas ny's pyrth den mara peys pel awronnd an dor stremys bras ov tewraga gans **mur** *nel* 'here is a dreadful shower. No man will abide it if it lasts long—around the earth (*or* from the depths of the earth) great streams pouring with much force' OM 1081-84

yma ov cul sacryfys ha'y pobel ef kekeffrys the'n keth dev na gans **mur** *tros* 'he is sacrificing and his people as well to that same God with much noise' OM 1556-58

aga fleyr a yl schyndye ha lathe **mur** *yethewon* 'their stench may harm and kill many Jews' PC 1547-48

lauar thy'mmo vy yn scon mars os myghtern yethewon cous gans **mur** *nel* 'tell me forthwith if you are king of the Jews. Speak out with great force' PC 1582-84

large   **GERYOW GWIR**

Wolcum oma meryasek me re glowes ov map wek ahanes covs **mur** *thadder* 'Welcome here, Meriasek. I have heard spoken of you, my dear son, much goodness' BM 526-28.

We thus find both G) **meur a joy** 'much joy' and G1) **meur joy** 'much joy':

G
yma thy'mmo cowyth da **mur a ioy** *sur yn tor-ma a'th tyryvas* 'I have great joy indeed, good friend, from your information' RD 1306-08.

G1
ha kemmys an gorthyo ef gans **mur** *ioy y tue the'n nef dre y thadder oberys* 'and all who worship him with great joy shall come to heaven, wrought by his goodness' RD 1219-24.

Indeed some examples of **meur a** + noun with the preposition **a** is suppressed, are indistinguishable from instances where **meur** is a prefixed adjective; see A) above.

Meur can also be used H) as a free-standing adverb meaning 'greatly'

H meur 'greatly'
the vanneth thy'm **mur** *a blek ha banneth ov mam inweth* 'your blessing will please me greatly and my mother's blessing also' OM 455-56
An tas dev re bo gorthyys synsys **mur** *on th'y gare* 'May God the Father be worshipped; we are greatly bound to love him' OM 1125-26
A vrry assos gentyl my a'd car **mur** *ru'm peryl rag the worthebow ev tek* 'O Uriah, how obliging you are. I love you greatly upon my peril, for your answers are kind' OM 2152-55
the tas kera thy lawe re'n danvonas the'th servye rak **mur** *thotho ty a plek* 'your most beloved Father—praised be he!—has sent us to serve you, for you please him greatly' PC 166-68
my re thysyryas fest **mer** *dybry genogh why haneth boys pask kyns ov bos marow* 'I have very greatly desired to eat the Passover meal with you tonight, before I die' PC 718-20
ny vennaf pel ymbreyse rag nyns yv a vaner vas the voy denuyth ny'm gorse kyn facyen **mur** *renothas* 'I will not praise myself for long, for the custom is not a good one. No man would revere me the more, though I should brag greatly, by my father' PC 1677-80
ha pryns heb par ew ef ha **mer** *the breysya drys suel a welys heb mar* 'and a peerless prince is he and greatly to be praised beyond anyone I have seen in truth' BK 2242-44
mer *tha vlamya yth osta* 'you are greatly to blame' CW 161.

GERYOW GWIR   **large**

Generally speaking, however, the ordinary word for 'large, great, big' is not **meur** but **brâs**. Brâs is used A) as a predicative adjective; B) as an attributive adjective; C) as an adverb meaning 'greatly' and D) as a noun, often in the plural, meaning 'large person, adult' and in the plural 'gentry':

A **brâs** *as attributive adjective* 'large, great'
Du sur dre virtu an tas 3ynny a 3yttyas gweras en mab dre y skyans **bras** *pan gemert kyg a werhas* 'God surely through the power of the Father for us prepared help, through his great wisdom, the Son, when he took flesh of a virgin' PA 3ab
ha me ad wra arluth **bras** *ow honore mar mynnyth* 'and I shall make you a great lord, if you will honour me' PA 16d
angus **bras** *ha peynys tyn ha gloys creff as kemeres* 'great anguish and bitter pains and mighty torment overtook her' PA 221d
noe dre the thadder **bras** *ty a bew ov grath nefre* 'Noah, because of your great goodness, you will always have my favour' OM 973-74
rag lyf **bras** *my a thoro a gutho ol an norveys* 'for I shall bring a great flood, which will cover all the earth' OM 981-82
a traytor **bras** *sur map gal the gafus gynen yv mal* 'O great traitor, sure son of a criminal, we are glad to get you' PC 1177-78
cothys of yn edrek **bras** 'I have sunk into great remorse' PC 1440
ha me ynweth a'n guelas ha ganso ef company **bras** 'and I also saw him and a great company with him' RD 555-56
y fue ow manegow plat spygys **bras** *dre ow dywle* 'my gauntlets of plate were great spikes through my hands' RD 2589-90
Yma eff in meneth **bras** *del glowevy sur myl pas theworth an grond awoles* 'He is, as I hear, on the great mountain indeed, a thousand paces from the ground below' BM 1956-58
Rag henna gwregh drehevall in ban agas colonow hag egerogh y a leis the receva abervath inna kerensa **bras** *the thu* 'Therefore raise up your hearts, and open them wide to receive into them great love for God' TH 16
I say Arthur is my nam, myghtern **bras** *ha galosak* 'I say, Arthur is my name, a great and powerful king' BK 1399-400
mars es den po [neb] beast **bras** *dowte ahanas thym yma* 'if you are a man or some great beast, I am afraid of you' CW 1594-95
An poble erra zetha en tolgo a wellaz gollow **broaze** 'The people who were sitting in darkness, have seen a great light' Rowe
Ha Deu gwras an pusgaz **broz** 'And God made the great fishes' BF: 52
dreffen en tacklow **broaz**, *ma an gy mennow hetha go honnen* 'for in great matters they often stretch themselves' ACB: E e 4 *verso*.

B **brâs** *as predicative adjective* 'large, great'
En scherewys a sorras rag bonas crist honoris ha bos y ober mar **vras** 'The scoundrels became angry that Christ was honoured and that his work was so great' PA 31ab
y beynys o cref ha **bras** 'his pains were strong and great' PA 56c

255

large GERYOW GWIR

I feynys o ***bras*** *ha creff yn ioy ʒeʒy trylys yw rag mygternes yw yn nef ʒe vos gorʒijs hy yv gyw* 'Her pains which were great and strong have been turned for her into joy, for she is queen in heaven; she is worthy to be revered' PA 226ab
pur wyr y gallos yv ***bras*** 'in very truth his power is great' OM 1155
yn amendys a'd pehosow orden bos gureys temple golow ***bras*** *ha ledan* 'to atone for your sins command that a bright temple be built, great and spacious' OM 2259-61
dev teka bren rag styllyow ha compos y denwennow ***bras*** *ha crom y ben goles* 'God, what a fine piece of timber for rafters, and straight its sides, great and curved its base' OM 2441-43
kyn fe the thyvvregh mar ***bras*** *my a's kylm re sattenas* 'though your arms be never so great, I'll bind them by Satan' PC 1189-90
an emperour ef sawse maga tek bythqueth del fue kyn fe y cleues mar ***bras*** 'it would heal the emperor as clean as ever he was, though his disease be never so great' RD 1658-60.

C ***brâs*** *as an adverb* 'greatly, very'
yn egyp whyrfys yv cas ov popel vy greuyys ***bras*** *gans pharow yv mylyges* 'in Egypt trouble has arisen: my people greatly aggrieved by Pharoah, who is accursed' OM 1416-17
the colon yw cales ***bras*** 'your heart is very hard' OM 1525
me a grys ny re peghas hytheu ***bras*** *worth y lathe* 'I believe that we have sinned greatly today in killing him' PC 2993-94
yn cref ***bras*** *me re peghes* 'very greatly have I sinned' RD 1569
desesijs ***bras*** *off defry kekefrys ha nos ha deth* 'I am greatly diseased indeed both night and day' BM 1771-72
Dadn an mean ma deskes ***broaz*** *dean* 'Under this stone lies a very learned man' BF: 48.

D ***brâs*** *as a substantive* 'great person, adult'; *in the plural* 'gentry'
lauaraf theugh a tus vas kekyfrys byan ha ***bras*** *lemmyn gureugh ol ov sywe* 'I say to you, good people, both small and great, now do you all follow me' OM 1672-74
lemyn ol byan ha ***bras*** *knoukyough ef del dyndylas may cosso y tynwennow* 'now everyone, small and great, beat him as he has deserved, so that his sides tingle' PC 2082-84
kefrys ***brosyen*** *ha kemyn parusugh the voys gena* 'likewise great persons and common, get ready to go with me' BM 3215-16
mar kyllons heb feladov thage bevnans bones dreys cavs thynny eff a vya in ihesu map marya the cresy byen ha ***brays*** 'if they can be without fail brought back to life, it would be a cause for us, small and great, to believe in Jesus, son of Mary' BM 4115-17
cresowh ow bosaf prince creif hag inweth thewhy cheften bean ha ***brase*** 'believe that I am a powerful prince and also chieftain to you, small and great' CW 116-18
den in mes bean ha ***brase*** *chattall ethyn ha bestas myns a ve in lester dres* 'let us disembark, small and great, cattle, birds and beasts, all who were brought into the ark' CW 2481-83.

Rarely **bian ha meur** is used for **bian ha brâs**:

> *Crist indelma a leuer ov sywa neb a vynna forsakyans* **byen ha muer** *teryov trefov an bys ma y days hay vam y nessevyn hay cothmans hag eff a gvayn roov cans* 'Christ thus says: Whoso wishes to follow me, let him forsake, be he great or small, lands, farms of this world, his father his mother, his family and his friends, and he will gain a hundred gifts' BM 382-88.

Overall, then, it would seem that in Cornish the ordinary word for 'great, big, large' is **brâs**, e.g. in **best brâs** 'great animal', **gorhel brâs** 'great ship', **puscàs brâs** 'great fishes' and **an brâssa meyn** 'the biggest stones'. The modern neologism **Bardh Meur** 'the Great Bard, the Grand Bard' would seem to be an unobjectionable example of **meur** in a personal title. The expression **An Gerlyver *Meur**, on the other hand, is perhaps more questionable. **An Gerlyver Brâs** might have been a better designation.

LATER

In English the word 'later' can either be an adjective or an adverb. It is an adjective in sentences like 'I'll take a later train' or 'the later programmes weren't as funny'. It is an adverb, for example, in 'I'll see you later' or 'When he returned later he was very drunk'. In Cornish the two senses need to be translated in different ways. The adjective 'later' is to be translated **dewetha**, which also, of course, can mean 'latest'. The adverb can be variously rendered, e.g. (**a**)**wosa hebma**, (**a**)**wosa hedna**.

Unfortunately there appear to be no examples of the form **dewetha** by itself with comparative sense. All the attested examples are superlative in meaning, i.e. they must all be translated 'last, latest' rather than 'later':

A **dewetha** 'later, latest, last' *(adjective)*
> *Tus vas, in* **dewetha** *sermon ha homelye i fe declarriis thewgh why pandra ew an egglos ha fatell ylly bos aswonys* 'Good people in the last sermon and homily it was declared to you what is the Church and how she can be recognized' TH 35a

> *hag ena eff a wethas y stall pemp blethan warnegans bys in* **dewetha** *blethan, honna o an xiiii- as a reign Nero* 'and there he kept his post twenty five years until the last year, that was the 14th year of the reign of Nero' TH 47

> *ha kepar dell rug eff nena promysya, indella wosa henna eff a rug y perfumya, evyn an* **dewetha** *nois a rug eff bos in company gans y aposteleth therag y virnans* 'and as he then promised, so thereafter he performed it, even the last night when he was in company with his apostles before his death' TH 51a-52

later   **GERYOW GWIR**

An tirmyn o an nois therag eff the suffra myrnans, the signifia thynny fatell o an bois na defferis bys in **dewetha** *deth a ve agan Sovyour conuersaunt gans y appostlis* 'The time was the night before he suffered death, to indicate to us that that food had been deferred until the latest day that our Saviour was in company with his apostles' TH 52

me agis pys panadra ew hemma? pan vo an **dewetha** *gyrryow clowis a onen a vo in y gwely marnance: ha paris the verwall* 'I beg you what is this? When the last words have been heard by someone on his deathbed, and he is ready to die' SA 59.

Notice incidentally that the first vowel in **dewetha** is usually **e**, whereas in the related etymon **dyweth** 'end', the vowel is usually **y**.

The only place in the texts where the comparative form **dewetha** is found is in the temporal adverb **bëtte dhewetha**:

Rag charite ew inweth the gara pub den oll tha ha bad, cothman hag yskar. ha penagull a cause an geffa den in contrary, whath **bette thewetha** *the thon blonogath da ha colonnek the pub den* 'For charity is also to love everyone good and bad, friend and foe; and whoever has cause to the contrary, still nonetheless to bear good and cordial will to everyone TH 21a

nyns ugy crist ow leverall inweth, fatell ra scribes ha pharises setha in chare moyses, **bette thewetha** *eff a vyn an bobill the folya aga lessons?* 'Does not Christ also say, that scribes and pharisees sit in the chair of Moses; nonetheless he wishes the people to follow their lessons?' TH 34.

In **bëtte dhewetha** the comparative adjective is preceeded by **dhe**, which renders it an adverb, i.e. 'never the later' > 'nonetheless'; cf. **bÿttele** 'nonetheless' and **bytegyns** 'nonetheless'.

The literal meaning of **wosa henna**, **wosa hemma** is 'thereafter, hereafter' but not infrequently it can also be translated 'later' as can be seen from the following examples:

B **wosa hemma**, **wosa henna** 'later' *(adverb)*

ty a wra **woge hemma** *gorre an tus alena bys yn tyreth a thynwa lanwes leyth ha mel kefrys* 'you will later take the people thence to the land flowing with milk and honey also' OM 1427-30

my a worhenmyn yn scon ha **wose henna** *evyn pep ol adro draght a wyn rag comfortye y golon* 'I will command shortly later, let each one of us all around drink a draught of wine to comfort his heart' OM 2625-28

a thomas ass osa fol hen yv agan crygyans oll ihesu cryst woge merwel y vones gorrys yn pry **woge henna** *dassergky the pen try dyth ha seuel* 'O Thomas, how foolish you are; that is the belief of us all, that Jesus Christ after dying that he was buried, that later he rose again at the end of three days and arose' RD 953-58

thy'n kyns ef a leuerys ol annotho del whyrys yn nor bys ma ra'gan prenna y fyrwy hag arte y tassergky **woge henna** 'beforehand he told of all that would happen to him in this world, that he would die to redeem us and again he would rise again later' RD 1189-94

omma lemen fondya plays dre voth ihesu a vercy sur me a vyn **awose helme** *eglos the worthya crist deth ha nos* 'here now by the will of Jesus of mercy surely I shall found a church later, a church to worship Christ day and night' BM 720-24

pandra ew an keth taclennow na, eff a vith **awosa hemma** *desquethis thewgh dre weras a thu* 'what those same things are, he will later demonstrate to you by the help of God' TH 16

Awosa henna *ny a redd fatell rug lyas onyn an disciplis a crist scryffa aweylys* 'Later we read that many of the disciples of Christ wrote gospels' TH 37a

Bohogogneth abreth du remoconn then cur yth yv **wose helma** 'Poverty in God's name is later elevation to the court of heaven' BM 2010-12

Sul voy ancov a rellogh the larchya preysys fethogh kemendis **wose helma** 'The more deaths you cause, the more generously will you be commended later' BM 2351-53.

It is clear, therefore, that we should translate our two examples as follows:

Me a vydn agas gwelas wosa hebma 'I'll see you later'
Pàn wrug ev dewheles wosa hedna, ev o pòr vedhow 'When he returned later he was very drunk'.

LAY WASTE *see* WASTE

TO LEND

There are no attested words for 'to lend' in Cornish, although several have been suggested: A) **cola**; B) ***lêna**; C) ***lendya** and D) ***prestya**. Let us look at these in turn.

Cola means 'to listen to' and is followed by the preposition **worth**, **orth**. Here are a very few examples:

A **cola**

A out warnes drok venen worto pan wrussys **cole** *rag ef o tebel ethen neb a glewsys ov cane* 'Oh, fie upon you, evil woman, that you listened to him, for he was a wicked bird that you heard singing' OM 221-23

Ellas vyth pan ruk **cole** *mar hogul worth ov eskar kemys druk vs ov cothe ha dewethes hag avar yma ken thy'm the ole* 'Alas that I listened so credulously to my enemy. So much evil is happening both early and late; I have cause to weep' OM 629-30

Coyl *ortheff vy meryasek me ath desyr dre tekter bonyl ty a feth edrek* 'Listen to me, Meriasek, I request you nicely, or you will regret it' BM 407-09

lend

Ov breder duen ny the dre ny vyn an den ma **cole** *dotho orth neb a vyn da* 'My brothers, let's go home; this man will not listen to someone who wishes good for him' BM 2848-50

Taw Taw eva yth os foole ny vynnys **kola** *orthe da me a ragtha ty an owle ow husyll mar gwreth naha* 'Silence, silence, Eve. You are a fool. You will not listen to what is good. I garantee you will regret it, if you reject my advice' CW 664-67.

In all the above instances **cola worth** means 'to listen to, to harken to'. The meaning 'to lend' was surmised by Nance from a survival of traditional Cornish recorded from Mount's Bay in 1875: *Paj·i kulaa· tuvee· unpolee·un du moi·jonaa·y* which was said to mean 'Tom Becaleck, lend me your stick to go to Penzance' (*Handbook*: 249). Nance seems to have thought that *kulaa· tuvee·* was from Cornish **col do vy*. This, is surely impossible. First because *cola* means 'listen', not 'lend'. Second because *cola* is followed by *worth* not *dhe*; and third because the interpretation leaves unexplained the stressed long syllable in *kulaa·*. We are, I think, compelled to admit that this surving sentence is still largely unexplained. Since it is the only evidence we have for **cola** with the sense 'to lend', we must, I fear, abandon such a correspondence. There is no evidence that **cola** could mean 'to lend' in Cornish.

*Lêna 'to lend' would be a borrowing from Middle English *læne, lene*. As such it is unobjectionable. The Modern English form is *lend* with an inorganic *d*. Such a verb would almost certainly have been borrowed as ***lendya** in later Middle Cornish and is also acceptable. ***Prestya** would be a borrowing from Middle French *prester*, Modern French *prêter*. Since, however, the Breton word is *prestañ* < Middle French *prester*, one might expect the equivalent Cornish word to be ***presta** rather than ***prestya**. ***Prestya** might also be thought of as a derivative of the Middle English noun *prest* 'loan'.

All in all, it seems that the best words for 'to lend' in revived Cornish are either ***lêna** or ***lendya**. There is no warrant for **cola** 'to lend'.

LEPER, LEPROSY

For 'leper' Nance suggests A) **clâv dyberthys** (UC *claf dyberthys*); B) **clâv** (UC *claf*); C) **clavorek**; D) ***lover**; and E) **leper**. Let us look at these five terms in turn.

A **clâv deberthys**

claff deberthys *eff yv sur ny welys in beys namur den vyth del ywa dyghtijs* 'he is a separated leper indeed; I never saw in the world many a man treated as he is' BM 1413-15

*Rag kerense arluth neff gueres dyn orth agen gref **clevyon deberthys** ny yv* 'For the love of the Lord of heaven, assist our misery; we are separated lepers' BM 3128-30.

In both cases we know that the sick men are lepers because they are **dyberthys** 'separated', that is to say they live apart from society as was medieval custom (and indeed as was enjoined in the Mosaic law). It must be admitted, however, that by itself **clâv dyberthys** does not mean 'leper', but 'separated sick man', and the status as a leper is therefore only implicit.

The word **clâv** *m.*, means 'sick person' only, as can be seen from the following attestations of the plural **clevyon**:

B clâv, clevyon

*arluth whek ny amount man an pyt a wrussyugh certan lemyn moy dysenour thys rag ov keusel yth eder aban eth e the'n teller bos **clevyon** dretho sawayys* 'lord what you did is of no avail indeed, but is more dishonour for you, since people are declaring that since it went there sick people are being healed thereby' OM 2791-96

***Clevyon** pendra govsugh why us nygis dyugh ortheff vy lefrugh in hanov du* 'Sick men, what do you say? Have you business with me? Tell it in God's name' BM 3125-27

*I tendeles y cara lues den guan in bys ma pur guir eff a confortyas dal ha bother evrethyon palgy ha dyvers **clevyon** ny wothen covs mar lues* 'He deserved to be loved; many weak men in this world very truly he comforted: blind and deaf, cripples, palsied and various sick men; we cannot say how many' BM 4479-84.

In all three instances the word **clevyon** means 'sick people, patients' in general. It does not mean 'lepers'.

The word **clavorek** is attested four times:

leprosus, **clafhorec** 'leprous; leprous person' OCV §386

Gweth oge ys contreuuer pylf, **clovorak** 'You are worse than a worthless leprous counterfeiter' BK 178-79

Jovyn, pen cog, du bothorag, gwyth ve orth drog! Te, **glovorag**, *re 'foga caugh!* 'Jovyn, blockhead, a god hard of hearing, preserve me from ill! You leprous one, may you have shit!' BK 1247-50

A Du, danvon anfugy war an raf **glovorak** *na* 'O God, send misfortune upon that leprous fellow' BK 2301-02.

In each case **clavorek** can be understood as an adjective rather than a substantive. In the three last attestations above **clavorek** is used as an epithet of abuse rather than as an accurate description.

The commonest term for 'leper' is **leper** *m.*, *plural* **lepers**:

leper   GERYOW GWIR

D **leper**

*yma ortheff lovrygyan cothys ha ny won fetla ellas ellas yth oma gyllys **leper** del leuer pup ol hager ny gar den gueles ov fas* 'leprosy has fallen upon me and I don't know how. Alas, alas, I have become a leper, hideous as everyone says; no man wants to look at my face' BM 1356-61

*An power han auctorite na kepar dell ve va fuguris in la goyth thyn ordyr a prontereth, the judgia **lypers** ha the punyssya oll an re na na vynna obeya an prontirion* 'That power and authority, just as it was figured in the old law to the order of priests, to judge lepers and to punish all those who would not obey the priests' TH 38a

*Rag kerensa Marya ha'y Mab a'th pernas i'n pren, saw ve a'n drog us o'm kyk ha neffra me a'th vynyk. **Leper** of a'n troys the'n pen* 'For the sake of Mary and of her Son who redeemed you on the cross, heal me of the evil in my flesh and ever will I bless you. I am a leper from my foot to my head' BK 788-92

***Leper** a ros the Ke an fentan Chy Soor ha peder eraw dyer* 'A leper gave St Kea the spring of Chy Soor and four acres of land' BK 822 [stage direction].

Leper can also mean 'leprosy'

*Kepar del e'th purnas ker, Jesu re bo the vethak a'n **leper** cref anhethek* 'Just as he redeemed you dearly, may Jesu be your healer of the powerful chronic leprosy' BK 804-06.

The other attested term is the collective plural **lovryjyon**:

*yma ortheff **lovrygyan** cothys ha ny won fetla ellas ellas yth oma gyllys leper del leuer pup ol hager ny gar den gueles ov fas* 'leprosy has fallen upon me and I don't know how. Alas, alas, I have become a leper, hideous as everyone says; no man wants to look at my face' BM 1356-61.

For 'leper' in the revived language **leper**, **lepers** should perhaps be the default term. The adjective **clavorek** can also be used for 'leprous'. For 'leprosy' one can use either **lovryjyon** or **leper**.

LIKE, AS

The word **kepar** is an adjective meaning 'like, similar, equal'. A common way of saying 'like' as a preposition is to use **kepar ha(g)**. There are many examples:

A **kepar ha(g)**

*a'y frut a wrello dybry y fethe **kepar ha** dev* 'whoever would eat of its fruit would be like God' OM 230-31

*lemyn flerye ha peddry **kepar ha** seym py lyys haal* 'but stink and rot like fish oil or estuary mud' OM 2707-08

GERYOW GWIR   **like**

may hallons boys dewogys **kepar ha** *porhel bo lugh* 'that they may be bled like a pig or a calf' BM 1556-57

me a vyn the thalhenna hath ledya **kepar hag** *on der gallus du indelma* 'I will grab you and lead you like a lamb thus by the power of God' BM 4103-05

ha fatell ew oll an glory an broghter han lowender a vabden **kepar ha** *flowres in prasow* 'and that all the glory and splendour and joy of man is like the flowers in the meadows' TH 7.

Similarly **kepar dell** can be used as a conjunction meaning 'just as, as':

B kepar dell

arluth mar ny yl bos ken beȝens **kepar del** *vynny* 'Lord, if it cannot be otherwise, let it be as you wish' PA 57d

arloth dev an nef an tas **kepar del** *os luen a ras venytha gorthyys re by* 'Lord God, of heaven the Father, as you are full of grace may you ever be worshipped' OM 105-07

dev ha den **kepar del** *of sur an tas yma ynnof hagh ynweyth my ynno ef* 'as I am indeed God and man, indeed the Father is in me and I also in him' RD 2385-87

thygh oma y tuth heb bern **kepar del** *yv ov dute* 'I came here to you willingly as is my duty' BM 3197-98

kepar dell *ew scriffys in xviii chapter in genesis* 'as is written in the 18th chapter of Genesis' TH 6a.

Later, however, **kepar** has a tendency to metathesize to **pecar**:

C pecar

ha **pecar** *a ruk an nethewan e sensy, ha e recevia ef lymmyn, gans mustethas ganaw* 'and just as the Jews arrested him and receive him now with unclean mouth' SA 61

pekare *yth ew an sortow gorrys vnna der devyes in diffrans ha kehavall* 'similarly are the kinds put into them after a plan, as different and alike' CW 2199-201

Nenna chei a varginiaz rag vlethan moy, rag **pokaar** *gubber* 'Then they bargained for another year for the same wages' BF: 15

Mar pethum' Francan-belgan me ra bose **pocar** *dr'u Sousen-Curnow vith anar vrause* 'If I shall have it, Franco-Belgian I will be, as is Anglo-Cornish, it will be a great honour' BF: 31

ha gaue do ny gen pehazo **pecare** *ter era ny gava an pehadurrian war a gen pedne* 'and forgive us our sins as we forgive the sinners against us' BF: 41

Dellah Deew a traueth a wraaz deane **pocar** *a e honnen* **pocar** *a deew a traveth ew an gwraz bennaw ha gorrow a tra veth e ez gwraze* 'Thus God from nothing made man like himself; like unto God from nothing he made them, female and male' JKeigwin

n'ena agoz lagagow ra bos geres; ha why ra boaze **pocar** *a Deew a cothaz da ha droag* 'then your eyes will be opened and you will be like God knowing good and evil' Rowe

An dean yw devethez **pocar** *a ha onen anye, da othaz dha ha drôg* 'The man has become like one of us, to know good and evil' Rowe

Rag **pocar** *ez en pedd'n ha peege gungans me a vedd'n* 'For it is similar in the end and I shall pray for them' LAM: 224.

Since **pecar** is found in both SA and CW, it was clearly well established in the later Middle Cornish period. There is thus no need for users of Middle Cornish to proscribe it.

LION

For 'lion' Nance recommends ***lew** *m.*, *plural* ***lewas** and **lion** (UC *lyon*), *plural* **lions** (UC *lyons*). ***Lew** is not attested, being a respelling of Old Cornish: *leo*, ***leu*** 'lion' OCV §560. **Lion** on the other hand appears to be the only word in Middle Cornish:

*folle yn ta y whela ys del wra **lyon** y pray drey den yn peyn a calla* 'much more wildly than a lion his pray does he seek bring man to torment were he able' PA 21cd
*yma agys yskar an teball ell kepar ha **lyon** ow huga ow mos adro ow whelas rag agys devowrya* 'your enemy the devil like a lion roars prowling around trying to devour you' TH 3a-4
*Whath **luon** goyth in y ugo thys a ynclyn* 'Even the wild lion in his cave bows down to you' BK 1778-80.

Lion should perhaps be the ordinary word for 'lion' in the revived language.

TO LIVE, TO DWELL

In the revived language it is common to hear or to read sentences like **Me a drig in Bosvena** 'I live in Bodmin.' Such utterances are mistaken. **Me a drig in Bosvena** can only mean 'I shall remain/live in Bodmin'. This can be clearly seen from the following examples from the texts:

A **a drig**

*abel ty **a dryg** nefre awos ol the wyrthege yn tewolgow bras hep ioy* 'Abel, you will dwell for ever in spite of all your true tithe in great darkness without joy' OM 556-58
*rof thy's ov thour hel ha chammbour bethaf the wour warbarth ny **a dryg** nefre* 'I will give you my tower, hall and chamber. I shall be your husband. Together we shall live for ever' OM 2110-13
*gans an eleth yw golow yn nef agas enefow neffre **a tryg** hep ponow yn ioy na vyth dywythys* 'with the angels in light in heaven your souls will dwell for ever without pain in joy that will not end' PC 6-9

GERYOW GWIR live

*ha nena ny **a dryg** in du ha gans du, ha du **a dryg** innan ny ha genan ny ha in walascore heb deweth in neff gans crist ny a vith agan trigva rag neffra* 'and then we will dwell in God and with God, and God will dwell in us and with us and in in the kingdom without end in heaven we shall have our dwelling with Christ for ever' TH 30

*Rag heb dowt nyns es thyn trygva in crist, mas ny **a dryg** in vnyta ay Catholik egglos* 'For without doubt we have no dwelling place in Christ, if we will not dwell in in the unity of his catholic Church' TH 39a

*Penag oll a vo deberthys theworth an Catholicall egglos, kyn rella eff supposya y honyn the vewa neffra mar ware na mar worthy, whath an egglos a crist vnite an egglos a crist nyn sevith eff bewnas, mas an sorre a crist **a dryg** vghta* 'Whoever be separated from the catholic Church, though he suppose himself to never never so carefully nor worthily, yet of the Church of Christ, the unity of the Church of Christ he does not have life, but the wrath of Christ will remain over him' TH 40

*Howen, omma te **a dryg** rag dyfenn an pow orth bryg* 'Howel, here you will remain to defend the country from brigandage' BK 3205-06

*ef **a dryg** bys venytha yma ef barth awollas in pytt downe ow leskye* 'he will dwell for ever here below burning in a deep pit' CW 2032-34

*rag henna bys venary eve **a dryg** ena deffry in paynes bras avel ky* 'therefore he will remain for every in great torments like a dog' CW 2052-54.

If one wishes in Cornish to say 'I live in Bodmin' one must use the relevant part of **bos** 'to be' together with **trigys**, **tregys**, the verbal adjective of **triga**, **trega** 'to dwell': **yth oma trigys in Bosvena**. This syntax is amply corroborated in the texts:

B bos trigys

*War lyrgh mab den ʒe begha reson prag y fe prynnys yw ihesus crist ʒe ordna yn neff **y vonas tregys*** 'After mankind sinned, the reason he was redeemed is that Jesus Christ ordained that he should dwell in heaven' PA 7ab

*mar nyth wolhaff dre ow gras yn nef **ny veʒyth tregis*** 'if I do not wash you by my grace, in heaven you shall not dwell' PA 46c

*Vn venyn hardh a ynnyas war pedyr **y vos tregis** gans ihesus* 'A woman insistently urged against Peter that he dwelt with Jesus' PA 84ab

*ef a doys aʒesempys maga town ty del woʒye gans crist **na vye tregis** na bythqueth ef nan quelse* 'he swore immediately as deep an oath as he could that he had not dwelt with Christ nor had ever seen him' PA 85cd

*rys yw porris ʒe onon merwel rag pobyl an wlas pobyl ihesus y honon **na vons tregis** gans satnas* 'it is very necessary for one to die for the people of the country so that Jesus's own people should not dwell with Satan' PA 89cd

*yn nef **y feʒaff tregis** an barth dyghow gans am car yn sur thu ow tevones wy am gwylwyth heb neb mar* 'in heaven I shall dwell on the right with my parent; you shall see me coming without any doubt as true God' PA 93cd

*awotta an le mayʒ ese vmma **nyng ew ef tregis*** 'behold the place where he was; he does not dwell here' PA 255d

265

live   **GERYOW GWIR**

reys yv thy's mones ytho bys yn egip the pharo ha lauar my th'y warnye byth na wrella compressa ow tus **vs trygys** *ena rag dout mysshyf the gothe* 'you must go therefore to Egypt to Pharo and tell him that I warn him not ever to oppress my people who live there, lest mischief befall' OM 1421-26

A ty then myghtern pharo dev a'm danfonas thy'so the wofyn prak yv genes punscie y tus mar calas **vs trygys** *agy the'th wlas* 'You man, king Pharo, God has sent me to ask why you are intent on punishing his people so harshly who live within your kingdom' OM 1479-83

lauar thy'mmo kyns mones py tyller yma moyses ha py cost **yma trygys** 'tell me before you go where is Moses and in what region is he living' OM 1550-52

dun alemma the'n mor ruyth tus venenes ha flehys the'n tyreth a thythwadow yw reys gans dev caradow thyn ena rag **bos trygys** 'let us go hence to the Red Sea, men, women and children, to promised land, which dear God has given us to live there' OM 1622-26

guyn y vys **a vo trigys** *yn the seruys ragh tristys nyn dygemmer vynytha* 'happy is he who dwells in your service, for sorrow will never overcome him' PC 122-24

mar ny'th wolhaf dre ow ras yn nef **ny vythyth trygys** 'if I do not wash you by my grace, in heaven you shall not dwell' PC 857-58

en den ma war ow ene gans ihesu a nazare yn certan **a fue trygys** 'this man upon my soul certainly dwelt with Jesus of Nazareth' PC 1277-79

pan fy a'n bys tremenys gans cryst **y fythyth trygys** *agy th'y clos* 'when you depart from the world you shall live with Christ within his close' PC 3232-34

nep na crys ny fyth sylwys na gans dev **ny vyth trygys** 'who does not believe will not be saved nor will he dwell with God' RD 1109-10

yma tregys *in cambron den ov cul merclys dyson guel yv dyn moys dy us[kys]* 'there lives in Camborne a man doing miracles indeed; it is better for us to go there without delay' BM 687-89

py **ma tregys** *thym leferys bethyns dyson* 'where does he live? Let me be told immediately' BM 816-18

The ihesu re bo grasseys omma **yth ese tregys** *avel hermyt in guelfos* 'Thanks be to Jesus, here do I live like a hermit in the wilderness' BM 1962-64

tregys off *lemen heb wov berth in castel an dynas sur in peddre* 'I live now in truth in Castle an Dinas in Pidar indeed' BM 2209-11

Tregys vue *in lestevdar honna yma in menek* 'He lived in Lesteader; that is in Meneage' BM 2284-85

Ihesu eff re thendelas in gluas neff **bones treges** *ʒiso y fue servont lel* 'Jesus, he has earned to dwell in the kingdom of heaven; he was a faithful servant to you' BM 4337-39

mar ten ny indelma submyttya agan honyn in sight a thu ny a yll bos sure fatell ra eff in tyrmyn ay vicitacyon agan humbrag ny in ban then wlas **vgy** *y vab Jhesus crist inhy* **tregys**, *neb ew agan arluth ny* 'if we thus submit ourselves in the sight of God, we can be sure that he will in the time of his visitation lead us up to the kingdom in which his son, Jesus Christ dwell, who is our Lord' TH 11a

ha neb **a ve** *an prince an heynes, hen ew, prince an Jewys,* **tregys** 'and where the prince of the heathens, that is, the prince of the Jews, was living' TH 47a

266

The negys them menag a, py te a 'fyth edrega, **kyn fes tregys** *gans an Jowl!* 'Your business, tell me what it is, or you will regret it, though you dwell with the Devil!' BK 43-45

Yma tregys *in Kembra in Urbe Legionum* 'He lives in Wales in the City of the Legions' BK 1292-93

ena ty ***a vyth tregys*** *ha myns assentyas genas genas sche an naw order* 'there you shall live and all who agreed with you, with you of the nine orders' CW 246-48

En termen ez passiez ***thera trigaz*** *en St. Levan dean ha bennen en tellar creiez chei an Horr* 'Once upon a time there lived in St Levan a man and a woman in a place called the House of the Ram' BF: 15.

It is clear that the correct way to translate 'I live in London' in Cornish is **trigys oma/yth esof trigys in Loundres**. Notice that either the long or the short form of **bos** may be used with **trigys**. **Me a drig in Loundres** is perfectly correct, but it means 'I shall live in London' or 'I shall remain in London'.

M

MAN, MEN, PEOPLE

The ordinary word in Cornish for 'man', i.e. an adult human male, is **den**:

A **den** 'man'

*Mur a dus a leuerys ny dayl zys cam y naghe dre ze gows y3 ew prevys ze vos **den** a galyle* 'Many said, You should not at all deny it; by your speech it is proved that you are a man from Galilee' PA 85ab

den *glan yw a begh heb fall ynno eff dyfout nyng es* 'he is a man pure of sin without fail; there is not fault in him' PA 192c

*ny a'd wra ty **then** a bry haval d'agan face whare* 'I will make you, man, of clay, like unto our face indeed' OM 59-60

*A ty **then** myghtern pharo dev a'm danfonas thy'so* 'O you man, king Pharaoh, God has sent me to you' OM 1479-80

*pan veugh agey the'n cyte why a thyerbyn wharre **den** ow ton pycher dour glan* 'when you are within the city, you will meet a man straightway carrying a pitcher of pure water' PC 627-29

*dun war y lergh me a'th pys reys yv bos guyr lauarow agan arluth hep parow neb yv dev ha **den** keffrys* 'let us go after him, I beg you; the words of our peerless Lord must be true, who is God and man also' PC 663-66

*Heb na herre lafarov ny a vyn heb feladov moys then teller may me ve hag alena sur y dry **den** beneges ha worthy yv in meske age hense* 'Without further ado, we without fail with go to the place where he is, and bring him thence; he is a holy and worthy man among their kind' BM 2920-25

*The **den** yonk yth yv dufer bones in mesk arlythy* 'It is the duty of a young man to be among lords' BM 3171-72

*out dethy bethen marov gans flam tan mes ay ganov nys gorte myl **den** ervys* 'Curse upon her, we shall be killed by a flame of fire from her mouth; a thousand armed men cannot withstand her' BM 3945-47

*mar te **den** ha receva royow bras theworth y gothman po y soveran, mar te in by an by ha tyrry blonogath y soveran hay displesya, an fowt han disobediens dretho ew gwrys the vrassa* 'if a man receives great gifts from his friend of his sovereign, if soon thereafter he transgresses his sovereign's will and displeases him, the fault and the disobedience committed by him is the greater' TH 4a

*mar peth in **den** bo benyn corruptys gans pehosow yth ew re wan rag y purgya theworth pegh* 'if the man or woman is corrupted by sin, it is too weak to purge him of sin' TH 14

GERYOW GWIR   man

*Indelma an lell charite crist an discas may teffa pub **den** ha benyn cara du drys pub tra, ha cara peb y gyla, kyffris cothman hag yskar* 'Thus the true charity of Christ has taught us that each man and woman ought to love God beyond all things and everyone should love one another, both friend and foe' TH 22a

*me a wor inta, why the bredery tha vos maga benegas agis an **dean** gwyrryan Elias* 'I well know that you consider yourselves as blessed as the righteous man, Elijah' SA 60

*determys ove ʒa vn dra ha concludys magata tha wythyll vn **dean** omma a thore ha sleme ʒom servia* 'I am determined of one thing and have decided also to make a man here of clay and slime to serve me' CW 236-39

*En termen ez passiez thera trigaz en St. Levan **dean** ha bennen en tellar creiez chei an Horr* 'Once upon a time there lived in St Levan a man and a woman in a place called the House of the Ram' BF: 15

*Komeer weeth na raw'y ostia en chei lebma vo **dean** koath demithez da bennen younk* 'Take care not to lodge in a house where an old man is married to a young woman' BF: 16

*Demytho Jowan an **dean** tha Agnez an bennen* 'Marry John the man to Agnes the woman' ACB: F f 2 *verso*

*Me vee de more gen sara vee a pemp **dean** moy en cock* 'I went to sea with my father and five other men in the boat' LAM: 244.

The suppletive plural **tus** means 'men, adult males':

B **tus** 'men'

*An princis esa yn pow gans Iudas a thanvonas **tus** ven gweskis yn arvow kepar ha del ens ʒen gas* 'The princes who were in the land with Judas sent stout men dressed in armour as though they were going to battle' PA 64ab

***Tus** crist ʒe ves a fyas pep ay du pur voreʒek saw pedyr crist a holyas abell avel vn ownek* 'Christ's men fled each on his side very sadly, but Peter followed Christ afar like a coward' PA 77ab

*Ihesus a ve danvenys haʒeworth an prins annas gans **tus** ven aʒesempys bys an ebscop cayphas* 'Jesus was sent from prince Annas with stout men immediately to the bishop Caiaphas' PA 88ab

*ha ʒy notye drys an wlas sur a-ogas hag abell may teffe **tus** gans nerth bras er [y] byn rag gustle bell* 'and to make it known throughout the land far and wide so that men might come to wage war against him' PA 249cd

*Rag henna pylat a ros ʒen vorogyon aga ro may lavarsans ha dolos yn pub tyller dris an vro ʒe vos **tus** yrvys yn nos* 'Therefore Pilate gave to the soldiers their reward that they might say and claim everywhere throughout the country that armed men came by night' PA 250a-c

*moyses me a commond thy's ha the aron kekyfrys mayth ylleugh yn mes a'm glas **tus** benenes ha fleghys* 'Moses, I command you and Aaron also that you should depart from my kingdom, men, women and children' OM 1585-88

man   **GERYOW GWIR**

***tus** benenes ha fleghys ymons omma dyvythys ha'ga pyth degys ganse* 'men, women and children, they have come here and brought their belongings with them' OM 1611-13

*dun alemma the'n mor ruyth **tus** benenes ha flehys the'n tyreth a thythwadow yw reys gans dev caradow* 'let us go hence to the Red Sea, men, women and children, to the promised land which has been given us by dear God' OM 1622-25

*ov messyger kyrgh ov courser the varogeth ol **tus** ov chy deugh genef vy bryntyn ha keth* 'my messenger, fetch my courser to ride; all men of my house come with me, noble and common' OM 1959-62

*orden the'th **tus** hy knoukye gans meyn na hethens nefre erna varwa eredy* 'order your men to strike her with stones; let them not cease ever till she die indeed' OM 2675-77

*danvon **tus** th'y aspye mara'n kefons yn nep chy ha'n kelmyns treys ha dule ha'n hembrynkys bys thy'nny* 'send men to spy him, if they can find him in any house and let them bind him feet and hands and bring him to us' PC 581-83

*pur evn pan vo ow soppye me a thue th'agas guarnye ha gueytyeugh bos **tus** parys gans battys ha clythythow* 'exactly when he is having supper, I shall come to warn you, and be sure that men are ready with sticks and swords' PC 605-08

*ha nep as tefo gallos a vyth gans yowynk ha los henwys **tus** vras pup termyn* 'and whoever have power will be called great men by young and old always' PC 788-90

*lauar lemyn mars yv prys danuon genes **tus** ervys the gerghes an vyl losel* 'say now whether it is time to send armed men with you to fetch the vile scoundrel' PC 938-40

*mestrygy wolcom y'm tour iouyn roy theugh mur onour warbarth ol kyn gys merwel na wreugh vn tuch vyth letye athesempys fystyne kepar del ough **tus** vhel* 'masters, welcome in my tower. May Jovyn give you great honour together before you die; do not hesitate a moment; hurry immediately as you are noble men' PC 1711-16

***tus** vas owhy ha **tus** fuer, ha'm confessors* 'good men are you and wise men, and my confessors' BK 1621-22

*Wylcum, **tus** vas, owhy thymmo. Du danvon ras warnough adro, in ketap ol* 'Welcome, good men, are you to me. May God send his grace upon you all around' BK 1806-10

*Lowena thu'm arluth freth, gallosak drys **tus** an bys!* 'Welcome to my vigorous lord, powerful beyond men of this world!' BK 2554-55

*Der agis gweras gwren ef maraw gans **tus** ha boyis ywys, ru'm Arluth Du heb parow!* 'With your help let us kill him with men and boys indeed, by my peerless Lord God!' BK 3250-53

*enna ev a vettiaz gen trei vertshans a Trerin, **teez** pleaw, toaz dre mez an fear Ka'r Esk* 'there he met three merchants from Trerine, men of the parish, coming home from fair of Exeter' BF: 16

*Nena Herod perêg e gwellaz fatal o geaze gwreaze anotha gen an **teze** feere, yw engrez; ha thavanaz mehaz, ha lathaz oll an flehaz a era en Bethalem, ha oll an dro, en dadn deaw vloth coth, a tho an termen a reeg e gofen thur an **teez** feere* 'Then Herod, when he perceived he had been deceived by the wise men, was angry and sent out and killed all the children who were in Bethlehem, and all around, beneath two years old, from the time he enquired of the wise men' Rowe

*Eye vedn gwerraz dege **teez** Dendle peath a'n beaze* 'They will help their men earn their living' ACB: F f 3.

More rarely **tus** is used to mean 'people' of unspecified gender:

C) **tus** 'people'

*reys yv thy's mones ytho bys yn egip the pharo ha lauar my thy warnye vyth na wrella compressa ow **tus** vs trygys ena rag dout mysshyf the gothe* 'you must go therefore to Egypt to Pharaoh and tell him that I am warning him not to oppress my people living there, lest mischief occur' OM 1421-26

*ty a wra woge hemma gorre an **tus** alena bys yn tyreth a thynwa lanwes leyth ha mel kefrys* 'you shall hereafter bring the people thence into the land which flows with fullness of milk and honey' OM 1427-30

*guask gynsy dywyth an men hag y res gover fenten marth erhyth thotho hep fal may hallo **tus** ha bestes ha myns a vynno eve* 'strike the rock twice with it and a stream of a spring will run forth, if you command it, so that people and animals and whoever wishes may drink' OM 1844-48

*ef a allas dyougel del glowys y leuerel yn lyes le savye bewnens **tus** erel* 'he was able, as I heard said in many places, to save the lives of other people' PC 2873-76

*a **tus** vas why re welas a thasserghyens cryst del fue porthow yfarn a torras* 'O good people, you have seen how it was with the resurrection of Christ, the gates of hell broke' RD 2631-34

*So my a vyn agys desyrrya why, **tus** tha oll, the settia agys corfow hagys enevow hooll the thu galosek* 'But I will desire you, all good people, to set your bodies and souls entirely on Almighty God' TH 35

*Lymmyn omma, **tus** vas, kyn nag esogh why ow consyddra an plag a behosow athewethas in kith scisme a ve in agan mysk ny* 'Now here, good people, though you do not consider the plague of sins lately in the same schism that occurred among us' TH 40a

*rag ugge an **teez** goth tho merwal akar, ny a wele an **teez** younk tho e clappia le ha le* 'for after the old people die out, we see the young people speaking it less and less' BF: 25.

Usually, however, 'people' of both genders is rendered in Cornish by the word **pobel**:

D) **pobel** 'people'

*A[n] peynys a wotheuys ny ve ragtho y honan lemmyn rag **pobyll** an bys* 'The torments he suffered were not for himself but for the people of the earth' PA 6ab

*rys yw porris ʒe onon merwel rag **pobyl** an wlas* 'it is very necessary for one to die for the people of the country' PA 89c

*y **popel** ny vyth sparyys yssel y fethons guythys keffrys yn nos hag yn geyth* 'his people will not be spared, they shall be set to work abjectly both night and day' OM 1514-16

*Aron whek pyth a cusyl a reth thy'm orth am vresyl [h]a son a'n debel **bobel*** 'Dear Aaron, what counsel would you give about the strife and clamour of the wicked people?' OM 1813-15

*a ihesu ow map ellas yss yw hemma trueth bras bos the corf ker golyys gans tebel **popel** ogh ogh* 'O Jesu, my son, alas! What a great pity is this, that your beloved body has been wounded by evil people, oh, oh!' PC 3181-84

man   **GERYOW GWIR**

an antecryst yn lyes plu a treyl **pobyl** *thyworth dev yn pup le may kertho ef* 'the Antechrist in many parishes will turn the people from God wherever he goes' RD 247-49

a **pobyl** *omschumunys remembrogh agis sperys rag dovt cafus dampnasconn* 'O accursed people, remember your spirit lest you receive damnation' BM 1249-51

A war agys cam why **pobyl** *helma yv bevnans nobyl termen a thue* 'Go on your way, you people; this is a noble life for the future' BM 2022-24

Ima oma sur dragon ov latha **pobil** *dyson heb numbyr sur del clowa* 'There is here indeed a dragon killing people indeed without number surely as I hear' BM 3997-99

pobyl *rome orth ij vernans delyfrys yth yns oma* 'the people of Rome have been delivered from two deaths here' BM 4168-69

rag ny rug du agan creatya ny **pobill** *an bis heb reason* 'for God did not create us, the people of the world, without reason' TH 5

the hevelep ran an **bobill** *nyns o mas bean* 'to the appearance of some of the people it was only small' TH 5

Indell[a] ny **pobyll** *an bys surely nyg one mas gwels* 'Thus we the people of the world are surely nothing but grass' TH 7

cara agan cothmans nyns ew mas kepar dell ra an laddron, advltrers, denlath, hag oll an drog **pobill** *erell* 'to love our friends is only what the robbers, adulterers, murderers and all the other bad people do' TH 24

fatell ronns y tewlell drog **pobill** *in prison, kemeras in kerth aga pith, ha treweythow aga bewnans* 'how can they throw evil people in prison, take away their possessions and sometimes their life?' TH 24a

hen ew contulva an **bobill** *drys oll an bys* 'that is, the congregation of the people throughout the whole world' TH 31

An egglos an **bobill** *malignant ha drog* **pobill**, *hag inweth athewethas numbyr bras an scismaticals, an re na o drog* **pobill**, *ha yth ew in very dede an members han esyly an malignant egglos* 'The church of the malignant people and the evil people and recently a great number of schismatics, those were the evil people, and are in very deed the members and participants in the malignant church' TH 31A

Ha ny drog **pobyll** *a rug despisia oll y decreys, ha y ordynans eff ay justys* 'And we, evil people, despised all his decrees and his ordinance of his justice' TH 40-40a

Praga na russyn ny kyns y ymbrasia, ha ry grace the thu ragtha, rag y bosa an moyha precius jewall, han brassa, bythqueth a ve in myske **pobill** *mortall?* 'Why did we not embrace it and give thanks to God for its being the most precious jewel and the greatest that ever was among mortal people?' TH 54a

ha ef a vyn dos the judgia oll an **bobell** 'and he will come to judge all the people' SA 59

fatla vgy an **bobell** *ow leverall an kigg na ill recevia gifte Dew, henna ew bewnans heb dewath* 'how do people say that the flesh cannot receive the gift of God, that is everlasting life?' SA 63a

me a woer ny wrug an beys han **bobell** *myns es vnna tha voos mar gwicke destryes* 'I know, he did not make the world and all the people who are in it to be so quickly destroyed' CW 2381-83

An **poble** *erra zetha en tolgo a wellaz gullow broaze* 'The people who were sitting in darkness have seen a great light' Rowe

Ha ennah an suyaz e ruth veer a **boble**, *thor Alile, ha thor Decapolez ha thur Jerusalem, ha thur Judah, ha thur bar arall a Jordan* 'And then a great crowd of people followed him, from Galilee, and from Decapolis and from Jerusalem and from Judah and from the other side of the Jordan' Rowe

Ha Jesus geth oll a dro der Alale, deske et ago eglezow (an) gerryow Deew an gulasketh, sawyah oll sorto clevas, ha oll pesticks mesk an **boble** 'And Jesus went all around Galilee teaching in their churches the words of God of the kingdom, healing all sorts of disease, and all injuries among the people' Rowe

Whelas **poble** *tha trehe ithen* 'seek people to cut furze' ACB: F f 2

Ha enna ni e ved'n e ara amesk an **poble** *ez e gara* 'And there we will leave among the people who love him' LAM: 226

Ha me rig clowaz an **poble** *galarou, ta eth reas do chee eithick gwreag dah* 'And I heard the people complain that you have a wonderfully good wife' ACB: F f 3

Ol **poble** *eze war an oare a treegaz keno than Arleth gen gannaw looan* 'All people that dwell on the earth, sing to the Lord with joyful mouth' BF: 39

Ma peath hern pokar ol an beaz moy **poble** *bohodzack vel* **poble** *broaz* 'There is riches of pilchards like all the world, more of poor people than of substantial people' BF: 44

Oll an **poble** *en Porthia ha Marazjowan nevra ni ôr dho ganzingy* 'All the people of St Ives and Marazion will never be able to hold it' LAM: 228

Pobyll *abell bew castilly* 'People from afar inhabit castles' Scawen MSS

Nag es moye vel pager pe pemp en dreau nye ell clappia [Cornoack] leben, **poble** *coath pager egance blouth. Cornoack ewe all neceaves gen* **poble** *younk* 'There are not more than four or five in our town who can speak Cornish now, old people eighty years old. Cornish is all forgotten by the young people' LAM: 244.

When 'man' is a way of speaking about mankind (*Homo sapiens*), irrespective of gender, the expression used is **mab den**:

D **mab den** 'man, mankind'

War lyrgh **mab den** *ʒe begha reson prag y fe prynnys yw ihesus crist ʒe ord[na] yn neff y vonas tregys* 'After mankind sinned, the reason he was redeemed is that Jesus Christ decreed that he should dwell in heaven' PA 7ab

Mab den *heb ken ys bara nyn geuas ol y vewnans lemmen yn lauarow da a the ʒeworth an dremas* 'Mankind with bread only does not live all his life but with the good words which come from the Holy One' PA 12ab

In corff Ihesus yʒ ese hag ef yn crows ow cregy pymp myll strekis del iove ha pedergwyth cans goly ha tryvgons moy ganse ha pymʒek pur wyr ens y hag ol rag pur gerense worth **mab den** *ys goʒevy* 'In the body of Jesus there were when he was hanging on the cross five thousand strokes, as I have heard, and four times a hundred and sixty wounds and fifteen more they were, and all for love of mankind he suffered them' PA 227a-d

map den *a bry yn perfyth me a vyn y vos formyys* 'mankind I wish to be created perfectly from clay' OM 55-56

man GERYOW GWIR

ow spyrys ny dryc nefre yn corf **map den** *vyth yn beys ha reson yv ha prage rag y vos kyc methel gurys* 'my spirit shall not dwell for ever in the body of any one of mankind in the world and the reason and cause is that he was made soft flesh' OM 925-28

map den *hep ken ys bara byth nyn jeves ol bewnes leman yn leuarow da a thue thyworth [an] drenses* 'mankind with bread only does not live all his life but with good words that come from the Trinity' PC 65-68

an houl ny golse y lyw awos **map den** *the verwel na corf dasserhy the vew na dorgrys yn tyougel* 'the sun would not have lost its colour because a human being had died nor a body rise again to life nor an earthquake surely' PC 3083-86

ny fue ragtho y honan yn gothefys ef certan mas rak kerenge **map den** 'it was not for himself he suffered it indeed but for the sake of mankind' PC 3226-28

war y corf y whothefys yn certan mur a peynys rak sawye lynnyeth **map den** 'upon his body he suffered indeed many pains to save the lineage of mankind' RD 1808-10

myghtern of guyron ha cref kyns pegh **map den** *am sorras er ow fyn trauyth ny sef porth yfarn me a torras* 'I am a king righteous and strong; ere now the sin of mankind angered me; against me nothing stands; I broke the gates of hell' RD 2571-74

map den *my re wruk prenne gans gos ow colon na fe nep a wrussyn ny kyllys* 'mankind I have redeemed by my blood, lest anyone we had made should perish' RD 2622-24

mernans tyn eff a porthas eneff **map den** *gruk sawya ese in colmen satnas eff as dros the lowena* 'bitter death he bore; the soul of mankind he saved, which was in the bonds of Satan; he brought them to joy' BM 870-73

gans **mab den** *na ra mellya nefra awose helma abarth ihesu awartha* 'do not hereafter interfere with mankind in the name of Jesus above' BM 1128-30

Gesugh creys vfel ha clovr in hanov du dy lawe neb a formyas neff ha novr in bys ma gans y dule **map den** *a pry* 'Be silent, humble and meek, in the name of God, be he praised, who made heaven and earth, in this world with his own hands mankind of clay' BM 1312-16

Pur a wylste war an kee eneff **map den** *in bys mae* 'When did you see a soul of mankind left on the hedge in this world?' BM 1896-97

rag certen my yv mar claff ny gar **map den** *ov gueles* 'for certainly I am so sick, no human being wants to see me' BM 3100-01

An kyth cyrcomstans ma a alse bos geses in part du an tas rag eff a alsa creatya ha gull **mab den** *hebtha* 'This same circumstance could have been omitted on the part of God the Father, for he could have created and made mankind without it' TH 1

dre henna yth esa du ow notya ha shappya **mab den** *vgh oll an creatu[r]s erall myng a rug du creatya ha gull* 'through this he distinguishes and shapes mankind above all other creatures which God created and made' TH 2

en tas ew lene pacifies, satisfies ha greis contentys gans **mab den** 'the Father is fully pacified, satisfied and made content with mankind' TH 10a

rag neg ew lowr rag Christ the vos **mab dene***, ha the voese whippys, mas thagyn dry ny tha voese onyn gans ef* 'for it is not enough for Christ to be made a human being, and to be scourged, but to bring us to be one with him' SA 59a

GERYOW GWIR man

pana haker ew agen substance ny derag Dew an nef, an ena **mab den**, *neffra sawis mase dir criggyans da* 'how vile is our nature before God of heaven, the soul of man, never saved but by perfect faith' SA 60a

dirr vo an enef in kigg **mab deane** *an kigg yma causya an ena the vos junys the dew an neff* 'while the soul is in the flesh of mankind, the flesh causes the soul to be joined to the God of heaven' SA 60a

Corf Christ ew dibbris gans ganow **mab dean** 'The body of Christ is eaten by the mouths of mankind' SA 61

Ef ew an bolta **mab den** *a gampoller gans ganow* 'He is the boldest human being who is mentioned by mouth' BK 2319-20

Ay a vynta ge orth **mab dean** *pan vo gwryes a slem hager occupya rage sertayne ow rome ve na gevas peare omma in neve* 'Ah, do you wish for mankind, when they have been made of vile slime, to occupy indeed my space, I who have no equal here in heaven?' CW 254-58

Na reau latha **mâb dean** 'Do not kill a human being' BF: 55.

To translate '(human) person' one can say **person** *m., plural* **persons**:

E **person** 'person'

Ha dre pehosow mabden du a ve provokys warbyn an bys, may ruga cuthy ha dystrya gans lew Noye oll an bys, mas naye y honyn, y wreg, y iii mab haga iii gwreg, viii **person** *ens in holl myns a ve sawys* 'And by mankind's sin God was provoked against the world, so that he was saddened and destroyed all the world with Noah's flood, except Noah himself, his wife, his three sons and their three wives, eight persons in all they were who were saved' TH 7

Vn teball **person** *a yll tenna lyas onyn arell the lewdnes* 'One evil person can draw many others to wickedness' TH 25a

ny a res pub vr casa aga oberow haga offencys, so pub vr cara an **persons** 'we must always hate their deeds and offences, but at all times love the persons' TH 26

kyn rellens y groundya aga honyn apparantly war an scriptur benegas, whath yma thethy aga profession kemerys severally theworth neb drog then ha noghty **person** 'though apparently they ground themselves upon the sacred scripture, yet for them their profession has been taken severally from some evil man and worthless person' TH 32a

fatell vsy then Catholyk egglos an kythsam auctorite na only, rag discernya scripturs, han scripturs allowys dre an egglos, ny dalvea thetha bos refusyys gans particular **person** *vith* 'that only the catholic Church has this same authority, to interpret scripture and the scriptures permitted by the Church, they should not be rejected by any particular person' TH 38

Ith ew scryffys in viii-as chapter in actys an appostolis fatell rug Symon magus offra the ry mona the pedyr mar mynna pedyr ry power thotheff, penagull **person** *a rella eff ha gora y thewleff warnotha may teffans ha receva an spurissans* 'It is written in the eighth chapter of the Acts of the Apostles, that Simon Magus offered money to Peter if he would give power to him, that whichever person he might lay his hand on would receive the Holy Spirit' TH 46a.

Since **tus** can mean 'people' on occasion as well as 'men', it is not entirely suitable for use to distinguish men and women. The traditional language in such cases uses the singular A) **gour ha benen** or B) **gour ha gwreg**:

A **gour ha benen**

*ow corf yv re'n oferen kepar del leuerys theugh guyrthys lythys yn grovs pren dretho ef prynnys bytheugh ol ow tus **gour ha benen*** 'this is my body, by the mass, just as I have told you, sold, killed upon the cross, by it you will be redeemed, all my people, man and woman' PC 764-68

*drou e thy'mmo the tackye a vgh y pen gans mur greys may hallo pup y redye **gour ha benen** kekyffrys* 'bring it to me to fix above his head with great speed, that everyone may read it, man and woman also' PC 2807-10

*gosloweugh ol a tus vas bennath ihesu luen a ras theugh keffrys **gor ha benen*** 'listen, all you good people, the blessing of Jesus full of grace to you, both man and woman' PC 3217-19

*Saw thy'so y leuerys kepar del yw cryst yv pen **gor ha benen** yn chemma y fue gynen pur wyr hythyw* 'But he told it to you as it is; Christ, the head of man and woman, was with us very truly in this house today' RD 1394-98

*y fue gynen mar fest ygen lowenhas dotho ny thyalwhethas **gour na benen*** 'he was with us; very greatly he delighted us; neither man nor woman unlocked the door for him' RD 1443-46

*kens ol ef agan formyas ha gans y wos a prennas **gour ha benen*** 'first of all he created us, and by his blood he redeemed us, man and woman' RD 2430-32.

B **gour ha gwreg**

*moll[o]ʒ den ha **gour ha gwrek** a ʒe poran er ʒe byn peynys ad wra moreʒek yn yffarn down pub termyn* 'the curse of mankind, both man and woman, shall come right against you, pains will make you wretched in deep hell for always' PA 66cd

*wy agis beth **gor ha gruek** banneth crist ha meryasek banneth maria cambron* 'you will have, man and woman, the blessing of Christ and Meriasek, the blessing of Mary of Camborne' BM 2508-10

*E vannath genas, cosyn, du plegadow the **wor ha gwrek*** 'May his blessing be with you, cousin, a pleasant god, to man and woman' BK 651-53.

A new form ***denyon** 'men' has been suggested as a plural meaning 'men, adult males'. This is unnecessary. To translate 'ladies', 'gentlemen', or 'men', 'women' on public notices, for example, the elements in the phrases **gour ha benen** and **gour ha gwreg** can easily be pluralized as **gwer** 'men' and **benenes** 'women' or **gwrageth** respectively.

*Inweth S poull a commodias an **gwer** the cara aga gwregath kepar dell ra crist cara y egglos* 'Also St Paul commanded the husbands to love their wives as Christ loves his Church' TH 31

*Me a'n to theugh, re Gorran! pur welcum ough genan ny del on **guer** freth in casow* 'I swear to you, by St Gorran! you are very welcome with us as we are impetuous men in battles' BK 1362-64.

Alternatively one might use **gwesyon** 'fellows' and **benenes** 'women'. With **gwesyon** 'fellows, lads' compare:

*arvow lour thy'nny yma ha **guesyon** stout yn tor ma a'n chache vskys* 'we have arms enough now and stout fellows, who will catch him quickly' PC 614-16

*sav certan nyns o torn da danvon **guesyon** an par ma gans arvow thu'm kemeres* 'but certainly it was not a good deed to send men like these with arms to arrest me' PC 1298-300

*me a wor ple mons parys rag an **wesyon** ordenys war ow ene* 'I know where they are ready, arranged for the fellows upon my soul' PC 2579-81

*ogh govy ellas ellas guelas ov map mar dyflas gans tebel **wesion** dyghtys* 'Oh, woe is me, alas, alas, to see my son so dreadfully treated by wicked men' PC 2603-05

*tormentoris **guesyon** fol tormentoris dugh thym ol aberth mahum ha soly* 'torturers, mad fellows, come to me in the name of Mahound and Sol' BM 1170-72

*Ateve strepys in noth indelma guthel y coth then **guesyon** as tefe peth* 'Look, he has been stripped naked; thus one should treat fellows who have wealth' BM 1933-35.

There is no need for ***denyon**.

TO MARRY, MARRIAGE

The ordinary word for 'to marry' both of the espousing partners and of the administering priest, is **demedhy**, which is well attested:

A **demedhy**

*ny vanna omry then beys na **domethy** benytha* 'I will not devote myself to the world nor ever marry' BM 326-27

*Tav dymmovy meryasek ty a **thommeth** ov map wek the neb arlothes worthy* 'Hold your tongue, Meriasek. You, my dear son, shall marry some worthy lady' BM 328-30

***Domethy** mar ny re va tus a ra agan scornya* 'If he does not marry, people will mock us' BM 334-35

*Na govsogh ger war an beys benytha ov **domethy** the ken forthov sur ov breys yma syttis eredy* 'Do not speak any word in the world ever that I should marry. My mind is indeed surely set on other ways' BM 340-43

*pyth a an tyr han trevov us thynny heb feladov mar ny vynnyth **domethy*** 'where will the land and the settlements go that we posses without doubt, if you do not marry?' BM 369-71

*Komeer weeth na raw'y ostia en chei lebma vo dean koath **demithez** da bennen younk* 'Be careful not to lodge in a house where an old man is married to a young woman' BF: 16

marry   GERYOW GWIR

Kebmer uîth na ray ostia en tshei lebma vo dên kôth **demidhyz** *dho bennen iyngk* 'Be careful not to lodge in a house where an old man is married to a young woman' BF: 17

Demytho *Jowan an dean Tha Agnez an bennen* 'Marry John the man to Agnes the woman' ACB: F f 2 *verso*

Ha hemma urta ve, rago why Ha henna **demithe** *gy* 'And this is from me for you, and then marry them' ACB: F f 2 *verso*.

The verb **marya** 'to marry' is attested once:

B **marya**

the greffe y fyen ny y voys **maryys** *eredy ha moghheys agen roweth* 'we should be the stronger if he were married and our status increased' BM 311-13.

Speaking of the man, one can also say **kemeres dh'y wreg** 'to take as his wife':

kymmerr y 303 wrek *sconya ʒys ny vek* 'take her as your wife; she will not make to spurn you' CF 10.

In the revived language the default word for 'marriage, wedding' is ***demedhyans**. Curiously, this word is not attested. The only attested word for 'marriage, wedding' is **maryach**, **maryaj**:

yma **maryag** *galosek cowsys ʒyn rag meryasek mergh ʒe vyghtern gallosek* 'a mighty marriage has been mentioned to us for Meriasek, a daughter of a mighty king' BM 177-79

ty a thommeth ov map wek the neb arlothes worthy ha ny a veth the creffa der an **maryach** *benitha hag ol the lynnyeth defry* 'you shall marry, my dear son, some wordhy lady and we and all your family shall be the stronger for ever indeed through the marriage' BM 329-33

In kepar maner in aweyll yma agan savyour crist ow hevely y egglos the lyas tra, indan an hanow a regnum celorum, henew gwlascore neff, kepar ha the viterne a rug gull ha provya **mariag** *rag y vab* 'In the same way in the gospel our Saviour Christ likens his Church to many things, under the name of *regnum coelorum*, that is the kingdom of heaven, like a king who made and provided a wedding for his son' TH 31.

***Demedhyans** is a natural derivative of the verb **demedhy** 'to marry' and can hardly be proscribed. It should perhaps be remembered, however, that ***demedhyans** is not attested. The attested word is **maryach**, **maryaj**.

ME *see* **I**

TO MEAN, MEANING

There are three attested words for 'to mean': A) **styrya**; B) **mênya** and C) **sygnyfia**. Here are the attestations of them both:

A **styrya**

*yn erna crist a vynnas leuerell ely ely 3e **stirya** yw a gowsas arluth prag y hysta vy* 'then Christ wished to say Eli, Eli; what he said meant Lord, why did you forsake me?' PA 201bc

*hemma ew the **styrrya**, I wysce ath face te a thebbyr the vara* 'this means, in the sweat of your face will you eat your bread' TH 6

*hemma ew the **styrrya**, mabden genys a venyn, ny ra bewa omma mas termyn cut* 'this means, man born of women, he lives here only a short time' TH 7

*hemma ew the **styrrya**, neb a rug benega, han rena neb ew benegys, yth ens oll onyn* 'this means, he who blessed and those who are blessed are all one' TH 13

*Hemma ew the **styrrya** in mar ver dell ew lymmyn infancy passys in oys den, ha grace ew plenty res the vabden, han brasa royow promysys* 'This means, inasmuch as now infancy has passed in the age of man, and grace has been given in plenty to mankind and the greater gifts promised' TH 28

*hemm ew the **styrrya**, Na in tyller arell, na dre menes arell, ew heresy springys in man, ha scismes drehevys, mas rag nag us obedyens res thyn minister neb ew an pronter a thu* 'This means, nor in another place, nor through other means have heresies sprung up, and schisms arisen, but only because obedience has not been given to the minister who is the priest of God' TH 42a.

[Note: in the quotations from Tregear above I have translated **hemma yw dhe styrya** as 'this means'; literally it might be translated 'this is to be interpreted'.]

B **mênya**

*An rena ew the **venya**, vnderstonding, remembrans, ha blonogath gans lowar gyfte moy a gras* 'By those are meant understanding, remembrance and will, with many more gifts of grace' TH 1a

*An corfe a vabden in state a originall innocencye hen ew the **venya** yehas, nerth, comlines, gans qualites erell in vhella degre a perfection* 'The body of mankind in a state of original innocence, by which is meant health, beauty, strength, comeliness and other qualities in the highest degree of perfection' TH 2a

*ny rug eff leverall in pegh, mas in plurel number, in pehosow, hen ew the **venya** in mes a onyn y te mere* 'he did not say in sin, but in the plural number, in sins, by that is meant, out of one many come' TH 8a

*ny ra an yettys a yffarne prevayllya warbyn an egglos, dre an yeattys a effarne, yma eff ow **menya** error avell pan lavarra eff, an egglos catholyk neffra ny vith ouercommys gans error* 'the gates of hell will not prevail against the Church; by the gates of hell he means error, as though he were saying, the catholic Church will never be overcome by error' TH 17-17a

mean   **GERYOW GWIR**

Dre reson y bos an egglos an cyta vgy agan savyour ena ow **menya**, *han gantyll o ena cowsys anethy* 'Because the Church is the city which our Saviour means there, and the candle which was spoken of' TH 17a

Rag henna may hallogh why gothvas in pub poynt oll pandra vsy an catholyk egglos ow **menya** *haw cresy, eff a vith particularly disquethis ha settys in mes theugh wosa hemma* 'Therefore, that you may know in every respect what the catholic Church means and believes, it will be particularly demonstrated and set out for you later' TH 20

Gans agan gallus ha power, hen ew the **venya** *gans agan dewleff ha treys, gans agan lagasow ha scovornow, gans agan ganowow ha tavosow* 'By our ability and power, by which is meant with our hands and feet, with our eyes and ears, with our mouths and tongues' TH 21a

yma crist omma ow **menya** *certan company a bobill esa in myske an Jewys* 'Christ here means a certain company of people among the Jews' TH 26a

yma eff ow **menya** *na rellan ny cristonnyan desquethes agan honyn da ha virtus warves in sight an bys only* 'he means that we Christians should not display ourselves as good and virtuous externally in the sight of the world only' TH 26a

soo tyrry charite ew pan rella den **menya** *drog thy kyscristian* 'but the breaching of charity is when a man means ill to his fellow Christian' TH 30

ha neb a rella agys despisia why, yma worth ow despisia ve, ow **menya** *dre henna fatell vynna eff worth oll an bys gothvas ha confessia an auctorite an catholyk egglos* 'and whoever despises you, he despises me, meaning by that that he wanted the world to know and to confess the authority of the catholic Church' TH 35a

ymowns ow try tane strayng then alter a thu, hen ew the **venya**, *straynge discans, a vith lyskys gans an tane a neff* 'they bring strange fire to the altar of God, by which is meant, strange teaching, which will be burnt by the fire of heaven' TH 37

Ha pandra esa eff ow **menya** *the pedyr mas specyall privileg pan ruga promysya the ry thetho an alwetho a wlas neff in presons a oll an xii-ak?* 'And what did he mean to Peter except a special privilege when he promised to give him the keys of the kingdom of heaven in the presence of all the twelve?' TH 44a

henew, eff a rug omma **menya** *crist, yma ow sawya in very pen an egglos, ow* **menya** *pedyr, an decease a oll an corfe* 'that is, he here meant Christ; he heals at the very top of the Church, meaning Peter, the disease of all the body' TH 46

thyn kythsam egglos ma, ow **menya** *hag ow poyntya then sea bo stat a rome* 'to this same church, meaning and pointing to the see or state of Rome' TH 48

han tyrmyn a rug agan Savyour wosa y thethyrryans commyttya y thevas the vos megys, bys in epscop ma vs lemma in present tyrmyn ma ow **menya** *rag the wetha an catholik egglos* 'and from the time our Saviour, after his resurrection, committed his sheep to be fed until this bishop who is there in this present time, meaning to preserve the catholic Church' TH 49

Lymmyn pandra vsy hemma ow **menya**? 'Now what does this mean?' TH 52a

S Johan ena a rug aga expondia haga leveris, fattell rug crist, dre y tempill, **menya** *y corfe, an pith a vetha dre an Jewes gorys then mernans* 'St John then expounded them and said, that Christ by his temple means his body, that which woul be put to death by the Jews' TH 53

GERYOW GWIR   **mean**

an dall a welle han effreg a ra kerthes, han bothar a glew, han omlavar a cowse, ow **menya** *dre an dall, effreg, bothar, ha omlavar, an a re a ve therag dorne indella* 'the blind sees and the lame walks and the deaf hears and the dumb speaks, meaning by the blind, lame, deaf and dumb, those who were previously thus' TH 57a

dir girryow an tasow a vam egglos, eth esa ve ow **menya**, *a Justine, Irenae, Tertullian, Origene, Eusebius, Emisene, Athanasius, C[yri]ll, Epiphanius, Hierom, Chrisostom, Augustine, [Vig]ilius, Fulgentius [ha] lowarth onyn erall an tasow coeth* 'through the words of the fathers of mother Church; I mean Justin Martyr, Irenæus, Tertullian, Origen, Eusebius, [Eusebius] Emissenus, Athanasius, Cyril, Epiphanius, Jerome, [John] Chrysostom, Augustine, Vigilius, Fulgentius and many another one of the ancient fathers' SA 64

Materen Frink, thera vi a **menia**, *na venja hedda whath gun greevia* 'I mean the King of France; that still would not grieve you' LAM: 226.

A third verb **sygnyfia** 'to signify' is also frequently synonymous with 'to mean':

C **sygnyfia**

in hemma yma an drinsis ow **signifia** *pluralite, henew number a persons* 'in this the Trinity means plurality, that is a number of persons' TH 1a

dre hemma yth ew **signifies** *an vnite inweth agan nature ha substans* 'by this are meant the unity both of our nature and substance' TH 1a

yma ow **signifia** *an violacion han torva a cherite* 'he means the violation and the breach of charity' TH 28

hag eff a cowsys the pedyr only, ow **signifia** *an mater esa ef ow cowse anotha the pertaynya the pedyr chyfly ha principally* 'and he spoke to Peter only, meaning that the matter of which he spoke pertained chiefly and principally to Peter' TH 43

An tirmyn o an nois therag eff the suffra myrnans, the **signifia** *thynny fatell o an bois na defferis bys in dewetha deth a ve agan Sovyour conuersaunt gans y appostlis* 'the time was the night before he suffered death, to signify to us that that food had been deferred until the last day on which our Saviour was in the company of his apostles' TH 52

eff a luereis dre hemma, eff a rug **signifya** *pan kynde a virnans a re eff suffra* 'he said by this, he indicated what kind of death he would suffer' TH 53a

lymmyn rag **signifia** *an trelva an bara han gwyn thyn substans a corfe crist ha y gois* 'now to indicate the conversion of the bread and wine into the substance of Christ's body and his blood' TH 56-56a

kyn rellyn ny **signifia** *bara gwrys a eys in agan commyn eyth, whath in scriptur yma ow* **signifia** *pup kynde a foode, beva foode an corfe po food an ena* 'though we mean bread made from grain in our common speech, yet the scripture means every kind of food, whether food of the body or of the soul' TH 57a

ha rag henna na ruk Christ gylwall participation: rag malla ef **signifia** *brossa mater. ha eweth brassa conjunction in trethans* 'and therefore, did not Christ call it participation? So that he might mean a greater matter and also a greater union among them' SA 65.

mean

For 'meaning' Nance suggested ***styr** and ***sygnyfians** (UC *sygnyfyans*). Neither is attested. The attested words are A) **mênyng**; B) **sygnyfycacyon**; and C) **sens**. Here are the attestations:

A mênyng

*kynsa the wothfes fatell res thyn scripture bos vnderstondyys warlerth an generall **menyng** a egglos crist* 'first to know that the scripture must be understood according to the genereal meaning of Christ's Church' TH 18

*Ran an aweylors, onyn po arell, a rug y egery plenly an very **menyng** anotha* 'Some of the evangelists, one or another, very clearly explained the meaning of it' TH 53

*An **menyng** an gyrryow ma ew kemerys in lyas forth* 'The meaning of these words has been taken in many ways' TH 53

*Rag henna yma S Mark in x-as chapter ow declaria an very **menyng** anetha in vaner ma* 'Therefore St Mark in the 10th chapter declares the very meaning of them thus,' TH 53.

B sygnyfycacyon

*ymowns ow desyvya aga honyn, ow myskemeras an **significacion** an ger ma* 'they deceive themselves, misunderstanding the meaning of this word' TH 57a.

C sens

*hag yth esans ow pewa warlerth an letterall **sens** a la moyses mar compis in face an bys mayth ens accomptys dretha rag tus lell* 'and they lived according to the literal meaning of the law of Moses so punctiliously that they were considered by it to be faithful men' TH 26a

*In kynsa, du a ros power hag auctorite then catholik egglos the gafas an lell **sens** han vnderstonding an scriptur* 'In the first place, God gave power and authority to the catholic Church to receive the true meaning and understanding of the scripture' TH 36

*an egglos an jevas an lell **sens** an scriptur ha yth ew iudg a henna* 'the Church has the true meaning of the scripture and is judge of that' TH 36 fn.

For 'to mean' the authentic words are **styrya**, **mênya** and **sygnyfia**. For 'meaning' the attested words are **mênyng**, **sygnyfycacyon** and **sens**.

TO MELT

The only evidence for 'to melt' (intransitive) in Cornish is *Deliqueo… To melt, to thaw, to dissolve, &c. C. Dho **tedha** AB: 54a*. In some forms of Cornish this appears as ***teudha**, for which there is no evidence.

MENTION, TO MENTION

For the noun 'mention' Nance suggests ***menek**, which is unattested. The only attested term is **mencyon**, which occurs for the most part in the phrase **gwil mencyon** 'to make mention, to mention':

*nyns o sufficient the ryddia mab den a begh kepar dell vgy S paul thyn romans ow kull **mencion*** 'it was not sufficient to rid mankind of sin, as St Paul mentions to the Romans' TH 14-14a

*eff a drygas omma in nore, kepar dell vgy scriptur ow kull **mencion** adro then tyrmyn han oys a xxxiii-ans a vlethynnyow* 'he dwelt here on earth, as the scripture mentions, for the time and period of 33 years' TH 15

*Hag inweth yma eff ow leverell, Mar teffa den vith ha pregoth thyn kythsame barbarus nacions ma in aga eyth y aga honyn an **vencions** ma a heritickys in by an by y a vynsa stoppya aga scovurnow* 'And also he says, If anyone were to preach to these same barbarous nations in their own language of these statements of heretics, soon enough they would stop up their ears' TH 19

*yma Ireneus ow kull **mencion** anetha in vaner ma* 'St Irenaeus mentions them thus' TH 37

*Gans mere moy stroytya promysyow yma eff ow kull **mencion** then re a rella disobeya an auctorite an egglos* 'With many stricter promises he mentions to those who would disobey the authority of the Church' TH 37

*ha pan rug an bobyll gull mur aneth an myrakyll na, Pedyr a rug ena thetha narracion, kepar dell ew **mencion** gwrys in iiii-a, in v-es, ha in vi-as an actus appostolis* 'and when the people greatly marvelled at this miracle, St Peter recounted to them, as is mentioned in the third, fifth and sixth chapters of the Acts of the Apostles' TH 45

*Inweth eff a drellyas mer an bobyll then feith a crist, kepar dell ew gwrys **mencion** in xiiii chapter in seconde lever a Eusebius* 'Also he converted many people to the faith of Christ, as is mentioned in the 13th chapter of the second book of Eusebius' TH 46a

*Yma S Ambros ow kull **mencion** a virnans han martirdom a pedyr ha poulle in Rome* 'St Ambrose mentions the death and martyrdom of Peter and Paul in Rome' TH 47

*Whath, rag tochya thyn gyrryow ma, hem ew ow corffe vy, onyn vith an Aweylers nyg ues ow cull **mencyon** na declarasion war hemma* 'Moreover, about these words, This is my body, not one of the evangelists makes mention or declaration upon it' TH 53

*ha whath an girryow ma nyg us onyn vith an aweylers ow kull **mencion** vith* 'and moreover not one of the evangelists mentions these words at all' TH 53a

*Secondly, mars ugy onyn vith an Aweylers ow cull **mencion** a payne the vos dew then re a rella y receva vnworthy vnworthy yma S. paul ow leverell fatell ra an vnworthy recevans an sacrament ma dry iudgement ha dampnacion* 'Secondly, if any one of the evangelists mentions the pain that is due to those who receive it unworthily, St Paul says that the unworthy reception of this sacrament brings judgement and damnation' TH 53a

*maga pell dell vge a keth deane ma, Phoceus, lowarth gwyeth o gwyell **mention** a corf han gos agen arluth Dew, ema ef o tisquethas nyng o ef only deane ew sacrificed mas agen arluth christ e honyn, an gwrerer a pub tra oll* 'in as much as this same man, Phoceus, often mentions the body and blood of our Lord God, he shows that it was not only a man that was sacrificed but our Lord Christ himself, the creator of all things' SA 61.

Another way of saying 'to mention' is to use the verb **campolla**:

Vn ger na **campol** *a gryst ha mar qureth me ath wra trest* 'Do not mention a word of Christ, and if you do, I'll make youn unhappy' BM 903-04

han tresse meys gyngala dugol myhall byth henna in plu wyn noala sensys ha meryasek benytha inna purguir **campollys** 'and the third fair in September; that will be held in the blessed Parish of Noala at Michaelmas and Meriasek indeed will be mentioned for ever in them' BM 2200-04

Ty vyl pen pyst na **gampol** *crist theragovy* 'You vile blockhead, do not mention Christ in front of me' BM 2438-40

meryasek pan **gampollys** *an pap a ruk y presia* 'when I mentioned Meriasek, the pope praised him' BM 2791-92

Na vanna' heb the dolla, rag henna na **gampolh** *a. Te a'n kef rag an gwelha* 'I do not [wish], without deceiving you, therefore do not mention it. You will find it for the best' BK 2143-45

Ef ew an bolta mab den a **gampoller** *gans ganow* 'He is the boldest human being who is mentioned by word of mouth' BK 2319-20

The leud desyr a'm cuth por wyer. Na **gampoll** *a!* 'Your lewd desire truly disturbs me. Do not mention it!' BK 2952-54

Ha me rig clowaz an poble **compla** *[fatel ew reaz] do chee eithick gwreage dah* 'And I heard the people mentioning that you need a really good wife' LAM: 230.

Mencyon is the authentic term for the substantive 'mention'. 'To mention' in Cornish is either **gwil mencyon** or **campolla**.

MERCY

The native word for 'mercy' in Cornish is **tregereth** *f.*; cf. Welsh *trugaredd* 'mercy', Breton *trugarez* 'pity, mercy' and Irish *trócaire* 'mercy' < Celtic **trougakariya* 'love for the wretched'. I have been able to collect the following five examples:

ro thy'm the vanneth perfeth rag thy'm yma govenek cafes the gens **tregereth** 'give me your full blessing for I have hope to obtain mercy the sooner' OM 452

lauar annes ov bos vy a'm bewnens my th'y bysy a leuerel guyroneth thy'so a'n oyl a versy o dythywys thy'mmo vy gans an tas a'y **dregereth** *pan vef chacys* 'tell him that I am weary of my life; that I beg him to tell you the truth about the oil of mercy promised to me by the Father in his mercy when I was evicted' OM 700-05

arluth warnas **tregeryth** *goef a ra the serry* 'Lord, I beg you for mercy; unhappy the man who angers you' OM 1015-16

GERYOW GWIR mercy

ihesu kyn wruk the naghe luen **tregereth** *me a pys* 'Jesus, though I denied you, I beg full mercy' RD 1148-49

Costentyn rag the pyte a gemercys an flehys han **tregereth** *warnethe age lathe na vynsys me a vyn sur the sawye* 'Constantine, for the pity you took on the children and the mercy for them that you would not kill them, I shall surely heal you' BM 1836-40.

Much commoner, however, is the borrowed term **mercy**. It is used both generally and in the expression **an oyl a vercy** 'the oil of mercy' (a reference to the promised redemption of the world by Christ). Here are a few examples:

a das dev y'th wolowys grannt theth whythres my a'd peys neppeyth a oel a **vercy** 'O God the Father in your radiance grant to your handiwork, I beseech you, something of the oil of mercy' OM 325-27

Adam yn dyweth a'n beys my a wronnt oel **mercy** *they's ha the eua the wreghty* 'Adam, at the end of the world I shall grant the oil of mercy to you and to Eve your wife' OM 328-30

ellas my a wor henna bones ov fegh moy yn ta es **mercy** *dew* 'Alas, that I know, that my sin is considerably greater than the mercy of God' OM 590-92

moyses sur my re beghas hag a henna a elow **mersy** *war dev agan tas* 'Moses, surely I have sinned and for that I cry for mercy to God our Father' OM 1863-65

Arluth jhesu cryst a nef kymmer **mercy** *a'm enef del of ragos tormontyys* 'Lord Jesus Christ of heaven, have mercy on my soul, as I am tormented for you' OM 2721-23

yowynk ha lovs kyn fo tollys dre y deunos **mercy** *gylwys* 'young and old, though they be deceived by his temptations, let them call for mercy' PC 19-20

mercy *yw scos the nep a'n pys puppenagol a vo ef* 'mercy is a shield to him who begs it, whoever he may be' PC 22-3

asson whansek ol the pysy lettrys ha lek war thu **mercy** 'how eager we all are, lettered and lay, to pray to God for mercy' PC 37-38

dev a **mercy** *the pup huny sur yth ywe* 'he is indeed a God of mercy for everyone' PC 237-38

ye mar vur me re peghas ow querthe crist luen a ras the'n yethewon the lathe moy yv ys **mercy** *an tas* 'Yea, so greatly have I sinned betraying Christ full of grace to the Jews to be killed; it is greater than the Father's mercy' PC 1519-22

the ihesu gras luon yv a ras hag a **vercy** *fos ny torras na war tharas ny thue thy'nny* 'thanks to Jesus; he is full of grace and mercy; he broke no wall nor does he come to us by a door' RD 327-30

mercy *pysaf pup termyn yn certan a luen golon* 'I pray for mercy always indeed from the bottom of my heart' RD 1156-57

rak ty yw dev gallogek the pup a vo othommek warnos a pysse **mercy** 'for you are a powerful God for all who are in need, who beg you for mercy' RD 2376-78

mercy *war crist y creya boys crystyan menna heb wov* 'I cry to Christ for mercy; I want without a lie to be a Christian' BM 1816-17

mercy GERYOW GWIR

Penys purguir yv ov luyst ha creya pup vr war crist **mercy** *rag ov fehosov* 'My desire in very truth is to fast and to pray to Christ always for mercy for my sins' BM 1824-26

mercy *neb a gemerre* **mercy** *an gueres puppreys* 'whoever has mercy, mercy will heal him always' BM 1842-43

an ladron a veth pelleys ran the guel forthov treylys **mercy** *du mar crons goven* 'the robbers will be banished, some converted to better ways, if they ask God for mercy' BM 2083-85

Mercy *du prest yv parys the vap den mara'n wyla* 'The mercy of God is always ready for man if he seek it' BM 2743-44

Du a wrappyas pub nacion in discregyans may halla eff kafus **mercy** *war oll* 'God wrapped every nation in unbelief, that he might have mercy upon all' TH 7a

mar ten ha menegas agan pehosow du ew lene a **vercy**, *just ha fethfull the gava thyn agan pehosow ha thegan glanhe a bup filth* 'if we confess our sins, God is full of mercy, just and faithful to forgive us our sins and to cleanse us of all filth' TH 8

ha gesow ny the repentya ha mekya ha humblya agan honyn hartely ha crya **mercy** *war thu* 'and let us repent and abase and humble ourselves heartily and cry to God for mercy' TH 9-9a

Gesow ny inweth the aswon an exceding **mercy** *a thu thenny desquethis* 'Let us also recognize the limitless mercy of God shown to us' TH 11a

neb a vynna gylwall thy remembrans an dader a thu golosak in y **mercy** *a vgh pub tra thyn ny desquethis heb y thyrfyne, neb as tevas spot vith a gras, eff a ill bos methek ay vnkyndenys ha disobediens warbyn du* 'whoever wishes to remember the goodness of almighty God in in his mercy shown to us above all things without our deserving it, whoever has any modicum of grace, he can be ashamed of his unkindness and disobedience towards God' TH 30a

A arluth len a **vercy**, *pana confort ha commodite ew hemma ragan ny an cristonnyan, the gafus crist tregys innan ny!* 'O Lord, full of mercy, what comfort and usefulness is that for us Christians, to find Christ dwelling in us!' TH 39

Ne nahaf Du a **vercy**, *ragtho kyn fena maraw, na raf pur wyer* 'I will not deny the God of mercy, though I be killed for it, I will not in very truth' BK 579-81

Der weras Christ ha'y **vercy** *te ru'm grug saw ha ru'm dros a ver bonvas* 'By the help of Christ and his mercy you have healed me and brought me out of great affliction' BK 812-14

ow folly yth ew mar vras haw holan inweth pur browt ny vanaf thaworth an tase whylas **mercy** *sure heb dowte* 'my folly is so great and my heart is also very proud; I do not wish to seek mercy from the Father indeed without doubt' CW 1522-25

pan deffa an oyle a **vercy** *te a vith kerrys then ioye than nef vghall a vghan* 'when the oil of mercy arrives, you will be brought to bliss, to high heaven above' CW 2075-77

Both **tregereth** and **mercy** are authentic, but **mercy** is much the commoner of the two.

For **gromercy** 'many thanks' *see* **THANKS**.

MESSENGER

There are two words in the texts for 'messenger': A) **cannas, cadnas**, plural **canasow** and B) **messejer**, plural **messejers**. **Cannas** on occasion can mean 'message' rather than 'messenger':

A **cannas, cadnas**

*Thy gour hy a ʒanonas a crist kepar del welse yn kerdh delma dre **gannas** nyng ew ragos se laʒe Cryst* 'She sent to her husband about Christ as she had seen, in this way by a messenger: It is not for you to kill Christ' PA 123ab

*gorthyans thy's a thev a ras pan danfensys the **cannas** rag pharo th'agan guythe* 'glory to you, O God of grace, that you sent your messenger to protect us from Pharaoh' OM 1669-71

*Wel thov fare messyger rag **cannas** os hep danger nynsus fout ynnos guelys* 'Farewell, messenger, for you are a messenger without grudge; no fault is seen in you' OM 2291-93

*messyger **cannas** gentyl del os ov seruont hep gyl dus yn rag del y'm kyrry* 'emissary, gentle messenger, as you are my guileless servant, come forth as you love me' OM 2401-03

*ow **cannas** whek the'n beys covth lowenna tekca gothfy ihesu ov map kevarwouth vgy warnaf ow pygy* 'my sweet messenger, descend to the world; as joyful and finely as you can direct my son, who is praying to me' PC 1041-43

*lyʒt foude **cannas** paramour ke lauar thu'n dev doctour dos the gous er byn ihesu* 'Light Foot, devoted messenger, go, speak to the two doctors to come to speak against Jesus' PC 1632-34

*heil a heil madama vras danfon the pilat **cannas*** 'hail, oh hail, great madam. Send a messenger to Pilate' PC 1935-36

*aban ywe yndella me a vyn danfon toth da ow **cannas** rag y warnye* 'since it is thus, I will send my messenger straight away to warn him' PC 1953-55

*me a'th pys arluth a ras a thanfon thy'nny **cannas** may ben nepith aswonfas fatel yw thy's* 'I beseech you, Lord of grace, to send us a messenger, that we may have some knowledge of how it is with you' RD 767-70

*omma wharee ny redufe gans an **gannas*** 'hither I have come quickly with the message' BM 1431-33

*Keugh ahanan, **cannas** flowr! ha kerth Ke thym bys o'm towr, rag eth esaf in awhyr* 'Depart hence, choicest messenger! and bring Ke to me in my tower, for I am in anguish' BK 1031-33

*theworth Lucy **canhasow** danvenys on dris leas gwlas rag nygyssas orthewhy* 'we are messengers sent from Lucius to you across many lands to negotiate with you' BK 1891-95

***Canhasow** on devethys prevath heb son drys lyas gwlas rag nygyssas orthawhy* 'We messengers have come privately without hullaboo across many lands to negotiate with you' BK 1899-903

*Ha thewgh grasow, a **ganhasow!*** 'And thanks to you, O messengers!' BK 2008-09

messenger   **GERYOW GWIR**

Maseger, pen **canhasow**, *deugh 'rag in un thyena* 'Delegate, chief of messengers, come forth panting' BK 2348-49

Canhas, *welcum os sertan* 'Messenger, you are welcome indeed' BK 2396

Farwell, **canhas** *plegadaw!* 'Farewell, pleasant messenger!' BK 2409

Canhas, *farwel!* 'Messenger, farewell!' BK 2443

Welcum, **canhas** *ker!* 'Welcome dear messenger!' BK 2458

Bienvenu, **canhas** *sauns peer!* 'Welcome, messenger without peer!' BK 2504

Canhas *gentyl, na borth dowt. Awos Arthor ny a rowt* 'Gentle messenger, fear not. We will vanquish in spite of Arthur' BK 2520-21

Welcum os, flowr **canhasow**, *welcum melwith, ru'm ena!* Welcome are you, choicest messenger, a thousand times welcome, upon my soul!' BK 2530-31

Ow **canhas** *ker, ke thegy bys in Rom gans pen Lucy* 'My dear messenger, go to Rome with the head of Lucius' BK 2838-39

Canhas *sauns per drys pub mab Grek os hag ylyn* 'You are a peerless messenger above every Greek man and pure' BK 2894-96

A **canhas** *mas, da re fary, ha this mer gras bys venary* 'O good messenger, may you fare well, and many thanks to you for ever' BK 2917-20

Canhas, *des rag desempys!* 'Messenger, come forth at once!' BK 3017

Welcum, **canhas**, *re Jowan!* 'Welcome, messenger, by St John!' BK 3038

Canhas, *guarn an anprevion na vyth hueth war ow holan erna vons e dyskevrys* 'Messenger, warn the miscreants that there will be no joy in my heart until they are unmasked' BK 3158-60

Canhas *of, so mot Y gon, theworth Arthur danvenys gans dynnerth stowt ha calys* 'I am a messenger, so mote I go, sent from Arthur with a greetings stout and hard' BK 3165-67

y a vythe ryall ha splan **canhasawe** *them danvenys rage ow servia bys vickan* 'they will be royal and bright, messengers sent for me, to serve me for ever' CW 28-30

me yw **cannas** *dew ankow omma dretha appoyntys* 'I am the messenger of God, death, appointed by him' CW 985-86

Cadnas 'messenger' Bodewryd MS.

B **messejer**

wel thew fare **messeger** *fystyn dywhans gans en ger a thesempys* 'fare thee well, messenger; hasten eagerly with the word immediately' PC 1641-43

messeger *ke alemma leuerel thu'm arluth gura ihesu na wrella damnpnye* 'messenger, go hence to tell my lord not to condemn Jesus' PC 1956-58

messeger *er the laute yv guyr thy'm a leueryth* 'messenger, upon your honour, is what you tell me true?' PC 2205-06

danveneugh why the pyladt gans **messeger** *may tanfonno thyugh yn scon cryst myghtern an yethewon* 'send to Pilate with a messenger that he should soon send you Christ, the king of the Jews' RD 1594-97

messeger *me a'th pys ke aberth yn pow the wandre vn pols byan* 'messenger, I beg you, go into the country to wander for a little while' RD 1633-35

messeger *ny thebbraf bos bones marow an profos a alse sur ow yaghe* 'messenger I shall not eat food since the prophet who could have cured me is dead' RD 1685-87

meseger *scon alemma kegy gans ov mab kerra bys yn mester a grammer* 'messenger, do you go hence immediately with my most beloved son to the master of grammar' BM 34-6

Messeger *na 3ovt an cas my an dysk na vo yn gvlas gramarion vyth ay parov* 'Messenger, have no fear in the matter; I will teach him so that there will not be in the kingdom any grammarian to equal him' BM 90-2

Maseger *athesempys kergh thym an epscop omma han doctour brays kekefrys* 'Messenger, immediately fetch here for me the bishop and the great doctour also' BM 1378-80

Wolcum **maseger** *ylyn oys oma war ov ena* 'Welcome are you, pure messenger, here upon my soul' BM 1400-01

maseger *tek lauer thymo in preytha then emper tek pendrus werys* 'fair messenger, tell me I pray you what has happened to the fair emperor' BM 1409-12

Maseger *gans mur a greys kergh seluester thym uskys* 'Messenger, with great speed fetch Silvester to me quickly' BM 1733-34

Dus in rag ov **maseger** *ke thym the pap seluester* 'Come forth, my messenger; go for me to Pope Silvester' BM 2722-23

Yma an bollys parys **maseger** *kemer y dis der lescyans ov arluth* 'The bulls are ready. Messenger take them into your hands by my lord's licence' BM 2769-71

Maseger *wolcum yth os lemmen ens tus then guelfos the kerhes dyn meryasek* 'Messenger, you are welcome. Now let men go to the wilderness to fetch Meriasek to us' BM 2793-95

dus oma ov **maseger** *ha kergh uskys sylvester the covs gena a fur spas* 'come here, my messenger, and fetch Silvester to talk with me for a short while' BM 3977-79

Ow **maseger** *Cuf-e-Das, joy war the vody ha ras!* 'My messenger, Cuf-e-Das, joy and grace upon your person!' BK 876-77

Maseger, *pen canhasow, deugh 'rag in un thyena!* 'Messenger, chief of legates, come forth panting!' BK 2348-49.

It is clear from the above examples that **cannas** and **messejer** are sometimes used in the same passage to refer to the same person. Either is legitimate for use in the revived language.

MILLION

The default word for 'million' in revived Cornish appears to be **milvil** f. This is attested twice:

myl vyl *dyaul a vye guan er-y-byn ef* 'a million devils would be weak against him' RD 132-33

yth ese gynef moy ages **myl vyl** *enef yn bros pur dek* 'I had with me more than a million souls in a very nice broth' RD 140-42.

million

The word **milyon** 'million' is also attested:

*reys yw theugh mones certan the tenne pilat yn ban yn mes a'n dour gorreugh ef yn schath the'n mor and y schal yf yow ther for try **mylyon*** our 'you must go indeed to pull Pilate up out of the water. Put him in a boat going to the sea, and I will give you for him three million gold coins' RD 2253-58.

There is no reason to proscribe **milyon** 'million' in the revived language.

MIRACLE

For the noun 'miracle' Nance suggests A) **mêstry** (UC *maystry*); B) **marthus** and C) **myrakyl**. **Mêstry** does not really mean 'miracle', but rather 'great power, authority, domination'. This can be seen from the attested examples:

A) **mêstry**

*Ke ʒe ves omscumvnys ʒe ʒyveyth veth yn tewolgow the **vestry** a vyth leʒys neffre war an enevow* 'Depart, accursed one, to a wilderness into darkness; your power will be lessened for ever over souls' PA 17cd

*In meth crist o du ha den arte ʒy abestely golyough ha pesough yn ven rag own an ioul hay **vestry*** 'Christ, who was God and man, said again to his apostles, Watch and pray assiduously for fear of the devil and his power' PA 57ab

*Ha dew a thuk dustuny yn clewsons ow leuerell pur wyr y fenne terry an tempel cref hay wuʒell war lyrgh henna dre **vestry** yn tressa dyth heb fyllell dre nerth bras yn drehevy* 'And two bore witness that they had heard him indeed saying that he would break down the mighty temple and rebuild it on the third day by great power, without fail by might he would raise it up' PA 91a-d

*a ny woʒas ow **mestry** bos ʒymmo may fes leʒys bo delyffris ʒe wary* 'do you not know that I have authority to have you killed or released to freedom?' PA 144cd

*In meth Ihesus yn vrna **mestry** vyth te ny vea waraff ve drok vyth na da ken onan ʒys nan rolla* 'Jesus then said, You would have no authority over me, either good or bad, had not another One given it to you' PA 145ab

*beʒens ʒe ves defendis y vonas mygtern ʒynny ha beʒens ena gorris y fense bos dre **vestry*** 'let it be struck out that he is our king, and let it be put there that he wished to be by power' PA 188bc

*kyns yn ta ef a ylly tus a bup drok ol sawye lemmyn gans ol y **vestry** ragon ny wor omweʒe* 'before now he well could heal men of every ill; now with all his power he cannot protect himself from us' PA 194bc

*mars oge crist mab dauy des an grows heb pystege ha ny a grys ʒe **vestry** hag ad syns mester neffre* 'if you are Christ the son of David, come down from the cross unharmed and we will believe in your power, and will consider you master for ever' PA 197bc

GERYOW GWIR   miracle

yn vr na byth leuerys ef ʒe sevell dre **vestry** 'then it will be said that he has risen by power' PA 240d

vn eskar bras thy'm yma war ov thyr ov gul **mestry** 'I have a serious enemy threatening my kingdom' OM 2143-44

ty a verow sur cowal awos the thev nay **vestry** 'you will die utterly in spite of your God and his power' OM 2737

ay **vestry** *ef ny ren bram yn dyspyt th'y das hay vam an voren a vyth lethys* 'of his power I do not give a fart; the girl will be killed in spite of his father and mother' OM 2739-41

the **vestry** *a vyth leyhys neffre war an enevow* 'your power will be diminished for ever over souls' PC 143-44

ha'n **maystri** *bras ol a'm bo my re'n collas quyt dretho* 'and all the great power I had, I have lost it utterly through him' PC 148-49

maydes ihesu an guas prout re wruk re **maystry** *yn dre hagh ef thy'n re leuerys kyn fe an temple dyswrys yn tri dyth y'n dreafse* 'help! Jesus, the proud fellow, has been greatly bragging in the town and he has told us that though the temple were destroyed, in three days he would build it again' PC 362-66

ef re thyswrug an marhas yma ow kul **maystry** *bras rak mennas cafos enor* 'he has destroyed the market swaggering greatly, because he wanted to receive honour' PC 376-78

maras ose map dev mur dyeskyn a'n vynk the'n lur ha dyswe ran a'th **veystry** 'if you are the son of great God, come down from the ledge and show some of your power' PC 2867-69

ol agan **maystry** *me a grys ny daluyth bram* 'all our authority, I believe, will not be worth a fart' PC 3077-78

Me yv empour ha governour conquerrour tyr arluth worthy mur ov **mestry** 'I am an emperor and a governor, a conqueror of territory, a worthy lord; great is my authority' BM 930-34

The afles a bredireth, te fals goky, thymmo ve pan leveryth kymmys **mestry** *a'th Du gyntyl* 'You are thinking of your own detriment, you false idiot, when you speak to me of your noble God's so great power' BK 160-64

War ow horf mar qureth **maystry**, *mes a'n bys ma pan ylhy, te a'n kef war the forth hyr* 'If you exercise power over my body, when you depart from this life, you will in the long run suffer for it' BK 582-84

Drys Bryttyn rag ow onor ha der **vestry** *ha der wyr me a'm byth ef* 'Over Britain for my honour and by power and by right I shall have it' BK 1645-47.

It is, I think, apparent from these examples, that **mêstry** does not mean 'miracle', and can therefore be left out of consideration here.

Marthus *m.*, does mean 'miracle, wonder'. The plural **marthusow** can also have singular sense:

B **marthus**

vn flough yonk gwyn y ʒyllas eyll o ha y ny woʒyens scruth own mur askemeras rag an **marthus** *re welsens* 'they saw a young child in white raiment. He was an angel and they did

291

miracle

not know it. Horror, fear overcame them, because of the miracle they had witnessed' PA 254cd

mars os dev a nef golow dysqua lemman **marthusow** *may allyf vy y weles* 'if you are God from bright heaven, show me as miracle now, so that I may perceive it' PC 81-3.

There is another (possibly) plural word, however, **marthùsyon, marthùjyon, marthujyon** which means 'wonder, wonders; astonishment' and also 'astonishing':

C **marthùsyon, marthùjyon, marthujyon**

ov arluth myghtern salmon yma mur a **varthogyon** *a'n keth gyst ma warvethys* 'my lord, king Solomon, much astonishment has occurred through this same beam' OM 2545-47

a a arluth ker bynyges yma thy'm mur **varthegyon** *pyv a yl henna bones ahanan ny vyth onon* 'Oh, oh, dear blessed Lord, I am greatly astonished who that can be. It will not be one of us' PC 769-72

bos trest thywhy pendra wher ha ponfosyk agas cher mayth ough serrys nag ues ioy yges colon lemyn dar nep **marthegyon** *vs wharfethys* 'what has happened to you to be sad and your mood downcast that you are angry, so there is no joy in your hearts, except some wonder has occurred?' RD 1255-60

Kepar dell rug an tas a neff dre wondres **marthugian** *hag aneth forth gull Adam an kynsa den bethqueth a ve in kepare maner eff a rug Eva in strang maner a forth* 'Just as the Father of heaven by remarkable wonder and supernatural way made Adam, the first man who ever was, similarly he made Eve in a strange way and manner' TH 2a

han kythsam tra na a alsa bos **marthuggian**, *pan esa kyffrys bartholomew ha nychodemus present, hag y a welas an oberow a crist ha inweth a glowas y dyscans* 'and that same thing might have been remarkable, when both Bartholomew and Nicodemus were present, and they saw the works of Christ and also heard his teaching' TH 37a-38

yma S Cyrill ow commondya thetha sessia heb gull **marthussyan** *crist the ry power an par na* 'St Cyril recommends that they cease to marvel that Christ bestowed power like that' TH 38a

Ith ew **marthussyan** *the welas fatell rug an re na esans y ow kemeras rag aga doctors bras, ha scollmeisters, y a rug aga abusia, seducia, ha ga mockya, evyn in kethsame mater ma an primace* 'It is remarkable to see that those whom they took as their great doctors and schoolmasters, they abused, seduced and mocked them, even in this same matter of the primacy' TH 49a

hemma yth ew **marrudgyan** *bras yth esaf ow pose gorthys ny won pylea* 'this is a great wonder; I am being carried I know not whither' CW 2124-26.

The commonest word for 'miracle' in the texts is **merkyl** *m.*, *plural* **merclys**:

D **merkyl**

toul an welen ol yn tyen the'n dor vskys ty a wylfyth sur yn pyrfyth **merkyl** *tek gurys* 'throw the rod entirely to the earth quickly; indeed you will see a fine miracle perfectly done' OM 1447-50

yma tregys in cambron den ov cul **merclys** *dyson* 'there lives in Camborne a man who does miracles indeed' BM 687-88

na ve y vose guir sans mar lues **merkyl** *dyblans byth ny russe* 'were he not a true saint, he would indeed not perform so many miracles' BM 2051-53

ledyogh vy the veryasek me re glowes galosek y vose in y **verclys** 'lead me to Meriasek. I have heard that he is mighty in his miracles' BM 2525-27

ha pan rug an bobyll gull mur aneth an **myrakyll** *na, Pedyr a rug ena thetha narracion* 'and when the people wondered greatly at that miracle, Peter there gave them an account' TH 45

an consent a mar lyas ha mar ver pobill, nacions, ha gwlasow a ra gwetha an auctorite an egglos, ow talleth gans **myraclis**, *norysshys gans govenek, encresshys gans charite, ha confyrmys gans antiquite* 'the consent of so many and so great peoples, nations and countries will keep the authority of the Church, beginning with miracles, nourished by hope, enlarged by charity and confirmed by antiquity' TH 49

Du re vynnas ragon ny guthyl **marclus** *pur thefry* 'God has wished to do miracles for us very truly' BK 861-62

MERKYL 'a miracle' ACB: T 2 *verso.*

For 'miracle' the best terms are **marthus** and **merkyl**.

MONEY

For 'money' Nance recommended **arhans** (UC *arghans*), and for the most part revivalists have followed him. Unfortunately Nance was mistaken, since **arhans** in traditional Cornish does not mean 'money' but 'silver'. I have collected the following examples:

A **arhans** 'silver'

Alene yn hombronkyas vghell war ben vn meneth ha 3030 y tysquethas owr hag **arghans** *gwels ha gweth* 'From there he led him high up to the summit of a mountain and showed him gold and silver, grass and trees' PA 16ab

an **arghans** *a gemeras rag corf crist ʒe rysseve ef as tewlys dre sor bras ʒen eʒewon yntreʒe* 'the silver he accepted to receive for the body of Christ, he threw them in great wrath at the Jews among them' PA 103bc

fenten bryght avel **arhans** *ha pedyr streyth vras defry ov resek adyworty* 'a bright spring like silver and four great streams indeed flowing from it' OM 771-73

yn enour the'n pren may fe my a vyn bos garlont gureys a **arhans** *adro thethe rag gothvos pyt vo y hys* 'so that it might be an honour for the tree, I desire that a garland of silver be made around it to know what is its width' OM 2095-98

money   GERYOW GWIR

nyns us gyst vyth ol hep wow vas the dra vyth sur ragtho nag yn wlas ma yn nep pow saw vn pren gans garlontow a **arhans** *adro thotho* 'there is no beam at all inded good for anything about it either in this kingdom or in any country apart from a tree with silver garlands about it' OM 2496-500

aban nag vs ken maner an **arhans** *kettep dyner me a's deghes war an luer* 'since there is not other way I will hurl every penny of the silver onto the floor' PC 1513-15

en **arhans** *me a gymer hagh a's guyth kettep dyner yn certan rak an termyn* 'I will take the [pieces of] silver and will keep them, every penny, indeed for the time' PC 1537-39

awos cost **arhans** *nag our greugh y tenne mes a'n dour* 'in spite of the cost of silver or gold, pull it out of the water' RD 2231-32

An pelle **arrance** *ma ve resse, gen mere hurleyey, creve, ha brasse, do Wella Gwavas, an deane gentle* 'This silver ball was given by many strong and great hurlers to William Gwavas, the gentleman' BF: 38

Kymero 'wyth goz lavrak pouz goz **argan**, *ha guz aur* 'Take care of your heavy trousers, you silver and your gold' BF: 58.

The word for 'money' in traditional Cornish is **mona**:

B **mona** 'money'

Iudas fals a leuerys trehans dynar a **vone** *en box oll beȝens gwerthys avos den rag y ranne the vohosogyon yn bys* 'False Judas said, 300 pence of money, let the whole box be sold for man's sake to share it among the poor of the world' PA 36a-c

y fons vnver yn treȝe kepar ha del wovyny xxx a **vone** *yn vn payment y wrens ry* 'They were agreed among themselves, that as a payment, just as he asked, they would give 30 pieces of money' PA 39cd

ow box mennaf the terry a dal mur a **vone** *da war the pen y thenewy ha war the treys magata* 'I will break my box, which is worth much good money, pour it over your head and on your feet also' PC 485-88

dek warn ugens a **mone** *me ny vennaf cafus le yn guyryoneth* 'thirty pieces of money; I will not accept less in truth' PC 593-95

me re peghes marthys trus guyr gos dev pan y'n guyrthys rak henna an guella vs dascor myns **mone** *yv pys* 'I have sinned very perversely, when I bartered God's blood; therefore the best thing is to relinquish all the money that has been paid' PC 1505-08

ha my a's pren thyworthy's otte an **mone** *parys thy'so the pe* 'and I will buy it from you; here is the money ready for you' PC 1555-57

ha me a vyn then benenes ry **mona** *boys ha dewes the perna* 'and I will give the women money to buy food and drink' BM 1671-73

Nans yv preys aspya pray due yv an **mona** *rum fay* 'Now is the time to look for plunder; the money is gone, by my faith' BM 1872-73

Me a weyl guas in gon hyr pronter ef a hevel suyr yma **mona** *gans henna* 'I see a fellow in a long gown; he certainly appears to be a priest; that man has money' BM 1902-04

sav dascor ol the **vona** *boannyl the quartona oma me a ra heb let* 'but hand over all your money or I'll cut you into quarters here without hesitation' BM 1917-19

GERYOW GWIR   **mortal**

Ith ew scryffys in viii-as chapter in actys an appostolis fatell rug Symon magus offra the ry **mona** *the pedyr mar mynna pedyr ry power thotheff, penagull person a rella eff ha gora y thewleff warnotha may teffans ha receva an spurissans* 'It is written in the eighth chapter of the Acts of the Apostles that Simon Magus offered to give Peter money, if he would give him power, that whoever he laid his hands on would receive the Holy Spirit' TH 46a

I costyans showre a **vona** *an keth tacklowe es omma* 'They cost a lot of money, the same things that are here' CW 2445-46

Nenna dzhei a dorhaz an dezan, ha thera nâu penz en dezan. Ha an **mona** *andzhei a gavaz; ha'n bara dzhei a dhabraz* 'Then they broke the cake, and there were nine pounds in the cake. And the money they got and the bread they ate' BF: 19

Loan Blethan Noueth, ha bennen joungk; ha **mona** *lour gans goz gureg* 'Happy New Year and a young wife and enough money with your wife' BF: 45

Ni venja pea a **munna** *seer ez boaze whelees car thurt an tir* 'We would certainly pay the money that is being sought from far afield' LAM: 226

Dry dre an **mona**, *ha perna muy* 'Bring home the money and buy more' ACB: F f *verso*
Pecunia... Money, coin, a sum of money, money's worth, one's whole estate or revenue. C. **Monnah** AB: 115c.

In the light of the above examples, it might be wise perhaps for revivalists to use **mona** for 'money', and to confine the use of **arhans** to 'silver'.

MORTAL

For 'mortal' Nance suggested ***marwyl**, which is not attested. For 'immortal' he suggested ***dyvarow**, which is not attested either. The attested words are **mortal** and **imortal**:

A **mortal**

ha remembra agan **mortall** *genesegeth a russyn kemeras theworth Adam an kynsa den a ve gwrys* 'and to remember our mortal birth, which we received from Adam the first man who was created' TH 6a

may hallan bos delyuerys theworth an miserabill stat ha captiuite a veny ynna towlys dre agan **mortall** *yskar an teball ell* 'so that we can be delivered from the miserable estate and captivity that we were thrown into by our mortal enemy, the devil' TH 10

an second person in dryngys du o ymmortall, eff a ve den **mortall**, *hag yth o gwrys in pub part kepar hag onyn ahanan ny* 'the second person in God the Trinity was immortal, he became a mortal man, and was made in every way like one of us' TH 15

wosa an tyrmyn cut a vethyn ny omma in present ha **mortall** *bewnans ma, ny an gevith ganso eff eternall bewnans* 'after the short time that we shall be here in this present and mortal life, we shall have with him eternal life' TH 26

Praga na russyn ny kyns y ymbrasia, ha ry grace the thu ragtha, rag y bosa an moyha precius jewall, han brassa, bythqueth a ve in myske pobill **mortall**? 'Why did we not rather

295

embrace it, and give thanks to God for it, since it is the most precious jewel, and the greatest that ever was among mortal people?' TH 54a.

B **imortal**
parda ef a rug an ena **immortall**, *hen ew tra an parna a rella contenewa neffra heb deweth* 'indeed he made the soul immortal, that is something of the kind that will continue for ever without end' TH 2a

an second person in dryngys du o **ymmortall**, *eff a ve den mortall, hag yth o gwrys in pub part kepar hag onyn ahanan ny* 'the second person in God the Trinity was immortal, he became a mortal man, and was made in every way like one of us' TH 15.

TO MOVE, MOVEMENT, MOTION

The verb **gwaya** is both transitive and intransitive and means 'to move' in a physical sense:

A **gwaya**
Ny a vyn y carhara purguir na ala **guaya** *na luff na troys* 'we will shackle him indeed so that he can move neither hand nor foot' BM 3573-75

Hy rum lathes gans hy gwyns re vahum wek pen an sens alemma num bus **gvaya** 'She has killed me with her breath by sweet Mahound, chief of the saints; from now on I shall not be able to move' BM 4096-98

mar teffa an holl brodereth obeya according then commondmentys a thu, ny vynsa den vith styrrya na **gwaya** *warbyn an colleges* 'if the entire brotherhood had obeyed the commandments of God, no one would have stirred or moved against the colleges' TH 42a

ha kepar ha men po carrak na yll bos **gwayys**, *eff a rug contynewa ha gwetha an fram han weight an holl egglos a crist* 'and like a stone or rock that cannot be moved, he continued and supported the frame and the weight of all the Church of Christ' TH 45a-46

mar pe an holl fraternity han bredereth, according then commondement a thu, obedient, ny vynsa den vyth **gwaya** *na styrrya warbyn an brederneth a crist* 'had the whole fraternity and brotherhood, according to the commandment of God, been obedient, nobody would have moved or stirred against the brotherhood of Christ' TH 48a

ha spiriz Deu reeg **guaya** *var budgeth an dour* 'and the spirit of God moved upon the face of the water' BF: 51

ha kanifer es **guaya** *var an aor* 'and everything which moves upon the earth' BF: 53.

The substantive 'move, movement' is rendered by ***gway**, **gwayow**:

Th'agan palas gwel ew thyn revertya gans cannow tek ha predery, ren Austyn! a'gen **gwayow** 'It is better for us to return to our palace with beautiful songs and to consider, by St Augustine, about our moves' BK 2061-64.

The verb **muvya**, **môvya** 'to move' is used in a metaphorical sense:

move

B **muvya**, **môvya**

*ihesus crist a ve **mevijs** may fynnas dijskynna yn gwerhas ha bos genys gans y gyk agan perna* 'Jesus Christ was moved so that he wished to descend into a Virgin and be born, to redeem us by his flesh' PA 4b-d

*my a vyn kyns es dybarth **muvya** omma certan tra rag dader hag honester 3e varyasek* 'I will before leaving move a certain matter for goodness and decency to Meriasek' BM 259-62

*Rag an scriptur ny theth bethqueth dre an blonogeth a then, mas tus benegas a gowses kepar dell ens y **moviis** dre an spuris sans* 'For never did the scripture come by the will of man, but blessed men spoke as they were moved by the Holy Spirit' TH 18

*So pella agys henna, omma y thyll bos **movyes** questyon* 'But more than that I will here move a question' TH 29a

*Surely, ny vynsan cresy an aweyll, na ve an Catholyk egglos the ry thym experiens, ha ow **movya** thotha* 'Certainly I should not believed if the catholic Church had not given me experience, and moved me to it' TH 37a

*Rag henna yth ewa scriffys in kynsa chapter in actus appostolus, fatell rug pedyr in contynent awosa an ascencion a crist sevall in ban in cres an elect pobyll han feithfull, thega **movya** y the thewys onyn rag bos in rome esa Judas ynna* 'Therefore it is written in the first chapter of the Acts of the Apostles, that Peter stood up in the assembly after the ascension of Christ in the midst of the elect and faithful people to move them to choose someone to fill the vacancy left by Judas' TH 44a

*An kynsa tra vsy worth ow **movya** ve the predery ha the cresy, an epscop a rom the vos pen war oll re erall* 'The first thing which moves me to consider and to believe that the bishop of Rome is the head over all the others' TH 50.

Curiously **remuvya** 'to remove' is used in a physical sense:

C **remuvya**

*botler my a worhemnyn ha'th cowyth guytheugh why y ma na vons yn nep maner **remmvys** the gen tyller* 'butler, I command you and your companion: guard them, so that they are not by any means removed to another place' OM 2042-46

*Emperour na myghtern glas na sodon kyn fo mar vras a fyl aga **remmvve*** 'Emperor nor king of a country, nor a sultan, be he never so great, will fail to remove them' OM 2055-57

*yn certan mar **remvfe** y pen crak me a torse kyn couse vyth mar huhel* 'certainly, if he removes his head, bang, I would break it, though he speaks never so haughtily' RD 396-98.

The substantive **remôcyon**, however, appears to mean 'promotion':

*Bohogogneth abreth du **remoconn** then cur yth yv wose helma* 'Poverty in God's name is promotion to the court of heaven hereafter' BM 2010-12.

No word for 'motion' is attested in the texts, however.

MURDER, TO MURDER, MURDERER

The substantive 'murder' is rendered in Middle Cornish by **denlath**. By the sixteenth century, however, this appears to have given way to **mùrder**. [**Denlath** can also mean 'murderer(s)'; see below.]

A **denlath**

*Onon esa yn preson barabas yth o gylwys presonys o ef dre dreyson ha rag **denlath** kekyffris* 'One who was in prison, he was called Barabbas. He had been imprisoned for treason and also for murder' PA 124ab.

B **mùrder**

*envy, **murdyr**, methewnep, glotny ha re an par ma* 'envy, murder, drunkenness, gluttony and things of this kind' TH 16a

*An chiff poynt a ra den tyrry charite ew **murdyr**, han punisment a henna yn myske an Jewys o judgment* 'The greatest way in which a man violates charity is murder, and the punishment for that among the Jews was judgement' TH 27

*yma crist warth y declarya the vos fowt bras ha grevos war y wull equall ha kepar ha **murder*** 'Christ declares it to be a great and grievous fault, making it equal and like murder' TH 28a

*nyng es dean vytholl in byes tha wythell an kethe **murder** mes te haw mabe cotha cayne* 'there is no one in all the world to do the same murder apart from you and my eldest son, Cain' CW 1250-52

*gansa y ny vyth ankevys an **murder** bys venary* 'by them the murder will not be forgotten ever' CW 1348-49

*rag an **murder** o mar vrase ny yll dew thymo gava* 'for the murder was so great that God cannot forgive me' CW 1365-66.

'To murder' as distinct from **ladha** 'to kill', is rendered in traditional Cornish by **moldra**:

*yma debron thum ij vregh mar bel ov boys ov powes heb **moldra** an crustunyon* 'there is an itch in my arms that I have been so long refraining from murdering the Christians' BM 1187-89

*eff a ra prest the golhy may festa sav eredy heb **moldra** flogh vyth in bys* 'he will readily wash you so that you may be healed without murdering any child at all' BM 1716-18

*Dar, ny worthebys mynrew prag e **fuldrys** ow cosyns ha subjectia neb a bew ow thyr!* 'What, did the greaybeard not answer why he murdered my kinsmen and subject those who possess my land!' BK 2285-88.

'Murderer' can be rendered by **denledhyas**:

*Neb a rella seperatya vn den, theworth an holl, the part vith, eff ow provys the vos flogh an teball ell, ha very **denleythyas*** 'Whoever separates one man from the whole to any part, he is proven to be the child of the devil and a very murderer' TH 32a.

It is noteworthy that **denlath** 'murder' can also be used to mean both 'murderer' and 'murderers':

*Dauid ny wreth thy'mo chy yn certen bys venary the vos **denlath** yv anken ty re thyswrug eredy hevelep tho'm face vy vrry nep o marrek len* 'David, you will not build my house for me indeed for ever. It is a grief that you are a murderer. You have killed indeed a likeness to my face, Uriah, who was a faithful soldier' OM 2333-38

*nyns ew mas kepar dell ra an laddron, advltrers, **denlath**, hag oll an drog pobill erell* 'it is no different from what is done by thieves, adulterers, murderers, and all the other evil people' TH 24.

MUST

The Cornish word **res** (UC *res*) means 'necessity', and can be used with parts of the verb *bos* 'to be' to express the idea 'I must, you must, he must,' etc. Here are some examples from the texts:

A **res yw**

*yn meth pylat worth an myns an pegh peuas **ris yv** ry* 'Pilate said, the reward must be given in proportion to the sin' PA 117c

*gorhemmyn dev dres pup tra **res yv** y vos coullenwys* 'the commandment of God must be fulfilled above all things' OM 654-55

*yn cres a'n chy **res vye** kafus gyst cref na vo guan* 'in the middle of the house one would have to find a strong beam that would not be weak' OM 2481-82

***res yv** thy'so y thyffras kemerr'y a thysempys* 'you must relieve him; take it immediately' PC 2619-20

*Siluester lowena dys then emperour dones uskys **reys yv** thywy in certeyn* 'Hail to you, Silvester. You must come to the emperor quickly indeed' BM 3986-88

*A remembrance, **a vea res** thetha bos, in keth sacrament na rag an marow* 'Of remembrance, that it should be made in that same sacrament for the dead' SA 66

*An gorhemmyn ew henna, ha **ris ew** gul e thevys war bayn cregy ha tenna* 'The commandment is this, and one must perform his ordinance on pain of being hanged and drawn' BK 2373-75.

Res is also a defective impersonal verb in the present-future:

B **y res**, **ny res**

*lays es yn pow adro may **rys** y laʒe yn scon mygtern neb a omwrello* 'there are laws in the surrounding country that it is necessary soon to kill anyone who claims to be a king' PA 121cd

*Ena pylat a gewsys yndelma ʒen eʒewon me ny won bonas kyfys yn den ma byth acheson may **rys** y vonas leʒys* 'Then Pilate spoke thus to the Jews, I know no reason to have been found in this man for which he must be killed' PA 141a-c

must   **GERYOW GWIR**

An debel dus a gewsys ʒynny sur yma laha may **rys** *y vonas leʒys rag mab du ef a omwra* 'The evil men spoke, We indeed have a law by which he must be killed because he claims to be the son of God' PA 143ab

Cafes moy thy's aban **res** *try heys the bal kemery* 'Since you must have more, take three spade lengths' OM 391-92

serry orthyf ny **res** *thy's* 'you do not have to be angry with me' OM 2524

gothe mernans dyn **a reys** *byth ny yller y sconya ov bredereth* 'we must suffer death; it cannot be denied for ever, my brethren' BM 1753-55

ny remembrons an charych **a reys** *dethe ry harlych therag crist pan deer then vrueys* 'they do not remember the charge that they must give exactly, when one comes before Christ to judgement' BM 2831-33

ny **res** *the then vith bos deseviis* 'no man need be deceived' TH 25a

ny **res** *desquethes theugh an plagys a russyn ny suffra a thea leff du ragtha* 'there is no need to demonstrate to you the plagues we have suffered from the hand of God for it' TH 51

ny **res** *thynny dowtya an pith a rug eff ry* 'there is no need for us to doubt what he gave' TH 52

Gans gweras theworta ef ny **rys** *thymmo bos ameys* 'With assistance from him I need not be dismayed' BK 1178-79

Ni **rys** *this ow congurya!* 'You do not need to beseech me' BK 2364

Ny **res** *theugh bos duwenyk awos lavarow drog-den* 'You need not be wretched because of an evil man's utterance' BK 2659-60.

From the earliest period **res** can also be a personal verb and thus can follow a noun or personal pronoun.

C *me a res

penys **a reys** *ragh y terros may fo leheys mvr a y gallos* 'fasting is necessary against his destruction so that much of his power may be reduced' PC 43-44

ow dyskyblon ysethough hag omma pols powesough hedre vyma ov pygy ol sav peder ha jamys ha johann an try **a reys** *mones gynef yredy* 'my disciples sit and rest awhile here, while I am praying, you all but Peter, James and John; the three must go with me indeed' PC 1011-16

guyryoneth **a reys** *bos dreys aberueth yn mater ma* 'the truth must be brought into this matter' PC 2447-48

pendra leuer an podren **a reys** *dym mones dotho* 'what does the wretch say? Must I go to him?' BM 3323-24

Rag why **a res** *vnderstondia ha cresy fatell ew an dewses spuris ha not substans a corffe* 'For you must believe and understand that the Godhead is spirit, not substance of body' TH 1a

crist **a res** *in pub poynt oll bos havall thy bredereth* 'Christ must in every point be like his brethren' TH 13

han offendars **a res** *bos rebukys ha correctys in dew tyrmyn* 'and the offenders must be rebuked and corrected in due time' TH 25a

*Rag an kythsame ii cawse ma ny cristonyan **a res** thyn supposia an yocke a crist the vois wheg* 'For these two same causes we Christians must consider that the yoke of Christ is sweet' TH 28

*why **a res** theugh gothfas an presens agan sauyour Jhesu crist in kith sacrament ma an aulter* 'you must know the presence of our Saviour Jesus Christ in this same sacrament of the altar' TH 55a

*Te **a res** thys lavurrya bys o'm arluth desempys* 'You must travel to my lord immediately' BK 1047-48.

Notice that the personal verb, e.g. **me a res** is on occasion followed by the prepositional pronoun, **me a res dhybm**.

Res as a personal verb also has an imperfect form **resa**.

*ha pan ruga colynwell pub tra according then scriptur han prophetes, an pith **a resa** bos colynwys anotheff the rag y pascion, nena eff a suffras myrnans colonnek* 'and when he had completed everything according to the scriptures and the prophest, that which had to be fulfilled by him before his passion, then he suffered a willing death' TH 15.

'I must' can either be **res yw dhybm** or **me a res**. 'I need not' can be rendered **ny res dhybm**. When one wants to say 'one really must, it is essential' the words **res** and **porres** are used. When **porres** is used with **res**, **res** is either the noun 'necessity' as in A above, or the defective verb as in B above or a personal verb as in C above.

D res + porres

*Mas lemmyn **rys yv porris** batayles kyns ys coske* 'But now it is essential to do battle before sleeping' PA 51a

reys yw porris heb strevye both ow ʒas ʒe vos sewijs 'it is esssential that my Father's will be followed without struggling' PA 73d

rys yw porris ʒe onon merwel rag pobyl an wlas 'it is essential that one should die for the people of the land' PA 89c

*rag sustene veuans thy'n **rys yw porrys** lafurrye* 'to sustain our life it is very necessary for us to work' OM 682-83

res yv porrys an sprus ma pan dremenna an bys ma yn y anow bos gorrys 'it is essentially that these pips be put in his mouth when he passes from this world' OM 874-76

rays yw purryes lavyrrya ha gones an beise omma 'it is essentially to work and to cultivate the earth here' CW 1079-80

*Rag **porrys rys o** ʒoʒo gase y ben ʒe gregy* 'For it was unavoidable for him to let his head hang' PA 207a

*reys yv y wruthyl **porrys*** 'it is essential to do it' OM 648

*rys yv thy'm **porrys** coske possygyon yn pen yma* 'I really must sleep for there is heaviness in my head' OM 1905-06

*reys yv y vos guyr **porrys*** 'it is really necessary that it be true' PC 1074

*ha me [a] wra y iugge aban **reys** thy'mmo **porrys*** 'and I will judge him since it is esstential for me' PC 2226-27

must GERYOW GWIR

*Eff **a res purris bos** y very corfe eff hay gois in dede* 'It must of necessity be his very body and his blood indeed' TH 52.

Nance suggests that **porres** is a compound of **pur**, **pòr** 'very, utter' and **res** 'necessity'. It might also be for ***par res** 'by necessity, perforce'. With **par** 'by, through' compare: *the ʒerevas **par** lauarow* 'to tell by words' PA 1c; *evough why **par** cheryta 'drink by charity'* PA 47b; ***par** hap y wrussen fye* 'by chance I might flee' OM 1352. Certainly when **porres** is attested by itself it is an adverb meaning 'of necessity':

*rag Ihesus crist ʒen mernans y a vynne **porrys** dry* 'for they wished to bring Jesus Christ to his death by necessity' PA 117b
*En eʒewon a vynne **porrys** y vonas leʒys* 'The Jews wished that he would perforce be killed' PA 118a
*ytho why a vyn **porrys** bos agas myghtern crousys* 'therefore you wish of necessity that your king be crucified' PC 2359-60.

Any of the three **res yw porres**, **y res porres** and **ev a res porres** is legitimate in the revived language.

N

NATION
For 'nation' Nance recommended **kenedhel** (UC *kenethel*). The word **kenedhel** is unattested in Middle Cornish, being a respelling from Old Cornish: *generatio*, **kinethel** 'generation' OCV §159. *Generatio* in Latin, however, does not mean 'nation', but rather 'generation, family; procreation, begetting.' The attested word for 'nation' in Cornish is **nacyon** *m.*, *plural* **nacyons**:

*kyn nag o ov poscessyon bras in meske sur ov **nascyon** me ren moghheys eredy* 'although my possessions were not indeed great among my nation, I have extended them truly' BM 2400-02

*densa ath conuersascon purguir yth oys aconty hag in meske ol the **nasconn** henwys oys pronter grassijs* 'right truly you are considered a good man in your converse and you have been called a gracious priest among all your nation' BM 2547-50

*densa dy conuersasconn sur in mesk ol y **nascon** ny a wor guir y vose* 'surely I know that he is a good man of his converse truly among all his nation' BM 2917-19

*Densa ath conuersasconn ty yv in meske the **nascon** ha sevys an gois worthy* 'A good man among your converse you are among your nation and sprung from noble blood' BM 2944-46

*lemen pen oys theth **nasconn*** 'now you are the chief of your nation' BM 3016

*pensevyk yv thy **nascon** mentenour fay crustunyon socour the lues huny* 'he is a prince to his nation, the defender of the Christian faith, succour to many' BM 3022-24

*Fy dis hag oll theth **nasconn** fy mylwyth then crustunyon* 'Fie to you and all your nation! A thousand times fie to the Christians!' BM 3509-10

*Du a wrappyas pub **nacion** in discregyans may halla eff kafus mercy war oll* 'God wrapped every nation in unbelief that he might have mercy upon all' TH 7a

*In the haes thege oll an **nacions** an bys a veth benegys* 'In your seed all the nations shall be blessed' TH 13

*lyas barbarus **nacion**, ow crege in crist, a ra ry crygyans heb screffa vith arell na scriptur mas an pith vs scriffis in aga colonow* 'many barbarous nations believe without any other writing or scripture than what is written in their hearts' TH 19

*Mar teffa den vith ha pregoth thyn kythsame barbarus **nacions** ma in aga eyth y aga honyn... y a vynsa stoppya aga scovurnow* 'If anyone were to preach to these same barbarous nations in their own language... they would stop up their ears' TH 19

nation GERYOW GWIR

Agan Savyour dre I thevyne skeans a rug percevya fatell o va necessary the onyn bos vgh an holl multytude an pith o, hag ew, numbyr a lyas **nacion** 'Our Saviour by his divine wisdom perceived that it was necessary for one to be over the multitude, what was, and is, a number of many nations' TH 44a

an consent a mar lyas ha mar ver pobill, **nacions**, *ha gwlasow a ra gwetha an auctorite an egglos* 'the consent of so many and so great peoples, nations and countries will preserve the authority of the Church' TH 49

Nebas e won ow **nacion** *i'n bys ma* 'Little I know my nation in this world' BK 35-36

ha re Astrot ha Jovyn in dyspyt the'th **nassyoyn**, *the vaw the honen a'th crog* 'and by Astrot and Jovyn in spite of your nation your own servant will hang you' BK 464-66

Lowena arag **nation** *theso drys an re erall!* 'Hail before the nation to you beyond the others!' BK 1988-89.

Nacyon is attested 16 times and in three different texts, while **kenedhel** is unknown in Middle Cornish and does not mean 'nation', but 'generation.' **Nacyon** should perhaps therefore be the ordinary word for 'nation' in the revived language.

NEVER, EVER

Cornish, like the other Celtic languages, distinguishes '(n)ever' in the past from '(n)ever' in the future. In Irish, for example one says:

A 'never' in the past
Níor chuala mé a leithéid de sheafóid **riamh** 'I have never heard such nonsense'
B 'never' in the future
Ní dhéanfaidh mé dearmad air **go deo** 'I will never forget it'

and in Welsh one says:

A 'never' in the past
Ni chlywais **erioed** *y fath lol* 'I have never heard such nonsense'
B 'never' in the future
Ni anghofiaf i **byth** *mohono* 'I will never forget it.'

In Cornish '(n)ever' in the past is **bythqweth** (later **byscath**), whereas '(n)ever' in the future is **nefra**, and the distinction is maintained until the death of the language at the end of the eighteenth century:

A **nefra** 'ever, never'
yn meȝens y nyn gorȝyn na ny goth thyn y worȝye na ken mygtern ny venyn ys Cesar caffos **neffre** 'they said, We do not revere him nor should revere him nor will we ever have any king but Caesar' PA 148cd

GERYOW GWIR   never

pub er te ʒen gura lewte be va den yonk bo den coth orʒaff mar mynnyth cole **neffre** *gans an fals na soth* 'you man, whether he be young or old, show loyalty; if you will listen to me, never be employed by a false man' PA 175cd

mars oge crist mab dauy des an grows heb pystege ha ny a grys ʒe vestry hag ad syns mester **neffre** 'if you are Christ the son of David, come from the cross unharmed and we will believe in your power and will ever consider you master' PA 197bc

adam plos a thesefse warnan conquerrye **neffre** *lemyn ef yv agan guas* 'vile Adam, who would have hoped to lord it over us for ever, now he is our servant' OM 908-10

Noe rag kerenge orthy's my ny gemere **neffre** *trom dyal war ol an beys na dre thyal pup lathe* 'Noah, for your sake I shall never unannounced take vengeance upon all the world nor by vengeance kill everybody' OM 1207-10

war gas vy the thehesy gans morben bom trewysy the'n vyl hora war an taal **neffre** *na wrello dybry lemyn flerye ha peddry kepar ha seym py lyys haal* 'watch out! Let me let strike with a mallet a nasty blow upon the vile whore on the forehead, so never will she eat, but stink and rot like fish oil or marsh mud' OM 2703-08

gans an eleth yw golow yn nef agas enefow **neffre** *a tryg hep ponow yn ioy na vyth dywythys* 'with the angels who are bright your souls will dwell for ever without pain in everlasting joy' PC 6-9

neffre *ef the thasserghy me ny fynnaf y grygy bew hedre ven* 'as long as I live I will never believe that he has risen' RD 1046-48

mar ny wreta y crygy byth ny thueth **neffre** *the'n ioy sur vs yn nef* 'if you do not believe, never will you come to the joy indeed which is in heaven' RD 1088-90

yn vr na ny reys thy'nny na den byth ol yn teffry caffus **neffre** *na moy ovn* 'then we or any other man do not need ever to fear any more' RD 2169-70

ny fylleth hedre ven bev ath porpos gene **neffra** 'you will not ever fail in your purpose by me as long as I live' BM 55-6

lowena ʒum mam defry enour ha dader **neffra** 'greetings to my mother indeed and kindness always' BM 209-10

us dour omma in oges rag **nefre** *nahen dewes nyns a om ganov defry* 'is there water near here, for never will any other drink enter my mouth indeed' BM 655-57

thys best me a worhemyn moys then guelfos gans mab den na ra mellya **nefra** *awose helma* 'to thee, beast, I command to go into the wilderness; do not henceforward interfere with mankind ever' BM 1126-29

dre an yeattys a effarne, yma eff ow menya error avell pan lavarra eff, an egglos catholyk **neffra** *ny vith ouercommys gans error* 'by the gates of hell he means error, as though he were saying that the catholic Church will never be overcome by error' TH 17a

rag heresy, pub vr a rug hag a ra raynya, ha bys worfan an bys, kepar dell rug athewethas tevy ha raynya, ha inweth lurkya in cornettyow priveth, so **neffra** *agry gonsa y honyn* 'for heresy always did and will reign, and until the end of the world, as it recently grew up and reigned, and also lurked in private corners, but will never agree with itself' TH 34a

hag eff a groweth in ascra y vam egglos, hag eff a vith sure na ra crist, an very spowse a sans egglos **neffra** *y ankevy* 'and he will lie in the bosom of his mother Church, and he will be sure that Christ, the very spouse of holy Church, will never forget him' TH 39a

never

[*h*]*enna ew tha leverall, pana haker ew agen substance ny derag Dew an nef, an ena mab den,* **neffra** *sawis mase dir criggyans da* 'that is to say, How disfigured is our substance before God of heaven; the soul of mankind never saved but through good faith' SA 60a

Me a lever, ru'm besow! **neffra** *ny'n gevyth esow a venna Du e weras* 'I declare by my ring! Never will he experience want whom God wishes to help' BK 873-75

Erna vony unwerhys, **neffra** *ny veth da ow cher* 'Until we are reconciled, never will my mood improve' BK 1035-66

The omthegyans ew worthy comtys in mysk arlythy. **Neffra** *ny vyth ankevys* 'Your behaviour is considered noble among lords. Never will it be forgotten' BK 1615-17

Mar kowsyth moy a Arthor o'm goith ve, te fals bribor! **neffra** *ny thibbryth bara* 'If you speak more of Arthur in my presence, you false vagabond, never will you eat bread' BK 3185-87

neffra *na thowt a henna adam wheak ow harenga* 'never be afraid about that, Adam, my love' CW 753-54

rag henna woʒa hemma **nefra** *ny wren rejoycya mes pub ere oll ow murnya heb ioy vyth na lowena der tha wadn ober omma* 'therefore after this never will we rejoice, but always we'll be mourning without any joy or gladness because of your evil deed here' CW 1271-75

rag yth ota droge eball na vyn **nefra** *bonas vase* 'for you are an evil colt who will never be any good' CW 2398-99

rag mar vras yw dallethys **neffra** *ny vithe dowethis me an to war ow honssyans* 'for so large is it begun, it will never be finished, I swear upon my conscience' CW 2406-08

Ne vedn e **nevra** *dvz vês a ȝyndan* 'He'll never get out of debt' AB: 230c.

B **bythqweth** 'never, ever'

pedyr te am nagh tergweth **bythqueth** *arluth na vef ȝys* 'Peter, you will deny me three times, that ever I was lord to you' PA 49c

pedyr arta a gowsas **bythqueth** *me nyn aswonys* 'Peter spoke again, Never did I know him' PA 84d

en deȝyow a vyth guelys hag a ȝe sur yntreȝon may fyth torrow benegis **bythqueth** *na allas d[m]ȝon* 'they days will be seen and are coming among us when wombs that were never able to conceive will be blessed' PA 169bc

ellas vyth pan yu kyllys Abel whek ov map kerra na **bythqueth** *pan vef formys* 'alas for ever that dear Abel, my favourite son, is lost, or ever that I was created' OM 614-16

govy vyth pan vef genys a dor ov mam dynythys na **bythqueth** *pan denys bron* 'woe is me that I was born, brought forth from my mother's womb or that ever I sucked the breast' OM 1753-55

dre goth y wruk leuerel kyn fe dyswrys an temple yn tri dyth y'n drehafse **bythqueth** *whet na fe ve guel* 'through pride he said that though the temple be destroyed, in three days he would build it, that is was never better' PC 381-84

bythqueth *bay thy'm ny ryssys ha homma vyth ny sestyas aban duthe yn chy thy's pup vr ol amme thu'm treys* 'you never gave me a kiss and this woman has not ceased, since I entered your house, to kiss my feet continuously' PC 522-25

me a'th worthyp hep lettye ny fuf den thotho **bythqueth** *na ny wylys ru'm leaute kyns lymman y lyv na'y feth* 'I will answer you immediately: I was never his man nor upon my word did I see his complexion or his face' PC 1237-40

saw an corf na byw a pe an emperour ef sawse maga tek **bythqueth** *del fue kyn fe y cleues mar bras* 'but that body were it alive, he would heal the emperor as beautifully as he ever was, though his sickness be so great' RD 1657-60

my ny wylys yn wlas ma **bythqueth** *dyllas d[n] sevt na sur* 'I have never seen in the kingdom clothes of that colour' RD 2549-51

Ellas emperour debyta mar mennyth oma latha flehys **bythqueth** *na pehes* 'Alas, pitiless emperor if you intend to kill here children that never sinned' BM 1591-93

me a wyl lemen in tek **bythqueth** *ny welys clerra* 'I now see beautifully; never did I see more clearly' BM 2624-25

Bythqueth *ny vue vays in pov aban vys crystyan heb wov* 'Never was there good in the land since you became a Christian indeed' BM 3968-69

Kepar dell rug an tas a neff dre wondres marthugian hag aneth forth gull Adam an kynsa den **bethqueth** *a ve in kepare maner eff a rug Eva in strang maner a forth thegen heveleb ny eff a rug Eva an kynsa benyn* **bethqueth** *a ve* 'As the Father of heaven created Adam, the first man who ever was, in a remarkable and wonderful way, in a similar way he made Eve in a strange mode and manner in our likeness; he made Eve the first woman who ever was' TH 2a

So an catholicall egglos, kyn rug an heretickys y henwall papisticall egglos, henna ew egllos an pab, whath awos oll a henna ny rug **bethqueth** *receva ken hanow agys catholyk egglos, ha egglos an cristonyan* 'But the catholic Church, though the heretics called her the papistical Church, that is the Church of the pope, still in spite of all that she never received any other name than the catholic Church and the Church of Christians' TH 32a

pana bugell a ruge **bithquath** *maga e thevas gans e members e honyn?* 'which shepherd ever fed his sheep with his own limbs?' SA 59

Henna suer ew tra anath ha tra na wharva **bythquath**, *del clowas ve, in neb gwlas* 'That indeed is a wonder and a thing which never happened, as I have heard, in any land' BK 852-54

Gove **bythquath** *e welys! Ny lowenhaf o'm tyrmyn* 'Alas ever to have seen it! I shall not rejoice in my day' BK 1208-09

Lowena thu'm gwelha gour a ve **bythquath** *a Gurnow!* 'Hail to the best hero who ever came from Cornwall!' BK 1914-15

soweth **bythqwathe** *bos formys* 'alas ever to have been created!' CW 1265

rag henna mos alema me a vyn ny won pylea rag **bythqwath** *me nyn kerys* 'therefore I shall go hence, I don't know where, for I never liked him' CW 1287-89

bythqwath *me nyn beyf moy dewan* 'never did I have more sorrow' CW 1393

ha sure me ew an kensa **bythqwath** *whath a ve dew wreag* 'and indeed I am the first man ever to have had two wives' CW 1453-54

rag na rigga ve **beska** *gwellaz skreef Bretten coth veeth* 'for I never saw any ancient British writing' BF: 27

E ve welcumbes, me ore gwir ha the vethes tha Careesk maga sow **besca** *ve pesk* 'He was welcomed, I know well, and reached Exeter as safely as ever was a fish' LAM: 224

No rig avee **biscath** *gwelles lever cornoack* 'I never saw a Cornish book' LAM: 244.

never   GERYOW GWIR

It is clear from the above examples that **nefra** may not be used with preterite verbs. Unfortunately this misuse is prevalent in the revived language. The following sentences have all appeared in print:

Ny vuf vy brewys ***nefra** *an keth* 'I was never injured the same'
Mars o ev edhenn, ***nevra** *ny wrug vy klywes travyth a'n par kyns* 'If it was a bird, I never heard anything of the kind before'
***Nevra** *ny wruga vy mos ena* 'I never went there' [for *ena* read *dy*]
Wel, ***nevra** *ny leveris bos Kernewek Kemmyn fonemek yn tien* 'Well, I never said that KK was wholly phonemic.'

In each case **nefra** should have been **bythqweth**.

NOBLE

The default word in Cornish for 'noble' is **bryntyn**, which is well attested:

A **bryntyn**

ol tus ov chy deugh genef vy **bryntyn** *ha keth* 'all men of my house come with me, both noble and unfree' OM 1961-62

messyger ke gorhenmyn ol the'n masons yn cyte may tyffons vmma myttyn war beyn cregy ha tenne the wul fos a vyyn **bryntyn** *hag a lym yn creys an dre* 'messenger, command all the masons of the city to come here tomorrow morning on pain of being hanged and drawn to build a wall of fine stones and of mortar in the middle of the town' OM 2279-82

oyeth or oyeth ynweth syglewyugh **bryntyn** *ha keth* 'hear now, hear, attention, noble and unfree' OM 2419-20

ny goth aga bos gorrys yn arghov rak bos prennys ganse mernans den **bryntyn** 'they ought not be put in the treasury, because the death of a noble man was bought with them' PC 1540-42

Heyl ov arluth costentyn kekefrys gal ha **brentyn** *oma yth on devethys* 'Hail, my lord, Constantine, both villein and noble we have come here' BM 1527-28

mar mynnogh arluth **brentyn** *me a dregh y vreonsen hag an dewoys knak oma* 'if you desire, noble lord, I will cut his throat and bleed him here on the spot' BM 1650-52

A dyr **bryntyn** *the wonys teurant re bo confoundys, hedre vema orth e geys* 'A tyrant has been deprived of fine land to cultivate, while I was enclosing it' BK 1180-82

parys ove arluthe **brentyn** *tha vlanogathe lavartha* 'I am ready, noble lord; tell me your will' CW 2242-43.

As can be seen from the above examples, **bryntyn** can also mean 'fine', as well as 'noble'.

The word **nôbyl** is sometimes used as a noun to refer to the noble, an obsolete gold coin worth one third of a pound sterling:

B **nôbyl** (coin)

*ix **nobyl** a calame a russe sokyr thynny* 'nine nobles from the first of May would be of help to us' BM 3338-39

*Me a's dros genawgh i'n dowr, ha gwreugh leas **nobyl** owr, a ysmegow pur gostly!* 'I have brought them with you into the water, and make many gold nobles, you very costly preparations!' BK 1168-70

*Duk Borgayn, awos e frap, ny yl poral thymmo scap, orth ow **nobyl** ny spyn groet* 'The Duke of Burgundy, for all his striking, a pig cannot get away from me; he does not spend a groat for my noble' BK 2449-51.

Nôbyl is increasingly used, however, as an adjective meaning 'noble':

C **nôbyl** 'noble'

*ov arluth by godys day parys yv an stede gay yn weth an courser melyn kefrys hakney ha palfray ynmons yn **nobyl** aray* 'my lord, by God's day, the fine steed is ready, the dun courser also, hackney and palfrey, they are in noble array' OM 1963-67

*Drefen ov boys corff hep par ha dovtijs gan an bobil ov hanov in guir heb mar yv costyntyn the **nobil** emprour worthy* 'Because I am a person without peer and feared by the people, my name in very truth is noble Constantine, a worthy emperor' BM 1153-57

*Heyl costenten the **nobil** del on ny the lel bobil devethys yth on warbarth* 'Hail, Constantine the noble, as we are your loyal people, we have come here together' BM 1172-74

*Heyl costentyn the **nobyl** molothov mur a bobyl rag the plesya me rum bue* 'Hail, Constantine the noble, I have received curses from many people in order to please you' BM 1578-80

*A war agys cam why pobyl helma yv bevnans **nobyl** termen a thue* 'Oh, on your way you people; this is a noble life for the future' BM 2022-24

*tus **nobil** in stallasconn deth gore yv devethys* 'noble men have come to install you' BM 3017-18

*Heyl dyugh duk **nobil** magus me ham crosser presagus re duth dywy 3e sportya* 'Hail to you, noble Duke Magus, I and my crozier-bearer Praesagus have come to you to go hunting' BM 3930-32

*adam hag eve, dre an singular daddar han speciall favoure a thu golosek, creatis **nobyll** ha worthy creaturs hag in stat a perfect innocencye* 'Adam and Eve, by the singular goodness and special favour of Almighty God, created noble and worthy creatures and in a state of perfect innocence' TH 12

*Aban dallathas an bys, **noble** marrak, me a grys, ny ombrevys in dan scoys* 'Since the world began, a nobler knight, I believe, never proved himself behind a shield' BK 1631-33

*Lucyfer te ew henna sure a bashe myns es in nef creatys **nobell** omma yth ota [a] nature creif* 'Lucifer, you are he indeed who surpasses all who are in heaven. Created noble are you of a strong nature' CW 148-51

noble   **GERYOW GWIR**

ha by god nyng es ʒym dowte tha dastya an keth avall haw dremas a wor thym grace tha weyll vyadge mar **nobell** 'and by God I do not fear to taste the same apple, and my husband will give me thanks for completing such a noble enterprise' CW 705-08
'th erama suppoga andelna tho an liha rag an Bretten ha an Curnowean, voz an Frenkock feen parrez tho cummeraz war an iel ha an Sousenack **nobla** *war e gilla* 'I suppose thus at least for the Bretons and the Cornish, because of the fine French, ready to take the place of the one, and the nobler English upon the other' BF: 29.

The phrase **Costentyn the nobyl** which is attested three times is English, not Cornish, although it occurs in Cornish, rather than in English, speech. Even omitting those three instances, it is apparent that the adjective **nôbyl** is commoner than **bryntyn**.

NOSE

In some forms of Cornish the default word for 'nose' is ***tron**. This is a pity, because ***tron** is unattested in the texts, being a respelling of **trein** 'nasus [nose]' OCV §29. **Tron** is cited by ACB: Z 4 *verso*, where it is asserted that, **tron**, originally 'nose', means 'promontory' in toponyms; cf. also CPNE: 235. The OCV also cites *naris, **friic** 'nostril' OCV §30. The dual **dewfrik** is attested in CW:

*goer sprusan in y anowe han thew arall kekeffrys bethans gorrys in ye **thywfridg*** 'put a pip in his mouth and let the other two be put in his nostrils' CW 1852-54
*an eall a ornas thyma pan vo dewath theth dythyow gorra sprusan yth ganow han thew arall pur thybblance in tha **thewfreyge*** 'the angel commanded me, when your days were over, to put a pip in your mouth and the other two in your nostrils' CW 1928-33.

In the plural **frigow** is the ordinary word for 'nose':

*kynth us ganso sawer poys gor dotho nes the **frygov*** 'although it has a nasty smell, bring your nose near it' BM 1453-54
*lemen pan ywe messent me an set ryb the **frygov*** 'now that it stinks, I will set it near your nose' BM 3398-99
*ha del ve thym kyns ornys an dayer sprusan yw gorrys in y anow hay **fregowe*** 'and as I was ordered before, the three pips have been put in his mouth and nose' CW 2085-87
***freegaw**, freeg* 'nose, nostrils' Bodewryd MS
Naso... that hath a great nose. C. **Frigau** *brâz* AB: 97a
Nasus... A nose. C. **Frigau**, †*trein* AB: 97a
NASUS, W. Truyn, C. **Frigau**, †*trein* AB: 295a
freggow 'nose' Gwavas
freggow *broaze* 'great nose' Gwavas.

GERYOW GWIR   number

In the revived language in the interests of authenticity the default word for 'nose' ought perhaps to be **frigow**. There is no real warrant for **tron** 'nose'.

NUMBER, TO NUMBER

In the revived language the default word for the substantive 'number' has always been **nyver**. This word is certainly attested:

A **nyver**

Pub teʒ oll neb a vynne leuerel pymʒek pater a leun golon rag gorʒye pascon agan arluth ker yn blyʒen y a vye ha bederow keneuer hag a owleow ese yn gorf Ihesus worth **neuer** 'Whoever would every day say fifteen paters from the bottom of his heart to adore the passion of our dear Lord, in a year there would be as many prayers in number as there were wounds in Christ's body' PA 228a-d

Abel rag the offryn ker ty a vyth genen nefre ha dewolow hep **nyuer** *pup vr orthys ov scrynkye* 'Abel, for your offering, you will be with us for ever and devils without number perpetually grimacing at you' OM 567-70

dens omma hage mammov tremmyl orth **nyver** *heb wov* 'let them come here and their mothers, three thousand in number indeed' BM 1538-39.

Much commoner, however, is **nùmber** (UC *nomber*):

B **nùmber**

tus benenes ha fleghys ymons omma dyuythys ha'ga pyth degys ganse moy ys cans vyl yn **nomber** 'men, women and children, have come here bringing their possessions with them, more than 100,000 in number' OM 1611-14

Danvenogh sovdrys in pov the kuntel an flehyggyov ea **numbyr** *a tremmyl* 'Send soldiers into the country to collect the little children, yea, three thousand in number' BM 1514-16

Ima oma sur dragon ov latha pobil dyson heb **numbyr** *sur del clowa* 'There is indeed a dragon here killing people verily without number, surely as I hear' BM 3997-99

in hemma yma an drinsis ow signifia pluralite, henew **number** *a persons* 'in this the Trinity signifies plurality, that is a number of persons' TH 1a

Inweth fatell rug an den benegas ma confessia y pehosow fattell ens mar ver in **number** 'Also that this holy man confessed his sins, that they were so great in number' TH 8a

Mark inta me a ve conceviis in pehosow ny rug eff leverall in pegh, mas in plurel **number**, *in pehosow* 'Mark well, I was conceived in sins. He did not say in sin, but in the plural number, in sins' TH 8a

henn ew the vos excludys ha debertis theworth an **number** *an elect, pobill dewysys* 'that is, to be exclude and separated from the number of the elect, chosen people' TH 22a

An egglos an bobill malignant ha drog pobill, hag inweth athewethas **numbyr** *bras an scismaticals* 'The church of the malignant and evil people, and also recently the great number of the schismatics' TH 31a

311

number GERYOW GWIR

fatell o va necessary the onyn bos vgh an holl multytude an pith o, hag ew, **numbyr** *a lyas nacion* 'that it was necessary for one to above the whole multitude, which was and is, the number of many nations' TH 44a

theth hays a wra incressya heb **number** *tha accomptya* 'and your seed shall increase without number to be reckoned' CW 1320-21

han bys yth ew incresshys drethaf ve hag ow flehys heb **number** *tha vos comptys* 'and the world by me has been increased and my children are to be reckoned without number' CW 1988-90.

Curiously the verb A) **nùmbra** 'to number' is less common than B) **nyvera** 'to number':

A **nùmbra**

Inweth fatell rug an den benegas ma confessia y pehosow fattell ens mar ver in number ha mar teball the vnderstondya in maner the wothfas the vttra ha thega **numbra** 'Also that this holy man confessed his sins, that they were so many in number and so evil to understand, in a way to know and utter and to number them' TH 8a.

B **nyvera**

neb a vynna a ylly **neuera** *oll y yscren hay skennys kyc ha gwyzy pan esa yn crows pren* 'whoever wished could number all his bones, and his sinews, flesh and veins when he was on the cross' PA 183cd

ny yllons bos **nyfyrys** *an tus yv marow ywys* 'they cannot be numbered, the men who are dead indeed' OM 1544-45

ha me ynweth a'n guelas ha ganso ef company bras orth y sywe lyes guas ny yllons bos **nyfyrys** 'I also saw him and with him a great company following him, many fellows, they cannot be numbered' RD 555-58.

In the revived language the default word for 'number' should be either **nùmber** or **nyver**. For 'to number' **nyvera** is perhaps to be preferred to **nùmbra**.

O

TO OBEY, OBEDIENT, OBEDIENCE

For 'to obey' Nance recommends **obeya** (UC *obaya*) and **bos gostyth dhe**. **Obeya** is well attested:

a ny vynta **obeye** *the thev a wruk the formye hag a formyas nef ha'n beys* 'will you not obey God who created you and who created heaven and earth?' OM 1505-07

the ȝethov sur **obaya** *nefre ny vanna orthogh* 'I will never obey a Jew for you' BM 3535-36

ha pan o va kyllys ny vynna an corfe **abeya** *an ena, nan ena ny vynna* **obeya** *du* 'and when it was lost the body would not obey the soul, nor would the soul obey God' TH 4

ha then re na an remenant a res thetha kyffrys golsowes diligentlty, ha **obeya** *humbly* 'and the rest must also listen diligently to those and humbly obey them' TH 33a

the judgia lypers ha the punyssya oll an re na na vynna **obeya** *an prontirion* 'to judge lepers and to punish all those who would not obey the priests' TH 38a

hag eff a wothya an auctorite an egglos, ha rag henna eff a rug **obeya** *gans vvelder* 'and he knew the authority of the Church and therefore he obeyed with humility' TH 39

In dede nyns es tra vith moy a yll supressy[a] heresy ys an gouernans an egglos, mar petha estemys accordyng the henna, hag **obeyys** *kepar dell vsy S Ciprian ow recordya* 'Indeed there is nothing else which can suppress heresies more than the government of the Church, if it is esteemed accordingly, and obeyed as St Cyprian records' TH 42

mar teffa an holl brodereth **obeya** *according then commondmentys a thu, ny vynsa den vith styrrya na gwaya warbyn an colleges po company a prontyrryan* 'if all the brotherhood had obeyed according to the commandments of God, no man would have stirred or moved against the colleges or the company of priests' TH 42a

ha henna the vos reputyes kepar ha vicar crist, the lettya ha suppressya hereses, han gouernar na the vos **obeyys** *gans oll an cristonnyan* 'and that man to be reputed as the vicar of Christ, to prevent and suppress heresies, and that governor to be obeyed by all Christians' TH 42a

mas rag y bos an prounter a thu despisiis ha nag ewa **obeys** 'but because the priest of God is despised and he is not obeyed' TH 48a.

Dysobeya 'to disobey' is also found in TH:

obey

*ha dre an deda na a russens ow **dissobeya** du, I a gollas an originall innocency stat a vongy in aga creasion* 'and by that deed they committed disobeying God they lost the original innocence, a state they had in their creation' TH 4

*yma eff ow kull mencion then re a rella **disobeya** an auctorite an egglos* 'he mentions those who disobey the authority of the Church' TH 37

*Pella yma an martyr benegas S. Ciprian in tressa epistill yn y kynsa levyr ow cowse warbyn sertayn re a rug **dysobeya** ha despisia Cornelius, an epscop a rome* 'Moreover the blessed martyr St Cyprian in the third epistle in his first book speaks against certain people who disobeyed and despised Cornelius, the bishop of Rome' TH 48a

*Rag yth ew gwelys nanns ew myll blethan ha moy, fatell rug oll an re na a rug **disobeya** an sea han stall a rome a rug cotha in abominably heresy* 'for it has been seen for a thousand years and more that all those who disobeyed the see and stall of Rome fell into abominable heresy' TH 49a

*Arta inweth pana anken ha miseries a rug cotha in agan mysk ny thea ban russyn **dysobeya** an sea han stall a rome* 'Again also what affliction and miseries have come about in our midst since we disobeyed the seet and stall of Rome!' TH 51.

For 'obedient' Nance recommends A) **gostyth** and B) **uvel** (UC *huvel*). **Gostyth** is attested and does indeed mean 'obedient'.

A gostyth

*y rof hynwyn the'n puskes porpus sowmens syllyes ol thy'm **gustyth** y a vyth* 'I give names to the fish: porpoise, salmon, eels; they shall all be obedient to me' OM 135-37

*Rag ty the gola worty ha tolle the bryes len nefre **gustyth** th'y gorty me a orden bos benen* 'because you listened to her and deceived your faithful spouse I ordain that woman be perpetually obedient to her husband' OM 293-96

*a vyn ef bones **gostoyth** thymmo ve kepar del goyth ha chastya u golan?* 'will he be obedient to me as he ought and chasten his heart?' BK 2227-28

*rag ty tha gulla ortye ha tulla tha bryas leel nefra **gostyth** thy gorty me a ordayne bos benyn* 'because you listened to her and deceived your faithful spouse, I ordain that woman shall be perpetually obedient to her husband' CW 892-95.

In BK, however, **gostoyth** is a most frequently a substantive meaning 'obedient person(s), subject(s), vassal(s)':

A1 gostoyth 'subject(s), vassal(s)'

*Both day and night the **wostoyth** on, ow arluth stowt* 'Both day and night we are your subjects, my brave lord' BK 1672-74

*Penag na vyn bos the **wostoyt** saw kowsa tyn hag anhostoyt, ny a'n gor quit mes a'n bys* 'Whoever will not be your subject but speak sharply and disobediently, we will pur him utterly out of the world' BK 1853-57.

*The sogys ha'th **wostoyth** on* 'We are your subjects and your vassals' BK 2593

*Ny re dueth theugh, ru'm ena! the **wostoyth** a'n gulasow pel, Arthor rag e thevenya* 'We have come to you, upon my soul! your vassals from far lands, to hack Arthur' BK 2601-03

*Del os arluth cref ha gwan, the **wostoyth** on devethys* 'As you are the lord of strong and weak, we your vassals have come' BK 2698-99

*An lahys te a lel-syns ha guyer the ol the **wostoyth**, guyryow eglos myns del ens* 'You will faithfully maintain the laws and right for all your vassals, the rights of the Church as they were' BK 3105-07.

Uvel means 'humble' rather than 'obedient':

B uvel

*Humilis, **huuel** 'humble'* OCV §430

*ihesu ov corfe ham spyrys ol ov nerth ham cowgegyow rof ʒeth gorthye hag ath peys **vvel** ha clour nefra na vena yn nor trelyes ʒe lust an bys me* 'Jesus, my body and my spirit, all my strength and my mind I give to worship you and beseech you humbly and gently that never may I be turned on earth to the lust of this world' BM 148-53

*Meryasek yv flogh fur cortis hag **vvel** yn sur drys oll flehys an pow ma* 'Meriasek is a wise, courteous child and humble indeed beyond all children of this country' BM 181-83

*Indelma ny a yll disky in scriptur the vos **vvell** ha myke warlerth an examplys a dus tha* 'Thus we can learn in scripture to be humble and meek following the examples of good men' TH 10

A common word for 'obedient' is **obedyent**:

C obedyent

*An corfe a then nena o **obedient** then ena, han ena oll holly **obedient** the thu* 'the body of man then was obedient to the soul and the soul then was wholly obedient to God' TH 2a

*fynally mar ten ny ha contynewa fleghys **obedyent**, in ascra agan mam Sans egglos, ny a vith megys gans an bos a lell feith ha bewek* 'finally if we continue obedient children in the bosom of our mother, holy Church, we will be fed with the food of a true and lively faith' TH 41

*ha the henna mar pe an holl fraternity han bredereth, according then commondemente a thu, **obedient**, ny vynsa den vyth gwaya na styrrya warbyn an bredereth a crist* 'and if the whole fraternity and brotherhood had been obedient to that man, no one would have stirred or moved against the brotherhood of Christ' TH 48a

*Syr king, dar ny vynnowgh why (leverough expedient!) ry ken gorthyb the Lucy ha bonas moy **obedient** ys indella?* 'Sir king, what, will you not (speak expediently!) give a different answer to Lucius and be more obedient than that?' BK 2138-42.

obey   GERYOW GWIR

For 'obedience' Nance recommends ***obeyans** (UC **obayans*) which is not attested. **Obedyens** is attested, however, as is **dysobedyens** 'disobedience':

A **obedyens** 'obedience'
beva dre commondment du, bo dre neb one͡[n ny ew] dre **obediens** *kylmys the seruya ha specially dre commondment du* 'whether it be by the commandment of God or by someone, we are bound to serve and especially by the commandment of God' TH 5

Na in tyller arell, na dre menes arell, ew heresy springys in man, ha scismes drehevys, mas rag nag us **obedyens** *res thyn minister neb ew an pronter a thu* 'Neither in another place nor by other means have heresies arisen and schisms occurred, except because obedience has not been given to the minister, who is the priest of God' TH 42a

Ha wosa henna in destruccion, ha agy the proces a dyrmyn arta bos lowenek the trelya thega dew **obediens** 'And after that into destruction, and within the passage of time again be happy to return to their due obedience' TH 49a

Merowgh inweth war germany, ha kemerogh examp[yl] anethy, fatell russans prosperya agy thetha aga honyn, aban russens declynya theworth an **obediens** *an sea han stall a rome* 'Look also at Germany, and be instructed by her, how they have prospered among themselves since they have declined from the obedience of the see and stall of Rome' TH 49a

B **dysobedyens** 'disobedience'
mar te den ha receva royow bras theworth y gothman po y soveran, mar te in by an by ha tyrry blonogath y soveran hay displesya, an fowt han **disobediens** *dretho ew gwrys the vrassa* 'if a man receives great gifts from his friend or his sovereign, and if shortly thereafter he happens to violate his sovereign's will and displease him, the fault and the disobedience become all the greater' TH 4a

An dra a rug Adam hag Eva dybbry nyns o mas avall, so whath an debry an kyth sam avall na in kyth case na, o **disobediens** *bras warbyn du* 'The thing which Adam and Eve ate was only and apple, but the eating of that same apple in that same case was great disobedience to God' TH 4a

ha in kythsame chapter na yma S Powle ow leverall in kepar porposse dre an **disobediens** *a vn den mer a theth the vos pehadorryan* 'and in that same chapter St Paul says to the same effect through the disobedience of one man many came to be sinners' TH 4a

me a dryst why a vith circumspect the avoydia oll kynde pehosow ha **disobediens** *kyn fe an dra vith mar nebas in y nature y honyn* 'I trust that you will be circumspect to avoid all kinds of sins and disobedience, be the matter never so small in its own nature' TH 5

eff a ill bos methek ay vnkyndenys ha **disobediens** *warbyn du* 'he can be ashamed of his unkindness and disobedience against God' TH 30a.

Obeya is attested in three different texts. There can, I think, be no reason to avoid its use. Similarly **obedyent** 'obedient' is in TH and BK and was clearly part of the lexicon of Middle Cornish, and in consequence, there is no need to avoid it. **Disobeya**, **obedyens** and **dysobedyens** are all confined to Tregear's homilies, but that does not mean we have to avoid them entirely.

TO OFFEND

The two most suitable words to render 'to offend' in Cornish are A) **sclandra** and B) **offendya**. **Sclandra** means 'to reproach, to accuse' as well as 'to scandalize, to offend':

A **sclandra**

*arluth leuerel dy'm gura marsof vy an keth henna na vo den aral **sclandrys*** 'Lord, tell me whether I am that same man, lest another man be reproached' PC 741-43

*kyns bos vn nos tremenys why a vyth pur wyr **sclandrys** ahanaf ketep map bron* 'before one night has passed you will be ashamed of me indeed, every one of you' PC 890-92

*ha kyn fons y ol **sclandrys** neffre awos bos lethys my ny wraf the thyflase* 'and though they be all offended, never even were I killed, will I turn away from you' PC 899-91

*mal myscheff regis doga ov **sclandra** mar mynnogh why ha leferel ov bosa omma cruel* 'Blast, may mischief carry you off, if you will reproach me and say that I am cruel here!' BM 3745-49.

The commonest, and best word for 'to scandalize, to offend' is **offendya**:

B **offendya**

*y volungeth mars ywa y **offendye** ny vynna kyn fen marow yn tor ma* 'if it is his will I will not offend him though I die now' OM 1329-31

*a vap whek yth of cuthys ow colon yv marthys claf thy'so gy del lauaraf **offendye** dev ny vynnaf* 'my dear son I am grieved. My heart is wondrous sick. As I tell you, I will not offend God' OM 1336-39

*Both du nyns us **offendia** an corff in beth y wora gruegh lemen in hanov du* 'We must not offend God's wish; put the body in the grave now in the name of God' BM 4529-31

*ny a rug theth **offendia** ge, arluth, ny a rug theth naha ge* 'we have offended you, Lord; we have denied you' TH 10

*whath gesow ny the remembra pana displesure a russyn ny gull warbyn du, pesqueth a russyn ny y **offendya*** 'yet let us remember what displeasure we have caused God, whenever we offended him' TH 24

*Ha mar ten ny ha consyddra henna neb a rug agan **offendia** ny nyg usy ow deservya the gafus gyvyans theworthan* 'And if he consider him who has offended us, that he does not deserve to obtain our forgiveness' TH 24a

offend   **GERYOW GWIR**

mar towns y ha suffra du the vos **offendys** *rag lak a correccion* 'if they allow God to be offended for lack of correction' TH 25

ny a res then aga correctia, haga cawsia y the vos correctis dre dew ponisment, may fo du han commonwelth the lee hurtys dretha, hag **offendys** 'we must correct them, and cause them to be corrected with due punishment, so that God and the commonwealth may be less hurt by them, and offended' TH 26

An epscob benegas ma, a rug percevya fatell rug an Emperour **offendya** *grevously* 'This blessed bishop perceived that the emperor had offended grievously' TH 39

rag henna gwrens tues dowtya an tase dew tha **offendya** *der neb maner for in beyse* 'therefore let people fear to offend God the Father in any manner of way at all' CW 2167-69.

Since **offendya** is found in four separate texts, there can be no objection to its use.

For 'offender' *see* '**CRIME, CRIMINAL**'.

TO OFFER

For the verb 'to offer' Nance recommends *****kynnyk** and **profya**. *****Kynnyk** was suggested by Welsh *cynnig* and Breton *kinnig*, but is unattested in Cornish. **Profya** 'to proffer, to offer' is attested:

A **profya**

kowyth **profyyn** *an styllyow mars ens compes the'n fosow may haller age lathye* 'friend, let us offer up the rafters to see if they fit the walls, so that they may be fixed' OM 2471-73

Ov arluth dywy mur grays ov **profia** *dotho dadder* 'My lord, much thanks to you offering him kindness' BM 484-85

thy handla sur eff am gays myr pur whar in ketelma ow sywa eff a levays truspys vyth ny ra **profia** 'he will let me handle him. Look, very gently thus he ventures to follow me. He will not offer any violence' BM 1113-16

Gul truspys thym ny **profias** *nag eff nyn geveth dregen* 'He did not offer to do violence to me, nor shall he have hurt' BM 1123-24

Ser arluth by sen iowan my an kemer pur lowan mar mynner dym y **profia** 'Sir Lord, by St John, I will take it very gladly if people wish to offer it to me' BM 2878-80

me am be wondrys fancye orth y wellas in weathan ha the vy in curtessye y **profyas** *avell cothman mere a dacklow ram lowta* 'I had wonderful pleasure seeing him in the tree and in courtesy he offered me as a friend many things upon my word' CW 761-65.

In TH and SA, however, the ordinary word for 'to offer' is **offra**:

B **offra**

Eff ew an vhell prownter han prounter heb deweth a rug **offra** *y honyn the thu* 'He is the high priest and the eternal priest who offered himself to God' TH 11

*Rag nyg one ny kylmys the vos circumcisis, na the **offra** in ban the thew ley, oghan, devas, ha gyffras* 'For we are not bound to be circumcised nor to offer up to God calves, oxen, sheep and goats' TH 27a

*An epscob benegas ma, a rug percevya fatell rug an emperour the offendya grevously, ny rug eff sparya the omskumenesa, kyn ruga **offra** y honyn the vos recevys obediently* 'This blessed bishop perceived that the emperor had offended grievously; he did not spare to excommunicate him, though he offered himself to be received obediently' TH 39

*Ith ew scryffys in viii-as chapter in actys an appostolis fatell rug Symon magus **offra** the ry mona the pedyr* 'It is written in the eighth chapter of the Acts of the Apostles that Simon Magus offered to give money to Peter' TH 46a

*na rug agan savyour **offra** thethy an sacrament only, mas ow **offra** henna eff a leueris inweth thethy, Kemerogh ha debrogh, kemerogh hag evogh* 'that our Saviour did not merely offer them the sacrament, but offering that he said to them as well, Take and eat, take and drink' TH 52a

*A ra tus vsya **offra** bois ha dewas the re rag purpos vith arall* 'Do men usually offer food and drink to people for any other purpose?' TH 52a

*neb a vge **offra** an affection in satisfaction eth ew moy the vose consideris, dell ew an quantite an oblation* 'whoever offers from the heart in [a matter of] satisfaction, is more to be considered than the size of the offering' SA 64

*whath eth ew gwrys satisfaction, thethans rag neb a vo **offrys**, accordyng the quantyte aga devotion* 'yet it becomes a satisfaction for those for whom it is offered according to the extent of their devotion' SA 64

*na illen denaha an nenevow tha vos y relevis dir an devotion aga hvthmans ew bew, pan vo **offrys** an sacrafice a Corf Christ* 'we cannot deny that the souls are relieved through the devotion of their living friends, when the sacrifice of Christ's body is offered' SA 66.

In some of the above examples **offra** is used of a sacrificial or other religious offering. The verb **offryna/offrynya** 'to offer' seems to be used at all periods in a religious context:

*Caym hag abel ov mebbyon eugh sacryfyeugh in scon yn meneth the'n tas a'n nef hag ol agas gwyrthege thotho gvetyeugh **offrynne** ha'y lesky del yrghys ef* 'Cain and Abel, my sons, go, sacrifice soon on the mountain to the Father of heaven and be sure to offer to him all your true tithe and to burn it as he commanded' OM 437-42

*rag leverel yn preve my ny vynnaf **offrynne** ol ov dege yn certan* 'speaking privately, I will not offer up all my tithe indeed' OM 499-501

*bugh **offrynne** my a vyn whare war an alter na* 'I will immediately offer a cow upon that altar' OM 1185-86

*ffesont onan fat ha da then tas dev a'n nef guella my a **offryn** hep lettye* 'I will without delay offer a pheasant, a fat and good one, to God the Father from best heaven' OM 1192-94

offer   **GERYOW GWIR**

goth dek scon my a **offryn** *the dev war ben ov dewlyn hag a'n gor war y alter* 'soon I will offer a fair goose to God upon bended knee and will put it on his altar' OM 1195-97

my a **offrynn** *mallart da yn gorthyans the tas dev ker* 'I will offer a good duck in worship to dear God the Father' OM 1199-200

yn enour thotho hep fal my a **offryn** *scon aral ha chappon da war ov fyth* 'in honour to him without fail I will offer immediately another and a good capon, on my faith' OM 1204-06

the vap ysac a geryth y **offrynne** *reys yv thy's war veneth a thysquethaf* 'your son Isaac, whom you love, you must offer up upon a mountain I shall show you' OM 1279-81

ow map ysac **offrynnys** *ef a vyth war an meneth* 'my son Isaac, he will be offered up upon the mountain' OM 1287-88

dun alemma rag **offrynna** *an sacryfys* 'let us go hence to offer the sacrifice' OM 1307-08

me a leuer ov map thy's dev thy'mmo vy a erghys may fy thegy **offrynnys** *thotho ef war an alter* 'I will tell you, my son: God has ordered me that you be offered to him upon the altar' OM 1325-28

yn gorthyans thotho omma **offrynnye** *an keth mols ma* 'I will offer this same wether in honour to him here' OM 1383-84

omma pen tarov schylwyn **offrynnya** *sur me a vyn* 'here a whitish bull's head I shall offer indeed' BM 3391-92

Thum du **offrynnyaff** *pen margh tan ha gore in the argh present worthy* 'To my god I offer a horse's head; take it and put it in your chest, a worthy present' BM 3400-02

Thum du iovyn benygas me a **offren** *iij bran vrays* 'To my blessed God Jovyn I will offer two large ravens' BM 3406-07

Thum du iovyn in y fath me a **offren** *lawen cath* 'To my god Jovyn in his face I will offer a tom-cat' BM 3412-13

Rag henna an arluth Dew ow leverall ema in nawaile a S. Luke, rag an wethvas a ruke **offrennia** *ii mittes, hy a dowlas in offering a Dew moy agis y oll* 'Therefore the Lord God says in the gospel of St Luke, for the widow offered two mites, She cast into the offering of God more than them all' SA 64.

In the revived language 'to offer' is best rendered **profia** or **offra**. **Offryna** can be used in a religious context.

OFTEN

Nance cites *inter alia* A) **lies gweyth** (UC *lyes gwyth*); B) **lies torn** (UC *lyes torn*); C) **lies treveth** (UC *lyes treveth*) and D) **lies tro** (UC *lyes tro*) as ways to render English 'often'. Only some of these are attested:

A **lies gweyth**

sav rak peder caradow **lyes guyth** *me re bysys na dreyle y gousesow awos ovn bones lethys* 'but for beloved Peter often I have prayed that his mind would not turn for fear of being killed' PC 883-86 *me a'n clewas dyougel* **lyes guyth** *ov leuerel an temple y wre terry hag arte y threheuel* 'I often heard him say indeed that he would destroy the temple and rebuild it' PC 1307-10

lyes guyth *y wruk bostye thy'so gy del lauara terry the'n dor an temple yn try deth y wul arta maga ta bythqueth del fue* 'often he boasted, as I tell you, that he would raze the temple in three days and build again as good as it ever was' PC 2439-43

Maria me reth pesys rag ov map sur **lues guyth** 'Mary, I have beseeched you often indeed for my son' BM 3615-16

ny bydgyaf gwelas mabe dean gans ow both in neb termyn mes company **leas gwyth** *a bub beast* 'I will not endure to see mankind willingly ever, but often the company of every animal' CW 1670-73.

B lies torn

The only instance of **lies torn** is in **lies torn dâ** 'many good turns':

lyes torn *da yn bys-ma re wruk the vohosugyon* 'he has done many good turns to the poor in this world' PC 3107-08.

Lies torn 'often' does not appear to be attested.

C lies treveth

lyes trefeth *y'n clewys ma na yl y thynaghe map dev pur ha den keffrys a vaghteth gulan dynythys* 'often I heard him so that he cannot deny it: the son of holy God and a man also, born of a pure virgin' PC 1722-2.7

D ***lies tro** does not seem to occur.

Nance does not appear to mention **lies termyn** which is found six times:

E lies termyn

So **lyas tyrmyn** *an froward nature a then a ra* **lyas tyrmyn** *predery an offencys han displesure gwrys thotha dre y yskerans* 'But often the perverse nature of man often thinks of the offences and displeasure done to him by his enemies' TH 24

Whath kyn fe va **lyas tyrmyn** *assays ha teball pynchis, whath an feith a rug prevaylya woteweth* 'Still though it be often tried and in dire straits, still the faith has prevailed in the end' TH 34

ha **lyas tyrmyn** *ny a red in aweyll fatell rug agan saviour Jhesus crist cowse the abosteleth warlyrth an vaner ma* 'and often we read in the gospel that our Saviour, Jesus Christ spoke to the apostles in this manner' TH 35a

Indella gans kepar reuerens yma S Augustyn **lyas tyrmyn** *ow submyttya oll y judgment hay oberow then Catholik egglos a crist* 'Thus with similar reverence St Augustine submits all his judgements and his works to the catholic Church of Christ' TH 37a

ha kyns oll hemma ew the vos notys, fatell rug du thea dalleth an bys, **lyas tyrmyn** *apperya the vabden* 'and first of all, this should be noted, that God from the beginning of the world often appeared to mankind' TH 55.

In the light of the above examples, **lies termyn** could perhaps be added to the expressions used in the revived language to say 'often'.

OINTMENT

For 'ointment' Nance gives A) **ely** (UC *yly*); B) ***uras**; C) **unyent** and D) **onyment**. **Ely** does not signify 'ointment' *per se*, but rather 'salve, medicament, remedy':

A **ely**

Benyn dyr vur cheryte y box ryche leun a **yly** *a vgh crist rag y vntye hy a vynnas y derry* 'a women for great charity wished to break a rich box full of unguent over Christ to anoint him' PA 35ab

An goys na dagrennow try dre y ij lagas y3 eth nyg o comfort na **yly** *a wrello y holon hueth* 'Of that blood three drops went through her eyes; there was no comfort of salve that would make her heart joyful' PA 225ab

ha mar scon del y'n guylly ef ath saw hep ken **yly** *ol a'th cleues yn tyen* 'and as soon as you see it, it will heal you completely, without other remedy, of all your malady' RD 1694-96

in nomine patris et filij virtu crist rebo **yly** *a dus gvan dygh in tor ma* '*In nomine Patris et Filii*, may the virtue of Christ be a remedy, O disabled men, for you now' BM 555-56

Inweth an dour ov fenten rag den varijs in certen peseff may fo eff **ely** *thy threy arta thy skyans* 'Also the water, my spring, I pray that it may be a remedy for a deranged man to bring him again to his senses' BM 1005-08

ihesu arluth a selwyans sav an den ma heb **ely** 'Jesus, Lord of salvation, heal this man without salve' BM 3077-78

in hanov map maria me a vyn the degelmy neb a yl hag a ylly ressawhya gy heb **yly** 'in the name of the son of Mary I will untie you; may he who can and will heal you without salve' BM 3841-44

Ihesu a ruk neff ha nor me a peys omma in clor re therbara dis 3ehes mones ha doys may hylly kepar del yl heb **yly** *sawya oll the esely a pup galer ha cleves* 'Jesus, who made the heaven and the earth, I beseech him here gently: may he grant you health that you may come and go, as he can without salve heal all your limbs of every affliction and disease' BM 4219-25

the oll an re na a vo claff, not then re ew yagh, rag an re ew claffe an gevas othom ay **elyow** 'to all those who may be sick, not to those who are healthy, for the sick have need of his remedies' TH 8a

rag ysmegennow costly us thym heb mar ha lyas denteth **ely** *rag corf ha rag esyly* 'for of course I have costly embrocations and many dainty salves for body and for limbs' BK 1118-21

*Plenteth lowr a **ylleow** rag pub maner annyow heb dowt e kefyr genas* 'Abundance enough of salves for every kind of ailment without doubt will be found in your possession' BK 1138-40.

*****Uras** is not attested, being a respelling of **urat** 'unguentum, ointment' OCV §287. **Unyent** is attested once:

B unyent
*ef eth 3en corff o marow gans **vnnient** 3030 esa ha spycis a vur rasow* 'he went to the body, which was dead, with ointment which he had and spice of great virtue' PA 234cd

The ordinary term for 'ointment' in the texts is **oynment, onyment**:

C onyment, oynment
*Nycodemus a vras corff Ihesus hay esely **oynment** o a gymmys ras may we3e corf heb pedry* 'Nicodemas anointed the body of Christ and his limbs; it was ointment of such power that it preserved a body from corruption' PA 235ab

*In keth gythna pur avar han houll nowyth drehevys tyr marea cleyr ha whar a 3eth 3en beth leuerys ha ganse **oynment** heb par* 'On that same day very early, when the sun had just risen, the Three Maries came clearly and mildly to the aforementioned tomb and they brought peerless ointment' PA 252a-c

*me a vyn mos the vre ow arluth treys ha devle gans **onement** ker yn certan* 'I shall go to anoint my Lord, feet and hands with rich ointment indeed' PC 473-75

*pyth yv an ethom vye an **oynment** ker y skullye ef a galse bos guyrthys a try cans dyner ha moy* 'what need was there to waste the expensive ointment? It could have been sold for 300 pence and more' PC 533-36

*en keth **oynement** a scollyas warnaf rak ow anclythyas hy a'n gruk dre kerense* 'she poured the same ointment over me for my burial; she did it for love' PC 547-49.

The default word for 'ointment' in the revived language should perhaps be **oynment**.

ONLY

There are three ways in Cornish to render the adverb 'only'. Let us examine them in turn:

The first is to use a negative followed by **marnas**, **ma's**, **mès**, or **bùs** all of which mean 'but' or 'except'. This idiom is the equivalent of the English 'nothing... but', for example in 'He needed nothing but a new job', which is the same as 'he only needed a new job'. In Cornish one might say **Ny'n jeva ev othem ma's a ober nowyth** 'He had no need except of a new job' i.e. 'He only needed a new job'. Such expressions are common in the texts:

A **marnas, ma's, mès** or **bùs**
nyns a den vyth vynytha a'n keth re-na the'n tyr sans **marnas** calef ha iosue 'Only Caleb and Joshua of those same men will ever go to the Holy Land' OM 1878-80
pendra wrama **marnes** drethos vernona *ny'm byth* gueres 'what shall I do? I will get succour only from you, Vernona' RD 2219-21
pan ve luen ov 3os a wyn **ny gara** covs **mes** laten 'when my cup is full of wine I like to speak Latin only' BM 80-1
dres an gluas y comondyaff du **mas** crist gorthys **na ve** ha me a ra mar pewaff the lays ihesu cresyae 'throughout the kingdom I command that only Christ be worshipped as God and if I live I shall cause the laws of Jesus to be believed' BM 1862-65
In ov nesse hevys ruen **ny eve** cydyr na gwyn na dewes **marnes** dour pur 'in my horsehair undershirt I drink as beverage neither cider nor wine but only pure water' BM 1968-70
marnes dadder **ny govsy** 'he spoke only goodness' BM 4463
Rag henna yth ewa poynt bras a error, the supposya **na rug** crist kemeras y gyge **mes** a gyge an wyrhes maria y vam 'Therefore it is a great fallacy to suppose that Christ took his flesh only from the flesh of the Virgin Mary his mother' TH 12a
nena **ne ra** an pronter vsya girreow e honyn, **mas** girreow Christ 'then the priest does not use his own words, only the words of Christ' SA 62
ha lebben **nag ez buz** nebbaz en pow ma 'and now there is only a little in this country' BF: 27.

The second way of saying 'only' is found in Lhuyd, who uses the expression **yn udnyk** (*en ydnek, en ydnik* in Lhuyd's orthography) 'only, merely'

B **yn udnyk**
nyz **en ydnik** líaz kanz ʒêr, mez enuêdh guîr-nàtyr pẏ lavarnanz priez an Tavaz Brethonek 'not only many hundreds of words, but also the true nature or native pronunciation the British language' AB: 222
Mi a ụôr pordha nag ero huei a skrefa an ʒerrio-ma del skrefam mî ʒen dzh, *mez* **en ydnek** ʒen an uẏnyn letheren g 'I know full well that you do not write these words as I write with *dzh*, but only with the single letter *g*' AB: 223
mez hedda a kodha **en ydnek** heruedh skrefyanz an Ẓouznak 'but that occurs only according to the orthography of English' AB: 223
*Tîz a ôr pordhâ kouz Ẓouznak po'n Tavaz yu'n arbednek ha'***n ydnek** reyzyz lebmyn en an Glaskor nei 'Men can very well speak English, or the language which in particular and only is necessary now in our country' AB: 224.

The difficulty with **yn udnyk** is that the expression does not occur outside Lhuyd's preface in AB. It seems that **yn udnyk** may simply be based on Welsh **yn unig** 'only' and is most probably not traditional Cornish at all.

GERYOW GWIR **only**

The third way of saying 'only' in traditional Cornish is to use the English borrowing **only**. Here are a very few examples:

C **only**

*Ov flehys eugh why de dre ha thymmo na regh grasse mas **only** the crist avan* 'My children, go home and do not give thanks to me but only to Christ above' BM 3150-52

*why a ra vnderstondia nag o an heveleb a then havall the thu in bodily symblans, hen ew the leverall in y gorffe **only*** 'you will understand that the similarity of man to God was not in bodily semblance, that is to say in his body only' TH 1a

*ny a ra the well vnderstondia an mercy a thu, ha fatell vgy agan salvacion ow tos dre crist **only*** 'we will better understand the mercy of God, and that our salvation comes only through Christ' TH 10

*mar tewgh why ha cowse da **only** an rena neb ew agys brederath ha cothmans, pana vattar bras ew henna?* 'if you speak well only of those who are your brothers and friends, what great matter is that?' Th 22

*Ny rug crist cara y cothmans **only**, mas inweth y yskerens* 'Christ did not love only his friends, but also his enemies' TH 22a

*so an auctorite an egglos a rug amyttya an peswar aweylar **only**, luk, mark, mathew, ha Jowan* 'but the authority of the Church admitted only the four evangelists, Luke, Mark, Matthew and John' TH 37a

*ha **only** mab dew, agyn arluth han saviour, ew ascendis then nef* 'but only the son of God, our lord and saviour, has ascended into heaven' SA 59

*ha gvle ny e gorf ef, not der faith **only**, mas eweth in very deed* 'and to make us his body, not only through faith but also in very deed' SA 59A

*not **only** [e] touchia, bus e thibbry* 'not only to touch him, but to eat him' SA 60a

*nyng o ef **only** deane ew sacrificed mas agen arluth christ e honyn* 'it was not only a man that was sacrificed, but our Lord Christ himself' SA 61

***Only** Peder a leveris ema genas ge girreow bewnans heb dewath* 'Only Peter said, With you are found the words of eternal life' SA 63

*bus **only** an owriek Chrisostom* 'but only golden Chrysostom' SA 66

*y praytha thymma lavar a wrug [dew] cowsall thagye **only** heb dean arall vyth omma* 'Pray tell me, did God speak to you only without any other man here?' CW 2348-50.

Only is attested in total almost 40 times. It is found in four different texts (BM, TH, SA and CW) and it would thus appear to have been an integral part of spoken Cornish from the early sixteenth century onwards.

> NOTE: the expression **heb ken** 'without cause' is found in the Middle Cornish texts, which some commentators by comparison with Breton *hepken* 'only' have taken to mean 'only' in Cornish. The analogy is hardly justified:

only   **GERYOW GWIR**

> *ha buxow leas **hep ken** ha tummasow kekyffris ʒe gryst a dro ʒe ʒewen gans nerth bras a ve syttis* 'and many blows without cause and buffets were laid with great force upon Christ about his face' PA 138cd
>
> *a debel venyn hep ras ty ru'm tullas sur **hep ken*** 'O graceless evil woman, you have indeed deceived me without cause' OM 250-51
>
> *Eua prag y whruste sy tulle the bryes **hep ken*** 'Eve, why did you deceive your husband without cause?' OM 277-78
>
> *ty dyowl gvra ov gorthyby prag y tolste sy **hep ken** worth hy thempte the dyrry an frut erbyn ov dyfen* 'you devil, answer me. Why did you without cause deceive her, tempting her to pluck the fruit against my prohibition?' OM 301-03
>
> *a thu aso why bylen ov lathe guyryon **hep ken** whet vyngeans warnogh a gouth* 'O God, how wicked you are, killing a just man without cause. Yet vengeance will fall upon you' PC 2624-26
>
> *map den **hep ken** ys bara byth nyn jeves ol bewnes* 'mankind without more than bread will not live wholly' PC 65
>
> *ef a'th saw **hep ken** yly ol a'th cleues yn tyen* 'he will heal you wholly without any other salve of all your sickness' RD 1695-96

The adverbial expression **heb ken** means 'without a cause, gratuitouly'. Here **ken** is the noun 'cause, reason.' In the last two examples, however, **ken** is the adjective 'different, other' and must precede a noun or a noun phrase: **heb ken yly** 'without a further remedy, without any other remedy' and **heb ken ys bara** 'without anything other than bread'. **Heb ken** in traditional Cornish, then, is never an adverb meaning 'only'.

Generally speaking 'only' in traditional Cornish is rendered by negative + **marnas**, **ma's**, **mès** or by **only**.

OPEN

For the adjective 'open' Nance suggests ***igor** (UC *ygor*), a word that is unattested. The attested word **opyn** means both 'open' and 'openly':

A **opyn**

> *Coyl ortheff vy meryasek me ath desyr dre tekter bonyl ty a feth edrek **open** dys me a leuer* 'Listen to me, Meriasek, I wish you by fairness, or you will regret it; openly I tell you' BM 407-10
>
> *kerys oys purguir gans du prevys **open** oma yv theragon in teller ma* 'you are indeed loved by God. It has been openly proved before us here' BM 675-77
>
> *grua scon agen begythya **opyn** guelys yv omma nag us du mas ihesu ker* 'baptize us soon; it has been seen openly that dear Jesus is the only God' BM 4151-53

GERYOW GWIR open

so yth ev **opyn** *ha manifest therag lagas du neb a well oll an prederow preveth a vab den* 'but it is open and manifest before God's eyes, who sees all the private thoughts of mankind' TH 28.

The adverb in TH and SA is **openly**

B **opynly**

Rag henna yma Salamon ow declaria **openly** *in Ecclesiasticus nag es vn den gwyrryan war an nore* 'Therefore Solomon declares openly in Ecclesiasticus that there is no righteous man upon the earth' TH 8

An gyrryow a S poull ew in delma, maga ver dell yll bos gothvethis gans du, ew **openly** *gothvethis ha gwelys ynans y* 'The words of St Paul are as follows: Inasmuch as it can be known by God, is openly known and seen in them' TH 14

may halla an gwyr bos progowthis ha gothvethis **openly** '...that the truth may be preached and openly known' TH 17a

mar lyas del ra devydya aga honyn theworth an kysam egglos ma **openly** *gothvethis the vas an egglos a crist... whath ny rowns y inta vnderstondia an scripture lell* 'as many as divide themselves from this same Church, openly known to be the Church of Christ... still will not properly understand the true scripture' TH 17a

han pith vsy oll cristoneth **openly** *ow disky, hag a rug dysky a dyrmyn the dyrmyn* 'and that which all Christendom openly teaches, and has taught from age to age' TH 19a-20

yth ew **openly** *gothvethis in marver dell rug crist promysya an conforter* 'it is openly known in as much as Christ promised the Comforter' TH 36

Christ ew devethis, not dir subtelnath, bus **openly** *the kenever a whelha ha vo o sevall rebta* 'Christ has come, not by subtlety, but openly, to whomever will see and will stand beside him' SA 60.

The default word for 'to open' in Cornish is **egery** (UC *ygery*), which can also mean 'to expound':

C **egery** 'to open'

thy's yth arghaf a dyreyth gas adam the'th **egery** 'to you, O land, I command that you let Adam open you' OM 380-81

vgor *daras the pryson ha gor ihesu ynno scon pols the powes* 'open the door of your prison and put Jesus in it quickly to rest for a while' PC 1870-72

pan wruk an bara terry ha'n scryptor y **egyry** 'when he broke the bread and expounded the scripture' RD 1324-25

an carn [n]a a **ygoras** *del o destnys thotho ef* 'that mass of rock opened, as was destined for him' RD 2335-36

Dore in mes the garov theorthys an carharov prest me a den ha dyso an darasow **vgoreff** *heb feladow* 'Put forth your legs; I will draw the fetters from you and will open the doors for you without fail' BM 3685-89

open   **GERYOW GWIR**

*hy purguir am degolmas han dares dym **egoras*** 'she very truly loosed me and opened the door for me' BM 3772-73

*Rag henna gwregh drehevall in ban agas colonow, hag **egerogh** y aleis, the receva abervath inna kerensa bras the thu* 'Therefore lift up your hearts and open them wide to receive into them great love for God' TH 16

*why a ra da bys may teffa an jeth hag **egery** han vurluan **agery** in agys colonow* 'you will do well until the day break and the morning star open in your hearts' TH 18

*Indella eff a eth thy virnans heb gull travith er aga fyn, na **egery** y ganow the cows ger vith a throckoleth* 'Thus he went to his death without doing anything against them nor opening his mouth to speak any evil' TH 23

*Rag yth off purposyys dre weras a thu, the **egery** ha the thisquethas penadra ew an kythsame egglos ma* 'For I intend with God's help, to expound and to demonstrate what this same Church is' TH 31

*Ran an aweylors, onyn po arell, a rug y **egery** plenly an very menyng anotha* 'Some of the evangelists, one or another, expounded clearly the meaning of it' TH 53.

The verbal adjective **egerys** may also be used to render the adjective 'open':

D **egerys** 'opened, open'

*En beȝow yn lower le apert a ve **egerys** han corfow esa ynne a ve yn ban drehevys* 'The graves in severel places were open wide and the bodies which were in them were raised up' PA 210ab

*syr arluth ker cuf colon **egerys** yv an pryson wythout[e] les* 'Sir lord, dear heart, the prison is open without a lie' PC 1877-79

*rak an porthow hep dyweth a vyth **ygerys** ynweth sur mayth ello aberueth an myghtern a lowene* 'for the eternal gates will be open also so that the King of Joy may enter in' RD 100-04.

The adjective 'open' in Cornish, then, is either **opyn** or **egerys**. 'Openly' is **opyn** or **opynly**.

P

PAIN
There are several words in Cornish to express the idea of 'pain'. A) *pl.* **ponow**; B) **dolor**, *plural* **dolors**; C) **torment**; and D) **pain**, *plural* **painys**.

A **ponow**
*ha rag henna desempys ny a'th deg bys gorfen bys yn **ponow** the wrowethe* 'and therefore we will carry you immediately to lie in pains until the end of the world' OM 902-04

*yn nef agas enefow neffre a tryg hep **ponow** yn ioy na vyth dywythys* 'your souls will dwell for ever in heaven without pain in joy that will not end' PC 7-10

*lafurye a wra pup prys rak dry den the vos dampnys the **ponow** na fe sylwys* 'he works always to bring man to be condemned to pain that he be not saved' PC 15-7

*an enefow a **ponow** y's dros omma the'n golow* 'the souls out of pain he brought here to the light' RD 219-20

*ef a'n gevyth genen ny a pup drok maner **ponow*** 'he will have with us pains of every nasty kind' RD 2345-46

*rag raunsona mabden hay thelver thea **ponow** ha thea captiuite* 'to ransom mankind and to deliver him from pains and from captivity' TH 15

*In preson cref me a'n colm e gans cronow in mosatter ha **ponow*** 'I shall bind him in a strong prison with bonds in filth and pains' BK 406-08.

B **dolor, dolors**
*An fals brybours dre bur **tholowrs** ru'm grug muscog* 'The false charlatans through sheer pain have driven me mad' BK 747-49

*An ryboth Myghtern Breatayn, thotha ef ny ra **dolor*** 'The villainous King of Britain, on him he will not inflict pain' BK 2398-99

*Lowena thu'm arluth flower! Na berthewgh kueth na **dolor*** 'Greeting to my choicest lord! Bear neither pain nor sorrow' BK 2620-21

*An pen, algat, kyn fe **dolors**, the ol an stat a'n senators ew danfenys* 'The head at any rate, though it be a pain, has been sent to all the estate of the senators' BK 2864-68

*Elhas bos rys thymmo dry thys nowothow a **tholor**!* 'Alas that I have to bring you news of pain' BK 3126-27

*Ow servantes, maru'm kerough, a'gys dyhowgh prederowgh ha bethough war na glowo agys **dolors** onyn vith a'gys amors* 'My servants, if you love me, think of your right flank and be careful that none of your friends hears any one of your pains' BK 3259-63.

pain GERYOW GWIR

C **torment**

*ha whath moy wy a glewyth a **dormont** crist del wharfe* 'and still more you shall hear of Christ's pain as it happened' PA 132d

*an scherewes a dregas yn yffarn yn **tormont** creff* 'the wicked remained in hell in great pain' PA 213d

*yn **tormont** mar a'th welaf gynes me a vyth marow* 'if I see you in pain, with you I shall die' PC 1029-30

*peder ny wo[th]ys y[n] fas vn prygwyth gynef golyas kyns ys dos ow **tormont** tyn* 'Peter, can you not watch with me one moment before my bitter pain comes?' PC 1054-56

*vs whet the'th corf galarow na **tormont** orth the greffye* 'are there still pangs in your body or pain grieving you?' RD 487-88

*rak an **tormont** a'n gefe y'm colon yma neffre cvthma na'm gas* 'because of the pain he had there is sorrow in my heart; so that it never leaves me' RD 694-96

*ha paynys intollerabill ha **turmontys*** 'and intolerable pains and torments' TH 15a

*Ef a'm pernas gans e wos, gothaf **torment** mayth ew own* 'he redeemed by his blood, so that it is right for me to suffer pain' BK 429-30.

D **pain, painys**

*folle yn ta y whela ys del wra lyon y pray drey den yn **peyn** a calla neffre ny vnsa moy ioy* 'much more madly than a lion his prey does he seek to bring man to pain; if he were able never would he desire more joy' PA 21cd

*Maras ew 3e voth ow 3as gura 3en **payn** ma ow gasa* 'If it is your wish, my Father, let this pain pass from me' PA 55a

*Colon den a yll crakye a vynha prest predery an **paynys** bras an geve han dyspyth heb y dylly* 'The heart of man might crack, that would consider the great pains he suffered and the undeserved mockery' PA 139ab

*Caym ny vethyth yndella rag the lathe den mar qura ef a'n gevyth seyth kemmys a **paynys** in norvys ma* 'You will not be thus for if any man kill you, he will have seven times as much pain in this world' OM 597-600

*deus mei miserere herweth the grath hath pyte na'm byma **peyn** yn gorfen* 'have mercy on me, O God, according to your grace and pity, that I do not have pain in the end' OM 2252-54

*ellas a cryst ow map ker yn mur **payn** pan y'th welaf ellas dre kveth yn clamder the'n dor prag na ymwhelaf* 'alas, O Christ, my dear son when I see you in great pain; when I see you why do I not collapse on the ground in misery?' PC 2591-94

*rag y fynner mara kyller gans **paynys** mer ow dyswul glan* 'for people wish if they can with great pains to destroy me utterly' PC 2600-02

*dasserhy sur ef a wruk ha mur a **paynys** re thuk war y corf ker* 'surely he rose again and he has borne many pains upon his dear body' RD 1279-81

*arluth pylat yv marow dre **payn** ha dre galarow y honan yth ymwanas* 'lord, Pilate is dead; through pain and misery he stabbed himself' RD 2063-65

*gorth quik iovyn ha soly bo ty a vyrwe eredy oma dre **peynys** garov* 'worship Jovyn quick and Soly or you will die here indeed by grim pains' BM 1231-33 *ny won awose merwel a vetha* **peyn** *thum ena* 'I do not know when I die whether my soul with suffer pain' BM 1635-36

mar corthyyth an plos myngov neb a thuk **peynis** *anwhek sur in grovs pren* 'if you worship the dirty liar who bore nasty pains indeed upon the cross' BM 2379-81

ha **paynys** *intollerabill ha turmontys* 'and intolerable pains and torments' TH 15a

may hillyn gwelas ha percevya fatell esa the crist mer a garensa worthan ny pan ruga suffra kymmys **paynys** *ragan ny* 'so that we may see and perceive that Christ bore much love for us when he suffered so many pains for us' TH 15a

Pan o promysys thetha an **payne** *rag tyrry an vhella degry a charity* 'When the pain was promised to them for breaking the highest degree of charity' TH 27

Rag henna an quantite an oblation ma ew sufficient rag oll an **payn** 'Therefore the quantity of this oblation is sufficient for all the pain' SA 64

Dar, nyng ewa dyenys in mosogter ow penys in **paynys** *ha callacter?* 'What, isn't he gasping, fasting in filth and pains and hardship?' BK 507-09

Rag an **payn** *us thotha gwrys the voy eth ew lowenhys* 'For the pain inflicted on him the more he is gladdened' BK 716-17

rag henna bys venary eve a dryg ena deffry in **paynes** *bras avel ky* 'therefore for ever he will remain there in great pains like a dog' CW 2052-54

dyne ny warbarth a gowetha tha effarnow alema then **paynes** *a thewre nefra* 'let us go together hence, comrades, to hell to pains that will endure for ever' CW 2067-69.

For 'to pain, to inflict pain, to hurt' one can use A) **tormentya**; B) **painya**; C) **hùrtya** and D) **grêvya** (for this last see s.v. '**GRIEVE**').

A tormentya

Hag y worth y **dormontye** *y cuзens y ben gans queth* 'And paining him they covered his head in a cloth' PA 97a

Arluth jhesu cryst a nef kymmer mercy a'm enef del of ragos **tormontyys** 'Lord Jesus Christ, have mercy upon my soul, as I am pained for you' OM 2721

my re thysyryas fest mer dybry genogh why haneth boys pask kyns ov bos marow ha **tormentys** *yn garow kyns avorow hanter deth* 'I have greatly desired to eat the paschal meal with you tonight before I die and pained grimly before noon tomorrow' PC 718-22

gruegh y **tormontya** *besy crist mar ny veth denehys* 'hurt him assiduously if Christ is not denied' BM 973-74

etho mos th'y **dormente***, nyng ew ken the accowntya agys guthyl e thesyr* 'thus to go to hurt him, it is not to be considered other than doing his desire' BK 539-41

ha angy droaze thotha oll an glevyan, ha rimah o comeraz gen pup sort clevyas ha **tormentyaz** 'and they brought to him all the sick, and those who were suffering every kind of illness and pained' Rowe.

B painya

Ragon menough rebekis ha dyspresijs yn harow yn growys gans kentrow fastis **peynys** *bys pan ve marow* 'For us often rebuked and despised, harshly fixed to the cross with nails, pained until he died' PA 2cd

pain   **GERYOW GWIR**

*Ha crist yndelma **peynys** aberth yn crows pan ese yn vaner ma y pesys rag an keth re ren crowse* 'And Christ thus tormented, when he was on the cross, he prayed for the very ones who had crucified him' PA 185ab.

C **hùrtya**

*may fo du han commonwelth the lee **hurtys** dretha* 'that God and the commonwealth may be less pained by them' TH 26

*pandra rug an sea postall a rome theth **hurtya** ge* 'what did the apostolic see of Rome do to pain you?' TH 48

*ha pandra rug an sea postall a hierusalem theth **hurtya** ge* 'and what did the apostolic see of Jerusalem do to pain you?' TH 48

*Lædo, To hurt, to wrong, to injure, to do displeasure to, to offend, to trouble or grieve, to annoy. C. Dho droaga, dho **hertia*** AB: 75b.

It would seem that the commonest word for 'pain' is **pain**, **painys**. For the verb 'to pain' **tormentya**, **painya**, or **hùrtya** can be used.

TO PAINT

For 'to paint' Nance suggests **paintya** (UC *pêntya*) and ***lywa**. ***Lywa** is unattested, but **paintya** is found:

*yma S paul worth agan **payntia** ny in mes in colors in leas tellars in scriptur* 'St Paul paints us in colours in many places in scripture' TH 7a.

In the interests of authenticity, **paintya** should perhaps be the default word for 'to paint' in the revived language.

PARADISE

There are two forms of the word for 'paradise' in Cornish: A) **paradhys** (later **paravys**) with the stress on the second syllable, and B) **paradîs** with the stress on the first syllable and a secondary stress on the third syllable.

A **paradhys**

*why a geyl of lowene a rys thyugh yn **parathys*** 'you will lose my joy which I gave you in paradise' OM 319-20

*Cherubyn kemmer clethe fystyn trogha **parathys*** 'Cherub, take a sword and hasten towards paradise' OM 331-32

*the **parathys** scon yth af rag gruthyl ol both the vrys* 'I shall go quickly to paradise to do all the wish of your heart' OM 339-40

*seth ov map my a thanfon the yet **parathys** in scon* 'Seth my son I shall send to the gate of paradise soon' OM 690-91

GERYOW GWIR   **paradise**

pan wruge dres ov defen mes a **parathys** *lowen an el whare a'n gores* 'when he broke my prohibition, the angel gladly put him out of paradise immediately' OM 922-24

Praga a rug du ry thewhy commondment na rellowgh dybbry a bup gwethan in **parathis** 'Why did God give you a commandment that you should not eat of every tree in paradise?' TH 3a

Rag hedda Arleth Deew devenas eve arage thor **paraves**, *tha gonez an noare, thor neb ve va comeres* 'Therefore the Lord God sent him forth from paradise to cultivate the earth from which he had been taken' Rowe

Na 'ra komerras hannaw Deew en vaine rag na vedn an Arleth gon cawas en **paraves** *rag comeras e hanow en vaine* 'Do not take the name of God in vain, for the Lord will allow us into paradise for taking his name in vain' Rowe.

B **paradis**

te a vyth yn keth golow yn **paradis** *genama* 'you shall be in the same light in paradise with me' PA 193d

eugh lemmyn yn **paradis** *kepar del ygys prynnys marthys yn tyn* 'go now into paradise as I redeemed you wondrous painfully' RD 179-81

whath pelha agys helma inweth eff a woras mabden the trega in **paradise** 'yet more than this he also put mankind to dwell in paradise' TH 2

mas an frut an wethan vs in nes in cres **paradis** *du agan defennas na rellan tuchia na myllia gynsy* 'but the fruit of the tree close to the middle of paradise, God forbade us to touch or interfere with it' TH 3a

wosa an towle agan hyndasow adam hag eva pan rug an tas aga dryvya in mes a **paradice** 'after the faith of our ancestors, Adam and Eve, when the Father drove them out of paradise' TH 13

Kepar ha dre an gyrryow a thu ny a wore py le a ve **paradise** *plyngys* 'Just as by the words of God we know where paradise was planted' TH 32

rag tha garenga lemyn me a vyn gwyll **paradice** 'for your sake I will now make paradise' CW 359-60

now adam ma ow lordya avell duke in **paradise** 'now Adam is ruling like a duke in paradise' CW 456-57

nyns ew helma **paradice**, *a nagew adam nag ew* 'this is not paradise, oh, no, Adam, no' CW 1048-49

pana gwarter yth ama ser tha whylas **paradice** 'which way, sir, shall I go to seek paradise?' CW 1741-42

des nes then yet seth ha myer te a weall oll **paradice** 'come near to the gate, Seth, and look; you will see all paradise' CW 1797-98.

Both **paradhys** and **paradîs** are legitimate forms for the revival, but they need to be distinguished.

payment

PAYMENT

For 'payment' some commentators recommend ***talas** m.*, a coinage based on the root **tal-** 'pay'. There is no need for such a neologism, since **pêmont** 'payment' is well attested in the traditional language:

*y fons vnver yntreʒe kepar ha del wovyny xxx a vone yn vn **payment** y wrens ry* 'they were agreed among themselves, just as he asked they would give thirty piece of money as a payment' PA 39cd

*Rum fay ny alla peragh besse teka **pemont** nansyv wesse* 'Upon my faith I cannot ? a fairer payment now is ?' BM 1475-76

*prederugh helma deth brus **pemont** thymmo gruegh in suyr* 'consider this on the day of judgement you will surely make payment to me' BM 1923-24

*pan vo an vrus wy a wour an **pement** na hyns ny veth* 'when Judgement comes you will know; the payment will not be any sooner' BM 1931-32

*raghyl yv in y **pemont** argya orto ny ammont* 'he is a scoundrel in his payment. It is no use arguing with him' BM 3331-32.

In the interests of authenticity **pêmont** should perhaps be preferred to ***talas** to express the idea of 'payment'.

PEOPLE see MAN

TO PLEASE

There are two verbs in Cornish for 'to please': A) **plegya** which is followed by **gans** or **dhe**; B) **plêsya** followed by a direct object. I have collected the following examples:

A **plegya gans/dhe** 'to please'

*genes mar a **plek** ha tanha y kymmerr y 303 wrek* 'if she pleases you, here, take her as your wife' CF 7-10

*In meth ihesus yn vr na mara kewsys falsury ha na **blek** genas henna ha fals te dok dustuny* 'Then Jesus said, If I spoke falsehood and that did not please you and it is false, bear witness' PA 82ab

*the vanneth thy'm mur a **blek** ha banneth ov mam inweth* 'your blessing pleases me greatly and my mother's blessing as well' OM 455-56

*Ryght wel yseyd cowyth whek the wheyl yn ta, thy'm a **blek*** 'Right well said, dear comrade; your work pleases me well' OM 2459-60

*the tas kera thy lawe re'n danvonas the'th servye rak mur thotho ty a **plek*** 'your dearest Father, praise him, has sent us to serve you for you please him greatly' PC 166-68

*an chy yn ta thy'm a **plek*** 'the house pleases me well' PC 683

*lauar fur mur thy'm a('m) **plek*** 'a wise saying that will greatly please me' PC 1737

GERYOW GWIR please

*me a'th pys gynes mar **plek** war iouyn gylwel mercy ha na gous kemmys whetlow* 'I beg you if it pleases you to call upon Jovyn, and do not speak so much nonsense' PC 1896-98

*hag yn ur na sur hep wow ty a **plek** the'n arlythy* 'and then without a lie you will please the lords' PC 1899-900

*agis norter yv mar dek mayth ogh keris gans lues hagis manerov a **plek** kefrys the letrys ha lek* 'your nurture is so fair that you are loved by many, and your manners please both lettered and lay' BM 287-90

*ha gensy y feth tra dek maners trefov castylly theth tus ha dyso mar **plek** me a leuer pyv ew hy* 'and there will be fine possessions with her, manors, settlements, castles for your people and for you; and if it pleases you, I will tell you who she is' BM 304-07

*benyges yv in pup plays y oberov dym a **plek*** 'blessed is he in every place; his works are pleasing to me' BM 3873-74

*Nawothow ema gena' na **pleg** the why, me a grys* 'I have news, which will not please you, I believe' BK 934-35

*ny **bleig** thym sight anotha* 'the sight of it does not please me' CW 747

*hebma yth ew sawer wheake hag in weth sacrifice da pur wyer noy ef thybma a **blek*** 'this is a sweet smell and a goodly sacrifice; truly, Noah, it pleases me' CW 2493-95.

B **plêsya** 'to please'

*ny yllons bos nyfyrys an tus yv marow ywys nyns yw **pleysys** dev isrel* 'they cannot be counted, the men who are dead indeed. The God of Israel is not pleased' OM 1544-46

*nyns yw aga dev **pleysys** genes gy pan os punsys ty ha'th pobel mar calas* 'their God is not pleased with you, when you and your people are punished so severely' OM 1562-64

*ke ha dus pan vy **plesyes** myns may hyllen sur esyes ty a vyth yn pup termyn* 'come and go when you please. As much as I can do, you will be accommodated indeed at all times' BM 139-41

*gans golyas ha gans pynys me a garsa crist 3e **plesya** a newyth hag a henys* 'with watching and with fasting I want to please Christ in youth and in old age' BM 164-67

*Me agis pesse mester mara pewy sur **plesijs** mones 3e dre heb awer 3e vyras ov 3as vskys* 'I would ask you, master, if you are please, to let me without ado go home to visit my father quickly' BM 193-96

*mar kyssys yn ta spedie me yv sur 3e well **plesijs** an keth tra na* 'if you left to speed well, I am the better pleased of that same fact' BM 218-20

*Welcom ogh agan soueran yn keth plass ma pur certan **plesijs** one agis gwelas* 'Welcome are you, our sovereign, in this same place. Certainly we are pleased to see you' BM 246-48

*Ny yv **plesijs** hag a vyn boys revlijs drethogh certeyn ha meriasek kekefrys* 'We are pleased and will be ruled by you indeed and Meriasek will be as well' BM 313-16

*Mar peth stat the den arel grueys annotho dyogel ov liche wek me yv **plesijs*** 'If an estate is made over to another man, I am well pleased with that, my dear liege' BM 422-24

please   GERYOW GWIR

*Heyl costentyn the nobyl molothov mur a bobyl rag the **plesya** me rum bue* 'Hail, Constantine the noble, I have the curses of many people for pleasing you' BM 1578-80

*ihesu pup vr ol ov desyr yv in bys ma the **plesia*** 'Jesus, my desire in this world is always to please you' BM 2544-45

*ny a vyn ompredery forth rag y treyla defry ken **plesijs** me ny vethe* 'we will think of a way to turn him indeed, otherwise I shall not be pleased' BM 2857-59

*ihesu crist map maria reth gedya del vo **plesijs*** 'may Jesus Christ, the son of Mary, guide you as he is pleased' BM 3014-16

*Lemmen oll ny yv **plesijs** meryasek y voys sacrys epscop thynny* 'Now we all are pleased that Meriasek has been consecrated bishop for us' BM 3019-21

*guel **plesijs** me a vya so mot y go ty the drega in tre oma genevy* 'I should be better pleased, so mote I go, that you remain at home with me here' BM 3181-84

*A vam grua del vy **plesijs** neb ath worth a veth esijs kyn fensi polge ov cortes* 'O mother, do as you are pleased; whoever reveres you shall be eased, though they be waiting for a while' BM 3653-55

*arlythy del vugh **plesijs** gruegh why lemen* 'lords, do as you are pleased now' BM 4522-25

*ha eff a ros thethe gouernars da hag orders, dretha may alsans bewa ha **plesya** du* 'and he gave her good governors and orders, that they might live by them and please God' TH 40

*devethis yth of omma gans adam ow thase thewhy indella marth ewgh **plesys*** 'I have come here with Adam, my father, to you thus, if you are pleased' CW 1780-82

*ca veha a vlethan veth mar hir, ni veea **plaises**, me ore guir* 'though the year be never so long, we would be pleased, I know well' LAM: 226.

Plêsya is clearly a borrowing from English 'to please' and it becomes increasingly common in the texts. The verb **dysplêsya** 'to displease' has been discussed above.

POET

The word ***pridit*** 'poet' occurs in OCV §263. It appears as **prydyth** in Middle Cornish:

*Beal syr, Du don vous bonjor, moun senior, [re'n] **prydyth** mort!* 'Fair sir, God give you good day, my lord by the dead poet' BK 2496-97

The reference seems to be to Virgil, the poet par excellence of the medieval period.

It has been suggested that OC ***pridith*** would have given Middle Cornish ****prysyth***. This is an erroneous suggestion, now disproved by the attestation in BK. The **-d-** is preserved unassibilated by the adjacent **r**; cf. **gweder** 'glass', **Peder** 'Peter' and **peder** 'four (*fem.*).'

POISON, TO POISON

For the substantive 'poison' Nance suggests ***gwenyn**, **venym**, **poyson** and. ***Gwenyn** is unattested as such, being a respelling of the first element of *guenoinreiat* 'veneficus, poisoner' OCV §312. Both A) **venym** and B) **poyson** are attested, however:

A **venym**

*Ellas moyses ogh tru tru shyndyys of gans cronek dv ha whethys gans y **venym** ov coske yn hans yn hal* 'Alas, Moses! Oh, woe, woe! I have been harmed by a black toad and swollen by his poison sleeping yonder on the moor' OM 1777-80

*Arluth beneges re by del ose dev hep pehes sawyys yv ov ysyly ol a'n **venym** ha'm cleves* 'Lord, may you be blessed as you are God without sin. My limbs are all healed of the poison and of my disease' OM 1795-78.

B **poyson**

*I a vsse crafft ha deceyt, an **poyson** a serpons yma in dan aga gwessyow* 'They practise craft and deceit, the poison of serpents is under their lips' TH 7a

*Rag edyfya spiritually an holl corffe in feith ha rag lell defence then holl corffe theworth an **poyson** a heresy* 'Spiritually to build up the whole body in faith and for the proper defence of the whole body from the poison of heresy' TH 42.

For 'to poison' Nance suggests ***gwenyna**, **venymya** and **posnya**. ***Gwenyna** is unattested. The other two verbs are found once each:

A **venymya**

*gans nader yth of guanheys hag ol warbarth **vynymmeys** afyne trois the'n golon* 'I have been stung by a snake and poisoned entirely from the foot to my heart' OM 1756-58

B **posnya**

*an dour ha'n eys yv **posnys** mayth ens mur a tus dyswreys ha bestes certan y'th wlas* 'the water and the grain have been poisoned, so that many of the men and animals in your kingdom have been killed indeed' OM 1559-61.

The substantive 'poison' can be rendered by either **venym** or **poyson**. 'To poison' is either **venymya** or **posnya**.

POSSIBLE, IMPOSSIBLE

For 'possible' Nance suggests **a yll bos** (UC *a yl bos*) and possybyl. **A yll bos** is simply a relative clause meaning 'which can be'. **Possybyl** is remarkably well attested in Cornish, however, as is its opposite **impossybyl**, **ùnpossybyl**:

possible   **GERYOW GWIR**

A **possybyl**

*ow thas whek luen a ras da **possybil** yv thy's pup tra* 'my dear Father, full of fair grace, for you everything is possible' PC 1031-32

*nyns ew **possibil** thy power, neb a rug pub tra a dravith* 'is it not possible for his power, who made everything from nothing?' TH 54

*na ren ny in mar vhell mater predery nag ewa **possyble** thagyn gwrear* 'let us not think in so high a matter that it is not possible for our Creator' TH 57.

B **impossybyl**, **ùnpossybyl**

*Ith ew **Impossybyll** the then rych entra in gwlascur neff* 'It is impossible for the rich man to enter the kingdom of heaven' TH 53

*thotheff nyng ew travith **impossible*** 'for him nothing is impossible' TH 56a

*ha ny russans y remembra tam vith nag o travith **impossible** gans du* 'and they did not remember that nothing was impossible with God' TH 57

*ha rag gothfas henna whath the vos kyffris bara ha y corfe eff inweth war vnwith ew **impossibli*** 'and to know that still was both bread and his body also at the same time is impossible' TH 58

vnpossyble yth ewa an dower na tha vose kevys 'it is impossible for that water to be found' CW 2384-85

vnpossyble nyng ew tra tha wrear all an bys ma 'nothing is impossible to the Creator of this world' CW 2386-87.

There is clearly no need to avoid either **possybyl** or **ùnpossybyl**.

POWER, POWERFUL

The default word in revived Cornish for 'power' is **gallos**, the verbal noun of the verb 'to be able', while the default word for 'powerful' is **galosek**, **galojek**. **Gallos** 'power' is certainly well attested. Here is a random selection of examples:

A **gallos**

gallus o grontis ȝeȝe ȝe weȝyll aga mynnas 'power had been granted to them to do as they wished' PA 70b

*ha leuerough bos gevys ol ow sor beȝens lowen ham **gallus** y vos grontijs ȝoȝo ȝe urusy an den* 'and tell him that all my wrath has been remitted; let him be glad and that my power has been granted to him to judge the man' PA 113cd

*gurens dev y voth ha'y vynnas pypenag vo yn y vreys pur wyr y **gallos** yv bras yn nef hag yn tyr kefrys* 'let God do his will, whatever is in his mind. Very truly his power is great in heaven and on the earth also' OM 1153-56

*war ethyn bestes popprys **gallos** a fyth warnethe* 'over birds, animals—always will you have power over them, OM 1213-14

GERYOW GWIR   **power**

*Syr arluth ker del vynny my a wra prest hep ynny ol thu'm **gallus** vynytha* 'Dear sir lord as you wish I shall straightway do without urging all to my power for ever' OM 2147-49

*yowynk ha lovs kyn fo tollys dre y denuos mercy gylwys scon y **gallos** a vyth lehys* 'young and old, though they be seduced by his persuasion, let them call for mercy; soon his power will be lessened' PC 19-21

*ha nep as tefo **gallos** a vyth gans yowynk ha los henwys tus vras pup termyn* 'and those who have power will by old and young be called great men always' PC 788-90

*leuereugh thy'mmo whare mars yv den a galile hag a **gallus** erodes* 'tell me immediately whether he is a man of Galilee and of Herod's jurisdiction' PC 1599-61

*ha fattel duthys yn ban dre the **gallus** the honan ha war the corf mar drok stuth* 'and how you came up by your own power when your body is in such a sorry state' RD 2568-70

*ihesu arluth map guirhays dyswe the **gallus** ryall lemen oma* 'Lord Jesus, son of a Virgin, show your royal power here now' BM 552-54

***Gallus** ha confort an tas re bo genes pup termen* 'May you have the power and comfort of the Father always' BM 2735-36

*maria me reth cervyes thum **gallus** bythqueth defry* 'Mary, I have served you to my utmost power indeed' BM 3595-96

*an dragon y ra fethe der ov **gallus** defry yth eseff orth y care ny vanna y ankevy* 'he will vanquish the dragon by my power indeed. I love him. I will not forget him' BM 4021-24

*eff as led avel on doff ha der **gallus** du in prof as comond then dysert dovn* 'he will lead it like a tame lamb and by the power of God as proof will command it deep into the wilderness' BM 4028-30

*Charite ew the gara du gans oll agan colan, gans oll agan bewnans, gans oll agan **gallus**, ha gans oll agan nerth* 'Charity is to love God with all our heart, all our life, with all our power and with all our strength' TH 21

*Why a welle an **gallus** a geir Christ fatla vgy ow conys* 'You see the power of Christ's word, how it works' SA 62a

*Rag henna mars ees mar ver **gallus** in geir agen arluth Christ tha gwiel pith nyng o derag dorne, paseil moy **gallus**, the gonys ha changya an pith nag o derag dorne* 'Therefore if there is such great power in the word of our Lord Christ to create that which was not there before hand, by how much the more is there power to work and to change something that was not beforehand' SA 62a

*Laver an pyth a vynhy gans the golan the uny, ha te a vith ef heb mar mar pyth o'm **gallus** evy* 'Say what you will desire in your heart, and of course you will have it, if it is in my power' BK 1075-77

*Mara pethaf dywenhys, me a'm bues **gallos** i'n bys ha'm yskerans a throkfar* 'If I am afflicted, I have power in the world and my enemies will fare badly' BK 1410-12.

Notice, incidentaly, how reluctant are the scribes to lenite the initial consonant of **gallos** to **allos**.

Power 'power' is found in both BM and TH:

B power

*maria whek peys genef byth nan geffa an iovl keth warnaf **power** nan beys ov escare arall* 'dear Mary, pray for me that the caitiff devil will never have power over me nor the world, my other enemy' BM 158-61

*in kepar maner ny a res thy casa an teball ell hay **power** ha then vttermost thegen gallus avoydya y temptacions* 'in the same way we must hate the devil and his power and to the uttermost of our power avoid his temptations' TH 3a

*eff ny rug cessia dre crefte ha dre questonow adro the eva neb o an gwanha in **power** han medalha vessell bys may rug gull thethy terry commondment an tas* 'he did not cease by craft and with questions around Eve, who was the weaker in power and the softer vessel, until he made her break the commandment of the Father' TH 4

*Saw eff a ros thynny notabill qualitys ha **powers*** 'But he gave us remarkable qualities and powers' TH 5

*Rag nyng esan ny ow cara Du mar ver dell one ny kylmys the cara, gans oll agan colonow, agan mynde ha **power*** 'For we do not love God as much as we are bound to love, with all our hearts, our mind and power' TH 9a

*tus a russa supposia mar teffa du aga suffra aga naturall the vsya aga naturall **powers** y a vynsa optaynya salvacion in ta lovr heb gweras vith arell in party du* 'men would have supposed, if God had allowed them to use their natural powers, they would have obtained salvation well enough without any other assistance on the part of God' TH 13a

*Rag y fe gwelys gans an bobyll in tyrmyn na tacklennow invisibly, han eternall **power** a thu* 'For at that time things were seen invisibly and the eternal power of God' TH 14

*nyns o in **power** thega gwetha mes a pegh indella* 'it did not posses the power to keep them thus from sin' TH 14

*henn re grantya thynny an **power** an tas, an mab, han Spuris sans* 'may the power of the Father, the Son and the Holy Spirit grant us that' TH 16

*Gans agan gallus ha **power**, henew the venya gans agan dewleff ha treys, gans agan lagasow ha scovornow* 'With our ability and power, that means with our hands and feet, with our eyes and ears' TH 21a

*hag in aga actys ha dedys y a rug y pursuya gans oll aga nerth haga **power** then myrnans* 'and in their acts and deeds they pursued him to death with all their force and power' TH 23

*An vhall **powers** ew ordeynys gans du, not the vos dowtys gans an re ew da, mas the punsya an drog pobill gans an gletha* 'The sovereign powers have been ordained by God, not to be feared by those who are virtuous, but to punish evil people with the sword' TH 25

*Eff a ros thy abosteleth **power** bras, ha auctorite bras, kepar dell vsy S Mathew ow recordya* 'He gave his apostles great power and great authority, as St Matthew records' TH 35a

*hag eff a ros thethy **power** war teball spurugian* 'and he gave her power over evil spirits' TH 35a

*In kynsa du a ros **power** hag auctorite then catholik egglos the gafas an lell Sens han vnderstonding an scriptur* 'In the first place God gave power and authority to the catholic Church to find the true sense and interpretation of scripture' TH 36

GERYOW GWIR   power

*yma auctorite arell res gans du, hen ew **power** the relessia ha the pardona an penytent pehadur* 'another authority has been given by God, namely the power to release and to pardon the penitent sinner' TH 38a

*An **power** han auctorite na, kepar dell ve va fuguris in la goyth thyn ordyr a prontereth* 'That power and authority, as it was prefigured in the Old Law to the order of priests' TH 38a

*yma S Cyrill ow commondya thetha sessia heb gull marthussyan crist the ry **power** an par na* 'St Cyril commands them to cease being astonished that Christ gave power of that kind' TH 38a

*Crist a rug ry **power** ha appoyntya ran the vos appostels, ran profettys, ran aweylers, ran beguleth devas* 'Christ gave power and appointed some as apostles, some prophets, some evangelists, some pastors of sheep' TH 42

*Rag agan Savyour Jhesu crist a ros an kynsa **power** ha auctorite the pedyr ha war an **power** ma eff a rug buldya y egglos* 'For our Saviour Jesus Christ gave the first power and authority to Peter and upon this power he built his Church' TH 45a

*Ith ew scryffys in viii-as chapter in actys an appostolis fatell rug Symon magus offra the ry mona the pedyr mar mynna pedyr ry **power** thotheff* 'It is written in the eighth chapter of the Acts of the Apostles that Simon Magus offered to give Peter money, if Peter would give him power' TH 46a

*an pith ew spiritual, ha not ow longya thyn regall **power**, hen ew **power** mytern* 'that which is spiritual, and does not belong to the royal power, that is power of a king' TH 51

*nyns ew possibil thy **power**, neb a rug pub tra a dravith* 'is it not possible for his power, who made everything of nothing?' TH 54

*fatell o va gwrys kyge dre an galus han **power** a thu* 'that he became flesh through the might and power of God' TH 56

*Crist an prontyr invisibli a ra trelya creaturs visibili dre y ger dre y secret **power** then substans a corfe ha gois* 'Christ the priest invisibly converts visible creatures by his word, by his secret power to the substance of body and blood' TH 56.

The default word for 'powerful' is **galosek**, **galojek** (UC *gallosek*, *gallojek*). This adjective is common at all periods:

*may fe y tus ol gesys the wul thotho sacryfys del yv ef **gallosek** bras* 'that all his people should be allowed to make sacrifice to him as he is very powerful' OM 1492-94

*a tas dev **gallosek** fest the gorhemynnadow prest sur ny a wra* 'O mighty Lord God we will straightway assiduously do your request' PC 157-58

*arluth **gallosek** ha cref worto an porthow ny sef* 'powerful and mighty lord, the gates will not stand against him' RD 118

*rak ty yw dev **gallogek** the pup a vo othommek warnos a pysse mercy* 'for you are a mighty God to all who are in need, who call upon you for mercy' RD 2375-77

*mar luen oys a corteysy me ath ra den **galosek*** 'you are so full of courtesy, I will make you a powerful man' BM 299-300

power

kyn fo brays y devethyans ef a dryk pennoth in hans nyn guel an rych **galosek** 'though his origins are great, he will remain bare-headed yonder; the rich powerful man will not see him' BM 439-41

neb a vynna gylwall thy remembrans an dader a thu **golosak** 'whoever wishes to call to mind the goodness of mighty God' TH 30a

ma[y] halla an nenaf bos mekys worth Dew **golosak** *ha [e] vab ras agen saviour Jesus Christ* 'that the sould may be nurtured by mighty God and his gracious Son, our Saviour Jesus Christ' SA 60a

*Gothvith in ta bos an Tas ol***gallogak***, a rug pub tra, tas Christ Jesu* 'Understand well that the Father almighty, who made everything, is the Father of Christ Jesu' BK 217-20

Lowena this, myghtern freth, gwerror fers ha **galosak***!* 'Greeting, stalwart king, a fierce and mighty warrior' BK 1996-97

*me ew henwis dew an tase ol***gollousacke** *dres pub dra* 'I am called God the Father, almighty above all things' CW 12-13.

The word **dyspusant** means A) 'powerless' in BM, but B) 'powerful' in BK:

A) **dyspusant** 'powerless'
mar calla y tebelfar drefen y voys sur heb mar erbyn fay crist **dyspusant** 'if I can, he will fare badly because indeed he is powerless agains the faith of Christ' BM 2281-83

B) **dyspusant** 'powerful'
Thewhy me a worhemmyn: bethough pur glor. Me ew body **dyspusond***, Augel, myghtern in Scotland.* 'I command you: be very meek. I am a mighty person, Augel king of Scotland' BK 1277-80

Henna ew kowsys efan hag a golan **dyspusant***. Me a vyn mos ahanan. Del ough myghtern sofusant, na vethough pell!* 'That is publicly spoken and from a mighty heart. I shall go hence. As you are a sufficient king, do not be long!' BK 2436-40.

For 'power' one can use either **gallos** or **power**. 'Powerful' can be rendered by **galosek**, **galojek**. Because **dyspusant** is ambiguous, it needs to be used with great care.

PRAISE, TO PRAISE

The customary word for 'praise' as a substantive in the revival is **gormola** m., *plural* **gormolys**. This is attested:

A **gormola**, *plural* **gormolys** 'praise
Gormolys thys ha grasow ha war the gorf lowena, joy hag awen 'Praises to you and thanks and happiness, joy and delight upon your person!' BK 2532-34

GERYOW GWIR   praise

Lowena ha lun yehas thu'm arluth ha **gormolys** *drys kenevar us genis!* 'Joy and complete health to my lord and praise beyond everyone who is with you!' BK 2677-79

Welcum, arlythy gwlasaw! **Gormolys** *theugh ha grasaw, rag why a'm car, me a wel* 'Welcome, lords of kingdoms! Praises to you and thanks, for you love me, I see' BK 2707-09

Gen ol an **gormola** *brez ve dotha garres ew ni, ha neidges ewartha* 'With all the praise of mind that he had, we are left, and [he is] flown aloft' BF: 59

Mêr a **gormola** *tha why war tîr ha môr ha en pub chy* 'Much praise to you on land and at sea and in every house' Bilbao MS

Laus… Praise, laud, commendation… C. **Gormola** AB: 77b

The English borrowing **prais** is attested more than once in TH, however:

B **prais** 'praise'

Ima an profet Dauit in peswar vgans ha nownsag psalme ow exortya oll an bobyll the ry **prayse** *hag honor the du* 'The prophet David in Psalm 99 exhorts all the people to give praise and honour to God' TH 1

Rag in dede neb a rella predery an creacyon a vabden ha pondra in ta in y remembrans a behan o agan dallath ny wore gull ken ys ry honor, lawde ha **preysse** *the du* 'For indeed, whoever thinks of the creation of mankind and ponders well in his remembrance what our origins were, he cannot do otherwise than give honour, laud and praise to God' TH 1

Indella yma S Pawle ow confessia y honyn pandra o eff anotha y honyn pub vr ry **prayse** *hag onor thy mester crist* 'Thus St Paul confesses himself what he was in himself, always giving praise and honour to Christ his master' TH 8

Han office a epscobow han re an jeffa cure a enevow ew the ry laude ha **preise** *the oll an dus da rag aga oberow da* 'And the office of bishops and those who had the cure of souls is to give laud and praise to all the good people for their good works' TH 25

Thotheff, gans an tas han Spuris sans re bo honor, **preysse** *ha glory heb deweth* 'To him with the Father and the Holy Spirit be honour, praise and glory without end' TH 41.

The usual word for 'to praise' in the revived language is **gormel**, *preterite* **gormolas**. This verb is well attested:

A **gormel** 'to praise'

heth ov lefer a fysek dok hy in dan the gasel ha grua thegy ov **gormel** *ov boys fecycyen connek* 'fetch my medical textbook; carry it under your arm and praise me saying I am a skilful doctor' BM 1418-21

ny gowsy mas honester pur guir a fur a thadder lues re ruk y **gormel** 'he spoke nothing but seemliness in very truth; many have praised him for much goodness' BM 2239-41

S. Johan baptist, a ve benegas in breis y vam ha **gormelas** *kyns y bos genys* 'St John the Baptist was blessed in his mother's womb and praised before he was born' TH 8

praise GERYOW GWIR

*ef am sett yn ban vhall hag am **gormall** meare heb dowt* 'he will set me up high and will greatly praise me without doubt' CW 710-11

*keno than Arleth gen gannaw looan **gormollow** eaue gen owyn preezyo eaue a rage* 'sing to the Lord with joyful mouth; praise him with fear, praise him forth' BF: 39

*preezyo **gormall** ha beniggo e hannawe da stella* 'laud, praise and bless his good name always' BF: 39.

As common, however, is **praisya**:

B **praisya** 'to praise'

*ef a gara crist gwelas rag kymmys y3 o **praysys*** 'he liked seeing Christ, because he had been so praised' PA 109b

*Sul voy ancov a rellogh the larchya **preysys** fethogh kemendis wose helma* 'the more deaths you cause, the more generously will you be praised, commended hereafter' BM 2351-53

*Indelma ny a yll disky in scriptur the vos vvell ha myke warlerth an examplys a dus tha, ha the exaltia, glorifia, **presia**, ha honora Du vth pub tra* 'In this way we can learn in scripture to be humble and meek according to the examples of good men, and to exalt, glorify, praise and honour God above all things' TH 10

*gesow ny oll gans vn accorde the ry thotheff agan voyses gans ioy pub vr **presya** ha magnifya an kyth arluth ma* 'let us all with one accord give him our voices with joy, always praising and magnifying this same lord' TH 11-11a

*ha pryns heb par ew ef ha mer the **breysya** drys suel a welys heb mar* 'and he is a prince without equal and greatly to be praised above all men I have seen without doubt' BK 2242-44

*Pandr'ota te indar fol, pan i'n **preysyth** araga'?* 'What are you if not a fool, when you praise him in front of me?' BK 2245-46

*Te a thindel the **breysya*** 'You deserve to be praised' BK 3056

*domynashon yn tew ma ow **praysya** hag ow laudia ow hanow nefra heb gyll* 'Dominion on this side praising and lauding my name for ever indeed' CW 56-8

*keno than Arleth gen gannaw looan gormollow eaue gen owyn **preezyo** eaue a rage* 'sing to the Lord with joyful mouth; praise him with fear, praise him forth' BF: 39

***preezyo** gormall ha beniggo e hannawe da stella* 'laud, praise and bless his good name always' BF: 39.

'Praise', the substantive, is either **gormola** or **prais**. For 'to praise' in the revived lanuage we can use either **gormel** or **praisya**.

PRESENCE, PRESENT, TO PRESENT

There are several ways of rendering 'presence' in Cornish. One can, for example, use **lôk** < Middle English *lok*.

A lôk

*dreugh an prysners ol y'm **lok** a thesempys* 'bring all the prisoners into my presence' PC 2329-30

*yma thymo servysy orth ov gorthya pur vesy in dyweth a thue ʒum **lok*** 'I have servants who worship me assiduosly, who in the end will come into my presence' BM 3373-75.

The word **presens** can also be used:

B presens

*dre reson y the justyfia aga honyn dre aga contyrfett benegitter therag an **presens** an bobill* 'because they justify themselves by their bogus holiness before the presence of the people' TH 9

*Ith ew scryffys fatell rug pedyr kemeras warnotha in **presens** a oll an appostlys the gowse in aga hanow y oll then bobyll* 'It is written that Peter took upon himself in the presence of all the apostles to talk in their name to the people' TH 44a

*why a res theugh gothfas an **presens** agan sauyour Jhesu crist in kith sacrament ma an aulter* 'you must know the presence of our Saviour Jesus Christ in this same sacrament of the altar' TH 55a

*mas y **presens** in sacrament ew an attent the vos spirituall foode thynny* 'but his presence in the sacrament is for the purpose of being spiritual food for us' TH 56

*an chorll adam y drygva a vyth abarth awartha in onyn an clowsters na neb na vyth tam lowena mes in tewolgow bras ena ow kelly **presens** an tase* 'the churl Adam, his dwelling-place will be above in one of those cloisters where there will be no joy, but in great darkness, bereft there of the presence of the Father' CW 2024-29.

When 'present' is a noun, BM uses **present**:

A present (noun)

*Thum du ny vanna boys gorth mahum kemer dys pen horth gorovrys y gernygov na gymer meth am **present*** 'To my god I do not want to be recalcitrant. Mahound receive a ram's head with gilded horns. Do not be embarrassed by my present' BM 3394-97

*Thum du offrynnyaff pen margh tan ha gore in the argh **present** worthy* 'To my god I offer a horse's head; take and put it in your chest, a worthy present' BM 3400-02.

The same word is always an adjective in Tregear's homilies:

B present (adjective)

*Rag henna the concludia rag an **present** termyn ma helma a vith rag agys exortia why* 'Therefore to conclude for the present time, this will be to exhort you' TH 5

*mar men an cristonnyan in kythsam **present** termyn ma folya ha sewya an kythsam trade ma* 'if Christians in this same present time follow and pursue this same practice' TH 19a *wosa an tyrmyn cut a vethyn ny omma in* **present** *ha mortall bewnans ma, ny an gevith ganso eff eternall bewnans* 'after the short time we will be here in this present and mortal life, we will have with him eternal life' TH 26

ha indella theworth crist bys an **present** *dith ma vn feith a rug pub vr sevall stedfast* 'and thus from Christ until this present day one faith always stood steadfast' TH 34

han kythsam tra na a alsa bos marthuggian, pan esa kyffrys bartholomew ha nychodemus **present** *hag y a welas an oberow a crist* 'and that same thing could have been remarkable, when both Bartholomew and Nicodemus were present and they saw the works of Christ' TH 37a-38

yth esa apostles erall ena **present**, *ha in aga myske yth esa henna esa crist pub vr ow kull mer anotha* 'other apostles were present there and among them was he whom Christ always made much of' TH 43

bys in epscop ma vs lemma in **present** *tyrmyn ma* 'unto this bishop who is here in this present time' TH 49

na cafus naneyll y vam an wyrhes maria **present** *ena gonsa, na onyn vith ay disciplis mas an xii apostell only* 'nor have either his mother, the Virgin Mary present with him, nor any of his disciples but the twelve apostles only' TH 52a

ha rag henna eff ew **present** *in sacrament in dan an forme a bara ha gwyne* 'and therefore he is present in the sacrament under the form of bread and wine' TH 56.

'To present' is rendered by the verb **presentya** in BK and CW:

Ow canhas ker, ke thegy bys in Rom gans pen Lucy ha por harth the'n senators trybut Bretayn **presant** *a in dyscharg thymmo nefra* 'My dear messenger, go to Rome with the head of Lucius and very forcibly to the senators present it as Britain's tribute in discharge for me for ever' BK 2838-42

tha adam kerras pur greyf me a vyn the sallugye han avall y **presentya** 'I will go very vigorously to Adam to greet him and to present the apple' CW 720-22.

PRIEST

The default word for 'priest' in the revived language is ***oferyas**, a word which is not attested, being a respelling of *presbiter, henbrenchiat plui uel* **oferiat** 'leader of a parish, priest' OCV §106. The ordinary word for 'priest' in Middle and Late Cornish is **pronter**, **prownter**, *pl.* **pronteryon**. This word almost certainly derives from the Insular Celtic *premiter*, a variant of Latin *presbyter* 'priest'; cf. Old Welsh *premter* 'priest' and Old Irish *cruimther* 'idem', although the stressed vowel appears to have been contaminated by some other etymon. I have collected the following examples:

Rag y vos war **bronteryon** *mester bras aberth yn wlas gurris ve yn y golon yndelma gul may cowsas* 'Because he was a great master over priests in the land, it was put in his heart to do thus, so he said' PA 89ab

GERYOW GWIR priest

pronter *boys me a garse corff iheus thy venystra mar myn ov descans servya* 'I should like to be a priest to administer the body of Christ, if my learning is found sufficient' BM 522-24

*Yma oma in penwyth nebes a weyst a carnebre vn **pronter** ov cuthel guyth* 'There is here in Penwith a little to the west of Carnbre a priest doing work' BM 783-85

***pronter** ef a hevel suyr yma mona gans henna* 'he seems to be a priest; he will have money on him' BM 1903-04

*hag in meske ol the nasconn henwys oys **pronter** grassijs* 'and among all your nation you are called a gracious priest' BM 2549-50

*Eff ew an vhell **prownter** han **pronter** heb deweth a rug offra y honyn the thu* 'He is the high priest and the eternal priest who offered himself to God' TH 11

*may teffa eff inna hag ordenya **prontiran** in pub cita, han **prontyryan** han epscobow ny vethans dysdaynys, na nebas regardys* 'that he might there ordain priests in every city, and the priests and bishops were not disdained nor little regarded' TH 33a

*kepar dell rug S paule ordeynya Tymothe ha Tyte, Ea, ha moy epscobow ha **prontyrryan** in y tyrmyn* 'just as St Paul ordained Timothy and Titus, yes, and more bishops and priests' TH 33a

*rag nag us obedyens res thyn minister neb ew an **pronter** a thu* 'for no obedience is given to the minister who is the priest of God' TH 42a

*Rag an tyrmyn an **prontyr**, ha rag an tyrmyn an judge* 'At one moment the priest and at another time the judge' TH 42a

*ny vynsa den vith styrrya na gwaya warbyn an colleges po company a **prontyrryan*** 'no man would have stirred or moved against the colleges or company of priests' TH 42a

*Nens ew na hene cowse y bos hereses drehevys ha scismes springes ha tevys, mas rag y bos an **prounter** a thu despisiis* 'There is no other cause for heresies to have arisen and schisms to have sprung up and grown, except that the priest of God is despised' TH 48a

*ha rag nag us onyn kemerys in egglos the vos an vhell **pronter*** 'and since not one is accepted in the Church to be the high priest' TH 48a

*an re na ew an coleg po company a **prontyryan*** 'they are the college or company of priests' TH 48a

*nena ne ra an **pronter** vsya girreow e honyn, mas girreow Christ* 'then the priest does not use his own words but the words of Christ' SA 62

*an pith ew benegys gans **prontyrryan*** 'that which is blessed by priests' SA 65a

*inter dowla an **pronter*** 'in the hands of the priest' SA 66

*ny a welas an pensevik **pronter** ow tose then [ha] offra gois agan arluth Christ* 'we saw the prince priest coming to us and offering the blood of our Lord Christ' SA 66

*Drake **Proanter** East, the Toby Trethell* 'Drake Parson of St Just to Toby Trethell' ACB: F f 2 *verso*

*E a roz towl Dho **Proanter** Powle, Miz-du ken Nadelik* 'It gave a fall to the priest of Paul in November before Christmas' ACB: F f 4.

*Dew reffa sowia an Egles ni ha an **prounterian** da eze et angy* 'May God save our Church and the good priests that are among them' LAM 226

*an **prounter** ni ez en plew East* 'Our parson who is in the parish of St Just' LAM 228

prince　　　　　　　　GERYOW GWIR

In view of the above examples, **pronter**, **prownter** should perhaps be preferred to *****oferyas** as the word for 'priest'.

PRINCE

The common word for 'prince' in the revived language is **pensevyk**, which is certainly attested:

princeps, **pendeuig** 'prince' OCV §169
yma **pensevyk** *an gluas dysplesijs pur guir genas the days hath vam kekefrys* 'the prince of the land is displeased with you in very truth and your father and mother as well' BM 488-90
pensevyk *yv thy nascon mentenour fay crustunyon socour the lues huny* 'he is prince to his nation, defender of the faith of Christians, succour to many' BM 3022-24
Me yv turant heb parov in dan an hovle **pensevyk** 'I am a peerless tyrant, prince under the sun' BM 3208-09
neg esa ow desquethas theugh elath nanyle arth elath, mas an very corf agen master ha **pensevike** *oll* 'I show you neither angels nor archangels but the very body of our master and prince of all' SA 60a
ny a welas an **pensevik** *pronter ow tose then [ha] offra gois agan arluth Christ* 'we saw the prince priest coming to us and offering the blood of our Lord Christ' SA 66
lucyfer ew ow hanowe **pensevicke** *in nef omma* 'Lucifer is my name, prince here in heaven' CW 119-20
Proceres... The head men of a town, as governours, rulers, and officers... C. **Pendzhiviȝion**, *arludhi* AB: 128c.

The word **pryns** 'prince', *plural* **pryncys** is much more common, however:

An **princis** *esa yn pow gans Iudas a thanvonas tus ven gweskis yn arvow* 'The princes who were in the land sent with Judas strong men in armour' PA 64ab
saw pedyr crist a holyas abell avel vn ownek ȝe dyller an **prins** *annas* 'but Peter followed Christ afar like one afraid to the place of prince Annas' PA 77bc
En **prins** *scon a leueris te crist lauar ȝym plema ȝe dus mar voldh* 'The prince quickly said, You Christ, tell me, where are your people so bold?' PA 78ab
Ihesus a ve danvenys haȝeworth an **prins** *annas gans tus ven aȝesempys bys an ebscop cayphas* 'Jesus was sent from prince Annas with stout men immediately to the bishop Caiaphas' PA 88ab
han dus esa ol yn dre ha **pryncis** *yn pow ynweth ha mur a bobyll ganse aȝyghow sur hag agleth the gryst y tons ȝy syndye ha ȝe dry ȝen dor gans meth* 'and the men who were all in the city and princes in the land also and much people with them on the right and the left, indeed they came to Christ to harm him and to pull him down in shame' PA 97b-d

GERYOW GWIR   prince

ow map lyen kergh annas an **pryns** *may hyllyf clewas pyth yw an gusyl wella* 'my chaplain, fetch Annas, the prince, that I may hear what is the best plan' PC 553-55

lowene thy's syr **pryns** *gay* 'greetings to you, splendid sir prince' PC 563

heil **pryns** *annas thywhy jammas mur lowene* 'hail, prince Annas; great joy to you always' PC 933-34

ha why annas ov def ker dyswethough bos **pryns** *somper rak dyswyl an cristenyon* 'and you, Annas, my dear son-in-law, show that you are a peerless prince to destroy the Christians' PC 977-79

ha hayl thy'so syr cayfas ha hayl thy'so **prins** *annas* 'and hail to you, sir Caiaphas and hail to you, prince Annas' PC 1708-09

epscop **pryns** *doctor ha maw the'n iustis pylat arte eugh ganso yn kettep pen* 'bishop, prince, doctor and servant again take him every one away to the magistrate Pilate again' PC 1794-96

lemyn **pryns** *ha mestrygy hag epscop cayfas deffry why re thros thy'm an den ma* 'now prince and masters and bishop Caiaphas, you indeed have brought this man to me' PC 1850-52

ov benneth thy's belsebuk del ose **pryns** *ha chyf duk* 'my blessing to you, Beelzebub, as you are prince and chief duke' PC 1925-26

heil pilat syre iustis stout heil syre cayphas epscop prout heil **pryns** *annas heil doctors ha mestrygi* 'Hail Pilate, brave Sir Justice, hail Sir Caiaphas, proud bishop, hail prince Annas, hail doctors and masters' PC 2343-46

why **pryncys** *a'n dewolow scon egereugh an porthow* 'you princes of the devils, open the gates at once' RD 97-98

arluth cref ha galosek hag yn bateyl barthesek rak henna ygor hep mar why **pryncis** 'a strong and might lord and marvellous in battle, therefore open surely you princes' RD 108-11

ef yv gallosek yn cas ha myghtern a lowene why **pryncis** 'he is mighty in battle and a king of joy, you princes' RD 122-24

parlet mar stovt **prence** *war an vebyen lyen nyns us in breten vyen ov parov pur guir heb dovt* 'such a stalwart prelate over the clerics, there is not in Brittany my equal in truth without doubt' BM 515-18

ty a crek in cloghprennyer rag perel **prence** *hag emperour* 'you will hang on the gallows by the peril of prince and emperor' BM 923-24

Ser **prence** *yv why us omma* 'Sir prince, is it you that is here?' BM 3473

the helghya heb feladov the **prince** *par del yv dufer moys me a vyn* 'to hunt without fail as is the duty of a prince I shall go' BM 3898-900

Inweth eff a yll leverall, an **prince** *an bys a theth, hag inno ve ny gafas travith* 'Also he can say, the prince of the world came, and in me he found nothing' TH 11

may teffa ena growetha ha powas an pen han dalleth a benegytter, ha neb a ve an **prince** *an heynes, hen ew,* **prince** *an Jewys tregys, ena an* **princes** *a Sans egglos a res thetha growetha* 'so that the end and the beginning of sanctity might lie and rest there, and where the prince of the heathens, that is the prince of the Jews dwelt, there the princes of holy Church must lie' TH 47a

ha thea ban rug **princes** *temporall kemeras warnetha an office na* 'and since temporal princes took upon themselves that function' TH 51

prince   **GERYOW GWIR**

Hayl, **pryns** *of myght uhal i'n tron!* 'Hail, prince of might, high on the throne!' BK 1670-71

Hayl, **prins** *heb par, te a bew ol!* 'Hail, prince without peer, you possess all!' BK 1790-91

Lowena the'n ryelha **pryns** *a allos ombrevy!* 'Hail to the most regal prince who was able to prove himself!' BK 1980-81

ha **pryns** *heb par ew ef ha mer the breysya* 'and a peerless prince is he and greatly to be praised' BK 2242-43

Pax nunc, prelyatores, **prynsys***, dukys, marrogyon* 'Peace now, warriors, princes, dukes, knights' BK 2380-81

Leud ema owth umbrevy mar goyth pan ra ankev **pryns** *mar ryall* 'She is proving herself to be wicked when she so quickly forgets such a royal prince' BK 3001-03

myghale **pryns** *ow chyvalry han elath an order nawe* 'Michael, prince of my chivalry and the angels of the nine orders' CW 291-92.

Both **pensevyk** and **pryns** are attested, but overall the scribes appear to have preferred **pryns**.

PROMISE, TO PROMISE

In the texts there are a number of words meaning 'promise' as a substantive: A) **dedhewadow**; B) **ambos** and C) **promys**.

A **dedhewadow**

dun alemma the'n mor ruyth tus benenes ha flehys the'n tyreth a **thythwadow** *yw reys gans dev caradow thyn ena rag bos trygys* 'let us go hence to the Red Sea, men, women and children, to the Land of Promise, which has been given to us by loving God to dwell there' OM 1626-22

Rag na worsys ov hanow harag an flehysygow a Israel dyscryggyon ny's goryth hep falladow the'n tyr a **thythewadow** *ty na the vroder aaron* 'Because you did not revere my name before the unbelieving children of Israel, you will not lead them indeed to the Land of Promise, you nor your brother Aaron' OM 1867-72.

B **ambos**

Noy rak kerenge orthy's my a wra thy's **ambos** *da luen dyal war ol an beys ny gemeraf vynytha* 'Noah, for your sake I will make you a fair promise: complete retribution of the world I shall not ever take' OM 1231-34

ambosow *orth tryher gureys annethe nynses laha* 'contracts made with a victor, there is no law with regard to them' OM 1235-36

benneth maghom re'th fo prest rak certan lell os ha trest ha stedfast y'th **ambosow** 'may you always have the blessing of Mahound, for certainly you are loyal and trusty and steadfast in your promises' PC 947-49 *yn dan **ambos** yth eses ha ken na fe da genes gul the seruys ty a wra* 'you are under contract for certain and though you may not like it, you will do your duty' PC 2259-61

*Lemmyn, Ke, ow mata guyu, an **ambos** kepar del ew, ke ge duwans the barkya* 'Now Ke, my worthy mate, as is the contract, go you immediately to enclose land' BK 1150-52

*Suer heb kelas, in syrrys neb a'n gwelha ny'n dythursa pyth ellya war **ambos** e wohelas* 'Sure to be frank, whoever might see him angry, would not care where he went, on the condition of avoiding him' BK 2321-24

C **promys**

*Oll the **promes** hath teryov guethy lemen avel kyns* 'All your promise and your lands, keep them now as before' BM 2594-95

*yma an scriptur ow concludia oll in dan pegh rag may halla an **promys** dre an feth a Jhesu crist bos res the oll an re na a lell greys* 'the scripture includes all under sin so that the promise by the faith of Jesus Christ might be given to all those who truly believe' TH 7a

*fatell ew an **promes** ny colynwys, a rug du promysya wosa an towle agan hyndasow adam hag lynnyath eva* 'that our promise is fulfilled, which God promised after the fall of our forefathers Adam and the lineage of Eve' TH 13

*Arta yma du ow kull an second **promys** gans an venyn* 'Again God makes the second promise to the woman' TH 13

*oll an **promysyow** ma a thu ny vea colynwys in crist* 'all these promises would not have been fulfilled in Christ' TH 13a

*Saw an dra ma ew strayng the ran an bobyll, dre reson du the wortas mar bell heb colynwel an **promyses*** 'But this thing is strange to some people, because God waited so long without fulfilling the promises' TH 13a

*ha then kythsam eglos ma crist a rug **promys** in xvi chapter a Johan* 'and to this same Church Christ made a promise in the 16th chapter of John' TH 17

*Thyn kythsam eglos ma eff a rug an **promys** arall, scriffis in xxviii chapter a mathew* 'To this same Church he made another promise, written in the 28th chapter of Matthew' TH 17

*ha ny an jeva **promes** a brassa royow dell vouns y* 'and we got a promise of greater gifts than they' TH 28

*Inweth awosa y assencion thyn neff, according thy **promes**, eff a thanvonas then dore an spuris sans war ben y abosteleth* 'Also after his ascension into heaven, according to his promise, he sent down the Holy Spirit upon the head of his apostles' TH 36

*ha according thy **promys**, in agan tyrmyn ny* 'and according to the promise in our time' TH 40a

*Gesow ny the consyddra fatell rug agan savyor Crist omma in bys gull solem **promys** a vois* 'Let us consider that Christ, our Saviour here in the world made a solemn promise of food' TH 51a

*ha wosa henna in dede eff a ros henna according the **promysse*** 'and thereafter indeed he gave that according to the promise' TH 51a

promise

*Ow kull an **promys** eff a leverys kepar dell ew scriffes in vi-as chapter in aweyll a S Johan* 'Making the promise he said, as is written in the seventh chapter of the gospel of St John' TH 51a

*Mar tene ny comparia an gyrryow cowsys gans crist pan rug eff gul an **promes** a vois* 'If we compare the words spoken by Christ when he made the promise of food' TH 52

*In **promes** eff a leverys fatell vynna eff ry thynny y gyge ha ow performya an **promes** eff a ros henna* 'In the promise he said that he would give us his flesh and performing the promise he gave that' TH 52

*Arta ow kull an **promes**, eff a rug affyrmya fatell o an kyg a vynna eff ry thynny the vaga warnotha, fatell vetha an kithsam kyge na a vetha rys rag an bewnans a oll an bys, ha in performans ay **promys** eff a leueris fatell o an dra esa eff ow ry y gorfe eff y honyn* 'Again making the promise he affirmed that the flesh he would give us to feed on, that that very same flesh would be given for the life of the whole world, and in performance of his promise he said that the thing that he was giving was his own body' TH 52

*praga a russa agan savyour cowse kepar dell rug eff cowse in **promys** gwrys a henna?* 'why would our Saviour speak as he did in a promise made of that?' TH 54

*hay **bromas** o mar wheake may wruge eve thyma cola ny thowtys war ow ena a falsurye* 'his promise was so sweet that he harkened to me. Upon my soul I feared no falsity' CW 776-79

*hay **bromas** yth o largya mar gwrean tastya an frut na avell dew ny a vea* 'and his promise was generous: if we tasted that fruit, we would be like God' CW 780-82

*an **promas** me ny roof oye y dristya ny vannaf vye dowt boos tulles* 'I don't give a fig for the promise; I won't trust it for fear of being deceived' CW 1379-81

*saw whath wos an **promes** na mere yth esaf ow towtya y bedna ʒym ny vyn ef* 'but in spite of that promise, I greatly fear that he will not give me his favour' CW 1539-41

It can be seen from the above examples that **dedhewadow** is attested only in the phrases *an **Tir/Tireth a Dhedhewadow*** 'the Land of Promise, the Promised Land'. **Dedhewys** is attested once only and in the phrase *dedhewys heb keweras* 'an unfulfilled promise, an unfulfilled contract'. **Ambos** means 'contract, agreement' rather than 'promise' *per se*. **Promys**, *plural* **promyssyow** or **promyssys**, is the commonest word for 'promise'.

For 'to promise' three verbs are found in the texts: A) **ambosa**; B) **dedhewy** and C) **promyssya**:

A **ambosa**

*agensow my a'n guelas an arluth nan gefes par ha gynef y tanfonas y te theugh pane veugh war kepar ha del **ambosas*** 'recently I saw him, the Lord who has no equal, and he sent message by me, that he will come to you when you are not expecting, as he promised' RD 911-15.

B **dedhewy**

hag ef rag own ny ylly gans ihesu kewsel ger vas henna o poynt a falsury **deʒewys** *heb koweras* 'and he for fear could not speak a word of help for Jesus; that was a false claim, promised but not fulfilled' PA 83cd.

lauar annes ov bos vy a'm bewnens my th'y bysy a leuerel guyroneth thy'so a'n oyl a versy o **dythywys** *thy'mmo vy gans an tas a'y dregereth pan vef chacys gans an el yn pur thefry* 'tell him I am weary of my life, that I beg him to tell you the truth of the oil of mercy, which was promised to me by the Father in his pity when I was banished by the angel in very truth' OM 700-07

ov thas ev coth ha squytheys ny garse pelle bewe ha genef ef a'd pygys a leuerel guyroneth a'n oyl dotho **dythywys** *a versy yn deyth dyweth* 'my father is old and tired; he does not want to live any longer and he has begged you through me to tell the truth of the oil of mercy promised to him on the last day' OM 737-42

ef yv an oyl a versy a fue the'th tas **dythywys** 'he is the oil of mercy promised to your father' OM 815-16

a maria eugh yn scon leuereugh th'y thyskyblon ha the pedar par del **dythywys** *thethe ef a thue the galile pur wyr hep mar* 'O Mary, go quickly; tell his disciples and Peter as he promised, he will come to Galilee truly without doubt' RD 793-98

y **tethewys** *nansyv meys mones in hans then prasov erbyn duk magus a breys* 'I promised a month ago to go over to the meadows to meet worthy Duke Magus' BM 3918-20.

C **promyssya**

fatell ew an promes ny colynwys, a rug du **promysya** *wosa an towle agan hyndasow adam hag lynnyath eva* 'how is that promise fulfilled, which God promised after the fall of our ancestors Adam and the lineage of Eve?' TH 13

Eff a **promysyas** *fatell vetha onyn genys mes an stok han has a Eva, a re overcommya agan eskar ny an teball ell* 'He promised that one would be born of the stock and seed of Eve, who would overcome our enemy, the devil' TH 13

Eff a **promysyas** *the viterne Dauid fatell re haes inweth dos anotheff* 'He promised to king David that a seed would also come from him' TH 13a

na ny yll bos decevys in maner vith a forth dre gwryoneth necessary kepar dell rug crist **promysya** *in xvi chapter a mathew* 'nor can she be deceived in any kind of way by necessary truth, as Christ promised in the 16th chapter of Matthew' TH 17

Rag crist a **promysyas** *fatell vynna eff bos gans y egglos rag neffra* 'For Christ promised that he would be with his Church for ever' TH 20

nena yma crist ow **promysya** *ha ow assurya thyn, fatell vsy eff worth agan cara ny* 'then Christ promises and assures us, that he loves us' TH 26

Pan o **promysys** *thetha an payne rag tyrry an vhella degry a charity, ha yth ew thynny* **promysys** *an punisment na rag tyrry an lyha degre a cherite* 'Since they were promised punishment for breaking the greatest degree of charity, and that punishment is promised to us for breaking the least degree of charity' TH 27

han gela ew an braster a rewarde **promysys** *thynny vght an Jewys* 'and the second is the size of the reward promised to us above the Jews' TH 27a

promise   **GERYOW GWIR**

In mar ver dell ew lymmyn infancy passys in oys den, ha grace ew plenty res the vabden, han brassa royow **promysys** 'In as much as the infancy of man's age has passed, and grace in plenty has been given to mankind, and the greater gifts promised' TH 28

rag lymmyn nanelle possessyon an bys, na pith an bys, na bewnans here, na gweras a flehes, na victory warbyn agan gostly eskerens, ew **promysys***, mas an wlascore a neff* 'for now neither worldly possession, nor worldly wealth, nor long life nor the help of children, nor victory over our spiritual enemeies have been promised but the kingdom of heaven' TH 28

an spuris a wrioneth han spiris a vnite **promysys** *dre crist then egglos catholyk* 'the spirit of truth and the spirit of unity promised by Christ to the catholic Church' TH 32

Whath yma S Agustyn in kythsame tellar na ow **promysya** *an punysment a thu* 'Yet St Augustine in that self same place promises God's punishment' TH 32a

kepar dell rug crist **promesya** *in vaner ma* 'as Christ promised in this way' TH 36

yth ew openly gothvethis in marver dell rug crist **promysya** *an conforter* 'it is openly known, in as much as Christ promised the Comforter' TH 36

eff a ve **promvsiis** *thethans y ha thega successors neb a ve, neb ew, ha neb a vith in egglos* 'he was promised to them and to their successors who were, who are and who will be in the Church' TH 36a

In gyrryow ma nyg usy eff mas ow **promysya** *an auctorite ma thotheff* 'In these words he promising to him only this authority' TH 44

Ha pandra esa eff ow menya the pedyr mas specyall privileg pan ruga **promysya** *the ry thetho an alwetho a wlas neff in presens a oll an xü-ak?* 'And what did he mean for Peter except a special privelege when he promised to give him the keys of the kingdom of heaven in the presence of all the twelve?' TH 44a

ha kepar dell rug eff nena **promysya***, in della wosa henna eff a rug y perfumya* 'and as he promised then, thus thereafter did he perform' TH 51a

ragan ny ne rug eff refusia the suffra mirnans, henna o mirnans in growsse, na nyns o warbyn y vrys, neb a rug **promysya** *indella dry y only mercy* 'for our sakes he did not refuse to suffer death, that was death on the cross, nor was it contrary to his mind, who promised thus by his mercy only' TH 54a

an serpent der falsurye am temptyas tha wuthell hena hag y **promysyas** *tha vee y fethan tha well nefra* 'the serpent falsely tempted me to do that and promised me that I should ever be the better for it' CW 887-90.

In the revival either **dedhewy** or **promyssya** can be used for 'to promise'.

PROUD

For 'proud' the default word in the revived language has always been **gothys**. This is certainly attested:

A **gothys**
Adam ty a ve **gothys** *pan eses yn paradys avel harlot ov lordye* 'Adam you were proud when in paradise you lorded it like a scoundrel' OM 899-901

GERYOW GWIR   **proud**

lauar thy'm del y'm kerry pan vernans a'n geve ef ha fetel ve fe lethys rag ef o stout ha **gothys** *hag a ymsensy den cref* 'tell me, as you love me, what death took him and how he was killed, for he was courageous and proud and considered himself a mighty man' OM 2218-22

Taw lucyfer melegas in gollan del os tha **gothys** *rag skon ty a tha baynes heb redempcyon thyma creys* 'Silence, accursed Lucifer, as you are proud in heart, for soon you will go to pains without redemption, believe me' CW 283-86.

rag y bosta melagas hag in golan re **othys** *der reson thys me a breif* 'because you are accursed and too proud in your heart, I will prove it to you by reason' CW 305-07.

A commoner word, however, is **prowt**:

B prowt

Gromersy arloth hep par ny a yl lour bones **prout** *ny's teve tus vyth hep mar roow mar tha by myn hout* 'Thank you, lord without equal, we can be proud enough. No men ever had such good gifts by my hood' OM 2595-98

out warnas a pur vyl scout hep thout pestryores stout kyn fy mar **prout** *ty a'n pren* 'Damn you, very evil harridan, without doubt an obstinate witch; be you never so proud you will pay for it' OM 2667-69

heyl syr cayfas epscop stovt maydes ihesu an guas **prout** *re wruk re maystry yn dre* 'Hail, Sir Caiaphas, stalwart bishop. Help us, Jesus, the proud fellow, has done too much bluster in the town' PC 361-63

yma vn guas marthys **prout** *ol an cyte ow trylye theworth mahomm by myn hout hagan lahes ov syndye* 'a remarkably arrogant fellow is turning all the city from Mahound by my hood and harming our laws' PC 577-80

ef a geus lauarow stout hag a leuer the pup **prout** *certan y vones map dev* 'he speaks bold words and tells everyone proudly that he certainly is the son of God' PC 1665-67

heil pilat syre iustis stout heil syre cayphas epscop **prout** 'hail, Pilate, bold Sir Justice, hail Sir Caiaphas, proud bishop' PC 2343

Rag henna ny ve mas nebas an dus **prowd**, *an dus fure, an dus dyskys, an dus perfect han pharyses, a ve sawys dre crist* 'Therefore it was only a few of the proud men, the wise men, the learned men and the pharisees who were saved by Christ' TH 9

Gesow ny the veras war agan treis, ha gwren leverall, then dore, lost peacok... **prowt**, *then dore, colonow* **prowt** 'Let us look upon our feet, and let us say, Down, proud peacock's tail, ... down, proud hearts' TH 9

Kyn fen gaysys gans pobyl Christ, nyng ew mar **bowrth** 'Though I be mocked by the people of Christ, he is not so proud' BK 1229-31

Aragas e feth lethys, rag an pylf **prowt** *ru'm cuthys ve, duk Bitini, Pollitetes, gwerryor stowt* 'In your presence he will be killed, for the proud good-for-nothing has afflicted me, the duke of Bithynia, Pollitetes, a brave warrior' BK 2702-06

ty am gweall ve creif omma whath pur **browt** *ow trebytchya* 'you see me strong here still, stumbling proudly' CW 269-70

ow folly yth ew mar vras haw holan inweth pur **browt** *ny vanaf tha worth an tas whylas mercy sure heb dowte kyn nam boma lowena* 'my folly is so great and my heart also is very

proud

proud; I will not seek mercy from the Father surely without doubt, though I shall not enjoy happiness' CW 1522-26

*ow holan whath yth ew **prowte** kynth oma ogas marowe* 'my heart is still proud, though I am almost dead' CW 1689-90.

For 'proud' in the revived language both **gothys** and **prowt** would seem acceptable.

PUBLIC HOUSE

For 'public house' many revivalists use *dewotty. This word is not attested, having been coined by Nance on the basis of Welsh *dioty, diwoty* 'ale-house.' **Dewotty** is unnecessary, since there are two attested words for 'ale-house, tavern, pub', namely A) **tavern** and B) **hostlery**:

A tavern

*in **tavern** sur ov eva ymons pur ruth age myn* 'they are indeed in the pub drinking with their mouths all red' BM 3308-09

*Caupona… A Tavern, an Ale-house… A. [& C.] **Tavargn**; Hostleri* AB: 47a
*Taberna… A tavarn or victualling house… C. Tshy **tavarn*** AB: 160b.

B hostlery

*Caupona… A Tavern, an Ale-house… A. [& C.] Tavargn; **Hostleri*** AB: 47a
***Hostleri**, a Tavern; Alehouse* Borlase
***HOSTLERI**, an inn, an alehouse, a victualling house* ACB: R 2.

In the interests of authenticity it might be wise to replace *dewotty with **tavern** or **hostelry**. The word **hostlery** incidentally is probably to be stressed on the second syllable.

TO PUNISH, PUNISHMENT

For 'to punish' Nance recommends *kessydhya and pùnyshya (UC *punsya*). *kessydhya is not attested, being based on *sure gossythyans* at CW 1122 (see below). **Pùnyshya** is well attested:

A pùnyshya

*A ty then myghtern pharo dev a'm danfonas thy'so the wofyn prak yv genes **punscie** y tus mar calas* 'You man, King Pharaoh, God has sent me to you to ask why you are minded to punish his folk so severely' OM 1479-82

*mar ny wreth ymamendye ef a wra tyn the **punssye*** 'if you don't mend your ways, he will punish you cruelly' OM 1526-27

GERYOW GWIR **punish**

nyns yw aga dev pleysys genes gy pan os **punsys** *ty ha'th pobel mar calas* 'their God is not pleased with you, when you and your people are punished so severely' OM 1562-64

ty a vyth **punsys** *pur tyn rag the throg a ver dermyn gans arluth nef awartha* 'you will be punished very cruelly for your evil soon by the Lord of heaven above' OM 1600-02

An office arell ew the rebukya, correctya ha **punsya** *vicys* 'The other duty is to rebuke, correct and punish vices' TH 25

Rag yth ew an office a charite magata the rebukya, **punsya** *ha correctia drog pobyll* 'For the duty of charity also is to rebuke, punish and correct evil people' TH 25

An vhall powers ew ordeynys gans du, not the vos dowtys gans an re ew da, mas the **punsya** *an drog pobill gans an gletha* 'the authorities are ordained by God, not to be feared by those who are good, but to punish the evil people by the sword' TH 25

ha the **punyssya**, *ha correctya, an obstynat han froward pehadure* 'and to punish and correct the obstinate and perverse sinner' TH 38a

the judgia lypers ha the **punyssya** *oll an rena na vynna obeya an prontirion* 'to judge lepers and to punish all those who would not obey the priests' TH 38a

ha according thy promys in agan tyrmyn ny agan **punyssya** 'and according to his promise to punish us in our time' TH 40a

na thowt perill war ow honesty benyn vas pokeean y whressan fyllell hag y fea peth pur vras ha me gweffa tha vos **punyshes** 'fear no danger upon my honesty, madam, otherwise I should fail, and it would be a great sin, and I more worthy to be punished' CW 583-87.

Notice that the word **pùnyshya** is stressed on the first syllable.

Chastia 'to chastise' can also on occasion be translated as 'to punish', though 'to subdue' is often a better rendering in English:

B **chastia**

mar mynnough me an **chasty** *ol war barth y[n] nycyte hag an delyrf ʒe wary* 'if you wish, I will punish him altogether in folly and will release him' PA 127cd

mar ny vethe **chastijs** *a vahum ny veth sensys moy es ky heb faladov* 'if he is not subdued, Mahound will be no more revered than a dog without fail' BM 810-12

reys yv dywy lafurya rag **chastya** *an crustunyon dres ol gluas rome alemma* 'it is necessary for you to go forth to subdue the Christians through the country of Rome from here' BM 1179-81

Mars ew the ras, pan o'm **chastyys**, *heb mar in ta e won, te a'm car* 'If it is your grace that you should punish me, I know without doubt that you love me' BK 482-84

ny a **jasty** 'we will punish' BK 690

a vyn ef bones gostoyth thymmo ve kepar del goyth ha **chastya** *y golan?* 'will he be obedient to me as he should and subdue his heart?' BK 2226-28.

The word **kessydhyans** 'punishment' is attested once:

punish   GERYOW GWIR

A **kessydhyans** 'punishment'
*te rom lathas cayne ow brodar yn bys ma rag tha wreans ty a berth sure **gossythyans*** 'you have killed me, Cain my brother, in this world for your deed you will suffer sure punishment' CW. 1119-22.

Tregear uses the English borrowing **pùnyshment**, *plural* **pùnyshmentys**:

*Nyns ew plagys ha **punyshmentys**, teball anetha aga honyn, mar pethans kemerys in forth tha* 'Plagues and punishments are not evil of themselves, if they are taken in good part' TH 24a

*haga cawsia y the vos correctis dre dew **ponisment**, may fo du han commonwelth the lee hurtys dretha* 'and to cause them to be corrected by apt punishment, so that God and the common weal are less hurt by them' TH 26

*An chiff poynt a ra den tyrry charite ew murdyr, han **punisment** a henna yn myske an Jewys o judgment* 'The greatest way man can rupture charity is murder, and the punishment for that among the Jews was judgement' TH 27

*an lya tra a ra den tyrry charite ew bos angry, han **punysment** a henna appoyntys thynny gans crist ew judgment* 'the least thing by which a man can rupture charity is to be angry, and the punishment for that ordained by Christ for us is judgement' TH 27

*ha yth ew thynny promysys an **punisment** na rag tyrry an lyha degre a cherite* 'and that punishment has been promised for us for rupturing charity to the smallest degree' TH 27

*han **punysment** dew ragtha a vith brassa inweth according the gyrryow crist in v-as chapter a S mathew* 'and the punishment due for it will be greater according to the words of Christ in the fifth chapter of St Matthew' TH 28a

*Ha dre gusyll ny a res thyn vnderstondia brassa **punysment** dell o judgment* 'And by council we must understand punishment greater than judgement' TH 28a

*ny rug eff in oll y lawys apporcion **punysment** vith rag parricide* 'in all his laws he apportioned no punishment at all for parricide' TH 29

*Whath yma S Agustyn in kyth same tellar na ow promysya an **punysment** a thu* 'Yet St Augustine in that very place promises the punishment of God' TH 32a.

Nance assumed that ***sure gossythyans*** 'sure punishment' at CW 1122 was a real word, albeit from an unrecognized root. It seems more probable, however, that ***sure-gossythyans*** is a misreading for ****sure gorythyans***, where ****gorythyans*** is the lenited form of ****kerydhyans*** 'rebuke, chastisement' (see s.v. '**REBUKE**' below). **Keredhy** is cognate with Welsh *ceryddu* 'to chastise, to rebuke'. If ****kessydhyans** is indeed a ghost-word, then Tregear's **pùnyshment** would seem to be the only attested word in Cornish for 'punishment'

PURSE

Some commentators recommend borrowing Breton *yalc'h* 'bourse' into revived Cornish as ***yalgh** f. This suggestion has little to recommend it. In the first place an earlier ***yalgh** would have become ***yal** in Cornish (cf. **cal** < ***calgh** 'penis' and **Calesvol** < ***Calesvolgh** 'Excalibur'). Secondly, and more importantly, Cornish already has a word for purse, namely **pors**, *plural* **porsys**:

> *due yv an mona rum fay mester in agen mesk ny aspyen gvas gans **pors** poys* 'upon my faith, the money is gone, master, among us; let us look for a fellow with a heavy purse' BM 1873-85
>
> *deyskyn then dor mata ha the **borse** mes ath ascra me am beth hath margh uskis* 'dismount mate, and I'll have your purse from your bosom and your horse quickly' BM 1887-89
>
> *ser parson bona dyes me a vyn changya **porses** be my fay kyns mos lema* 'Sir parson, good day; I will change purses by my faith before going hence' BM 1905-07
>
> *gedyogh dym quik y **pors** eff an geveth godys cors neb a covs erbyn raffna* 'guide his purse to me quick; he will have God's curse who speaks against robbery' BM 2089.

The Cornish word **scryp** is a borrowing from Middle English *scrip*, *scrippe*, means 'a small bag, a pilgrim's satchel'. It occurs twice:

> *leuerough ow dyskyblon mara fyllys theugh trauyth pan wruge ages danvon hep lorgh na **scryp** nos na deyth* 'tell me, my disciples, whether you lacked anything night or day when I sent you out without staff or scrip' PC 911-14
>
> *lemman lorgh nep a'n geffo gorrens y **scryp** dyworto* 'now whoever has a staff, let him put from him his scrip' PC 919-20.

Scryp could be used in the revived language as an alternative to **pors**. The word ***yalgh** is phonetically questionable and unnecessary.

Q

QUESTION

For 'question' as a noun Nance suggests **govyn**, **govynadow** (UC *govynnadow*) and **qwestyon** (UC *questyon*). **Govyn** is not used in the texts as a noun. A possible exception is *An vyghternath par **govyn** a nug thygo drys tenuyn ha'th soccors oll, pub huny* 'The kings by request will fly to you over valleys and your allies, every one' BK 2527-29. In this passage ***par govyn*** is an editorial emendation for ***por gevyn*** and is quite possibly not what the author had in mind. **Govyn** certainly means 'to ask, to request', but there is no certain evidence that it was ever used in traditional Cornish as a noun meaning 'question, enquiry'.

Govynadow is attested once only. At PC 599-601 Caiaphas is replying to Judas Iscariot, who has just demanded 30 pieces of silver (***dek warn ugens a mone***) as his price for betraying Christ together with an escort to assist in the arrest. Caiaphas shows Iscariot the money and replies:

A govynadow

*sur ol the **wovynnadow** ty a fyth yn guyr hep gow otensy gynef parys* 'sure without doubt you will have your demand entirely. Look I have them ready here'.

Govynadow does not, then, seem to mean 'question, enquiry' but rather 'demand, stipulation'.

The only word in the texts for 'question' is **qwestyon** *m.*, plural **qwestyons**, **qwestyonow**:

B qwestyon

*ha worto pan wofynnyf nep **question** by god ys fo blam vyth ny gafaf ynno* 'and when I ask him any question, by God's foe I find no blame in him' PC 1855-57

*ena wy a gyff in lel guas ovth eria heb **question** esel yv then tebel el* 'there you will truly find a fellow being defiant. Without question he is a limb of the Evil One' BM 967-69

*rag henna eff ny rug cessia dre crefte ha dre **questonow** adro the eva* 'therefore he did not cease by craft and by questions around Eve' TH 4

GERYOW GWIR   question

fattla mar teffa ha contradicion ha varians chansya the vos drehevys war **questyon** *bean?* 'how would it be if a contradiction and difference of opinion happened to arise over a minor question?' TH 19

Omma me a vyn govyn vn **questyon** *the vos assoyles* 'Here I will ask a question to be solved' TH 24a

So pella agys henna omma y thyll bos movyes **questyon** 'But further here a question may be advanced' TH 29a

Rag gurryp thyn kythsam **questyon** *ma, yth ewa the vos notyys fatell rug agan savyoure Jhesu Crist in kythsame tyllar ma in scriptur agan forbyddya ny a bup kynde a vncharitablynes, ha travith ken* 'For an answer to this same question, it should be noticed that our Saviour Jesus Christ in the very same place in scripture forbade all kinds of uncharitableness to us and nothing otherwise' TH 29a

fatla mar pith contencyon ow consernya ran an **questonow** *menys, ny vea eff necessary the trelya ha sewia an auncyent egglosyow?* 'How would it be, if there is a dispute concerning some of the minor questions, would it not be necessary to turn and follow the ancient Churches?' TH 36a

yma Justinus an martyr benegas ow affirmya an **question** *ma* 'Justin, the blessed martyr, affirms this question' TH 57

yth ugy S Chrisostum in kepar maner war an vi a Johan ow leverell pan deffa an **questyon** *ma* 'St John Chrysostom similarly on the sixth chapter of St John says, When this question arises' TH 57

An Sperys Sans gallosak ew heb **queston** *i'n Dryngys, Du marthojak, tryga parson, ow kysragnya* 'The mighty Holy Spirit is without question in the Trinity, marvellous God, a third person, jointly reigning' BK 248-52

ha mer thuwon ew heb **queston**... *dyswryans mab den i'n bys* 'and much anguish is without question... the ruin of mankind in the world' BK 1028-30

Ny worthebe' thotha toching the'n **questons** *eral* 'I will not answer him concerning the other questions' BK 2127-28.

Qwestyon is found in four separate texts and should perhaps, in the interests of authenticity, be the ordinary word for 'question' in the revived language. It should also be noticed that 'to ask a question' is either **govyn qwestyon** or **môvya qwestyon**.

R

TO READ, READER

From the Old Cornish period onwards Cornish has always used the Old English root *ræd-* for 'to read' and for any derivatives. Thus we find both *lector*, **redior** 'reader' OCV §117 and *lectrix*, **rediores** 'female reader' OCV §118. Here are some examples of the verb **redya** 'to read' from Middle Cornish:

pan eth pylat ʒy **redye** *scyle nyni o nagonon* 'when Pilate went to read there was no reason' PA 187c

En lybell a ve tackis worth en grous fast mayʒ ese hag a vgh pen crist gorrys may hylly peb y **redye** *rag bos Ihesus crist crowsys ogas ʒe forth an cyte gans leas y fe* **redijs** *y vonas mygtern ʒethe* 'the charge was fixed to the cross upon which he was and put above Christ's head, so that everyone might read it. Because Christ was crucified near to road from the city, it was read by many that he was their king' PA 189a-d

crist a besys del **redyn** *yndelma yn luas le ow eneff me a gymyn arluth yntre ʒe ʒewle* 'Christ prayed, as we read so in many places, I commend my soul, Lord, into your hands' PA 204cd

yn er na del **redyn** *ny y[n] lyffrow del yw scrifys ʒen neʒyn gwyls rag nyeʒy tellyryow esa paris* 'then, as we read, as is written in scripture, there were ready for the wild birds places to nest' PA 206bc

puppenak ma fo **redys** *an awayl kywhethlys hy a vyth pur wyr neffre* 'wherever the gospel is read, she will be spoken of indeed for ever' PC 550-52

drou e thy'mmo the tackye a vgh y pen gans mur greys may hallo pup y **redye** *gour ha benen kekyffrys* 'bring it to me to fix above his head with great speed, so that everyone can read it, man and woman alike' PC 2807-10

perfect ef a wore **redya** *grammer angeffa deffry y vyea tek* 'he can read perfectly; if he knew grammar it would be good' BM 19-21

ger vyth a scryve pluven whath me ny won ʒe **redya** 'I still cannot read a single word of writing by pen' BM 71-2

A dyves del **redyn** *ny rych lour o in pup termen* 'As we read about Dives, he was always rich enough' BM 446-47

Neffrev pesy bo **redya** *in eglos eff a vetha* 'he used always to be praying or reading in Church' BM 4461-62

Rag ny ren ny **redya** *in teller vith in scripture fatell rug du schappya na furnya mabden* 'For we do not read in any place in scripture how God shaped and formed mankind' TH 2

GERYOW GWIR   read

*ha rag henna ny a **rede** in lyas tyllar in scriptur lowar notabyll lesson warbyn pehosow coth ha vicys inweth* 'and therefore we read in many places in scripture a number of noteworthy lessons against established sins and vices as well' TH 6

*yth ew **redys** in genesis fatell rug du ry thyn oll tytyll ha henow in agan hyndas Adam* 'it is read in Genesis that God gave us all titles and names in our forefather Adam' TH 6

*kyn fowns y vith mar diligens ow **redya** an scrypture, awos oll a henna whath ny rowns y in ta vnderstondia an scripture lell* 'though they be never so diligent in reading scripture, in spite of all that they do not properly understand the scripture' TH 17a

*So keneuer a wothfa **redya** ha vnderstondia a yll gwellas fatell ra ran y vsya gloriusly* 'But as many as can read and understand, can see that some use it gloriously' TH 32a

*Awosa henna ny a **redd** fatell rug lyas onyn an discriplis a crist scryffa aweylys* 'Thereafter we read that many of the disciples of Christ wrote gospels' TH 37a

*kepar dell ren ny **redya** in tryssa leuer an myterneth* 'as we read in the third book of Kings' TH 50a

*Te a **redias** oll an oberow an noruys* 'You have read all the working of the world' SA 61a.

Lhuyd, wishing to avoid, the English borrowing **redya**, devised *lenner 'reader', *lenneryow (Lh. *lennerio*) on the basis of Breton. Modern revivalists have suggested extracting ***lenna** 'to read' from Lhuyd's *lenner 'reader. It has further been suggested that **redya** 'to read' and ***lenna**, might be used in different contexts. **Redya** would then be the ordinary word for 'to read', whereas ***lenna** could be used for 'to read in public, to read aloud'. There is no basis for this distinction.

In the *Old Cornish Vocabulary*, as already noted, we find both ***redior*** 'reader' and ***rediores*** 'female reader'. OCV dates from the early twelfth century, and is based on a Latin-Old English glossary from the tenth century. In the period of the tenth to twelfth centuries very few men would have learnt to read and even fewer women. **Rædestre** 'female reader' in Old English and **rediores** 'female reader' in Cornish almost certainly meant both to the Anglo-Saxon glossarist and his Cornish imitator, a nun who read aloud to the other members of her community while they were eating. In the medieval period there was hardly any other context in which the idea of a female reader would have suggested itself. If this is so, ***rediores*** and ***redior*** from the beginning of recorded Cornish would have referred to those who read aloud. In which case ***redya*** is the correct word to translate 'to read aloud', not the unattested ****lenna***. The suggested distinction between reading quietly to oneself and reading aloud is unwarranted. Until the advent of mass-literacy in the last few centuries, 'to read' in many languages meant 'to read aloud'. **Lenna** 'to read' and its derivatives are both unnecessary and inauthentic. The Cornish for 'to read' is **redya**; 'a reader' is **redyor** *m.* or **redyores** *f.*

REASON, TO REASON

For the substantive 'reason', when it means 'cause, motivation' Nance suggests A) **skyla**; B) **prag** (UC *prak*); C) **praga**; D) **ken**; and E) **rêson**. Let us look at these in turn:

A **skyla** 'reason'

*Ha ʒeso y tanvonas y allus crist rag iudgye ha ny ad cusyll na as lemyn y voth heb sewye yn meth pylat **scyle** vas me ny gafe rum lewte* 'And to you he has sent his authority to judge Christ and we advise you: do not fail to obey his wish. Pilate said: Upon my honour I find no good reason' PA 116a-c

*Pylat a vynsse gwyʒe bewnans Ihesus dre goyntis hag a leuerys ʒeʒe yndelma del yw skrifis lemmyn merough pe nyle an dus a vyth delyffris po cryst leuerough **scyle** po barabas den blamys* 'Pilate wished to preserve Jesus's life by cleverness and said thus to them: As it is written now look which of the men will be released, either Christ, give a reason, or Barabbas, a convicted man' PA 125a-d

*pylat a gewsys arte dreʒough why beʒens leʒys rag ynno me ny gaffe **scyle** vas may fo dampnys* 'Pilate spoke again: Let him be killed by you, for I find no good reason in him that he should be condemned' PA 142cd

*Ef a thuk an grous ganse pur wyr henn o ay anvoth ny wrens y na hen **scyle** lymyn sywye aga both* 'He bore the cross with them; very truly that was against his will; they give no other reason than to follow their wish' PA 175ab

*pan eth pylat ʒy redye **scyle** nyn io nagonon prest y keffy pan vyre henma yw mygtern eʒewon* 'when Pilate went to read it there was no reason. Always when he looked he found: This man is King of the Jews' PA 187cd.

Notice first that all the examples come from PA. Note also that **skyla** can function as a verb:

*natur **scyle** me a syns arluth da mar pyth peynys ol y sogete kyn fons syns rag y beyn ʒe vos grevijs* 'nature causes, I consider, if a good lord is pained, all his subjects, though they be saints, to be afflicted for his pain' PA 211cd.

B **prag** 'reason'

I can find no example.

C **praga** 'reason'

*ow spyrys ny dryc nefre yn corf map den vyth yn beys ha reson yv ha **praga** rag y vos kyc methel gurys* 'my spirit will never dwell in the body of any human in the world and the reason and wherefore is because he was created soft flesh' OM 925-28

*ha reason ew ha **praga** rag y voos kyg medall gwryes ha pur vrotall gans henna* 'and the reason and wherefore is that he was created soft flesh and very weak as well' CW 2221-23 *pyrra foole ne ve gwelys me a levar theis* **praga** 'a more thorough fool was never seen. I will tell you the reason' CW 2400-01.

Praga really means 'why' and in the last of the above examples **praga** could equally well be translated 'why, wherefore?'

D **ken** 'reason'

kemys druk vs ov cothe ha dewethes hag avar yma **ken** *thy'm the ole daggrow gois yn gvyr hep mar* 'so much evil is happening both late and early. I have reason to weep tears of blood in truth without doubt' OM 628-31

ny a vyn mos the besy whare war an arluth ker del ywe luen a versy may rollo yn nep teller dour the eve thethe y na allons yn nep maner kafus **ken** *the thyscrysy* 'I will go straightway to pray the dear Lord, as he is full of mercy, that he may give them somewhere water to drink so that they cannot in any way find cause to disbelieve' OM 1820-26

my ny welaf **ken** *yn bys may fe an keth den ma guyv dre reson the vos lethys* 'I cannot find any reason in the world that this same man be reasonably considered deserving of being put to death' PC 1589-91

my ny gafaf ynno **ken** *may cothfo thy'm y lathe* 'I find in him no reason for which I ought to put him to death' PC 1797-98

ny gafaf vy **ken** *ynno na blam the vones lethys* 'I find no reason in him nor guilt that he should be put to death' PC 2157-58

arlythy war ow laute ny gafaf **ken** *th'y lathe na blam vyth ol ynno of* 'lords upon my word, I find no reason to kill him nor any guilt in him' PC 2213-15

the pygy certan mensen tarye lemmyn na wrelles rak yma thy'mmo vy **ken** 'I would beseech you now not to delay, for I have a reason' RD 444-46.

E **rêson** 'reason'

War lyrgh mab den ʒe begha **reson** *prag y fe prynnys yw ihesus crist ʒe ordna yn neff y vonas tregys* 'After man sinned, a reason why he was redeemed is that Jesus Christ ordained that he would dwell in heaven' PA 7ab

reson *o rag ol an wlas ef a woʒye y verwy* 'a reason was for all the country he knew he would die' PA 56d

me ny gafa moys kyns **reson** *gans gwyr ʒy vrvsy* 'I do not find any more than previously a reason to condemn him justly' PA 117d

En eʒewon a vynne porrys y vonas leʒys **reson**[s] *y a rey ragthe mes war fals yʒ ens growndys* 'The Jews wished urgently that he should be killled. They gave reasons for it, but they were based on falsehood' PA 118cd

kymmes drok a wothevyth ha te **reson** *vyth adres er aga fyn na gewsyth* 'you suffer so much wrong and you do not utter any contrary reason against them' PA 120ab

In meth pylat me ny won ʒen trayteur esa ganso yn crist cafos byth **reson** *merwell prag y reys ʒoʒo* 'Said Pilate to the traitor with him, I cannot in Christ find any reason why he should die' PA 121ab

reason

*yn meth pylat me ny won **reson** prag y fyt dd[m]pnys* 'said Pilate, I know no reason why he should be condemned' PA 128b

*yn meth pylat byth **reson** ʒe laʒe nyng es keffys* 'Pilate said, No reason to kill him has been found' PA 128d

*ow spyrys ny dryc nefre yn corf map den vyth yn beys ha **reson** yv ha prage rag y vos kyc methel gurys* 'my spirit will never dwell in the body of any human in the world and the reason and wherefore is because he was created soft flesh' OM 925-28

*ha dyswe thy'm nep **reson** a'th tyskes omma dyson may hyllyn gynes dysky* 'and show me some reason from your teaching here soon that we may learn from you' PC 1248-50

*my ny welaf ken yn bys may fe an keth den ma guyv dre **reson** the vos lethys* 'I see no cause in the world why this same man deserves by reason to be killed' PC 1589-91

*me a'n conclud yredy ma na wothfo gorthyby vn **reson** thu'm argument* 'I will refute him readily so that he will not be able to answer a single reason to my argument' PC 1659-61

*pup pystryor y cothe dre **reson** da y leysky* 'every magician ought by good reason be burnt' PC 1766-67

*ytho dre pup **reson** da ny goth thotho bos crousys* 'therefore for every good reason he ought not to be crucified' PC 2389-90

*yn certan mara pyth gurys sur warlergh an keth dev ma ny fyth ef neffre dyswrys dre pur **reson** vynytha* 'certainly if it be done according to these same two, he will never be undone by sheer reason henceforth' PC 2451-54

*dyswrys a vyth ol iudy ha kellys an lagha ny dre **reson** sur me a'n pref* 'all Judea will be undone and our law ruined. By sure reason I shall prove it' RD 10-12

*dre pur natur ha **reson** pan wreth hepcor an bevnens hep guthyl na moy cheyson a hugh an eleth ha'n sens ty a thue the nef thu'm tron* 'by pure nature and reason when you relinquish life without giving any other cause, you will come to heaven to my throne above the angels' RD 458-62

*ny geusyth mes a **reson** pleth esos ioseph caugyon ha'th cowyth nychodemus* 'you do not speak unreasonably. Where are you, Joseph, you wretch, and your companion, Nicodemus?' RD 643-45

*erbyn **reson** yv in beys heb hays gorryth thymo creys bones flogh vyth concevijs in breys benen heb awer* 'it is contrary to reason in the world that without male seed, believe me, any child be conceived in a woman's womb freely' BM 844-47

*Sav bytegyns in spyt thy dyns me an gorthyb gans **reson*** 'But nonetheless in spite of you I will answer it with reason' BM 3455-57

*byth nyns off the omager na der **reson** vyth danger dyso ny ruk* 'I am not your vassal at all nor did I ever by reason do you homage' BM 3482-84

*rag ny rug du agan creatya ny pobill an bis heb **reson*** 'for our God did not create us people of the world without reason' TH 5

*rag an meyne ef a creatyas heb **reson**, an brut beastas heb **reson**, Saw eff a ros thynny notabill qualitys ha powers* 'for the stones he created without reason, the brute beasts without reason, but he gave us notable qualities and powers' TH 5

*ha pelha agys henna eff a blanges innan ny particularly **reson** hag vnderstonding* 'and further than that he planted in us in particular reason and understanding' TH 5

GERYOW GWIR   reason

ny a ledyas agan bewnans in pehosow, contrary the **reason** *ha gwryoneth* 'we led our lives in sins, contrary to reason and truth' TH 10

ha the thysky gwryoneth, skyans ha **reason** 'and to learn truth, wisdom and reason' TH 17

ow supposia fatell ewa warbyn **reason** *bos res the vabden cara y yskar* 'assuming that it is contrary to reason that it should be necessary for a man to love his enemies' TH 23a

warbyn oll an kithsam **reasons** *ma ny a res thyn kemeras wyth* 'against all these same reasons we must be on our guard' TH 23a-24

yma dre **reson** *batallyow bras theworthan ny requyrys* 'it is reasonable that great battles are required from us' TH 28

henn ew, yma lyas tra a ra dre **reson** *da ow gwetha ve in lays an egglos catholik* 'that is, there are many thing that keep me for good reason within the laws of the catholic Church' TH 49

Han **reason** *na ew mar vras ha a force an par na ken na ve scripture vith na cowse vith arell* 'And that reason is so great and of such force, otherwise there would be no other scripture nor talk' TH 50a

ha yma **reson** *da ow confirmya, an neyl henn ew owne, hay gela ew feith* 'and good reason confirms, the one is fear and the other is faith' TH 51a

So na ren suffra agan goostly ysker dre carnall **reasons** *thegen dry ny mes agan lell crygyans the heresy* 'But let us not allow our spiritual enemy through carnal reasons to bring us out of true faith to heresy' TH 54a

Desympys gorthyb thymmo ha gas clowas **reson** *da* 'Answer me at once and let me hear good reason' BK 150-51

In kethtella der **reson** *da onyn ew Christ, Du ha den, ow Arluth guew, neb a formyas nef ha'n bys* 'In that way by good reason one is Christ, God and man, my worthy Lord, who created heaven and earth' BK 201-05

An Tas ha'n Mab der **reson** *porrys ew Du* 'The Father and the Son by reason are of necessity God' BK 264-65

In kethtella der **reson** *Arluth Nef in try ferson ew un Du heb dowt i'n cas* 'In the same way by reason the Lord of Heaven in three persons is one God without doubt in the matter' BK 287-89

A'th dewou ne gowsave erbyn **reson***, na raf heb mar* 'I shall not speak of your gods contrary to reason, indeed I shall not' BK 643-45

ha thu'm arluth magata te a vith suer pub seson, hag amyndya ef a ra y'th kevar del vo **reson** 'and to my lord also you will be sure at all times, and he will improve with respect to you as will be reasonable' BK 914-17

Lowena ha sansolath th'agan arluth pub seson, ha fues ha skeantolath ha governans ha **reson** 'Joy and sanctity to our lord at all times, and prosperity and wisdom and authority and reason' BK 1538-41

Dun the glowas e **reson***, rag an matters govynnys* 'let us go to hear his reason for the matters requested' BK 2082-83

Del vo **reson***, me a ra gans weras Du ha yehas* 'As will be reason, I will act with the help of God and good health' BK 3110-11 *rag y bosta melagas hag in golan re othys der* **reson** *thys me a breif* 'for I will prove by reason to you that you are accursed and too proud in heart' CW 305-07.

It will be noticed in the examples above that **rêson** can mean both 'cause, motivation' and 'rational thought'. Clearly **rêson** is the commonest word in traditional Cornish for all senses of the noun 'reason'.

Rêson is also used in TH and in BK in the phrase **dre rêson** 'because, because of':

yth o tra eysy lowre the forberya ha **dre reson** *a henna y offence o the vrassa* 'it was an easy enough thing to refrain from and because of that his offence was the greater' TH 4

Rag henna ny ve mas nebas an dus prowd, an dus fure, an dus dyskys, an dus perfect han pharyses, a ve sawys dre crist, **dre reson** *y the justyfia aga honyn dre aga contyrfett benegitter therag an presens an bobill* 'Therefore only a few of the proud men, the wise men, the learned men, the perfect men and the pharisees were saved by Christ, because they justified themselves by means of their bogus sanctity before the presence of the people' TH 9

Saw an dra ma ew strayng the ran an bobyll, **dre reson** *du the wortas mar bell heb colynwel an promyses* 'But this thing is strange to some of the people, because God waited so long without fulfilling the promise' TH 13a

rag henna yth esans y heb excusse, **dre reson** *pan wothyans aswon du, ny rens y honora, na y gorthya kepar ha du* 'therefore they were without excuse, because when they knew God, they did not honour him, nor worship him as God' TH 14

travith mas sore, anger, han vingians a thu, **dre reson** *eff thegan dyluer ny vnwyth theworth pegh dre y vercy* 'nothing but the wrath, anger and vengeance of God, because he delivered us once from sin by his mercy' TH 15a

Dre reson *y bos an egglos an cyta vgy agan savyour ena ow menya, han gantyll ew ena cowsys anethy* 'Because the Church is the city which our Saviour means there and the candle which is spoken of there' TH 17a

Rag henna ow cothmans, **dre reson** *y bosow gwarnys theragdorne, bethow ware* 'Therefore, my friends, because you have been warned in advance, beware' TH 18

ran a gothas theworta, **dre reason** *a termes ha talys nowith faynes, ha* **dre reason** *inweth y the gemeras warnetha an gothfos* 'some fell away, because of new-fangled terms and tales, and because also they assumed knowledge' TH 18a

fatell rons y dos in crehyn devas, **dre reson** *y bosans y ow pretendya an gyrryow a thu ha gans henna ow dalhe lagasow an bobyll* 'that they come in the skins of sheep, because they claim the words of God and thus they blind the eyes of the people' TH 19a

ha **dre reson** *nag es fawt vith mar vras dell ew then cotha in mes gans agan kyscristyan ha tyrry kerensa ha cherite* 'and because there is no fault greater than falling out with our fellow Christian and rupturing love and charity' TH 26a-27

gans moy payne dell rug an Jewys, **dre reson** *ny the receva moy grace dell rug an Jewys* 'with more pain than the Jews bore, because we received more grace than did the Jews' TH 28

GERYOW GWIR — reason

*Ha whath nyns ugy agan savyowre ow hynwall na moye degreys, partly **dre reson** y bos an payne an kythsame tressa degre ma tane effarne* 'And yet our Saviour does not name any more degrees, partly because the pain of this same third degree is the fire of hell' TH 29

*han kyhsame egglos ma, **dre reson** y bossy sanctifies ha benegys* 'and this same Church because she is sanctified and blessed' TH 31

*hen ew the leverell an vnyuersall egglos, dre **reson** nag ussy ow lurkya in cornettow* 'that is to say the universal Church, because she does not lurk in corners' TH 31a

*pella is hemma **dre reson** y bos S paule lynwys an Spurissans, eff a attendias fatell vynna oll an heretikys gylwall thetha an auctorite an aposteleth* 'more than this, because St Paul was filled with the Holy Spirit, he noticed that all the heretics wished to invoke for themselves the authority of the apostles' TH 33

*rag henna ny a goth thyn cresy then Catholyk egglos, **dre reson** crist y honyn thy hevely the roois towlis in more* 'therefore we should believe in the catholic Church, because Christ himself likened her to a net cast into the sea' TH 34

*Oll an re ma sure, gans mere moy, a theth warnan ny **dre reson** y bosen gyllys in mes thean chy a thu* 'All these indeed and many more have come upon us because we have strayed from the house of God' TH 40a

*ha **dre reson** y vosa mar sure in feith, an egglos a ve buldys warnotha* 'and because he was so sure in faith, the Church was built upon him' TH 45a

*Pedyr ew gylwys carrak **dre reson** eff the vos an kynsa a rug laya an fowndacion* 'Peter is called Rock because he was the first to lay the foundation' TH 45a

*Ken rug oll an x tryb a Israell departia athewarth Roboam mab Salamon, whath **dre reson** y bosa gwrys dre an blonogeth a thu, yth o cryff ha fyrme heb aucthorite vith arell* 'Although all the ten tribes of Israel separated from Rehoboam the son of Solomon, yet because he had been made by the will of God, he was strong and firm without any other authority' TH 50a

*Ha whath **dre reson** ran athewethas a rug talkya vaynly ha curiously an kythsam seconde part ma* 'And yet because some recently have talked vainly and bizarrely of this same second part' TH 55

*ha whath ny rug den vith dowtya **dre reson** y bos du an gwrear anetha* 'and yet no man doubted because God was their creator' TH 57

*Whath **dre reson** in scriptur, an dra esan ny ow reseva, pan deffan then sacrament, ew gylwys bara, rag henna lyas onyn an gevith fantasy an par na* 'Yet because in scripture that which we receive, when we come to the sacrament, is called bread, therefore many have a fantasy of that kind' TH 57

*kepar hag Adam ew gylwys dore, **dre reson** y bosa gwrys a dore* 'just as Adam is called clay, because he was made from clay' TH 57a

*Henna o e lavarow, ha **der reson** ha drefan e vos mer goyth govynnys, ef a leverys efan, e fethowgh why dybynnys th'y aquyttya* 'Those were his words, and because and since it was so impudently demanded, he said publicly that you would be beheaded to pay it' BK 2268-73.

In Cornish 'to have lost one's reason' is **bos mes a'y rewl:**

reason   GERYOW GWIR

*Meryasek dyugh lowena den **mes ay revle** us gena ha tus re ruk ov heskey may rellen y dry oma the voys socrys genogh wy* 'Greetings, joy to you, Meriasek. I have with me here someone who has lost his reason, and men advised me to bring him to you here to be helped' BM 3816-20.

For 'to reason, to dispute' the best translation is **rêsna**

*Pana vater a vea hemma thynny omma besy the **resna** warnotha, fatell ylly du po ell apperia in hevelep a den* 'What matter would this be for us here to dispute about it assiduously, whether God or an angel can appear in the likeness of a man?' TH 55
*ny amount thymma **resna** genas noy me a hevall* 'it is no use for to reason with you, Noah, it seems' CW 2395-96.

REBEL, TO REBEL, REBELLYON

The attested word for the substantive 'rebel' is **rebel**:

*in dyspyt in kyg e thyns, mara'n mettya', an **rebel** gu ha fals dell ew, me a'n dyel heb lettya* 'in spite of his gums, if I meet him, the wretched rebel and false as he is, I shall be avenged on him without delay' BK 2280-84.

For 'to rebel' Nance recommends ***omsevel**, **gùstla** (UC *gustla*) and ***rebellya**. ***Omsevel** is not attested. **Gùstla** occurs in the phrase ***rag gustla bell*** 'to wage war' at PA 249d and does not therefore mean 'to rebel'. ***Rebellya** is not attested but the noun **rebellyans** 'rebellion' is found:

*myghale pryns ow chyvalry han elath an order nawe an **rebellyans** ma deffry than doer ganso mergh ha mawe* 'Michael, prince of my chivalry, and the angels of the nine orders, this rebellion indeed, down with it, horse and boy!' CW 291-94.

TO REBUKE, A REBUKE, REPROOF

For the verb 'to rebuke, to reprove' some revivalist use **keredhy**. This is certainly attested:

A **keredhy**
*war y lergh guel yv mones ken sur ny a veth blamyes ha **kerethys** eredy* 'it is better to go after him, otherwise we shall certainly be blamed and rebuked indeed' BM 3248-50
*Awota ve devethys, ha'm dyns terrys mes a'm pen ha kronkyys ha **kerethys** ove* 'Here I have come, with my teeth broken in my head and I have been beaten and rebuked' BK 837-39
*Ny goyth thewgh bos **kerethys**, whyl ye be swynys so light* 'You should not be rebuked, while your swains be so light' BK 2220-21

GERYOW GWIR — rebuke

Kin fena dyanhethys, ny'th curyn ow crabanow, na rownys, kyn fena lethis, rag own bonas **kerethis** *gans suel a ugar ganow* 'Though I be evicted, my hands will not crown you, they will not, though I be killed, for fear of being rebuked by all who open their mouths' BK 3090-94.

reprêva, reprovya is also attested:

B reprêva, reprovya

out warnaugh a thevv adla pendra wreugh ov **repryfa** *ha my omma yn ov hel* 'out upon you, you two rogues! What do you rebuke me and I here in my hall?' OM 1499-501

na **repreff** *tus vohosek dymo a vo devethys* 'do not rebuke poor men who have come to me' BM 3120-21

Inweth eff a yll leverall, pew vs a hanow why a yll ow **reprovia** *vel rebukia ve rag pegh* 'Also he can say, Who among you can reprove or rebuke me for sin?' TH 11

So rag an wyckyd han drog requestys ma eff a ve grevously rebukys ha **reprovys** 'But for these wicked and evil requests he was grievously rebuked and reproved' TH 46a.

It seems, however, that the commonest word in the texts for 'to rebuke' is **rebukya**:

C rebukya

Ragon menough **rebekis** *ha dyspresijs yn harow yn growys gans kentrow fastis peynys bys pan ve marow* 'For us often rebuked and spurned grimly; fastened with nails to the cross; tormented until he died' PA 2cd

ena y an **rebukyas** *therag an try may3 esa annas pylat ha cay[p]has* 'there they rebuked him when he was before the three, Pilate, Annas and Caiaphas' PA 112ab

Gans mur a Iucters yn wlas ef a ve veyll **rebukis** *kavanskis ef a whelas rag own y vonas le3ys* 'he was vilely rebuked by many justices in the kingdom; he tried to evade for fear of being killed' PA 156ab

Inweth eff a yll leverall, pew vs a hanow why a yll ow reprovia vel **rebukia** *ve rag pegh* 'Also he can say, Who among you can reprove or rebuke me for sin?' TH 11

Hag indelma eff a vsyas y honyn, ow exortya y yskerens ha ow **rebukya** *aga fautes* 'And thus he behaved, exhorting his enemies and rebuking their faults' TH 22a

dre kerensa eff a rug **rebukya** *aga theball bewnans* 'through love he rebuked their evil life' TH 23

Ea ha the **rebukya** *ha correctia dre an gere a thu an offences ha fawtys an drog pobill* 'Yes, and to rebuke and correct by the word of God the offences and faults of evil people' TH 25

An office arell ew the **rebukya**, *correctya ha punsya vicys* 'The other function is to rebuke, correct and punish vices' TH 25

Rag yth ew an office a charite magata the **rebukya**, *punsya ha correctia drog pobyll* 'For it is the function of charity also to rebuke, punish and correct evil people' TH 25

Inweth S paule the Tymothe ow **rebukya** *pegh constantly* 'Also St Paul to Timothy, constantly rebuking' TH 25

rebuke

*han offendars a res bos **rebukys** ha correctys in dew tyrmyn* 'and the offenders must be rebuked and corrected in due time' TH 25a

*may thillans **rebukya** an drog pobyll han trespasces han offendars a lays du* 'so that they may rebuke the evil people and the trespasses and the offenders of the laws of God' TH 29a

*yth ew gwris da aga **rebukya**, may hallans bos methek ha kemeras sham aga fawtys* 'it is well done to rebuke them, so that they may be embarrassed and be ashamed of their faults' TH 29a

*so yma cherite ow commondia thyn **rebukya** malefactors ha drog tus* 'but charity commands us to rebuke malefactors and evil men' TH 30

*Yma S paule ow **rebukya** in y epistill thyn Corinthians, neb a ve in kythsam case na* 'St Paul in his epistle to the Corinthians rebukes them, who were in that same situation' TH 33

*So an apostyll benegas S paul as **rebukyas** in vaner ma* 'But the blessed apostle Paul rebuked them as follows' TH 33

*Eff a commondias Tite the exortya ha **rebukya** gans oll ferventnes a commondia* 'He commanded Titus to exhort and rebuke with all the eagerness he could command' TH 33a

*So rag an wyckyd han drog requestys ma eff a ve grevously **rebukys** ha reprovys* 'But for these wicked and evil requests he was grievously rebuked and reproved' TH 46a

*An arluth a thysquethas an cruelte a Judas, pan rug an arluth Dew e **rebukya**, whath na ruk Judas e vnderstandya* 'The Lord demonstrated the cruelty of Judas, when the Lord rebuked him; yet Judas did not understand him' SA 65a.

Given that **rebukya** is attested three times already in PA, our earliest long text, it was clearly borrowed from Middle English into Cornish at an early date. If it has been an integral part of the Cornish lexicon since the fourteenth century, there is no reason to avoid it in the revived language.

There is no attested form in the texts to translate the English substantive 'rebuke, reproof' that is based on the root seen in **keredhy**. The ordinary words for 'rebuke, reproof' are either A) **repref** or B) **rebuk:**

A **repref**

***repreff** na cam nygis beth* 'reproof nor wrong you shall not have' BM 1770

*Nyng ew **repref** tho'm ehan hag awos own, me a dyrhas i'n forest a Rosewa* 'There is no reproof to my kindred and because I was afraid, I landed in the forest of Rosewa' BK 96-9.

B **rebuk**

*eff a suffras ragan ny lyas **rebuk*** 'he suffered for us many rebukes' TH 24

*dre hemma ny a yll gwelas ha persevya fatell ew kynde an par na an **rebukys** an re an jevas auctorite* 'by this we can see and perceive the rebukes of those in authority are kinds like that' TH 29a *may hallans bos methek ha kemeras sham aga fawtys ha dre* **rebukys** *amendia aga lewde bewnans* 'that they may be embarrassed and ashamed of their faults and by rebukes emend their wicked lives' TH 29a

han kithsame kende me a **rebukys** *ew da ha lawfull* 'and this very same kind of rebukes are good and lawful' TH 29a.

TO RECEIVE, RECEIVER

For 'to receive' many revivalists use the verb **degemeres**. This is attested:

A degemeres

guyn y vys a vo trigys yn the seruys ragh tristys nyn **dygemmer** *vynytha* 'happy is the man who lives in your service, for sorrow will never receive him' PC 122-24

dre rychyth ha chevalry den a veth **degemorys** *in ban in meske arlythy ha ganse prest enorys* 'through riches and chivalry a man will be received into the midst of lords be always honoured by them' BM 432-35

der rychyth pur eredy den a veth **degemerys** *in ban in mesk arlythy ha ganse prest enorys* 'by sheer riches indeed a man will be received into the midst of lords and always honoured by them' BM 2572-75.

It appears, however, that the commonest word for 'to receive' in Cornish is **recêva, recêvya**:

B recêva, recêvya

an arghans a gemeras rag corf crist ʒe **rysseve** *ef as tewlys dre sor bras ʒen eʒewon yntreʒe* 'the silver he had got for them to receive Chirist's body, he threw them in great anger at the Jews in their midst' PA 103bc

Ena vn lowarth ese ha ynno [beth] o parys den marow rag **receve** 'There was a garden there and in it a tomb had been prepared to receive a body' PA 233ab

hay dew myr orth ov offryn ha **ressef** *thy's ov dege* 'Oh, God, look at my offering and receive for yourself my tithe' OM 505-06

arluth dev ker klew ov lef ha gor vy the lowene ha'm spyrys thy'so **ressef** *in manus tuuas dumine* 'Lord, dear God, hear my voice and carry me to bliss and receive my spirit to you. Into your hands, O Lord' OM 1895-98

ov arluth my a'n te thy's re'n ordyr a **recevys** 'my lord, I swear it to you by the order of chivalry I received' OM 2159-60

aban vynnyth yndella y **resseve** *my a wra yn gorthyans the'n tas a'n nef* 'since you wish it thus, I will receive it in honour of the Father of Heaven' OM 2617-19

en tas dev roy thy'n bos gwyw the wos ker the **resceue** *dre the voth yn geth hythyw* 'God the Father grant us to be worthy to receive his dear blood through your will today; PC 829-31

dismas iesmas deugh yn ban ihesu ynweth baraban agas brus the **resseue** 'Dismas, Jesmas, come up, Jesus also and Barabbas, to receive your judgement' PC 2337-39

receive   **GERYOW GWIR**

iosep whek **resceu** *e thy's hag y'n cendal glan mayly'e* 'dear Joseph, receive him to you and wrap him in the clean linen cloth' PC 3155-56

eno ny a'n **receuas** *vthyk yw clewas y lef tan ha mok ha potvan bras yn carna neffre y sef* 'there we received him. It is terrible to hear his voice. Fire and smoke and great heat in that rock-heap will remain for ever' RD 2339-42

an men re ruk inclynya in tyr rag the **receva** *gras the ihesu galosek* 'the stone has bent down to the earth to receive you, thanks to mighty Jesus' BM 1094-96

meryasek yv dewesys sav eff ny vyn del glowys y **receva** *eredy* 'Meriasek has been chosen but he will not receive it indeed, as I have heard' BM 2875-77

corff ov arluth del deleth hythyv me re **recevas** 'as is fitting, today I have received the body of my Lord' BM 4253-54

corff crist inweth **receva** *vngijs gans henna defry* 'to receive the body of Christ, anointed therewith also indeed' BM 4281

mar te den ha **receva** *royow bras the worth y gothman po y soveran* 'if a man happens to receive great gifts from his friend or sovereign' TH 4a

discans vith a vo contrary the thiskans an abostoleth han catholik egglos generall **recevis** *in sans egglos* 'any teaching which is contrary to the teaching of the apostles and the catholic Church generally received in holy Church' TH 19a

lymmyn why a well pan benefittys ha dadder a russyn ny **receva** *thea rome* 'now you see what benefits and good we have received from Rome' TH 51

onyn an chyff duty ew the preparya agan honyn the vos worthy rag **receva** *an Sacrament an aulter* 'one of our chief duties is to prepare ourselves to be worthy to receive the sacrament of the altar' TH 51a

Penagull a rella **receva** *anotha ha na vova worthy, yma ow tybbry ha ow heva y damnation y honyn* 'Whoever receives of it and is not worthy, he eats and drinks his own damnation' TH 51a

ha fatell rug abraham aga **receva** 'and that Abraham received them' TH 55

ow **receva** *an corfe han gois agan savyour Ihesu crist* 'and having the whole manhood receiving the body and blood of our Saviour Jesus Christ' TH 56

Eliseus a rug **recevia** *e mantall kepare e lell ha meer inheritance* 'Elisha received his mantle like his true and great inheritance' SA 60

ha pan vova **recevis** *[g]enas, kee thath tre ha gwra golhe theth enaff theworth [o]ll mvstethas a pehosow* 'and when he has been received by you, go home and wash your soul from all filth of sin' SA 60a

Indella emowns y dishonora Christ pan vonsy y **recevia** *ef ha e corf benegas ef gans dowla mustethas* 'Thus they dishonour Christ when they receive him and his blessed body with unclean hands' SA 61

ha e **recevia** *ef lymmyn gans mustethas ganaw* 'and receive him now with unclean mouth' SA 61

neb vge o **recivia** *corf dew gans dowla mustethas eth ew ef gilty an gos agen arluth dew* 'he who receives the body of God with unclean hands, he is guilty of the blood of our Lord God' SA 61

eth esan ny o **recevia** *dan an lell mystery kigg ay corf benegas* 'we receive under the true mystery the flesh of his blessed body' SA 61

GERYOW GWIR — record

*te a **recevas** an shap a myrnans Christ, indella eth esta eva e presivs gois* 'you received the shape of the death of Christ, thus you drink his precious blood' SA 63

*rag henna te a **receves** an Sacrament* 'for this you received the Sacrament' SA 63

*Dir henna eth os diskys, te the **recevia** pith ew corf Christ* 'Through this you are taught, you to receive that which is the body of Christ' SA 63

*fatla vgy an bobell ow leverall an kigg na ill **recevia** gifte Dew* 'how can the people say: the flesh cannot receive the gift of God?' SA 63a

*[not] ef the **recevia** pith ow badd [mas ef a] **recevyas** Corf Dew warlerth badd maner* 'not that he received what is bad, [but that he] received the body of God in a bad manner' SA 65a

*ha'y dengys us **recevys** in Du parfyt, me a grys, a'n Worthyas Ker Marya* 'and his manhood, which is received in perfect God, I believe, from the Blessed Virgin Mary' BK 157-59.

Recêva might well be used as the ordinary word for 'to receive' in the revived language.

TO RECORD

For 'to record' Nance recommends A) **cofhe** and B) **recordya**. The first of these seems to be attested three times:

A cofhe

*why a'm **cofua** vy hep gow pys[quyth] may fe ve evys* 'you will without doubt remember me, whenever it is drunk' PC 827-28

*hag honor bras in pelder bys venytha heb duwath sertan heb flos, a thallath bys may fen **cofuys**: a wll corf ny glowys cows* 'and great honour continually for ever without end surely without trifling, from the beginning of the world that we may be reminded: no talk was ever heard of a better person' BK 1932-37

*Flowran a skyentolath ha gallosak in leawte os war pub ous, a thallath bys, may fen **cofuys**: a wel corf ny glowys cows* 'The flower of wisdom and mighty in loyalty you are at all times since the beginning of the world, that we may be remined: no talk was ever heard of a better person. BK 1940-45.

Recordya is more frequently found:

B recordya

*del **recorde** agen latha* 'as our law records' BM 1629

*yma ow **recordia** an severall gwra a then, magata ay gorffe worta y honyn* 'it records the several creations of man, also of his body by itself' TH 2

*kepar dell lavar an Abostyll pedyr ow **recordia** in. v. chapter yn kynsa pystyll* 'as the apostle Peter says, recording in the fifth chapter in the first epistle' TH 3a

*may rug du repentya eff the wull mabden kepar dell vgy an scripture ow **recordya*** 'so that God repented of having created man, as the scripture records' TH 7

record   **GERYOW GWIR**

yma eff ow dysky fatell ra drog gerryow ha drog prederow deservya condemnacion ow **rekordya** *inweth fatell ren ny gull accompt ha rekyn a bup ger cowses in sovereth* 'he teaches that evil words and evil thoughts deserve condemnation, recording also that we will give account and reckoning in every word spoken in jest' TH 9

Eff a leuerys the Abraham kepar dell ew **recordys** *in xxii a geneses* 'He said to Abraham as is recorded in the 22nd chapter of Genesis' TH 13

Ima S paul ow **recordia** *in v chapter then galathians* 'St Paul records in the fifth chapter to the Galatians' TH 16a

kepar dell vsy Oecumenius inweth ow **recordia** 'As Oecumenius records' TH 27a

Eff a ros thy abosteleth power bras ha auctorite bras, kepar dell vsy S Mathew ow **recordya** 'He gave to his apostles great power and authority, as St Matthew records' TH 35a

kepar dell vsy S Ciprian ow **recordya** 'as St Cyprian records' TH 42

kepar dell vsy Justinus an martyr ha den auncient ow **recordia** *in y seconde Apologie* 'as Justin Martyr and an ancient man records in his second *Apologia*' TH 46a

Ireneus inweth in y kynsa lever Contra Hereses ow **recordya** *henna* 'Irenaeus also in his first book *Contra Hereses* recording that' TH 46a

ha hemma yma S Jherom ow **recordya** *in dalleth ay story* 'and this St Jerome records in the beginning of his history' TH 47

Indelma yma S Ambros ow leverall ha the henna yma Egesippus ow **recordya** 'Thus St Ambrose says, and to that Hegesippus records' TH 47a

In v-as a Josue yth ew **recordys** *fatell rug onyn sodenly apperya the Josue* 'In the fifth chapter of Joshua it is recorded that someone suddenly appeared to Joshua' TH 55a

In iii chapter a Daniell yth ew **recordys** *an iii flogh the vos in furnyas in flam* 'In the third chapter of Daniel it is recorded that the three children were in the furnace of flame' TH 56a

Ow! Me a wothya, parda! the vota ow **recordya** *ow bosa den eredie* 'Oh, I knew, by God, that you were recording that I was a man indeed' BK 351-53

Turba gentis future a **record** *the vonas flowr* 'A crowd of future people record that you are the choicest' BK 1564-65

rag voydya an peril na scryffes yma thym pub tra a thallathfas an bys ma may fova leall **recordys** *a vyns tra es ynna gwryes* 'to avoid that danger everything is written for me since the beginning of the world, that it might accurately be recorded of every thing that has been done in it' CW 2170-74

Since **recordya** is attested in four different texts, it was clearly an essential part of the Cornish lexicon. There is no reason, therefore, to avoid it.

Covath 'record' (substantive) is attested twice in the idiom **ny asaf an covath** 'I do not forsake the record, the memory', i.e. 'I shall remember':

A **covath**

an **couath** *bvth ny hassaf mar qureth thy'm an sacryfys* 'I shall never abandon the memory of it, if you make the sacrifice to me' OM 1281-84 *a ow map ker na porth a wher dev a'th weres ef dev a ras an* **covath** *ny has termyn vyth nes* 'my dear son, do not be dismayed; God will assist you. He, a God of grace, will not forsake the memory of you at all at any time' OM 1359-60.

Record 'record' is also found twice:

B **record**

yn **record** *yn tokyn len ov guarak a fyth settyys yn ban yn creys a'n ebren na allo bones terreys* 'as a record as a true token my bow will be set up in the middle of the sky, so that it cannot be broken' OM 1243-46

lemyn me es goer in badn hag in nyell sure bys vickan an **record** *a vythe heb fall pur wyer kevys* 'now I will put them up and in one or the other for ever the record will be found in truth without out fail' CW 2202-05.

REDEEMER, TO REDEEM, REDEMPTION

The word **dasprenyas** 'redeemer' is attested:

ha venytha me a grys the vos a werghes genys map dev agan **dysprynnyas** 'and for ever I shall believe that you were born of a Virgin, the son of God, our Redeemer' PC 402-04

del os formyas the'n nef ha'n lur ha **dysprynnyas** *thy'nny pup vr cryst ow sylwyas clev mar a'th dur thy's daryvas del garsen mur* 'as you are Creator of heaven and earth and redeemer for us always, Christ my Savior, hear me if you will, as I should greatly like to tell you' RD 843-46.

Dasprenyas is related to the verb **dasprena** 'to redeem', which is also attested:

ow arluth cryst dr'y vercy a wruk ow **dysprenne** *vy mes a yfarn yn teffry* 'out Lord Christ by his mercy from hell delivered him indeed' RD 215-17

der thowgys e tathorhas e honnyn par del vynnas, ha'y lel servantes **dyspernys** 'in his divinity he rose again as he wished himself and redeemed his loyal servants' BK 310-13.

For 'redeemer' Tregear uses **redêmer**:

ha gans perfect colonow the reiosya in sight agan creator ha **redemar** 'and with perfect hearts to rejoice in the sight of our Creator and Redeemer' TH 1

dysquethys ha declarys in Crist Jhesu agan arluth ha **redemer** 'shown and declared in Christ Jesus, our Lord and Redeemer' TH 11.

For 'to redeem' TH and SA use **redêmya**:

redeemer   **GERYOW GWIR**

eff a rug agan **redemya** *dre an pascion han myrnans ay vnvab eff Jhesu crist agan savyour ny* 'he redeemed us by the passion and death of his only Son, Jesus Christ, our Saviour' TH 16

Kyffrys an creasion a vabden, ha fatell veva **redemys** 'Also the creation of man and how he was redeemed' TH 30a

Jhesu crist, neb a rug agan **redemya** 'Jesus Christ, who redeemed us' TH 30a

wath dir grace christ ema remaynea the **redemya** *an redemtion* 'yet by the grace of Christ the redemption remains to redeem' SA 63

whath ema ef ow conys an prys tha **redemya** *ny* 'still it works to pay the price to redeem us' SA 63.

For the substantive 'redemption' Nance's first choice is ***daspren**, which is unattested. The only word in the texts is **redempcyon**:

kepar ha dell ewa sufficiant cawse agan **redempcion** 'as though it is sufficient cause of our redemption' TH 1

eff ewe an arluth an gefas plenty a **redempcion** 'he is the Lord who has plenty of redemption' TH 10a

Hen ew the vnderstondia agan **redempcion** *ny* 'That is to say, our redemption' TH 12

wath dir grace christ ema remaynea the redemya an **redemtion** 'yet by the grace of Christ the redemption remains to redeem' SA 63

rag skon ty a tha baynes heb **redempcyon** *thyma creys* 'for soon you will go to torments without redemption, believe me' CW 285-86

why a weall matters pur vras ha **redempcon** *granntys der vercy a thew an tase tha sawya neb es kellys* 'you will see great matters and redemption granted by the mercy of God the Father to save those who are lost' CW 2542-45.

In the revived language 'redeemer' can be either **dasprenyas** or **redêmer**. 'To redeem' is either **dasprena** or **redêmya**. 'Redemption' should perhaps be **redempcyon**.

TO REJOICE

As has been noted s.v. '**ENJOY**' the Cornish verb **lowenhe** means 'to rejoice, to be glad'. Another way of saying 'to rejoice', however, is to use the verb **rejoycya**:

ha thy servya in lowendar ha gans perfect colonow the **reiosya** *in sight agan creator ha redemar* 'and to serve him in joy and with perfect hearts, to rejoice in the sight of our Creator and Redeemer' TH 1

te neb vgy ow **reiosya** *in la, dre transgression an la yth esas ow dyhonora du* 'you, who rejoice in the law, by transgression of the law you dishonour God' TH 14a

GERYOW GWIR remember

*Ha dre an reson ma y honyn an martyr S Ciprian yma ow **reiossya** in mer y epistlis* 'And by this very reason the martyr St Cyprian rejoices in many of his epistles' TH 50a

*rag henna woʒa hemma nefra ny wren **rejoycya** mes pub ere oll ow murnya heb ioy vyth na lowena* 'thereafter after this we will never rejoice, but always mourning without any joy or happiness' CW 1271-74

*Ef a lathas ye vrodar ny gemeras yddrag vyth mes y **regoyssyas** pur vear hag a sor an tas tre vyth yn serten ef ny synges* 'He killed his brother. He was not at all sorry but rejoiced greatly and cared nothing certainly for the anger of the Father' CW 2047-51.

The verb **rejoycya** is attested in two texts. There is no reason to avoid it.

TO REMAIN

Although **gortos** is the ordinary word for 'to remain', the borrowing **remainya** is attested in three separate texts:

*rag y bos an forme a bara ow **remaynya** whath in henna yma... inweth gylwys bara* 'because the form of bread remains... it is still called bread' TH 57a

*wath dir grace christ ema **remaynea** the redemya an redemtion* 'still by the grace of Christ the redemption remains to redeem' SA 63

*ena ornys thies ew place gans an tas theso heb gowe tha **ramaynya** rag season* 'there a place has been ordained for you by the Father without a lie to remain for a while' CW 2072-74.

There is no reason to reject **remainya** out of hand.

TO REMEMBER, REMEMBRANCE

'To remember' is sometimes translated **perthy cof**, literally 'to bear remembrance':

A **perthy cov**

*arluth **porth cof** yn deyth dyweth am enef vy* 'Lord, remember my soul at the last day' OM 1272-73

***pertheugh cof** ol an tokyn a leuerys kyns lemyn thywy why a gowethe* 'Remember, you all, of the token I have told you before now, O friends' PC 1081-83

*y'n gylwys map dev yn prof ahanaf may **portho cof** pan deffe th'y wlascor ef* 'I called him Son of God in proof moreover that he might remember me when he came to his kingdom' RD 271-73

*ha dres henna **porth cof** lauar confort yn ta thymmo pedar mur yu kyrys* 'and further remember, say, comfort well Peter for me who is greatly loved' RD 890-92

*hag arta **perthugh coff** guel pendrellen the comondya* 'and in the future remember better what I command' BM 1064-65

remember GERYOW GWIR

ov sovdrys duen warnetha pur theffry kyns tremena ahanan y a **perth coff** 'my soldiers, let us attack them. They will very surely remember us before they die' BM 2484-86

omskem[i]nys lower yth ove nyng ew reis skemyna moye nyth anea **perth ge cove** *na ow dama in teffrye* 'I am cursed enough. There is no need to curse more. I will not annoy you, remember, nor my mother indeed' CW 1213-16

noy mabe lamec gylwys ove arluthe brase oll **perthew cove** *yth of omma in bys ma* 'Noah son of Lamech am I called, a great lord, remember you all, am I in this world' CW 2232-34

Perhgoh *the giwthe sanz an dyth Sabboth* 'Remember to keep holy the Sabbath day' ACB: E e 3 *verso*

En Hâv, **perkou** *Gwâv* 'In Summer, remember Winter' ACB: E e 4.

For 'I remember' one can also say **yma cov dhybm**:

B **yma cov dhybm** 'I remember'

ha whaeth **ma ko them***, pe nag oma buz dro tho wheeath bloah coth, na olga ma e clappia na skant e guthvaz* 'and yet I remember when I was about six years old I could not speak it nor hardly understand it' BF: 27

Ma ko them *cavaz tra a'n par ma en lever Arlyth an Menneth* 'I remember finding something like this in the book of Lord Montaigne' BF: 29

nag ez ko them *tho guthva[z] meer en tavaz Curnooack lebna tose tho gawas tra gweele en bez* 'I do not remember understanding much in the Cornish language until I came to get business in the world' BF: 29.

Bewnans Ke has two examples of the 2nd plural imperative of ***kevena** 'to remember':

C **kevena** 'to remember'

E fyth lyas, **kevenough***, in e chy a thyvers tyr* 'There will be many, remember, in his house from various lands' BK 1359-60

Saw **kevennough***, del ew a goyth leverys: por theffry ny vith kerys neb mar te va re venowgh* 'But remember, as has been said from of old: in very truth anyone will not be loved if he comes too often' BK 1598-601.

The commonest way of saying 'to remember', however, is to use the verb **remembra**:

D **remembra** 'to remember'

Grefons ha cleves seson mar an geveth lel crystyan hav **remembra** *in plas ma ihesu arluth cuff colan y grefons gura sewagya* 'If a loyal Christian have a complaint and a seasonal sickness and remembers me here, O Jesus, dearly beloved Lord, assuage his complaint' BM 1000-04

a pobyl omschumunys **remembrogh** *agis sperys rag dovt cafus dampnasconn* 'O accursed people, remember you spirit lest you receive damnation' BM 1249-51

GERYOW GWIR   remember

*Pesugh mercy war ihesu ha **remembrogh** agis du* 'Beg mercy from Jesus and remember your God' BM 2160-62

*ny **remembrons** an charych a reys dethe ry harlych therag crist pan deer then vrueys* 'they do not remember the charge that they will have to give exactly before Christ when one comes to judgement' BM 2831-33

*Myns an geves charge a cur **remembrogh** helma lemen eff a ree reken in sur* 'Everyone who has the care of souls, remember this now: he will give a sure account' BM 2834-36

*An kythsame poynt na **remembres** in ta ew sufficient cawse ha ground then ny the renowncya ha naha pehosow* 'That very same point well remembered is sufficient cause and ground to us to renounce and resist sins' TH 3

*hemma ew pelha inweth thegys exortya why the **remembra** pana miseri ha drockoleth a theth the mabden dre begh* 'this is further also to exhort you to remember what misery and evil came to mankind through sin' TH 5

*an patriark benegas Abraham a **remembras** ay thalleth* 'the blessed patriarch Abraham remembered his beginning' TH 6-6a

*hag y a re dehesy dowst ha lusew drys aga pennow ha war aga pennow pan rellens **remembra** ha lamentya aga pehosow haga drog bewnans* 'and they used to throw dust and ashes over their heads and upon their heads when they remembered and lamented their sins and their evil living' TH 6a

*ha fatell russens **remembra** aga henwyn, aga thytyll, aga vile ha corrupt nature* 'and that they remembered their names, their title, their vile and corrupt nature' TH 6a

*yma an lyver a skyantoleth ow **remembra** thyn may teffan ha tenna then dore an pryde vs ew raynya ynnan, ha **remembra** agan mortall genesegeth a russyn kemeras theworth Adam an kynsa den a ve gwrys* 'the book of Wisdom reminds us that we should cast down the pride that reigns in us and remember our mortal birth which we received from Adam, the first man who was ever created' TH 6a

*A te dore, **remember** y bosta, dore, dore* 'O you clay, remember that you are clay, clay' TH 7a

***Remymbrow** fatell rug pegh agan dry ny in kynsa thea an favour a thu* 'Remember that sin brought us first from God's favour' TH 16

*whath gesow ny the **remembra** pana displesure a russyn ny gull warbyn du, pesqueth a russyn ny y offendya* 'yet let us remember what displeasure we have caused God, every time we offended him' TH 24

*Me a vyn agys exortya why the **remembra** an wytnys ma a sans egglos* 'I will exhort you to remember the witness of holy Church' TH 46

*ha ny russans y **remembra** tam vith nag o travith impossible gans du* 'and they did not remember in any way that nothing was impossible with God' TH 57

*gas ve the **remembra** fatla or ve in ta tha honora* 'let me remember how I can honour you well' SA 59

*pesqwythe mays gwella why hy **remembra** ahana'* why me a wra bys venarye 'as often as you see it indeed, I shall remember you for ever' CW 2502-04.

Notice also that in the quotation from TH 6a above *yma an lyver a skyantoleth ow **remembra** thyn* can be translated 'the Book of Wisdom reminds us'.

remember

This means that Cornish speakers can say, for example, **Me a godhvia remembra dhywgh bos dyfednys debry hag eva i'n lyverjy** 'I should remind you that eating and drinking are forbidden in the library'. The word **cov** itself means 'memory, remembrance' and is so used:

A **cov** 'remembrance'
my a vyr scon orth honna hag a'n acord a vyth ***cof*** *gans lyf ny wraf bynytha lathe an dus guyls na dof* 'I will look at once at that and will have remembrance of the covenant. Never again will I kill the people, wild or tame' OM 1251-54
guyn y vys pan ve gynys a allo gul thy's servys a'y ***cof*** *ny'n gas* 'happy the man that he was born who can do you service. He does not let it from his memory' OM 1476-78
Gweth ve y'th ***cof*** *ha'm noe a ra the rewlya* 'Keep me in remembrance and my nephew will rule you' BK 2745-46
ha boz gwethys enna bys vican yn ***cof*** 'and to be kept there for ever as a remembrance' JKeigwin.

A commoner word for 'remembrance', however, is **remembrans**:

B **remembrans** 'remembrance'
Rag in dede neb a rella predery an creacyon a vabden ha pondra in ta in y ***remembrans*** *a behan o agan dallath* 'For indeed whoever considers the creation of man and ponders well in his remembrance what our beginning was' TH 1
An re na ew the venya, vnderstonding, ***remembrans****, ha blonogath gans lowar gyfte moy a gras* 'Those mean understanding, remembrance and will, with many other gifts of grace' TH 1a
why a ra perfectly done in agys ***remembrans*** *fatell ve an holl nature a then kyffrys in corffe hag in ena defolys ha kyllys dre originall pegh* 'you will perfectly carry in your remembrance that the whole nature of man both in body and in soul was corrupted and lost through original sin' TH 12
henn o ***remembrans****, vnderstonding, blonogeth, gans moy royow erall an par na* 'that was remembrance, understanding, will, together will further different gifts of that kind' TH 12
neb a vynna gylwall thy ***remembrans*** *an dader a thu golosak in y mercy a vgh pub tra thyn ny desquethis heb y thyrfyne* 'whoever wishes to call to his remembrance the goodness of mighty God in his mercy above everything shown to us without our deserving it' TH 30a
mar tewgh why gylwall thegys ***remembrans****, pew ew an guyde han gouernar an egglos* 'if you call to your remembrance who is the guide and the governor of the Church' TH 36
ema Chrisostom ow scryfa than philipians a ***remembrance****, a vea res thetha bos, in keth sacrament na rag an marow* 'Chrysostom writing *To the Philippians* of remembrance, which they should have in that same sacrament for the dead' SA 66.

TO REPENT, TO REGRET

For 'to repent' Nance recommends A) **codha in edrega**, B) **kemeres edrek** and C) **repentya**. He also points out that D) **edrek a'm beus** (UC *edrek a'm bus*) and E) **yma edrek dhybm** (UC *yma edrek dhym*) can be used for 'I repent'.

A

cothys of yn edrek bras 'I have greatly repented [*literally*: I have fallen into great repentance]' PC 1440

B

ha rag an pehas us grueys **kemerogh** *luen* **edrega** *ha bethugh war na dreylogh ze pegh na moy* 'and for the sin committed, repent fully and be careful not to turn any more to sin' BM 2749-52

Ef a lathas ye vrodar **ny gemeras yddrag** *vyth mes y regoyssyas pur vear* 'He killed his brother; he did not repent at all, but rejoiced very greatly' CW 2047.

C

Pur a wylste war an kee eneff map den in bysmae ov **repentya** *rag y throk* 'When did you ever see a soul of man in this world discarded on the hedge repenting of his evil?' BM 1896-98

In dede pub den dre aga drogkoleth ha naturall prones o mar ver declynes the behosow, may rug du **repentya** *eff the wull mabden kepar dell vgy an scripture ow recordya* 'In deed everybody by their wickedness and natural tendency had so far descended to sin, that God repented that he had created mankind, as scripture records' TH 7

Rag henna gesow ny the venegas agan honyn the thu kepar dell ony in dede miserably wrytches, pehadoryan, ha gesow ny the **repentya** *ha mekya ha humblya agan honyn hartely ha crya mercy war thu* 'Therefore let us confess ourselves to God, as we are indeed miserable wretches, sinners, and let us repent and prostrate and humble ourselves earnestly and cry to God for mercy' TH 9-9a

surely ymowns in gwan cas, mas y a rella gans speda ha in du tyrmyn **repentya** *ha gull penans* 'surely they are in a miserable condition, unless they with speed and in due time repent and do penance' TH 32a

yn vr na der vaner da mara pethowgh **repentys** *an kethe plage a wra voydya* 'then if you have repented properly the same plague will be averted' CW 2343-45.

D

*rag why re sorras an tas m'***agys byth** *luen* **edrege** 'for you have angered the Father so that you will repent fully' OM 357-58

me a'th cusyl a grysy ha ma[r] ny wreth yn teffry **ty a fyth** *sur* **edrek** *tyn* 'I advise you to believe and if you do not indeed you will repent bitterly' RD 1130-32

Coyl ortheff vy meryasek me ath desyr dre tekter bonyl **ty a feth edrek** 'Listen to me, Meriasek, I require you to politely, or you will repent' BM 407-09

repent   **GERYOW GWIR**

The negys them menag a, py **te a 'fyth edrega**, *kyn fes tregys gans an Jowl!* 'Tell me your business, or you will regret it, though you dwell with the Devil!' BK 43-45

an bargayne **ny vyth eddrack** 'he will not regret the deal' CW 717

nymbes yddrag *vythe yn beise* [*gans*] *owe doarn ke thewe lethys par del oma gwicker coynt* 'I do not repent at all, though he has been killed by my hand, as I am a sharp dealer' CW 1141-43

awos latha abell lowte na whath vs molathe en tase **nymbes yddrack** *vyth in beys* 'I do not regret at all having killed the lout Abel in spite of the Father's curse' CW 1504-06

der henna me a angras ha pur vskys an lathas **nymbes yddrag** *a henna* 'therefore I got angry and very quickly killed him; I do not regret that' CW 1683-85

kyn wrug adam pegh mar vras **ef an geva yddrage** *tyn* 'though Adam committed such a great sin, he repented grievously' CW 2042-44.

E

yma thy'm *sur* **edrek** *tyn rak the naghe gy lemmyn* 'indeed I greatly regret having denied you now' PC 1155-56

pan **us dywhy edrega** *y raff agis benyga* 'since you repent, I will give you my blessing' BM 2175-76

malbew **yddrag es thyma** *an chorle abell vs latha* 'I have damn all regret about having killed the churl Abel' CW 1290-91

tety valy bram an gathe **nyng es yddrag thymo** *whath awos an keth ober na* 'fiddlestick! The cat's fart! I do not regret that same deed' CW 1305-07

hag **eddrag thothef yma** *bythquath mabe dean tha vos gwryes* 'and he repents of ever having created mankind' CW 2339-40

Me a wor ow bos camblys, saw pur wyer rag an tryspys **ema thymmo eddrag** *tyn* 'I know I am guilty but the wrong doing I bitterly regret' BK 1072-74.

Although Nance does not mention it, there is another way of saying 'he repented': **edrek a'n kemeras**, literally 'repentance seized him'. There is one attested example:

Eddrek *mur an kemeras rag an ober re wresse* 'He repented greatly for the deed he had done' PA 220a

Several things are apparent from the above examples. There appears to be no semantic difference between **edrek** and **edrega**, so one can say either **kemeres edrek** or **kemeres edrega**, **y'm beus edrek** or **y'm beus edrega**, **yma edrek dhybm** or **yma edrega dhybm**. The two expressions **y'm beus edrek** and **yma edrek dhybm** appear to mean 'I regret' as much as 'I repent (of)'. The only ambiguous way of expressing the idea of repenting of one's sins rather than simply regretting something, is to use the verb **repentya**.

REPROVE *see* **REBUKE**

TO REQUIRE

For 'to require' Nance suggests **dervyn**; ***gorholy** and **reqwîrya** (UC *requyrya*). The verb ***gorholy** is not attested. **Dervyn** does not mean 'to require', but rather 'to deserve':

A **dervyn**

*rag eff y honyn ny rug **dyrfyn** an myrnans nan payne na, a ruga suffra, rag eff bythqueth ny pehas* 'for he himself did not deserve that death or pain, which he suffered, for never did he sin' TH 15a

*Ha gwren ny consyddra pan a royow a russyn receva rag theworth du, heb ny thega **dyrfyn*** 'And let us consider what gifts we have received from God without deserving them' TH 24a

*an dader a thu golosak in y mercy a vgh pub tra thyn ny desquethis heb y **thyrfyne*** 'the goodness of mighty God in his mercy about everything shown to us without our deserving it' TH 30a

*Why a **thyrfyn** cafas gras drys kenever us in wlas* 'you deserve to be thanked above all men in the land' BK 3045-56

*dew a **therfyn** bos gwerthyes gans an gwella frute pub preys* 'God deserves to be worshipped with the best fruit always' CW 1097-98.

Reqwîrya, on the other hand, is well attested:

B **reqwîrya**

*ny a vyn the **requyrye** ha warbarth ol sur crye crucifige* 'we will all require you and all together cry Crucify!' PC 2474-76

*why a res gothfas hemma, fatell rug du **requiria** innan ny certan taclennow the vos colynwys* 'you must know this, that God required in us certain things to be fulfilled' TH 16

*an kythsam ii poynt ma ew the vos **requyrys** in agan part ny* 'these two same points are to be required on our part' TH 16a

*mar te cherite **requyria** the predyry, the cowsse da ha the wull da the bub den, da ha bad* 'if charity requires us to think, to speak well and to do good to all men, good and bad' TH 24a

*yma charite ow **requyrya** eff the vos deberthis theworth an commonwelth* 'charity requires that he be separated from the community' TH 25a

*pan vsy agan Savyowre ow **requyrya** theworthan ny may teffan ny ha passia an scribes han pharises in gwryoneth ha iustice* 'since our Saviour requires from us that we excel the scribes and pharisees in truth and justice' TH 26a

*Kemerogh wyth lymmyn, tus mas, fatell vsy crist ow **requyria** theworthan ny perfect cherite, rag yma crist ow **requiria** theworthan ny the wetha charite ha na rellan tyrry agan charite, kepar dell rug an scribis han pharases in tyrmyn coth* 'Take note now, good people, that Christ requires from us perfect charity, for Christ requires from us to maintain charity and that we should not rupture our charity, as did the scribes and pharisees in ancient times' TH 27

rag henna yma dre reson batallyow bras theworthan ny **requyrys** 'therefore great battles are quite reasonably required from us' TH 28

kyn fo an pith vs **requyris** *the worthen vith mar calis the vos gwris* 'though the thing required from us be never so difficult to do' TH 28

Why a glowas pana kerensa pana perfect charite vsy agan saviour ow **requiria** *the vos ynnan ny* 'You heard what love, what perfect charity does our Saviour require to reside in us' TH 30

hemma ew thegys exortia why ha in hanow du thegys **requiria** *the regardia an primaci han supremite a rome avell aucthorite appoyntys gans crist* 'this is to exhort you and to require you in the name of God to regard the primacy and the supremacy of Rome as the authority appointed by Christ' TH 51

yma ü tra in agan part ny **requyrys** 'two things are required on our part' TH 51a

ha mar petha indella me a vidn ye **requyrya** *a thewla an kethe dean na y woose a theffa scullya* 'and if it is so, I will require it from the two hands of that same man who sheds his blood' CW 2519-22.

Reqwîrya is attested in three different texts. It was clearly an essential part of the Cornish lexicon. There is no reason to avoid it in the revived language.

REVERENCE

When 'reverence' is broadly synonymous with 'respect, honour, prestige', it can be translated into Cornish in several ways. Perhaps A) **roweth**; B) **worshyp**; and C) **reverons** are the most obvious. Let us look in turn at how these three are used in the traditional language:

A **roweth**

awos ol **roweth** *adam bys thy'n vmma yn vn lam ef a vyth kyrhys* 'in spite of all the reverence owed to Adam, he will be fetched here to us at one single leap' OM 884-86

the greffe y fyen ny y voys maryys eredy ha moghheys agen **roweth** 'we would be the stronger if he were married indeed, and our prestige increased' BM 311-13

Pan othem vs thysogy a naha **roweth** *an beys* 'what necessity is there for you to deny the honour of the world?' BM 354-55

kyn fo mar fur an **roweth** *oll ny a thue the helma* 'though the prestige be so great, we all shall come to this' BM 4539-40

Pan 'th esta dowt, a **rowath***, re Jovyn! ema trewath ha pytta thym ahanas* 'Since you doubt, your Honour, by Jovyn, I feel sorrow and pity for you' BK 614-16

*Lowena ha lune-***rowath** *theso war ver lavarow* 'Joy and full reverence to you in a few words' BK 1578-79

GERYOW GWIR   reverence

E fyth **ruweth***, ha suwyna i'th tylu weth* 'There will be honour and prosperity in your household yet' BK 1745-46

Honester ha poteste ha **rowath** *ha dignite th'agan arluth pob seson!* 'Seemliness and power and reverence and dignity to our lord at all times!' BK 2687-89

Rowath *anbeis* 'worldes joy' Bodewryd MS.

B worshyp

arluth lemmyn a's dysken dyragough noth y fyen ny's vye **worshyp** *yn cas* 'lord, if I took it off in your presence, I should be naked; you would not have respect in the matter' RD 1943-45

grammer an geffa deffry y vyea tek ha **worshypp** *wosa helma* 'if he were to learn grammar it would be fine and reverence hereafter' BM 20-2

nyns yv **worschyp** *theth ehen the conseyt in pur certen ov map preder forthov guel* 'it is not reverence to your kindred, your conceit very truly; my son, consider better ways' BM 360-62

indelle te a alse gul **worschyp** *mur theth nesse ha boys selwys* 'thus you could do great reverence to your kinsmen and be saved' BM 2039-41

berth in eglos sent sampson bethens eff consecratis gans **worschyp** *ha revte* 'let him be consecrated within the church of St Samson with reverence and pomp' BM 2983-85

Ow negys ny wothvethys na **worship** *te ny 'fethyth* 'You shall not know my business nor will you get respect' BK 46-7

Marrogyan, leverugh why pan **worshyp***, er agys fith, a wothya Arthor the ry rag an trubut solathyth a stoppyas ef?* 'Knight, by your faith, tell me what respect was Arthur able to give in compensation for the tribute he has already stopped?' BK 2252-56.

C reverons

reuerons *thy'so a vam ker henor mur ha lowene* 'reverence to you, dear mother, great honour and joy' RD 495-96

Honour ʒyvgh master worthy ha benytha mur **reuerens** 'Honour to you, worthy master, and for ever great reverence' BM 82-3

Lowena ʒum tas worthy ha **reuerens** *bys bynyʒa* 'Joy to my worthy father and reverence for ever' BM 207-08

Reuerens *ʒyvg ser duk worthy par del ovgh corf a galloys* 'Reverence to you, worthy Sir Duke, as you are a person of power' BM 232-33

Welcum omma lych ryall del ogh pen ha princypall dreson ny ol yn tyan worthy rag cawas **reuerens** 'Welcome here, royal liege, as you are head and principal over us all entirely, worthy to receive respect' BM 252-55

Meryasek dyso **reuerans** *keris gans du a seluans gon guir lemen the vota* 'Meriasek, reverence to you; I now know that you are loved by the God of salvation' BM 569-71

Ser ʒurle lowene dywhy ha **reverens** *then hole colgy bras ha byen* 'Sir Earl, greetings to you and reverence to all the great college, great and small' BM 2896-98

meryasek **reverons** *dywhy* 'Meriasek, reverence to you' BM 3148

reverence   **GERYOW GWIR**

Hebasca thywhy ov mam mur **reverons** *the varia* 'Comfort to you, my mother. Great reverence to Mary' BM 3753-54

meryasek dyso **reverans** *sensys ovy theth gorthya* 'Meriasek, reverence to you. I am bound to worship you' BM 3852-53

agen part yv mones pur guir gans **reverans** *thy wore in doyr dywans* 'it is our duty to go very truly to put him in the ground straightway with reverence' BM 4376-78

Indella gans kepar **reuerens** *yma S Augustyn lyas tyrmyn ow submyttya oll y judgment hay oberow then Catholik egglos a crist* 'Thus with similar reverence St Augustine often submits all his judgement and his works to the catholic Church of Christ' TH 37a

penagoll mean a vo va gothvethis ha aswones yth ewa the vos recevys, ha kemerys gans **reuerens** 'whatever way it is known and recognized, it is to be received and accepted with reverence' TH 50a

Saw **refrens** *ahanogh why, orthowgh kefrys ef a fy re'n keth Du a woneth a* 'But saving your reverence, he also cries Fie upon you by the same God which he serves' BK 945-47

drefan eve thom controllya ha me y vrodar cotha ny wrug **refrance** *thym in beys* 'because he controlled me though I was his older brother; he showed me no reverence at all' CW 1680-82.

Roweth is perhaps closest in sense to English 'prestige'. **Worshyp** means 'respect, honour', while **reverons** is similar in semantic range to English 'reverence'.

REWARD, TO REWARD

There are several words in the texts to translate the English substantive 'reward', chief among them A) **reward**; B) **gweryson** and C) **gober**. **Gober** also means 'wage' and I discuss the word under 'wage, wages' below. **Reward** is better attested than **gweryson**:

A **reward**

neb a kuntel an moghya an geveth an grays brassa ea ha **reward** *purfeth* 'he who collects the most will get the greatest thanks, yes and a perfect reward' BM 1544-46

Rag mar tewgh why ha cara an re vsy worth agys cara why, pana **rewarde** *a vethow why?* 'For if you love those who love you, what reward will you get?' TH 22

So mar ten ha gull ken, y myth crist, nyg esan ow kull bithwell agys an pharises, publicans, han hethens, ha ny an Jevith agan **reward** *gansans y* 'But if we do otherwise, says Christ, we do no better than the pharisees, publicans and heathens, and we will have our reward along with them' TH 22a

han gela ew an braster a **rewarde** *promysys thynny vght an Jewys* 'and the other is the size of the reward promised to us above the Jews' TH 27a.

reward

B **gweryson**

*mara kyl bones yagheys ty a fyth the lyfreson hag an our the **weryson*** 'if he can be healed, you will get your freedom and the gold of your reward' RD 1675-77

*A caffan neb a wothya y'n gevea **gwereson** may fe the well* 'If I could find someone who did know how, he would get a reward so that he would be better off' BK 528-30.

Either **gwereson** or **reward** can be used in the revived language for 'reward'. It should perhaps be noted that both words are borrowed from Middle English.

For the verb 'to reward' Nance suggests **tylly**, ***gobra** and **rewardya**. **Tylly** does not mean 'to reward', but 'to pay' and is not really an apt translation. ***Gobra** is unattested. **Rewardya** on the other hand, occurs in six different texts:

Rewardya 'to reward'

*My a'd pys now messyger dog manerlich ov baner del vynny bos **rewardyys*** 'I beg you now, messenger, carry my banner bravely, as you hope to be rewarded' OM 2199-201

*messyger rag the seruys the **rewardye** my a ra* 'messenger, for your service I shall reward you' OM 2309-10

*ru'm fay ty yv cowyth da the **rewardye** my a wra* 'upon my faith, you are a good companion. I will reward you' PC 611-12

*ha **rewardys** ty a vyth a thyworthyf vy ru'm fyth sur kyns pen vys* 'and you will be rewarded upon my faith surely before a month is passed' PC 1644-46

*ytho pyth yv the cusyl worth an dra na the wruthyl lauar lemmyn ha ty a vyth **rewarddys*** 'so what is the advice to be done for that matter? Tell me and you will be rewarded' RD 25-8

*ty a yl cafus mur gras the lauarow mars yns guyr ha ty a fyth **rewardys*** 'you can receive much thanks, if your words are true, and you will be rewarded' RD 1699-700

*dyskovgh ef yn maner dek ha wy a vyth **rewardys*** 'teach him in a fair manner and you will be rewarded' BM 88-9

*thymo mar myn boys methek in ta y feth **rewardys*** 'if he will be my doctor, he will be well rewarded' BM 2528-29

*yma ov quan **rewardya** y servysy rum ene* 'he poorly rewards his servants upon my soul' BM 3261-62

*Lemmen yth ogh **rewardis*** 'Now you have been rewarded' BM 3364

*Rag yth ew an office a charite magata the rebukya, punsya ha correctia drog pobyll, magata dell ewa the chesya, **rewardia** ha defendia an re na ew da ha innocent* 'For it is the duty of charity both to rebuke, punish and correct evil people, as much as it is to cherish, reward and defend those who are good and innocent' TH 25

*welcom eva os benynvas marsew an nowothow da te a vythe **rewardyes*** 'you are welcome, Eva, madam; if the news is good, you will be rewarded' CW 730-32.

reward

It would seem that **rewardya** is the ordinary word for 'to reward' in the traditional language. It would perhaps be sensible for the revived language to imitate the texts in this respect.

RICH

For 'rich' Nance suggests **rych**, **golusak** and **kevothak**. *****Golusak** is not attested as such, but is a respelling of ***wuludoc***, the lenited form of *****goludoc** at OCV §296, where it glosses *dives* 'rich'. **Goludoc** is exactly parallel with Welsh *goludog* 'rich'. Apart from this single attestation in Old Cornish, however, the word is not found.

*****Kevothak** is not attested either, but is a respelling of OC ***chefuidoc***, which occurs in the phrase ***duy chefuidoc***, glossing *Deus omnipotens* 'Almighty God' at OCV §1. The Welsh cognate of OC ***chefuidoc*** is *cyfoethog* and both ***chefuidoc*** and *cyfoethog* are related to OIr *cumachtach* 'powerful', Modern Irish *cumhachtach* 'powerful'. Welsh *cyfoethog* means both 'powerful' and 'rich', and it seems that Nance believed, or perhaps hoped, that Old Cornish ***chefuidoc*** might have meant 'rich' as well.

There is no example outside OCV of either *****goludoc**, *****golusak** 'rich', or *****kevothak** 'powerful'. Moreover there is no evidence at all that OC ***chefuidoc*** 'powerful' ever meant 'rich'. In the Cornish texts the only word for 'rich' is **rych**, which is very well attested:

*Benyn dyr vur cheryte y box **ryche** leun a yly a vgh crist rag y vntye hy a vynnas y derry corf ihesus rag comfortye* 'A woman for sheer charity wanted to break a rich box full of ointment over Christ in order to anoint Jesus to comfort his body' PA 35ab

*Henna pylat pan welas kymmys cawsys er y byn rowtors ha tus **ryche** yn wlas resons mar fol ha mar dyn* 'When Pilate saw that, so much spoken against him, rulers and rich men in the land uttering such frenzied and bitter reasons' PA 100ab

*I a wyskis crist gant queth han purpur **rych** o dyskis rag y thry 3en dor gans meth* 'They dressed Christ with a cloth and the rich purple was taken off in order to humiliate him with shame' PA 136ab

*An queth tek a ve dyskis han purpur **ryche** a vsye hay bowys y honon gurris a dro 3030 hy a ve* 'The fair garment was removed and the rich purple he was wearing, and his own robe was put on him' PA 161ab

*adro 3y gorff y trylyas sendall **rych** yn luas pleg* 'he wound rich linen around his body in many folds' PA 232c

*obereth dremas a dyff yn er na **rych** ef a vyth* 'the work of a good man will grow, he will be rich then' PA 259c

*eugh growetheugh ov arlut may haller agas cuthe gans dylles **rych** del deguth the vyghtern a dynyte* 'go, lie down, my lord, that you can be covered with rich clothes, as is fitting for a king of dignity' OM 1923-26

cytes **rych** *trevow a brys castilly bras hagh huhel ol an re ma ty a fyth ow gorthye mara mennyth* 'rich cities, important towns, great and high castles—all these you shalll have if you worship me' PC 132-35

me a ordyn y wyske yn purpyr **rych** *ru'm laute kepar del goth the vyghtern* 'I ordain that he be dressed in rich purple by my faith, as is fitting for a king' PC 2121

kyn fo brays y devethyans ef a dryk pennoth in hans nyn guel an **rych** *galosek* 'though great is his lineage, he will remain hatless yonder. The powerful rich man will not see him' BM 439-41

A dyves del redyn ny **rych** *lour o in pup termen* 'As we read of Dives, he was always rich enough' BM 446-47

dar soposia a reta den **rych** *nefra mones then neff da ny yl* 'what? Do you imagine that a rich man can never enter into goodly heaven?' BM 459-61

An scriptor leferel grua den **rych** *then neff dyogel mage fur weyll yv dotha moys avel capel gorhel der trov nasweth* 'The scripture says that a rich man to the heaven indeed, it is as great a labour for him as a ship's cable through the eye of a needle' BM 464-68

indellan den **rych** *besy the vohosogyan guet ry in cheryte part ath peth* 'thus the rich man, assiduously be careful to give in charity to the poor part of your wealth' BM 471-73

eff a alse der y rays selwel **rych** *ha bohosek heb boys marow* 'he could by his grace have saved rich and poor without dying' BM 876-8

kefrys **rych** *ha bohosek pur guir a yll lemen mones then feryow* 'both rich and poor in very deed can now go to the fairs' BM 2183-85

henwys oys pronter grassijs the **ryche** *ha bohosogyon* 'you have been called a gracious priest to rich and poor' BM 2551-52

yma **rych** *ha bohosek ov teserya meryasek epscop pur guir may fo va* 'rich and poor desire that Meriasek be bishop in very truth' BM 2695-97

inweth myterneth gwlasow, subiectys, tus ientyll, **rych** *ha behosek ymowns ow tos omma thyn bys haw mos in kerth alemma arta ny woryn pyscotter* 'also kings of countries, subjects, gentlefolk, rich and poor, they come here into the world and depart hence again we know not how soon' TH 6a

in mar vere dell rug an appostlis y gasa athellar kepar ha dell vo va tresure **riche** *a oll gwryoneth* 'inasmuch as the apostles left it behind as though it were the rich treasury of all truth' TH 19

Ith ew impossybyll the then **rych** *entra in gwlascur neff* 'It is impossible for the rich man to enter into the kingdom of heaven' TH 53

Ith ew calys rag an re **rych** *vsy ow tristya in aga substans the vos sawyys* 'It is hard for the rich who trust in their own wealth to be saved' TH 53

Gromersy a'n gwelha tas, Arthor **rych** *a ryowta, y'th chy ny thefyk penlas* 'Great thanks of the best father, Arthur rich in royalty, in your house liquor never fails' BK 1554-56

rych *os ha fuer ha'th gallas mer heb dowt i'n cas* 'you are rich and wise and your power is great without any doubt in the matter' BK 1697-99.

Since **rych** is the only word for 'rich' in Cornish literature and is found in six separate texts, it ought perhaps be the ordinary word for 'rich' in the revived language.

river   GERYOW GWIR

RIVER

For 'river' Nance suggests **avon** *f.*, *plural* ***avenow** and **ryver** *m.*, *plural* **ryvers**. ***Avon** 'river' is not found, since in the few attested forms the intervocalic segment is [w] rather than [v]. OCV has flumen, ***auon*** 'river' OCV §731. Lhuyd cites ***auan*** 'river' on a number of occasions:

A **awan** 'river'

*C. Terneuan, a side; Terneuan an **auan**, the bank of the River* AB: 3b
W. Avon, A river; Corn, ***Auan*** AB: 22c
Amnis... A River, a Brook, &c. C. ***Auan*** AB: 42c
Flumen... A river, stream or water-course; a floud. C. ***Auan*** *bras* AB: 60b
*Ripa... A bank of a river... C. Torneuan an **auan*** AB:141a
Rivus... A river, a brook. C. ***Auan*** AB: 141b
Torrens... A land flood, a torrent. C. ***Auan*** AB: 165a.

Notice also that the name ***Awen-Tregare*** (1698) refers to Tregeare Water by Truro (CPNE: 14). **Awon, awan** 'river' is not otherwise attested.

The word for 'river' in river-names is invariably **dowr**, literally 'water':

B **dowr** 'river'

*arluth yn trok a horn cref yn **dour tyber** ef a sef er y anfevs* 'lord, he shall stay to his misfortune in a chest of strong iron in the River Tiber' RD 2135-37
*teuleugh ef yn trok a horn yn **dour tyber** yn nep corn may fo buthys* 'throw him in a chest of iron into the River Tiber in some creek that he may drown' RD 2162-64
*den dreys **dour tyber** nyns a yn certan na vo marow* 'no man passes over the River Tiber without being killled' RD 2214-15
*yn **dour tyber** ef a fue yn geler horn gorrys dovn* 'he was placed deep in the River Tiber in a coffin of iron' RD 2319-20
An duk a'n gevith pur wyer rag e laver ol an tyr a ***Thowr Hombyr*** *the Scotland* 'For his labour the Duke very truly will get all the land from the River Humber to Scotland' BK 3235-37.

When the word is used by itself, rather than in a river name, the word for 'river' appears to be **ryver** *m.*, *plural* **ryvers**:

C **ryver** 'river'

war an meneth dyogel hag orth an ***ryuer*** *surly a josselyne chapel guthel me a vyn rag gorthya maria wyn* 'upon the mountain indeed and by the river truly of Josselin I shall build a chapel to revere the Virgin Mary' BM 1140-44
Neb a crisse ynna ve kepar dell levar an scribis, ***ryvars*** *a thowre a ra resek in mes anetha y* 'Whoever believes in me, as the scribes say, rivers of water will flow from them' TH 53.

When speaking of rivers outside hydronymy, **ryver** would perhaps seem to be the word of choice for the revived language.

ROMANS

For the substantive 'Roman' Nance gives **Roman** *m.*, *plural* **Romanas**. The plural *****Romanas** is unattested but revivalists have followed Nance this form. The attested plural, however, is **Romans**:

Rag henna yma S Powle in y epistyll then ***romans*** *in v chaptyr ow leverall* 'Therefore St Paul in his epistle to the Romans says in the fifth chapter' TH 4a

S Pawle thyn ***romans*** *an iii-a chapter Pub den oll keffrys Jew ha Jentyll ew pehadoryon* 'St Paul to the Romans, the third chapter: All men both Jew and Gentile are sinners' TH 7a

yma S pawle in kynsa chapter thyn ***romans****, ow affirmya playn fatell wothya an bobyl mer an gwrythyans a thu* 'St Paul in the first chapter to the Romans plainly affirms that the people knew much of the acts of God' TH 14

kepar dell vgy S paul thyn ***romans*** *ow kull mencion* 'as St Paul mentions to the Romans' TH 14a

Yma S poule indelma ow declaria thyn ***romans*** 'St Paul declares thus to the Romans' TH 25

An ***Romans*** *a vyth wystyys* 'the Romans will be ravaged' BK 2136

Merough ple ma an ***Romans*** *ow settya ragow' myrnans* 'Look where the Romans are plotting death for you' BK 2808-09

Ha na ore den veeth durt peniel reeg an kol ma kensa dose, durt an ***Romans*** *meskez gen a Brittez* 'And no one knows from which this loss first came, from the Romans mixed with the Britons' BF: 29.

Romans would seem to be more authentic than **Romanas** 'Romans'.

ROOM

Some revivalists use **stevel** as their default word for 'room'. This derives from *triclinium*, ***steuel*** 'dining-room' OCV §933, the only attestation of the word. As Graves has pointed out, *steuel* looks like the plural of an unattested **stauel*; cf. Welsh *ystafell* < Latin **stabellum*. If so, ***steuel*** is the plural of an unattested singular. In the Cornish texts, however, the attested word for 'room' is **rom**, *plural* **rômys**, which can also mean 'space, position':

Rag henna fystyn ke gura gorhel a blankos playnyys hag ynno lues trygva ***romes*** *y a vyth gylwys* 'Therefore hurry, go, make a ship of planed planks with many dwellings in it. They shall be called rooms' OM 949-52

x GERYOW GWIR

Rag yma an scriptur ow prevy fatell rug agan savyour appoyntya Pedyr thyn kyth vhell **rome** *ma* 'For the scripture proves that our Saviour appointed Peter to this same high position' TH 42a

thega movya y the thewys onyn rag bos in **rome** *esa Judas ynna* 'to move them to chose one to occupy the position in which Judas had been' TH 44a

ena eff a rug contynewa Epscop in.kythsame **rome** *na xxv-ans a blethynnyow* 'then he continued bishop in that same position 25 years' TH 46a

fatell rug agan savyoure appoyntya pedyr in brassa **rome** *ys onyn vith an abosteleth erell* 'that our Saviour appointed Peter to a greater position than any other of the apostles' TH 47a

Ay a vynta ge orth mab dean pan vo gwryes a slem hager occupya rage sertayne ow **rome** *ve nagevas peare omma in neve* 'Oh, do you want man, who was made from vile slime, indeed to occupy my room in heaven, I who am without equal?' CW 254-58

Sow an keth adam yw gwryes me a wore heb dowte in case tha golenwall an **romys** *es yn nef der ow goth brase a voyd drethaf hawe mayny* 'But the same Adam has been created, I know for certain, to fill the rooms in heaven left empty by me and my household through my great pride' CW 461-65.

The attested word for 'bedroom' is **chambour**, **chamber**:

rof thy's ov thour hel ha **chammbour** *bethaf the wour warbarth ny a dryg nefre* 'I will give you my tower, my hall and bed-chamber. I will be your husband and together we shall live for ever' OM 2110-12

Arlothas, guyn avel gurys, dun the'n **chamber***, me a'th pys, may hyllyn omacountya* 'Lady, white as crystal, let us go to the bedchamber, I beg you, that we may give account of ourselves' BK 2981-83

Cubiculum... A bed-room, a lodging-room; C. **Tshombar** AB: 52c.

The default word for 'room' in the revived language ought perhaps be **rom**, **rômys**. 'Bedroom' can be expressed by the word **chambour**.

ROUND, CIRCULAR

For the adjective 'round' Nance gives two options, **crèn** (UC *cren*) and **rônd** (UC *rond*). **Crèn** is not actually attested in the Middle Cornish texts, being known only from a single entry in Lhuyd:

Rotundus... Round, circular... C[ornish] & Ar[moric] **Kren**, **kern** AB: 141c.

Apart from that single entry, there appears to be no other evidence for **crèn**, **kern** 'round' in Cornish. In the texts on the other hand the word for 'round' is **rônd** or **rownd**:

*Thum du iovyn benygas me a offren iij bran vrays marthys **rond** age mellov* 'To my god, blessed Jovyn, I offer three great ravens with very round joints' BM 3406-08

*Ha genz hedna Dzhûan genz e golhan, trohaz der an tol mêz a kein gûn an manah pîs pyr **round*** 'And thereupon with his knife John cut through the hole out of the back of the monk's habit a completely round piece' BF: 18

*Ha genz hedna gen a holhan me a trohaz pîs, der an tol mes a kein gûn an manah; pîs pyr **round*** 'And thereupon with my knife I cut a piece, through the hole out of the back of the monk's habot, a completely round piece' BF: 18.

The abstract noun is **rowndenep** 'roundness':

*Yn howl yma **rowndenab** ha golow splan ha tomdar bras* 'There is roundness and light and great heat in the sun' BK 283-85.

Another word used for 'round' or 'circular' is *****kelhek** or *****kelghyek**. *****Kelgh** 'circle' and *****kelhek** or *****kelghyek** 'round, circular' are unattested. It would seem, therefore, that **rônd** or **rownd** is a more authentic word for the revived language than **kern**, **crèn** or *****kelhek**, *****kelghyek**.

S

SAKE, FOR THE SAKE OF
To render 'for the sake of' many revivalists use **abarth**. This, however, does not mean 'for the sake of' so much as 'in the name of', as can be seen from the following examples:

A **abarth** 'in the name of'
drehevyn ef **abarth** *dev yn ban lemyn re got ev* 'let us raise it in the name of God. Now it is too short' OM 2539-40
dus yn mes **abarth** *an ioul vynytha ny efyth coul marrow cowal ty a vyth* 'come out in the devil's name; never shall you drink broth; you will die utterly' OM 2700-02
abarth *ow thas bynyges th'y thyller arte glenes kepar del ve* 'in the name of my blessed Father let it adhere to its place exactly as it was' PC 1152-54
ru'm fay cowyth my a wra ragos moy es yndella dys yn rak **abarth** *iovyn* 'upon my faith, friend, I will do more for you than that. Come on in Jovyn's name' PC 1231-33
tormentours **abarth** *a'n iaul fysteneugh th'agas kregy* 'Tormentors, hurry in the devil's name, hang you!' PC 2045-46
Bohogogneth **abreth** *du remoconn then cur yth yv wose helma* 'Poverty in God's name is promotion to the court of heaven hereafter' BM 2010-12
Abarth *Christ, an mab gwelha, me a vyn mos gans mer grys the ge an gowr ryelha* 'In the name of Christ, the best son, I shall go with great haste to the house of the most royal hero' BK 1282-84
Ahanan eugh **abarth** *an Tas ha'm negys gwreugh lemmyn in fas* 'Go now hence in the name of the Father and do my business well now' BK 1867-70.

The ordinary way of saying 'for the sake of' in Cornish is **rag kerensa**:

B **rag kerensa** 'for the sake of'
Noy **rak kerenge** *orthy's my a wra thy's ambos da luen dyal war ol an veys ny gemeraf vynytha* 'Noah, for your sake, I will make a good covenant for you: I will not take vengeance ever upon all the world' OM 1231-34
fatel fue cryst mertheryys **rak kerenge** *tus a'n beys why a welas yn tyen* 'that Christ was put to death for the sake of the men of the world you have seen completely' PC 3220-22

ny fue ragtho y honan yn gothefys ef certan mas **rak kerenge** *map den* 'it was not for himself he suffered it indeed but for mankind's sake' PC 3226-28

mur a peyn a wothefys **rak kerenge** *tus a'n bys del yw myghtern a gallos* 'much pain he suffered for the sake of the men of the world as he is king of might' RD 832-34

rag kerensa *an passyonn a porthes ihesu ragan pynys hyȝyv y fanna* 'for the sake of the passion which Christ bore for us I will fast today' BM 123-25

Rag kerense *crist an neff me a vyn agis pesy na gemerre den vyth greff na duwen am govys vy* 'For the sake of Christ of heaven I will beg you that no man suffer grief nor woe on my account' BM 403-06

me a vyn mones uskys wath de thesky dadder moy **rag kerense** *an drensis na temptyogh vy the foly* 'I shall go quickly to learn more goodness yet for the sake of the Trinity. Do not tempt me to folly' BM 498-501

Me ath peys a luengolon ty the vynnes ov sawya **rag kerense** *an passconn a thuk ihesu in bys ma* 'I beseech with all my heart that you will deign to heal me for the sake of the passion which Jesus suffered in this world' BM 2598-601

rag kerensa *crist map ras myr thynny bohosogyon* 'for the sake of Christ, son of grace, look to us, poor fellows' BM 2640-41

Na govsugh an dynyte **rag kerense** *crist avan* 'Do not speak of the dignity for the sake of Christ above' BM 2956-57

rag kerense *crist avan ny ages pesse certan gul gueres dyn dyogel* 'for the sake of Christ above, we would beg you to help us indeed' BM 3110-12

Rag kerense *arluth neff gueres dyn orth agen gref clevyon deberthys ny yv* 'For the sake of the Lord of heaven, help us in our misery; we are separated lepers' BM 3128-30

rag kerense *ihesu wek lauer dym a then grassyes py caffsen ua meryasek* 'for the sake of dear Jesus, tell me, O gracious man, where I might find Meriasek' BM 4195-97

rag kerense *an passconn a porthes ihesu ragonn meryasek grua thym gueras* 'for the sake of the passion which Jesus bore for us, assist me, Meriasek' BM 4208-10

oll an royow ma ew res thynny dre y vercy eff frely ha **rag kerensa** *agan saviour Jhesus crist, neb o an pure one a thu heb defullya* 'all these gifts have been given to us freely by his mercy and for the sake of our Saviour, Jesus Christ, who was the pure and undefiled Lamb of God' TH 10a

Ea, ha the forsakya pub tra oll in bys **rag kereensa** *du* 'Yea, and to forsake everything in the world for the sake of God' TH 21a

ny a gothyn gava thotha **rag kerensa** *du* 'we should forgive him for the sake of God' TH 24a

neb a rug ry y vn vab eff the suffra myrnans **rag kerensa** *y egglos* 'who gave his only Son to suffer death for the sake of his Church' TH 31a

Lymmyn sure one ny fatell rug an abosteleth a crist suffra myrnans **rag kerensa** *crist* 'Now we are sure that the apostles of Christ suffered death for the sake of Christ' TH 36a

prag a reta gelwall an sea han stall an apostelath an sea ha stall a pestilence, mars esta worth y wull **rag kerensa** *an dus* 'why do you call the see and stall of the apostles the see and stall of pestilence, if you do it for the sake of men?' TH 48

Rag kerensa *Marya ha'y Mab a'th pernas i'n pren, saw ve a'n drog us o'm kyk ha neffra me a'th vynyk* 'For the sake of Mary and her Son, who redeemed you on the cross, heal me of the evil in my flesh and I shall ever bless you' BK 788-91.

Rag kerensa should perhaps be the ordinary way of rendering 'for the sake of' in the revived language.

SALMON

For 'salmon' some revivalists use **eog**. This word is actually unattested being a respelling of **ehoc** from *Iscius vel salmo,* **ehoc** at OCV §543. The only word for 'salmon' found in the texts is **sowmens**, the plural of ***sowmen** 'salmon':

y rof hynwyn the'n puskes porpus **sowmens** *syllyes ol thy'm gustyth y a vyth* 'I give names to the fishes: porpoise, salmon, eels, they shall all be obedient to me' OM 135-37

In the interests of authenticity, **sowmen** should perhaps be the ordinary word for salmon in the revived language.

SALVATION

There are two words in the texts for 'salvation': A) **selwans**; B) **salvacyon**:

A **selwans**

Ha ȝymmo gras ha skyans the ȝerevas par lauarow may fo ȝe thu ȝe worthyans ha **sylwans** *ȝen enevow* 'And to me grace and knowledge to recount in words, that it may be for God's glory and for the salvation of souls' PA 1cd

ef a yrhys thy'm kyrhas a mount tabor gueel a ras ma'm bethen drethe **sylwans** 'he commanded me to fetch rods of grace from Mount Tabor that we might have salvation through them' OM 1956-58

aban of seuys a'n beth gothfetheugh y's byth **sylwans** *ha pup crystyon ol ynweth a vynno pygy gyfyans* 'since I have risen from the tomb, know that you will have salvation and all Christians also who will pray for forgiveness' RD 1573-76

ihesu arluth a **selwans** *gront helma der ȝe vercy* 'Jesus, Lord of salvation, grant this by your mercy' BM 1009-10

ha then ena sur megyans yth yv rag cafus **selwans** *ol then ene* 'and to the soul surely nourishment it is to obtain salvation all for the soul' BM 2025-27

Gorthyans the crist a **selwans** *der syluester in tor ma pobyl rome orth ij vernans delyfrys yth yns oma* 'Glory to Christ of salvation, by Silvester now the people of Rome from two deaths, they have been saved here' BM 4166-69

GERYOW GWIR salvation

mere worthyans than drenges tase ow crowntya thymmo **sylwans** *woʒa henma kenth ew pell* 'Much glory to the Father of the Trinity, granting me salvation hereafter though it is far distant' CW 1940-42.

B salvacyon

sav an devgys a vynnays arta y vones prennys the **saluascon** 'but the Godhead wished that he should again be redeemed to salvation' BM 884-86

Maria myternes neff maria agen eneff peys men geffe **saluasconn** 'Mary queen of heaven, Mary, pray that our souls may obtain salvation' BM 1246-48

Ihesu arluth cuff colon ihesu gront thyn **saluasconn** *rag oma reys yv merwell* 'Beloved Lord Jesus, Jesus, grant us salvation for we must die here' BM 1258-60

duen alema kescolon ihesu map a **saluasconn** *regen guerese pub deth* 'let us go hence with one acord. May Jesus, Son of salvation, assist us every day' BM 1756-58

A rag oll an golyov a thuk crist cleth ha dyov the vap den rag **saluasconn** 'Oh for all the wounds which Christ sustained, left and right, for salvation for mankind' BM 3049-51

nyg es daddar innan na in agan oberow nyg es gweras na **salvacion** 'there is no goodness in us nor in our works is there any help or salvation' TH 10

ha fatell vgy agan **salvacion** *ow tos dre crist only* 'and that our salvation comes only through Christ' TH 10

In kepar maner theworth du yma ow tos thynny oll daddar ha **salvacyon** 'Similarly from God comes all goodness and salvation to us' TH 11a

tus a russa supposia mar teffa du aga suffra aga naturall the vsya aga naturall powers y a vynsa optaynya **salvacion** *in ta lovr* 'men would think that if God had allowed them to use their natural powers, they would have obtained salvation well enough' TH 13a

So yth ew pleyn the vos attendys fatell esa ethom the vabden the gafus specially succure ha gweras the worth du, rag optaynya eternall **salvacion** *han bewnans heb deweth* 'But it is plain to see that mankind needed to get special succour and help from God to obtain eternal salvation and the life without end' TH 13a

rag may hallans dretha attaynya an bewnans heb deweth ha eternall **salvacion** 'that they might through it attain the life without end and eternal salvation' TH 17

mas an catholyk eglos an jevas an gothfas a pub tra oll necessary rag **salvacion** 'but the catholic Church has the knowledge of all things necessary for salvation' TH 17

ymowns in sure in forth a **salvacion** 'they surely are on the way to salvation' TH 20

an donatists neb a rug denaha an catholick egglos, hag a ascribia an feith a crist, hag oll **saluacion** *thethy aga honyn only* 'the Donatists, who denied the catholic Church, and who ascribed the faith of Christ and all salvation to themselves only' TH 32.

In the revived language, if one is talking of salvation in either a religious or secular context, either **selwans** or **salvacyon** can be used.

sanctify

TO SANCTIFY

Some revivalists recommend the verb ***sans'he*** for 'to sanctify'. Such a verb is unattested. The attested A) **sona** and B) **benega** both mean 'to bless', and are thus fairly close synonyms:

A **sona**

*Rag bones ol tek ha da in whed dyth myns yw formyys aga **sona** ny a wra may fe seythves dyth hynwys hen yw dyth a bowesva* 'Because all that has been created in six days is fair and good, we will bless them so that the seventh day may be named, that is a day of rest' OM 141-45

*a thev lemyn gwyn ov beys ov bos **sonys** hep whethlow* 'O God, now happy I am that I am indeed blessed' OM 465-66

*A das colon caradow ny vynnaf lettya pella my a'd pys ov **sona** gura kyns ys mos hep falladow* 'O father, dear heart, I will not delay any further. I beg you to bless me before I leave without fail' OM 721-24

*lemyn agan **sone** gura kyns ys bones anhethys* 'now bless us before we are housed' OM 1721

*Me agis **son** an barth cleth drok hag anfusy inweth guetyogh vsia* 'I will bless you on the left side; also take care to make use of evil and misfortune' BM 3420-22

*In hanow Du me a's **son** ma na relhans theso bern ha nask e, abarth Jowan!* 'In the name of God I shall bless them so that they do you no harm and yoke them, in the name of St John' BK 858-60

*my d[s] **sone** gans ow ganow* 'I will bless them with my mouth' CW 74

*an ry ma ew oll teke gwryes me as **sone** warbarth heb gowe* 'these are all created fair. I will bless them together without a lie' CW 112-13

*rag bonas oll teake ha da yn whea dyth myns es formys aga **sona** me a wra may fon sythvas dyth henwys an dyth sure a bowesva* 'since all that has been created in six days are fair and good, I will bless them that the seventh day be named the sure day of rest' CW 413-17.

B **benega**

*pan us dywhy edrega y raff agis **benyga*** 'since you have repentance I will bless you' BM 2175-76

*Arluth neff ren **benyga*** 'May the Lord of heaven bless him!' BM 4541

*S. Johan baptist, a ve **benegas** in breis y vam ha gormelas kyns y bos genys* 'St John the Baptist was blessed in his mother's womb and praised before he was born' TH 8

*hemma ew the styrrya, neb a rug **benega**, han rena neb ew **benegys**, yth ens oll onyn* 'that means, he who blessed and those who are blessed are all one' TH 13

*Arluth, thewhy lowena! Te a yl ow **benega*** 'Lord, greeting to you! You can bless me' BK 1105-06

*Ha Deu rêg gi **benigia*** 'And God blessed them' BF: 53.

Notice also that the verbal adjective **benegys** (***benegas***) is widely used as an adjective to mean 'blessed'. For 'to sanctify' *per se* one can also use either

sacra 'to consecrate' or **consecrâtya** 'to consecrate'; see above s.v. 'CONSECRATE'.

The only attested word for 'to sanctify', however, is **sanctyfia** which is attested twice:

*hag vnwith rag oll in sacrament ay wosse suffrys vel scollis war an growspren, gans an oblacion na eff a rug perfect rag neffra neb o **sanctyfyes*** 'and once for all in the sacrament of his blood suffered or shed upon the cross, by that oblation he made perfect for ever him who was sanctified' TH 11

*han kyhsame egglos ma, dre reson y bossy **sanctifies** ha benegys inweth purchasiis dre mernans agan savyoure Jhesus crist, yth ew hy the vos kerys gans du an tas a neff* 'and this same Church because she is sanctified and blessed, also purchased by the death of our Saviour Jesus Christ, she is to be loved by God the Father of heaven' TH 31.

Since **sanctyfia** is attested while ***sans'he** is not, **sanctyfia** is perhaps to be preferred.

SAXONS

We have already seen that the native Cornish for 'Romans' in the plural was **Romans**, rather than ***Romanas**. In the same way the Cornish for 'Saxons' is **Saxons**:

*ha vi c. blethan wosa crist an **Saxons** a ve spredys drys oll an wlas* 'and 600 years after Christ the Saxons had spread across all the country' TH 51

*Me re thanvanas deffry duk an **Saxens**, Chellery, the whelas myns a geffa a bagans in Germany* 'I indeed have sent to the duke of the Saxons, Childerich, to seek as many as he can find of pagans in Germany' BK 3229-32.

In the interests of authenticity **Saxons** should perhaps be preferred to ***Saxonas**.

SCOT, SCOTLAND

For 'Scot, man from Scotland' Nance suggests ***Alban**, plural ***Albanas**. Neither singular nor plural is attested. The attested word is **Scot**:

*Pes, seniors, je vow commaund, yonk ha loys, Gothal ha **Scot!*** 'Peace, sirs, I command you, young and old, Irishman and Scot!' BK 1258-59

*Na thowtyans rag sham na Cornow na **Scot*** 'Let him not fear for shame either Cornishman or Scot' BK 2486-87.

Scot

Cf. *ha'n Kelezonek po'n* **Skot**-*Vrethonek* 'the Gaelic or Scot-British' AB: 222.

For 'Scotland' Lhuyd uses **an Alban** once: *en Ehual-dir* **an Alban** *hag en G'laskor Uordhyn* AB: 222. *An Alban is clearly based on Welsh *yr Alban* 'Scotland'. The name **Scotlond** is now attested three times in traditional Cornish:

Me ew body dyspusond, Augel, myghtern in **Scotland** 'I am a powerful person, Augel king of Scotland' BK 1279-80

An duk a'n gevith pur wyer rag e laver ol an tyr a Thowr Hombyr the **Scotland** 'The duke very truly will get for his labout all the land from the River Humber to Scotland' BK 3235-37

Now, myghtern **Scotland**, *Augel, ha Syr Gawen ew maraw* 'Now the king of Scotland Augel, and Sir Gawain are dead' BK 3284-85.

It should also be pointed out that the ordinary word for 'Scotland' in Welsh is *Sgotland f. Yr Alban* is literary only. In the interests of authenticity, perhaps **Scotlond** should be used in revived Cornish instead of ***Alban**, or at least, in addition to it.

SEAGULL

For 'seagull' Nance recommends **gwylan**, *plural* ***gwylanas**. This derives from *alcedo*, **guilan** 'kingfisher, seagull' OCV §507. Lhuyd gives us:

Gu̱llan, A gull AB: 240c

Mi 'rig guelaz an Karnou idzha an **gu̱llez** *ha'n idhen môr aral kîl ẏ ʒe neitho* ' I saw the rocks where the gulls and other sea birds make their nests' AB: 245a

We seem to be dealing here with two different words. The first **gu̱llan** 'gull' is presumably the reflex of OC **guilan**. The second is the plural **gu̱llys**, which is apparently a borrowing from English 'gull, gulls.'

SECOND

In lists the ordinal 'second' is **nessa**, literally 'next'. Generally speaking, however, the Cornish for 'second' is **secu̱nd**:

A **nessa** 'next, second in a series'

*Kensa, vrt an hagar uall iggeva gweell do derevoll warneny... **Nessa**, vrt an skauoll crackan codna iggeva setha war... Tregya, vrt an gurroll iggeva gweel gen askern skooth davas* 'First by the storm he cause to rise up against us... Second, by the break-neck stool he sits on... Third, by the ship he makes with a sheep's shoulder-bone' BF: 9

GERYOW GWIR second

*Ha Deu kries an ebron neve, ha gethihuer ha metten vo **nessa** jorna* 'And God created the vault of heaven, and evening and morning were the second day' BF: 52

*Kensa blethan, byrla a' baye, **Nessa** blethan, lull a' laye, Tridgya blethan, comero ha doga, Peswarra blethan, mollath Dew war ef reeg dry hy uppa* 'The first year, hug and kiss, The next year, lullaby; The third year, take and bring; The fourth year, the curse of God on him that brought her here' ACB: F f.

B **secùnd** 'second'

*yn **secund** dyth y fynna gruthyl ebron nef hynwys* 'On the second day I will make a firmament called heaven' OM 17-8

*in meys est an viijves deth an **secund** feer sur a veth sensys in pov benytha* 'in August the eighth day the second fair will indeed by held in the land for ever' BM 2196-98

*an gerryow a thu an tas, kowses warlerth an maner an bobill, the thew an mab an **second** person ha then spuris sans* 'the words of God the Father spoken according to the manner of people to God the Son, the second person and to the Holy Spirit' TH 1

*whi a ra vnderstondia an **second** chapter an lever a Moyses gylwys Genesis* 'You will understand the second chapter of the book of Moses called Genesis' TH 1a

*ha conserning ena mabden yth ew scriffes in **second** chapter in Genesis* 'and concerning mankind then it is written in the second chapter in Genesis' TH 2

*eff appoyntias thean dalleth an bys y vn vab eff, an **second** person in dryngys, the vos savyowre an bys* 'he appointed from the beginning of the world his only Son, the second person of the Trinity, to be the saviour of the world' TH 12a

*an very mab du an **second** person in dryngys according the blonogath y das, a gemeras warnotha an nature a then* 'the very Son of God, the second person in the Trinity accord to the will of his Father, took upon himself the nature of man' TH 12a

*yma Sent powle in **second** chapter thyn hebrues ow leverell* 'St Paul in the second chapter to the Hebrews says' TH 13

*Arta yma du ow kull an **second** promys gans an venyn* 'Again God makes the second promise to the woman' TH 13

*an **second** person in dryngys du o ymmortall* 'the second person in God the Trinity was immortal' TH 15

*hen ew Jhesu Crist, an **second** person in dringys* 'that is Jesus Christ, the second person in the Trinity' TH 15a

*yma pedyr in kynsa chapter in **second** pistyll ow ry thyn ny certayn ha sure rulle* 'St Peter in the first chapter of the second epistle gives us a certain and sure rule' TH 17a

*ha in y tressa chapter the Thimothe in **second** pistill yma eff ow cowsse indelma* 'and in the third chapter to Timothy in the second epistle he speaks thus' TH 18a

*han **second** ew havall the hemma* 'and the second is similar to this' TH 20a

*ha S pawle a gylwys an galathians, fooles ha tus heb vnderstonding, in **second** chaptur in epistill scriffis thyn Galathians* 'and St Paul called the Galatians fools and men without understanding in the second chapter of the epistle to the Galatians' TH 29a

*han kynsa ew antiquite, hen ew cotheneb, an **second** ew vniversalite han tryssa ew vnytie* 'and the first is antiquity, that is age, the second is universality, and the third is unity' TH 34a

second   GERYOW GWIR

*dre an **second** ny a yll vnderstondya fatell ew lell feith ha discans an egglos an pith ew only vniversall in pub gwlas dyskys ha cresys* 'through the second we understand that the true faith and teaching of the Church is only that which is universal taught and believed in every country' TH 34a

*han **second** circumstance the vos omma consyddrys, ew fatell rug agan sovyour govyn worth pedyr very ernysch* 'and the second circumstance to be considered here is that our Saviour asked Peter very earnestly' TH 43-43a

*kepar dell vsy Justinus an martyr ha den auncient ow recordia in y **seconde** Apologie* 'as Justin, martyr and father, records in his second Apology' TH 46a

*dell ew gwrys mencion in xiiii chapter in **seconde** lever a Eusebius* 'as is mentioned in the 13th chapter of the second book of Eusebius' TH 46a

*Tuchia an **seconde**, ken na vo travith na hene mas an generall cregians an chatholik egglos* 'Concerning the second, though it is nothing other than the general belief of the catholic Church' TH 55

*ran athewethas a rug talkya vaynly ha curiously an kythsam **seconde** part ma* 'some recently have talked vainly and curiously of this same second part' TH 55

*So lymmyn rag procedya in rag the declaria an **seconde** tra the vos consyddrys in sacrament benegas an aulter* 'But now to proceed further to declare the second thing to be considered in the blessed sacrament of the altar' TH 55a

*in **second** degre y fithe gwryes try order moy yn sertan* 'in the second degree there will be made three more orders certainly' CW 51-2

*lebmyn yn **second** jorna gwraf broster athesempys* 'now on the second day I will make a firmament immediately' CW 80-1.

Secùnd 'second' is attested in four different texts, OM, BM, TH and CW. It should perhaps replace **nessa** in the revived language as the default word for 'second'.

SERVANT

The Cornish word for 'servant' is **servont**. The plural is sometimes **servons**. More frequently, however, the plural is **servysy**, **servyjy**, as though from an unattested singular *****servyas**:

A servons

*nyns yv ow gulas a'n bys ma hag yn certan a pe hy ov **seruons** byth ny'm gasse* 'my kingdom is not of this world and if it were indeed, my servants would never have left me' PC 2010-12

*eugh ow dew el thu'm **seruons** lel yn pryson evs* 'go, my two angels to my faithful servants who are in prison' RD 315-16

*yma ov **servons** ov toys* 'my servants are coming' BM 2329

*rag vyngia purguir me yv war y **servons** eff certen* 'I am minded to take vengeance indeed upon his servants certainly' BM 2383-84

GERYOW GWIR servant

Lymmyn ny vanna ve na moy agys gylwell why **servantes** *mas cothmans* 'Now I will not longer call you servants but friends' TH 35a

ken fene ny oll an dythyow agan bewnans kepar ha **servans** *gober* 'though we be all the days of our lives like hired servants' TH 41

der thowgys e tathorhas e honnyn par del vynnas, ha'y lel **servantes** *dyspernys* 'by deity he rose again himself as he wished, and he redeemed his faithful servants' BK 311-13

Aragough na ren gwelas the **servantes**, *tues vras ha coyth, bos wottywath drog telys* 'Before your face let us not see your servants, great and wise men, being badly recompensed in the end' BK 754-56

Servantes, *gwysyon a the bleysyon ha pejadaw* 'Servants, lackeys go to oblation and to begging' BK 763-65

Ow **servantes**, *maru'm kerough, a'gys dyhowgh prederowgh ha bethough war* 'My servants, if you love me, think of your right flank and beware' BK 3259-61.

B **servysy**

pysyn may fyyn **servysy** *th'agan arluth hep parow* 'let us pray that we may be servants to our peerless Lord' OM 235-36

gorthyans ha gras the dev ow thas luen a vercy pan danvonas yn onor bras thy'm **servysi** 'glory and thanks to God my Father, full of mercy, in that in great honour he has sent me servants' PC 169-72

saw ol the len **servygy** 'save all your faithful servants' PC 277-79

an tas dev roy thy'n bos guyv the vos len **seruysy** *thy's* 'God the Father grant us to be worthy to be faithful servants to you' PC 712-13

rak the weres yv parys the'th **seruygy** *yn bys ma* 'for your help is ready for your servants in this world' PC 2707-08

thomas ty a the eynda hag ena pregoth a wra yn ow hanow ha gura thy [m] moy **seruygy** 'Thomas, you will go to India and there preach in my name and make more servants for me' RD 2458-60

ha nep na vynno crygy ny yl bos a'm **seruysy** *yn certan awos an beys* 'and who will not believe cannot be one of my servants certainly for all the world' RD 2469-71

yma ov quan rewardya y **servysy** *rum ene* 'badly does he reward his servants, upon my soul' BM 3261-62

yma thymo **servysy** *orth ov gorthya pur vesy* 'I have servants worshipping me very assiduously' BM 3373-74

sav mercy y raff pesy hag onen ath **servysy** *nefra bethe heb awer* 'but I shall beg for mercy and shall be one of your servants for ever without grief' BM 3800-02

theorth crist lel map guirhas rag ov **servesy** *in beas war thu pesy me a ra* 'from Christ, true Son of a Virgin, I shall pray to God for my servants in the world' BM 4274-76

... **servygy** '...servants' BK 675

sirvigy 'servants' Bodewryd MS.

In the revived language if **servont** is the singular, both **servons** and **servysy** may be used for the plural. There is no evidence for a singular ***servyas**.

serve

TO SERVE, SERVICE

For 'to serve' some speakers use **gonys**. This verb really means 'to till, to cultivate' but can mean 'to serve' on occasion:

A gonys

maria a ***wonetheff*** *dywhy re wrontya ʒehays* 'Mary, whom I serve, may she grant you health' BM 3140-41

maria ***gonys*** *a raff thy fesy gans colen claff rag ov map me a vyn moys* 'I serve Mary; with a sore heart I will go to pray to her for my son' BM 3588-90

ihesu crist ny sefeth greff in bys ma ath lel ***wonys*** 'Jesus Christ will have no grief in this world from your faithfully serving him' BM 3890-91

Fals du ema ow ***conys*** 'he serves a false god' BK 399

Saw refrens ahanogh why, orthowgh kefrys ef a fy re'n keth Du a ***woneth*** *a* 'Saving your reverence, he says Fie to you also by the same God that he serves' BK 945-47.

The commonest word for 'to serve', however, is **servya**:

B servya

Adam an tas dev guella a yrghys thy's growethe gans the bryes ker eva rag cafus flogh the'th ***servye*** 'Adam the best Father has bidden you lie with your dear spouse Eve to get a child to serve you' OM 644-47

ny a thynyth vn flogh da thy'n a ***seruyo*** 'we will engender a good child who will serve us' OM 664-65

an tas a'n nef caradow roy thotho grath th'y ***seruye*** 'the dear Father of heaven give him grace to serve him' OM 679-80

guyn bys bones thym fethys lafur ha duwon a'n bys fest pel my re'n ***seruyas*** *ef* 'happy I am that I have conquered the labour and trouble of the world; very long have I served it' OM 849-52

nyns us den ort ov ***seruye*** *len ha guyryon me a greys* 'there is no man serving me loyally and truly, I believe' OM 929-30

drefen luen ty thu'm ***seruye*** *ov cres a fet venary* 'because you have fully served me, you will have my peace for ever' OM 1019-20

mara qureth aga lettya na allons len y ***servya*** *me a leuer yn tor ma vynions cref a goth warnas* 'if you prevent them from faithfully serving him, I tell you now harsh vengeance will fall upon you' OM 1495-98

guyw yv yn len the ***servye*** 'it is worthwhile to serve you faithfully' OM 2608

guyw yv prest ***servye*** *yn ta pur wyr epscop an par ma rag gentel yv del weleugh* 'it is right in truth to serve well a bishop of this kind, for he is gracious as you see' OM 2776-79

ow eleth sevegh yn ban evgh alemma ahanan the ***seruye*** *ow map kerra* 'my angels, rise up; go hence from here to serve my dearest son' PC 151-53

the tas kera thy lawe re'n danvonas the'th ***servye*** 'your dearest Father, praised be he! has sent us to serve you' PC 166-67

GERYOW GWIR serve

yn creys me re ysethas avel seruont ow **seruye** 'I have sat in the midst like a servant serving' PC 803-04

rak an keth den ma bythqueth ny'n **servyes** *war ov ene* 'for this same man never upon my soul have I served' PC 1284-85

en keth guas ma yth ese gans ihesu worth y **seruye** 'this same fellow was with Jesus serving him' PC 1405-06

iesu crist gwyth vy pupprys lel ʒeth **servye** *om dyʒyow* 'Jesus Christ, keep me always faithfully to serve you in my days' BM 146-47

pronter boys me a garse corff ihesu thy venystra mar myn ov descans **servya** 'I should like to be a priest to administer the body of Christ, if my learning will serve' BM 522-24

hag omma darber ʒehas then ij den ma may fo guelys ov boys in beys orth the **servya** 'and here provide health for these two men, that it may be seen that I serve you in the world' BM 2645-49

maria me reth **cervyes** *thum gallus bythqueth defry* 'Mary, I have served you as best I could always indeed' BM 3595-96

meryasek in ov bewnans me a vyn prest the **servya** 'Meriasek, in my life, I will always serve you' BM 3850-51

ow exortya oll an bobyll the ry prayse hag honor the du ha thy **servya** *in lowendar* 'exhorting all the people to give praise and honour to God and to serve him in joy' TH 1

be va dre commondment du bo dre neb one ny dre obediens kylmys the **seruya** 'whether it be through the commandment of God or through someone whom we are by obedience bound to serve' TH 5

hagan hooll bewnans res thy **servia** *eff a vght pub tra* 'and in all our life given to serving him above all things' TH 21a

ha the vos quiet agan honyn the **servia** *du in y egglos catholik* 'and to be quiet ourselves to serve God in his catholic Church' TH 51

Fy the Jovyn ha Beryth hag Astrot plos ha the gymmys a govyt ha dyeth ha nos aga **servya** 'Fie upon Jovyn and Beryth and dirty Astrot and upon as many as yearn to serve them day and night' BK 273-77

Omden, gas the folneb! **Serf** *Du avan!* 'Begone, stop your folly! Serve God above!' BK 281-82

*Jesu Christ, mab Marya, roy thym gras the'th lel-***servya** 'Jesus Christ, son of Mary, give me grace to serve you faithfully' BK 781-82

Parys on the'th unadow rag the **servya** *pub termyn* 'We are ready at your desire to serve you always' BK 2036-37

Nyng ew ow thowl **servya** *an Jowl* 'It is not my intention to serve the Devil' BK 2937-38

canhasawe them danvenys rage ow **servia** *bys vickan* 'messengers sent to me to serve me for ever' CW 29-30

determys ove ʒa vn dra ha concludys magata tha wythyll vn dean omma a thore ha sleme ʒom **servia** 'determined I am of one thing and decided as well to make a man of clay and slime here to serve me' CW 236-39

adam me a levar theys tha vabe seth ew dowesys genaf prest thom **servya** *ve* 'Adam, I tell you, your son Seth has been chosen by me to serve me always' CW 1402-04

serve **GERYOW GWIR**

*me a **servyas** pell an beyse aban vema kyns formys* 'I have served the world long since I was first created' CW 1974-75

*nyng es dean orthe ow **seruya** len ha gwyrryan sure pub pryes* 'no man serves me faithfully and truly indeed always' CW 2224-25

*Lebben Jooan e na vengha **servia** na velha* 'Now John did not want to serve any longer' BF: 16

*Lebmen Dzhûan e na vendzha **servia** na velha* 'Now John did not want to serve any longer' BF: 17

*Amedh Dzhûan, me a ve **servia** ha lebmen theram moz drê dho a urêg* 'Said John, I have been serving and now I am going home to my wife' BF: 17

*Che ra gorthy tha Arleth Deew hag eu e honnen che ra **servya*** 'You shall worship your Lord God and him only shall you serve' Rowe

*ha gweel thangy ul **servia** Dewe, [h]an poble en kaniffar plewe* 'and make them serve God and the people of every parish' LAM: 226.

For the substantive 'service' Nance recommends **gwryth**, **gonys**, ***gonesegeth**, and **servys**:

Gwryth is attested three times:

A **gwryth**

*rak henna the'n bys y tuyth rag don dustiny ha **guryth** the'n lendury yn pup prys* 'therefore I came into the world to bear witness and service to good faith always' PC 2022-23

*ple ma haneth a wor den vyth may caffen wheth cryst len a **wryth*** 'where tonight (does anyone know?) where I might find Christ full of works?' RD 849-50

*a vynynryth na tuche vy nes na na wra **gruyth** na fo the les* 'O woman, do not touch me at all nor do a deed that would not be of advantage' RD 875-76.

The sense of **gwryth** is uncertain. In the three attestations it seems to mean 'action, deeds' as much as 'service'.

Gonys: this is a verbal noun meaning 'to cultivate, to work, to worship'. I can find no example in the texts of a substantival use with the sense 'service'.

***Gonesegeth** is not attested, having been devised by Nance on the basis of Welsh *gwenidogaeth* 'administration' and Breton *gounidigezh* 'cultivation'. There is no evidence that a form ***gonesegeth** ever existed in Cornish, or that it meant 'service'.

Servys 'service' is widely attested in the texts:

B **servys** 'service'

*Ihesus crist a leueris ʒe thu ny goth thys temptye yn neb ehan a **seruys** lemmyn prest y honore* 'Jesus Christ said: You should not tempt your God in any kind of service, but always honour him' PA 15ab *besy yw ȝys bos vuell ha seruabyll yth* **seruys** *manno allo an tebell ogas ȝys bonas trylys* 'it is essential for you to be humble and obedient in your service so that the evil one cannot be turned near you' PA 19cd

en gyth o deyow hablys may fenne ihesus sopye gans an re yn y **seruys** *war an bys re ȝewesse* 'the day was Palm Sunday when Jesus wished to sup with those in his service in the world that he had chosen' PA 41cd

Kyn fallens ol me a veth yn meth pedyr yth **seruys** 'Though they all fail, I shall be, said Peter, in your service' PA 49a

Ihesus crist a wovynnys worth an bobyll a ȝeth dy gans an fals yn y **seruys** *pandra yw a vynnough wy* 'Jesus Christ asked the people who had come thither with the false one in his service, What is it you want?' PA 67ab

ganso drys nos yȝ olyas yn y **seruys** *neb o len* 'with him through the night there watched one who was faithful in his service PA 237c

guyn y vys pan ve gynys a allo gul thy's **servys** 'happy the man to have been born who can do you service' OM 1476-77

messyger rag the **seruys** *the rewardye my a ra* 'messenger, for your service I will reward you' OM 2309-10

the vos epscop yn temple an lahe the venteyne **servys** *the dev the gane* 'to be bishop in the temple, to maintain the law, to sing service to God' OM 2601-03

kymmer the vytour whare ha byth yn the **servys** *len* 'take your mitre now and be faithful in your service' OM 2615-16

mar man dev rag an guella my a leuer yn templa whare **seruys** *thotho ef* 'if God wishes it for the best, I shall straightway say service for him in the temple' OM 2620-22

guyn y vys a vo trigys yn the **seruys** *ragh tristys nyn dygemmer vynytha* 'happy the man who dwells in your service, for sadness will never overtake him' PC 122-24

the rewardye my a wra rak the **servys** 'I shall reward you for your service' PC 612-13

ysetheugh yn kesoleth rak scon why a fyth **seruys** 'be seated in peace for soon you shall receive service' PC 715-16

ha ken na fe da genes gul the **seruys** *ty a wra* 'and though you do not want to, you shall do your service' PC 2260-61

nebes **seruys** *ty a wra tan syns y'th dorn an giu na* 'you shall do a little service; here take that spear in your hand' PC 3009-10

Ov flehys wek eugh why dre ov banneth genogh neffre na letyogh vy am **servys** 'My dear children, go home. My blessing to you always. Do not hinder my service' BM 2676-78

mar mynnogh oma neb preys thymo comendya **servys** *awos areth me an gruae* 'if you commend service to me ever here, I will do it for wages' BM 3199-201

ny a ra bohes venogh syluester **servys** *dywhy* 'seldom, Silvester, do we service for you' BM 4161-62

Rag meth na vethens gegys a'y **servys** *the omdenna* 'For shame, let him not be permitted to withdraw from his service' BK 1844-45

ha pub onyn thy thecree a vyth gorris thom **service** *pan vidnaf ve comanndya* 'and everyone according to its decree will be put to my service when I command it' CW 34-6

me a vyn thewhy poyntya **service** *tha[n eyl] hay gela rage rowlya eys ha chattell* 'I will appoint service for you, for the one and the other to rule grain and cattle' CW 1062-63 *nyng es tra in bys ma gwryes mes thewhy a wra* **service** 'there is nothing created in this world but that will do you service' CW 2515-16

Mose tha an more en **serves** *an Vaternes* 'Go to sea in the Queen's service' Bilbao MS.

It is quite apparent from the citations from OM 2601-03 and 2620-22 that **servys** is exactly the right word for a church service. It also seems that the default word for 'service' in any of its senses should be **servys** in the revived language. The ordinary word for 'to serve' is **servya**.

TO SHAKE

The two ways of translating 'to shake' in Cornish are with A) **crena** and B) **shakya**.

A **crena**

3eworte vn lam beghan y3 eth pesy may halle 3y 3as ynweth vgy a van hag ef rag own ow **crenne** 'he went a little distance from them to pray also to his Father who is above and he was shaking for fear' PA 53cd

a thev a ras serponnt yv hy evth hy guelas ovn a'm bus vy **crenne** *a wraf* 'O God of grace, it is a snake, dreadful to look upon. I am afraid; I am shaking' OM 1451-53

yma an dor ow **krenne** *seuel vnwyth ny yllyn* 'the ground is shaking; we cannot even stand' PC 2995-96

rak ovn desefsen merwel me a **crennas** 'for fear I thought I would die. I shook' RD 1771-72

eff a deerbyn trestyns hag a guayn pur sempel los may **kerna** *purguir y dyns* 'he will meet sadness and will obtain a right ?simple loss, so that his teeth will chatter' BM 2255-57

y a **gren** *age barvov* 'they will shake their beards' BM 2309

ny a **gren** *agen barvov mar ny omthegen the guel* 'we will shake our beards if we do not behave better' BM 3450-51

Why a **gren** *agis barvov treytours kyn gul indella* 'you will shake your beards, traitors, before doing that' BM 3529-30

Saw ny vyth gwyth gweth ys fol, pan i'n **crennif** *Calesvol, me a'n dyhals* 'But he will not dare deeds worse than a fool, when I shake it — Excalibur, I shall cleave him in two' BK 3268-70.

B **shakya**

aga fen y a **sackye** *hag a gewsy pur debell worth Ihesus rag y angre* 'they shook their heads and spoke vilely to Jesus to annoy him' PA 195bc

Parys oll onn in arvov y a **schaky** *age barvov neb a settya er the byn* 'We are all ready in arms; they will shake their beards, whoever attacks you' BM 2312-14

ha mar ver **shackys** *ha tossys may rug lyas onyn seperatya aga honyn theworty* 'and greatly shaken and tossed, so that many separated themselves from her' TH 30a

ha na ven ny alemma rag kepar ha flehes ow **shackya** *gans pub waffe* 'and let us not from now on be like children shaking with every gust of wind' TH 42
Gorah an vose tha **shakiah** *an kala* 'Put the maid to shake the straw' ACB: F f *verso*.

Crena, **kerna** and **shakya** can both be used for 'to shake'. **Crena** is perhaps the better verb for 'to tremble'. Though notice also the following in SA:

rag eth ony megys gans an kethsam tra vgy an elath ow gwelas ha ow **trembla** 'for we are nourished by the very same thing which the angels see and tremble' SA 59.

SHAME, TO SHAME

There are two main ways of expressing the idea of 'shame': A) **meth** and B) **sham**:

A meth

ha mur a bobyll ganse a ȝyghow sur hag a gleth the gryst y tons ȝy syndye ha ȝe dry ȝen dor gans **meth** 'and many people with them on the right and on the left, they came to Christ to harm him and to bring him low with shame' PA 97cd

In meth pylat why a vyn drys pub tra me ȝy laȝe agis mygtern **meth** *yw ȝyn na veȝens clewys neffre* 'Pilate said, You want above all things that I should kill your king. It is shame to us; let it not ever be heard' PA 148ab

mar tue nep guas ha laddre en gueel theworthyn pryve **meth** *vyth ol d'agen ehen* 'if some fellow comes and steels the rods from us privily, it will be shame to all our kindred' OM 2064-66

arluth golhy mara qureth ow treys thy'm y ffye **meth** *hedre veyf byv yn certan* 'Lord, if you wash my feet for me, it would be shame for me as long as I live surely' PC 845-47

my ny fethaf sur rak **meth** *dos yn mysk ow brudereth* 'I dare not for shame come among my brethren' PC 1429-30

rak an harlot a geus freth pur wyr ynno nyns us **meth** 'for the scoundrel talks glibly; indeed there is no shame in him' PC 1832-33

hag yndella mara qureth neffre ny fyth scham na **meth** *saw mur a ioy* 'and if you do thus, never will you have disgrace nor shame but much joy' PC 1901-03

tav thegy lemmyn rak **meth** *gans ihesu nyns os pryveth* 'Silence now, for shame. You are not in Jesus' confidence' RD 1091-92

marth yv gynef na'th ues **meth** *ow keusel gow* 'I am astonished you are not ashamed to speak falsehooood' RD 1391-92

teweugh rak **meth** *dew adla ymthysquethas ny vynna the plussyon auelough why* 'Silence, for shame, two scoundrels; he did not wish to appear to dirty wretches like you' RD 1495-97

drok den a fue sur bythqueth a wul drok ny'n gefe **meth** *yn y thythow* 'he was an evil man always indeed; he had no shame of doing ill in his days' RD 1782-84

pilat gynef nyns yw **meth** *awos guyske sur an queth a fue yn kerghyn ihesu* 'Pilate, I have no shame about wearing the garment indeed that was about Jesus' RD 1935-37

shame

meth *yv gans ol the cufyon tha vones omma dyson avel begyer desethys* 'it is shame to all your loved ones that you indeed are seated here like a beggar' BM 2019-21

na gampol crist theragovy ha mara queth ta a feth **meth** *hath ost defry* 'do not mention Christ in front of me, and if you do you will have shame and your army indeed' BM 2439-43

na gymer **meth** *am present lemen pan ywe messent me an set ryb the frygov* 'be not ashamed of my present, but since it is fetid, I shall set it against your nose' BM 3397-99

A aswonsyn ve the stat, ne setsan warnas algat, na russan rag **meth** *an bys* 'had I known your state, I should not have attacked you at all, I should not for fear of shame in the world' BK 606-08

Rag **meth** *na vethens gegys a'y servys the omdenna* 'For shame, let him not be permitted to withdraw from his service' BK 1844-45

The leudnys gas rag **meth** *an bys* 'Give over your lewdness for the shame of the world' BK 2209-10

Hy a chans hy athdrevy orth **meth** *ha cas ha dyal* 'She is risking being rewarded by shame and hatred and revenge' BK 3004-05.

B **sham**

hag yndella mara qureth neffre ny fyth **scham** *na meth saw mur a ioy* 'and if you do thus, never will you have shame nor disgrace but much joy' PC 1901-03

ogh ellas gouy tru tru gueles thy'so a ihesu kemmys **sham** *ha vyleny* 'Oh, alas, woe, woe, pity, pity, to see so much shame and mistreatment done to you, O Jesus!' PC 2627-29

me a wysk wythowte blam mars ens garow the voy **scham** *the'n fleryys* 'I will strike without blame. If they are rough, the greater the shame for the stinking wretch' PC 2737-39

marregyon theugh ny won blam rak thy'mmo y fye **scham** *gul drok thywhy* 'Soldiers, I impute no blame to you, for it would be a shame to do you harm' RD 657-59

out govy na vuff marov kyns doys a dor ov dama govi rag **schame** 'Ouch, woe that I did not die before emerging from my mother's womb. Woe is me for shame!' BM 795-97

ath deryvas **schame** *yth yv pan othem o the vap du boys lethys avel carov* 'shame it is for your narration. What need was there for the Son of God to be slain like a stag?' BM 879-81

rag in mater ny coth **schame** 'for in the matter there is no need for shame' BM 1626

yth evel gena y voys **schame** *sur moy es honester* 'it seems to me to be a shame rather than an honest matter' BM 3026-27

benythe num bethe **schame** *awoys gul drok* 'never am I wont to be ashamed for doing evil' BM 3371-72

A arluth agan Du ny, thynny yth ew worthy the vos accomptys **shame** *ha confucion* 'O our Lord God, to us it is right to ascribe shame and confusion' TH 9a-10

yth ew gwris da aga rebukya, may hallans bos methek ha kemeras **sham** *aga fawtys* 'it is well done to rebuke them, so that they may be embarrassed and be ashamed of their failings' TH 29a

Gwyth ve orth **sham** *ha re vysmer, kyn tus a'th vlam hag a lever na'th usta ras* 'Keep me from shame and excessive disgrace, otherwise people will blame you and say you have no grace' BK 1237-41

Gas cres, rag **scham**! 'Silence, for shame!' BK 2204

Na thowtyans rag **sham** *na Cornow na Scot* 'Let him not fear for shame, either Cornishman or Scot' BK 2486-87

shame *ew genaf tha glowas ow cregy then gyrryaw na* 'I am ashamed to hear you believing those words' CW 637-39.

As can be seen from the two sets of attestations 'to be ashamed' is either **kemeres meth** or **kemeres sham**. The adjective 'ashamed' is **methek**:

Myterne Davith o **methek** *rag y pehosow, so nyns o ef* **methek** *the confessia y pehosow* 'King David was ashamed for his sins, but he was not ashamed to confess his sins' TH 8a

Ha na esow ny the vos **methek** *the confessia nag ony mar perfect dell vea res thyn* 'And let us not be ashamed to confess that we are not as perfect as we ought be' TH 9a

na esow ny the vos **methek** *the confessia agan foly* 'let us not be ashamed to confess our folly' TH 9a

yth ew gwris da aga rebukya, may hallans bos **methek** *ha kemeras sham aga fawtys* 'it is well done to rebuke them, so that they may be ashamed and be embarrassed for their failings' TH 29a

eff a ill bos **methek** *ay vnkyndenys ha disobediens warbyn du* 'he can be ashamed of his unnatural behaviour and his disobedience against God' TH 30a

nyng ew marth, kyn fen **methak** *ha serrys hag anhethak* 'it is not astonishing, though I be ashamed and angry and discomforted' BK 1012-13.

The verb 'to shame' is **shâmya**:

ellas mar pethen **schamys** *wath preder a guel forthov* 'alas if we are put to shame! Consider better ways' BM 420-21

A, Du a vyn **shamys** *ow bos ha'm gar syttys der hi ben* 'Oh, God wants me to be put to shame with one leg crossed over the other' BK 3301-02.

For the revived language one can recommend **meth** 'shame', **sham** 'shame'; **kemeres meth** and **kemeres sham** 'to be ashamed'; **methek** 'ashamed' and **shâmya** 'to shame'.

SHARP, TO SHARPEN

The default word for 'sharp' is **lymm**:

A lymm

gew a ve yn y ȝewle gans an eȝewon gorris ha pen **lym** *rag y wane ȝe golon Ihesus hynwys* 'a spear was put in his hands by the Jews with a sharp point to pierce to the heart of holy Jesus' PA 217cd

en gew **lym** *ef a bechye pur ewn yn dan an asow dre an golon mayȝ e[ȝ] e* 'the sharp spear he was thrusting very exactly under the ribs so that it went through the heart' PA 218cd *otte spern grisyl gyne ha dreyn **lym** ha scharp ynne a grup bys yn empynyon* 'look, here I have horrible thorns with sharp and keen prickles on them, which will penetrate into the brain' PC 2118-20

*gans gu **lym** y a'n guanas dre an golon may resas the'n dor an gos a cothas* 'with a sharp spear they pierced him, so that it ran through the heart; the blood fell down' RD 1117-19

*yn le basnet war ow fen curyn a spern **lym** ha glev* 'instead of a helmet on my head a crown of sharp and keen thorns' RD 2581-82

*gans gu **lym** in tenewon del russons y y guana* 'with a sharp spear in the side as they pierced him' BM 2604-05

*Marrak **lym**, orth both ow brys, uhal-worthyys of i'n bys* 'A keen knight, to my heart's desire, highly revered in the world' BK 1648-49

*Hayl, arluth grym, del os gallant ha'th skyans **lym**!* 'Hail, fearsome lord, as you are brave and your wits sharp!' BK 1740-42

*Fers of ha **lym**, ha, soccors grym, asa allaf bos galant!* 'I am fierce and keen, and, fearsome friends, how valiant can I be!' BK 2714-16

*Theugh e tof ve glu ha **lym*** 'I shall come to you bitter and sharp' BK 3204.

The adjective **sherp**, **sharp** is also used:

B **sherp**, **sharp**

*yma omma dev clethe parys gans ov cowethe cales ha **scherp** kekeffrys* 'Here are two swords prepared by my companions, hard and sharp also' PC 925-27

*otte spern grisyl gyne ha dreyn lym ha **scharp** ynne a grup bys yn empynyon* 'look, here I have horrible thorns with keen and sharp prickles on them, which will penetrate into the brain' PC 2118-20

*teulyn grabel warnotho **scherp** ha dalgenne ynno byth na schapye* 'let us throw a sharp grapnel upon him and hold him that he will never escape' RD 2268-70

*Drys an gwlasow scon heb ardag, rys ew rowtya **sherp** avel spern* 'Across the kingdoms soon without delay it is necessary to swagger sharp as thorns' BK 1662-65.

'To sharpen' is **lemma**, **lebma**:

*Gora an dens harraw tha an gove tha **lebma*** 'Put the harrow tines to the smith to sharpen' ACB: F f 2

*Acuo… To Whet or Sharpen; … C. Dho **lebma*** AB: 41b.

Lhuyd also suggests that 'sharp' is **lemmys**, i.e. 'sharpened' AB: 41b. **Lemmys** 'sharp' is presumably to be used of knives and other implements that have been whetted to sharpness.

For the revived language one can recommend **lymm/lybm** 'sharp', **sherp/sharp** 'sharp'; **lemma/lebma** 'to whet, to sharpen' and **lemmys/lebmys** 'sharp (of blades, etc.)'.

SHOP

For the substantive 'shop' many revivalists favour the word ***gwerthjy**. This word is unattested having been devised by Nance from **gwertha** 'to sell' and **-chy** 'house'; cf. the Welsh neologism *gwerthdy* 'shop'. There is, however, no need for such an item, since **shoppa** 'workshop, shop' (< Middle English *shoppe*) occurs in place-names, e.g. *Ponson Joppa* and *Parc Joppa*. The Middle English word *shoppe* meant both a workshop and a shop open to the public, where wares were sold. It is likely, therefore, that *shoppe*, when borrowed into Cornish **shoppa**, had a similar semantic range.

Two further points should be noted. First, the ordinary Welsh word for 'shop' is *siop*. Second, Caradar, always uses **shoppa**, *plural* **shoppys** in his writing in preference to ***gwerthjy**:

*Tom Temayne o kyger agan treveglos-ny, ha'y **shoppa** o chy coth war ryn an vre* NWB: 6

*Yth esa Jowan Typconyn, marchont, a Stretyn Myghal, yn treveglos Tegarrack, ow treghy kyk mogh pan dheuth an wycoryon ajy dhe'n **shoppa*** NWB: 22

*Un jeth, ha hy ow tos yn mes a'n **shoppa** ha canstel a daclow presy yn dan hy bregh, slynkya war an cawns a wruk* KmK: 41

*Desempys an bel a nyjas crak! erbyn fenester onen a'n **shoppys*** KmK: 47.

I can find no example of ***gwerthjy** in Caradar's writing.

SHORT

For the adjective 'short' many revivalists, following Nance and Caradar, use the word **berr** (UC *ber*). **Berr**, however, is found only A) in Lhuyd's englyn and B) in set phrases, **a verr spîss**, **a verr termyn**:

A **berr** in Lhuyd's englyn

*An lavar kôth yu lavar guîr, Bedh dvrn rê **ver**, dhvn tavaz rê hîr; Mez dên heb davaz a gvllaz i dîr* 'What's said of old will always stand: Too long a tongue , too short a hand: But he that had no tongue, lost his land' AB: 251c.

B1 **a verr spîss**

*na allaf sparie na moy hep gul dyel **a ver speys** war pep ol sur marnas ty* 'so that I cannot spare from making requital shortly on everyone surely except you' OM 946-48

*myshyf a goth warnotho yn certan hag **a ver spys*** 'disaster will fall upon him indeed and very shortly' OM 1539-40

*lauar thy'mmo **a ver spys** py nyl o mogha sengys an keth den ma the care* 'tell me quickly which of them was the more bound to love that same man?' PC 509-11

*lauar thy'nny me a'th pys the volungeth **a ver spys*** 'Tell us, I beg you, your wish shortly' PC 2052-54

short   **GERYOW GWIR**

*gura gueres thy'm **a ver spys** del os sylwyas* 'work assistance for me quickly as you are a saviour' RD 1721

*myr worto hag **a ver spys** a'th trok ty a vyth yaghays* 'look upon it and quickly you will be healed of your complaint' RD 1729-30

*arluth ker hag **a ver spys** thywhy ef a vyth kerghys* 'dear lord, he will be brought to you and quickly' RD 1785-86

*how ty geyler dus yn rak ha mar ny thueth me a'th tak hag **a ver spys*** 'ho, you gaoler, come forth and if you don't, I'll soon throttle you' RD 1989-91

*Ke a'n gevith yselder in carharow **a ver spys*** 'Ke will be humiliated in fetters shortly' BK 404-05

*Christ ow Arluth me a bys re'th weresa **a ver spys*** 'Christ my Lord I shall pray; may he help you shortly' BK 802-03

*Me a's musyr **a ver spys** maga ledan avel hyer* 'I will measure them soon as wide as long' BK 821-22.

B2 **a verr termyn**

*lemyn yn hast me a'th kelm fast **a ver termyn*** 'now in haste I will bind you fast without delay' OM 1361-62

*cous er the fyth **a ver termyn** pandra synsyth y'th luef lemyn* 'speak by your faith quickly. What are you holding in your hand?' OM 1441-42

*pur parys th'y worhemmyn ny a thy **a ver termyn** agan dev wythoute fal* 'very readily at his command we will go there without delay, the two of us without fail' PC 1653-55

*leuereugh **a ver termyn** py hanow yv a'n iaudyn thy'mmo a thanfonas e* 'say without delay what is the name of the scoundrel he has sent me' PC 1690-92

*y tue warnough vyngeans tyn man gueller **a ver termyn** ha war the fleghys keffrys* 'harsh vengeans will come upon you so that it will be seen shortly and upon your children also' PC 2199-201.

The englyn is very early Middle Cornish. In the other Middle Cornish texts, **berr** is not used other than in two set phrases. **Berr** is not the default word for 'short' (and 'shortly'), which is **cot**:

C **cot** 'short'

*yn scon dyswreys ef a vyth ha the'n mernans **cot** gorrys* 'soon he will be destroyed and shortly put to death' OM 1521-22

*kyns ys trehy war an pren re **got** o a gevelyn* 'before cutting the timber, it was too short by a cubit' OM 2519-20

*drehevyn ef abarth dev yn ban lemyn re **got** ev a gevelyn da yn guyr* 'let us lift it up in the name of God. Now in truth it is too short by a good cubit' OM 2539-41

*an nyl torn y fyth ro hyr tres aral re **got** in guyr ken fo mar len musurys* 'at one moment it is too long, another time too short, even though it be measured correctly' OM 2548-50

***cot** yv the thythyow thegy nahen na grys* 'short are your days. Do not believe otherwise' RD 2037-08 *ren arluth then beys am ros me a ra pur* **cot** *y guyns* 'by the Lord who brought me into the world, I will render his breath very short' BM 2252-53

ny ra bewa omma mas termyn **cut** 'he lives here a short time only' TH 7

rag henna degow in kerth in agis colonow an lesson **cut** *ma* 'therefore take away in your hearts this short lesson' TH 26

ha wosa an tyrmyn **cut** *a vethyn ny omma in present ha mortall bewnans ma* 'and after the short time that we shall be here in this present and mortal life' TH 26

merow war agys bewnans in kythsame lesson bean **cut** *ma* 'look upon your life in this same short lesson' TH 28a

an moar brase yn **cutt** *termyn adro thom tyre a vyth dreys* 'the great sea in a short time will be brought about my land' CW 88-89

yma thymma hyrathe bras rag gothevas pandra vea in **cutt** *termyn ages negys* 'I have a great longing to know in a short time what your errand would be' CW 590-92.

In the revived language, the default word for 'short' should perhaps be **cot**, rather than **berr**.

SIGHT

When 'sight' means 'vision, range of vision' it can be translated by A) **golok**:

A **golok**

out warnas harlot pen cok scon yn mes quyk a'm **golok** 'Damn you empty-headed rogue. Soon, quick out of my sight!' OM 1529-30

me a wra thy's mur a throk ha dyspit somot y go hag ath whyp war an **wolok** 'I will do you much harm and spite, so mote I go, and will whip you across your sight' PC 2098-100

ken teffo yges **golok** *thotho ny yllough gul drok sur me a grys hedre vo yn y gerghen* 'though he come into your sight, you cannot do him any harm surely, I believe, while it is about him' RD 1862-65

thotho ny ylleugh gul drok hedre ve ygys **golok** *yn pur deffry* 'you will not be able to do harm to him, as long as he is in your sight in very deed' RD 1914-16

myryn orto vn **golok** *kyn na vo hy rag y leys* 'let us look one look upon him, though that be no advantage to him' BM 3386-87

In mes a'm **golag** *omden, rag nu'm pleg the lavarow* 'Withdraw out of my sight, for your words do not please me' BK 304-05

In mes a'm **golak** *omden!* 'Get out of my sight!' BK 474

A, harlot, re by leskys! Desympis gweyf ow **golog***!* 'Oh, scoundrel, may you be burnt! Leave my sight at once!' BK 569-70

Voydough ha coyth, degowgh an toyt mes a'm **golok** 'Get out and smartly, take the cup out of my sight' BK 750-52

Desempys gueyf ow **golok** *ha dyspyt the vab the das!* 'Get out of my sight immediately in spite of the son of your father!' BK 993-94

sight GERYOW GWIR

Ya, ou **golag** *ew garow* 'Yea, my sight is harsh' BK 1407
Eugh a'm **golak** *in neb tol!* 'Get out of my sight into some hole!' BK 2343
Desempis guef ow **golog**, *rag, te tyllyk, ny'th cara'* 'Get out of my sight immediately, because, I don't like you, you ragamuffin' BK 3183-84
Ens mes a'm **golag** *uskys py me a'n lath desempys, re Syn Thomas a gara'!* 'Let him leave my sight quickly or I'll kill him forthwith, by St Thomas whom I love!' BK 3188-90.

When 'sight' means 'view, vista' it can be translated by **vu**:

B vu

dismas iesmas yn vn **fu** *theugh dyuythys* 'Dismas, Jesmas in one view [has] come to you' PC 2350-51
y carsen guelas an **fvu** *anotho y voth mar pe* 'I should like to see the sight of him, were it his wish' RD 469-70
ny allaf guelas an **fu** *anotho ef yn nep tv* 'I cannot see the sight of him in any direction' RD 741-42
ro thy'm an gras par may feyf gvyw the gafos spas gynes hythev sur yn nep plas may bome **vu** *ha guel a'th fas* 'give me grace that I may be worthy to get a chance to be with you somewhere today, that I may have a view and a sight of your face' RD 840-42
galsen y[n] ta the'n kense **fu** *map maria henwys ihesu* 'well could I [recognize him] at the first sight, the son of Mary called Jesus' RD 863-64
ewgh mes a'm **veu** *hag omdennowgh* 'get out of my sight and withdraw' BK 1954-55.

The word **syght** [sɪxt] is used in the texts to translate 'sight' in all its senses:

C syght

ihesu crist mytern glorijs roy y **syght** *dotho heb fal* 'Jesus Christ, glorious king, give him his sight without fail' BM 548-49
Benedicite pana **syght** *am buevy haneth in noys* 'Benedicite, what a sight I had tonight in the night' BM 1725-26
sav noswyth a thyuvne **syght** *coynt y welys certen* 'but at night while awake I saw a curious sight indeed' BM 1785-86
teka **syght** *war ov ena ny welys in ov dethyov* 'a fairer sight upon my soul I never saw in all my days' BM 1814-15
peys gevyans warna losel bo voyd am **syght** *a pur hond* 'beg me for forgiveness, rogue, or get out of my sight, you utter cur' BM 2413-14
fout **syght** *numbus ommeras* 'for lack of sight I cannot help myself' BM 2560
ihesu crist y **syght** *grua dry den dem ma del yth pesa* 'Jesus Christ, bring his sight to this man as I beseech you' BM 2618-19
trewethek **syght** *yv helma gueles den yonk tek certan cheynys in keth vaner ma* 'a pitiful sight is that, to see a young man indeed chained in this way' BM 3823-25
mar thue in **syght** *me an gor yma omma pobil lor rag y latha eredy* 'if it comes into sight, I know it, there are enough people here to kill it indeed' BM 3939-41
ny gar namur in bys ma doys in ov **syght** *nam guelas* 'not many in this world want to come into my sight or see me' BM 4215-16

ha then neff eff a verays lowenek in **syght** *thynny* 'and he looked to heaven joyfully in our sight' BM 4433-34

ha gans perfect colonow the reiosya in **sight** *agan creator ha redemar* 'and with perfect hearts to rejoice in the sight of our Creator and Redeemer' TH 1

an venyn a welas y bos an frut da the thybbry ha teg the **sight** *y lagasow ha pleasant the veras warnetha* 'the woman saw that the fruit was good to eat and fair to the sight of her eyes and pleasant to look upon' TH 3a

rag nyns us den bew a vith keffys iust in the **sight** *ge, arluth* 'for there is no man alive who will be found just in thy sight, O Lord' TH 10a

mar ten ny indelma submyttya agan honyn in **sight** *a thu ny a yll bos sure, fatell ra eff in tyrmyn ay vicitacyon agan humbrag ny in ban then wlas vgy y vab Jhesus crist inhy tregys* 'if we thus submit ourselves in the sight of God, we can be sure, that he will in the time of his visitation lead us up to the kingdom where his son Jesus Christ dwells' TH 11a

yma eff ow menya na rellan ny cristonnyan desquethes agan honyn da ha virtus, warves in **sight** *an bys only* 'he means that we Christians should not show ourselves good and virtuous externally in the sight of the world only' TH 26a

ny a res thyn bois da ha virtuus in **sight** *a thu* 'we must be good and virtuous in the sight o God' TH 26a

ny bleig thym **sight** *anotha* 'I don't like the sight of it' CW 747

nang ew mear a for pur wyer aban gylsen **sight** *an tyre* 'it is now a long way very truly, since we lost sight of the land' CW 2448-49

hag an golam in pur sure me as danven pur vskys **sight** *an noer mar kill gwelas* 'and the dove I will send very surely out quickly to establish whether she can see sight of the land' CW 2453-55.

It would seem from the above lists that the commonest word in traditional Cornish for 'sight' is **syght**, and can thus hardly be proscribed.

SIGN

For the substantive 'sign' Nance recommends A) ***arweth**; B) **sin** (UC *syn*); and **tôkyn** (UC *tokyn*). Let us look at these three in turn:

A ***arweth** 'sign'

This word is unattested in Cornish, having been devised by Nance on the model of Welsh *arwydd* 'sign' and Breton *arouez* 'sign'. The element **-arwedh-**, however, is attested once in the verb **kevarwouth**, the 2nd singular imperative of ***kevarwedha** 'to direct, to guide': *lowenna tekca gothfy ihesu ov map* **kevarwouth** *vgy warnaf ow pygy* 'as joyfully and as finely as you can, direct Jesus, who is praying to me' PC 1042-44. Otherwise ***arweth**, **-arwedh-** is unknown in Cornish. The two attested word for 'sign' are A) **sin** and B) **tôkyn**.

sign

B **sin** 'sign'

Syne *an grovs kymer genys ha ty as led del vynneys poren theth voth ʒe honen* 'Take the sign of the cross with you and you will lead them as you wish exactly according to your will' BM 4057-59

syne *an grovs theragon scoen degeugh aberth maria* 'carry before us quickly the sign of the cross in the name of Mary' BM 4066-67

nyns ew ottrys na settys in mes dre ***signn*** *vith, mas only conceviis secretly in golan* 'it is not uttered or set out by any sign, but only conceived secretly in the heart' TH 28

henna ew the vttra aga anger dre ***sygne*** *ha tokyn* 'that is to utter their anger by sign and token' TH 28a

dre racha ny a yll vnderstondia an ***signe*** *warves vttrys in mes dre anger* 'by *racha* we can understand the outward sign uttered in anger' TH 28a

ha yth ew the vos dowtys maga vur avell ***signe*** *vith arell a vlonogath Du* 'and it is to be feared as greatly as any other sign of God's will' TH 50a

An gyrryow ma scryfys a vea res bos a laha in keth ***sign*** *ma .+.* 'These words should be written besided this sign .+.' SA 66a

ha grenz angye boaz rag ***seenez*** *ha rag termeniow ha ragg jornehow ha ragg blethednyow* 'and let them be for signs and for times and for days and for years' JKeigwin

ha gwrens gi bos rag ***signezou****, rag termen, ha rag dethiou ha blethaniou* 'and let them be for signs, for time, for days and years' BF: 52.

Notice in the last citation from John Boson's translation of *Genesis* 1, that the plural ***seenez*** (i.e. **sînys**) has been recharacterised with a second plural suffix to give ***signezou*** (i.e. **sînesow**).

C **tôkyn** 'sign'

ty a wylfyth an ***toknys*** 'You will see the signs' OM 716

yn record yn ***tokyn*** *len ov guarak a fyth settyys yn ban yn creys a'n ebren* 'as a record, as a true sign my rainbow will be set up in the middle of the heavens' OM 1243-45

honna a vyth ***tokyn*** *da a'n acord vs gureys hep fal* 'this shall be a good fair sign of the agreement made without fail' OM 1247

yn guyrder an thyr guelenyv dysquythyans ha ***token*** *a'n try person yn drynsys* 'in truth the three rods are a manifestation and sign of the the three persons of the Trinity' OM 1732-35

rag an thyyr guelen defry a ve gans dauyd plynsys hag a ivnnyas the onan yv ***token*** *da yn certan a'n try person yn drynsys* 'for the three rods indeed, which were planted by David, and have joined into one, are a splendid sign indeed of the three persons of the Trinity' OM 2656-60

tokyn *thyugh mar ny thyswe kyn fe dyswrys an temple the'n dor quyt na safe man me a'n dreha sur arte* 'if no sign appears to you, though the temple be razed to the ground so that it is not standing, I will build again surely' PC 343-46

me a thysk theugh ***tokyn*** *da* 'I will teach you a good sign' PC 971

hep dout henna my a wra rag thy'm yma ***tokyn*** *da rak y gafus* 'without doubt I shall do that, for I have a good sign for arresting him' PC 983-85

GERYOW GWIR   **small**

pertheugh cof ol an **tokyn** *a leuerys kyns lemyn* 'all remember the sign I mentioned before now' PC 1081-82

yn **tokyn** *y vos goky ha myns a geusys foly ma na veath y avowe hethough cercot a baly thotho me a vyn y ry* 'as a sign that he is foolish and all he has spoken folly, so that he dares not admit it, fetch a surcoat of satin; I will give it to him' PC 1781-85

saw yn **tokyn** *ov bos gulan a gous ihesu nazare me a wolgh scon ow dule a wel though kettep onan* 'but as a sign that I am clean of the blood of Jesus of Nazareth I will forthwith wash my hands in the presence of all' PC 2497-500

in **tokyn** *a gerensa amma thyugh ol me a vyn in hanov map maria* 'as a sign of affection I will kiss you all in the name of the Son of Mary' BM 4325-27

henna ew the vttra aga anger dre sygne ha **tokyn** 'that is to utter their anger by sign and token' TH 28a

yma Justinus an martyr benegas ow affirmya an question ma, fatla yth ew **tokyn** *a thiscrygyans* 'Blessed Justin Martyr affirms this question: how it is a sign of unbelief. TH 57

Dell eugh tus fuer, ordnowgh aragof uskis peswar myghtern curunys gans clethythyow a owr per in **tokyn** *me the fetha ow yskerans in pub tu* 'As you are wise men, decree before me immediately four crowned kings with swords of pure gold as a sign that I have vanquished my foes on all sides' BK 2022-27

Ens peswar myghtern worthy the thon arag Gwynnever deaw gopyl a gelemmy, dof gans pluf gwyn, rag an vyghternes real in **tokyn** *hy bos uval ha whek ha tek hag ylyn* 'Let four worthy kings go to bear before Gwinevere two pairs of tame doves with white plumage, for the regal queen as a sign that she is modest, sweet and pure' BK 2043-49

token *warnas me a wra henna gwelys pan vova ny vethis gans dean towches* 'I will set a sign upon you; when that is seen, no man will touch you' CW 1181-83

hay verck y settyas omma in corne ow thale rag **token** 'and his mark he set here in the corner of my forehead as a sign' CW 1643-44.

Together the two etyma **sin** and **tôkyn** can be used to translate any of the various senses of the English word 'sign'. There is no need for the unattested word ***arweth**.

SIGNIFICANT *see* IMPORTANT

SMALL

The word for 'small' in Unified Cornish is *byghan*. Oddly enough this form is not attested in the traditional texts, though it does occur in place-names. The attested spellings in Middle Cornish are A) **beghan**; B) **byhan**; C) **byan**, **byen** and D) **bean**. Late Cornish forms include **bîan** (Lhuyd) and **beean**

small

A **beghan**

*ʒeworte vn lam **beghan** yʒ eth pesy may halle* 'he went a little distance from them that he might pray' PA 53c

*nyng ew ow faynys **beghan** vs lemyn war ow sensy* 'not small are the pains that now are holding me' PA 166b.

B **byhan**

*my ha'm gurek ha'm flogh **byhan** bysy vyth the sostene* 'I and my wife and my small child will need to be fed' OM 397-98

*Mab dev o neb a wylsys avel flogh **byhan** maylys* 'Whom you saw was the Son of God wrapped up like a little child' OM 809-10

*reys yv thy'so lafurrya vn pols **byhan** alemma* 'it is necessary for you to travel a little from here' OM 1268-69

*yma thy'mmo yn certan the wruthyl vn pols **byhan** takclow pryve* 'I must for a little while do private things' PC 90-2

[Cf. ***behan*** *na bras* 'small nor great' BK 1312; *Parvus… Little, small… C. Bîan &* ***bihan*** AB: 113c].

C **byan**, **byen**

*flogh **byen** nowyth gynys* 'a little new-born child' OM 806

*kekyfrys **byan** ha bras* 'both small and great' OM 1673

*kekyffrys **byan** ha bras* 'both small and great' OM 1695

*tormentors bras ha **byan*** 'tormentors great and small' OM 2682

*lemyn ol **byan** ha bras knoukyough ef del dyndylas* 'now all small and great, beat him as he has deserved' PC 2082-83

*en prysners bras ha **byan** dre why thy'm kettep onan* 'the prisoners, great and small, bring them to me every one' PC 2250-51

*marregyon heil heil thywhy **byan** a bras* 'soldiers, hail, hail to you, small and great' PC 2347-48

*longys reys yv thy's gyne vn pols **byan** lafurye* 'Longinus, you must journey with me a little way' PC 3003-04

*drefen agis governans rewlys on brays ha **byan*** 'by your governance we are ruled, great and small' BM 256-57

*dun yn palys ʒe setha bras ha **byan** pub huny* 'let us go into the palace to sit, everyone great and small' BM 266-67

*dugh lemen bras ha **byen*** 'come now, great and small' BM 1346

*benen gans the flogh **byen*** 'woman with your little child' BM 1550

*orth flehys gruergh ha **byen*** 'to children innocent and small' BM 1692

*Out gony bras ha **byen*** 'Oh, woe to us great and small!' BM 2092

*cavs thynny eff a vya in ihesu map marya the cresy **byen** ha brays* 'it would be a cause for us, small and great, to believe in Jesus the Son of Mary' BM 4114-17.

[This list is not exhaustive].

-D bean

*nag o offence **bean** mas very grevaws ha poos* 'it was not a small offence but very grievous and serious' TH 4
*nyns o mas **bean*** 'it was only small' TH 5
*the vos drehevys war questyon **bean*** 'to be raised upon a small question' TH 19
*mas tra **vean** ha fawt **bean*** 'but a small matter and a small sin' TH 28a
*in kyth same lesson **bean** cut ma* 'in this same small short lesson' TH 28a
*parcell **bean** a aphrica* 'a small part of Africa' TH 32
*cresowh ow bosaf prince creif hag inweth thewhy cheften **bean** ha brase* 'believe that I am a mighty prince and also chieftain to you, small and great' CW 116-17
*den in mes **bean** ha brase* 'let us go out, small and great' CW 2481
*'Ma lever **bean** rebbam* 'I have a small book beside me' BF: 29
[Cf. *beez **beean*** 'little finger' Bodewryd MS].

E bîan

*Calculus... A little Pebble or Gravelstone; C. Mêan **bîan** AB: 45b*
*Equuleus... A horse-colt. C. Ebal, Marh **bîan** AB: 57b*
*Linter... A boat made of a hollow tree; a wherry, a sculler; a trough. C Gurhal **bîan**, kok AB: 80a*
*Parvus... Little, small... C. **Bîan** & bihan AB: 113c*
*An lÿzûan **bîan** ʒen i'ar nedhez* 'The small plant with the twisted stalk' AB: 245a.

In KS 'small' is written **bian**. In UCR it was *byan*. There is little warrant for ***byghan**.

SMELL

There are several attested words for the noun 'smell': A) **sawour**, **saworen**; B) **odour**; C) **blas**; D) **fler**.

A sawour, saworen

*byneges yv an guel-ma pan vs **sawor** sur mur da ov tevos annethe y* 'blessed are the rods since a fragrant smell is coming from them' OM 1739-41
*an re me ev guel a ras rag ny glewsyug yn nep plas **sawor** an par ma bythqueth* 'these are rods of grace and for you never smelt anywhere a smell of this kind ever' OM 1989-91
*kynth us ganso **sawer** poys gor dotho nes the frygov* 'although it has a fetid smell put your nose near it' BM 1453-54
*whecter **sawer** gans Ke* 'Ke has a fragrance of smell' BK 517 [note]
*hebma yth ew **sawer** wheake hag inweth sacrifice da* 'this is a sweet smell and also a good sacrifice' CW 2493-945
*Odor... A savour, scent, or smell; an odour C. **Sauarn** AB: 105c.*

smell

B odour
*an luef a'm gruk me a wel ha'y **odor** whekka ys mel ow tos warnaf* 'I see the hand which made me coming upon me and its odour sweeter than honey' RD 143-45.

C blas
*kemereugh corf a'n drok was vgy ow flerye gans **blas** yw myligys* 'take the body of the evil fellow that stinks with an accursed stench' RD 2159-61.

D fler
*odor, **flair** 'smell' OCV §775
aga **fleyr** a yl schyndye ha lathe mur yethewon* 'their stench may injure and kill many Jews' PC 1547-48.

Lhuyd's ***sauarn***, if it is not an error, is presumably a singulative i.e. *****saworen** f*. **Sawour** can refer to both a fragrant and an unpleasant odour. The same is probably true of **odour** and **blas**. **Fler** means 'nasty smell, stench' only. With **fler** compare A) the substantive **flerynjy** 'smell, stench' and B) the verb **flêrya** 'to stink':

A flêrynjy 'stench'
*mars cryst a weres deffry ef a lath gans **fleyryngy** ol ow glascor* 'unless Christ help us indeed he will with his stench kill all my kingdom' RD 2132-35.

B flêrya 'to stink'
*gans pegh mar vr ev **flerys** na allaf sparie na moy* 'it is stinking with such great sin I can no longer spare' OM 945-46
*gas vy the thehesy gans morben bom trewysy the'n vyl hora war an taal neffre na wrello dybry lemyn **flerye** ha peddry* 'let me let fly with a mallet wretchedly on the vile whore's forehead so that she may not eat but stink and rot' OM 2703-07
*me a gesul bos ganse prennys da gwon yn nep le rag anclathva crystunyon ma na vons y ov **flerye*** 'I counsel that with them be bought cheaply waste land somewhere as a graveyard for Christians, so they will not be stinking' PC 1543-46
*mars ens garow the voy scham the'n **fleryys*** 'if they are rough, the greater shame to the stinking fellow' PC 2738-39
*rak lowene ny gen bo yn le may fuen lemmyn potvan ha lesky ow **flerye** ov movsegy kepar ha kuen* 'for we had no joy where we were but burning and scorching, stinking and giving off bad odours like dogs' RD 168-72
*war ow fay mur me a'n cas an plos **fleryys*** 'upon my faith I hate him greatly, the dirty stinking fellow' RD 1889-90
*kemereugh corf an drok was vgy ow **flerye** gans blas* 'take the body of the evil fellow who stinks with a stench' RD 2150-60.

Notice incidentally that **blas** means 'smell, scent' only. There is no evidence that it meant 'taste, flavour'. See further s.v. '**TASTE**'.

SNAKE

The word **sarf** 'serpent, snake' is attested twice:

A **sarf**
*A das kuf y'th wholowys an **sarf** re ruk ow tholle* 'O beloved Father in your glory, the snake deceived me' OM 285-86

*vn **sarf** in guethen yma best vthek hep falladow* 'there is a snake in the tree, a dreadful animal without doubt' OM 797-98.

No plural is attested, though Nance speculated that the plural would have been either ***syrf** or ***sarfy**.

The word **nader** means 'snake, viper' and is well attested, mostly from Lhuyd:

B **nader**
*Vipera uel serpens uel anguis **nader*** 'viper or serpent or snake' OCV §612

*gans **nader** ythof guanheys hag ol warbarth vynymmeys afyne trois the'n golon* 'I have been stung by a viper and altogether poisoned from my foot to my heart' OM 1756-58

W. Neidir, A Snake; Cor. **Naddÿr** AB: 15b
Anguis... A Snake; an Adder; C. **Naddÿr** AB: 42c
Coluber... An Adder; C. **Nadar** AB: 49a
*Ophioglosson... Adder's tongue. C. Tavaz **nadar*** AB: 107c
Serpens... A Serpent, any creeping vermin that creeps upon it's belly. C. **Nadar** AB: 149b
Vipera... A viper. C. **Nadÿr**, †*nader* AB: 174c.

By far the best attested word for 'snake, serpent', however, is **serpont**, *plural* **serpons**:

C **serpont**
*a thev a ras **serponnt** yv hy evth hy guelas ovn a'm bus vy* 'O God of grace, it is a snake, horrible to see. I am afraid' OM 1451-52

*Inna yth ew scriffes fatell rug an wyly **serpent** an tebell ell dos the eva* 'In it is written how the wily serpent, the devil came to Eve' TH 3

*Nena myth an **serpent** then venan, No ny rewgh merwell* 'Then the serpent said to the woman, No, you shall not die' TH 3a

*an poyson a **serpons** yma indan aga tavosow* 'The poison of snakes is under their tongues' TH 7a

snake   **GERYOW GWIR**

An tyrmyn na eff a leverys thyn **serpent** *kepar dell ew scriffis in tryssa chapter a genses* 'Then he said to the serpent as is written in the third chapter of Genesis' TH 13

marth ha casak hag asan ky ha cathe ha logosan deffrans ethan ha **serpentis** 'horse and mare and ass and cat and mouse, various birds and snakes' CW 406-08

an tas a rug der entent in myske oll prevas in bys formya preve henwis **serpent** 'the Father intentionally among all reptiles of the world created a reptile called serpent' CW 496-98

an **serpent** *o re wylly ragas she in keth torn ma* 'the serpent was too wily for you at that same moment' CW 816-17

an **serpent** *der falsurye am temptyas tha wuthell hena* 'the serpent by falsehood tempted me to do that' CW 887-888

serpent *rag aga themptya mer a bayne es thyes ornys* 'Serpent, because you tempted them, much pain is ordained for you' CW 906-07

han **serpent** *tregans yna nefra ny the alena rag yth ew malegas bras* 'and let the serpent dwell there ever, for from now on it is greatly cursed' CW 933-35

gans an Jowle y fowns tulles der an **serpent** *malegas dell welsowgh warbarth omma* 'they were deceived by the Devil, by means of the accursed serpent as you have together seen here' CW 1003-05

henna yth ew trewath bras der an **serpent** *malegas ny tha vonas mar gucky* 'that is a great shame that we were were so stupid through the accursed serpent' 1006-08

rage yth o ef re wylly pan eth in **serpent** *agye rag tha dulla* 'for he was too wily when he entered in the serpent in order to deceive you' CW 1028-30

me a weall sure vn gwethan ha **serpent** *vnhy avadn marow seigh hy avalsa* 'I see indeed a tree and a serpent up in it; it would seem to be dead and dry' CW 1808-10

han **serpent** *na a welta yth ew an very pryf na a wrug an iowle tha entra vny hy rag temtya theth vam eva* 'and that serpent which you see is that very reptile in which the Devil entered to tempt your mother, Eve' CW 1816-20

me a wellas gwethan moy ha **serpent** *in ban ynny marow seigh hy afalsa* 'I saw a further tree and a serpent up in it. It seemed dead and dry' CW 1916-18.

The default word for 'snake, serpent' in the revived language should perhaps be **serpont**, *plural* **serpons**. **Nader** can be used for 'adder, viper'.

SPITE, IN SPITE OF, DESPITE

There are three ways of saying 'in spite of, despite': A) **awos**; B) **in despît dhe**; C) **in spît dhe**. Here are some examples from the texts:

A awos

awos *a gallo na wra tra vyz* 'in spite of all he can do, do nothing' CF 34

ov arluth ker salamon ***awos*** *lavur na dewon nefre ny fallaf theugh why* 'my dear lord Solomon, in spite of labour or sorrow never will I fail you' OM 2404-06

awos *gotheuel ancow ny nahas hy lauarow wostalleth na wosteweth* 'in spite of suffering death she did not retract her words at the beginning or at the end' OM 2760-72 *ha kyn fons y ol sclandrys neffre **awos** bos lethys my ny wraf the thyflase* 'though they all be offended, never will I turn from you, in spite of being killed' PC 899-901

awos *lauarow trufyl ny grysaf thy's* 'in spite of empty words, I shall not believe you' RD 1055-56.

B in despît dhe (wàr, in)

yn dyspyt th*'y thewlagas my a wyth an gueel a ras yn ierusalem nefre* 'in spite of his eyes, I shall keep the rods in Jerusalem for ever' OM 2058-60

yn dyspyt th*'y das hay vam an voren a vyth lethys* 'in spite of his father and mother the girl shall be killed' OM 2740-41

*henna my a wra wharre re maghom arluth pup le **yn dyspyt the**'n casadow* 'that I will do forthwith by Mahound, lord of all places, in spite of the wretch' PC 993-95

*kychough ef yn vryongen ha dalynnough mur cales ma na allo pertheges **yn dyspyt** ol th'y eghen* 'catch him by the throat and hold him so hard that he cannot rant in spite of all his efforts' PC 1008-10

*my a's kylm re sattenas warbarth auel lader pur hag a'th wor bys yn cayphas **yn dyspyt the**'th devlagas* 'I will bind them together by Satan, like a thorough robber and will send you to Caiaphas in spite of your two eyes' PC 1190-94

*anon syre somotty thryue to the deth they schal blyue **yn dyspyt th**'aga hehen* 'anon sir, so may I thrive, to the death they shall remain, in spite of all their efforts' PC 2525-27

yn dyspit the *vap the vam kenter scon dre the devtros my a's guysk may fo drok lam* 'in spite of your mother's son soon I will strike a nail through your two feet so you will get a nasty shock' PC 2780-82

*wath **in dyspyt war** the dyns me a worth kepar ha kyns neb a ruk an gol han sul* 'yet in spite of your teeth, I will worship as before him who made holiday and Sunday' BM 3558-60

in dyspyt the*'th nassyoyn, the vaw the honen a'th crog* 'in spite of your nation, your own servant will hang you' BK 465-66

in dyspyt in *kyg e thyns, mara'n mettya', an rebel gu ha fals dell ew, me a'n dyel heb lettya* 'in spite of him gums, if I meet him, the lying and false rebel that he is, I will be avenged on him without delay' BK 2280-84

*kyn fe an Joule war e scoyth, ny a'n dywoys avel goyth, **in dyspyt th**'y gerans pell* 'thought he Devil were upon his shoulder, we will bleed him like a goose, in spite of his distant relatives' BK 2730-32.

C in spît dhe

*me a vyn y thyscuthe hag **yn spyt thotho** true war y fas ha'y devlagas* 'I will strip him and in spite of him spit upon his face and eyes' PC 1393-95

*a harlot **yn spit the**'th fas gans ov scorge tys ha tas me a'th wysk may fo drok pyn* 'O scoundrel, in spite of your face I will strike you with my scourge, stroke after stroke, so that you'll suffer agony' PC 2105-07

*genen ny certan ty a **yn spyt the** vap the thama a fals iaudyn* 'you will certainly go with us in spite of your mother's son, O false knave' RD 1794-96

spite   **GERYOW GWIR**

> *hanter an elath genaffa assentyes yth yns sera thom mayntaynya* **in spyte thys** *dell welta ge* 'half of the angels agree with me, sir, to support me in spite of you, as you see' CW 272-74
>
> *han keth place mannaf gwetha whath* **in spyta theis** 'and I will keep the same place in spite of you' CW 314-15
>
> *ha pur vskes gwraf an pratt then serpent* **in spyte thy** *face* 'and very quickly I'll do the trick on the snake in spite of her face' CW 518-19.

As can be seen above **in despît dhe** and **in spît dhe** are often used in phrases like **in despît dhe vab dha vabm** 'in spite of your mother's son', i.e. 'despite you', **in spît dhe'th fâss** 'in spite of your face', etc. Expressions of this kind really mean 'whether you like it or not'. Compare also the following:

> *arlothes ker my a wra agas nygys fystyne* **dyspyt the** *vyrgh the dama mar ny'n guarnyaf scon wharre* 'dear madam, I will hasten your business; scorn to your mother's daughter, if I do not warn him soon straightway' PC 1965-68
>
> *Desempys gueyf ow golok ha* **dyspyt the** *vab the das!* 'Immediately leave my sight and scorn to your father's son!' BK 993-94.

It seems, nonetheless, that **in spît dhe** and **in despît dhe** are as common as **awos** to mean 'despite, in spite of'. They can hardly be proscribed in the revived language.

TO SPRING UP, TO ARISE

The default verb in the texts for 'to arise, to spring up' is **sordya**. **Sordya** is borrowed from Middle English *sourden* 'to arise, to originate'< Old French *sordre* < Latin *surgere*.

A **sordya**

> *bresell cref a ve* **sordijs** *en grows pu elle ʒy don* 'a vigorous dispute arose about the cross, who was going to carry it' PA 160c
>
> *Ternoys y* **sordyas** *bresel gans an eʒewon goky* 'On the next morning there arose a dispute among the foolish Jews' PA 238a
>
> *Ny* **sowrd** *clevas in mab pron na ra unwyth e lawsa* 'No sickness arises in any mother's son that it will not at once relieve' BK 1124-25.

When speaking of water springing up from a well Cornish uses the verb **spryngya** and this verb is used metaphorically as well:

B **spryngya**

*Indella crist a gemeras warnotha an kythsame nature na a rug **speringia** ha dos thea Adam hag eva then wyrhes ker maria* 'Thus Christ took upon himself that same nature which sprang and came from Adam and Eve to the Blessed Virgin Mary' TH 12a

*ha dre henna ny a well nag ew an egglos tevys ha **springis** in ban athewethas* 'and by this we can see that the Church did not grow or spring up recently' TH 34a

*ha mes an kyth fyntan na y ra **spryngya** thynny ha innan ny mer a benegyttar a bewnans* 'and from that same spring there will arise for us and in us much sanctity of life' TH 41

*hemm ew the styrrya, Na in tyller arell, na dre menes arell, ew heresy **springys** in man, ha scismes drehevys, mas rag nag us obedyens res thyn minister neb ew an pronter a thu* 'that is to say, Not in another place nor by other means has heresy arisen and have schisms occurred, but because obedience is not shown to the minister who is the priest of God' TH 42a

*Nens ew nahene cowse y bos hereses drehevys ha scismes **springes** ha tevys, mas rag y bos an prounter a thu despisüs* 'There is no other discussion of heresies have arisen and schisms sprung up and grown, except that the priest of God is despised' TH 48a

*A Christ, re be benegas! Attomma fyntan **spryngys*** 'O Christ, may you be blessed! Look a well has sprung up' BK 785-86.

The verb **spryngya** is a borrowing from English, like **sordya**. There is no reason to proscribe it.

STATE

When 'state' means 'condition' there are several ways of conveying the idea in Cornish: A) **stuth**; B) **plît** and C) **stât** (this can also mean 'state' in a political sense).

A **stuth**

*ha fattel duthys yn ban dre the gallos the honan ha war the corf mar drok **stuth*** 'and how did you come up by your own power when your body was is such a bad state?' RD 2568-70.

B **plît**

*ellas claf yv ow colon the vos yn **plyt** a par na* 'alas, my heart is sick that you should be in stuch a state' PC 2637-38

*govynneugh orth an geiler kyns ol pan **pleyt** yme fe* 'ask the gaoler first of all what state he is in' RD 2052-53

*pahan **pleyt** yma pilat yn le may ma* 'what state is Pilate in where he is?' RD 2058-59.

C **stât**

*Der y peth grueys den ryel ha gorys then **stat** vhel* 'By his wealth made a royal man and elevated to the high state' BM 436-37

state

An corfe a vabden in **state** *a originall innocencye* 'The body of mankind in a state of original innocence' TH 2a

the vos verefies in den rag tuchia an **estate** *ay originall innocenci* 'to be verified in man concerning the state of his original innocence' TH 3

So in mer ver dell ew an **stat** *na kyllys, ha mabden dre an koll a henna cothes in extreme miseri ha wretchednes* 'But in as much as that state has been lost and mankind through the loss of that fallen into extreme misery and wretchedness' TH 3

fatell ve mabden dres theworth an kyth **stat** *na benegas the miserabill* **stat** *a throkolleth* 'that mankind was brought from that blessed state to the miserable state of wickedness' TH 3

Pegh o an cawse a rug the oll an vssew a Adam ha Eva the vos genys in **state** *a thampnacion* 'Sin was the cause that led to all the issue of Adam and Eve's being born in a state of damnation' TH 3

hag in **stat** *a eternall dampnacion* 'and in a state of eternal damnation' TH 4

fatell ruga delyuera mabden dre mervelous maner thean **stat** *a thampnacion* 'that in a wonderful way he delivered mankind from the state of damnation' TH 5

Ith esa thyn profet Job experience an miserabyll **stat** *a mab den* 'The prophet Isaiah had experience of the miserable state of mankind' TH 7

ha ny worta vn tam in vn **stat** 'and does not remain at all in one state' TH 7

may hallan bos delyuerys theworth an miserabill **stat** *ha captiuite a veny ynna towlys* 'that we might be delivered from the miserable state and captivity into which we had been cast' TH 10

creatis nobyll ha worthy creaturs hag in **stat** *a perfect innocencye* 'created noble and worthy creatures and in a state of perfect innocence' TH 12

an pith ew an gwanha part a ve dres then **stat** *a mortalite dre an meanys a originall pehosow* '... what is the weakest part was brought to the state of mortality by the means of original sin' TH 12

ha then **stat** *an bewnans heb deweth* 'and to the state of eternal life' TH 12

ha the restoria mabden arta then **stat** *a ras* 'and to restore mankind again to the state of grace' TH 12a

in **stat** *a anken heb deweth hag in* **stat** *a miseri* 'in a state of endless wretchedness and in a state of misery' TH 16

So in contrary part, neb na grise hemma ima certainly in **stat** *a dampnacion perpetually* 'But on the contrary, whoever does not believe this is certainly in a state of damnation for ever' TH 20

May thill pub den heb error aswon y honyn, pana **stat** *ha condicion vsa ynna ow sevall* 'That every man may without error know himself, in what state and condition he stands in' TH 23

Ha pub tra arell ow longia then **stat** *an testament nowith* 'And everything else belonging to the state of the New Testament' TH 27a

whath ny ve recevys erna ruga suffra penans hyre kyns eff the gafus y **stat** *ha bos absoluys* 'yet he was not received until he suffered long penance, before he got his state and was absolved' TH 39

then **stat** *a den perfect, warlyrth an measure an lene oys a crist* 'to the state of a perfect man, according to the full age of Christ' TH 42 *kepare ha mytearne, o setha in [d]an queth a* **stat** 'like a king sitting under the robe of state' SA 60

Te gwas, py **stat** *e 'th esta kyns te the thos thu'm pow ma?* 'You, fellow, what state were you in before you came to this my country?' BK 590-91

Ow **stat** *o del vynnas Christ* 'My state was as Christ wished' BK 593.

It is clear from the above examples that the commonest word for 'state, condition' in the texts is **stât**.

STEP

Neither **camm** (UC *cam*) nor **cammen** is ever used to mean 'step'. **Camm** (UC *cam*) is used: A) as an adverb meaning 'in any way' or B) in the phrase **wàr gabm** or **wàr y gabm** 'steadily, at a steady pace', whence **ke wàr dha gamm** 'steady on, hang on a moment'.

A **camm** 'at all, in any way'

Gans gloteny ef pan welas **cam** *na ylly y dolla en tebell el a vynnas yn ken maner y demptye* 'When he saw that he could not in any way beguile him by gluttony, the devil wished to tempt him in another way' PA 13ab

Mur a dus a leuerys ny dayl ȝys **cam** *y naghe dre ȝe gows yȝ ew prevys ȝe vos den a galyle* 'Many said, You should not in any way deny it; by your speech it is proved that you come from Galilee' PA 85ab.

B **wàr gamm** 'steadily'

ty a whyth auel caugh guas whyth **war gam** *vyngeans y'th glas* 'you blow like a careless fellow; blow steadily, vengeance in your guts!' PC 2715-16

ty uyl losel guask **war gam** *ha compys yfl mot thow the* 'you vile scoundrel, strike steadily and evenly, evilly may you thrive!' PC 2735-36

Ay tevdar ke **war the gam** 'Ho, Teudar, steady on!' BM 1048

A thermas ke **war the gam** *nyns yv onest thys heb nam dones the rag arlythy ha ty noth the corff ol trogh* 'Good sir, steady on! It is not decent without doubt for you to come before lords all naked and your body all broken' BM 3043-46

Ser turant ke **war the gam** *bythqueth ny vue map the vam genys wath then eretons* 'Sir Tyrant, steady on! Never was your mother's son born yet to the inheritance' BM 3467-69

Ay turant ke **war the gam** *molleth du the vap the vam* 'Ho, Tyrant, steady on. God's curse upon the son of your mother!' BM 3737-38

Arlythy eugh wy **war gam** *crist ha maria y vam dua rag agen gueras* 'Lords, steady on. Christ and his mother will come to our aid' BM 3974-76.

With **wàr gamm** cf. Middle Welsh *ar y cam, ar gam* 'at a walking pace'.

step

The word **cammen** may have originally meant 'a single step', but it is not found in this sense. It is used only to mean 'at all, in any way' (cf. **camm** above):

ov arlothes sur gyne dre thynnargh agas pygys na wrellough **cammen** *lathe an profus a nazare* 'my lady indeed by me greets you and begs you not in any way to kill the prophet of Nazareth' PC 2194-97
me a vynse y wythe ha ny yllyn **cammen** *vyth* 'I would have preserved him but I could not in any way' PC 3125-26
ellas the vos mar wokky **cammen** *na vynnyth crygy* 'alas that you are so foolish that you will not in any way believe' RD 989-90
den na gresso dyougel an keth den na the selwel **cammen** *vyth na yl wharfos* 'a man who does not believe, for that same man in no way can it happen that he will be saved' RD 2478-80
my ny won p'ywe **cammen** 'I do not know at all who he is' RD 2493.

The only words for 'step, pace' in the texts are A) **stap** and B) **pass**:

A **stap**
ser turant agys pagys sur ny vynnons fovt wagys vn **stap** *lafurye adro* 'sir tyrant, your pages will not for lack of wages travel around a single step' BM 3284-86.

B **pass**
M **pas** *sur yv an meneth theworth an grond byteweth* '1000 paces indeed is the mountain from the ground to begin with' BM 1147-48
Yma eff in meneth bras del glowevy sur myl **pas** *theworth an grond awoles* 'He is on the great mountain, as I hear, indeed a thousand paces from the ground below' BM 1956-58
Oma yma meryasek ov corthya du galosek poren in top an meneth myl **pas** *in ban alemma* 'Here Meriasek is worshipping almighty God exactly at the summit of the mountain a thousand paces hence' BM 1974-77
dovn yv an caff may ma hy cans **pas** *del glowys ha moy crist guyth ny orth tewolgow* 'deep is the cave, so that it is a hundred paces as I have heard and more. Christ protect us from darkness!' BM 4071-73
An mens tyrath a barkys, hedre ven ow cul tronkys, me a ro thys perpetual in dyswyllyans an trespas, ha moyha **pas** *te a vith dihogal* 'The amount of land you enclose, while I am taking a bath, I will give you as atonement for the wrong, and a greater space of land you will have indeed' BK 1087-92

It would seem from the above examples that the ordinary word for 'step' in the revived language should perhaps be **stap**. 'Pace' should probably be **pâss**.

TO SUCCEED, SUCCESS

For 'to succeed, to be successful' many revivalists use **soweny**. This is certainly attested:

A **soweny**

*ny vyn dev gul vry ahanaf na **sowyny** an peyth a wrehaf ny wra* 'God will not take notice of me nor make prosper what I do' OM 519-21

*ha pup vr chatel abel y a **sowyn** myl blek guel* 'and always Abel's cattle succeed a thousand times better' OM 522-23

*venytha na **sowyny** tan hemma war an challa* 'may you never prosper! Take that on the jaw!' OM 539-40

*me a'n dalhen fest yn tyn ha gans ow dornow a'n guryn na **sowenno*** 'I will grab him very firmly and with my hands grapple him so that he will not thrive' PC 1131-33

*Neb a gemer ovn a thu ny **sowen** henna neb tu* 'Whoever is afraid of God, he never anywhere will succeed' BM 1914-15

*byth ny yllyn **soweny** boys agen gober hep pee* 'we can never succeed that our wages are unpaid' BM 3336-37

*molothov kentrevogyan thywhy **sowyny** a ra* 'the curses of neighbours will make you succeed' BM 3424-25

*Scaf ove ha **sowenys*** 'I am quick and successful' BK 3032

*me a wore ny **sewenaffa** nefra yn beyse* 'I know I shall never succeed in the world' CW 1285-86

*ny **sowynaf** gon yn ta nefra in byes* 'I shall not succeed, I know well, in the world' CW 1358-59

*an noer sure ny **sowenas** in for m[a]y wruge eave kerras* 'the earth indeed has not thriven in the way that he walked' CW 1766-67.

The verb **spêdya**, however, is rather more common:

B **spêdya**

*pyth a vynnough why ʒe ry ha me a ra ʒeugh **spedye** ow cafos crist yredy* 'what will you give me if I make you succeed in arresting Christ indeed?' PA 39ab

*Dew ʒen crist a ʒanvonas ʒe berna boys ha dewas an keth rena a **spedyas** han soper a ve paris* 'Two men Christ sent to buy food and drink. Those same men succeeded and the supper was prepared' PA 42ab

*Then eʒewon pan doʒye y leuerys hag y ow tos me a gris yn ta **spedye** om negis haneth yn nos* 'When he had come to the Jews he said as they came, I hope to succeed well in my business this very night' PA 63ab

*ny amont travyth hemma cayphas ny yllyn **spedye** yma ol tus a'n bys ma yn certan worth y sywe* 'this is no use, Caiaphas, we cannot succeed. All the people of this world certainly follow him; PC 439-42

*leuereugh thy'mmo whare pandra vynnogh thy'm the ry ha me a wra thygh **spedye** ow cafus crist yredy* 'tell me forthwith what will you give me and I will make you succeed in finding Christ indeed' PC 585-88

succeed   **GERYOW GWIR**

bythaf bysy sur war an dra hag yn teffry byth ny falla ow nygys vy **spedye** *a wra* 'I will be active in the matter and indeed I will never fail. My business will succeed' PC 1932-34

syth cans ha syth myl blythen vn den kyn fo ow kerthes ow tos kyn **spedye** *yn geyth dev vgans myldyr perfeyth omma ny alse bones* 'if a man should be travelling for 7700 years, though he succeed in coming in one day forty miles, he could not reach here' RD 2495-98

me a bys du karadow roy ӡynny yn ta **spedya** 'I will beseech beloved God that he grant us well to succeed' BM 74-5

mar kyssys yn ta **spedie** *me yv sur ӡe well plesijs an keth tra na* 'if you left well to succeed, I am the better pleased by that same thing' BM 218-20

henna gans y destrowhy a yl bos **spedijs** *defry* 'that by destroying him can indeed be made to succeed' BM 469-70

Bys dotho me agys led dre voth ihesu ny a **sped** *ganso agen nygysyov* 'I will lead you to him. By the will of Jesus we will succeed in our business with him' BM 2530-32

hebogh why sur na menogh ny a **sped** *mater in pov ma* 'without you seldom do we succeed in a matter in this country' BM 2693-94

Ov arluth dywhy mur grays mar uskis why the vynhays **spedia** *sur ov negysyov* 'lord, great thanks to you, that you were willing so quickly to make my business succeed' BM 2775-77

ov negesyov **spedijs** *dour the porpos yma gena* 'I have succeed precisely to purpose in my affairs' BM 2788-89

lebmyn pan ew thymo gwryes neve ha noore orth both ow bryes han naw order collenwys han kynsa jorna **spedyes** *my a[s] sone gans ow ganow* 'now that I have made for myself heaven and the earth to my desire and finished the nine orders and have succeed with the first day, I will bless them with my mouth' CW 70-4.

It is apparent that it is legitimate to use either **soweny** or **spêdya** for 'to succeed'.

For the substantive 'success' Nance recommends A) **sowynyans**; B) **sowena**; C) **spêda** (UC *speda*). Here are the attestations of all three:

A **sowynyans**

ha gans an merthus **sawynans** *o both Dew ol gallouseck... the talvega ga kolonnow leall, ha ga perthyans* 'and of the wonderful success with which it hath pleased Almighty God... to reward their loyalty and patience' JKeigwin

B) **sowena**

E fyth ruweth, ha **suwyna** *y'th tylu weth ha wyrthynva* 'there will be stateliness and success in your household yet and laughter' BK 1745-48

Ehaz ha **sewen[a]** *whath do chee ha tha henwath* 'Health and prosperity to thee and thy posterity' Ustick MSS. [Note: this word appears as **sewen** in the manuscript; cf. **karens** for **karensa** in the Hutchens memorial. It is unlikely that there was ever a word **sewen**, ***sowen** 'success'].

C) spêda

*Tremenys yv dyogel lemen genen an chanel may fe holmyv **spede** dek* 'Passed indeed by us the Chanel has been so that it may be—this is fair speed' BM 1088-90

*ymowns in gwan cas, mas y a rella gans **speda** ha in du tyrmyn repentya ha gull penans* 'they are in a poor position, unless they will success and in due time repent and do penance' TH 32a.

Spêda is also used in the phrase **god spêda** 'Godspeed, may success attend you':

***god spede** gonesugy gonys a wreugh pur vysy thy'm del hevel* 'godspeed, workmen, you are working very busily for me, it seems' OM 2447-49

*now **god speda** theis ow thase me a wrug oblashion brase* 'now godspeed to you, may father. I have made a great oblation' CW 1187-88.

For 'to succeed' either **soweny** or **spêdya** can be used in the revived language. **Sowynyans**, **sowena** and **spêda** are all authentic ways of rendering 'success'.

SWAN

For 'swan' many revivalists use ***alargh**, plurals **elergh**, ***elerhy**. This word is unattested. The only attestation of anything similar is *olor vel cignus*, ***elerhc*** 'swan' OCV §509. The form ***elerhc*** here is really a plural, which appears to be used as a singular; cf. Welsh *alarch* 'swan' and Breton *alarc'h* 'cygne, swan'. Lhuyd cites the word †*Elery* 'A Swan' AB: 53b, 106c and 241b, and says that it is 'now disus'd by the Cornish' AB: 4b.

The only attested word for 'swan' in the texts is **swàn**:

*lemyn hanwaf goyth ha yar a sensaf ethyn hep par the vygyens den war an beys hos payon colom grvgyer **swan** bargos bryny ha'n er moy drethof a vyth hynwys* 'Now I name goose and hen, which I consider peerless birds to feed a man in the world, duck, peacock, dove, partridge, swan, kite, crows and the eagle, further will be named by me' OM 129-34.

The default word for 'swan' in the revived language should perhaps be **swàn**, *plural* ***swanys**.

TO SWEEP, TO BRUSH

For 'to sweep' Nance suggests ***scuba**, which is based on Welsh *ysgubo*, *sgubo* 'to sweep' and Breton *skubañ* 'balayer'. Curiously Nance seems to have missed the attested word:

Verro... To brush, scower or sweep... C. Dho **skibia** AB: 172a.

The Cornish for 'to sweep, to brush' would seem to be **scubya**, rather than ***scuba**.

T

TABLE

The default word for 'table' in the revived language has always been **moos** (UC *mos*) *f.* This word is attested from the Old Cornish period onwards.

> *Mensa,* **muis** 'table' OCV §843
>
> *Han gwyn esa war en* **foys** *ef a rannas yntreʒa* 'And the wine that was on the table he shared among them' PA 45a
>
> *may wrylleugh yn lowene keffrys dybry hagh eve war ow* **mos** *yn vhelder* 'that you may in joy both eat and drink at my table on high' PC 811-13
>
> *maria del won the bos berth yn bys ma onan a'y* **uos** 'Mary, as I know that you have been one of his table in this world' RD 859-60
>
> *Ov arluth lich a esa omma purguir an kynsa hav thays theragtho inweth ham mam ger in pen an* **voys** 'My liege lord will sit here indeed the first, and my father before him also and my dear mother at the head of the table' BM 278-81
>
> *An feith a res thyn ny kafus in agan colonow, pan deffan thyn* **vois** *a crist* 'The faith which we should have in our hearts when we come to the table of Christ' TH 51a
>
> *yma eff ow ry thyn kusyll diligently rag examyna ha trya agan honyn kyns ny the thos then* **vois** *a thu* 'he gives us advice diligently to examine and try ourselves before we come to the table of God' TH 53a-54.

Unfortunately **moos** (UC *mos*) is similar both to **mos** 'to go' and with lenited initial to **vos** 'to be' and **voos** (UC *vos*) 'food'. As a result it seems that **moos** was in the later period replaced either by A) **tâbel** or B) **bord**:

A **tâbel** 'table'

> *henna ew the leverall, gas ve the remembra fatla a rave in ta tha honora, ha pana* **tabell** *esta ow setha* 'that is to say, Let me remind you how I honour you well, and what sort of table you are sitting at' SA 59.

B **bord** 'table'

> *Mensa... A table or board to eat on; ... C.* **Bord**, †*mius* AB: 88c.

In the revived language both **tâbel** and **bord** are legitimate alternatives to **moos**, and they have the advantage of being less ambiguous than **moos**.

tame   **GERYOW GWIR**

TO TALK see TO CONVERSE

TO TAME
Nance recommends A) **dova**; B) ***dofhe**; C) **tempra**; and D) ***wharhe**.
Of these four verbs only A and C are attested:

A **dova**
*Domo... To tame, to subdue, to vanquish, to overcome, to break (a horse, &c.)... C. Dho **dova**, dho terhi (marh, &c.)* AB: 55b.

C **tempra**
*ham kyke yv escar teball pur ysel me an **temper*** 'and my flesh is an evil enemy; I will tame him to bring him low' BM 162-63

*Yma in pov falge cregyans ov cul dym angyr an iovle mar tur na pel ov bevnans me as **temper** by my sovle* 'There is in the land a false belief that is making me damned angry. If my life lasts a while I will tame it' BM 1161-64.

It seems that in the revived language **dova** and **tempra** are the best verbs to translate 'to tame'

TO TASTE
For 'to taste' Nance suggests A) ***blasa**; B) ***sawory**; and C) **tâstya**. Neither ***blasa** nor ***sawory** is attested. **Tâstya** is the only word in the texts:

C **tâstya**
*honna yw ol the vlamye a dorras an avel tek hag a'n dug thy'm the **dastye*** 'she is all to blame who plucked the fine apple and brought it to me to taste' OM 266-68

*ty re gam wruk eredy ha re'n dros the vur anken pan russys thotho dybry ha **tastye** frut a'n wethen* 'you have transgressed indeed and have brought him to great misery when you induced him to eat and to taste the fruit of the tree' OM 281-84

*Eff a considras y pehosow compys theworth an wreythan, oll an buddes an barrow, oll an effect, ow **tastya**, ow gwellas, ow predery* 'He considered his sins complete from the root, all the buds, the boughs, all the effect, tasting, seeing, considering' TH 8a

*Judas a ruk **tastia** corf an arluth* 'Judas tasted the Lord's body' SA 65a

*ef a **tastyas** kigg an arluth Dew* 'he tasted the flesh of the Lord God' SA 65a

*mar pyth y frute hy **tastys** te a vyth dampnys ractha* 'if its fruit is tasted, you will be damned for it' CW 377-78

*me a levar thys eva mar gwreth **tastya** an frute ma es oma war an wethan maga fure te a vea avell dew es awartha* 'I tell you, Eve, if you taste this fruit which is on the tree, you will be as wise as God who is above' CW 618-22

GERYOW GWIR — tent

dew a ornas contrary na theffan **tastya** *henna* 'God ordained on the contrary that we should not taste that' CW 630-31

genas a peva **tastys** *maga fure te a vea yn pub poynt sure avella* 'if it were tasted by you, you would be in every way as wise as he' CW 640-42

me a ra in pur serten ny allaf ra pell perthy pan vo reys **tastya** *anothy* 'I shall indeed. I cannot long endure, since one has to taste of it' CW 689-91

ha by god nyng es ʒym dowte tha **dastya** *a[n] keth avall* 'and by God I do not fear to taste the same apple' CW 705-06

mar gwreth **tastya** *anotha eve a drayle theʒo tha leas moy eas myllyow a bynsow* 'if you do taste of it, it will turn out to you of more value than thousands of pounds' CW 738-40

hay bromas yth o largya mar gwrean **tastya** *an frut na avell dew ny a vea* 'and his promise was generous: if we were to taste of that fruit, we should be like God' CW 780-82

syr war nebas lavarow **tast** *gy part an avallow po ow harenga ty a gyll* 'sir, in a word, taste part of the apples or you will lose my love' CW 830-32

hy a dorras an avall teake hag an dros thym tha **dastya** 'she plucked the fair apple and brought it to me to taste' CW 879-80

adam eva na pegha ha deffan an tas terry mernans ny wressans **tastya** 'had Adam and Eve not sinned and broken the Father's prohibition, they would not have tasted death' CW 994-97

a vs kyek an bestas na na a veast na lodn in beyse ny wressan bythqwath **tastya** 'hitherto flesh of those animals or of any beast or animal in the world we have not ever tasted' CW 1470-73

ny **dastyans** *an payne bras* 'they shall not taste the great torment' CW 2063.

For the substantive 'taste, flavour' the only attested word is Lhuyd's **saworen** (*sauarn*), which can mean 'savour' as well as 'odour' (see s.v. 'SMELL' above).

The word **blas** is attested once and does not mean 'taste, flavour'. The verb *****blasa** is not known. In the revived language the word for 'to taste' should perhaps be **tâstya**. The noun 'taste, flavour' is best rendered **saworen**.

TENT

For 'tent' Nance suggests A) *****tylda**; B) **scovva**; and C) †**tenta**. The word *****tylda** is not attested, having been derived by Nance from the verb **tyldya** 'to cover, to roof':

my a vyn lemyn **tyldye** *guartha an gorhyl gans queth* 'I will now cover the top of the vessel with a cloth' OM 1073-74.

The word **scovva** (< ***scodva** 'place of shade') is attested, but it means 'shelter' rather than 'tent':

moyses whek ny a dreha ragon chy pols the wonys rag ny a yl gul **scovva** *ov cortes bos goskesys* 'dear Moses, we will build ourselves a shelter, to till for a season while we wait to be put under cover' OM 1715-18.

It is not clear where Nance found Old Cornish **tenta**. The word *tentus* or *tentum* 'tent' is not infrequently found in Latin stage directions in the Cornish dramas. Perhaps that was Nance's source. The only attested word for 'tent' in Cornish, however, appears to be **tent**:

Gwel corf in **tent** *nag in towr whath ny glowys skovernow e vos genys a'gan hunyth in Christonath, a nowyth nag a henys* 'A better person in tent or in tower never yet did ears hear that such had been born of our generation in Christendom recently or of old' BK 1916-21.

Since **tent**, *plural* ***tentys**, is the only attested word for 'tent' in traditional Cornish, it might be wise to use it in preference to any other item.

THANK YOU
There are several ways of saying 'thank you, thanks' in the texts A) **Dùrdala dhe** (< **Duw re dallo dhe**); B) **meur ras dhe**; and C) **gramercy dhe**.

A **Duw re dallo dhe**
Durdala de*why, syra* 'Thank you, sir' Borde
Durdala tha *why* 'Thank you' Carew.

B **meur ras dhe**
Gromercy agen lych da ***mur gras*** *y wothen nefra* ***thywy*** *agis bolnegeth* 'Thank you, our good liege. We thank you for your good will' BM 308-10
Syr Teuthar, ***mer gras theso****!* Sir Teudar, thank you!' BK 1081
A canhas mas, da re fary, ha ***this mer gras*** *bys venary, a caradow!* 'Good messenger, may you fare well, and thanks to you always, dear friend!' BK 2917-21
Me a wor ***theso mer gras*** *rag the thos thu'm arhadow* 'I give you thanks for coming at my command' BK 3073-74
mear a rase thewhy *sera ow ry cusyll zym mar stowte* 'thank you sir, for giving me such sound advice' CW 702-03
mear a ras thewhy *eall due* 'thank you, angel of God' CW 1872
a das kere ***mere rase thewhy*** *agis dyskans da pub preyse* 'dear father, thank you for your sound teaching always' CW 1953-54

GERYOW GWIR thank you

***Meras ta** du* 'thank God' Borlase.
***Meras ta** why* 'I thank you' Borlase.

C **gramercy**
*A das a nef **gramercy** the gorf ker gorthys re bo* 'O Father of heaven, thank you, may your person be worshipped' OM 407-08
***gromersy** arluth a brys rag the roow prest yv da* 'thank you, worthy lord, for your gifts are always good' OM 2313-14
*agas enour **gromersy** a vynnough the wul thy'mo* 'thank you for your honour you will do me' OM 2382-85
*serys **gromersy** ynweth mara pewaf why a veth ov chyf prive guyththysy* 'sirs, thank you also. If I live you will be my chief bodyguards' OM 2395-97
*ha largys ha **gromersy** ny a yl bos fest mery rag cafus ro an par na* 'Oh largesse, and thank you! We can be very merry for getting a gift like that' OM 2465-67
***Gromersy** arloth hep par* 'Thank you, peerless lord' OM 2595
***grant mercy** syre iustis ef a vyth sur anclethys yn le na fue den bythqueth* 'thank you, sir justice. He will indeed be buried where no man was ever before' PC 3133-35
***grant merci** syr iustis vynytha syngys of thy's* 'thank you, sir justice. We are obliged to you for ever' RD 95-6
***Gramercy** 3ywy warbarth* 'Thank you to you together' BM 258
***Gromercy** meryasek wek* 'Thank you, Meriasek' BM 286
***Gromercy** meryasek wek mar luen oys a corteysy* 'Thank you, Meriasek; you are so full of courtesy' BM 298-99
***Gromercy** agen lych da mur gras y wothen nefra thywy agis bolnegeth* 'Thank you, our good liege. We thank you for your good will' BM 308-10
*Tewdar gyntel, **gromercy** a'th veneson* 'Gentle Teudar, thank you for your blessing' BK 641-42
***Gramersy** theso, dremas!* 'Thank you, good man!' BK 823
*Teuthar gentel, **gramersy!*** 'Gentle Teudar, thank you!' BK 1093
***Gromersy** a'n gwelha tas, Arthor rych a ryowta* 'Thanks of the best Father, Arthur rich in nobility' BK 1554-55
***Gromersy**, arluth cortys, flowran ol an arlythy* 'Thank you, courteous lord, flower of all lords' BK 1594-95
***Gramersy**, arluth glorius, the peb eth os plegadow* 'Thank you, glorious lord, to all you are pleasant' BK 1626
***Gramercy**, ow arluth gay* 'Thank you, my splendid lord' BK 3060
***Gramersie**, gentyll Howen* 'Thank you, gentle Howel' BK 3214
*myhall sera thewgh **gramercy*** 'By St Michael, sir, thank you' CW 599
Gad marshe 'I thank you' RSymonds
gyra-massi *Diolch ichwi* 'Thank you' Lhuyd, *Geirlyer Kyrnweig*: 84.

Although **Meur ras dhywgh**, **meur ras dhis** are the default forms for 'thank you' in the revived language, it must be admitted that **gramercy** is better attested in the traditional language. Moreover the citations above

thank you   GERYOW GWIR

from Symonds (1644) and Lhuyd's Cornish glossary (1707) indicate that **gramercy** survived in speech well into the Late Cornish period. **Gramercy** could perhaps be more widely used in the revived language.

TO THREATEN

The default word for 'to threaten' in the revived language has always been **godros**. Until the discovery of *Bewnans Ke* it was poorly attested:

A **godros**
rak ny yllyn yn nep tre tryge dres nos del vs an yethewon wheth pur vr worth agan arveth hag ow **koddros** 'for we cannot stay in any town over night as the Jews are still at all times harrassing us and threatening' RD 2406-08

Avond, mar qurer y **woodros** *ha me, myghtern Orcados, a'n socker gans ol ow gwlas* 'Forward, if he is threatened, and I, king of Orkney, will come to his aid with all my kingdom' BK 1426-28

Myr, ow **codres** *y'm sesya!* 'Look, he was seizing me while threatening me!' BK 2238.

A commoner word for 'to threaten' is **braggya**:

B **braggya**
Ty horsen [n]agen **brag** *ny* 'You whoreson, don't threaten us!' BM 1228

Na **vragyogh** *brays lafarov y a veth purguir marov rag cafus sur age goys* 'Don't threaten bigmouth, they will certainly die so we can get their blood' BM 1597-99

Te falge horsen [n]am **brag** *vy avond tellek theth cregy* 'You false whoreson, don't threaten me. Be gone, ragamuffin, hang you!' BM 3491-92

byth na wyle neb ur **braggye** *an crustunyon* 'never seek at any time to threaten the Christians' BM 3506-08

So in marver dell russens wilfully tyrry lays Du, hay ordynans, eff as **braggyas** *in vaner ma.* 'But in as much as they wilfully broke the laws of God, and his ordinance, he threatened them like this' TH 40.

Perhaps **braggya** might be used alongside **godros** to mean 'to threaten' in the revived language.

TOP

The noun **gwartha** 'top' is attested only once:

A **gwartha**
my a vyn lemyn tyldye **guartha** *an gorhyl gans queth* 'I will now cover the top of the vessel with a cloth' OM 1073-74.

A far commoner word for 'top' in the texts is **top**:

B **top**

*At eve fast bys in **top** nov mata make fast the rop* 'Look it is firm up to the top. Now mate, make fast the rope' BM 599-600

*Oma yma meryasek ov corthya du galosek poren in **top** an meneth* 'Here Meriasek is worshipping mighty God on the very top of the mountain' BM 1974-76

*ha in guryn po an **top** an pen, eff a ra framya yehas the oll an mymbyrs erell* 'and in the crown or the top of the head, he provides health for all the other members' TH 46

*now in **toppe** an wethan deake yth esa vn virgyn wheake* 'now in the top of the fair tree there was a sweet virgin' CW 1907-08.

Either **gwartha** or **top** can be used for 'top, upper part' in the revived language.

TRADITION

For 'tradition' Nance suggests ***hengof**. This word is unattested in Cornish, being based upon Breton *hengoun*. The attested word for 'tradition' is **tradycyon**, *plural* **tradycyons**:

tradycyon 'tradition'

*ny a vea res thyn nena sewya an order in **tradicions**, delyuerys drethens y then re a rellans y commyttya an ordyr an egglos thetha* 'should we then not follow the order in traditions delivered by them to those to whom they commited the order of the Church?' TH 19

*then **tradicions** na lyas barbarus nacion, ow crege in crist, a ra ry crygyans heb screffa vith arell na scriptur mas an pith vs scriffis in aga colonow* 'to those traditions many barbarous nations who believe in Christ give credence without any other writing or scripture apart from what is written in their hearts' TH 19

*hag in marver dell rug an phariseys gans aga pestilens **tradicions**, fals **tradicions** ha interpretacions ha gloses* 'and in as much as the pharisees with their pestilent traditions, false traditions and interpretations and glosses' TH 22

*Dar ny vea necessary thyn folya an ordyr an kythsame **tradicion** a russans dyluer then rena neb a russens kymmyn an egglos?* 'What, would it not be necessary for us to follow the order of the very same tradition which they deliverd to those to whom they committed the Church?' TH 37

*y myth Ireneus, ny a res thyn sewya, observia, ha gwetha an **tradicions** an auncient egglos* 'Irenaeus says, we must follow, observe and maintain the traditions of the ancient Church' TH 37

*ha nag en ny kylmys the wetha **tradicion** vith* 'and that we are not bound to maintain any tradition' TH 37.

Tradycyon is well attested; ***hengof** is not attested at all. In the interests of authenticity **tradycyon** should perhaps be more widely used in the revived language than it is at present.

TO TRANSFORM, TO TRANSFIGURE

To render these verbs in Cornish some commentators suggest *****treusfurvya**. Such a neologism is unnecessary since **transformya** and **transfygura** are both attested:

A **transformya**

*henna ew the leverall Bara nyng ew figure, mas **transfvrmys** the Corf Christ ha henna ew kygg Christ* 'that is to say: bread is not a figure, but is transformed into the body of Christ, and that is Christ's flesh' SA 66a

*enoch me a levar thyes owe bothe tha vos indelma may fosta qwyck **transformys*** 'Enoch, I tell you my wish is thus: that you be quickly transformed' CW 2110-12.

B **transfygura**

*In xvii a mathew, ny a rede fatell ve crist **transfiguris*** 'In the 17th chapter of St Matthew we read that Christ was transfigured' TH 56a.

The attested **transformya** and **transfygura** are perhaps preferable to the modern neologism.

TRIBE

For 'tribe' Nance suggests A) **kenedhel** (UC *kenethel) f.*; B) **ehen** (UC *eghen*); C) *****lyth** ; and D) **trib** (UC *tryb*). As has been mentioned under 'nation' above **kenedhel** means 'generation, begetting' and is not really a suitable translation for 'tribe'. **Ehen** means 'kind, sort' in a general sense (see s.v. 'KIND' above). **Ehen** is hardly suitable to translate 'tribe'.

*****Lyth** is not attested as such, being a respelling of *progenies uel tribus,* **leid** 'progeny or tribe' OCV §158. There is no other example. The attested word in Middle Cornish is **trib**:

*Ken rug oll an x **tryb** a Israell departia atheworth Roboam mab Salamon, whath dre reson y bosa gwrys dre an blonogeth a thu, yth o cryff ha fyrme heb aucthorite vith arell* 'Though all the ten tribes of Israel departed from Rehoboam son of Solomon, yet because he had been created by the will of God, he was strong and firm without any other authority' TH 50a.

Trib would seem to be the best word for 'tribe' for use in the revived language.

TRUTH

The default form for 'truth' in the revived language is **gwiryoneth** (UC *gwyryoneth*). It must be admitted, however, that forms with **gwiryon-** (UC *gwyryon-*) in the first syllable are attested only in PC and RD; moreover PC is not consistent in using **gwiryoneth** exclusively. In the other texts 'truth' is either B) **gwironeth** or C) **gwrioneth**.

A gwiryoneth

*me ny vennaf cafus le yn **guyryoneth*** 'I will not take less in truth' PC 595-96

*nyns yu lemmyn vyleny awos **guyryoneth** keusel* 'it is only mistreatment for speaking the truth' PC 1275-76

*mar keus ken es **guyryoneth** my a'n te thy's war ow feyth ef a'n pren kyns tremene* 'if he speaks other than truth, I swear it to you upon my faith, he shall suffer for it before he dies' PC 1468-70

*lauar thy'nny **guyryoneth** hep feyntys na falsury* 'tell us the truth without feigning or falsehood' PC 1477-78

*syre ny a'n gor wharre the pylat fast bys yn tre hag ef syngyns **guyryoneth*** 'sir, we will take him forthwith to Pilate right into the town and let him decide the truth' PC 1799-801

*me a worthyp thy's warre an **guyryoneth** yredy* 'I will forthwith answer the truth to you verily' PC 1973-74

*lauar th'ymmo er the fyth pandra yv ol **guyryoneth** pan geusyth mur annotho* 'tell me by your faith what is all truth, since you speak much of it?' PC 2028-30

***guyryoneth** a reys bos dreys aberueth yn mater-ma* 'truth needs to be brought into this matter' PC 2447

*yn **guyryoneth** an den-ma yv map dev a'n nef avan* 'in truth this man is the son of God in heaven above' PC 3079-80

*thy's lauaraf **guyryoneth*** 'I tell you the truth' RD 407

*an **guyryoneth** kyn clewyth awos tra uyth ny'n cregyth* 'although you hear the truth, on no account will you believe it' RD 1384-85

*nyns yv gulan lemmyn mostys an **guyryoneth** lauara* 'it is not clean but dirty; I speak the truth' RD 1927-28

*yn **guyryoneth** me a grys kynyuer peyn vs yn beys thotho by ny vye re* 'in truth I believe, all the torments in the world woul not ever be too much for him' RD 2054-56

B gwironeth

*my th'y bysy a leuerel **guyroneth** thy'so a'n oyl a versy o dythywys thy'mmo vy* 'that I pray him to tell you the truth about the Oil of Mercy that was promised to me' OM 701-04

*ha genef ef a'd pygys a leuerel **guyroneth** a'n oyl dotho dythywys a versy yn deyth dyweth* 'and he asked you through me to tell the truth about the Oil of Mercy promised to him on the last day' OM 739-41

*me a leuer **guyroneth*** 'I speak the truth' PC 735

truth GERYOW GWIR

*ty re'n leuerys iudas an **guyroneth** ru'm leaute* 'you have said it, Judas, the truth upon my word' PC 759-60

*yth esan ow desyvya agan honyn han **gweroneth** nys ugy genyn* 'we deceive ourselves and the truth is not in us' TH 8

*concernya an **gweranath** an kig h[an] gois agen arluth Christ* 'concerning the truth of the flesh and blood of our lord Christ' SA 61

*An **gwîranath** ew an gwella, En pob tra, trea, po pella* 'The truth is best in everything at home or further away' ACB: F f 4.

C gwrioneth

*mes mara kewsys yn ta han **gwreoneth** y synsy prag om gwysketh yndelma* 'but if I spoke well and adhered to the truth, why do you thus strike me?' PA 82cd

*thynny yth ew worthy the vos accomptys shame ha confucion, ha theso ge arluth **gwryoneth*** 'it is right to consider it shame and confusion for us, and to you, Lord, truth' TH 9a-10

*contrary the reason ha **gwryoneth*** 'contrary to reason and truth' TH 10

*theso ge yma ow pertaynya **gwryoneth*** 'to you pertains truth' TH 10

*Rag henna ny wothya du dre **gwryoneth** ha iustus, receva mabden arta thy favowre* 'Therefore God was not able by truth and justice to receive mankind into his favour again' TH 12

*kynth ew an gothvas an **gwryoneth** necessary the attaynya an bewnans heb deweth* 'although the knowledge of the truth is necessary to obtain everlasting life' TH 14

*ha te a wore dre an la an forme a sciens ha **gwryoneth*** 'and you know through the law the form of science and truth' TH 14a

*the well establysses in gothfas a **wryoneth** ha the wandra in **gwryoneth*** 'better established in the knowledge of the truth and to walk in truth' TH 14a

*ha the thysky **gwryoneth**, skyans ha reason* 'and to learn truth, knowledge and reason' TH 17

*pan deffa an spuris na a **wryoneth**, eff a thiske theugh oll **gwryoneth*** 'when that Spirit of truth comes, he will teach you all truth' TH 17

*na ny yll bos decevys in maner vith a forth dre **gwryoneth*** 'nor can be deceived in any manner of way by truth' TH 17

*yma S paul in iii chapter the Tymothe ow kylwall an egglos catholyk an pyllar han grownd a **wryoneth*** 'St Paul in the third chapter to Timothy calls the catholic Church the pillar and the ground of truth' TH 17a

*hen o an **gwryoneth** an catholyk feith a rug eff cowse anotha* 'that was the truth of the catholic faith of which he spoke' TH 18a

*Ny dall thynny whelas an **gwreoneth** in myske re erell* 'We need not seek the truth among others' TH 18a

*in marvere dell rug an appostlis y gasa athellar kepar ha dell vo va tresure riche a oll **gwryoneth*** 'in as much as the apostles left it behind as though it was a rich treasure of all truth' TH 19

*hag ena dysky an **gwryoneth*** 'and there learn the truth' TH 19 *ha dre **gwryoneth** mar mynnyn ny judgia compis hag in ta* 'and by truth if we judge accurately and well' TH 21

*rag pub ober a **wryoneth** ew contaynys in charite* 'for all the works of truth are contained in charity' TH 21

*fatell ma **gwryoneth** ha justice in kysam text ma ow signifia pub kynde oll a virtu ha daddar* 'that truth and justice in this same text signify every kind of virtue and goodness' TH 26a

*Rag henna pan vsy agan Savyowre ow requyrya thewarthan ny may teffan ny ha passia an scribes han pharises in **gwryoneth** ha iustice* 'Therefore, since our Saviour requires of us that we should pass the scribes and pharisees in truth and justice' TH 26a

*ha the vos pyllar an **gwryoneth** in oll agen dawnger* 'and to be a pillar of the truth in all our danger' TH 30a

*hen ew an spuris a **wrioneth** han spiris a vnite promysys dre crist then egglos catholyk* 'that is the Spirit of truth and the Spirit of unity promised by Christ to the catholic Church' TH 32

*eff a ra deneya ha forsakya an very truth **gwryoneth*** 'he will deny and foresake the very truth' TH 33a

*Ima oll an re na ow cotha theworth an **gwryoneth*** 'All those fall away from the truth' TH 37

*Eff a ra agys ledya in oll **gwryoneth*** 'He will lead you into all truth' TH 38

*alemma rag the vos constant ha feithfull in **gwryoneth*** 'henceforth to be constant and faithful in truth' TH 54a

*rage eth o e **gwreonath**, ha moy presius agis owr veith* 'for it was in truth and more precious than any gold' SA 60

*Amen: henna ew **gwryonath*** 'Amen, that is truth' SA 61a

*me a levar thewgh dell goeth an **gwreanathe** a bub tra* 'I will tell you, as is right, the truth about everything' CW 1891-92

*E **wreeanath** ol termen ma seval kreaue* 'His truth at all times stands strong' BF: 39

Gureoneth 'truth' Borlase.

Although **gwiryoneth** is the default way of spelling 'truth', the variants **gwironeth** and **gwrioneth** should perhaps be allowed also.

TO TRY, TO TEST

The simplest way to translate 'to try, to attempt' is to either to use **whelas**, **whylas** 'to seek' or the verb **assaya**, itself a borrowing from Middle English *assaien* 'to essay, to try'.

A **assaya** 'to essay, to try'

*ny vern tra vyth **assaye** how guereseugh cowethe ov corre tvmbyr yn ban* 'To try does not matter at all. Oh, help me comrades to offer up the timber' OM 2477-79

try   **GERYOW GWIR**

*guel yv thy'n ym**assaya** yn plath certan kyns mones* 'it is better for us to try ourselves here before we go' PC 2302-03

***asaye** ow arluth ker govynneugh orth an geiler kyns ol pan pleyt yme fe* 'try, my dear lord, ask the gaoler first in what condition he is' RD 2051-53

*Whath kyn fe va lyas tyrmyn **assays** ha teball pynchis, whath an feith a rug prevaylya woteweth* 'Yet though it was often tried and in severe difficulty, still the faith prevailed in the end' TH 34

*hag in yr na gwraf **assaya** 3a vos m[este]r war an trone* 'and now I shall try to be master upon the throne' CW 200-01

*sowe Eva manaf **saya** hy ew esya tha dulla* 'but I shall try Eve; she is easier to deceive' CW 470-71.

The English borrowing **tria** is also well attested:

B **tria** 'to try'

*Job, an moyha den a ve **tryys** ha prevys, a thowtyas y oberow* 'Job the man who was most tried and proved doubted his works' TH 8

*Yma try meynes rag **trya** an egglos a crist, po an dyscans, han kynsa ew antiquite, henew cotheneb, an second ew vniversalite, han tryssa ew vnytie* 'There are three ways to try the Church of Christ or the teaching, and the first is antiquity, that is, its age, the second is universality, and the third is unity' TH 34a

*An peswora yma eff ow ry thyn kusyll diligently rag examyna ha **trya** agan honyn, kyns ny the thos then vois a thu* 'Fourth, he gives us advise diligently to examine and try ourselves before we come to God's table' TH 53a-54

*Heb **trya** fest ny vith scaf e thuscuthy* 'Without trying hard it will not be easy to alleviate' BK 1417-18

*keffrys me ham cowetha der gletha a vyn **trea** ow bosaf moy worthya agis an tase sure pub pryes* 'also I and my companions by the sword will test that I am more worthy than the Father indeed at all times' CW 316-19

*Ha po chee & tha wreag an moiha looan varbarr; nenna g'reu **trea** an dezan ha na henz* 'And when you and your wife are the happiest together, then try the cake and not before' BF: 16

*Tento... To assay, to prove, to tempt... C. Dho **trîa** AB: 162a.*

Tria would seem to be a useful alternative to **assaya**.

U

TO UNDERSTAND, UNDERSTANDING

The default word for 'to understand' in revived Cornish has always been **confedhes, convedhes**. It is perhaps not generally realized, however, that this word is confined to CW and Late Cornish:

convedhes 'to perceive, to understand'

ow voice oll yta changis avel mayteth in tevery me ne vethaf **confethes** *om bos ynaff fallsurye* 'behold my voice is all changed like a maiden indeed; I shall not be found out that there is falsehood in me' CW 530-33

sera ny won **convethas** *ages dewan in neb for agen deaw vabe 3a thew grace yth ins pur vew byth na sor whath nyng ew pell* 'sir, I cannot understand your grief in any way; our two sons, thank God, were very much alive—do not be angry—a little while ago' CW 1232-35

me ny allaf **convethas** *y bosta ge ow hendas na care vyth thym in teffry* 'I cannot understand that you are my grandfather or any relative of mine indeed' CW 1609-11

marcke dew warnaf ew settys te an gweall in corne ow thale gans dean pen vo **convethys** *worthaf ve sertan ny dale bos mellyes avs neb tra* 'God's mark has been set upon my. You see it in the corner of my forehead. When it is perceived by man, it is not worth meddling with me for any reason' CW 1617-20

distructyon yma ornys pur serten war oll an beise may fyth consumys pub tra henna yth ew **convethys** *der an discans es thymma reis gans an tas es a vghan* 'destruction has been ordained in very truth for all the world, so that everything will be consumed. That has been understood by the teaching given to me by the Father above' CW 2150-55

an howle han loor kekeffrys oll warbarth ew **confethys** *than purpose na mowns ow toos* 'the sun and the moon also, all together they are perceived, to that purpose they are coming' CW 2159-61

Der taklow minniz ew brez teez **gonvethes***, avelan tacklow broaz; dreffen en tacklow broaz, ma an gymennow hetha go honnen; bus en tacklow minnis, ema an gye suyah hâz go honnen* 'Through small things are men's minds perceived, rather than by great things, because in great things they often exert themselves, but in tiny thing they follow their own nature' ACB: E e 4 *verso*.

understand   GERYOW GWIR

In two of the quotations above **convedhes** seems to mean 'to perceive' rather than 'to understand'. This is not astonishing, since **convedhes** is a late reshaping of the verb **canfos, canvos** 'to perceive'; cf. Welsh *canfod* 'to perceive, to see'. The Cornish verb **canfos** is now attested in *Bewnans Ke*:

canfos 'to perceive'
*Ema Arthur devethys ha ny gansa **canfethys** *'Arthur has come and we have been perceived by him' BK 2794-95
*Rag kueth, pan i'n **canfethis**, me re jangyas ow holor* 'For grief, when I perceived it, I changed my hue' BK 3129-30.

It is noteworthy that Lhuyd does not cite either **canfos** or **convedhes** as meaning 'to understand'. Under *intelligo* 'To perceive or understand' at AB: 72a Lhuyd gives Cornish ***adzhan*** i.e. **aswon, ajwon**. **Aswon** 'to understand' is used by John Boson in a letter to Williams Gwavas in April 1710:

aswon 'to recognize, to understand'
*ha rag hedna ni el guelas ha **adzhan** an tavas kernuak dha boz tavaz koth ha triuadh ew dha boz kellez* 'and therefore we can see and understand that the Cornish language is an ancient tongue and it is a pity it should be lost' BF: 46.

It was probably because **confedhes, convedhes** meant 'to perceive, to notice, to find out' as much as 'to understand', that TH and SA use the borrowed verb **ùnderstondya, ùnderstandya**. Together TH and SA use this verb 35 times. Here are a few examples:

ùnderstondya 'to understand'
*lymmyn rag may hallogh **vnderstondia** an mater ma the well ha the pleynnya, why a ra **vnderstondia** nag o an heveleb a then havall the thu in bodily symblans, hen ew the leverall in y gorffe only. Rag why a res **vnderstondia** ha cresy fatell ew an dewses spuris ha not substans a corffe* 'now in order that you may understand this matter better and more plainly, you will understand that man's likeness to God was not in bodily appearance, that is to say in his body only. For you must understand and believe that the Godhead is spirit and not substance of body' TH 1a
*dre hemma eff a ros thyn ny the **wondyrstondia** fatell vs iii person in drynsys* 'by this he gave us to understand that there are three persons in the Trinity' TH 1a
*henna ew the **vndyrstondia** dre dybbry an avall* 'that is to be understood, by eating the apple' TH 5
*nynses onyn a ra **vndyrstondia**, nynses onyn ow sewya ha folya Du* 'there is not one who understands, there is not one following and emulating God' TH 7a
*mar tene ny consyddra hag **vnderstondia** in ta, ny a ra the well **vnderstondia** an mercy a thu, ha fatell vgy agan salvacion ow tos dre crist only* 'if we consider and understand well, we will understand the mercy of God, and that our salvation comes through Christ only' TH 10

GERYOW GWIR   **understand**

*Omma why a well fatel rug pedyr exortya pub den oll, kynsa the wothfes fatell res thyn scripture bos **vnderstondyys** warlerth an generall menyng a egglos crist, So not warlerth an priveth interpretacion a then vith severall, na company, hag in iii-a chapter in kythsam pistyll ma, yma pedyr ow leverall pelha fatell vs in pystlys a S paule lyas tra calys the vos **vnderstondiis*** 'Here you see that Peter exhorted every man, first to know that the scripture must be understood according to the general meaning of the Church of Christ, but not according to private interpretation of any man or company, and in the third chapter of this same epistle, St Peter says further that there are many things in St Paul's epistles that are difficult to understand' TH 18

*yma an apostyll pedyr ow leverall omma an very cawsse praga vgy tus ow cam**vnderstondia** scripture* 'the apostle Peter here mentions the very cause why men misunderstand scripture' TH 18

*dre racha ny a yll **vnderstondia** an signe warves, vttrys in mes dre anger* 'by racha we can understand the external sign uttered in anger' TH 28a

*me a rug supposya fatell o va da ha mytt rag may hallowgh **vnderstondia** vn tra arell a thadder ha benefitt* 'I supposed that it was good and meet that you might understand one further matter of value and benefit' TH 30a

*So keneuer a wothfa redya ha **vnderstondia** a yll gwellas fatell ra ran y vsya gloriusly* 'But as many as can read and understand may see that some use it gloriously' TH 32a

*An dra ma, tus vas, why a yll in ta **vnderstondia** y bosa lell, mar tewgh why gylwall thegys remembrans, pew ew an guyde han gouernar an egglos henew the **vnderstondya** an spurissans* 'This matter, good people, you will properly understand to be true, if you recall, who is the guide and governor of the Chruch, that is to be understood as the Holy Spirit' TH 36

*ny oll ew kylmys the percevya ha **vnderstondia** innan agan honyn* 'we are all bound to perceive and understand within ourselves' TH 51

*So rag **vnderstondia** an girryow ma, Hemmew ow corffe ve* 'But to understand these words: This is my body' TH 53a

*Mar tewhy demandea, praga a ruke an egglos dewys mar galys vnderstandyng an keth artickell ma girryow an scripture a yll bos eaisy **vnderstandis*** 'If you ask why did the Church choose such difficult understanding of this same article, the words of scripture can be easily understood' SA 64

*whath na ruk Judas e **vnderstandya**, ef a tastyas kigg an arluth Dew* 'Still Judas did not understand it; he tasted the flesh of the Lord God' SA 65a

TH and SA also use the noun **ùnderstondyng**, **ùnderstandyng** 'understanding':

*Rag an **vnderstonding** a henna gesowgh ny the gafus recourse then tryssa chapter a genesis* 'For the understanding of that let us have recourse to the third chapter of Genesis' TH 3

*rag ny rug du agan creatya ny pobill an bis heb reason, skyans hag **vnderstonding*** 'for God did not create us, people of the world, without reason, knowledge and understanding' TH 5

understand GERYOW GWIR

ha pelha agys henna eff a blanges innan ny particularly reason hag **vnderstonding**, *ha lowar qualite arell kyffrys in corfe hag in ena* 'and more than that he planted in us in particular reason and understanding and many other qualities of both body and soul' TH 5

An golow a nature ynnan ny, na an gothvas han **vnderstonding** *a vlonogath du der speciall dyswythyans innan ny, nyns o abyll thegan gweras ny* 'The light of nature in us, nor the knowledge and understanding of the will of God by special revelation were unable to help us' TH 13a

So whath awos oll aga gothfas ha **vnderstonding**, *y a gotha[s] in abomynabill ydolatri* 'But yet in spite of their knowledge and understanding, they fell into vile adolatry' TH 14

Henna ew rag lak ha fowt gothvas hag **vnderstonding** 'That is for lack and want of knowledge and understanding' TH 18

Whath rag dowt mar te ran ahanow why dowtya an **vnderstonding** *an scriptur ma, omma why a glew fatell ma S Austyn ow scriffa anotha* 'Still lest for fear, if some of you dobt the understanding of this scripture, here you will hear how St Augustine writes of it' TH 32

Rag lymmyn athewethas pub den sempill heb **understonding** *na skyans a re supposia fatell yllens y bos iudges in maters a contrauercite* 'For now recently every simple man without understanding or wisdom supposes that they can be judges in matters of dispute' TH 37

Mar tewhy demandea, praga a ruke an egglos dewys mar galys **vnderstandyng** *an keth artickell ma girryow an scripture a yll bos eaisy vnderstandis* 'If you ask why did the Church choose such difficult understanding of this same article, the words of scripture can be easily understood' SA 64.

It should be pointed out here that nouns and adjectives in **-yng** from English are well established in Cornish from an early period, for example: **connyngh** 'cunning' PC 1458; **faryng** 'faring, conduct' PC 375; **mornyngh** 'mourning' RD 438; *whek* **smyllyng** 'sweet-smelling' OM 1743 and **tochyng** 'touching, concerning' BK 1137.

In view of the prevalence of both **ùnderstondya** and **ùnderstondyng** in TH and SA, it would be unwise and indeed inauthentic to proscribe either of them.

UNITY

For 'unity' Nance suggests ***unsys**, a word that is not attested but rather has been devised on the basis of Welsh *undod* 'unity'. The only attested word for 'unity' is **unyta**:

dre hemma yth ew signifies an **vnite** *inweth agan nature ha substans* 'by this is signified the unity also of our nature and substance' TH 1a

hag anethe hy kemeras dynsys ha joynyas y honyn then dusys in **vnite** *a person* 'and from her he took humanity and joined himself to the Deity in unity of person' TH 12a *hag eff a rug kylmy the thugys an corfe han ena a then, in **vnite** a person in strang forth ha maner an par na* 'and he bound to the Godhead the body and the soul of man, in unity of person in a strange way and manner of that kind' TH 15

*hen ew an spuris a wrioneth han spiris a **vnite** promysys dre crist then egglos catholyk* 'that is the Spirit of truth and the Spirit of unity promised by Christ to the catholic Church' TH 32

*An second ew vniversalite ha'n tryssa ew **vnytie*** 'The second is universality and the third is unity' TH 34a

*Rag heb dowt nyns es thyn trygva in crist, mas ny a dryg in **vnyte** ay Catholik egglos* 'For without doubt we have no dwelling place in Christ unless we dwell in the unity of the catholic Church' TH 39a

*Indella ny vith nag onyn sawys theworth dampnacion, mas an re vsy in **vnite** an egglos a crist* 'Thus no one will be save from damnation, except those who are in unity with the Church of Christ' TH 39a

*Penag oll a vo deberthys theworth an Catholicall egglos kyn rella eff supposya y honyn the vewa neffra mar ware na mar worthy, whath an **vnite** an egglos a crist nynsevith eff bewnas, mas an sorre a crist a dryg vghta* 'Whoever is separated from the catholic Church, even though he considers himself to live never so carefully nor worthily, yet he will not have the life of the unity of the Church of Christ, but the wrath of Christ will hang over him' TH 40

*bys may teffan ny oll ha dos warbarth in vn **vnyte** a crisgians ha feith* 'till we all come together in a unity of belief and faith' TH 42

*the wetha **vnyte** hag ordyr da the vos gwethis in egglos* 'to maintain unity and for good order to be maintained in the Church' TH 45

*ha theworth henna eff a rug ordeynya ha disquethas an dalathvas an **vnite** the procedya* 'and from that he ordained and showed the beginning of the unity to pursue' TH 45a

*rag preservya an **vnytye** in y egglos* 'to preserve the unity in his church' TH 46

*ganso eff ny ew kylmys in catholik **vnite*** 'by him we are bound in catholic unity' TH 48.

In view of the prevalence of **unyta**, it would seem preferable to the unattested ***unsys**.

TO USE

The word **devnyth** 'material' is attested once in the expression **gwil devnyth a** 'to make use of, to use':

A **gwil devnyth**

*ha hen yv emskemunys rak ny allas den yn beys anotho **gul defnyth** vas* 'and that one is accursed for no man in the world has been able to make good use of it' PC 2546-48.

On the basis of **gwil devnyth** some commentators have suggested a verb ***devnydhya** 'to use', cf. Welsh *defnyddio* 'to use'. Such a coinage is unnecessary, since the verb **ûsya** 'to use' is common.

use GERYOW GWIR

B ûsya

*An queth tek a ve dyskis han purpur ryche a **vsye** hay bowys y honon gurris adro 3030 hy a ve* 'The fair cloth was taken off and the rich purple he was wearing, and his own coat, it was put about him' PA 161ab

*Rag gwan spyr[n] hag ef yn ten caman na ylly gwyӡe war nans na bosse y ben rag an arlont a **vsye*** 'For thorn pricks as he was spread out he could not in any way prevent his head from leaning downwards, because of the wreath he was wearing' PA 205ab

*ny re bue tus ongrasyas ha re **vsias** hager gas raffna ladra pur lues feyst* 'we have been graceless men and have used an ugly business to rob, to steal from very many' BM 2142-44

*drok hag anfusy inweth guetyogh **vsia** ha pyle bohosogyan* 'evil and misfortune be careful to use and pillage poor people' BM 3421-23

*bredereth **vsyogh** dader han vohosogyen pub vr bethugh sokyr an re na* 'brethren, employ goodness and the poor, always be assistance to them' BM 4260-62

*guyn na syder ny **vsya*** 'he used neither wine nor cider' BM 4451

*sow in creacion a vabden an tas a **vsias** solempnyty bras* 'but in the creation of man the Father used great solemnity' TH 1

*ha yth ew redys inweth in scriptur fatell rug Judith, Hester, Job, Jheremye, gans mere moy tus benegas ha benenas in testament coth a rug **vsia** gwyska yscar ha canfas garow* 'and it is read in scripture also that Judith, Esther, Job, Jeremiah and many other holy men and women in the Old Testament used to wear sackcloth and rough canvas' TH 6a

*mar teffa du aga suffra the **vsya** aga naturall powers y a vynsa optaynya salvacion in ta lovr heb gweras vith arell in party du* 'if God had allowed them to use their natural powers, they would have obtained salvation well enough without any other assistance on God's part' TH 13a

*ha the **vsya** agan honyn jentyll the pub den* 'and to practice kindness to all men' TH 21a

*Hag indelma eff a **vsyas** y honyn, ow exortya y yskerens, ha ow rebukya aga fautes* 'And thus he employed himself, exhorting his enemies and rebuking their faults' TH 22a

*In kepar maner neb a rella don colan tha ha mynde, hag **vsya** in ta y tavas, hay oberow the bub den, cothman hag yskar, eff a yll gothfas dre henna, fatell vs thotha cherite* 'Similarly whoever bears a good heart and mind and employs his tongue well and his works to all men, friend and foe, he can know thereby that he possesses charity' TH 23a

*na the refraynya theworth kyge porrell, na the wetha taclenow wo **vsyys** in la moyses* 'nor to refrain from pork or to keep things that were practised in the law of Moses' TH 27a

*So keneuer a wothfa redya ha vnderstondia a yll gwellas fatell ra ran y **vsya** gloriusly* 'But anyone who can read and understand can see that some use it gloriously' TH 32a

*yth yns accomptes gans S paull oll warbarth carnall ha pell vnworthy the **vsya** an hanow a egglos* 'they are all together considered by St Paul to be carnal and greatly unworthy to use the name of Church' TH 33

*Dar, ny ren ny redya fatell rug S paule **vsya** an kythsam auctorite ma, pan rug omskemenegy Hymmenyus* 'Why, do we not read that St Paul used this same authority when he excommunicated Hymenaeus?' TH 39 *dar, ny rug an epscob benegas S Ambros **vsya** an auctorite ma in pub poynt war an Emporowre Theodosius?* 'why, did not the blessed bishop St Ambrose use this authority in every particular against the emperor Theodosius?' TH 39

*An kithsam epscob ma a **vsyas** an auctorite res thotha gans du* 'This same bishop used the authority given to him by God' TH 39

*Surly ny russa an egglos a crist dos then dishonor han disordyr a wylsyn ny, na ny vea vices ha drokoleth mar fre **vsyys*** 'Surely the Church of Christ would not have come to the dishonour and disorder we have seen, nor would vices and wickedly be so freely employed' TH 39

*Lymmyn an circumstans consydrys da a rug agan saviour **vsia** worth an institucion an kith Sacrament benegas ma* 'Now the circumstances well considered which our Saviour used at the institution of this same holy sacrament' TH 52

*ha rag henna pan ve an sacrament institutys, henna a ve gesys ha na moy **vsyys*** 'and therefore, when the sacrament was instituted, that was relinquished and was no longer used' TH 52a

*A ra tus **vsya** offra bois ha dewas the re, rag purpos vith arall, mas may teffans eva dybry hag eva anotha?* 'Do men usually offer food and drink to people for any other purpose than that they should eat and drink of them?' TH 52a

*ha gans very vylle termes ow jestia gansa, ha in moyha vylla a rug **vsya** an presyvs corfe ha gois agan savyour Jhesu crist in sacrament ma an aulter* 'and with very vile terms mocking it, and in the most vile used the precious body and blood of our Saviour Jesus Christ in this sacrament of the altar' TH 55a

*An egglos catholyk a ra **vsya** an ger ma transsubstantiation* 'The catholic Church uses this word Transubstantiation' TH 56a

*ny a res honora an corffe han gois agan sauyour Jhesu crist in sacrament an aulter, kepar dell rug lell cristonyan **vsya** pub vr oll* 'we must honour the body and the blood of our Saviour Jesus Christ in the sacrament of the altar, as were faithful Christians accustomed always to do' TH 58

*Na esyn **vsya** argumentys, mas **vsya** exampels Christ* 'Let us not use arguments, but use the examples of Christ' SA 61a

*nena ne ra an pronter **vsya** girreow e honyn* 'then the priest will not use his own words' SA 62

*genas ny vannaf flattra na ny vanaf **usya** gowe* 'I will not use cajolery with you nor will I employ falsehood' CW 648-49

*na gwyne ny **vsyan** badna* 'nor do we use any drop of wine' CW 1471-74

*Soleo... To be accustom'd or wont... C. Dho **yuzia*** AB: 151c.

Notice that **ûsya** can mean both 'to make use of, to employ' and 'to wear, to practise' and 'to be accustomed to'. The sense 'to be accustomed to' is still seen in English expressions like 'I used to speak Cornish every day' and 'I used not drink much coffee'. The other senses are now archaic in English, but the Cornish verb **ûsya** preserves them.

Given that **ûsya** is so widespread in the texts, it seems preferable to use it as the ordinary word for 'to use'.

V

VALLEY

For 'valley' revived Cornish has always used **nans**, **nansow**. Outside toponyms, however, this word is very rare indeed and is attested twice and only once in Middle Cornish:

vallis, **nans** 'valley' OCV §719

In erna ȝen menyȝyow why a ergh warnough coȝe yn ketella an **nanssow** *wy a bys ragas cuthe* 'Then you will command the mountains to fall upon you; similarly you will beg the valleys to cover you' PA 170ab.

In the texts later than PA the words for valley are **tnow**, *plural* **tenwyn** and **valy**:

A **tnow**

Me a gergh erba rasaw drys keel, drys gwel, drys prasaw, drys ***tnow***, *drys gun, drys mene* 'I shall fetch herb of grace over bower, over field, over meadows, over valley, over moor, over mountain' BK 1159-61

byth ny falla' ve an fals orth e houlya, drys ***tenuyn*** *ha menythyow* 'never will I fail following him, the renegade, over valleys and mountains' BK 2313-14

An vyghternath par govyn a nug thygo drys ***tenuyn*** *ha'th soccors oll, pub huny* 'The kings by request will fly to you over valleys and all your allies, every one' BK 2527-29.

B **valy**

me a vyn heb falladowe vn dean formya in ***valy*** *ebron devery* 'I shall without fail create a man in the valley of Hebron indeed' CW 338-40.

In the interests of authenticity, perhaps **tnow**, **tenwyn** and **valy** should be more widely used.

VENGEANCE, TO AVENGE

For 'vengeance' Nance recommends A) **hardygras**; B) **dial** (UC *dyal*) and C) **venjyans**. **Hardygras** is attested once only but the other two words are more frequently found:

A **hardygras**

*mahum darber **hardygrath** ʒe neb a ruk ov throbla* 'Mahound, apply vengeance on him who troubled me' BM 948-49.

B) **dial**

*gans pegh mar vr ev flerys na allaf sparie na moy hep gul **dyel** a ver speys war pep ol sur marnas ty* 'with sin so greatly does it stink that I can no longer spare to work vengeance soon upon everyone apart from you' OM 945-48

*Noe rag kerenge orthy's my ny gemere neffre trom **dyal** war ol an beys na dre thyal pup lathe* 'Noah, for your sake I will not ever wreak vengeance upon all the world nor by vengeance kill everybody' OM 1207-10

*Noy rak kerenge orthy's my a wra thy's ambos da luen **dyal** war ol an beys ny gemeraf vynytha* 'Noah for your sake I will make a fair covenant for you: I will never wreak utter vengeance upon the world' OM 1231-34

*honna a vyth tokyn da a'n acord vs gureys hep fal kyn fynnyf war an bys ma tevlel vyngeanns na **dyal** my a vyr scon orth honna hag a'n acord a vyth cof* 'that will be a good sign of the agreement made without fail. Though I wish to wreak vengeance or retribution upon this world, I will quickly look at that and the agreement will be remembered' OM 1247-52

*pilat a'n lathas hep fal warnotho telywgh **dyal** rak ef o crist myghtern nef* 'Pilate without fail killed him. Wreak vengeance upon him, for he was Christ, king of heaven' RD 1752-54

*a du an neff tayl **dyel** warnogh a tus ongrassyes* 'O God in heaven wreak vengeance upon them, graceless men!' BM 1595-96

*Ny re dueth a'gan gwlasow the ge in socker ryal mayth hylly towlal **dyal** war the yskar in fasow* 'We have come from our kingdoms to you as royal assistance, that you may wreak vengeance upon your enemy in his threats' BK 2632-25

*Hy a chans hy athdrevy orth meth ha cas ha **dyal*** 'She risks being rewarded with shame, hatred and revenge' BK 3004-05

*Drog-chauns war an kynwelas, na alsan ny teulal **dyal*** 'Evil luck upon the encounter, that I could not wreak vengeance' BK 3278-79

*Warnotha, Du, tal **dyel**!* 'Upon him, O God, inflict vengeance!' BK 3284.

C) **venjyans**

*han tebel el hager bref yn y holon a worre war y mester **venions** cref y to Ihesus mar laʒe* 'and the devil, evil serpent, put it into her heart that stiff vengeance would come upon her master if he were to kill Jesus' PA 122cd

*Y thewleff pylat a wolhas hag a leuerys ʒeʒe glan off a wos an dremas rag ay woys **venions** a ʒe* 'Pilate washed his hands and said to them, I am clean of the good man's blood, for from his blood vengeance will come' PA 149ab

*honna a vyth tokyn da a'n acord vs gureys hep fal kyn fynnyf war an bys ma tevlel **vyngeanns** na dyal my a vyr scon orth honna hag a'n acord a vyth cof* 'that will be a good sign of the agreement made without fail. Though I wish to wreak vengeance or retribution

vengeance

upon this world, I will quickly look at that and the agreement will be remembered' OM 1247-52

*What **vyngeans** thy's a pen pyst ple clevsta gelwel dev cryst gans den yn bys ma genys* 'What! Vengeance on you, fool. Where did you hear God called Christ by a man born in this world?' OM 2641-43

*leuereugh athysempys the wrek pilat an iustis certan y tue **vyngeans** bras war y gour mar pyth lethys ihesu cryst an lel profys* 'tell the wife of Pilate the justice immediately, that certainly great vengeance will come upon her husband if Jesus Christ, the true prophet is killed' PC 1919-23

*pur wyr y tue **vyngeans** tyn mar pyth an guyryon dyswrys warnough war agas fleghys* 'very truly bitter vengeance will come upon you and your children if the righteous man is destroyed' PC 1937-39

***vengyans** the nep a'n sparryo* 'vengeance on any man who spares him!' PC 2078

*y tue warnough **vyngeans** tyn man gueller a ver termyn ha war the fleghys keffrys* 'bitter vengeance will come upon you and upon your children also, so that it will soon be seen' PC 2199-201

*mar tue **venians** vyth ragtho warnan ny ef re gotho ha war ol agan fleghas* 'if any vengeance for it come, let it fall upon us and upon all our children' PC 2501-03

*a thu aso why bylen ov lathe guyryon hep ken whet **vyngeans** warnogh a gouth* 'O God, how villainous you are killing a righteous man without case. Yet vengeance will fall upon you' PC 2624-26

*ty a whyth auel caugh guas whyth war gam **vyngeans** y'th glas* 'you blow like a reckless fellow; blow steadily, vengeance upon your guts!' PC 2715-16

*a harlos yn kettep guas hertheugh **vynyons** yges glas py ken why a's byth drok lam* 'O scoundrels, push every one—vengeance on your guts—or you will have disaster' PC 3073-75

*tormentores thy'mmo deugh py yn sur **vyngeans** ha geugh why agas byth kyns dos haf* 'tormentors, come to me, or certainly you will suffer vengeance and woe before summer comes' RD 1761-63

***vyngens** re'n geffo amen ha drok thyweyth* 'may he suffer vengeance—amen—and an evil end' RD 2085-86

*wharre ny a'n ten yn ban mur **venions** ha calas ran ef a whylas* 'Straightway we will pull him up. Great vengeance he sought and a hard lot' RD 2259-61

*pana dra a ren ny gwettyas theworth du alymma rag mar teny ha peha hay ankevy eff, forsoth, travith mas sore, anger, han **vingians** a thu* 'What will we expect from God from now on if we sin and forget him? Indeed nothing but wrath, anger and the vengeance of God' TH 15a

*ha the gemeras **vingians** an drog pobill* 'and to take vengeance on evil people' TH 25

*rag henna oll an **vengens** a allaf tha brederye me a vyn goneth dewhans* 'therefore all the vengeance I can image, I shall work immediately' CW 430-32

*hemma o **vengeance** pur vras ha just plage ornys thyma soweth an pryes* 'this was very great vengeance and a just plague ordained for me—alas the time!' CW 1657-59

*hag adam **vengens** thotha lymbo ew ornys thotha, ea ragtha ef ha[y] gowetha* 'and Adam, vengeance upon him. Limbo has been ordained for him, yes for him and his companions' CW 2060-62

GERYOW GWIR   vengeance

ha then tas gwren oll pegy na skydnya an keth ***vengeans*** *in neb termyn warnan ny nagen flehys* 'and let us all pray to the Father that the same vengeance does not descend upon us nor upon our children' CW 2207-10

vengens *war tha ben krehy nynges omma dean in wlase a greys thys malbe vanna* 'vengeance upon your scurvy pate! There is not a man here in the country who will believe you, devil the bit' CW 2326-28

mar ny wrewh ***vengence*** *pur vras a skydn warnough kyns na pell* 'and if you don't, great vengeance will descend upon you before long' CW 2368-69

Mille ***vengeance*** *warna thy* 'A thousand vengeances take thee' Carew.

As is clear from the above citations, **gwil dial wàr**, **kemeres dial wàr** and **tôwlel dial wàr** are ways in Cornish of saying 'take revenge on, be avenged on'. **Kemeres venjyans wàr** is also found. It is also apparent that the noun **venjyans** is very commonly found in the texts.

For 'to avenge' Nance recommends A) **diala** (UC *dyala*) and B) **venjya**. **Diala** seems to mean 'to mistreat, to hurt':

A **diala**

an laddron a'n ***dyalas*** *dre lyes torment ahas ha dre mur a galarow* 'the brigands were vindictive towards him with many torments and by much pain' RD 1426-28

ihesu a whylyth deffry marow yw gallas yn pry nep o agan arluth ny ha pylat a'n ***dyallas*** 'Jesus whom you seek is indeed dead. He has been buried who was our Lord and Pilate mistreated him' RD 1653-56

arluth ot omme an guas del gleseugh a ***thyallas*** *an profus ihesus dampnyas the vos gorrys yn grous pren hag ynhy ef a verwys* 'lord, here is the fellow, as you heard, who mistreated the prophet Jesus. He condemned him to be put on the cross and on it he died' RD 1803-07

out warnas ty harlot was ihesu ty a ***thyallas*** *ow arluth ker* 'Damn you, you scoundrelly fellow. Jesus you mistreated, my dear Lord' RD 1965-67

Lyvyryns theugh prag ema ow quarellya drys ow thyr, ha prag e rug ***dyelha*** *ow cosyns heb mur awher* 'Let him say why he is laying a claim against my country and why he mistreated my cousins without being much bothered' BK 1836-39

ha fals dell ew, me a'n ***dyel*** *heb lettya* 'and false though he is, I'll be avenged on him without delay' BK 2283-84

Arthor, pryck bost, a'n prenwyth tost ha whath pelha in suer ny a'n ***dyelha*** 'Arthur, the empty boaster, will pay for it soon and still further surely we shall be avenged upon him' BK 2576-79

Me, Evander, duk Syry, a'n ***dyelha*** 'I, Evander, duke of Syria, shall be avenged upon him' BK 2693

Owt! Ny vith vas, me a grys, na ny vyan ***dyelhis***, *na ve both Du a'n gwelha* 'Out! It will not be well, I believe, nor would I be mistreated, were it not the will of the highest God' BK 3271-73.

vengeance

B **venjya**

*rag **vyngia** purguir me yv war y servons eff certen* 'for I am minded to take vengeance upon his servants indeed' BM 2383-84
*pendra deseff an map devle dar **vyngya** war thuk kernov* 'what does the devil's son presume? What, to be avenged on the Duke of Cornwall?' BM 2395-96.

Venjya would seem to be the best verb to express the idea of being avenged upon someone. Otherwise one can use **gwil/kemeres/tôwlel dial wàr** or **kemeres venjyans wàr**.

VERY

For 'very' used adverbially before an adjective or another adverb Nance recommends **pur**. This he believed was to be pronounced [py:ɹ], i.e. exactly like the full adjective **pur** 'pure'. It is likely, however, that Nance may have been mistaken in this matter, and that **pur** before adjectives and adverbs, although written <pur>, was pronounced with a weakened vowel i.e. schwa [pəɹ]. This latter form then appears often to have been rounded by the following **-r** to have given **pòr** [pɔɹ]. The unrounded form **per** is found occasionally:

A **pèr** 'very'
*Nenna e eath car rag Frink rag debre an tacklow ewe **per** trink* 'Then he went away to France to eat the things that are very bitter' LAM: 226
*Ha Deu guelles kanifer tra vo gwres gen e vonnin, ha mero tho vo **perth** da* 'And God saw everything that had been made by himself, and behold it was very good' BF: 53.

The rounded form **pòr**, however, is well attested:

B **pòr** 'very'
*Mars eugh the Arthor **por** wyr, ow thowl ew monas genowgh* 'If you are going to Arthur very truly, my intention is to go with you' BK 1357-58
***por** theffry ny vith kerys neb mar te va re venowgh* 'very truly someone will not be loved if he comes too often' BK 1600-01
*Bethans **por** war!* 'Let them be very careful!' BK 1739
*War ow forth hyr, **por** gentyll ew ha'y uos presyus hag honorys a ve va guyw* 'In the long run, he is very noble and precious is his blood and honoured it was worthily' BK 2013-17
*Henna ew kowsys garow hag a golan stowt **por** wyer* 'That is spoken harshly and from a courageous heart very truly' BK 2404-05

GERYOW GWIR   very

*Nyng es den mar stowt a vyrhe der hot, na'n guren ny **por** dam* 'There is not a man so stowt who would look through a helmet that we will not render very tame' BK 2483-85

*A'y gavow a brederha neffra ny vith da e ger, na vith **por** wyer* 'Who ponders his sorrows never will he be cheerful, he won't very truly' BK 2761-63

*Ow canhas ker, ke thegy bys in Rom gans pen Lucy ha **por** harth the'n senators trybut Bretayn present a* 'My dear messenger, go to Rome with the head of Lucius and very forcefully present it to the senators as Britain's tribute' BK 2838-40

*The leud desyr a'm cuth **por** wyer* 'Your wicked desire afflicts me very truly' BK 2952

*Ny thebbra' boys na nu'm deg troys, ny raf **por** wyr* 'I shall not eat food, I shall not walk, I shall not very truly' BK 2967-69

*Me a ra, syra, **por** wyr* 'I shall, sir, very truly' BK 3028

*Mar ny vethaf curunys, in tan **por** doun te a lysk* 'If I am not crowned, in very deep fire you will burn' BK 3095-96

***Por** wyer o'm gallos ema kekeffrys gul drog ha da* 'Very truly it is in my power to do both evil and good' BK 3112-13

*Rag fraga an arleth ni ewe deawe **por** tha* 'For why our Lord is a very good God' BF: 39

*Etho ve **por** loan tha gwellas why a metten ma* 'I am very glad to see you this morning' ACB: F f *verso*.

In the light of the above quotations, it might be sensible for revivalists to use **pòr** rather than **pur** for 'very' before adjectives and adverbs.

When 'very' is an adjective preceding its noun, Cornish uses **very**:

*an **very** mab du an second person in dryngys according the blonogath y das, a gemeras warnotha an nature a then* 'the very Son of God, the second person of the Trinity according to the will of his Father, took upon himself the nature of man' TH 12a

*mas eff a gemeras an nature a then an **very** substans an wyrhes ker maria y vam* 'but he took the nature of man, the very substance from the Blessed Virgin Mary his mother' TH 12a

*not an ymaginacion a then, mas an **very** gyrryow ha exampill agan Savioure Jhesu crist* 'not the imagination of man, but the very words and example of our Saviour Jesus Christ' TH 21

*An re ma ew an **very** gyrryow agan savyoure ow tochia an kerensa agan kyscristian* 'These are the very words of our Saviour concerning the love of our fellow Christians' TH 22

*hag eff a vith sure na ra crist, an **very** spowse a sans egglos neffra y ankevy* 'and he will be sure that Christ, the very spouse of holy Church, will never forget him' TH 39a

*Ith ew the vos cresys gans oll cristonnyan heb dowt vith y bos in sacrament an aulter an **very** corfe ha gois a crist* 'It is to be believed by all Christians without doubt that the very body and blood of Christ subsist in the sacrament of the altar' TH 54

*ha gvle ny e gorf ef, not der faith only, mas eweth in **very** deed* 'and to make us his body, not by faith only, but also in very deed' SA 59a *neg esa ow desuethas theugh elath nanyle arthelath, mas an **very** corf agen master ha pensevike oll* 'I am not showing you angels nor archangels, but the very body of our master and prince of all' SA 60a

*Pan glowaf the lavaraw, gwryth ow thavas ew pur vans rag **very** scruyth* 'when I hear your words, I become wholly tongue-tied for very horror' BK 973-74

*Rag **very** spyt dyswrys of quit* 'For very spite I am quite destroyed' BK 1016-17

*ty a weall allow ow thryes pan deth ve a baradice en an **very** prynt leskys pan ve an noer malegas* 'you will see the tracks of my feet, when I came from paradice, burnt in the very print when the earth was cursed' CW 1748-51.

It is also to be noted that Tregear never uses **pur**, **pòr** for 'very' before adjectives and adverbs, but instead employs **very** itself:

*Du a wellas pub kynd a ruga gull, ha yth ens **very** da* 'God saw everything he had made and they were very good' TH 3

*ha nena ny a ra whare persevya nag o offence bean mas **very** grevaws ha poos* 'and then we will immediately perceive that is was not a small offence but very grievous and weighty' TH 4

*S Ireneus martyr benegas inweth, **very** ogas eff a ve then tyrmyn an abosteleth* 'St Irenaeus also, a blessed martyr, he was very near to the time of the apostles' TH 18a

*han kyth tra na a yll bos prevys **very** pleyn dre an scripture* 'and that same thing can be proved very plainly by means of scripture' TH 42a

*fatell rug agan sovyour govyn worth pedyr **very** ernysch, mars ega eff worth y gara gara eff moy ys onyn arell an abosteleth* 'that our Saviour asked Peter very earnestly, whether he loved him more than anyone else among the apostles' TH 43-43a

*ow reylya in moyha spytfully a ylly bos, ha gans **very** vylle termes ow jestia gansa* 'railing the most spitefully as possible, and in very vile terms mocking it' TH 55a.

Expressions like **an very geryow** 'the very words', **rag very scruth** 'for very horror', etc. can legitimately be used in the revived language. There is no need, however, to imitate Tregear and to replace **pòr** 'very' with **very**.

VICTORY

For 'victory' Nance suggests A) *****tryhans** (UC *tryghans*); B) *****budhygoleth** and C) **vyctory**. The noun *****tryhans** is unattested, being derived from an equally unattested verb *****tryhy** 'to conquer'. This was devised by Nance on the basis of the root seen in **tryher** 'despot, superior' at OM 1235. B) *****budhygoleth** is also unattested, having been devised on the model of Welsh *buddugoliaeth* 'victory'. The root on which *****budhygoleth** was based seems to be unknown in Cornish apart from the saint's name **Budhek**, found , for example, in *****plu vuthek** 'Budock' at OM 2462.

The Cornish for 'victory' is **vyctory**, which is attested in four different texts:

C **vyctory** 'victory'
*myghtern of a lowene ha'n **victory** eth gyne yn arvow ruth* 'I am king of joy and I won the victory in arms of red' RD 2520-22
*gorthyans the crist caradov grontia dym an **vyctory*** 'glory to beloved Christ for granting me the victory' BM 2497-98
*rag lymmyn nanelle possessyon an bys, na pith an bys, na bewnans here, na gweras a flehes, na **victory** warbyn agan gostly eskerens, ew promysys mas an wlascore a neff, dre an gweras a thu, ha **victory** warbyn an dywolow* 'for now neither worldly possessions nor wordly wealth, nor long life nor the assistance of children nor victory agains our spiritual enemies are promised, but the kingdom of heaven, by the help of God, and victory against the devils' TH 28
*hag eff an jeva an thorne vhella han **victuri*** 'and he had the upper hand and the victory' TH 34
*Pys the Vab ras, hethew ma'm byf an **victory*** 'Beseech your gracious Son, that today I may have the victory' BK 2814-15.

The Cornish for 'victory' is **vyctory**, which may well have been stressed on the second syllable.

VINEYARD

For 'vineyard' Nance suggests ***gwinlan** (UC *gwynlan*) on the basis of Welsh *gwinlan* 'vineyard'. The word actually used in Cornish is attested, however:

vynyard 'vineyard'
*pan rug du dre y profet Esay settya in mes thynny pycture ay egglos in dan an hanow a **vyneyarde*** 'when God through his prophet Isaiah set out for us a picture of his Church under the name of vineyard' TH 40
*me a vyn kemeras theveis an ke aw **vyneyard**, may halla peryssya* 'I will take away the fence of my vineyard, that it may perish' TH 40
*hag eff a suffras an drog pobyll the denna thyn dore an paell han kee ay **vyneyarde*** 'and he allowed evil people to pull down the fence and hedge of his vineyard' TH 40a.

Since **vynyard** is attested three times, it should perhaps be the ordinary word for 'vineyard' in the revived language.

VIOLENCE

For 'violence' Nance *inter alia* suggests ***garowder**. This abstract noun, based on the adjective **garow** 'rough, harsh', is not actually attested.

violence

A further possibility is the word **froth**, which occurs once only in JCH and seems to mean 'disturbance, disharmony':

ha na ve idn ***frôth*** *na mikan na tra uar an nôr vez* 'and there was no disturbance nor malice or anything in the world' BF: 19.

Froth is probably a variant of **fros** (< dialect 'froze') 'tumult, disturbance'. The shift of final **-s** > **-th** is quite common in Cornish, cf. ***fath*** 'face' (for ***fas***) OM 1412, PC 1401, RD 1736, BM 944, 3412; ***grath*** 'grace' (for ***gras***) OM 5, 263, 495, 663, 669, 680, 974, RD 252, 821, BM 346, 2082, etc.

The suggestion that **frôth** is somehow cognate with Welsh *ffrawdd* 'eagerness' and Breton *freuzh* 'havoc, disorder' cannot be sustained. Were Cornish **froth** related to *ffrawdd* and *freuz*, the stressed vowel would have been **e**, not **o**. Lhuyd would have written ****freth*** or ****fredh***.

In short, it seems that there is no one suitable word in Cornish to translate 'violence'. In which case speakers will need to resort to paraphrases, e.g. **gallos asper** 'harsh power', **mêstry garow** 'harsh domination' or the like. Or one could use various metaphors, e.g. **ev a spêdyas dre nerth dygabester** 'he succeeded by unrestrained might (i.e. by violence)', **y a ûsyas fors grysyl rag spêdya in aga thowlow polytyk** 'they used grim force (i.e. violence) to succeed in their political aims'.

VIRGIN

The word **gwerhes** (UC *gwerghes*) *f.* is used only in the singular when referring to the Blessed Virgin Mary and in the plural when talking of virgin martyrs. This can be clearly seen from the attestations of A) the singular **gwerhes** and B) the plural **gwerhesow**:

A **gwerhes** 'virgin'
ihesus crist a ve mevijs may fynnas dijskynna yn ***gwerhas*** *ha bos genys* 'Jesus Christ was moved that he descended into a virgin and to be born' PA 4bc
bynyges re bo an prys may fe a venen genys an ***wyrhes*** *ker maria* 'blessed be the time when he was born of a woman, the Blessed Virgin Mary' RD 152-54
y fue gynys a ***wyrhes*** *ker maria* 'he was born of the Blessed Virgin Mary' RD 1199-200
gorthya crist ker may hallen han ***werhes*** *flour maria* 'so that I may worship dear Christ and the choicest Virgin Mary' BM 630
maria mam ha ***guerhays*** *gueres ov pesy gena* 'Mary mother and virgin, help in praying for me' BM 706-07

GERYOW GWIR virgin

me a beys crist luen a rays in neff theywhy ren tala han **wyrhes** *maria splan* 'I beseech Christ full of grace in heaven that he may repay you and the bright Virgin Mary' BM 754-56

maria mam ha **guerhas** *the vercy du peys ragoen* 'Mary mother and virgin, pray for us for God's mercy' BM 2741-42

maria mam ha **guerhes** *maria da y wothes an charg peys da my ny nyns off* 'Mary mother and virgin, goodly Mary, you know that I am not pleased with the charge' BM 2973-75

Sens the vagyl in the leff in hanov crist us in neff ha maria **guirhes** *pur* 'Hold your crozier in your hand in the name of Christ who is in heaven and of Mary, a pure virgin' BM 3007-09

Maria mam ha **guerhes** *me a vyn the luenbesy* 'Mary mother and virgin, I will pray you earnestly' BM 3591-92

ihesu arluth map **guerheys** *y envy gor theorta* 'Jesus, Lord, son of a virgin, put his enemy from him' BM 3836-37

ihesu crist map maria ha genys a lel **werheys** 'Jesus Christ son of Mary and born of a true virgin' BM 4047-48

Ihesu avan map **guerhes** *splan thyugh ren tala* 'Jesus above, son of a bright virgin, may he repay you' BM 4246-48

Rag henna yth ewa poynt bras a error, the supposya na rug crist kemeras y gyge mes a gyge an **wyrhes** *maria y vam* 'Therefore it is a matter of error to suppose that Christ took his flesh only from the flesh of the Virgin Mary his mother' TH 12a

mar ny rug crist kemeras kygg an **wyrhes** *maria fatell ew an promes ny colynwys* 'if Christ did not take the flesh of the Virgin Mary, how is our promise fulfilled?' TH 13

nessa eff the gemeras dynsys han substans aye gyge in **wyrhes** *maria y vam* 'next, that he took humanity and the substance of his flesh in the Virgin Mary his mother' TH 13a

An here gurtas a crist the rag eff the thos the gemeras carnacion an **wyrhes** *maria nyns o awos lak blonogath da a thu the vab den* 'The long wait of Christ before he came to take incarnation of the Virgin Mary, it was not because of a lack of goodwill of God towards mankind' TH 13a

na vynnas crist then kythsam bankat benegas na cafus naneyll y vam an **wyrhes** *maria present ena gonsa, na onyn vith ay disciplis mas an xii apostell only* 'that Christ did not wish at that same blessed banquet to have either the Virgin Mary present there with him nor any one of his disciples but only the 12 apostles' TH 52a

An kithsam corfe na agan Savyour Jhesu Crist in substans a ve genys an **wyrhes** *maria* 'That same body of our Saviour Jesus Christ in substance was born of the Virgin Mary' TH 54a

Christ a ruge ry then en keith kigge na a ruge ef kemeras vrth an **werthas** *marya* 'Christ gave to us that same flesh which he took from the Virgin Mary' SA 59

Christ a gemeras kigg ha ve genys worth an **worthias** *maria* 'Christ took flesh and was born of the Virgin Mary' SA 61

agen arluth Jesus Christ a ve genis vrth an **Worthias** *Maria* 'our Lord Jesus Christ was born of the Virgin Mary' SA 61a

virgin GERYOW GWIR

ha'y dengys us recevys in Du parfyt, me a grys, a'n **Worthyas** *Ker Marya* 'and his humanity which was received in God without fault, I believe, from the Blessed Virgin Mary' BK 157-59

ha den parfyt mer e ras abarth e vam, **gwyrthyas** *pur* 'and a perfect man on the side of his mother, a pure virgin' BK 198-99.

B **gwerhesow** 'virgins'

Me a vyn, re'n **gwerhesow***! mos thu'm sofran alenha* 'I will, by the virgins, go thence to my sovereign' BK 1308-09

Re'n **gwerhesow***! te 'bew an bys the'th unadow* 'By the virgins, you possess the world at your will' BK 1717-19

Further words for 'virgin' are B) **maghteth** 'maiden, virgin' and C) **vyrjyn** 'virgin'.

B **maghteth** 'maid, maiden, virgin'

y vos ef re leuerys lyes trefeth y'n clewys ma na yl y thynaghe map dev pur ha den keffrys a **vaghteth** *gulan dynythys* 'he has said, I have often heard him, so he cannot deny it, that he is the Son of God and man also born of a pure virgin' PC 1723-27

rak del won sur map dev os pur yn beys gynys a **vaghtyth** *glan* 'for as I know surely you are the pure Son of God born in the world of a spotless virgin' PC 3025-27

maria mam ha **maghteth** *maras us dis chy na plaes oges oma grua ov gedya vy bys dy* 'Mary mother and virgin, if you have a house or place near here guide me thither' BM 634-37

Gorthyans the crist map **maghteth** 'Glory to Christ the son of a virgin' BM 1146

Christ mab an ughella Tas ew Du pur wyer ha den heb nam, a'n Spurys Sans concevyys hag a Varya genys, kekeffrys **mayghtath** *ha mam* 'Christ son of the highest God is pure God in very truth and spotless man, conceived by the Holy Spirt and born of Mary, both maid and mother' BK 170-75.

Durzona dewh, **mathtath** 'God speed you, maid' Borde

Mathtath*, [ro de vy] barow ha dewas* 'Maid, give me bread and drink' Borde

Mathtath *drewgh eyo hag amanyn de vi* 'Maid, bring me eggs and butter' Borde.

The first line of the Cornish song *Pelea era why moaz, moz, fettow, teag* printed by Pryce (ACB: F f 4 *verso*) is rendered in English 'Whither are you going pretty fair maid, said he'. Here the Cornish word *fettow* may be a variant of **maghteth**. If the original was *a vaghteth or *a vathtath, this could have been heard as *vattah or *vattow. By hypercorrection of the initial **v** to **f** this would give *fattow*, not very far from the attested form.

C **vyrjyn** 'virgin'

yma agan savyour crist ow hevely y egglos the lyas tra, indan an hanow a regnum celorum, hen ew gwlascore neff, kepar ha the viterne a rug gull ha provya mariag rag y vab, ha trewethow the *dege **virgin**, ha dre lyas maner forth an par na* 'our Saviour Christ likens his Church to many things, under the name *regnum caelorum*, that is the kingdom of heaven, like a king who made and provided a marriage for his son, and sometimes to a fair virgin, and by many other ways of that kind' TH 31

*an tas a rug der entent in myske oll prevas in bys formya preve henwis serpent hag yth ew wondrys fashes tha **virgin** deke pur havall* 'the Father deliberately created among all reptiles in the world a reptile called Serpent and it is wonderfully fashioned very like a fair virgin' CW 496-500

*now in toppe an wethan deake yth esa vn **virgyn** wheake hay floghe pur semely maylyes vny defran wondrys whans* 'now in the top of the faire tree there was a sweet virgin and her child was wrapped beautifully in her bosom, wondrous cause of longing' CW 1907-10.

As can be seen **maghteth** and **vyrjyn** can be used to refer the the Blessed Virgin, and to other virgin saints also. When speaking of virgins outside a religious context revivalists might be well advised to use either **maghteth** or **vyrjyn**, in preference to **gwerhes**, which in the singular refers exclusively to the Blessed Virgin Mary.

VOICE

The ordinary word for 'voice' is, of course, **lev**, plural **levow**. The borrowing **voys**, **voycys**, however, is widely attested:

voys 'voice'
*Otte **voys** mernans abel the vroder prest ov kelwel a'n dor warnaf pup teller* 'Behold the voice of the death of Abel your brother continually calling on me everywhere from the earth' OM 577-79

*arluth ny vynnons crysy na clewas ov **voys** avy awos me the gous thethe* 'Lord, they will not believe nor hear my voice, in spite of my speaking to them' OM 1435-37

*a pyth yv an keth dev na may reys thy'mmo yn tor ma a clewas ol y **voys** ef* 'Ah, what is that same God, that I must now hear all his voice?' OM 1485-87

*pepenag vo a'n barth wyr a cleufyth ov **voys** yn tyr sarsyn py yethow kyn fo* 'whoever is on the true side will hear my voice in the land though he be Jew or Saracen' PC 2025-27

*Yma oll an comen **voys** gans meryasek ov cul noyys may fo epscop eredy* 'All the common voice is making a noise in favour of Meriasek that he should indeed be bishop' BM 2710-12

*gesow ny oll gans vn accorde the ry thotheff agan **voyses** gans ioy* 'let us all with one accord give him our voices with joy' TH 11

*hen ew dre an **voyce** ma ny a ra vnderstondia mab Jonas, neb o thea Bethsaida, brothar Androw* 'that is, by this voice we will understand the son of Jonah, who was from Bethsaida, brother of Andrew' TH 45a

voice   **GERYOW GWIR**

*saw un **voys** whek a belder a-ughaf in uhelder ow kowsal cler a leveris pur ylyn: Devethys o the dirmyn* 'but a sweet voice from afar in the heavens above said very distinctly speaking clearly: Your time had come' BK 13-7

*ow **voice** oll yta changis* 'my voice, behold it is all changed' CW 530

*yta **voice** mernans abell thethe vrodar prest ow kylwall an doer warnas pub tellar* 'behold the voice of the death of Abel your brother continually calling upon you everywhere from the earth' CW 1155-57

*theth **voice** arluth a glowaf saw tha face me ny wellaf sure er ow gew* 'your voice, Lord, I hear, but your face I cannot see, alas' CW 1166-68.

The word **voys** 'voice' is attested in six different texts. It was clearly part of the vocabulary of spoken Cornish. There is no need to shun it in the revived language.

W

WAGES

The default word for 'wages' has always been **gober**. This word, however, can mean 'reward' as well as 'wages'. It is repeatedly used to mean 'wages' in Jowan Chy an Hordh, of course:

A **gober** 'reward, wages'

an deppro gans cregyans da **gober** *tek eff an geuyth* 'whoever eats it with strong faith will get a fair reward' PA 44d

pe dyth munys kewsovghwy let veth orth agis dysky ha mur nyns yv an **gobrov** 'what ever little utterance you speak will be a hindrance to teaching you and the rewards are not great' BM 96-98

Ty vav prag na ruste dre don agen wagys ome byth ny yllyn soweny boys agen **gober** *hep pee* 'You, boy, why haven't you brought home our wages here. We can never prosper that our remuneration hasn't been paid' BM 3334-37

ken fene ny oll an dythyow agan bewnans kepar ha servans **gober** 'though we be all the days of our lives like paid servants' TH 41

Na illansy bos seperatis in age **gober**, *pan vonsy o gwiell an ober warbarth* 'They cannot be separated in their rewards, since they do the work together' SA 61

yn termyn pan na eyagh **gober** *vyth boz gwelys* 'in a time when no reward could be seen' JKeigwin.

Ena chei a varginiaz rag trei penz an vlethan **gubber** 'Then they agreed on three pence for a year's wages' BF: 15

Meer Jooan meth a vaster; obba tha **gubber** 'Look John, said his master, here are your wages' BF: 15

Nenna chei a varginiaz rag vlethan moy rag pokaar **gubber** 'Then they agreed for another year for the same wages' BF: 15

Meer Jooan meth e vaster, obba da **gubber** 'Look, John, said his master, here are your wages' BF: 15

Meer Jooan meth e vaster obba tha (an) **gubber** 'Look, John, said his master, here are your wages' BF: 16.

The word **waja**, **wajys** 'wages' is also well attested:

wages

B **waja**, **wajys** 'wage, wages'

*the vantel gas yn gage my a'n byth rag ov **wage** ha ty a grek ren othas* 'leave your cloak as a pledge and I'll have it for my wage and you'll hang, by my father' PC 1186-88

*me a leuer an guyr thy's the pe yma ow **wagys** ny fynnaf tryge genes* 'I will tell you the truth; my wages are yet to be paid. I will not stay with you' PC 2256-58

*ny yllyn pee agen rent the guel awos y **wagis** mar ny veth thyn arluth guel ny venen bones na pel by my sovle dotho pagys* 'we cannot pay our rent better because of his wages. If he is not a better master to us, we will not be long, upon my soul, servants to him' BM 3264-68

*ser turant agys pagys sur ny vynnons fovt **wagys** vn stap lafurye adro* 'sir tyrant, your pages surely will not for lack of wages travel one step further' BM 3284-86

*guelheys yv ages nygys by my fay y feth **wagis** ha henna wy a clowyth* 'your business has been improved. Upon my faith there will be wages and that you will hear' BM 3316-18

*Ty vav prag na ruste dre don agen **wagys** ome* 'you, boy, why did you not bring our wages home here?' BM 3334-35.

The word **wajys** 'wages' is both well attested and unambiguous. It should perhaps be used alongside **gober** for 'wages'.

WALES

For 'Wales' Nance recommends ***Kembry** *f.*, even though he was aware that Lhuyd gives **Kimbra** with a final **-a** (i.e. schwa) rather than **-y**. In fact Lhuyd also writes **Kembra**. Here are the attestations of the name in Lhuyd's writing:

*ʒen a nei en **Kembra*** 'with us in Wales' AB: 222
*Tîz **Kimbra*** 'the Men of Wales' AB: 222
*Tîz **Kembra*** 'the Men of Wales' AB: 223
*Tîz Guenez **Kembra*** 'the Men of South East Wales' AB: 223
*ken yu hedda rêol por uîr en **Kembra*** 'though that is truly a rule in Wales' AB: 224.

Nance presumably assumed that Wales was ***Kembry** in Cornish with a final high front voewl in the second syllable because the Welsh form was *Cymru*, which is historically identical with *Cymry* 'Welshmen'. This is from pre-Welsh < *Kombrogî, plural of *Kombrogos 'fellow countryman, Welshman'.

There can be no doubt, however, that Lhuyd's form **Kembra**, **Kimbra** was authentic and that Nance was mistaken. This can be seen first from the personal names *Richard **Kembre*** 'Richard of Wales', *John **Kembre*** 'John of Wales' from 1327 (CPNE: 48), where the final **-e** of **Kembre** would by Lhuyd's time have developed as **-a**. Secondly, **Kembra** is now attested in Cornish literature itself:

a Dowl an Jowl in **Kembra** 'from the Devil's Drop in Wales' BK 1164
Yma tregys in **Kembra** *in Urbe Legionum* 'He lives in Wales in the City of the Legions' BK 1292-93.

It should also be pointed out the traditional word for 'Welsh language' is **Kembrek**: *Thera moy* **Gembrack** *peath rig ea gweele* 'What he did was more Welsh' (Oliver Pender, LAM: 238). The adjectival ending has been added directly to the stem **Kembr-**.

To sum up, the Cornish for 'Wales' is **Kembra** *f.*, not ***Kembry**. 'Welsh language' is **Kembrek**.

TO WANDER

For 'to wander' Nance suggests **gwandra** and ***rôsya** (UC *rosya). Nance appears to have devised ***rôsya** on the basis of a dialectal usage of the English verb 'to rouse', i.e. 'to move energetically'. Nance apparently took this form and ascribed to it the sense of Welsh *rhodio* 'to walk, to stroll'. Welsh *rhodio* and English 'to rouse' are unrelated, however, and there is no evidence that a verb ***rôsya** or ***rowsya** ever existed in Cornish.

The verb **gwandra** 'to wander, to walk' on the other hand is well attested:

gwandra 'to wander, to walk'
*Sa ban noe ow seruont ker dus gene pols the **wandre*** 'Get up, Noah, my dear servant and come with me a while to walk about' OM 933-34
*dvn alemma cowythe war menythyow the **wandre** ha the pigy* 'let us go hence, comrades, to roam upon the mountains and to pray' PC 107-09
*messeger me a'th pys ke aberth yn pow the **wandre** vn pols byan* 'messenger, I pray you, go into the country to wander about a little while' RD 1633-35
*dre an grace na eff a gotha thetha bos the well establysses in gothfas a wryoneth ha the **wandra** in gwryoneth* 'through that grace they should be the better established in the knowledge of the truth and to walk in the truth' TH 14a
*Walkyow ha **gwandrow** warlyrth an spuris* 'Walk and roam according to the spirit' TH 16a
*me a vyn mos tha **wandra** omma yn myske an flowrys* 'I will go and wander here among the flowers' CW 538
*sera ha me ow **gwandra** me a glowas awartha war an weathan ven eal wheake sure ow cana* 'sir, when I was wandering I heard above in the tree a sweet angel singing indeed' CW 757-60

wander

*ny won py theth tha **wandra*** 'I don't know where he has wandered off to' CW 1197
*me a vyn kyns es hethy mos alema ha **gwandra*** adro in powe 'I will forthwith go from here and wander about in the country' CW 1217-19
*rag henna saf y praytha ha gas cavow ʒa **wandra** me ne brederaf gwell for* 'therefore get up, I pray you, and let sorrow go wander. I cannot think of a better way' CW 1242-44
*cuntell warbarth ow fegans me a vyn mos pur vskys ha woʒa hemma dewans pell in devyth tha **wandra*** 'Gather together my possessions I will very quickly and after this immediately go into the desert to wander' CW 1293-96
*me a vyn mos tha **wandra** bestas gwylls tha asspeas* 'I will go roaming to spy out the wild animals' CW 1489-90
*Ha Jesus, **gwandra** reb a Môr Alale wellas deaw broderath Simnen criez Peder, ha Andrew e broder* 'And Jesus wandering by Lake Galilee saw two brothers, Simon called Peter, and Andrew his brother' Rowe.

The verb **gwandra** 'to wander' was so much part of the Cornish vocabulary that a noun was derived from it, **gwandryas** 'wanderer', *plural* **gwandresy**:

*lymmyn rag henna nyns owgh why strangers ha **gwandresy**, mas yth owhy citesens gans ans an syns* Now therefore you are no more strangers and wanderers, but you are citizens with the saints TH 33.

The Cornish for 'to wander, to roam' is **gwandra**. There is no need for the unwarranted verb ***rôsya**, *****rowsya**.

TO WANT TO

Revivalists have been taught that **me a vydn mos** means 'I want to go'. This is not really true. **Me a vydn mos** means quite simply 'I will go' with little if any implied volition. This can clearly be seen for example from the following examples:

A

*pronter boys me a garse corff ihesu thy venystra mar **myn** ov descans servya* 'I should like to be a priest to administer Christ's body, if my learning will serve' BM 522-24.

B

*So my a **vyn** agys desyrrya why, tus tha oll, the settia agys corfow hagys enevow hooll the thu galosek in sacryfice* 'But I will desire you, all good men, to set your bodies and souls entirely to Almighty God in sacrifice' TH 35

C

*Ne **vedn** e nevra dvz vês a ʒyndan* 'He will never get out of debt' AB: 230c

In A there is no volition implied in **myn** since the subject is *ov descans* 'my learning, my education', which cannot be definition desire anything. In B there is volition in the verb **desîrya**. There is none in *me a vyn*. Tregear is not saying 'I shall want to desire you to' but 'I shall desire you' In C the person spoken of may indeed wish to get out of debt, but is too poor to do so. No volition is implied.

In Cornish if one wishes to say, 'I want to go, I wish to go, I should like to go' one uses the conditional of the verb **cara** 'to love', i.e. **y carsen**, **me a garsa**, etc. This can be seen from the following examples:

y carsen, **me a garsa** 'I want, I should like'
*er y byn mennaf mones me a **garse** y weles ef yw dev luen a pite* 'I will go to meet him. I want to see him. He is God full of pity' PC 232-34
*a **garsesta** bynene mar mynnyth war ow ene me a gergh onan dek thy's* 'do you want a wench? If you do, upon my soul, I'll fetch you a pretty one' PC 2838-40
*dun alemma cowethe y weles me a **garse** owth astel ymthreheuel* 'Let's go from here, comrades. I want to see him vainly attempting to rise' RD 393-95
*y weles me a **garse** ha cous orth ow map ihesu* 'I want to see him and speak to my son Jesus' RD 435-36
*the voth sur mar pe genes guelas ow map y **carsen*** 'if it were your will, I would like to see my son' RD 441-42
*y **carsen** guelas an fvu anotho y voth mar pe* 'I would like to see the sight, were it his wish' RD 469-70
*cous ganso me a **garse** y volungeth mara pe* 'I would like to talk to him, if it were his wish' RD 744-45
*cryst ow sylwyas clev mar a'th dur thy's daryvas del **garsen** mur* 'Christ, my Saviour, if you care, I would very much like to tell you' RD 845-46
*gans golyas ha gans pynys me a **garsa** crist ʒe plesya* 'with vigil and with fasting I want to please Christ' BM 164-66
*bones sacris marrek du an order mur thym a plek benitha hedre ven byv me a **garse** lowenek* 'to be consecrated a knight of God of the great order which pleases me for ever as long as I live, I would like joyfully' BM 350-53
*pronter boys me a **garse** corff ihesu thy venystra* 'I would like to be a priest to administer the body of Christ' BM 522-23
*the kernov mars egh defry mones genogh y **carsen*** 'if you are going to Cornwall, I wish to go with you' BM 588-89
*rag mur y **carsen** defry guthel thymmo oratry in herwyth chy maria* 'for greatly I would like to build myself an oratory close to the church of Mary' BM 638-40
*Prag ymons y in ponfos ny ruk truspus thum gothfos dethe na the den in beys myns may hallen omguythe na ny **garsen** benythe gans weres du benegys* 'Why are they in sorrow? I never to my knowledge did them any wrong nor to any man in the world as far as I could, nor would I want to ever with the help of blessed God' BM 1987-91

*byth ny **garsen** gul da certen na y predery dyogel* 'I would never want to do good indeed nor to think it certainly' BM 2341-43

*yma drok turant in pow ny **garsen** orto metya* 'there is an evil tyrant in the land; I do not wish to meet him' BM 3206-07

*Me a **garsa** thotha ef dusquethas unwyth pew of* 'I want just want to show him who I am' BK 2067-68

*Me a **garsa** in tefry cafas gorthyb in certan* 'I want indeed to have an answer certainly' BK 2100-01

*me a **garsa** gul both the vrys, ow arluth ker* 'I wish to do the wish of your heart, my dear lord' BK 2851-53.

In Cornish **me a vydn y wil** means 'I will do it'. 'I want to do it' is best rendered **Me a garsa y wil**.

TO WAGE WAR, WARRIOR, WAR

The Cornish for 'to wage war, to make war' is **gwerrya**, which is attested once:

*menogh y car ewyas ha **guerrya** purthyogel* 'often he likes to ride out and to make war' BM 3453-54.

The Cornish for 'warrior' is better attested:

gwerrour 'warrior'

*Lowena this, myghtern freth, **gwerror** fers ha galosak!* 'Hail to you, stalwart king, a fierce and mighty warrior!' BK 1996-97

*Me, Excerces, ew **guerror** fers ha myghtern in Itury* 'I, Excerces, am a fierce warrior and king of Ituria' BK 2597-99

*Pollitetes, **gwerryor** stowt* 'Pollitetes, a courageous warrior' BK 2706

*Lemmyn, ow **gwerrors** gwelha, dun ahanan in un rowt* 'Now, my finest warriors, let us depart in a host' BK 2787-88

*Ow **guerrors** da ha worthy, prederough a'gys huneth, awell tus del russans y subjectia ol Christonath* 'My good and worthy warriors, remember your forebears, how as men they subjected all Christendom' BK 2800-03

*Marow ew Lucy heb gyl ha'y **werrors** in katap myl, mars an cowars re scapyas* 'Dead is Lucius without a lie and all the thousands of his warriors, unless the cowards have escaped' BK 2832-35.

Nance taught that the Cornish for 'war' was **bresel** *m*. or *f*., and revivalists have followed him. Nance was presumably influenced by Breton *brezel m.* 'war'. Although the word **bresel** is certainly attested in Cornish, it does not mean 'war', but rather 'dispute, disagreement, insubordination'. This can seen from the following examples:

bresel 'dispute, insubordination'

***bresell** cref a ve sordijs en grows pu elle ȝy don dre vur stryff y fe iuggijs ys degy crist y honon* 'A strong dispute was raised about the cross, who was going to carry it. As the result of much contention it was agreed that Christ himself should bear it' PA 160cd

*Ternoys y sordyas **bresel** gans an eȝewon goky lauarow tyn hag vghel fest yn foll y a gewsy* 'On the next day a dispute arose among the foolish Jews. Words sharp and loud very foolishly they uttered' PA 238ab

*Aron whek pyth a cusyl a reth thy'm orth an **vresyl** a son a'n debel bobel rag dewes mar nys tevyth yn certan y a dreyl fyth hag a worth dewow tebel* 'Dear Aaron, what advice to you give me about the dispute and murmuring of the evil people, for if they do not get drink, certainly they will turn their faith and will worship evil gods?' OM 1813-18

*rak ef a gergh thyworthy'n kemmys na worthyo iouyn hag a wra thy'n drok **bresul*** 'for he will carry off from us all who do not worship Jovyn, and will cause us an ill contest' PC 1916-18

*A consler cam, pyth ew cusyl orth an **wrusyl**?* 'O crooked advisor, what remedy is there agains the insubordination?' BK 967-69

*Nyng es myghtern in neb gwlas na wothvean, rennothas! dystogh lyha e **vrusyl*** 'There is no king in any country, whose insubordination, by my father, I could not immediately lessen' BK 1305-07

***Bressel**, a contest, an argument* ACB: L 3.

The expression **gùstla bell** occurs once in PA:

Ena pylat pan glewas yndelma y ȝe gewsell prederow an kemeras rag own y ȝe leuerell ha ȝy notye drys an wlas sur a ogas hag a bell may teffe tus gans nerth bras er [y] *byn rag **gustle bell*** 'Then Pilate, when he heard that they spoke thus, anxiety overcame him for fear that they would say and make it known throughout the country far and wide so that men with great force might come against him to cause a riot' PA 249a-d.

Gùstla is not otherwise known, but it may possibly be related to Welsh **gwst** 'labour, fighting'. It is more likely however, that **gùstla** is to be understood as ***gwystla** 'to pledge, to pawn, to chance', a verb derived from the root seen in *obses*, **guistel** 'hostage' OCV §174. The second element **bell** in the phrase **gùstla bell** might be a nonce borrowing from Latin *bellum* 'war'. In which case **gùstla bell** might best be translated 'to risk a war'. Unfortunately both the origin and sense of the phrase are so uncertain, that it would be unwise to base anything upon it.

Since there appears to be no unambiguous attested word in the texts for 'war', I recommend using the neologism ***gwerryans** 'warring, warfare, war', a noun based on the verb **gwerrya** 'to wake war' found in *Beunans Meriasek*.

waste

TO WASTE, TO LAY WASTE

For 'to waste' i.e. 'to squander' Nance recommends A) **scùllya** (UC *scullya*, *scollya*) ; B) **wastya**; and C) ***ufera**. This last verb is unattested, having been devised on the basis of **ufer** 'worthless'. **Scùllya** really means 'to pour out, to shed':

A scùllya

lauar lemyn ty jhesu pan [dokyn us] a vertu a thysquythysta thy'nny pan wreta mar coynt fara ow **scollye** *agan guara ha'n fer orth y tystrywy* 'say now, you Jesus, what token of authority will you show us that you behave so oddly, scattering our wares and destroying the market?' PC 337-42

me a vyn mos the vre ow arluth treys ha devle gans onement ker yn certan ha war y pen y **scullye** 'I will go to anoint my Lord, feet and hands, with expensive ointment indeed and to pour it over his head' PC 473-76

pyth yv an ethom vye an onyment ker y **skullye** *ef a galse bos guyrthys a try cans dyner ha moy* 'what is the need there would be to pour out the expensive ointment? It could have been sold for 300 pence and more' PC 533-36

en keth oynement a **scollyas** *warnaf rak ow anclythyas hy a'n gruk dre kerense* 'the same ointment which she poured over me for my burial, she did it for love' PC 547-49

eveugh lemyn ol an gwyn rag hemma yv ow gos fyn hag a vyth ragough **skullys** 'drink now all the wine for this is my fine blood which will be shed for you' PC 823-25

me a's ten gans ol ov nerth mayth entre an spikys serth dre an cen yn y grogen ha **scullye** *y ympynnyon* 'I will yank it with all my strength so that the sharp spikes may enter into his skull through the skin and scatter his brains' PC 2139-42

syr iustis me agas pys rak pask may fo dyllyfrys barabas hep **skullye** *y wos* 'sir justice, I beseech you for passover that Barabbas be released without shedding his blood' PC 2368-70

rak y wos a vyth **scollys** *rag ef yv map dev a nef del leuaraf an guyr thy's* 'for his blood shall be shed, for he is the Son of God of heaven, as I tell you the truth' PC 2460-62

mara tue in the ogoys eff a ra **scollya** *the goys ellas ateve ena* 'if he comes near you he will shed your blood. Alas, there he is!' BM 1106-08

guetyogh omprevy manly then cristunyan **scollya** *goys na sparyogh yowynk na loys* 'bear yourselves in manly fashion: do not hesitate to shed the blood of the Christians, young and old' BM 1194-96

broder povle duen alema the confortya costenten rag na **scollyas** *goys an flehas* 'brother Paul, let us go hence to comfort Constantine for he has not shed the children's blood' BM 1696-99

Drefen na russys **scollia** *goys then ynocens oma crist dys agen danvonas* 'Since you did not shed the blood of the innocents, Christ has sent us to you here' BM 1707-09

me am beth goys the golon **scollys** *omma war an ton kyns hy bos nos* 'I shall have your blood spilt here upon the grass before nightfall' BM 3494-96

Bo me a vyn **scollya** *the lyn oma war ton* 'Or I will shed your blood here upon the grass' BM 3503-05

aga threis ew paris rag **skollia** *goos* 'their feet are ready to shed blood' TH 7a *hag vnwith rag oll in sacrament ay wosse suffrys vel* **scollis** *war an growspren* 'and once for all in the sacrament of his blood tormented or shed upon the cross' TH 11

gwenys dre an assow then golon gans spera, hay woys precyous a ve **scollys** 'pierced through the ribs to the heart by a spear, and his precious blood was shed' TH 15a

Byner re gymmyrryf boys, mar ny **scollya**' *ve ow goys orth e socra, mar pyth rys* 'May I never take food, if I do not shed my blood assisting him, if it is necessary' BK 1458-60

ha mar petha indella me a vidn ye requyrya a thewla an kethe dean na y woose a theffa **scullya** 'and if it be thus, I will require it from the hands of that same man who sheds his blood' CW 2519-22.

'To waste, to squander' is perhaps better rendered by **wastya**:

A **wastya** 'to waste, to squander'

na ***wast*** *na moy lauarow rak gowegneth ny garaf* 'do not waste any more words, for I do not like falsehood' RD 905-06

rag henna theth[o] cregye me ny vannaf moy es kye na mendya ny venyn ny awoos theth gyrryan ***wastys*** 'therefore I will not believe you more than a dog, nor will amend because of your wasted words' CW 2359-62.

For 'to lay waste' Nance recommends ***dyfythya**, a word of his own devising. The attested word is **wastya** 'to waste, to squander' is used in this context also:

B **wastya** 'to lay waste, to ravage'

Pur doun ny a'n ***wyst*** *neb ur, ol maga stowt del omwre* 'Very profoundly shall we ravage him at some time, however nonchalant he pretend to be' BK 1842-43

An Romans a vyth ***wystyys****, ymstorvye pan na alhons* 'The Romans shall be ravaged, since they cannot starve themselves' BK 2136-37

Laver thu'm tas caradaw, me a'n ***west*** *ha ke napell* 'Tell my dear father, I shall ravage him [i.e. Arthur] and go a little distance' BK 2410-11.

Scùllya does not really mean 'to waste' but 'to pour out, to shed'. The ordinary word for 'to waste, to squander' is **wastya** and that is also used to mean 'to lay waste, to ravage'.

WAY

For 'way' Nance suggests A) **fordh** (UC *forth*) *f*.; B) **tres**; and C) **hens**. **Fordh** is the ordinary word for 'road, way' and is attested at all periods. Here are a very few examples:

rag henna ȝe bob dyȝgthtya ***forth*** *a rug the vos sylwys* 'therefore for everyone he provided a way to be saved' PA 7d

way   **GERYOW GWIR**

ny dyf guels na flour yn bys yn keth **forth** *na may kyrthys* 'no grass nor flower at all grows in the way I walked' OM 712-13

nag vs **forth** *thy'mmo ellas the vos sylwys ru'm leaute* 'there is no way, alas, for me to be saved, upon my faith' PC 1523-24

del leuaraf yn tor ma honna yv an **forth** *wella* 'as I say now, that is the best way' RD 581-82

ens pub the ʒeys thy gela nynsus oma **forth** *nahen* 'let everyone go to confess to his fellow; there is no other way' BM 607-08

han **furrow** *a cres y ny aswannas* 'and the ways of peace they have not recognized' TH 7a

kepar ha den a vo gyllys mes ay **forth** *in sowthan the belha ha the weusa* 'like a man who has gone astray from his way further and more mistaken' TH 17a

Fystyn! Na let! Ke a'th **forth***!* 'Hurry! Don't delay! Go on your way!' BK 2354

na gymmar dowt na mystrust mes an **for** *a vyth kevys* 'do not fear of be mistrustful, but the way will be found' CW 1744-45

Gwra owna guz **furu***, Hithow, po avorou, Ha why*[*l*] *boz dean dah whath* 'Mend your ways today or tomorrow and you can be a good man yet' ACB: F f 4.

The other two items are more problematic. **Tres** is attested once only and does not mean 'way' but 'occasion':

an nyl torn y fyth ro hyr **tres** *aral re got in guyr ken fo mar len musurys* 'at one moment it will be too long, on another occasion too short indeed, though it be so precisely measured' OM 2548-50.

There is no evidence at all that **tres** was ever used with the sense 'way, track' in Cornish.

The word **hens** 'way' is not attested at all as a noun. It has been conjectured from the presence of the root **-hins-**, **-ens-** in *camhinsic* 'injurious, unjust' OCV §§306, 403; *cammensyth*, **kammynsoth** 'injustice' TH 15, 15a and *eunhinsic* 'just' OCV §402. The word may also occur in the toponym ***Keballans*** (= King Harry Ferry) < ****caubalhint***; cf. Old Breton *Caubal hint* 'ferry'. Since we have no certain evidence that the simpled ****hens***, ****hyns*** ever occurred in Cornish, it is probably best to avoid it as far as possible. There is one place, however, where its use cannot be proscribed, namely in the neologism **hens horn** 'railway'.

If one wants to use an attested Cornish word for 'way, path' one can use **trûlergh** 'path, footpath' < *semita* ***trulerch*** 'footpath' OCV §712.

WELCOME, TO WELCOME

Outside towns in Cornwall it is quite common to see bilingual notices that read, for instance, 'Welcome to Camborne' in English and **Cambron a'gas dynergh** in Cornish, where **dynergh** is the 3rd person singular of **dynerhy** 'to greet'. It should be pointed out, however, that in the traditional texts the verb **dynerhy** is used of a messenger conveying a message of greeting to somebody in that person's own dwelling. This can be seen in the following:

dynerhy 'to greet'
*syre pilat lowene thy's genef yth os **dynerghys** gans cesar an emperour* 'sir Pilate, joy to you; you are greeted by the Caesar, the emperor, through me' RD 1627-29

*Banneth crist re bo genes **dynerugh** arlythy an gluaes thymo vy ha meryasek* 'May the blessing of Christ be with you. Greet the lords of the land for me and for Meriasek' BM 2781-83

*Lucy a'gys **dynnyrhes**, ut es potens in bono, saw e golan ew cuthys rag galaraw* 'Lucius greets you, as you are powerful in doing good, but his heart is afflicted by sorrow' BK 2389-92

*Myghtern Arthur a'th **tynnyrhys** ha thys gena' pen Syr Lucy, war ow ena! rag degevy ew danvenys* 'King Arthur greets you and to you by me is sent the head of Sir Lucius, upon my soul as his tithe' BK 2857-63.

The same is true of the noun **dynargh** 'greeting' which is taken to someone, not given to him on his arrival:

dynargh 'greeting'
*syr arluth theugh lowene ov arlothes sur gyne dre **thynnargh** agas pygys na wrellough cammen lathe an profus a nazare* 'Sir lord, joy to you. My lady certainly with a greeting sent with me has besought you that you should not in any way kill the prophet of Nazareth' PC 2193-97

*E tof, ru'm sergh a garaf suer! eth a **dynnergh** bys in Arthur* 'I swear by my sweetheart, whom I surely love, a greeting will go unto Arthur' BK 1735-38.

It is clear that **dynargh** does not mean 'a welcome' and **dynerhy** is not an apt translation for 'to welcome'. In Cornish the relevant words to translate 'welcome' are A) the adjective **wolcùm, welcùm** 'welcome' and B) the verb **welcùmma, wolcùmma** 'to welcome'. Both are well attested:

A **welcùm, wolcùm**
***wolcom** pilat by thys day* 'welcome, Pilate, by this day!' PC 379
***wolcom** by mahommys blout dues nes hagh yse gene* 'Welcome, by Mahomet's blood, come near and sit by me' PC 575-76

welcome **GERYOW GWIR**

wolcom *iudas par mon fay* **wolcom** *by maghomys lay* **wolcom** *mylwyth yn ow hel* 'welcome, Judas, by my faith, welcome by Mahomet's creed, a thousand times welcome in my hall!' PC 935-37
wolcum *fest ough yn chymma* 'you are very welcome in this house' PC 1207
wolcom *kayfas ru'm leaute ty hag ol the gowethe certan y'm hel* 'welcome, Caiaphas, by my loyalty, you and all your companions certainly in my hall!' PC 1579-81
wolcom *cayphas re iouyn and yk annas me cosyn hag ol agas cowethe* 'welcome, Caiaphas, by Jovyn, and also Annas, my cousin, and all your companions!' PC 1687-89
mars yv hemma an ihesu **wolcom** *yv re'n arluth dev* 'if that is the Jesus, he is welcome by the Lord God' PC 1699-700
mestrygy **wolcom** *y'm tour* 'welcome, masters, to my tower' PC 1711
wolcom *ens re'n arluth dev otte theugh myghtern ihesu athyragough ow seuel* 'they are welcome by the Lord God. Behold a king for you, Jesus standing before you' PC 2353-55
a pylat **wolcom** *os fest rak me a'th car dev yn test* 'O Pilate, you are very welcome for I love you, as God is my witness' RD 1811-12
wolcom *ow map os yn nef* **wolcom** *fest osy gynef yse thy'mmo athyow* 'welcome, my son, are you in heaven. You are very welcome with me. Sit on my right side' RD 2625-27
Meryasek **welcum** *yn tre ham luen vanneth y rof ʒys* 'Meriasek, welcome home, and I give you my full blessing' BM 216-17
Wolcum *ogh ov lyche worʒy* **wolcum** *ogh omma deffry wy hag ol agis pobell* 'Welcome are you, my worthy liege, welcome are you here indeed, you and all your people' BM 240-42
Welcom *ogh agan soueran yn keth plass ma pur certan plesijs one agis gwelas* 'Welcome are you, our sovereign, in this same place indeed. We are pleased to see you' BM 246-48
welcumma *den benary nefre ny ʒue yn ov chy kyn teff' ov ʒas am denes* 'never will a more welcome man come to my house, though it were my father who brought me up' BM 249-51
Welcum *omma lych ryall del ogh pen ha princypall dreson ny ol yn tyan* 'Welcome are you, royal liege, as you are the head and principal over us all entirely' BM 252-54
Wolcum *oma meryasek me re glowes ov map wek ahanes covs mur thadder* 'Welcome here, Meriasek. I have heard, my dear son, much goodness spoken of you' BM 526-28
Wolcum *oys genen dremas ny ath wor the pen an gluas dre voth du kyn pen sythen* 'Welcome are you with us, good man. We will take you to Land's End, God willing, within a week' BM 593-95
Wolcum *knyghtis euerych on* 'Welcome, knights, every one' BM 1178
Wolcum *maseger ylyn oys oma war ov ena* 'Welcome, bright messenger, are you upon my soul' BM 1400-01
A **wolcum** *ser epscop flour* **wolcum** *inweth ser doctour dugh inban me agis peys* 'Oh, welcome, sir choicest bishop, welcome also, sir doctor; come up, I beg you' BM 1434-36
Seluester **wolcum** *owhy* 'Silvester, you are welcome' BM 1767
Ser ʒurle ov arluth worthy oma **wolcum** *sur owhy* 'Sir earl, my worthy lord, you are welcome here indeed' BM 2704-05

GERYOW GWIR   welcome

Wolcum *yth os ov map wek den grassyes yv meryasek del glowys y acontia* 'You are welcome, my dear son. Meriasek is a gracious man, as I have heard recounted' BM 2763-65

Maseger ***wolcum*** *yth os lemmen ens tus then guelfos the kerhes dyn meryasek* 'Messenger, you are welcome now. Let men go to the wilderness to fetch Meriasek to us' BM 2793-95

Wolcum *ser ʒurle be thys day* ***wolcum*** *ser epscop worthy* ***wolcum*** *yv myns us genegh* 'Welcome, sir earl, by this day, welcome, sir worthy bishop, welcome is everbody who is with you' BM 2887-89

Wolcum *ser ʒurle caradov* ***wolcum*** *owhy epscobov* 'Welcome, beloved sir earl, welcome are you, bishops' BM 2902-03

Wolcum *oys ov servont len then guylfos mones lemen ny a vyn sur ʒe sportya* 'Welcome are you, my faithful servant; we will now go to the wilderness indeed to hunt' BM 3202-04

A ***wolcum*** *the dre gargesen* 'A, welcome home, you glutton' BM 3322

Now ***wolcum*** *ffadyr bischyp ny thue dragon me a dyp oges thyny* 'Now welcome, father bishop; no dragon will come near us, I think' BM 3936-38

eugh bo tregugh ***wolcum*** *vethugh kyn fewy sythen omma* 'go or remain, you will be welcome though you remain a week here' BM 4566-68

Wylcom*, gentyl Pen Taraw. Mer syngys of the'th cara del os body heb paraw* 'Welcome, gentle Bull Head. I am greatly bound to love you, as you are a peerless person' BK 394-96

Wylcom*, Ke, ha me a'th pys, orthave na vith serrys rag gule the voth me a vyn* 'Welcome, Ke, and I beg you, do not be angry with me for I will do your will' BK 1070-72

Welcum*, cosin, by my soul! Mos the Arthor ew ou thowl* 'Welcome, cousin, by my soul! To go to Arthur is my intention' BK 1346-47

Me a'n to theugh, re Gorran! pur ***welcum*** *ough genan ny del on guer freth in casow* 'I swear to you, by St Gorran! you are very welcome with us, as we are fierce men in battles' BK 1362-64

kyn tryken bys woyl Myhal, ***wylcum*** *ny a vyth ena* 'though we stay till Michaelmas, we shall be welcome there' BK 1377-78

Byanvenu, mes bels amors! Kyn fewhy cans pe pelha, ***welcom*** *mylwyth, ow sokors!* 'Welcome, my dear friends! Though you were a hundred or more, a thousand times welcome, my allies!' 1546-48

Benevenistis, domini! ***Welcom*** *ough genaf in suer* 'You are welcome, noble sirs. With me indeed you are welcome' BK 1618-19

Mylwyth ***welcum*** *ough gena'!* 'A thousand times welcome are you with me!' BK 1623

Welcum*, amors, owgh why pupprys!* ***Welcom****, sokers, drys tus an bes owhy heb mar!* 'Welcome, dear friends, are you always! Welcome, allies, beyond men in the world are you indeed!' BK 1730-34

Wylcum*, tus vas, owhy thymmo* 'Welcome, good men, are you to me' BK 1806

Wylcum *owhy arag ow sal,* ***wylcum*** *yns y, ha, re Vehal!* ***wylcum*** *ough ol* 'Welcome are you before those in my hall, welcome are they, and by St Michael, you all are welcome!' BK 1811-15

welcome   **GERYOW GWIR**

Senator mas, **welcum***, forsoyth, drefen the ras ha'th vos arluth a'n goys ryal* 'Welcome, good senator, indeed, because of your grace and because you are lord of the royal blood' BK 1904-08

Marrogyon flowr, **wylcum** *o'm tyr* 'Choicest knights, welcome to my country' BK 1946-47

Welcum *o'm gwlas, agys messag mars ew vas* 'Welcome to my country, if your message is good' BK 2010-11

Welcum *pan owgh devethys!* 'Welcome since you have come!' BK 2219

Canhas, **welcum** *os sertan* 'Messenger, you are welcome indeed' BK 2396

Welcum *oge, Gardyben! Ny thoutyaf an nowothow* 'Welcome are you, Gardyben! I do not doubt the news' BK 2428-29

Welcum*, canhas ker! Pan gerth ha pan ger?* 'Welcome, dear messenger! What expedition and what mood?' BK 2458-59

Welcum *os, flowr canhasow,* **welcum** *melwith, ru'm ena'!* 'You are welcome, choicest of messengers, a thousand times welcome, upon my soul!' BK 2530-31

Welcum *ough, arlythy mas, ha Du re thanvanna ras warnough in katap huny!* 'You are welcome, good lords, and may God send grace upon you every one!' BK 2570-72

Welcum *os, Myghtern Partys, ha Myghtern Egyp kefrys!* **Welcum***, Myghtern Babylon!* **Welcum***, Mightern Spain deffry!* **Welcum***, Myghtern Itury hag inweth Myghtern Lyby!* **Welcum** *in cres ow holan!* 'Welcome are you, King of the Parthians, and the King of Egypt also! Welcome, King of Babylon! Welcome, King of Spain, indeed! Welcome, King of Ituria and also King of Lybia! Welcome from the bottom of my heart!' BK 2640-46

Welcum*, arlythy gwlasaw! Gormolys theugh ha grasaw, rag why a'm car, me a wel* 'Welcome, lords of countries! Praise to you and thanks, for you love me, I see' BK 2707-09

Welcum*, canhas, re Jowan!* 'Welcome, messenger, by St John!' BK 3038

Welcum *os, ow ebscob mas!* **Welcum** *os heb falladow, mer* **welcum** *avel ow thas* 'You are welcome, my good bishop! You are welcome without fail, as welcome as my father' BK 3070-72

Welcum*, cosyn Chellery! Gans gweras ahanowgh why ow eskar a vith lethis* 'You are welcome, cousin Childerich! With your help my enemy will be killed' BK 3245-47

rag der tha ere yth falsa ty tha thos an nef totheta ha mara tethe alena pur **welcom** *yth ose genaf ha tha well ythe fythe cregys* 'for by what you say it would seem that you have come at speed from heaven, and if you come thence, you are very welcome with me and you will better be believed' CW 565-69

welcom *eva os benynvas mars ew an nowothow da te a vythe rewardyes* 'you are welcome, Eve, good woman. If the news is good, you will be rewarded' CW 731-33

welcom *os Seyth genaf ve pana nowethis es genas* 'welcome to me are you, Seth. What news have you?' CW 1885-86

Welcom *a whe, gwr[e]ac da* 'You are welcome good wife' Borde

ha **uelkom** *ti a vêdh* 'and you will be welcome' BF: 17

ha **uelkym** *ti a vêdh* 'and you will be welcome' BF: 17

ha **uelkym** *ti a vêdh* 'and you will be welcome' BF: 18.

B **welcùmma, welcùbma** 'to welcome'
*Adam adam pandra wreth prag na theth thu'm **wolcumme*** 'Adam, Adam, what are you doing? Why do you not come to welcome me?' OM 257-58
*Meriasek bedneth crist ȝys ha bedneth ȝe vam neffra gwyf os the vos **welcummys*** 'Meriasek, Christ's blessing to you and the blessing of your mother always. You are worthy to be welcomed' BM 224-46
*adam adam pandra wreth prage ny theth thom **welcomma*** 'Adam, Adam, what are you doing? Why do you not come to welcome me?' CW 867-68
*Pe reeg eve gurra trooze war tir e ve **welcumbes**, me ore gwir* 'when he set foot on land, he was welcomed, I know well' LAM: 224.

It is quite apparent that the Cornish for 'welcome' is **welcùm, wolcùm** and for 'to welcome' **welcùmma, wolcùmma**. On notices outside towns welcoming visitors, forms like **Yma Cambron worth agas welcùmma** or **Welcùm owgh why in Cambron** would be more authentic than **Cambron a'gas dynergh**.

TO WORK
For 'to work' Nance suggests A) **gonys** and B) **lavurya** (UC *lafurya*).
In the text **gonys** may mean 'to work'; its sense most often, however, is 'to cultivate, to till, to plough, to sow'. The following examples will exemplify these senses:

A **gonys** 'to work'
*awos bos claffy ȝewle toche vyth **gonys** ef na yll* 'because his hands are diseased he cannot work at all' PA 158b
***gonys** oll a wrens yn fast rag nag o crist attendijs* 'they were working firmly, for Christ had not been understood' PA 202d
*hethyw yw an whefes dyth aban dalletheys **gonys** may rug nef mor tyr ha gveyth bestes puskes golowys* 'today is the sixth day since I began to work, when I made heaven, sea, land and trees, animals, fish and heavenly bodies' OM 49-52
*god spede gonesugy **gonys** a wreugh pur vysy thy'm del hevel fossow da gans lym ha pry ha pen cref warnethe y gureugh drehevel* 'Godspeed, workmen. You will work very busily, it seems to me. Stout walls with mortar and clay with a strong head on them you will build' OM 2447-52
*hag yma pub vr oll ow travela haw **conys** gans oll an menys a ylla the **wonys** innan ny an pith a ruga **gonys** in agan hendasow adam hag eva* 'and he is always labouring and working with all the means he can to work in us what he wrought in our ancestors, Adam and Eve' TH 5a
*Rag henna mars ees marver gallus in geir agen arluth Christ, tha gwiel pith nyng o dera[g] dorne, paseil moy gallus, the **gonys**, ha changya an pith nag o derag dorne* 'Therefore if there is such great power in the word of our Lord Christ to create what did not exist

beforehand, how much the more power to work and change that was not beforehand' SA 62a

Mar crug an geir an tas an nef **gonis** *in taglenno erall, mer moy ema* **gonys** *in Sacramentes benegas* 'If the word of the Father of heaven work in other thing, much more does it work in the blessed Sacrament' SA 63

an ry ma yw fyne **gonethys** *ow bannath y rof thethy* 'these have been finely wrought. I give them my blessing' CW 104-05

me a vyn **goneth** *dewhans der neb for a vras envy* 'I will work immediately by some means of great resentment' CW 432.

B **gonys** 'to till, to plough, to sow'

an lyf-woth gurens ymdenne me a commonnd scon dotho th'y teller kyns ens arte noe **gonys** *may hallo* 'let the flood stream withdraw, I will soon command it. Let it return to its former place, that Noah may cultivate the ground' OM 1093-96

eug **gonetheugh** *termyn hyr powes ny'gys byth nep preys* 'go, till for a long time. You will have no rest at any time' OM 1221-22

pandra amount thy'n **gonys** *mar serryth orth den hep wow* 'what use is it for us to till if you are going to be angry with man indeed?' OM 1223-24

the worhenmyn a vyt gureys mos the **wonys** *my a wra ha'm gurek ha'm flehes kefrys* 'your commandment will be done. I shall go to till and my wife and my children also' OM 1256-57

A wylta kyrwas enos del vynnas Du whar ha dof orth an ewyow devethys gansa may hallan **gonys***?* 'Do you see stags yonder as God intended, having come gentle and tame to the yoke that I might cultivate with them?' BK 847-50

Me a vyn dallath **gonys***, rag mas ew ar thyaha* 'I will begin to plough, for good is peaceful cultivation' BK 868-69

Ke a thros an kyrwas the **wonys** 'Ke brought the stags to plough' BK 869 [stage direction]

In rag, Kyrnyk ha Kella! In hanow Du uhella, **gonethough** *heb bysmeras* 'Forward, Kyrnyk and Kella! In the name of the highest God, plough without reproach' BK 869-72

A dyr bryntyn the **wonys** *teurant re bo confoundys, hedre vema orth e geys* 'A tyrant has been deprived of fine land to cultivate, while I was enclosing it' BK 1180-82

in erbers i'n pow adro an lynes in tyawgal prag e tevons heb den vith th'aga **gonys** 'why do the nettles grow in the gardens about in the land indeed without anybody to cultivate them?' BK 2131-34

Praga i'gas kerthow why e tef lynas in erbers heb **gonys** *veth?* 'Why do nettles grow in your gardens without being cultivated?' BK 2295-97

rays yw purryes lavyrrya ha **gones** *an beise omma tha gawas theny susten* 'it is very necessary to labour and to cultivate the earth here to get food for us' CW 1079-81

Trehe ground beaten rag **gones** *sogall* 'To cut the pared and burnt ground to sow rye' Bilbao MS.

Gonys can also mean 'to serve, to worship' a saint or God. Examples of this sense will be found s.v. '**SERVE**' above.

Lavurya is the default word for A) 'to work, to labour', though it can also be used to mean B) 'to trudge, to walk laboriously'. For the connection between working and walking laboriously, compare the English word 'to toil' or the doublet 'travel' and 'travail'. Here are some instances of **lavurya** in both senses:

A **lafurya** 'to work'

mos the balas my a vyn rag sustene beunans thy'n rys yw porrys ***lafurrye*** 'I will go to dig. To sustain life for us it is very necessary to work' OM 681-83

pan vo ol thy'n ***lafurryys*** *agan wheyl a vyt mothow* 'when everything has been worked by us our work will be a failure' OM 1225-26

Wose cous ha ***lafurye*** *an vaner a vye da kemeres croust hag eve* 'After talking and working the custom would be good to have a bite and to drink' OM 1899-901

squyth of dre ver ***lafurye*** *powes my a vyn defry* 'I am tired through working much; I will rest indeed' OM 2049-50

dro ve gode chons re'th fo nans on ***lafuryys*** *ganso hag an yssyly pur squyth* 'bring it, may you have good luck. Now we are exhausted from labour with it and our limbs are very tired' OM 2822-24

lafurye *a wra pupprys rak dry den the vos dampnys the ponow na fe sylwys* 'he works continually to bring man to be damned to torments that he be not saved' PC 15-17

Heyll costentyn in the dour ***lafuryys*** *rag the pleysour adro in pov me re bue* 'Hail, Constantine, in your tower; I have been toiling for your pleasure about in the land' BM 1566-68

pan ***lafuryens*** *rag benefys ware y feth govynnys py lues puns a yl bos anethy grueys* 'when they labour for a benefice, forthwith the question is asked, how many pounds can be made from it' BM 2827-30

rays yw purryes ***lavyrrya*** *ha gones an beise omma tha gawas theny susten* 'it is very necessary to work and to cultivate the earth here to get food for us' CW 1079-81

Operor… To labour, to work, to travel… C. Dho ṣîl, dho ***laviria*** AB: 107c

Dera vi ***laviria*** 'I do labour' AB: 246a.

With **lavurya** 'to work, to labour' compare *Buz, gen nebas* ***lavirians****, Eye venjah dendle go booz, ha dillaz* 'But with a little work they would earn their food and raiment' ACB: F f 3.

B **lafurya** 'to walk, to travel'

A das dev yn vhelder bynyges re by nefre rag genes yn pup teller parys of the ***lafurye*** 'O Father, God on high, blessed may you be always, for I am ready to walk anywhere with you' OM 937-40

reys yv thy'so ***lafurrya*** *vn pols byhan alemma del lauaraf pur wyr they's* 'it is necessary for you to walk a little hence as I tell you the very truth' OM 1268-70

rys yv dy'mmo ***lafurye*** *the vn vatel yredy* 'I must travel to a battle indeed' OM 2176-77

485

work   **GERYOW GWIR**

thotho me a vyn y ry rag ef thy'm the **lafurye** 'I will give it to him, for he journeyed to me' PC 1785-86

longys reys yv thy's gyne vn pols byan **lafurye** *dre worhemmyn an iustis* 'Longinus you must walk a little with me by command of the justice' PC 3003-05

Ser epscop dywy mur grays **lafurya** *sur the ken gluas avesijs off alemma* 'Sir bishop, much thanks to you. I have been advised to journey to a different country hence' BM 575-77

Wolcum knyghtis euerych on reys yv dywy **lafurya** *rag chastya an crustunyon dres ol gluas rome alemma* 'Welcome knights, every one. You must journey hence to chastise the Christians throughout the realm of Rome' BM 1178-81

oma yth ese parys rag **lafuria** *pur ylyn alema in the nygys* 'here I am ready to journey brightly hence on your business' BM 1387-89

the costyntyn an emperour reys yv dygh **lafurya** *dour eff a erhys indella* 'you must travel to Constantine the emperor punctiliously. He has so ordered' BM 1748-50

y vollys a veth screfys ha waree grueys dis parys may hylly prest **lafuria** 'his bulls will be written and forthwith prepared for you so that you can quickly travel' BM 2766-68

myr an turant then guelfoys mara mynna **lafurya** *ha dus thagen guarnya ny* 'keep an eye on the tyrant, whether he will journey into the wilderness and come and warn us' BM 3270-72

sur ny vynnons fovt wagys vn stap **lafurye** *adro* 'surely they will not without wages take another step about' BM 3285-86

Te a res thys **lavurrya** *bys o'm arluth desempys* 'You must travel to my lord immediately' BK 1047-48

Pleth ew the doul **lavyrrya**? 'Where is it your intention to travel?' BK 1369

Operor... To labour, to work, to travel... C. Dho ʒîl, dho **laviria** AB: 107c.

Nance suggests that **obery** means 'to work, to work at'. This is questionable. The verb **obery** is incidentally very rare. Here are the only attested examples I can find:

an re ma yv **oberys** *del vynsyn agan honan* 'these have been wrought as we ourselves wished' OM 15-6

mar pue drok a **oberys** *trogh y hy gans the glethe* 'if it is evil that I wrought, slash her with your sword' OM 291-92

ha kemmys an gorthyo ef gans mur ioy y tue the'n nef dre y thadder **oberys** 'and as many as worship him shall with great joy come to heaven, wrought by his goodness' RD 1222-24.

The verb **obery** clearly does not mean 'to work' or 'to work at', but rather 'to accomplish, to bring about'. The default word for 'to work' in a general sense is **lavurya**. **Gonys** can be used for 'to work' in certain cases.

WORSE, WORST

The default words for 'worse' and 'worst' in revived Cornish have always been **gweth** and **gwetha** respectively; compare Welsh *gwaeth* 'worse' and *gwaethaf* 'worst'. **Gweth** 'worse' is well attested but **gwetha** 'worst' is very rare indeed.

A **gweth** 'worse'

*an ioul ynno re drecse may3 o **gweth** agis cronek* 'the devil had dwelt in him so that he was worse than a toad' PA 47d

*rag y scoth hy a grevye ha whath **gweth** a wre an pren war 3ellargh maran gorre* 'for his shoulder pained him and still worse it would hurt, if he put it back from the wood' PA 205d

*sau kyn fens y morthelek the **weth** vythons the'n cronek ha garow yn y thule* 'but though they be hammer-dinted, the worse they will be for the toad and rough in his hands' PC 2731-33

*dre mur hyreth yth of pur squyth ha'm corf the **weth** yscarn ha lyth* 'through great yearning I am exhausted and worse is my body, bone and limb' RD 847-48

*rag me re'th clowas ow ty the Jovyn plos **gweth** ys ky, drog-el ha dyawl casadow* 'for I have heard you swearing to dirty Jovyn, worse than a dog, an evil angel and detestable fiend' BK 115-17

***Gweth** oge ys contreuuer pylf, clovorak* 'You are worse than worthless, a scabby counterfeiter' BK 178-79

*Jovyn ew dyawl **gweth** ys ky, me a levar thotha Fy!* 'Jovyn is a devil, worse than a dog; I say Fie to him' BK 327-28

*Ef a vith **gweth**, re Christy's wel!* 'It will be worse, by Christ's weal!' BK 2146-47

*Saw ny vyth gwyth **gweth** ys fol, pan i'n crennif Calesvol, me a'n dyhals* 'But he will not dare deeds worse than a madman; when I shake it, Excalibur, I shall split him in two' BK 3268-70

*me an syns **gwethe** es bucka ny won py theth tha wandra* 'I consider him worse than a goblin. I don't know where he has wandered off to' CW 1196-97.

B **gwetha** 'worst'

*ha dun ny ganso toth bras bys yn epscop syr cayfas yn **guetha** prys er y gv* 'and let us go at speed to Sir Caiaphas the bishop to his woe unfortunately' PC 1128-30.

The word **gweth** is often ambiguous, because it is identical with **qweth** 'garment' with a lenited initial, and in spelling with **gweth**, the collective of **gwedhen** 'tree'. **Gweth** therefore survives best in unambiguous set phrases, i.e. **gweth ès cronak** 'worse than a toad', **gweth ès ky** 'worse than a dog', **gweth ès fol** 'worse than a madman' and **gweth ès bùcka** 'worse than a hobgoblin'. **Gwetha** 'worst' is identical in pronunciation and spelling with **gwetha**, a variant of **gwitha** 'to keep'. **Gwetha** 'worst' therefore appears to survive only in the phrase **i'n gwetha prÿs** 'in the worst time, unfortunately'.

It seems that for 'worse' and 'worst' the spoken language from the earliest texts preferred the less ambiguous form **lacka** for both 'worse' and 'worst':

alemma bys yn tryger war ow fay **lacka** *mester ny alsen y thyerbyn* 'from here to Trigg upon my faith I could not meet a worse master' PC 2274-76

Rag mellya gans tus vays del o meryasek henways mur ty a far the **lakka** 'For meddling with good men, as Meriasek was called, you will greatly fare worse' BM 2454-56

hag in stat a eternall dampnacion, an pith ew **lacka** *oll, ha in myrnans heb dywith kyffrys an corffe han ena* 'and in a state of eternal damnation, that which is worst of all, and in death without end both of body and of soul' TH 4

Mar wyr dell oui Jacca, ef a'n gevyth an **lacka** *hag in hast a vith maraw* 'As true as I am called Jack, he will suffer the worst and soon will be dead' BK 3297-99

me a vyth sure tha **lacka** *mes te thym a lavara en by and by* 'I shall surely be the worse for it, unless you tell me very soon' CW 611-13

me an kymmar in dysdayne mar ny vethaf ve prevys whath mere **lacka** 'I will take it in scorn, if I am not proved much worse' CW 1448-50

a lamec drog was yth os ha me inweth mear **lacka** 'O Lamech, you are a bad fellow, and I also much worse' CW 1655-56

ny a wele an teez younk tho e clappia le ha le, ha **lacka** *ha* **lacka** 'we see the young men speaking it less and less and worse and worse' BF: 25

Ma leiaz gwreage, **Lacka** *vel zeage, Gwell gerres, Vel kommeres* 'There are many wives worse than chaff, better left than taken' ACB: F f 3

ha muy dale moaz tha an gletha stella, an **lacca** *berra amesk an gwellah* 'I must yet go to the sword, the worst among the best' LAM: 226

Pejor… Worse, naughtier. C. **Laka** AB: 116a.

In view of the prevalence of **lacka** 'worse, worst', it should perhaps be used as much, if not more, than **gweth**, **gwetha** in the revived language.

Y

YOUNG

The customary word in revived Cornish for 'young' has always been the disyllabic form **yowynk**, yet **yowynk** is not the ordinary word in the texts. **Yowynk** occurs only in the two set phrases **yowynk ha hen** 'young and old' and **yowynk ha loos** 'young and grey':

yowynk ha lovs kyn fo tollys dre y denuos mercy gylwys 'young and old though he be deceived by his [the devil's] power let him implore mercy' PC 19-20

ha nep as tefo gallos a vyth gans *yowynk ha los* henwys tus vras pup termyn 'and whoever have power are called great men by young and old always' PC 787-90

na ve creya warnogh why kellys ol y fyen ny *yowynk ha loys* 'had it not been for appealing to you, we all should have been lost both young and old' BM 2169-71

ol ny a pys *yowynk ha hen* war thu pup prys mercy gan ken may fen guythys rak an bylen 'we all pray, young and old, to God for our cause that we may be protected from the evil one' PC 39-41

me a's guarn *yowynk ha hen* my ny gafaf ynno ken may cothfo thy'm y dampne 'I warn you you, young and old, that I find not cause why he should be condemned' PC 2031-33.

In most cases above the disyllabic form **yowynk** has been used *metri gratia*, i.e. to provide two syllables. Outside the set phrases **yowynk ha loos** and **yowynk ha hen**, the customary word for 'young' in Cornish of all periods is **yonk**. Though **yonk** itself also occurs in the expression **yonk ha loos**, when four syllables are not required:

pub er te ʒen gura lewte beva den *yonk* bo den coth orʒaff mar mynnyth cole 'always you man be loyal, whether a young man or an old man, if you will trust me' PA 175cd

worth an pen y a welas ʒen beth yw leueris kens vn flough *yonk* gwyn y ʒyllas 'at the head of the grave, which has been mentioned before, they saw a young child in white clothes' PA 254bc

a giglot of lynage ha ty mar *yonk* a'n age pendra wreta gans an guas 'O wanton by breed, and you so young in age, what are you doing with the fellow?' PC 1183-85

scullyas y wos rak *yonk* ha los 'he shed his blood for young and old' RD 333

den *yonk* whek guandre a wreth 'young man, you are wandering' RD 1639

489

young   GERYOW GWIR

ha flehys **yonk** *a gar boys* 'and young children love food' BM 116
esethugh oma purfeth han arlythy **yonk** *ha loys ran arak ran aberveth* 'sit here precisely and the lords young and old, some in the front, some inside' BM 283-85
The den **yonk** *yth yv dufer bones in mesk arlythy* 'It is the duty of a young man to be among lords' BM 3171-72
Vs vn den **yonk** *atoma me re ruk sur y sesia* 'Yes, behold a young man here; I have captured him' BM 3546-47
A then **yonk** *fetel esta* 'Young man, how are you?' BM 3659
trewethek syght yv helma gueles den **yonk** *tek certan cheynys in keth vaner ma* 'this is a pitiful sight indeed to see a handsome young man chained in this way' BM 3823-25
kerys o gans **yonk** *ha loys in bys ma dres arlythy* 'he was beloved by young and old beyond other lords in this world' BM 4477-78
yonk *ha loys, Gothal ha Scot* 'young and old, Irishman and Scot' BK 1259
ha guyw the wormoladow dris **yonk** *ha loys* 'and worthy to be praised beyond young and old in this world' BK 1629-30
harlygh robyowgh **yonk** *ha loys* 'vigorously rob young and old' BK 2378
ha abell ew ow mabe **younka** 'and Abel is my younger son' CW 1060
ha reeg laule thonz gworeuh whellaz seere râg an flô **younk** 'and said to them seek the young child surely' Rowe
ha zavaz derez leba era an flô **yonk** 'and stood over the place where the young child was' Rowe
ha kebar an flô **yonk** *ha e thama ha ke tha Egyp* 'and take the young child and his mother and go into Egypt' Rowe
Komeer weeth na raw'y ostia en chei lebma vo dean koath demithez da bennen **younk** 'Take care not to lodge in a house where an old man is married to a young woman' BF: 16
ny a wele an teez **younk** *tho e clappia le ha le* 'we see the young men speak it less and less' BF: 25
Idzha'n lêauh dhv'n dên **Yÿnk**-*na?* 'Has that young man got the ague?' AB: 242a
Cornoack ewe all neceaves gen poble **younk** 'Cornish has all been forgotten by the young people' LAM: 244.

It is noteworthy that the only comparative of **yowynk/yonk** attested in the texts is **younka** at CW 1060. We have no example of *__yowynca__. It is also apparent that **yonk**, not **yowynk**, is the usual word for 'young' in Middle and Late Cornish. **Yonk** should perhaps be the usual word in revived Cornish.

Appendix A

The Calendar

DAYS OF THE WEEK
The attested forms of the days of the week are as follows:

SUNDAY: Sul, De Sul
Dewsull *blegyow pan ese yn mysc y abestely y wreg ʒe re aneʒe mos ʒen dre ha degylmy an asen* 'On Palm Sunday when he was among his apostles he made some of them go to the town and untie the ass' PA 27a-c

*me a worth kepar ha kyns neb a ruk an gol han **sul*** 'I shall worship as before him who made the festival and the Sunday' BM 3559-60

*An mab leean ni e gana terwitheyaw war an **zeell*** 'Our cleric sometimes sings it on Sunday' BF: 39

*Perh co tra te guetha a **suile** benegas, wheha deth te ta guile whele, ha guil mens es des do wele, bus an Sithas deth eu an **Suil** de Arlith deu* 'Remember to keep the Sunday holy; six days you shall do labour and do as much as you have to do, but the seventh day is the Sunday of your Lord God' BF: 41

*Kova tha gwitha benigas **de'Zil**, weeah jorna ra whei gwra weal, ha gwra menz es thees tha guil, buz an sithas dêth eu **zîl** benigas guz Arleth Deui* 'Remember to keep Sunday holy; six days shall you do labour, and do as much as you have to do, but the seventh day is the holy Sunday of your Lord God' BF: 55

*En eglez ny **Zelio** Tri* 'In our church on three Sundays' ACB: F f 2 *verso*

Sunday; C, ***Dezil*** AB: 54c

Dezil*, Sunday* Borlase.

MONDAY: Lun, De Lun
munday; C. ***De lîn*** AB: 54c

Delin*, Monday* Borlase.

TUESDAY: Merth, De Merth
tuesday; ***De merh*** AB: 54c

Demer*, Tuesday* Borlase.

Days of the week   **GERYOW GWIR**

WEDNESDAY: Merher, De Merher

kyns ys **dumerher** *the nos eff a deerbyn trestyns* 'before Wednesday night he will encounter sorrow' BM 2254-55
Wednesday: C. **De marhar** AB: 54c
Demarhar, *Wednesday* Borlase

THURSDAY: Yow, De Yow

arta me a thue **deth yov** 'I will come again on Thursday' BM 1472
then guylfoys in pur certen me a vyn mones **deyow** *prest the helghya* 'to the wilderness in very deed I shall go on Thursday straight to hunt' BM 3158-60
Thursday; C. **De Ieu** AB: 54c
Du yow, *Thursday* AB: 232a
De Jeu, *Thursday* Borlase.

FRIDAY: Gwener, De Gwener

heȝyv sur yv **dugwener** *da yv sevell owrth vn pris* 'today indeed is Friday; it is good to forgo a meal' BM 120-21
Ha pub **gvener** *a vo sur drys an vlyȝan gul peyadov my a vyn kyns eva na ȝybbry mevr* 'And every Friday that will occur through the year indeed I shall pray before drinking or eating much' BM 126-29
Ov gol a veth suer in mes metheven an kynsa **guener** *rag nefre certen* 'My festival will surely be in June, the first Friday for ever indeed' BM 4302-05
Du guener *crist ihesu ker a ruk merwel ragon ny mayth off lowen* **du guener** *dascor ov ena defry thum selwadour ha* **du guener** *rag henna bethens ov gol vy nefra sensys gans ov flehys dour* 'On Friday Christ, dear Jesus died for us, so that I am happy to relinquish my soul on Friday indeed to my Saviour and on Friday therefore let my festival be always scrupulously kept by my children' BM 4316-23
Y leferys offeren **du guener** *vetten certen glorijs ha tek* 'He said mass on Friday morning, glorious and beautiful BM 4419-21
Friday; C. **De guenar** AB: 54c
De-guenar, *Friday* Borlase.

SATURDAY: Sadorn, De Sadorn

Saturday; C. **De Zadarn** AB: 54c
Dezadarn, *Saturday* Borlase.

THE SABBATH: Sabot, dëdh Sabot

may hallo cafus y vrus ha kyns dos **sabot** *lethys* 'that he may have his verdict and be put to death before the Sabbath comes' PC 1503-04
rag may hyllyn y settye yn grous kyng ys dos **sabot** 'that we may put him on the cross before the Sabbath comes' PC 2556-57

GERYOW GWIR **Months of the year**

Perhgoh the gwithe sanz an dyth **Sabboth**... *mez an sythvas dyth yw an* **Sabboth** *a'n Arluyth thy Dew* 'Remember to keep holy the Sabbath day... but the seventh day is the Sabbath of your Lord God' ACB: E e 3 *verso*
Periko bra chee gwitha sanz an Dyth **Sabbath**... *mez an seithas dyth yw an* **Sabbath** *a'n Arleth de Dew* 'Remember to keep holy the Sabbath day... but the seventh day is the Sabbath of your Lord God' ACB: E e 3 *verso*.

MONTHS OF THE YEAR

The following are the attested forms of the months of the year:

JANUARY: Genver, mis Genver
Januarius... The month of January. C. **ȝenvar** AB: 67a
Genvar, *January* Borlase
Mis Genuer, *January* Borlase.

FEBRUARY: Whevrel, mis Whevrel
Februarius... The month of february. C. **Huevral** [*cor.* **Huerval**] AB: 59a
Huerval, *February; corruptly for* **Huevral**, *id. Lh[uyd]* Borlase.

MARCH: Merth, mis Merth
Flô vye gennes an **Miz-merh,** *Ni trehes e bigel en miz-east; E a roz towl Dho Proanter Powle, Miz-du ken Nadelik* 'A child was born in March, we cut his navel in August; he gave a fall to the vicar of Paul in November before Christmas' ACB: F f 4
Martius... The month of march. C. **Mîz merh** AB: 86c
Merh, *a Daughter; it. March- Month* Borlase.

MAY: Mê, mis Mê
Maius... The month of May. C. & Ar. **Mîz mê** AB: 84b
Me, *May-month* Borlase
Mis Me, *May* Borlase.

JUNE: Metheven, mis Efen
Ov gol a veth suer in **mes metheven** 'My festival shall be surely in the month of June BM 4302-03
Junius... The month of June. C. **Mîz ephan** AB: 74b.

JULY: Gortheren, mis Gorefen
An wehes deth in **gortheren** 'The sixth day in July' BM 2069-70
vi deth in mys **gortheren** *vn feer a veth in certen thum desyr in ketelma* 'the sixth day in July there will be a fair indeed thus as I wish' BM 2194-96
Julius... The month July C. **Mîz gorephan** AB: 74a
Gorephan, *July;* **Miz Gorephan**, *the Month of July* Borlase.

Months of the year   GERYOW GWIR

AUGUST: Est, mis Est

*han gela veth **mys est** certen orth ov deser an viijth deth* 'and the other will be in the month of August indeed according to my desire, the eighth day' BM 2072-75

*in **meys est** an viijves deth an secund feer sur a veth sensys in pov benytha* 'in the month of August, the eighth day, the secund fair will be help in the country for ever indeed' BM 2197-99

*22 **East** 1711* '22nd August 1711' LAM: 238

*Adheworth Newlyn e'n Blew Paul on 22ves **mys Est**, 1711* 'From Newlyn in the Parish of Paul, the 22nd August, 1711' LAM: 238

*Flô vye gennes an Miz-merh, Ni trehes e bigel en **miz-east**; E a roz towl Dho Proanter Powle, Miz-du ken Nadelik* 'A child was born in March, we cut his navel in August; he gave a fall to the vicar of Paul in November before Christmas' ACB: F f 4

Augustus... August, C. ***East*** AB: 44a

***East**, August* Borlase.

SEPTEMBER: Gwydngala, mis Gwydngala

*han tresse **mys gvyngala*** 'and the third in September' BM 2076

*han tresse **meys gvyngala** dugol myhall byth henna* 'and the third in the month of September; that is Michaelmas' BM 2200-01

September... The month September. C. ***Mîz guedn-gala*** AB: 148c.

OCTOBER: Hedra, mis Hedra

*yn Castel Sudley yn dekvas dyth **mys heddra** in blethan myll whegh cans dewghans ha try* 'in Sudley Castle the tenth day of October in the year 1643' JKeigwin

*an kensa journa a messe **Heddra** an centle, en plew Paule, in Cernow teage* 'the first day of October was the meeting in the parish of Paul in fair Cornwall' BF: 38

October... The month october. C. ***Mîz-hedra*** AB: 105b.

NOVEMBER: Du, mis Du

*Flô vye gennes an Miz-merh, Ni trehes e bigel en miz-east; E a roz towl Dho Proanter Powle, **Miz-du** ken Nadelik* 'A child was born in March, we cut his navel in August; he gave a fall to the vicar of Paul in November before Christmas' ACB: F f 4

November... November C. ***Mîz diu*** AB: 100b

***Mis-Diu**, November; i.e. Black-month* Borlase.

DECEMBER: Kevardhu, mis Kevardhu

*Skrefis war an kenza dydh an **miz Kevardhiu** 1736* 'Written on the first day of December 1736' Bilbao MS

December... The month of December; C. ***Mís kevardhiu*** AB: 53c.

FESTIVALS AND HOLY DAYS

The following names for festivals and holy days are attested in the traditional texts:

NEW YEAR'S DAY (1st January): De Halan an Vledhen

Kyn fe mar freth du Halan an vlethan i'n kynsa deyth, me a gows war mab Malan ha ny'n sparya', wor ow fayth! 'Though so bold on the Calends of the year on the first day, I shall speak to the son of Belial and shall not spare him, upon my faith!' BK 1880-83.

EPIPHANY (6th January): Degol Stool

*Epiphania... Epiphany or twelfth day. C. **Degl stûl** AB: 57a.*

MAYDAY (1st May): Cala'Mê

*ix nobyl a **calame** a russe sokyr thynny* 'nine nobles on Mayday would be a help to us' BM 3338-39

ST JOHN'S EVE, MIDSUMMER (23rd June): Golowan

*Guâve en Hâve terebah **Goluan**, ha Hâve en Guâve terebah Nedelack* 'Winter in summer until Midsummer and Summer in Winter 'till Christmas' Ustick MSS.

MICHAELMAS (29th September): Degol Myhal, Gool Myhal

*han tresse mys gvyngala **dugol myhal** yv henna in plu noala neffrea an keth feriov ma a veth* 'and the third in the month of September, that is Michaelmas in the parish of Noala for ever the same fairs will be' BM 2076-79

*han tresse meys gvyngala **dugol myhall** byth henna in plu wyn noala sensys* 'and the third in the month of September, that will be Michaelmas held in the parish of holy Noala BM 2200-03

*Ny gans Arthor in e sal, kyn tryken bys **woyl Myhal**, wylcum ny a vyth ena* 'Though we stay with Arthur in his hall until Michaelmas, we will be welcome there' BK 1376-78.

ALL SAINT'S DAY (1st November): De Halan Gwâv

***Dew Whallan Gwa** Metten in Eglos De Lalant* 'One the morning of All Saints' Day in Lelant church' Exeter Consistory Court (1572)

CHRISTMAS (25th December): Nadelyk

*Flô vye gennes an Miz-merh, Ni trehes e bigel en miz-east; e a roz towl Dho Proanter Powle, Miz-du ken **Nadelik*** 'A child was born in March, we cut his navel in August; he gave a fall the the vicar of Paul in November before Christmas' ACB: F f 4

*Guâve en Hâve terebah Goluan, ha Hâve en Guâve terebah **Nedelack*** 'Winter in summer until Midsummer and Summer in Winter 'till Christmas' Ustick MSS.

*Natalis... C. **Nadelik; Deụ nadelik**, Natalis Christi* 'The birthday of Christ' AB: 97a.

Festivals and holy days   **GERYOW GWIR**

SHROVE TUESDAY: Enes
*Carnisprivium... Shrove-tide; C. **Enez** AB: 46b.*

PALM SUNDAY: De Sul Blejyow
***Dewsull blegyow** pan ese yn mysc y abestely y wreg ȝe re aneȝe mos ȝen dre ha degylmy an asen ha dry ganse* 'On Palm Sunday when he was among his apostles, he made some of them go to the town and untie the ass and bring it with them' PA 27a-c.

MAUNDY THURSDAY: De Yow Hablys
*en gyth o **deyow hablys** may fenne ihesus sopye gans an re yn y seruys war an bys re ȝewesse* 'the day was Maundy Thursday, when Jesus wished to sup those in his service he had chosen in the world' PA 41cd

*ke alemma servont ker kergh a'n fenten thy'm dour cler the thyghye bos thy'nny ny erbyn soper kepar del yv an vaner **duyow hamlos*** 'go hence, dear servant; fetch from the well clean water for me to prepare food for us for supper, as is the custom on Maundy Thursday' PC 649-54

*ema an doctors [ow leverall] nyn gegy cowse vith a **deow habblys** arr na theff[ensy th]an keth geyr ma* 'the doctors say: there is no talk of Maundy Thursday until they come to this same word' SA 66.

EASTER, PASSOVER: Pask, De Pask
*maner o ȝen eȝewon war **dyth pasch** worth an Iustis an preson govyn onon ha bos henna delyffrys* 'it was the custom of the Jews at the Passover to ask the guardian of the prison to free one man and that he was released' PA 124cd

*En eȝewon ny vynne bos an laddron ow cregy ternos rag **pasch** o ȝeȝe* 'The Jews did not wish that the robbers should be hanging for the next day was Passover for them' PA 229ab

*eugh yn dre hagh ordenegh bos **pask** thy'nny hep lettye* 'go into the town and order the Passover meal for us without delay' PC 617-18

*arluth cuf lauar thy'nny yn keth tre ma py fynny bos **pask** thy'nny ordyne* 'dear Lord, tell us where in this same town you want us to order the Passover meal' PC 621-23

*ragh yn nos haneth dybry bos **pask** omma ef a vyn* 'for this evening he will eat the Passover meal here' PC 671-72

*yv on **pask** thy'nny parys ma yllyn mos the soper* 'is the Passover lamb ready for us that we may go to supper?' PC 707-08

*my re thysyryas fest mer dybry genogh why haneth boys **pask** kyns ov bos marow* 'I have greatly wished to eat the Passover meal with you this evening before I die' PC 718-20

*bythqueth re bue vs geneugh war **pask** my the ase theugh vn prysner ha'y thelyffre* 'it has always been your custom at the Passover that I should yield to you a prisoner and release him' PC 2034-36

*a vynnegh ol assentye rak **pask** my thylyfrye ihesu myghtern yethewon* 'will you all agree fro the Passover that I hand over Jesus, king of the Jews?' PC 2037-39

*syr iustis me agas pys rak **pask** may fo dyllyfrys barabas hep skullye y wos* 'sir justice, I beg you that Barabbas should be released without shedding his blood' PC 2369-70

GERYOW GWIR Festivals and holy days

*thomas yth os pur woky drefen na fynnyth crygy an arluth the thasserghy **du pask** vyttyn* 'Thomas, you are very foolish, since you will not believe that the Lord rose again on Easter morning' RD 1105-08

*ow thesyre ew gans oll ow holan the dibbry an **pask** onn ma genogh* 'my desire is with all my heart to eat this Passover of lamb with you' SA 64a

*ema Tertullian ow leverall pana **pask** onn ow Christ wensys tha thibbry gans e apostelath* 'Tertullian says what sort of Passover of lamb Christ wished to eat with his apostles' SA 64a

*ef rag henna a ruge protestia, myre a thesyre the thybbry e **bask**, me a laver e **bask** e honyn rag nyng o met, ef the deserya mas e **bask** e honyn* 'he therefore professed his great desire to eat his Passover—I say his own Passover, for it was not meet for him to desire any Passover but his own' SA 64a

*Pascha... The passover, or the feast of Easter. C. **Pask*** AB: 113c
***Du pask**, Easter* AB: 232a
***Pâsk**, Easter; Pascha* AB: 241a.

WHITSUNDAY (PENTECOST): Pencost

*Ith ew scryffys fatell rug pedyr kemeras warnotha in presens a oll an appostlys the gowse in aga hanow y oll then bobyll war **du fencost** myttyn* 'It is written that Peter took upon himself in the presence of all the apostles to talk in the name of them all to the people on Whitsunday morning' TH 44a

*Corn. **Pencas**, Whitson-Tide* AB: 20a
***Penkast** [Corn.] Pentecoste* AB: 32bc
*Pentecoste... The fiftieth day after Easter, Whitsuntide. C. **Penkast*** AB: 116c
***Penkast**, Whitsontide; Pentecoste* AB: 241a.

Appendix B

Unnecessary Coinages

The following are words unattested in Cornish which have been coined by revivalists. They are all unnecessary, since in each case an attested word exists.

*AR 'battle, slaughter'.
For 'battle' one can use **cas** or **batel** (see '**BATTLE**' above). For 'slaughter' we have **ladhva** (*lathva*) in John Keigwin's translation of the letter of King Charles.

*ARGYANS 'argument'
This word is unattested. The attested form is **argùment**. See '**ARGUMENT**' above.

*ARWETH 'sign'
The attested words for 'sign' are **sin** and **tôkyn**. ***Arweth** is unnecessary; see '**SIGN**' above.

*BLASA 'to taste'
The authentic word for 'to taste' is **tâstya**. For the noun 'taste' we can use **saworen** *f*. See '**TASTE**' above.

*DAMPNYANS 'damnation'
The attested word is **dampnacyon**; see '**DAMNATION**' above.

*DENYON 'men'
This word has been suggested by some revivalists in the mistaken belief that **tus** means 'people', rather than 'men, adult males'. For notices where the genders are distinguished 'men' and 'women' can be rendered **gwer** and **benenes** or **gwesyon** and **benenes**. See '**MAN**' above.

*DEVNYDHYA 'to use'

This word appears to have been introduced in the 1980s on the basis of Cornish **devnyth** (UC *defnyth*) and by analogy with Welsh *defnyddio* 'to use'. The authentic word for 'to use' is **ûsya** (see '**USE**' above). **Devnydhyor** is sometimes used for 'consumer'. Since the traditional word for 'to consume' is **consûmya**, 'consumer' might better be rendered ***consûmyor** or ***consûmyores**.

*DEWOTTY 'public house'

This word was coined by Nance on the basis of Welsh **diotty**, *diowty*. The attested words are **tavern** and **hostelry** (see '**PUBLIC HOUSE**' above).

*DYVROA 'to exile'

Nance coined this word on the basis of OC *diures* and by analogy with Breton. The attested word, however, is **exîlya**; see '**EXILE**' above.

*ENWOSA 'to circumcise'

This word was coined by Nance on the basis of Welsh *enwaedu* 'to circumcise'. ***Trodrehy** 'to circumcise' was a further coinage used in the 2004 version of the New Testament in Kernewek Kemmyn. The attested word is **cyrcùmcîsya**; see '**CIRCUMCISE**' above.

*GOS 'is known'

This curious verbal form has been suggested as the present autonomous of **godhvos** 'to know'; cf. Middle Breton *gous* (Modern Breton *gouzer*). One wonders whether borrowing verbal forms into Cornish from Breton is really legitimate, particularly if such forms are not needed. The phrase 'is known' in Cornish is attested twice in the collocation **yw openly godhvedhys** 'is openly known':

maga ver dell yll bos gothvethis gans du, **ew** *openly* **gothvethis** *ha gwelys ynans y* 'as far as can be known by God, is openly known in them' TH 14

yth **ew** *openly* **gothvethis** *in mar ver dell rug crist promysya an conforter* 'it is openly know how greatly did Christ promise the Comforter' TH 36.

'Is known in Cornish' is (**yth**) **yw godhvedhys**. ***Gos**, on the other hand is neither authentic nor necessary.

*GWERTHJY 'shop'

This word was coined by Nance on the basis of the rare Welsh neologism *gwerthdy*. The word **shoppa** 'shop, workshop' is attested in place-names; see '**SHOP**' above.

*GWINREUNEN, *GWINREUN 'grape, grapes'
Nance coined ***gwinreunen** (UC *gwynrunen*) 'grape' on the basis of Welsh *gwinronyn, gwinrawn*. The form **grappys** is now attested however. See '**GRAPE**' above.

*GWINLAN 'vineyard'
Nance coined ***gwinlan** (UC ******gwynlan*) on the basis of Welsh *gwinlan*. **Vynyard** is now attested, however. See '**VINEYARD**' above.

*GWYNSELLA 'to fan'
Nance coined ***gwynsella** on the basis of Lhuyd's *guinzal* 'fan' and Welsh *gwyntyllu, gwyntyllio* 'to fan'. The attested word, however, is **fanya**; see '**FAN**' above.

*HEBASKHE 'to calm, to soothe'
Nance invented this word on the basis of Breton. The attested word is **comfortya, confortya**; see under '**COMFORT**' above.

*KELGHYEK 'circular, round'
Neither ***kelgh** 'round, circle' nor ***kelhek, *kelghyek** 'round, circular' are attested in the traditional language. **Kern, crèn** is attested once in Lhuyd. The ordinary word in the traditional language, however, is **rônd**; see '**ROUND**' above.

*LENNA 'to read'
Lhuyd coined the word ***lenner** 'reader' on the basis of Welsh. On that word revivalist have devised a word ***lenna** 'to read'. The Cornish for 'to read, to read aloud' is **redya**. 'A reader' is **redyor** or **redyores**; see '**READ**' above.

*POW SOWS, *BRO SOWS 'England'
Nance devised both ***Pow Sows** (UC ******Pow Saws*) and ***Bro Sows** (UC ******Bow Saws*). Neither is attested. **Pow an Sowson** is attested, however. See '**ENGLAND**' above.

*RÔSYA 'to wander'
Nance appears to have equated English dialect 'rouse' = 'to move energetically' with Welsh *rhodio* 'to stroll' and thus to have produced Cornish ***rôsya**. English 'rouse' and Welsh *rhodio* are unconnected. The ordinary Cornish word for 'to wander, to stroll' is **gwandra**; see '**WANDER**' above.

GERYOW GWIR   *Yêdhowek

*SANS'HE 'to sanctify'
Sans'he (UC *sanshe*) was coined by Nance. The Cornish for to 'sanctify, to consecrate' is either **sacra**, **consecrâtya** or **sanctyfia**; see 'SANCTIFY' above.

*SÊLYA 'to found'
This word was devised by Nance. The attested word for 'to found' is either **fùndya** or **grôndya**; see 'FOUND' above

*TALAS 'payment'
The word ***talas** first seems to have appeared in Snell and Morris, *Cornish Dictionary Supplement* 2 (1984). **Pêmont** 'payment', however, is attested five times in the texts. See '**PAYMENT**' above.

*TEMPTYANS 'temptation'
The Cornish word for 'temptation' is **temptacyon**, which is found in PC, BM, TH, CW and *Llyfr y Resolusion*. There is no need for ***temptyans**.

*TRODREHY see ***ENWOSA**

*TREUSFURVYA 'to transform, to transfigure'
Some commentators recommend ***treusfurvya** to render 'to transform, to transfigure'. Both **transformya** 'to transform' and **transfygura** 'to transfigure' are attested. ***Treusfurvya** is unnecessary. See '**TRANSFORM**' above.

*YALGH 'purse'
The word ***yalgh** has been suggested as the Cornish word for 'purse' on the basis of Breton **yalc'h**. The attested word for 'purse' is either **pors** or **scryp**. ***Yalgh** is unnecessary and is questionable from the phonetic point of view. See '**PURSE**' above.

*YÊDHOWEK 'Jewish, Hebraic'
Nance suggested ******Yedhowek* as the adjective deriving from **Yêdhow** 'Jew'. The adjective **Ebrow** 'Hebrew, Hebraic' is attested, however, and ***Yêdhowek** is unnecessary, though it could be used for 'Yiddish' i.e. Judaeo-German, both as an adjective and a noun.

Appendix C

Borrowed Verbs

In this list the KS spelling is given first; thereafter the manuscript spelling or spellings together with the source, the sense in English and the verb from which the item has been borrowed. An asterisk before a Cornish verbal noun implies that the verb is attested in the text in question, but not in the verbal noun. Notice also that one verb, **trebuchya**, appears to have been borrowed directly from Old French. By far the largest number of these loanwords come from Middle English—an indication of how long Cornish and English have been in intimate contact. In the lists below, borrowings from Old English, Old French, and Modern English are given before the longer list of borrowings from Middle English.

VERBS BORROWED FROM OLD ENGLISH
drùshya, drùshyan [*drushen* Pryce] 'to thresh' < OE *perscean*
fanja [**fanga* BK; *fanja* Pender] 'to get, receive' < OE *fang* 'possession, spoils' + *-a*
gravya [*grauio* OCV; **grauye* PC] 'to carve' < OE *grafan* 'to dig'
offrynna [*offrynne* OM; *offrynnya* BM; *offrennia* SA] 'to make a religious offering' < OE *offrung* 'offering' + *-a*
redya [*redye* PA, PC, BM; *redya* TH; **redia* SA] 'to read' < OE *rédan*

VERB BORROWED FROM OLD FRENCH
trebuchya [*trebytchya* CW] 'to trip, to stumble' < OF *trebucher* 'to stumble' [the following forms of the noun are attested in Middle English: *trepeget, trepget, trepgette, trebget, trebeget, trebgot, tripget, tripeget, tripgete, tripgette, tribget, treget*, Late ME *treibochet*. Compare OF *trebuchet, tribuchet*, Archaic French *trebechet, trepgette, trepgeut* & ML *trebuchetum, tribuchetum*, AL *tribechettum, tribegettum*]

VERBS BORROWED FROM MODERN ENGLISH
concystya [*concistia* TH] 'to consist' < NE *consist*
crambla [*grambla* Lh] 'to climb' < NE *cramble* 'to creep about in a winding fashion'; the Cornish word appears to have acquired permanent initial lenition

502

fria [*fria* Lh] 'to free' < NE *free*
fyckya [*fickya* Gwavas] 'to copulate' < Early NE *fuck* with unrounding of the dialectal vowel [y]
grysla [*grisla* Lh; *grizla* Lh] 'to snarl, to show the teeth' < NE *grizzle* 'to show the teeth; to laugh in a mocking fashion'
gwainya [*gvaynya* BM; *guaynia* Lh; *gwaynia* Pryce] 'to gain' < Early NE *gayne* 'to gain, to win', possibly influenced by *win*, *won*.
gwedhra [*guedhra* Lh] 'to dry out, to wither' < Early NE *wither*
inflamya [*inflammya* TH] 'to inflame' < NE *inflame*
intertainya [*yntertaynya* CW] 'to take into consideration, to welcome' < Early NE *entreteyne*
kenkya [*kenkia* LH] 'to contend' < NE *kink*, *kenk* 'twist, bend' + *ya*; the sense is probably 'to tangle with > to contend with'
perswâdya [*persuadya* TH] 'to persuade' < NE *persuade*
perùsya, perùjya [*porogga* Lh] 'to peruse, to read' < Early NE *peruse, porose*
plâgya [*plagya* CW; *plagia* TH] 'to afflict, to plague' < NE *plague*
preparya [*preparya* TH] 'to prepare' < Early NE *prepare*
pylya [*pelya* BM] 'to peel, to flay' < NE *peel*
sanctyfia [*sanctyfya* TH] 'to sanctify' < NE *sanctify*
sedûcya [*seducia* TH] 'to seduce' < Early NE *seduise*
stêvya [*stevya* PA] 'to hurry' < English dialect *stave* 'to move quickly'
tauntya [*tountya* BM] 'to taunt, to provoke' < NE *taunt*

VERBS BORROWED FROM MIDDLE ENGLISH

abâtya [*abatya* BK] 'to lessen' < ME *abaten*
abhorrya [*abhorrya* TH; *abhorria* SA] 'to abhor, to loathe' < ME *abhorren*
absolvya [*absoluya* TH] 'to absolve' < ME *absolven*
abûsya [*abusia* TH] 'to abuse' < ME *abusen*
acceptya [*acceptya* TH] 'to accept, to receive' < ME *accepten*
acowntya [*acontia* BM; *accontya* BK; *accontya* TH; *accowntya* BK; *acountya* BK; *accomptya* CW; *accomptya* TH; *accomtya* TH; *comtya* BK; *comptya* CW; *comptia* SA] 'to reckon' < ME *accounten*
acordya [*acordye* PA; *acordya* BM] 'to agree' < ME *accorden*
acûsya [*acusye* PC] 'to charge with an offence, to accuse' < ME *acusen*
afia [*afia* PC] 'to affirm' < ME *affien* 'to trust, to assure'
affyrmya [*affirmya* TH, SA] 'to affirm' < ME *affermen, affirmen*
agria [*agrea* TH; *agrya* TH] 'to agree' < ME *agreen*
alejya [*allegia* TH] 'to state, to claim' < ME *alleggen*
alowa [*alowe* BM; *allowa* TH] 'to allow, to let' < ME *allouen*
amendya [*amendye* OM, PC; *amendie* BM; *amendia* TH; *amendya* BK, CW; *amyndya* BK; *mendya* CW] 'to correct, to improve' < ME *amenden*
amowntya [*amontye* PA, PC, RD; *amonntye* OM; *amountye* OM; *ammontya* BM; *amontya* BK; *amowntya* CW] 'to add up, to mean' < ME *amounten*
amuvya [*amuvya* BM] 'to move, to experience emotion' < ME *ameven, amoven*

ancombra [*ancombra* PA; *ancumbra* BM] 'to trouble, to confuse' < ME *encombren*
andîtya [*andytya* BK] 'to indict, to accuse' < ME *enditen*
angra [*angre* PA; **angra* CW, Rowe] 'to be anxious; to annoy; to become angry' < ME *angren*
ania [*annya* BM] 'to bother, to annoy' < ME *annien*
anoyntya [**anoyntia* SA] 'to anoint' < ME *enointen*
anterya [*anterya* BK] 'to inter, to bury' < ME *enteren*
aperya [*aperia* BM] 'to damage' ME *apeiren*
apperya [*apperia* TH, SA; *apperya* TH] 'to appear' < ME *apperen*
appoyntya [**apoyntya* CW; **appoyntya* CW; *appoyntia* TH, SA; **apoyntia* SA] 'to appoint' < ME *appointen*
apposya [*apposya* BM] 'to examine' < ME *apposen*
aqwitya [**aquyttye* PC; *aquytya* BM; *aquyttya* BK; *acquyttya* CW] 'to recompense, to repay' < ME *aquiten*
arainya [**araynya* BK] 'to interrogate' < ME *arreinen*
argya [*argye* PC; *argya* BM] 'to argue' < ME *arguen*
ascendya [**ascendye* RD; **assendya* BM; *assendia* BM, TH; **ascendia* SA] 'to mount, to ascend' < ME *ascenden*
ascrîbya [*ascribia* TH] 'to ascribe' < ME *ascriben*
ascûsya [*ascusie* PC; *ascusia* BM; *excusia* TH] 'to excuse, to exonerate' < ME *ascusen, excusen*
aspia, aspias [*aspye* PA; **aspye* OM, PC, RD; *aspya* BM, BK; *asspeas* CW] 'to espy, to watch out for, to observe' < ME *aspien*
assaultya [**assaultya* TH] 'to assault, to attack' < ME *assauten, assaulten*
assaya [*assaye* OM; **assya* BM; *assaya* CW; *saya* CW] 'to try' < ME *assaien*
assentya [*assentye* PC, RD; **assentya* BM, CW; **asentya* BK] 'to agree, to consent' < ME *assenten*
assoylya [**assoylya* TH] 'to solve, to explain' < ME *assoilen*
assûrya [*assurya* TH] 'to assure, to guarantee' < ME *assuren*
attamya [*attamye* PA] 'to broach, to start' < ME *attamen*
attainya [*attaynya* TH] 'to attain' < ME *atteinen*
attendya [*attendia* BM; **attendye* PA; *atendye* RD; *attendya* BM, BK, CW] 'to pay attention to, to consider, to take care of' < ME *attenden*
avauncya [*afonsye* OM, *avonsye* OM; *avoncya* BK] 'to advance, to promote' < ME *avauncen*
avîsya [*avesya* BM; **avysya* BK; *avycya* CW; **avysshya* CW] 'to deliberate, to decide' < ME *avisen*
avowa [*avowe* PC] 'to swear, to admit' < ME *avouen* 'to swear, to promise solemnly'
avoydya [*avodya* BM; *avodia* BM; **avoydya* CW; *vodya* BM; *voyda* BK; *avoydia* TH; *avoydya* TH; **voydya* CW; *voydaya* SA] 'to depart; to avoid; to banish' < ME *avoiden*
bacbîtya [*bacbytya* TH] 'to backbite, to defame' < ME *bak-biten*
banyshya [**banysshya* TH] 'to banish' < ME *banishen*
bargenya [*barginia* NBoson; *bargidnia* Pryce, Lh] 'to bargain, to do a deal' < ME *bargainen*
bassya [**bassya* OM] 'to become shallow' < ME *bas* + *-ya*

batalyas [*batayles* PA; *batalyays* BM] 'to fight, to battle' < ME *bataillen*
betraya [*betraya* SA] 'to betray' < ME *bitraien*
blâmya [*blamye* PA, OM; *blamye PC, RD; *blamya* PA, BM, CW; *blamya TH] 'to blame; to condemn' < ME *blamen*
blessya [*blessya Symonds] 'to bless' < ME *blessen*
bocla [*bocla* TH] 'to buckle' < ME *bokelen, boklen*
bôstya [*bostye* PC, RD; *bostya* BM, TH, SA] 'to boast' < ME *bosten*
boxusy [*boxscusy* PA; *boxusy* PC] 'to strike, to whip'; cf. ME *box* 'blow' subs. + *usy*
bragya [*brakgye RD; *braggye* BM; *braggya TH] 'to threaten < ME *braggen* 'to boast'
byldya [*buyldya* CW; *buldya* TH; *byldya* TH] 'to build' < ME *bilden, buylden*
cachya [*cachye PA, OM; *cachye* PC; *catchah* Pryce] 'to seize, to catch' < ME *cacchen*
carya [*cariah* Pryce; *coria* Pryce] 'to carry' < ME *carien*
causya [*cawsya* TH; *cawsia* TH; *causya* SA] 'to cause' < ME *causen*
cessya [*sestya PC; *cessia* TH; *sessia* TH] 'to cease' < ME *cesen, cessen*
chainya [*chenya BM; *cheynya BM] 'to chain' < ME *chainen*
charjya [*chargya BM; *chargia TH; *chardgya CW; *charrdgya* CW] 'to charge, to command' < ME *chargen*
châssya [*chasye* PA; *chacye OM, PC; *chasshya CW; *chassya* CW] 'to chase, to harry' < ME *chacen*
chastia [*chastye PA; *chastya* BM, BK] 'to punish, to chastise' < ME *chastien*
chaunjya [*changya PA; *changya BK, CW, TH; *channgya CW; *changia* SA; *changya* BM, SA] 'to change, to alter' < ME *chaungen*
chauncya [*chungsya PA; *chansya BK; *chansia* TH] 'to chaunce, to venture' < ME *chauncen*
cherya [*cherya* BM, BK] 'to cheer, to comfort' < ME *cheren*
cheryshya [*chesya* TH] 'to cherish' < ME *cherishen*; see also **omjersya**
clappya [*clappia* NBoson, JTonkin, Bodinar] 'to jabber, to talk' < ME *clappen* 'to talk noisily'
clattra [*clattra* BM] 'to chatter, to babble' < ME *clateren*
clowtya [*cloutye RD] 'to patch' < ME *clouten*
clowtya [*clowtya BK, CW] 'to strike' < ME *clouten*
comendya [*kemendya* BM; *comendya* BM; *commendya* Borde] 'to recommend, to send one's compliments to' < ME *commenden*
comfortya [*comfortye* PA, OM; *comfortya Rowe; *confortye PA; *confortye* RD, BM; *confortya* BM; *confortia* BM; *confortya BK;] 'to comfort, to cheer' < ME *comforten*
comparya [*comparya* CW, TH] 'to compare' < ME *comparen*
comondya [*commondye* OM; *comondya* BM; *commondia* TH; *commondya* TH; *comanndya* CW; *commandia SA] 'to command' < ME *commaunden*
compella [*compella TH] 'to compel' < ME *compellen*
comprehendya [*comprehendya CW] 'to include, to encompass' < ME *comprehenden*
compressa [*compressa* OM] 'to oppress' < ME *compressen* 'to squeeze, to press'
comùnya [*communya BM] 'to communicate, to receive communion' < ME *communen*
comyttya [*commyttya TH] 'to commit' < ME *committen*

concernya [*concernya* TH, SA; *consernya* TH; *consernia* TH] 'to concern' < ME *concernen*

concêvya [*concevya* BM, BK, TH; *concyvya* BK] 'to conceive' < ME *conceiven*

conclûdya [*concludye* PC; **concludya* CW; *concludia* TH] 'to refute; to make a decision; to conclude' < ME *concluden*

confessya [*confessia* TH, SA] 'to confess' < ME *confessen*

confyrmya [*confirmya* TH; **confyrmia* TH; *confirmia* SA] 'to confirm' < ME *confirmen*

confùndya [*confundya* BM; **confoundya* BK; **confondya* TH] 'to confound, to frustrate' < ME *confounden*

conjorya [**coniorye* PC; *congurya* BK] 'to beseech, to charge' < ME *conjouren*

conqwerrya [*conquerrye* OM; *conquerya* BK] 'to conquer' < ME *conqueren*

consecrâtya [*consecratia* BM; **consecratia* SA] 'to consecrate' < ME *consecraten*

constrîna [*constryne* PC] 'to constrain, to compel' < ME *constreinen*

consûmya [**consumya* CW] 'to consume, to destroy' < ME *consumen*

consydra [*consydra* TH; *consyddra* TH; **considera* SA] 'to examine' < ME *consideren* 'to inspect, to examine, to observe'

containya [**contaynya* TH; **conteynya* TH] 'to contain' < ME *conteinen*

contentya [**contentya* CW, TH] 'to satisfy' < ME *contenten*

contynewa [*contenewa* TH] 'to continue, to persist' < ME *contineuen*

contraweytya [**contreweytye* PC] 'to ambush' < ME *countrewaiten* 'to guard against'

contradia [*contradye* PC] 'to gainsay' < ME *contradien* 'to deny'

controllya [**controllya* CW] 'to restrain, to control' < ME *countrollen*

convertya [*convertya* TH] 'to convert' < ME *converten*

convyctya [**convyctie* PA] 'to vanquish, to defeat' < ME *convicten*

correctya [*correctia* TH] 'to correct, to punish' < ME *correcten*

corrùptya [*corruptia* TH] 'to corrupt' < ME *corrupten*

costya [**costya* CW] 'to cost' < ME *costen*

covia [*covya* BM, BK] 'to hatch, to cherish' < ME *coveie* 'brood or covey of partridges' + *-a*

covytya [**covytya* BKl **covitya* Rowe] 'to cover' < ME *coveiten*

crackya [**crakye* PA; **crakkya* BM; **crackya* BK] 'to crack, to snap' < ME *craken*

creatya [**creatya* CW; *creatya* TH; **creatia* SA] 'to create' < ME *createn*

cria [*crye* OM, PC, RD; **creya* BM; *crya* BK, CW, Rowe; **crya* SA; **cryah* Rowe; **creia* NBoson; *kreia* Lh] 'to cry, to call' < ME *crien*

crôpya [*cropye* PA] 'to penetrate' < ME *gropen* with provection of the initial consonant in Cornish

crùllya [**kryllia* Lh] 'to curl' < ME *crullen* 'to curl'

crùppya [*cruppya* CW; *croppya* CW] 'to creep' < ME *crupen*, variant of *crepen* 'to creep'

cùssya [*cussia* TH; *cushah* Rowe] 'to curse, to swear < ME *cursen*

cyrcùmcîsia [**circumsicia* TH] 'to circumcise' < ME *circumcisen*

dampnya [**dampnye* PA, OM, PC, RD, BM; *damnya* CW; **dampnya* CW, TH] 'to condemn' < ME *dampnen*

dauncya [*donssye* RD; *donsia* BM; *donsya* BM; *downssya* CW; *daunsya* JKeigwin] 'to dance' < ME *dauncen*

GERYOW GWIR
dyghtya

debâtya [*debatya* BM] 'to quarrel; to debate' < ME *debaten*
decaya [*decaya* TH] 'to decrease, to diminish' < ME *decaien*
decernya [*decernya* BM; *desernya* CW, TH; *descernya* TH; *discernya* TH] 'to discern' < ME *discernen*
decêvya [**dessevie* PA; *desyvya* TH; *decevya* TH; **decevia* SA; *desevia* TH; *desevya* TH] 'to deceive, to defraud' < ME *deceiven*
declarya [*declarya* TH, SA] 'to declare' < ME *declaren* 'to relate, to proclaim'
declynya [*declynya* TH] 'to decline' < ME *declinen*
defâcya [**defashya* CW] 'to deform, to disfigure' < ME *defacen*
defâmya [*defamia* TH] 'to defame' < ME *defamen*
defendya [**defendye* PA; *defendia* TH; *defendia* SA] 'to forbid; to defend' < ME *defenden*
defolya [*daffole* PC; *dafole* RD; **dufolla* BK; *defollya* TH; *defullya* TH; **defoylya* TH] 'to injure; to defile' < ME *defoilen*
deformya [**deformya* CW] 'to deform, to disfigure' < ME *deformen*
defia [*defya* BM, BK, TH] 'to defie, to challenge' < ME *defien*
delyvra, delyfrya [**delyvra* PA, *delyfrya* PA, BM; *delyvrya* BM; *delyffra* PA; *delyfre* OM; *dylyfrye* PC, BM; *dyllyfre* PC; **delyvera* CW; **delyuera* TH] 'to release, to deliver' < ME *deliveren*
demondya [*demandea* SA; *dymandia* Lh] 'to demand, to ask for' < ME *demaunden, demanden, demonden*
deneya [*deneya* TH] 'to deny' < ME *denien, denaien*
descendya [**desendya* CW] 'to descend' < ME *descenden*
departya [*departia* TH; **departia* SA] 'to depart' < ME *departen*
deservya [*deservia* TH ; *deservya* TH] 'to deserve' < ME *deserven*
desirya [**deserya* PA; **desyrya* OM, PC, BM, Rowe; *desyrya* TH; *dysyrye* RD; *deserya* BM, SA] 'to desire, to require, to ask' < ME *desiren*
despîtya [*dyspytye* PC] 'to disparage, to speak ill of' < ME *despiten*
despîsya [*despisia* TH; *despisya* TH; *despicia* TH; *despisea* SA] 'to despise' < ME *despisen*
destria, destruya [**destrya* CW; *destrea* CW; *dystrya* TH; *dustruya* BM; **destria* Keigwin; *destrîa* Lh] 'to destroy' < ME *destrien, destruien*, variants of *destroien* 'to destroy'
determya [**determya* CW] 'to determine, to decide' < ME *determinen*, later *determe*
devorya [**deworya* BM; *devowrya* TH; *devorya* TH; *devourya* TH] 'to devour' < ME *devouren, deworen*
devîdya [*devydya* TH] 'to divide' < ME *dividen, deviden*
dôtya [*dotya* BM] 'to be silly, to act foolishly' < ME *doten*
dowtya [*dowtye* PA; *doutye* RD; *dovtya* BM; *dowtya* BK; **dowtya* CW] 'to doubt, to fear' < ME *douten*
draylya [**draylya* BM] 'to drag, to trail' < ME *trailen* with permanent lenition of the initial consonant
drîvya [*dryvya* TH] 'to drive' < ME *driven*
dropya [*dropye* PA] 'to drop, to drip' < ME *droppen*
dyghtya [*dy3gthtya* PA, *dygtya* PA; *dygtye* PC, **dyghtye* PC; *dyghtya* BM; **dyghtya* BK] 'to prepare, to arrange, to provide, to perform, to treat' < ME *dighten*

507

dyrectya [*dyrectya* TH] 'to direct, to guide' < ME *directen*
dysclôsya [**dysclosya* CW; *disclosya* CW] 'to reveal' < ME *disclosen*
dyscomfortya [**dyscomfortye* PA] 'to dishearten, to discourage' < ME *discomforten*
dyscrasya [**dyscrasya* BM] 'to affect with disease, to infect' < ME *discrasen*
dysdainya [*dysdaynya* TH] 'to disdain' < ME *disdeinen*
dysêsya [**desesye* PC; **desesya* BM; *dyseysya* BK; **dysaysya* BK] 'to distress, to hurt, to afflict with disease' < ME *disesen*
dyskevra [**dyskevra* BK; *dekyvra* CW; *dyskevera* CW] 'to unmask, to expose' < ME *discoveren*, *diskeveren*
dysobeya [*dissobeya* TH; *dysobaya* TH; *disobeya* TH] 'to disobey' < ME *disobeien*
dysonora [*dishonora* SA] 'to dishonour' < ME *dishonouren*
dyspraisya [*dyspresya* PA] 'to disparage' < ME *dispreisen*
dysplêsya [**dysplesya* BM; **dysplaysya* BK; *displesya* TH] 'to displease' < ME *displesen*
dysplêtya [**dyspleytye* PC, RD, BM] 'to unfurl' < ME *displaied* + ya
dysplewyas [*dysplevyas* PC] 'to display, to spread out' < ME *displaien*
dyspûtya [*dysputye* PC] 'to discuss, to dispute' < ME *disputen*
dyssembla [*dyssembla* TH; *dissembla* Lh] 'to dissemble' < ME *dissemblen*
dyssentya [*dessentya* TH] 'to dissent' < ME *dissenten*
dysseytya [*dyssaytye* PA] 'to deceive, to outwit' < ME *deceite* 'trickery, deceit' + *-ya*
dystempra [*dystempra* BM] 'to upset, to irritate' < ME *distemperen*
dystrybûtya [*distributia* SA] 'to distribute' < ME *distributen*
dystryppya [**dystryppya* PA, PC] 'to strip naked' < *dys*+ ME *strepen* 'to strip'
dyvlâmya [*dyvlamya* BK] 'to exonerate' < *dy* + ME *blamen*
edyfia [*edyfya* TH] 'to edify, to build up' < ME *edifien*
encressya [**encressya* OM; *incressya* CW; **incresshya* CW; **cressye* OM; *cressae* BM; *cressya* CW, SA] 'to increase, to multiply' < ME *encresen*
endewa [**endewa* TH; **enduwya* TH; **endewia* SA] 'to endow' < ME *endeuen*
endûrya [*endurya* TH] 'to endure' < ME *enduren*
enjoya [*enioya* TH; *inioya* TH] 'to enjoy' < ME *enjoien*
entendya [*entendie* TH; **intendia* TH] 'to intend' < ME *entenden*, *intenden*
entra [*entre* PC, *yntre* PC; *entra* BK, CW] 'to enter' < ME *entren*
erya [*errya* CW] 'to defy, to challenge' < ME *erren* 'to anger'
establyshya [**establyssa* TH] 'to establish' < ME *stablishen*
estêmya [**estemya* TH; **estymya* TH] 'to esteem' < ME *estemen*, *estimen*
êsya [*eysye* PC; **esya* BM; *aizia* Lh] 'to ease, to accommodate' < ME *esen*
exaltya [*exaltya* BM; **exaltya* CW; *exaltia* TH] 'to exalt, to honour' < ME *exalten*
examnya [*examne* PC, *examnye* PC, *examyne* PC; *examnya* CW, TH] 'to examine' < ME *examinen*, *exampnen*
excêdya [*excedia* TH] 'to exceed' < ME *exceden*
execûtya [*executia* TH] 'to carry out, to accomplish' < ME *executen*
exîlya [**exylye* OM] 'to exile' < ME *exilen*
exortya [*exortya* TH; *exortia* TH] 'to exhort' < ME *exhorten*, *exorten*
expowndya [*expondia* TH] 'to expound' < ME *expounen*, *expounden*
fâcya [*facie* PC; **fashya* CW] 'to brag; to show a face' < ME *facen* 'to show a bold face'

GERYOW GWIR gwardya

fanya [*fannye* PC] 'to winnow, to fan' < ME *fannen*
fara [*fara BM, BK; *faria* BM] 'to fare, to behave' < ME *faren*
fasthe [*fasthe RD] 'to confirm' < ME *fast* + *he*
fastya [*faste* PA; *fastie* PC] 'to fasten, to attach' < ME *fasten*
favera [*favera BM; *favera* TH] 'to favour, to show mercy on' < ME *faveren*
fia [*fygha BM; *fya BK] 'to say "fie" to, to disparage' < ME *fien*
fia [*fya PA; *fye* OM, BM; *feya* BM; *fya* BK] 'to depart, to flee' < ME *feien* 'to do away with, to remove'
flattra [*flattrye* PC; *flattre* RD; *flatra* BM; *flattra* CW, TH] 'to flatter, to beguile' < ME *flateren*, *flaterien*
floryshya [*florissya* TH; *florysshya* TH] 'to flourish' < ME *floryshen*
folya [*foulya* BK; *folya* TH] 'to follow' < ME *folien*, a variant of *folwen* 'to follow'
forberya [*forberya* TH] 'to refrain from, to forgo < ME *forberen*
forbydya [*forbydya* TH; *forbyddya* TH] 'to forbid' < ME *forbeden*, *forbidden*
formya [*formye* OM; *formye PC, RD; *formya BM, BK, CW, TH; *furmya TH] 'to create, to fashion' < ME *formen*
forsâkya [*forsakya BM; *forsakya* TH; *forsakia NBoson] 'to abandon, to repudiate' < ME *forsaken*
fowndya [*fondya* BM; *fundya* BM; *fowndya TH; *foundya TH] 'to found' < ME *founden*
frâmya [*framya* TH] 'to fashion' < ME *framen*
frappya [*frappia* BM] 'to strike' < *frapen*
fria [*frya BK] 'to fry' < ME *frien*
fynyshya [*fynsya* BM] 'to finish' < ME *finishen*
gêdya [*gedya* BM] 'to guide' < ME *giden*
gloryfia [*glorifia* TH] 'to glorify' < ME *glorifien*
gokya [*gokya* BK] 'to be foolish' < *gocky* 'foolish < English *gawky* 'foolish, literally cuckoo-like' + *ya* < ME *gok*, *gouk* 'cuckoo'
gordhya [*gorȝye* PA; *gorthye* OM, PC, BM; *gorthia* BM; *gorthya* BM, BK, CW, WGwavas; *gwerthya* CW; *gworria* CW; *gworthya* CW; *urria* Lh] 'to venerate, to worship' < ME *worthien*
governya, **governa** [*governye* OM; *governa* CW, TH; *gouerna* TH] 'to govern' < ME *governen*
graffya [*graffya TH] 'to graft' < ME *graffen*
grassya [*grassya PA, RD, BM; *grassia CW; *grassee* BM] 'to thank' < ME *gracen*
grauntya [*grontye PA; *gronntye* OM; *grontia* BM; *grontya CW, Keigwin; *grantye PC; *granntye OM; *granntya CW; *growntya PA; *grauntya CW; *grauntya* TH; *growntya* CW; *growntya TH] 'to permit, to grant' < ME *graunten*
grêvya [*grevye PA, OM, PC; *greffye* RD; *grefya* BM; *grevya CW] 'to injure, to afflcit, to weigh down' < ME *greven*
grôndya [*grondya* BM; *growndye PA; *groundye OM; *groundia* TH] 'to found, to base' < ME *grounden*
gwandra [*guandre* OM; *guandra* BM; *gwandre* PC, RD; *gwandra* CW, TH, Rowe] 'to walk, to wander' < ME *wandren*
gwardya [*gwardya* BK] 'to guard' < ME *warden*

509

GERYOW GWIR

gwarnya [*guarnye* RD; *guarnya* BM; *gwarnya* PA, Rowe; *gwarnye* OM, PC; *gwarnya* BK, CW, TH] 'to announce, to warn' < ME *warnen*
gwaya [*guaya* BM; *gwaya* TH] 'to move' < ME *weien* 'to weigh, to move'
gwerrya [*guerrya* BM] 'to wage war' < ME *werren*
gwetyas [*gueytyas* OM, PC, RD; *guetyas* BM; *gweytyas* BK, CW; *gwettyas* TH; *gwetias* TH] 'to be concerned, to be careful, to wait, to hope' < ME *waiten*
hackya [*hakya* OM] 'to hack' < ME *hakken*
handla [*handle* PC; *handle* RD; *handla* BM] 'to touch, to manipulate' < ME *handlen*
hangya [*hangya* BM; *hangya* TH] 'to hang' < ME *hangen*
hapnya [*happnya* TH] 'to happen' < ME *happenen*
happya [*hapye* PC] 'to happen' < ME *happen*
hastya [*hastia* BK] 'to hasten, to hurry' < ME *hasten*
hernessya [*hernessya* BM] 'to equip' < ME *hernessen* 'to equip'
hùmblya [*humblya* TH] 'to humble oneself' < ME *humblen*
hùrtya [*hurtya* TH; *hertia* Lh] 'to hurt, to pain' < ME *hurten*, *herten*
imbrâcya [*ymbracya* TH] 'to embrace' < ME *embracen*, *inbracen*
inclinya [*inclynya* BM; *inclenya* BM] 'to incline' < ME *enclinen*
inspîrya [*inspirya* TH] 'to inspire' < ME *enspiren*, *inspiren*
instrùctya [*instructia* TH] 'to instruct' < ME *instructen*
instytûtya [*institutya* TH; *institutia* TH] 'to institute, to establish' < ME *instituten*
jestya [*gestya* BK] 'to recite' < ME *gesten*
jùjya [*iudgye* PA; *iudgia* TH; *judgya* TH; *iugge* PC, *iuggye* PC; *iuggye* RD; *jugia* TH] 'to try, to judge' < ME *jugen*
jùnya [*yvunnye* OM; *ivnnye* OM; *jonya* TH; *joynea* TH; *jvnya* SA; *jvnia* SA; *dzhunia* Lh] 'to join' < ME *junen*
jùstyfia [*justyfia* TH] 'to justify, to acquit" < ME *justifien*
kesrainya [*kysragnya* BK; *kysraynya* CW] 'to reign jointly' < *kes-* + < ME *regnen*, *rainen*
kestalkya [*kestalkye* BM] 'to converse' < *kes-* + ME *talken*
knoukya [*knoukye* OM, PC, RD] 'to beat, to hammer' < ME *knokken*
lackya [*lakya* BK] 'to lack' < ME *lakken*
lâcya [*laʒye* PA; *lathye* OM; *lacie* PC] 'to fasten' < ME *las* 'cord, buckle' + *ya*
lamentya [*lamentya* TH] 'to lament' < ME *lamenten*
laudya [*laudia* CW] 'to laud, to praise' < ME *lauden*
launcya [*launcya* BK] 'to lance, to pierce' < ME *launcen*
lawa [*lawe* OM, PC, BM] 'to praise' < ME *louen*
laya [*laya* TH] 'to lay' < ME *leien*
lêdya [*ledya* OM, BM. TH; *ledia* Lh] 'to lead' < ME *leden*
lêshya [*lescya* BM] 'to leash (hounds)' < ME *lesse* 'leash' + *ya*
lettya [*lettya* OM, BM, BK, TH; *lettye* PC, RD] 'to delay; to hinder' < ME *letten*
londya [*londya* BM] 'to land, to disembark' < ME *londen*
longya [*longia* TH; *longya* TH] 'to belong' < ME *longen*
lordya [*lordye* OM; *lordya* CW] 'to hold sway' < ME *lorden*
lowsya [*lowsya* TH] 'to loose, to release' < ME *losen*, *lousen*
lùrkya [*lurkya* TH] 'to lurk' < ME *lurken*

lyftya [*lyftya* TH] 'to lift, to raise' < ME *liften*
magnyfia [*magnifya* TH] 'to magnify' < ME *magnifien*
mailya [*maylye* OM; **maylye* PC; **malya* BM; **maylya* CW] 'to wrap' < ME *mailen*
marya [**marya* BM] 'to marry' < ME *marien*
mêkya [*mekya* TH] 'to humble' < ME *meken*
mellya [*mellya* BM, CW; *myllya* BK; *myllia* TH] 'to meddle' < ME *medlen, mellen*
mentêna [**menteyne* OM; *menteyna* BM; *mayntaynya* CW; *mentanya* TH] 'to support, to maintain' < ME *maintenen*
mênya [*menya* TH; *meynya* TH; *menya* SA; *menia* JTonkin] 'to mean, to signify' < ME *menen*
menystra [*menystra* BM] 'to administer' < ME *ministren*
merkya, markya [*merkye* OM; *merkya* TH; **markya* TH] 'to mark; to notice' < ME *marken, merken*
metya [*metye* PA; *mettye* RD; *metya* BM; **mettya* BK; **mettia* NBoson] 'to meet, to confront' < ME *meten*
mevya, môvya [**mevie* PA; *movya* TH] 'to move' < ME *meven, moven*
mockya [*mockya* TH] 'to mock' < ME *mokken*
moldra [*moldra* BM; **muldra* BK] 'to murder' < ME *morderen*
monia [**monye* PC] 'to coin' < ME *monien*
mùrnya [*murnya* CW; *murnye* CW; *mornya* CW] 'to mourn, to lament' < ME *mornen*
myshevya [**myshevye* OM] 'to harm, to hurt' < ME *mischeven*
mystrestya [*mystrustya* CW] 'to mistrust' < ME *mistrusten*
napya [*napya* BM] 'to doze, to nap' < ME *nappen*
noryshya [**norysshya* TH] 'to nourish' < ME *norishen*
nôtya [*notya* PA; *notye* PC, RD; **notya* BM, TH] 'to perceive, to notice' < ME *noten*
nùmbra [*numbra* TH] 'to count, to number' < ME *nombren*
obeya [*obeye* OM; *obaya* BM; **obeya* TH] 'to obey' < ME *obeien*
observya [*observia* TH] 'to observe, to keep' < ME *observen*
obtainya [*optaynya* TH; *obtaynia* TH] 'to obtain' < ME *obteinen*
ocûpya [*occupya* CW] 'to occupy' < ME *occupien*
offendya [*offendye* OM; *offendia* BM, TH; *offendya* CW, TH] 'to do wrong; to displease' < ME *offenden*
offra [*offra* TH, SA] 'to offer' < ME *offeren*
omjersya [**omgersya* BM] 'make oneself at home' < *om-* + ME *cheryshen* 'to care for, to cherish'
omyttya [*ommyttya* TH] 'to omit' < ME *omitten*
onora [**onore* PA; **onovre* OM; *enora* BM; *honore* PA; **honora* BK; *honora* CW, TH, SA] 'to honour' < ME *honouren*
opya [*opea* CW] 'to open, to make vacant' < ME *ope*, variant of *open*
ordna, ordena [*ordna* PA; **ordna* OM, BK; *ordene* OM; *ordyne* PC, RD; **orna* BM, CW; **ordaynya* BK; *ordenya* TH] 'to order, to decree' < ME *ordeinen*
ôstya [*ostia* NBoson, Lh] 'to take lodgings, to stay' < ME *hosten, osten*
overcùmya [*overcummya* BM; *overcommya* TH; *ouercommya* TH; *ouercummya* TH] 'to overcome, to conquer' < ME *overcumen*
oversettya [*oversettya* BK] 'to overcome, to overthrow' < ME *oversetten*

owtya [*owtya* BK] 'to cry "alas"' < ME *out* 'alas' + *-ya*
pacyfia [**pacifia* TH] 'to pacify' < ME *pacifien*
paintya [*payntia* TH] 'to paint' < ME *peinten*
painya [*peynye* PA; *penya* CW] 'to inflict pain on, to punish' < ME *peinen*
parkya [*parkya* BK] 'to enclose land' < ME *park* + *-ya*
passya [**pasya* CW; **passhya* CW; *passya* TH; *passia* TH; **passia* NBoson, Lh] 'to pass; to surpass' < ME *passen*
pe [*pee* BM; *pea* Lh] 'to pay' < ME *paien*
pechya [**pechye* PA] 'to thrust, to pierce' < ME *picchen*
percêvya [*percevia* TH; *persevya* TH; *percyvia* SA] 'to perceive' < ME *perceiven*
performya [*performya* TH; *perfumya*] 'to perform' < ME *performen*
persecûtya [*persecutia* TH] 'to persecute' < ME *persecuten*
pertainya [*pertaynya* TH] 'to pertain, to belong' < ME *pertenen, pertainen*
peryllya [*peryllya* BM] 'to be in danger' < ME *peril* + *ya*
peryshya [**perisshya* TH; *peryssya* TH] 'to perish' < ME *perishen*
plainya [**playnye* OM; **playnya* CW; **pleynya* CW] 'to plane' < ME *planen*
plaintya [*plentye* PA] 'to plead, to lay a charge' < ME *plainten* 'to complain against'
plattya [*plattya* CW] 'to prostrate oneself, to lie flat' < ME *platten*
plauntya [*plontye* RD] 'to propagate, to plant (a false notion)' < ME *plaunten*
plêsya [**pleysye* OM; *plesya* BM; *plesia* BM; *pleycya* CW] 'to please' < ME *plesen*
plynchya [*plynchye* PA] 'to dodge, to avoid' < ME *blinchen*, with the initial consonant provected in Cornish
pockya [*pokkia* Lh] 'to push, to thrust' < ME *poken, pukken*
pondra [*pondra* TH] 'to ponder' < ME *ponderen* 'to weigh, to ponder
posnya [**posnye* OM] 'to poison' < ME *poisonen, poisnen*
pottya [**pottye* OM; **pottya* BM] 'to thrust, to choose, to put' < ME *putten*
poyntya [*poyntya* CW, TH] 'to establish, to cause to appear; to point' < ME *pointen*
practycya [**practisia* TH] 'to practice' < ME *practisen*
praisya [**praysye* PA; *praysya* CW; *preysya* BM; *preysya* BK; *presia* TH; **preezya* TBoson] 'to praise' < ME *preisen*
preferrya [*preferrya* TH] 'to prefer' < ME *preferren*
presentya [**presentya* BK; *presentya* CW] 'to present' < *ME presenten*
preservya [*preservia* TH] 'to preserve' < ME *preserven*
presûmya [*presumya* TH] 'to presume, to take for granted' < ME *presumen*
pretendya [*pretendya* TH; *pretendia* TH] 'to claim' < ME *pretenden*
prevailya [*prevaylya* TH; *prevayllya* TH; *preveylya* TH] 'to prevail' < ME *prevailen*
preventya [**preventya* CW] 'to anticipate' < ME *preventen*
procêdya [*procedya* BK, TH; *procedia* TH] 'to proceed < ME *proceden*
procûrya [*procuria* TH] 'to procure' < ME *procuren*
professya [*professia* TH] 'to pledge, to profess' < ME *professen*
profya [**profye* OM; *profia* BM; **profya* CW] 'to proffer, to offer up' (when building) < ME *profren* + *-ya*
promyssya [**promysya* CW; *promysya* TH; *promesya* TH; **promvsia* TH] 'to promise' < ME *promisen*

prononcya [*prononcia* TH; *prononcea* TH] 'to pronounce, to articulate' < ME *pronouncen*
prosperya [*prosperya* TH] 'to prosper' < ME *prosperen*
prosternya [*prosternya BK] 'to lay low' < the root of ME *prosternacioun* in the phrase *maken prosternacioun* 'to lie prostrate'
protestya [*protestia* SA] 'to protest' < ME *protesten*
provia [*provya* BM; *pruvya* BK; *provya TH, CW; *pruvya* BK; *pryvia* Lh] 'to provide' < ME *providen*
provokya [*provokya TH; *provyeha* Lh] 'to provoke' < ME *provoken*
prysonya [*presonya PA, CW; *prysonye* RD; *presonya* BK] 'to imprison' < ME *prisoun*, *presoun* + *ya*
pùnyshya [*punscie* OM; *punssye* OM; *punsya* TH; *punyshya CW; *punyssya* TH] 'to punish' < ME *punishen*
pùrchesya [*purchesya* TH; *purchasia* TH] 'to purchase' < ME *purchasen, purchesen*
pùrjya [*purgia TH] 'to purge, to cleanse' < ME *purgen*
pùrposya [*purposia* TH] 'to intend, to purpose' < ME *purposen*
pyla [*pyle* BM] 'to pillage, to rob' < ME *pilen*
pyltya [*pyltye* PA] 'to strike, to buffet' < ME *pilten*
pynchya [*pynchia TH] 'to pinch, to constrain' < ME *pinchen*
qwartrona [*quartrona* BM] 'to divide into quarters, to quarter' < ME *quartroun* 'quarter' + -*a*
rafna [*raffna* BM] 'to rob, to plunder' < ME *raven* 'plunder' noun + -*a*
rafsya [*rafsye RD] 'to seize, to ravish' < ME *ravishen*
railya [*reylya* TH] 'to rail, to speak vehemently' < ME *railen*
rainya [*regnya BM; *raynya* TH] 'to reign' < ME *regnen, rainen*
raunsona [*raunsona* TH] 'to ransom' < ME *raunsounen*
rebukya, rebûkya [*rebekia PA, *rebukya PA, *rebukya* TH, SA] 'to rebuke' < ME *rebuken*
recêva [*rysseve* PA, *receve* PA; *resseve OM; *resseue* PC; *receva* BM, TH; *receva BK; *recevya* SA; *recevia* SA; *recivia* SA] 'to receive' < ME *receiven*
reconcîlya [*reconcilia TH] 'to reconcile' < ME *reconcilen*
recordya [*recordya BM; *recordya* BK, TH; *recordya* CW; *recordia* TH] 'to remind, to state' < ME *recorden*
redêmya [*redemya* TH, SA; *redymya* TH] 'to redeem' < ME *redemen*
referrya [*referrya* TH] 'to refer' < ME *referren*
refrainya [*refraynya* TH] 'to refrain, to hold back' < ME *refreinen*
refûsya [*refusya* TH; *refusia* TH] 'to refuse' < ME *refusen*
regardya [*regardya* TH, SA; *regardia* SA] 'to consider' < ME *regarden*
rejoycya [*rejoycya* CW; *regoyssya CW; *reiosya* TH; *reiossya* TH] 'to rejoice' < ME *rejoisen, rejoicen*
rekna [*rekna* BM; *rekna BK; *reckna CW; *rekenna* TH] 'to reckon; to charge' < ME *rekenen*
remainya [*ramaynya* CW; *remaynya* TH; *remaynea* SA] 'to remain' < ME *remainen*
remedya [*remedya* BK] 'to remedy, to cure' < ME *remedien*
remembra [*remembra* BM, CW, TH; *remmembra* SA] 'to remember' < ME *remembren*

remuvya GERYOW GWIR

remuvya [*remuvye* OM, RD] 'to remove' < ME *remuen*
remyttya [*remyttya* TH] 'to remit, to surrender' < ME *remitten*
renowncya [*renowncya* TH] 'to renounce' < ME *renouncen*
repêrya [*reperya* TH] 'to repair, to revert' < ME *repairen*
repentya [*repentya* BM, TH; **repentya* CW] 'to repent' < ME *repenten*
reportya [*reportya* BK, TH] 'to report' < ME *reporten*
reprêva [*repryfa* OM] 'to reprove, to reproach' < ME *repreven*
reprôvya [*reprovia* TH] 'to reprove, to reproach' < ME *reproven* variant of *repreven*; see preceding
repûtya [*reputya* TH] 'to consider, to acknowlege' < ME *reputen*
reqwîrya [*requyrye* PC; *requyrya* CW; *requiria* TH; *requyria* TH] 'to require, to demand' < ME *requiren*
resna [*resna* CW] 'to discuss, to argue' < ME *resounen*
resortya [*resortya* BM] 'to resort to, to turn to' < ME *resorten*
restorya [*restoria* BM; *restoria* TH] 'to restore, to bring back' < ME *restoren*
retainya [*retaynya* TH] 'to retain, to keep' < ME *reteinen*
revertya [*revertya* BK] 'to return' < ME *reverten*
rewardya [*rewardye* OM, PC; **rewardye* RD; *rewardya* BM; **rewardya* CW; *rewardia* TH] 'to reward' < ME *rewarden*
rewlya [*revlye* OM; *reulye* PC; **rewlya* BM, *revlya* BM; *rewlya* BK, TH; *rowlya* CW; *rulya* TH] 'to rule, to govern' < ME *reulen*
robbya [**robya* BM, BK; *robbya* TH; *robbia* Lh] 'to rob' < ME *robben*
rollya [*rhyllio* Lh] 'to roll' < ME *rollen*
rôstya [**rostye* PC; *rostia* Lh] 'to roast' < ME *rosten*
rowtya [*rovtia* BM; *rowtya* BK, CW, Rowe; *rowtia* Rowe] 'to control, to rule' < ME *routen* 'to direct a pack of hounds by shouting'
ryddya [*ryddia* TH] 'clear, to rid' < ME *ridden*
ryndra [*ryndra* TH] 'to render, to yield' < ME *rendren*
sacra [**sacra* BM] 'to consecrate' < ME *sacren*
sacryfia [**sacryfye* OM; *sacrefie* PC] 'to sacrifice' < ME *sacrifien*
sarchya [*sarchia* TH, SA] 'to search' < ME *serchen*
satysfia [*satisfya* TH] 'to satisfy' < ME *satisfien*
sawya [*sawye* PA, OM, PC, BM; **sawye* RD; *sawya* BM, BK, CW, TH, SA; *sowia* JTonkin; *sawyah* Rowe] 'to save, to protect; to heal' < ME *sauf* 'safe; healed' + -*ya*
scaldya [**skaldya* BM] 'to scald, to burn' < ME *scalden*
scapya [*scapya* OM; **scapye* PC; **schapye* RD; **schappya* BM; **scappya* BM; **scapya* BK; *scappya* CW; **skapye* RD] 'to escape' < ME *scapen*
sclandra [**sclandre* PC; *sclandra* BM] 'to calumniate, to cause to falter' < ME *sclaundren*
scolkya [*scolchye* PA; *scolkye* PC] 'to skulk, to lurk' < ME *skulken*
sconya [*sconya* PA, OM, BM, BK; *sconye* PC] 'to refuse, to shun' < ME *schonen*
scorjya [**scorgya* PA, RD; **scurgya* TH] 'to scourge, to whip' < ME *scourgen*
scornya [*scornye* PA, RD; *scornya* BM, BK; *scorne* OM; **skornya* BK] 'to refuse; to despise' < ME *scornen*

scrynkya [*scrynkye* OM] 'to grimace, to snarl' < ME *scrinken* 'to flinch, to wince'
scùmbla [*scumbla* BM] 'to defecate' < ME *scombren*
scùrya [*scurrya TH] 'to scour, to polish' < ME *scouren, scuren*
sêlya [*selia SA] 'to seal' < ME *selen*
separâtya [*seperatya* TH; *seperatia SA] 'to separate' < ME *seperaten*
servya [*seruye* PA, PC; *seruya* CW, TH; *servye* OM, PC, BM; *servya* BM, BK, TH, Rowe; *servia* BM, CW, NBoson, Lh] 'to be of service, to serve' < ME *serven*
sêsya [*seysse* OM; *sesya* BM; *sesya BK; *sesia* Lh] 'take possession of, seize' < ME *seisen*
settya [*settya PA, *syttya PA, BM; *settya* OM, BM, BK, CW; *sittia SA] 'to set, to place, to put' < ME *setten*
sewajya [*sewagya* BM] 'to assuage' < ME *aswagen*
sewya [*sewya PA, CW; *sywe* OM, PC; *sewya* TH; *sewia* TH; *suyah Rowe; *suyah* Pryce] 'to follow, to accompany' < ME *seuen* 'to follow'
shackya [*sackye PA; *shakya* BM; *shackya* TH; *shakiah* Pryce] 'to shake' < ME *shaken*
shâmya [*schamya BM; *shamya BK] 'to shame' < ME *shamen*
shâpya [*shapya* CW; *shappya* TH; *schapye* OM; *schappya* TH; *schappia* TH] 'to shape' < ME *shapen*
shînya [*shynya* TH] 'to shine' < ME *shinen*
shyndya [*syndye* PA, OM, PC; *shyndye* OM, PC] 'to harm, to destroy' < ME *shinden*
slackya [*slackya CW] 'to lessen, to abate' < ME *slaken*
slynkya [*sklynkya* BM; *slynckya* CW] 'to creep, to crawl' < ME *slinken* (and a later form *sclink*)
sygnyfia [*signifya* TH; *signifia* TH, SA] 'to signify' < ME *signifien*
smertya [*smyrtya* TH] 'to smart, to hurt' < ME *smerten*
socra [*socra* BM, BK; *succra* CW] 'to succour' < ME *socouren*
somona [*somona* BK] 'to summon' < ME *somonden*
soposya [*soposia* BM; *seposia* BM; *soposya BK; *supposya CW; *supposia* TH; *supposya* TH; *suppoga* NBoson; *sybbosia* Lh] 'to suppose, to imagine, to assume' < ME *supposen*
sopya [*sopye* PA, PC] 'to sup, to eat supper' < ME *soupen*
sordya [*sordya PA] 'to arise, to originate' < ME *sourden*
sowndya [*sowndya* TH; *soundia SA] 'to sound' < ME *sounen, sounden*
sostena [*sostene* OM] 'to feed' < ME *sustenen*
sparya [*sparye* OM; *sparye PC, RD; *sparya BM, BK, JKeigwin; *sparya* CW] 'to spare, to forbear' < ME *sparen*
spêdya [*spedye* PA, PC; *spedye RD; *spedie* BM; *spedya* BM; *spedya CW] 'to succeed; to hasten' < ME *speden*
spêna [*speyna PA; *speyna* BM; *spyna BK] 'to spend, to exhaust' < ME *spenen*
spendya [*spendya TH; *spyndya TH] 'to spend' < ME *spenden*
spîtya [*speitia* Lh] 'to vex' < ME *spiten* 'to injure'
sportya [*sportya* BM, BK] 'to sport, to hunt' < ME *sporten* 'to enjoy oneself'
spryngya [*spryngya BK; *springya TH; *spryngya* TH; *speringia* TH] 'to spring up, to originate' < ME *springen*

sqwattya [**squattya* BM, CW; **squatya* CW; *skuattia* Lh; *squatchia* JBoson] 'to break, to crush' < ME *squatten*

stakena [**stakena* BK] 'to pierce with a stake' < ME *staken*

stâtya [*statya* BM] 'to convey property' < ME *(e)stat + -ya*

stewya [**stewya* BK; **styvya* BK] 'to bath, to bathe' < ME *steuen, stiwen* 'to bathe in hot steam or water'

storvya [**storuye* PA] 'to die, to perish' < ME *storven*

stowtya [*stowtya* BK] 'to be defiant, to rebel' < ME *stouten*

strechya [**strechye* PA, RD; *streche* OM, *streccha* OM; *strechye* PC; *strechya* BM, CW] 'to delay, to procrastinate' < ME *strecchen* 'to stretch, to increase'

strîvya [*strevye* PA; *stryvya* TH] 'to strive, to contend' < ME *striven*

stoppya [*stopya* BM; *stoppya* TH; *stoppia* JTonkin] 'to stop' < ME *stoppen* 'to obstruct, to stop'

stryppya [**streppya* BM] 'to remove the clothes' < ME *strepen*

studhya [*stethya* BM] 'to study' < ME *studien, stedien* 'to study' [the intervocalic *-th-* seen in the Cornish form probably arose inside English; cf. ME *fader* > NE *father*, ME *moder* > NE *mother*]

sùbjectya [*subjectia* BK] 'to subjugate' < *subjecten*

sùbmyttya [*submyttya* TH] 'to submit' < ME *submitten*

sùffra [*suffra* TH] 'to suffer' < ME *sufferen*

sùppressya [*suppressia* TH] 'to restrain, to subdue' < ME *suppressen*

swervya [*swarvia* TH; *swarvya* TH] 'to swerve, to turn aside' < ME *swerven*

sygnyfia [*signifia* TH, SA] 'to mean, to signify' < ME *signifien*

tackya [**tackie* PA, *tackye* PC; **tackye* RD] 'to tack, to nail' < ME *tak* 'a fastener' and ME *tachen* 'to fasten'

tacla [*takla* BM] 'to rig, to fit out' < ME *takelen*

talkya [*talkye* OM; *talkya* CW, TH] 'to talk, to converse' < ME *talken*

tarya [*tarye* RD] 'to tarry, to delay' < ME *tarien*

tâstya [*tastye* OM; *tastya* CW, SA; *tastia* SA] 'to taste' < ME *tasten*

tempra [*tempre* PC; **tempra* BM] 'to subdue, to calm' < ME *tempren*

temptya [*temptye* PA, PC, *temptya* PA, BM, CW; *tempte* OM; **temptye* RD; *temtya* CW; *temptia* TH; *demptya* Rowe] 'to tempt' < ME *tempten*

testyfia [*testifia* TH; *testifya* TH] 'to give testimony, to testify' < ME *testifien*

tormentya [*tormontye* PA; **tormontye* OM; **tormentya* PC; **tormente* BK; **tremowntya* CW; **tormentyah* Rowe] 'to torment, to torture' < ME *tormenten*

trailya [*tryle* PA; *treylye* OM, RD; *treyle* PC; *trylye* PC; *trelya* BK, TH; **trellya* TH; *trylia* BK; **treyllya* CW; **treylya* CW; **traylya* CW; **treylya* TH; **trilya* SA; *trailia* Lh; *traylyah* Rowe] 'to turn' < ME *trailen* 'to trail, to turn'

trainya [**treynye* RD] 'to dawdle, to delay' < ME *treinen* 'to drag, to delay'

traita [*trayta* PA; **traytya* BK] 'to betray' < ME *traien* 'to betray' contaminated with the form of the root seen in *traitour* 'traitor'

transformya [**transformya* CW; **transfvrmya* SA] 'to transform' < ME *transformen*

transfygura [**transfigura* TH] 'to transfigure' < ME *transfiguren*

travalya [*travalia* JBoson] 'to trudge, to journey' < ME *travailen*

travela [*trauela* TH; *trafla* TH] 'to labour, to travail' < ME *travailen*; variant of preceding
trembla [*trembla* SA] 'to tremble' < ME *tremblen*
trespassya [*trespascye* PC] 'to sin, to do a criminal act' < ME *trespassen*
trestya [*trestye* OM; *trestya* BM; *trystya* PC, BK; *trystya BM; *tristya* CW; *tristia* TH; *trustya* CW] 'to trust' < ME *trusten, tresten, tristen*
trettya [*trettya* BM] 'to tread, to trample' < ME *tret*, 3rd person singular of *treden* 'to tread'
tria [*trea* CW] 'to try' < 'to examine; to try' < ME *trien*
trobla [*trople PC; *trobla* BM; *trobla CW; *troubla SA, Rowe] 'to trouble' < ME *troublen*
tùchya [*tochye* PA; *tochia* TH; *tochya* TH, SA; *tochya BK; *tuchye RD; *tuchya BM; *tuchia* TH; *towchya CW; *touchia* SA] 'to touch, to harm; to mention' < ME *touchen*
tyldya [*tyldye* OM] 'to cover as with a tent' < ME *telden* 'to pitch a tent'
ùnctya [*vntye* PA] 'to anoint' < ME *ointen* contaminated with the form seen in ME *unctioun* 'unction'
ùnderstondya [*vnderstondia* TH; *vndyrstondia* TH; *vndirstondia* TH; *vnderstandia SA; *vnderstandya* SA] 'to understand' < ME *understonden*
ùsùrpya [*vrsurpia* TH] 'to usurp' < ME *usurpen*
ûsya [*vsye PA; *vsia* BM, TH; *vsya* SA; *usya* CW, TH] 'to use, to wear, to consume, to be accustomed to' < ME *usen*
ùttra [*ottra BK; *vttra* TH] 'to speak, to utter' < ME *outren*
varya [*varya BM] 'to be unstable' < ME *varien*
venjya [*vyngya* BM] 'to take vengeance on' < ME *vengen*
venymya [*vynymye OM] 'to poison, to envenom' < ME *venimen*
vexya [*vexya BM; *vexia* TH] 'to vex, to afflict' < ME *vexen*
viajya [*vaggya* CW] 'to voyage, to travel' < ME *viagge* 'journey' + *-ya*
violâtya [*violatia* TH] 'to violate, to assault' < ME *violaten*
walkya [*walkya TH; *walkia SA] 'to walk, to wander' < ME *walken*
warya [*warya BM] 'to beware, to be on one's guard' < ME *waren*
wastya, gwastya [*wastye RD; *wastya BK; *guastia* Lh] 'to waste, to squander, to lay waste' < ME *wasten*
whyppya [*whyppye PC; *whyppya* BK; *whippya SA] 'to whip, to scourge' < ME *whippen*
wolcùmma [*wolcumme* OM; *welcumma BM; *welcomma* CW; *welcumba JTonkin] 'to welcome, to greet' < ME *welcomen, welcumen*
wrappya [*wrappya TH] 'to wrap' < ME *wrappen*
wrestya [*restye* RD; *wrestia* TH] 'to wrest, to twist' < ME *wresten*

www.ingramcontent.com/pod-product-compliance
Lightning Source LLC
Chambersburg PA
CBHW022054150426
43195CB00008B/135